P9-CLI-221

COMPUTERIZATION MOVEMENTS AND TECHNOLOGY DIFFUSION

FROM MAINFRAMES TO UBIQUITOUS COMPUTING

Edited by Margaret S. Elliott and Kenneth L. Kraemer

Published on behalf of the
American Society for Information Science and Technology by

First printing, 2008

Computerization Movements and Technology Diffusion: From Mainframes to Ubiquitous Computing

Library of Congress Cataloging-in-Publication Data

Computerization movements and technology diffusion : from mainframes to ubiquitous computing / Edited by Margaret S. Elliott and Kenneth L. Kraemer.
p. cm. -- (ASIS&T monograph series)
Includes bibliographical references.
ISBN 978-1-57387-311-6
1. Technological innovations. 2. Electronic data processing. 3. Technology transfer--United States. I. Elliott, Margaret S., 1948- II. Kraemer, Kenneth L. III. Title. IV. Series.
T173.8.C67 2008
338.973'06--dc22

200705003

President and CEO: Thomas H. Hogan, Sr.
Editor-in-Chief and Publisher: John B. Bryans
Managing Editor: Amy M. Reeve
ASIST Monograph Series Editor: Samantha Hastings
VP Graphics and Production: M. Heide Dengler
Book Designer: Kara Mia Jalkowski
Cover Designer: Dana Kruse
Copyeditor: Dorothy Pike
Proofreader: Penelope Mathiesen
Indexer: Beth Palmer

Dedication

To Margaret's daughters—Allie, Bridget, and Mimi—and to her husband, Michael.

To Ken's wife, Norine Kraemer.

Contents

Part IV Death of Distance

Part V Freedom and Information Rights

Part VI Ubiquitous Computing

Part VII Conclusion

List of Figures and Tables

Acknowledgments

We wish to thank the authors for their outstanding contributions to this book. With their help, we have completed an excellent compendium of research papers that further the work of the late professor Rob Kling on computerization movements. We also wish to thank Samantha Hastings, the ASIST Monograph Series editor, who reviewed the initial and final draft of the book, for her helpful suggestions. We are grateful to John Bryans and Amy Reeve from Information Today, Inc. for their help in managing the publication of this book. And finally, last but not least, we give special thanks to Kathy Honda for her help in making the conference arrangements, communicating with participants, editing the papers, checking the page proofs, and keeping us on track throughout the preparations for the conference and for this book.

Foreword

Dr. Suzanne Iacono
Acting Division Director of the Computer and Network Systems
Division of the Computer and Information Sciences and Engineering
Directorate of the National Science Foundation

The views expressed in the foreword do not necessarily represent the views of the National Science Foundation or the United States.

This book is a significant contribution to scholarly study in Social Informatics and a tribute to a distinguished scholar, Rob Kling, who was professor at the University of California, Irvine from 1973 to 1996 and at Indiana University from August 1996 until his death in 2003. One of Rob Kling's major intellectual concerns, which I also shared, was articulating the notion of computerization movements (CMs), i.e., understanding how new computing technologies evolve and why they are adopted (or not) by organizations.

Dr. Peter Freeman[1] and I were both working in the Directorate for Computer and Information Science and Engineering (CISE) at the National Science Foundation at the time of Rob's death. One of the divisions in CISE—Information and Intelligent Systems—had supported Rob's work since the 1980s. That division funded a workshop that recognized the contributions of this noted scholar and brought together distinguished scholars and researchers to advance the study of CMs. Margaret Elliott and Ken Kraemer, editors of this book, organized the workshop and commissioned distinguished researchers in Social Informatics to write papers that focused on new contributions to the study of CMs.

A major issue in the study of CMs is, "How do new technologies evolve and why do organizations invest in them despite frequent failures to achieve stated objectives like increased productivity, enhanced collaboration, or fully effective virtual organizations?" A key proposition from this point of view is that adoption and diffusion of new technologies do not just depend on simple economic logic or managerial requirements, but on the broader social environment. Much of the research on diffusion of technological innovations has concentrated on adoption within single organizations and emphasized features of technology and organization that shape diffusion in response to economic needs. The macro-social and cultural environments surrounding the adoption of new technologies by organizations are largely ignored. Most studies also do not look at why or how organizations that implement the same information technology at the same time achieve different levels of success.

Rob and I long argued that the emergence of new technologies and their diffusion take place in a broader context of interacting organizations and institutions, which shape utopian visions of what technology can do and how it should be used. We called these broad environmental dynamics "computerization movements." A CM focuses on a type of computer-based system that advocates claim will be integral and instrumental in bringing about a new social order, e.g., a more collaborative or productive organization or even a new organizational form.

It is useful to reflect on the origin of these ideas. During the 1980s, Rob and I conducted a number of field studies in organizations that had invested heavily in Material Requirements Planning (MRP) systems. During the course of this research, we conducted in-depth interviews with MRP users, and discovered that most users believed the "hype" about MRP systems, i.e., what they could do for their organization in terms of reducing inventory, work in progress, and costs, despite the lack of any empirical evidence that those goals had actually been achieved. After we heard the hype in our interviews with Vice Presidents, Central Information Officers, Materials Managers, etc., we would ask them to provide proof of the benefits achieved from their investments in MRP systems, but none of them could. Rob and I talked about this anomaly continuously. We came to the conclusion that a reality gap existed between the ideology surrounding a new technology like MRP, which management bought into when they made their investments, and the actual practices that later ensued in an organization when they were using the new technologies. We began looking for further evidence of this gap with other technologies.

We examined technologies that had been developed and diffused during the period from the 1960s to the mid-1980s, and found that similar ideologies had arisen around urban information systems, artificial intelligence, computer-based education, office automation, and personal computing. We identified five mobilizing ideologies that we believed CM advocates in specific organizations employ when seeking to convince management to computerize their own organizations. Since few CM activists assert key ideological themes directly, we derived these ideologies from conversations with practitioners and developers, and from careful reading of books and articles about the benefits of these new technologies. The five mobilizing ideologies are as follows:

1. Computer-based technologies are central for a reformed world.

2. Improved computer-based technologies can further reform society.
3. More computing is better than less, and there are no conceptual limits to the scope of appropriate computerization.
4. No one loses from computerization.
5. Uncooperative people are the main barriers to social reform through computing.

Leigh Star was putting together a special issue of *Social Problems* and encouraged us to further develop these ideas, which resulted in our first paper on CMs (Kling & Iacono, 1988), where we argued that computerization in the United States had been strongly influenced by these mobilizing ideologies. We further noted that these ideologies were often offered by "CM activists" who were not employees of the computer vendors, but who were independent actors such as practitioners, academics, and journalists. We further distinguished between a general computerization movement in society in which activists proclaim "revolutionary" social changes and specific CMs focused on particular technologies and their benefits. We refined this work in two later papers in which we explored the concept of technological utopianism in the CM discourse (Iacono & Kling, 1996) and analyzed the Internetworking CM (Iacono & Kling, 2001).

This book builds on these earlier works in several important ways. First, it brings together 30 distinguished scholars from the U.S., Canada, and Europe, who each apply CM theory and concepts to their current areas of research. Thus, the book is unique in being the largest collection of research papers on CMs to date.

Second, it greatly extends our earlier contribution to CMs. It introduces new uses of the CM construct to characterize adoption decisions occurring in contemporary society. It provides richly textured descriptions of how public discourse within society creates utopian visions about the benefit of computer use. It uses the CM construct to better explain issues of mobilization and recruitment to various CMs. It shows how not only technology vendors, but also journalists, academics, visionaries, professionals, and users can all become "activists" promoting ideal visions of what the new technology is good for and how it should be used. And it shows that CMs greatly influence how people think about computing technologies and therefore help shape the technology adoption decisions of managers and users in organizations, and more broadly within society.

Third, the studies in this book show that the gap between the utopian visions promulgated by CM activists and the ways in which the technologies are actually used is very large indeed. This gap augers for change in the conduct of CM discourse as well as continuing research into new and emerging CMs.

Fourth, aside from the individual studies, the editors have analyzed the current socio-technical environment and have articulated today's key utopian visions surrounding new technologies. In the Introduction (Chapter 1), they identify five CM outcomes: productivity, democratization, death of distance, freedom and information rights, and ubiquitous computing. They then use examples from selected chapters to illustrate these themes. These themes also form the organizing framework for the body of the book (Chapters 2-19).

Finally, in the Conclusion (Chapter 20), the editors present a historical portrayal of CMs through comparative analysis of CMs during the four eras of computerization: Mainframe, PC, Internet, and Ubiquitous Computing. They generate new knowledge about the implications of ubiquitous computing by looking forward to examples of emerging technologies, and looking backward to earlier technologies for how they might inform this new era of ubiquitous computing. The editors conclude with these seminal points regarding the current and future state of CMs:

- There is a continuing gap between CM visions and the reality of technology use in organizations and society.
- CM rhetoric tends to shift from the utopian to the pragmatic with experience and contending discourse.
- Technologies that require a support infrastructure to be built as part of their implementation take longer to diffuse than those that can use existing infrastructures, resulting in a lower probability that a CM requiring a new infrastructure will lead to successful diffusion.
- The realities of day-to-day use of a CM's promoted technology cannot be predicted precisely in advance, but informed technology assessments can be made by better understanding of similarities and differences of emerging and earlier technologies. Such assessments can improve the success of a CM.
- The social context shapes technology use as much or more than the technology per se. New technology often reinforces existing organizational and social arrangements, rather than disrupting, changing, or transforming them. CMs that leverage the technology-organization linkage will be more successful than those that do not.

Finally, the editors develop a few key implications of their analysis for software designers, managers and professionals, organizational users, and CM scholars.

I am pleased to see the progress that the many chapters in this book, and the book as a whole, represent. I am grateful to the many scholars who contributed to the workshop, to the special issue of *The Information Society* critiquing Rob Kling's contribution to the field, and to this book on CMs. It was a great honor for me to have worked with Rob for so many years. His influence within the field of Social Informatics was ubiquitous, and remains so.

Endnotes

1. Peter was Assistant Director of the National Science Foundation and head of the Directorate for Computer and Information Science and Engineering (CISE) from 2002 until 2007. Peter and Rob were both Professors of Information and Computer Science at the University of California, Irvine during the early 1980s and were office neighbors for most of that time.

Part I

Introduction

Chapter 1

Computerization Movements and the Diffusion of Technological Innovations

Margaret S. Elliott and Kenneth L. Kraemer
University of California, Irvine

Abstract

What explains why organizations adopt computing technologies? Management and organizational research on diffusion of technological innovations has emphasized features of technology, organization, and environment that shape diffusion in response to some economic need. However, several computer scientists have argued that diffusion takes place in a broader context of interacting organizations and institutions that shape utopian visions of what technology can do and how it should be used. This broad environmental dynamic has been called a "computerization movement." A computerization movement is a type of movement that focuses on computer-based systems as the core technologies, which their advocates claim will be instruments to bring about a new social order. These advocates of computerization movements spread their message through public discourse in various segments of society such as vendors, media, academics, visionaries, and professional societies. Computerization visions often legitimate continuing large investments in technology based on the benefits promised by an ideal vision. However, there is often a gap between the vision and reality, which may be caused by limitations of the technology, social adaptation to the technology, or in the nature of the vision itself leading to failures or setbacks toward successful diffusion of the technology. This book examines this diffusion process across many platforms and contexts by examining computerization movements for the promotion of technologies ranging from small individual artifacts to large-scale computer-based systems. The chapters are organized across five themes representing key utopian vision regarding computerization movement outcomes: productivity, democratization, death of distance, freedom and information rights, and ubiquitous computing. In this chapter, we give a brief overview of these underlying themes, characterizing them as utopian visions of various computerization movements through the years, and discuss them in relation to their historical place in a particular era of computing identified as the Mainframe era, the Personal Computer era, the Internet era, or the Ubiquitous Computing era. Finally, we introduce the chapters in this book by illustrating the themes through examples from the case studies presented in the chapters in this book.

Introduction

What explains why organizations adopt computing technologies? This is the fundamental question addressed by this book. The management and organizational research on diffusion of technical innovations has tended to emphasize features of technology, organization, and environment that shape diffusion in response to an economic need (Thompson, 1965; Tornatzky & Fleischer, 1990). Environment has been conceived narrowly as constituting pressure for adoption due to firm, industry, or global competition. But several computer scientists have argued that environment needs to be conceived as a richer construct that captures more of the dynamics of diffusion within society (Kling & Iacono, 1988; King, et al., 1994). That is, diffusion takes place in a broad context of interacting organizations and institutions that shape visions of what the technology can do and how it should be used. Those socially constructed visions of the technology shape the perceptions of people in organizations and drive diffusion.

Innovation diffusion theory (Rogers, 2005) emphasizes the importance of the relationship between the features of technological innovations and the context of adopting organizations or societal groups in achieving diffusion of technology such as computers or information communication technologies (ICTs). Diffusion occurs when the innovation has reached a stage where an organization or society has adopted an innovation in practice. Sociologists and economists have theorized that diffusion in organizations is influenced by the specific context of the adopting organizations and by specific features of the technology or technological process being adopted (Rogers, 2005; Tornatzky & Fleischer, 1990; Zhu, Kraemer, & Xu, 2006). Examples of context might include organization size, adoption costs, technical background of potential users, or similar features. Various aspects of a technology, such as competitive advantage, return on investment, usability of the technology, or fit with work practices, might intervene in the diffusion process.

Although innovation diffusion theory is helpful in understanding the adoption and use of specific technologies in organizations, it does not address the broader societal context that influences technological diffusion, such as ideological beliefs or visions surrounding innovation. Many groups within society, such as vendors, media, academics, visionaries, and professional societies, are instrumental in promoting the adoption and diffusion of technology through *utopian visions* of what the technology can do to change or improve social or work life. Kling and Iacono (1988, 1995) have called this broad environmental dynamic a "computerization movement" (CM) to signal its separation from, yet affiliation with, technology and social movements more generally. A CM is a type of movement that focuses on computer-based systems as the core technologies, which their advocates claim will be instruments to bring about a new and better social order. CMs can be characterized as consisting of three components that interact with and shape each other (Iacono & Kling, 2001): (1) technological frames, (2) public discourse, and (3) organizational practice and use. Technological frames (Orlikowski & Gash, 1994) are composite understandings about how a technology works and could be used. These frames are built up in public discourse about a particular computer-based system in the form of mass media, scientific journals, public speaking, and trade journals (Iacono & Kling, 2001). Over time, a technological frame pervades and becomes the dominant frame representing a particular CM or group of CMs. Public discourse and technological frames influence how technology is used in organizational and inter-organizational contexts.

With this brief introduction, the remainder of this chapter elaborates on CMs and illustrates central themes that have emerged over the last fifty years. It first defines CMs as a concept and discusses the broader intellectual background from the social sciences and from previous CM research. Next, it presents a conceptual model of CMs that illustrates the principal components and their interactions. It then compares the CM construct as a research method to other theoretical approaches to the study of the adoption and diffusion of technology. After that, it identifies the following five technological action frames that have emerged in previous CM research and writing:

- Productivity
- Democratization
- Death of distance
- Freedom/information rights
- Ubiquitous computing

Finally, it explains each of these themes and uses examples from some of the chapters in the rest of the book to further illustrate and elaborate the themes, as well as to introduce the chapters.

CMs as a Concept

The notion of a CM was first defined by Kling and Iacono (1988) as a particular kind of social movement whose distinguishing feature is that advocates focus on computer-based systems as instruments to bring about a preferred social order. We characterize a CM as a specific kind of social and technological movement oriented toward the mobilization of bias for continuing investments in computer technology and related uses based on utopian visions of better social worlds. CMs advance computerization in ways that go beyond the effect of promotion by the industries that produce and sell computer-based technologies and services. CMs communicate key ideological beliefs about the favorable links between computerization and a preferred social order, which helps legitimate relatively high levels of computing investment or other resources (e.g., personal time, as occurs with the Free Software Movement [FSM]) for many potential adopters. These ideologies also set adopters' expectations about what they should use computing for and how they should organize access to it.

The CM construct refers to the loosely organized coalitions that promote technology and mobilize membership via professional or other organizations. Some CM organizations may be highly organized around a central group such as the Free Software Foundation (FSF), which promotes the FSM, or the National Information Initiative (NII), which promoted nationwide Internet access during the Clinton-Gore administration. Others are loosely linked subgroups of professional organizations, or informal groups. In addition, activists who write for broad national audiences, but who do not belong to professional organizations, contribute to technology diffusion through their creation, in public discourse, of utopian visions for technology use. These visions shape "technological frames" that form key ideas about how a technology works and how it could be used. Over time, the development and diffusion of new technologies can result in stabilization of the meaning of technologies in the form of dominant or master frames. These master frames promote large investments in the technology based on the benefits promised by the ideal vision.

There is often a gap between this vision and the way technology is realistically used by organizations and society. This may be due to limitations in the technology's performance, in social adaptation to the technology, or in the nature of the vision itself that leads to failure or to setbacks toward eventual success. As time goes by, contending discourse may evolve, through scientific studies and/or public journalism, showing how the actual use of technology does not match the expectations of the utopian vision. New dominant technological frames may emerge, replacing the original utopian vision with one more reflective of actual use of the technology. This reframing process may also result in the design of new technology.

Sociologists have used the term "movement" to study various types of collective behavior with the term "social movement" often used to refer to movements in general (Blumer, 1969). Movements can start out as general in nature (i.e., the women's rights movement) and evolve into specific movements based on the ideology of the general movement but with more specific objectives and supporting organizations. For example, the National Organization of Women (NOW), established in 1966, grew out of the broader women's rights movement, but focused on modern equality issues related to politics, and increased educational and employment opportunities. Similarly, CMs may be viewed as specific movements centered on a general CM that promotes mass computerization (Kling & Iacono, 1988). Distinguishing between the general and specific CMs provides a way of characterizing distinct wings of the larger, continually evolving computerization effort in the United States and elsewhere in the world, including developing countries. This distinction enables researchers to show how similar conceptions about modes of computerization found across many organizations or social settings can be understood in a more general way.

Specific CMs may generate specific counter-computerization movements (CCMs) that oppose certain modes of computerization, which their advocates view as bringing about an inappropriate social order (Kling & Iacono, 1988). There is no evidence of a general CCM forming in response to the general CM, but several specific CCMs have been identified (Kling & Iacono, 1988, 1995). For example, since 1990, the Computer Professionals for Social Responsibility (CPSR) group has served as an anti-war group opposing militant types of computer-based systems such as StarWars. It has also focused on other public issues of computerization such as workplace democracy and information rights. A general CCM is unlikely as it would have to rest on a technologically anti-utopian vision of all computerization in society. There are a few technologically anti-utopian books or articles (Mander, 1991), but no visible general CCM.

CM Background and Previous Research

Sociologists have studied a variant of CMs in the form of technological movements (McCarthy & Zald, 1977; Useem & Zald, 1982), such as the nuclear power movement in which particular technologies are central to a vision of a preferred social order. Technological movements are unique in comparison with typical social movements in that their mobilizing ideologies center on the promotion of an improved social order via the use of a particular family of technologies (Kling & Iacono, 1988). A key mobilizing resource of technological movements is the movement organization (McCarthy & Zald, 1977), which identifies their goals with a movement or counter-movement, and attempts to implement those goals. While movement organizations may play a role in promoting a CM, of utmost importance in mobilizing support for use of a particular computer-based system are the activists who write or speak for broad national audiences (Kling & Iacono, 1988) but may not necessarily belong to any particular movement organization. Such activists are illustrated by technology writers such as John Seely Brown, Howard Rheingold, and Nicholas Negroponte; business writers such as John Hagel and Arthur Armstrong; academics such as Jonathan Weisner and Sherry Turkle; and journalists such as Walt Mossberg; but there are legions of such activists at all levels within society. The fact that these activists have a positive influence on CM mobilization is a *key* distinguishing feature of CMs compared with other technological movements. The majority of CM mobilization for membership is advertised and successfully recruited through their public discourses in the mass media, professional organizations, public speeches, popular stories, television shows, and magazine articles (Kling & Iacono, 1988).

In previous research, Kling and Iacono (1988) analyzed CM ideologies of computerization based on a study of the historical trajectory of specific CMs. They examined the literature and did case studies of five CMs: artificial intelligence (AI), computer-based education, urban-based information systems (IS), office automation, and personal computers (PCs). They identified the following ideologies as characterizing each of the five CMs:

1. Computer-based technologies are central for a reformed world.
2. Improved computer-based technologies can reform society.
3. More computing is better than less, and there are no conceptual limits to the scope of appropriate computerization.
4. No one loses from computerization.
5. Uncooperative people are the main barriers to social reform through computing.

In later research (Kling & Iacono, 1995), they stated that the five ideological beliefs could be replaced by a simpler discussion by referring to them as forms of "technological utopianism." *Technological utopianism* is a rhetorical form that places the use of some specific technology, such as computers, as key enabling elements of a utopian vision. Later still

(Iacono & Kling, 1996), they expounded upon *technological utopianism* as a key device used by movement advocates to envision the renewal of society through technology.

Technological utopianism does not refer to the technologies themselves but to the analysis in which the use of specific technologies plays a key role in shaping an ideal or perfect world. For example, in 1993, when the White House issued an agenda for the NII, better known as the "Information Super Highway," readers were asked to imagine a world where people can live anywhere and telecommute to work. Without mention of the economic and political strife associated with computer networking, the NII report is a rich example of technological utopianism. Finally, in Iacono and Kling (2001), utopian visions are said to appear in public discourse and influence the emergence of *technological action frames*, which form key ideas about how a technology is used in micro-level contexts—currently and in the future.

The Concept of Frames in CMs

Snow and Benford (1988) originally defined frames as the conscious strategic efforts by groups of people to fashion shared understandings of the world that legitimate and motivate collective action. The concept of frames is used by social scientists of several disciplines—sociology, cognitive psychology, linguistics and discourse analysis, communication and media studies, and political science and policy studies—to describe and analyze the "interpretive schemas" people use to understand and act upon beliefs regarding the way things are now and how they should be changed in the future. The framing concept has been applied analytically and examined in empirical studies in sociology more extensively than in other areas (Benford & Snow, 2000; Snow, Rochford, Worden, & Benford, 1986; Snow & Benford, 1988, 1992).

Goffman (1974) first described frames as "schemata of interpretation" that enable people to identify occurrences within their life span and the world at large. Since frames help to make events meaningful to people, they serve as a guide to action. Collective action frames (Benford & Snow, 2000) serve as a simplifying mechanism combining individual attitudes and perceptions with negotiated shared meanings of the movement ideology. They serve to mobilize movement actors to recognize the need for change and to take action to make the necessary steps toward accepting an alternate way of doing things. Collective action frames are action-oriented sets of beliefs and meanings that support the goals of a social movement organization.

In their study of Internetworking as a CM, Iacono and Kling (2001) combine the sociological notion of "collective action frames" with the definition of "technological frames" (Orlikowski & Gash, 1994) to coin the term "technological action frames." Technological action frames are composite understandings that support high levels of investments in new technology and form the core ideas about how a technology works and how it could be used. They work at the macro-social level in motivating people to join a CM. Individuals and organizations then appropriate these frames into their micro-social contexts. These frames circulate in public discourses designed to mobilize membership in a particular CM. Iacono and Kling (2001) present a process of societal mobilization with the following three primary elements:

- Technological action frames – Multi-dimensional composite understandings that legitimate high levels of investment for potential users and form key ideas about how a technology is used, currently and in the future.
- Public discourse – Written and spoken public communications that develop around a new technology found in government discourses, the discourse of scientific organizations, mass media discourses, and organizational and professional discourses.
- Organizational practices – Ways that organizations and groups of individuals put technological action frames and discourses into practice in a micro-level social context.

These three elements are related in a recursive fashion, as illustrated by the arrows in Figure 1.1. To simplify our discussion of frames throughout this chapter, we refer to "technological action frames" hereafter as frames or technological frames. Moving from left to right in the figure, *technological frames* shape and structure *public discourse*, which then shapes and structures organizational use and practices related to the technology. Over time, the development and diffusion of new technologies can result in stabilization of the meaning of technologies in the form of *dominant* or *master frames*.

In turn, organizational practices can influence public discourse and result in a "reframing" process. This occurs when there is a gap between the *utopian vision* conveyed in public discourse and the actual organizational use of technology. As time goes by, *contending discourse* evolves in public discourse through scientific studies and journalism regarding this gap. Eventually, new *dominant frames* emerge, resulting in either new technology or new use of the same technology. This process is further described in the following section where we introduce the conceptual model of CMs.

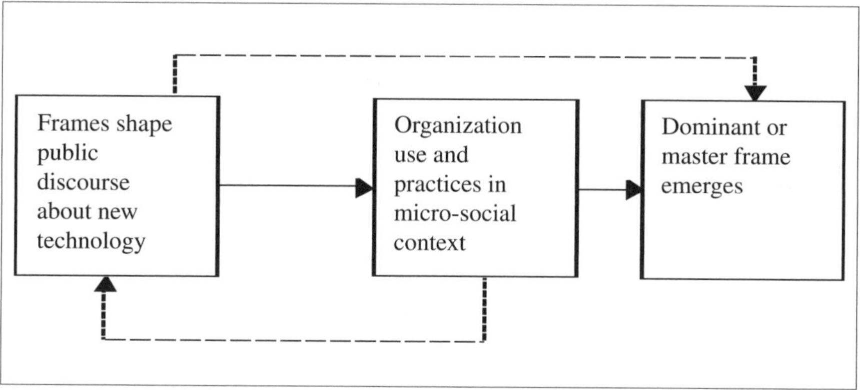

Figure 1.1 Computerization movements—relationship between discourse, dominant frames, and organizational use and practices

Conceptual Model of CMs

Using these primary elements, we developed a conceptual model of the life cycle of a CM and the various paths that it may take from emergence to finale. Figure 1.2 presents the basic model.

Moving from left to right in the figure, as new *computer technologies* are introduced into society, people in diverse organizations create *utopian visions* about these technologies. These visions are of improved social worlds enabled by the technology. The utopian visions are expressed in *public discourses* in the media, academic writings, user groups, industry associations, and professional societies and result in the emergence of dominant technological frames, which influence choices by organizations and individuals about technology adoption. These visions and technological frames serve to *mobilize individuals, organizations, and society* to invest in computer-based systems, thereby promoting *diffusion* of the technology broadly within society.

Depending upon the fit between the utopian visions and reality of technology use, the technology may fade, reach critical mass, or stimulate a new cycle. Similarly, the CM involved with the technology may fade, continue with the same *dominant frame*, merge with another CM, or face a CCM. As the CM continues, *contending discourse* may evolve in which the actual technology is described as not being used as in the original *utopian* vision. Continual *contending discourse* may eventually result in the replacement of the *dominant frame*, or may result in a new or revised technology. We discuss each of these key ideas next.

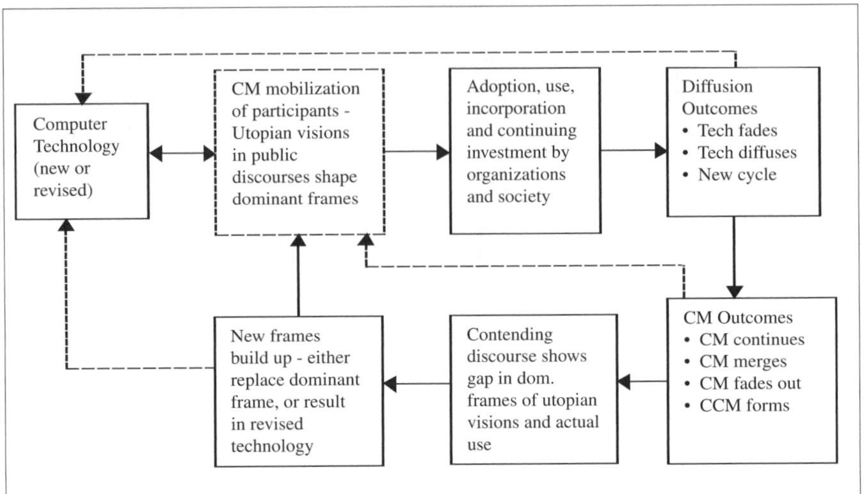

Figure 1.2 Conceptual model of life cycle of computerization movements

Computer Technology

Computer technology refers not only to the physical artifact of the computer but to the whole package of hardware, software, infrastructure, and organizational practices required for its effective use. Since the 1990s, user applications (software) and computer networks have become key technologies that are complex and increasingly required for effective use, but are mainly in the background. Typical users are not aware of the hardware and software that enable Internet connections. What they see is e-mail, instant messaging, and bulletin boards—primarily, software applications on the network. Increasingly, it is software that provides utility to users and thus it is not surprising that CMs have arisen around software such as enterprise systems and collaboration technologies. Organizational practices have also come to be recognized as key to successful use of software in order to achieve expected benefits. Thus, both software and organizational practices are part of the social fabric of the environment of use and therefore adoption and use of computing are more complex than with previous innovations such as the typewriter or the adding machine. This is perhaps the key reason that CMs have come to play a primary role in the diffusion of complex computer-based systems into social worlds within organizations and society.

Utopian Visions

CMs are most distinguished by their particular utopian visions about what the technology can do and how it should be used and organized.

These visions are "utopian" in the sense that they depict how things could be in ideal social worlds where the technology actually would do what it was supposed to do and both people and organizations would be perfectly attuned to the demands of the vision in terms of knowledge and skills, structure and control, and goals and objectives. The visions are sometimes far from reality. The technology does not work as envisaged, or perhaps does not work at all. People and organizations cannot or do not wish to make the required adaptations. If the vision is powerful, however, and people stay with the technology over time, the vision might eventually be achieved as a result of improvements in the technology, a subsequent new and related technology, or a unique organizational adaptation.

One such utopian vision can be seen in the FSM which advocates that software, in the form of source code and executable files, should be provided free to individual and organizational users rather than charging a price as in current practice. This concept is anathema to typical software development firms, which charge a price for proprietary software and generally include only executable files. Thus, typical users of software in organizations or individually rely on proprietary firms for software changes, which usually result in more fees. Although wider diffusion would be a result of free software, this is not the only purpose. The vision also appeals to a general and high ideal of "freedom." Richard M. Stallman, the leader of the movement (known as RMS in the free/open source software [F/OSS] communities), postulates many altruistic reasons why all people should give away source code, but they all come down to doing so in the name of freedom in keeping with the tenets of the Founding Fathers who wrote the U.S. Constitution. (See www.fsf.org for several essays articulating the benefits of free software.) In response, big business enterprises like Microsoft are claiming anti-utopian outcomes from free software such as the end of capitalism and the downfall of enterprise-oriented companies like Microsoft.

Mobilization of Participants Through Public Discourses

People are mobilized to join a movement by becoming aware of modes of computerization through activities and by-products of CMs: advocates, public speeches and written works, popular stories, television shows, and magazine articles (Kling & Iacono, 1988). Some CM advocates represent themselves and others represent organizations. Although various computer users and vendors contribute to creating interest in computerization, CMs help shape expectations and stimulate demand that traditional market analyses ignore. For example, the first PC hobbyists were part of a grassroots CM focused on building or buying home PCs, with CM membership spreading by word of mouth or electronic communication. In this way, they did not identify with the computer industry and were probably ignored by people marketing IBM PCs. CMs are centered on collaborations of individuals with diverse interests. Some CM participants are mobilized by outside influences such as popular press and friends and family, while others are motivated by organizations that advocate specific computer-based systems (such as AI).

Public discourse is essential in the mobilization of people to join a CM. Technological frames circulate in these discourses and are borrowed by agents who use them in their own organizational or societal contexts and discourses and, at the same time, often extend them (Iacono & Kling, 2001). In this way, the spreading of dominant frames in discourse at macro-levels of analysis (like professional associations) influences and shapes the micro-level context of discourse and practices. The four levels of public discourse outlined in Iacono and Kling (2001) include:

- Government discourses – Discourse circulated in government documents such as the NII agenda and on government Web sites devoted to promoting the use of computer-based systems in government settings.
- Scientific discipline discourses – Discourse produced in scientific fields from research on the development and use of computer-based systems in organizations and society. This discourse borrows heavily from the social science theory to explain what these new technologies might mean to the people who use them.
- Mass media discourses – Discourse taking place daily on television (shows such as CNN, Frontline, etc.), in newspapers and magazines, and over the Internet. Activists using mass media package their stories in such a way that the unfamiliar technology becomes more familiar and accessible.
- Institutional and professional discourses – Discourses that arise in individual organizational settings and in specific professional associations. The technological frames espoused by the government, scientific disciplines, and the media are operationalized within specific organizations and professional associations. This discourse also identifies which societal or professional problems can be alleviated through the use of specific computer-based systems. Within the micro-level settings, social groups struggle to understand the new technologies as they change or contend with the dominant technological action frame to fit their own preferences and goals. As a result, organizations may be restructured or professions redefined. While occasionally, best practices regarding the use of new technologies are discussed in trade magazines or business publications, more often discourses about actual practices are hidden within

organizations. Through historical analyses, ethnographic studies, and case studies of actual technology use, *contending discourse* arises and new technological frames are developed.

Contending Discourse

Contending discourses arise in the mass media, within scientific disciplines, and within organizations as scientific studies of the actual use of technology are published showing the gap between the intended use and actual use of the technology. These contending discourses, by framing technologies in alternative ways, can then have powerful influences on the development of new meaning about technology and the development of new technological frames. For example, the critical discourses about the work automation frame during the mainframe and PC eras developed into discourses about more collaborative technologies, resulting in new families of technologies such as computer-supported cooperative work (CSCW) and groupware (Kling & Iacono, 1988).

The Diffusion Process

Technological diffusion is a multi-stage process comprised of adoption, use, and widespread incorporation into organizations or society. Adoption, which is the first stage, refers to making the decision to use a new technology for personal or organizational purposes. Yet adoption does not always result in widespread use of the technology. It needs to be accepted, adapted, and assimilated into an organization or into general society such as in home computing. This is the second, or use, stage. Finally, the technology needs to be incorporated where it is institutionalized as an integral part of the individual's or the organization's activities.

This understanding of diffusion as a complex, multi-stage process helps to explain why CMs develop and why any particular technology may take decades to diffuse to its intended audience. As part of the diffusion process, improved new technologies may come along and displace the earlier ones. Alternatively, despite being better than the original technology, the new version may not displace earlier technologies because of the previous investments and due to the high costs of changeover.

Outcomes

Depending upon the fit between the utopian visions surrounding the technology and users' actual experience, the technology may fade, diffuse to critical mass, or influence the innovation of new technology that incorporates lessons learned from a failure. Once a technology reaches critical mass, it becomes institutionalized and several things can happen to the CM. The CM may fade out, continue and provide further support for diffusion, or merge with other CMs, creating discourses that promote new technological frames regarding the same or another technology.

A further outcome, which may occur at any point in the diffusion process, is that the utopian writings associated with specific CMs may spawn a CCM related to that CM's specific computer artifacts (hardware or software). The anti-utopian views of CCM advocates usually arise in response to a threat from the use and development of the specific technology promoted by a CM. Using the example cited earlier, Microsoft's purported efforts to downplay the advantages of free software with anti-utopian visions of the end of capitalism could be characterized as a CCM.

CM Compared with Other Research Methods

Most research on information technology (IT) and organizational change has concentrated on adoption and change within single organizations. The macro-social and cultural environment is largely ignored, and studies do not look at why or how organizations attempt to implement the same IT at the same time with different levels of success (Iacono & Kling, 2001). For exceptions to this, see Orlikowski (1992, 2000) and Orlikowski and Gash (1994). In the social movement literature, the emphasis is less on the social action and change in organizations and more on the wide-scale mobilization of participants for social change. In CM research, researchers bring together these bodies of study (Iacono & Kling, 2001). The analysis of CM research is at a macro-level, showing how the broader environment is critical to the adoption and diffusion of technology into social and work lives within society and between organizations. In this section we review other theoretical approaches to studying adoption and diffusion of technology at the individual and organizational levels. We then compare their strengths and weaknesses with those of the CM theoretical construct. Table 1.1 shows the five frameworks, their levels of analysis, and comparisons with CMs as a research framework.

Web of Computing

The web of computing framework (Kling & Scacchi, 1982) is a framework for use in a social analysis of computing at the organizational level. It has been used to show the complex network behind end-user computing. Web models view IS as complex social objects that are influenced by their context, infrastructure, and history. However, in their scope of analysis they are limited to within organizations. Web models (Kling & Scacchi, 1982) focus on the way that some focal computing resource is produced by a network of producers and consumers referred to as a production lattice. Web models examine both the social and economic organization of computing activities focused at the organization level of

Table 1.1 Computerization Movements Compared to Other Frameworks

Type of Analysis	Level of Analysis	Purpose
Computerization Movement	Societal	Show technology adoption as a social movement shaped by utopian visions of what technology can do
Web of Computing	Organizational level	Show complex network behind end-user computing activities
Structuration Theory	Organizational level	Show that technology use is an interactive social process
Actor-network Theory	Group	Focuses on technology adoption; shows end-users as social actors in global networks
Technology Acceptance Model (TAM)	Individual	Relates individual perceived ease of use and perceived usefulness to adoption

analysis. The production lattice for a particular computer-based system or resource consists of a social organization that is embedded in the larger picture (macrostructures) of the social and economic relations and is dependent on a local infrastructure. Web models enable the analysis of how the macrostructures relate to the local availability of technology resources at each node of the lattice. Web models view computing systems as a complex web of historical commitments and infrastructure changes throughout time. Thus, web models provide a social analysis of computing developments constrained by their organizational context, infrastructure, and history. They are most suited for complex computer-based systems and services that connect many different groups in the production lattice during development, operation, and use of a computer-based system. In a detailed presentation of web models and their use, Kling and Scacchi (1982) showed how using a web model enabled insight into the social and technically complex embedded computing developments within sample organizations.

Structuration Theory and Technology Use in Organizations

Structuration models portray technology as embodying structures (rules and resources) built in by designers during technology development and later appropriated by users of the technology (Orlikowski, 1992). Orlikowski (2000) developed a more advanced application of structuration theory to accommodate the constant redefinition of the meaning, properties, and applications of technology long after development.

Technologies such as screen displays do not structure human action until they are routinely mobilized in recurrent use patterns, which then produce and reproduce a particular structure of technology use. Structuration theory applied to technology use indicates that researchers and managers interested in estimates of technology performance prior to investment may get more meaningful results if they look for returns on the *use* of technology instead of just the *technology* itself. The application of structuration theory to technology is appropriate at the organizational level.

Actor-Network Theory

Actor-network theory (ANT) offers a framework for describing the process of technology adoption with emphasis on social construction as well as on technical innovation. Social interactions are viewed within a network society, providing a rich environment for viewing social networks. One of the most important contributions of ANT is that people along with their technologies comprise social networks known in ANT as actor-networks. This theory has been used by researchers to characterize the role of users of online IS as social actors in IS research (Lamb & Kling, 2003) and to analyze the socio-technological construction of China's strategy for the transformation of the telecommunications market (Gao, 2005). ANT is used as an analytical tool at the group level within organizations and societies.

Technology Acceptance Model

The technology acceptance model (TAM) proposed by Davis (1989) gives an explanation for user acceptance of IT. Adoption and diffusion of IT have been studied in depth by many researchers in the IS area. In the TAM model, adoption refers to the decision to accept, or invest in, a technology. The TAM model focuses on the individual level and states that an individual's adoption of IT is dependent on their perceived ease of use and perceived usefulness of the technology. The TAM model has been used to study the adoption of various technologies (Venkatesh & Morris, 2003; Venkatesh, 2000; Dasgupta, Granger, & McGarry, 2002) and to predict user acceptance of an IS (Davis, 1989; Venkatesh & Morris, 2003). Davis (1989) first proposed TAM when he verified that the perceived ease of use and perceived usefulness of an IS determine the behavioral intention of the user to use the system.

Advantages of Using the CM Framework

Using the CM framework enables researchers to use a macro-level analysis and historical picture of adoption and diffusion. This encourages researchers to use a deeper analysis of tacit and apparent attitudes and motivations for adoption and consequent diffusion of technologies in societal groups and organizations. The emphasis is on professional and public discourse which influences the creation of technological action frames that motivate people to purchase and integrate computer-based systems into their daily lives. Thus, analyzing the diffusion of technology through the CM lens shows that the spread of computer-based systems is more than just the by-product of ambitious marketing from high-tech companies.

Looking at macro-level issues related to diffusion of computer-based systems in organizations and society focuses the researcher on issues often missed when analyzing computer-based systems at the individual and organizational levels. The analyses of various computerization environments have come from careful scientific studies of work practices. These discourses are needed to help correct the many misrepresentations and misunderstandings about the nature of organizational restructuring and how new technologies influence work practices (Iacono & Kling, 2001).

Furthermore, using the CM construct affords the opportunity to examine computerization on a global level, which may be missed using another technique. For example, the web of computing is intended for analysis of the social and economic organization of computing activities without an analysis of the global influences related to software adoption and use. In the 2000s, global economic transactions are becoming more common, with e-commerce taking place over the Web. Analysis of general and specific CMs helps us understand the social forces behind the global information society of the future.

A disadvantage of using CMs as the focal point of social analyses of computing is that it may result in overlooking important aspects of the individual and organizational adoption of technology. For example, using an individual-level approach such as TAM can show the influence of individuals' perceptions regarding technology's usefulness on the success or failure of technology diffusion in an organization. Even though the "death of distance" technological frame may have a powerful influence on the rate of adoption of certain ICTs, individuals' perceptions regarding technology's usefulness (as shown by the TAM approach) may also be influential in success or failure of technology diffusion in any particular organization.

Dominant Technological Frames in Four Computerization Eras

We have shown the importance of CMs in the real world of diffusion of computing innovations. Our analysis of CMs indicates that the utopian visions underlying CMs are especially critical as they form the basis for the mobilization of individuals and organizations to use the technology and make continuing investments in it. We have shown how public discourse influences the derivation of technological frames in micro-social contexts of organizational and personal use, and how there usually is a gap between the actual use and the utopian visions projected in the discourse and frames. In our study of CM and computerization literature, we have found that five dominant technological frames—productivity; democratization; death of distance; freedom and information rights; and ubiquitous computing—have permeated the utopian visions found in public discourse over a period of four general computerization eras: mainframe, PC, Internet, and ubiquitous computing. Table 1.2 shows the eras, new technology introduced in each era, and corresponding dominant frames. These frames are used as the book's section headings, with papers grouped according to their connection with that particular frame. In this section we begin with a brief description of the eras and their dominant technological frames, followed by a section on each frame with discussions on existing CMs and on sample chapters in this book highlighting that particular frame. In the last chapter of this book, we give a comparative analysis of the dominant frames in each era, concluding with predictions for dominant frames and CMs in the ubiquitous computing era.

Eras of Computerization

In general, CMs have been instrumental in promoting computerization since the 1950s. As technology evolves through the years, new CMs emerge to support adoption and use of particular computer-based systems. We have identified four computerization eras and related CMs. The five technological frames represented by the various CMs discussed in this book are related to the four eras. Some frames such as *productivity* appeared in the CM literature during the mainframe era and are still being used to promote technology use today and into the future in the ubiquitous computing era. Two of the frames—*democratization* and *freedom/information rights*—began during the PC era and became emboldened by the advancement of the Internet era. The *death of distance* and *ubiquitous computing* frames were a direct result of the Internet era and continue to be discussed as an advantage of ICTs in the ubiquitous computing literature.

Technological advancements in the last 30 years have resulted in major cultural shifts in how people in businesses and homes view and use computer technology. Table 1.2 shows the growth of technology and the corresponding changes to CMs from the 1950s to the anticipated future. The mainframe era of the 1950–1970s gave way to the PC era. During the 1980s, IBM and Macintosh manufactured PCs that became popular with both home hobbyists and businesses. Around 1985, the

Table 1.2 Computerization Eras and Dominant Technological Frames

Computerization Era	New Technology	Dominant Technological Frame	Dominant Expected CM Outcome
Mainframe Era 1950s–1970s	Mainframes: ARPANET; Usenet; E-mail	Productivity	Organizational productivity; Better decision making; Improved efficiency
PC Era 1975–1990s	PCs; Unix boxes; PC apps; E-mail	Democratization	Democratization of organizations and society
Internet Era 1985–2005	Internet; Web; Web apps; ICTs; Free/open source software	Death of distance; freedom and information rights	Collaboration across teams, divisions, organizations, and business or social networks; Increased freedom and information rights
Ubiquitous Computing Era 2000 and beyond	PDAs w/ Web access; Mobile phones w/ Web access; BlackBerrys	Anytime, anywhere, anyhow computing and communications	Increased global access to information; Increased awareness of information rights, such as privacy

Internet era began with the creation of the ARPANET, the forerunner of the Internet, resulting in online communities exchanging messages on Usenet groups. By the late 1980s, e-mail was beginning to appear in select scientific and government communities, and more and more people were participating in Usenet groups.

In the 1990s, the advent of the World Wide Web (known as the Web) enabled virtual communities to evolve into social and work worlds such as the F/OSS movement. The Web is the universe of network-accessible information. It began as a networked information project at CERN, where Tim Berners-Lee developed a vision of what the Web could be with a prototype in 1992. The Web has a body of software that enables anyone to easily roam, browse, and contribute to Web sites through the use of hypertext and multimedia software.

The 2000s brought the use of advanced technologies for ubiquitous computing where people can connect to the Web through personal digital assistants (PDAs), mobile phones, and BlackBerry devices (for reading e-mail). As with most social movements, there is an ebb and flow to the support and popularity of CMs and sometimes the movement fades out altogether (Kling & Iacono, 1995). For example, the AI movement popular in the early 1990s has been replaced by intelligent agents, knowbots, and data mining. Meanwhile some movements, like the FSM and the open source software movement (www.opensource.org), have proliferated with the advent of the Web.

Productivity

The notion that computers and other ITs would improve productivity was the earliest vision behind CMs, and has been a continuing *dominant* frame to the present. In the mainframe era, when computing was the province of management information systems (MIS) departments in larger organizations, the emphasis was on organizational productivity through computerization of back-office activities and through automation of production. Computers were expected to substitute for people or to make people more productive by extending their capabilities. Similarly, they were expected to make equipment more productive through optimization of its operating features, performance time, output, and/or extending its life. In the PC era, the dominant frame was related to personnel work on personal and work group productivity and enhancing personal or group capabilities. In the current Internet era, the productivity promise is extended beyond organizations to interorganizational networks such as the value chains involving leading firms like Wal-Mart or Dell, Inc., and the hundreds of suppliers and business partners affiliated with them in bringing products to customers globally.

Vendors and reporters in the business and popular press produce public discourse about the benefits of computerization for decreasing costs or increasing productivity. Executives and others in organizations are often motivated to invest in new computer technology due to the expectations of increased efficiency created by these discourses. Academic research examining the claimed benefits was not conducted until the mid-1980s and until around 2000 was equivocal about whether computers actually improved productivity. Recent research has concluded clearly that it does, although not without considerable caveats regarding organizational complements such as reengineering, skills development, decentralized decision making, and the use of team structures. Despite the uncertainties surrounding the productivity payoff, firms continued to invest until the dot-com bust in 2001. The predominance of "productivity" as an underlying motivation, justification, and organizing frame to explain the success or failure of technological diffusion is nicely illustrated by two chapters in this book, Chapter 3, The Computerization Movement in the U.S. Home Mortgage Industry, and Chapter 4, Visions of the Next Big Thing.

A Long Way to Productivity: Automated Underwriting in Mortgage Banking

Chapter 3, the first chapter in the productivity section, by M. Lynne Markus, Andrew Dutta, Charles W. Steinfield, and Rolf T. Wigand, illustrates the importance of the productivity framing of the automated underwriting CM in the successful diffusion of such systems over a 20-year period. The authors suggest that three interrelated factors influence the success of this CM. One is the technological frames that are reflected in discourse about the innovation. The second is the reflection of these frames in intermediating organizations, such as industry associations, government enterprises, and leading firms in an industry. The third factor is information about the performance of the technology from early adopters and the emergence of a dominant frame resulting in a dominant design for automated underwriting. They show how over a 20-year period, the productivity theme is reflected in standardization efforts and technology development initiatives in mortgage banking. In addition, they show how reports of productivity gains by early adopters set the tone for later diffusion. And they show how the interests of some lenders beyond productivity resulted in rejection of successful technologies despite their productivity benefits. In this way, a gap developed between the utopian expectations of the productivity frame and the actual use of the technology.

They analyze articles from the *Mortgage Banking* journal from the 1980s to the present, providing a fascinating historical account of the diffusion of automated underwriting, how it was driven by the promise of greater productivity, and how it eventually fulfilled the promise. They show how this particular CM was successful due to more than just the economic needs of lenders to decrease loan defaults and reduce processing costs. It was influenced by institutional support in the public discourse of the leading industry association—the Mortgage Bankers Association (MBA) of America—and, eventually, by the technology's performance.

Surprisingly, until the mid-1990s, the mortgage process was mostly a manual, decentralized process, with thousands of mortgage lenders using their own guidelines to review borrowers' credit reports and documentation to determine creditworthiness for mortgage lending. Technology became a topic of interest in the mid-1980s, when there was a national increase in mortgage defaults. Both lenders and government-sponsored enterprises (GSEs) sought automated mortgage-scoring tools in order to more effectively measure borrowers' creditworthiness prior to lending, that is, to increase the productivity of loans.

Historically, the mortgage lending process involved an assessment by local savings and loan associations of borrowers' credit ratings, evaluation of property value, lending money to borrowers to purchase a home, and collection of mortgages. In order to overcome regional differences in mortgage rates, the U.S. government chartered two GSEs (Fannie Mae and Freddie Mac) to buy and securitize mortgages so that there would be a national market that ensured more competitive rates for consumers. Today, these federal corporations play a significant role in how primary lenders evaluate and approve loans because they now publish guidelines by which they will assess the loans they purchase. The MBA, the leading industry association for companies in the real estate finance business, worked closely with the GSEs to specify technology standards for automated underwriting.

Both Freddie Mac and Fannie Mae promoted this approach by developing computer-based systems to perform automated underwriting. By the late 1990s, they were promoting automated underwriting not only to reduce credit risks but also to reduce the costs of loan processing, and more and more underwriters started using these systems. Reports of productivity gains in professional discourse in the mortgage banking industry mobilized users through the *productivity technological frame*. However, there were setbacks along the way, creating a gap between the utopian vision of productivity in automated underwriting and the actual use by mortgage bankers.

To support automated underwriting on a large scale, mortgage lenders needed to supply credit data at the same time that they submitted loan applications for underwriting to Freddie Mac and Fannie Mae. Starting in 1995, these two government agencies provided underwriting software with a fee-based electronic data exchange network for lenders. The lenders reacted with skepticism about the costs and benefits, and were slow to adopt the system. Some lenders viewed the GSE's automated underwriting system as a way to tie them closer to the federal corporations, causing total dependence on the GSE's technology. Furthermore, other lenders were more interested in developing their own computer-based systems since they processed their own loans or sold them to investors (instead of selling them to Fannie Mae or Freddie Mac).

The lenders focused on underwriting systems that could provide them with borrowers' credit ratings at the "point of sale." The advent of the Internet promoted the development of such systems and, by 2002, a company proclaimed that by using the Internet, it could underwrite and fund online in less than four hours from start to finish. This discourse further fueled the technological frame of productivity gains by using computer-based tools and encouraged other lenders to adopt systems that bypassed mortgage brokers and federal corporations' systems.

The battle over the federal corporations' systems and lenders' systems and the attempt at standardization in automated underwriting is ongoing. But the case shows how the productivity theme in the automated underwriting movement changed course over the years, from appealing to national interest to self-interest to accommodating multiple systems. As automated underwriting has moved to the Internet, it appears to be evolving into the standard dominant frame and expectation of "how to process a mortgage loan." The story is still evolving on whether the mortgage banking industry may settle for a dominant design/technological frame or continue with competitive systems.

Productivity and PDAs

A second example of the productivity theme is illustrated in Chapter 4 by Jonathan P. Allen. He shows how various PDA products are proposed, manufactured, and eventually fail before two vendors create PDAs that reach mass diffusion.

Although hailed as tools for personal productivity as part of the early discourse regarding the utopian vision of the PDA CM, the earlier versions of PDAs did not meet users' needs and failed in the marketplace. From 1987 to 1998, three separate industries—PCs, telecommunications equipment, and consumer electronics—considered the PDA to be the "next big thing." During this period, North American and European manufacturers produced 71 versions of consumer-oriented PDAs. These failures are an example of what can happen if technology is not diffused (see Figure 1.2)—new frames evolve based on the failures of the previous models and a new technology or revised technology emerges in the form of the Psion and PalmPilot.

Allen shows how various PDA products were proposed and rejected until two companies, Psion and Palm, developed successful versions. In both cases, the companies resisted the temptation to follow the "frames" that were evident in discourse at that time—that PDAs would increase productivity for busy executives and workers who could not type by introducing pen-based input. Psion developed the Series 3 operating system and included keyboard as opposed to pen-based input. The Series 3 also had application programs and file systems.[1]

Palm Computing developed the PalmPilot as a "connected organizer"—having seamless connectivity with a PC and easy-to-use personal applications such as calendars and address books.[2] Rather than following the vision of the PDA industry that pen-based autonomous control was what executives wanted, Palm thought that a vision of users downloading files from their PDAs to PCs would resonate with busy executives and professionals. In addition, the company modified the strict pen-based input to include pen input one character at a time, using a specially modified alphabet.

Chapter 4 shows how a new technological frame can succeed in the face of a competing industry standard. The vision of the PDA CM was to fill a need of all those left behind by complex PCs, keyboards, and typing skills. The productivity theme in the initial vision for PDA usage promoted PDAs as a way to remain connected to both family and work "anytime, anywhere." Also, the thought was that executives and consumers who were keyboard phobic would be delighted to use the pen-writing devices. However, these initial PDAs failed to become adopted by large masses of consumers and hence some manufacturers gave up on this vision altogether (e.g., failed Newton by Apple). Then Palm and Psion developed their own visions for a PDA, partly based on the failure of the initial PDAs. Both the automated underwriting products and PDA products are still evolving. More recent versions of PDAs include sharing of files with a PC in addition to the ability to send and receive e-mails on a cell phone. The media reports recent trends with teens using cell phones, PDAs, and PCs to remain connected to their friends on a 24/7 basis using instant messaging (IM) from cell phones (Jones, 2005).

We now turn to CMs that serve to promote the acquisition of new technology to democratize groups of people in organizations and society.

Democratization

The second frame that underlies many CMs and shapes their utopian visions is democratization. Democratization is defined in Wikipedia (en.wikipedia.org/wiki/Democratization) as "the transition from authoritarian or semi-authoritarian systems to democratic political systems, where democratic systems are taken to be those approximating universal suffrage, regular elections, a civil society, the rule of law, and an independent judiciary." Democratization with regard to technology refers to the utopian vision that technology will transform organizations and societies into more egalitarian institutions by opening up new forms of communication (bottom up, interactive, two way, peer to peer). This theme occurs in the visions of various Internetworking CMs (Iacono & Kling, 2001) related to democratization within and between organizations, within local communities, and within societies. We show in case studies of specific CMs in several chapters in this volume that a gap exists between the achievement of democratization and reality.

Researchers and users have envisioned the use of computer-mediated communications (CMCs) as a means to facilitate democratic communication due to the pervasiveness of networking in organizations and because of the decontextualization inherent in such communication (Kiesler, Siegel, & McGuire, 1984). Social decontextualization refers to the lack of visual cues as to a person's true identity and facial expressions. For example, in a male-oriented discussion group, a female could "pretend" to be a male by joining an all-male discussion and consequently might be more accepted. As part of this vision, the use of CMCs such as groupware or decision support systems will transform an organization into a more open, democratic setting where there is a flattening of hierarchical boundaries. Research has shown that the use of e-mail in an organization can enable people who are peripheral to become more visible, and lower-level employees to communicate with upper managers more easily (Fountain, 2001; Sproul & Kiesler, 1991). However, adopting

CMC technologies does not guarantee democratization in an organization, as several chapters in this volume illustrate.

Another vision related to democratization, focused around e-mail and the Internet, is the grassroots effort to involve citizens in local government. The technological frame regarding democratization in this area involves communities having direct access to government officials, open access to government information, and easy, instant communication about issues that concern citizens. It is illustrated by the early movements to create electronic city halls such as the Santa Monica Public Information Network in California (Dutton & Guthrie, 1991) and by current e-government projects focused on citizen-government communication and information exchange such as citizens' open access to court schedules and case dispositions via Web site connections.

The e-government CM is one of the emergent Internet CMs that is being promoted in government discourse around the world, with the dominant frame of providing citizens with more access to government information. For example, a five-year study of e-government services (West, 2004) at both the state and federal level showed that in 2004, 56 percent had services that were fully executable online (e.g., no court visit necessary to obtain a document or information), up from 44 percent the previous year. In addition, of the 1,629 Web sites studied, 93 percent had e-mail addresses that the general public can use to request information, up from 91 percent previously. This vision of democratization of information for citizens assumes that people will eagerly use the Internet to access these e-government networks. As we will show with chapters in this section, reality does not always meet the CM visions.

Reinforcement vs. Democratization of Hierarchy

Chapter 6 in this volume, by Anabel Quan-Haase and Barry Wellman, shows that IM and e-mail usage in a heavily networked organization did not democratize the hierarchy as expected, but actually reinforced it. Thus, this shows another gap between a utopian vision and actual use of IM and e-mail in an organization. However, IM did foster trust, collaboration, a community of practice, and commitment to the organization. Quan-Haase and Wellman found that employees of a company called KME used IM for communication whether they were collocated or physically separated.

Thus, IM was used for both local and global communication. Employees used multiple media, often answering an IM and glancing at an e-mail while holding a face-to-face conversation. Even though people were collocated at KME, they preferred IM over face-to-face and telephone contact. Although the utopian vision of the democratization frame indicates that this increase in IM would result in more egalitarian relationships among higher- and lower-level personnel, that, in fact, did not happen at KME. If lower-level IT professionals were working with someone face to face and they received an IM from their supervisor, they responded immediately, whereas IMs from colleagues might be disregarded. This study showed that although democratization was not enabled using IM at KME, it did engender collaborative community and trust within and between departments while at the same time creating information overload and distraction while at work. The authors suggest that hierarchy and roles continue to influence interactions, even in the hyperconnected environment of KME. However, the organization is still more flexible and hyperconnected than a traditional bureaucratic organization.

Reinforcement but Not Democratization of Civic Engagement

In Chapter 7 by John M. Carroll, an example of using the Internet in the small in the Blacksburg Electronic Village (BEV) project is presented. Here the entire community was networked together with the utopian vision that the community would become more civic-minded and community-oriented. The results counter that assumption, showing that people in the Blacksburg community who made use of the Internet for civic purposes tended to already be activists in the community prior to the use of the Internet. Thus it did not change or democratize relationships, but reinforced previously existing ones.

The BEV project was an experimental project established in 1993 and backed by the Clinton Administration's NII initiative. The technological frame associated with this project was that the use of Internet technology would enhance the quality of life for residents of Blacksburg by electronically linking them to each other and to the Internet. It was created as a partnership among the town of Blacksburg, Virginia, the local telecommunications company, and Virginia Tech, and it was sponsored by both state and federal funds. By the early 2000s, adoption and use of the Internet were widespread in Blacksburg.

Carroll and a team of researchers designed an evaluation project to investigate the effects of the adoption of technology on the people of Blacksburg and Montgomery County. They evaluated peoples' use of the network by using a random sample of 870 Montgomery County residential addresses using a ten-item survey to classify the participants. Next they surveyed all participants with a lengthy questionnaire, logged Internet usage with some, and interviewed others. For this chapter, they focused on two key results from the wide range of variables collected: local activism and feelings of belonging. They found that the people in Blacksburg and the surrounding Montgomery County community "who make use of the Internet for civic purposes (for example, people who say they look for news online, or participate in local online groups) tend to be activists in the community (they feel they have ideas to improve the local community, they say they work with others to solve community problems, and so on)." In other words, people who were already connected to civic affairs continued to be involved, while those who were not connected to the community prior to the Internet use did not increase their civic activities. However, those who made use of the Internet for social purposes (e-mailing friends and family) reported a greater sense of community belonging.

The Death of Distance

The third frame that underlies CMs is the "death of distance." It refers to the utopian vision that computers, telecommunications, and various kinds of software tools would overcome the barriers of geography and distance, thereby enabling the virtual equivalent of working collocated. This frame was behind the telecommuting movement of the 1970s and 1980s. Then, the idea was to substitute ICT for transportation (Nilles, Carlson, Gray, & Hanneman, 1976; Nilles, 1983, 1998). Advanced ICT would be used to link headquarters offices in central cities with satellite offices in the suburbs. These offices could be shared by companies and workers and would reduce traffic congestion for cities, lower the cost of office space for companies, and reduce commute time and stress for workers, thereby making them more productive and effective. Governments and business leaders underwrote experiments with telecommuting in major cities throughout the U.S. and consultants made bold predictions and claims about take-up and success. But the movement never really caught on sufficiently to reduce urban traffic congestion to any measurable degree. The experiments also revealed that telecommunication was costly and unreliable; that the activities that could be relocated mainly involved information input or the MIS function; that management showed concerns about worker productivity (how do you know people are working if you can't see them); and that there were serious costs to employees in such remote work, including feelings of isolation and concerns about lack of visibility and therefore opportunities for promotion (Kraemer & King, 1982).

After 1995, when the Internet technology began to flourish, the rhetoric about geographically distributed collaboration changed to terms like CSCW, virtual teams, and online communities. Both academic publications and popular media began discussing and promoting virtual teams throughout the 1990s as more organizations invested in Internet technology and experimented with concepts like process reengineering, self-organizing teams, quality circles, and total quality management. The discourse during this period indicated that virtual teams will make organizations more efficient, will empower employees, and will transform business processes to be more successful (Townsend, DeMarie, & Hendrickson, 1998).

There are several current incarnations of the death of distance frame under work at home, distant/remote work, and distributed work. Each has subtle differences such that the visions appeal to different target markets. "Work at home" is an appeal to urban professionals, small businesses, and certain kinds of office workers who could achieve the ideal integration of work life and home life. It is promoted by housing developers for urban infill housing as well as suburban and exurban housing developments. Housing tracts and entire new communities are being developed that promote this vision, for example, Ladera Ranch in California (Venkatesh, Chen, & Gonzalez, 2003).

In contrast, remote work and distributed work are appealing to companies and office workers, but with important differences. Remote work is similar to the earlier telecommuting appeal whereas distributed work is an appeal to companies with knowledge workers whose expertise is distributed across multiple locations. The idea here is that ICT and collaboration technologies enable firms to bring the right mix of expertise to bear on projects regardless of their location. The promoters here are packaged software companies, computer scientists, and academics who see sales opportunities or who simply buy into the utopian vision because of its affinity with their own style of work.

Failure to Close the Distance Gap in Virtual Collaboration

The death of distance frame is illustrated in Chapter 9, by Sara Kiesler, Wai Fong Boh, Yuqing Ren, and Suzanne Weisband, in which they explore the distributed work CM. The authors examine the role that internetworking and collaboration tools played in a large company with different divisions in various locations around the U.S. The utopian vision was that the firm would be able to link and integrate distributed work groups to pull together the expertise needed for different projects, and that this would uniformly enhance the individual, the distributed groups, and the virtually integrated groups.

They studied the American Institutes for Research (AIR), a successful nonprofit organization that carries out applied research, consulting, and technical services. AIR employs more than 1,000 employees at seven major locations and a number of minor locations. Project teams originate and are managed from one site to perform the work for customers. The data are drawn from a large study of how managers decided to create dispersed projects from 1996 through 2000 (Boh, Ren, Kiesler, & Bussjaeger, 2005). In 1996, the Chief Operating Officer (COO) at AIR read a book on dispersed teamwork and decided to attempt to implement the use of CMC technology to augment the team project management at AIR. He hoped that this would enhance the firm's ability to utilize expertise across the growing firm. However, by 2003, computer-based tools for sharing files and collaborative work spaces were not yet fully developed and so failed to meet the firm's expectations. Managers did not see a strong connection between investments in technology, collaboration, and the bottom line. Contrary to the dominant frame of the virtual teams CM, the COO authorized investments in technology only as they could be demonstrated to support business operations.

The authors conclude that there are two visions of virtual teams—high-tech and low-tech. The high-tech version expects companies to invest in the "state of the art technology" in order to operate with virtual teams. In the low-tech world of AIR, the authors point out that the virtues of collaboration over distance appealed to managers but not necessarily with dependence on technology. For example, AIR had no teams connected by networked communications. Kiesler et al. conclude that the virtual teams rhetoric will continue to evolve and to motivate technology development despite limited achievement of the vision.

In Chapter 9, virtual teams in a low-tech environment breached vast distances by using CMC combined with face-to-face meetings to collaborate. Thus, the technology operates in the background for many users, making the death of distance a kind of reality that does not necessarily include the utopian vision.

Freedom and Information Rights

The fourth frame to emerge is related to freedom and information rights, which have been at the core of the U.S. society since its inception, with the ideology embedded in the U.S. Constitution and the Bill of Rights. Terms such as "freedom of speech" and "freedom of choice" are at the core of our individual liberties as part of being a U.S. citizen. In the U.S. democratic society, many freedoms we experience on a daily basis are taken for granted—vestiges of the free nation in which we live. In other societies people do not have the freedom that is inherent in the U.S. Constitution. The freedom theme is evident in the Internet CMs that foster information privacy and democratization. For example, e-government initiatives foster the freedom of individuals to access public information. This human right to access information to promote equity is also referred to as building and maintaining an "information commons" or public informational sphere (Schuler, 1996).

The freedom frame is instantiated in the FSM (DiBona, Ockman, & Stone, 1999; Williams, 2002), which promotes the freedom to run, copy, distribute, study, change, and improve source code. Free software is defined by the FSF (www.fsf.org) as software that is "free as in freedom, not as in beer" (also known as "libre" or "freedom" software). Richard M. Stallman (www.gnu.org) founded the FSF in 1985 to promote his concept of free software. His essays on the FSF Web site proselytize the importance of all software being free and promote the use of the "copyleft" principle—the copyleft license enables free software to be used, copied, studied, modified, and redistributed. His goal is nothing less than to eliminate proprietary software from the world someday. The FSF beliefs are encoded in the General Public License (GPL) and are based explicitly on the ideals of the American Revolution of 1776 (Elliott & Scacchi, forthcoming). In the GPL, the following definition of "free software" is listed:

> [A] matter of liberty, not price. To understand the concept, you should think of "free" as in "free speech," not as in "free beer." Free software is a matter of the users' freedom to run, copy, distribute, study, change, and improve the software. More precisely, it refers to four kinds of freedom, for the users of the software:
>
> - The freedom to run the program, for any purpose (freedom 0).
> - The freedom to study how the program works, and adapt it to your needs (freedom 1). Access to the source code is a precondition for this.
> - The freedom to redistribute copies so you can help your neighbor (freedom 2).
> - The freedom to improve the program, and release your improvements to the public, so that the whole community benefits (freedom 3).

Unlike other CMs discussed in this book, the FSM assumes that people have access to computing technology and instead promotes a new software development process and licensing concept. This community commons of free software is facilitated by the Internet CM since this enables free software communities to thrive, with contributors working together from all over the world to build, distribute, and maintain "free" software systems.

Although the FSM has been in action since 1985, its counterpart, the open source movement supported by the OSI (www.osi.org) was started in 1998. A group of free software developers decided to promote free software to businesses, changing the name to open source software and including software licenses with fewer restrictions so that companies could more easily combine "free software" with proprietary software. While the two movements differ somewhat in philosophy, their software is often referred to as free and open source software (F/OSS).

As the Internet has flourished and made a big impact on the way people process information, information-rights activists have formed several information rights-oriented CMs related to, and including, the FSM:

- Community networking – To promote universal access to enhance local community-based economic and social development.
- Free/open source software – To advocate the development and use of free/open source software over proprietary software.
- Informational privacy – To protect personal information.

The community networking CM was described in the section on democratization, and Carroll's chapter on the Blacksburg project is a fine example of community networking. The core belief system that has propelled this movement into action is that of universal access to the information/communication infrastructure and the widening panoply of information available over the Internet. The dominant frame is that providing universal access will promote social equity, as in closing the "digital divide," but it is also concerned with building and maintaining a virtual public space. As this space widens, attention is focusing on the informational privacy movement by government and individuals.

The informational privacy movement started in the 1960s with the growth of massive computerized data banks of personal information. Alan Westin explicated the rights ideal in his books, *Privacy and Freedom* (1967) and *Databanks in a Free Society* (Westin & Baker, 1972), providing this definition of informational privacy: " ... the chain of individuals, groups, or institutions to determine for themselves when, how, and to what extent information about them is communicated to others (Westin, 1967)." Through the years it has grown into a powerful movement due to the increasing encroachment of privacy with the commercialization and expansion of the Internet. Identity theft through accessing records on the Internet and stealing credit card information has flourished, with sophisticated hackers accessing online database systems and personal computers.

Information Rights as a Freedom

In Chapter 12, Andrew Clement and Christie Hurrell suggest that the three information rights-oriented CMs listed previously may potentially merge to form a future information rights movement comparable to the emergence of the environmental movement formed from several separate movements. They suggest that although currently fledgling, all three movements will eventually coalesce based on alliances to form one overarching information rights movement. They explore the similarities (and differences) between the nascent information rights movement and the much more fully developed environmental movement.

They first give a historical account of the rise of the environmental movement in North America, starting with the post-World War II period to the present. They trace how the wilderness movement with its emphasis on preserving remote wilderness areas, the campaign to preserve wetlands, and the growing concern for personal and community health all converged to form the environmental movement. They claim that "what unites these three broad areas of environmental concern is their grassroots social and political drive: they were not typically tied to particular power groups or political parties." The environmental movement succeeded in bringing a wide range of disparate advocacy efforts into one unified movement for social reform by forming an agenda that integrated the themes of commons, ecology, and environment. They suggest that this principle could be applied to community networking, F/OSS, and informational privacy to form a new information rights movement.

Clement and Hurrell suggest that the software used in community networking to date includes proprietary, homegrown, and shared, but that there is growing interest in using F/OSS to support this "grassroots" effort. Although the F/OSS movement was not formed around concern for information privacy, the two movements do share a strong and fundamental commitment to the ideal of personal "freedom." Clement concludes that these three CMs all share a focus on human rights issues beyond their focus on computerization. Similar to advocacy organizations in the early stages of the environmental movement, these movements presently work in relative isolation from each other. Drawing on lessons from the environmental movement, he suggests that these three CMs could form a more unified force by developing an integrative conceptual frame centered on their common themes of freedom, commons, and privacy, and by joining forces with non-computer movements such as civil liberties or global justice. This chapter, in addition to its identification of a new and important theme, is a nice illustration of how computerization and other movements might merge and become more powerful influences in society.

Freedom as in Free and Open Software

In Chapter 13, the antecedents for success of the FSM are explicated. Margaret S. Elliott traces the historical growth of this movement and what factors have led to its ongoing success and diffusion into traditional methods of software development. This chapter explores how the ubiquitous computing era facilitates the success of this movement by providing vast opportunities for the spread of the FSM ideology and for global access to the movement's software and articles on free software. The stages of a typical social movement are traced using four stages: social unrest, popular excitement, formalization, and institutionalization. To accommodate the unique aspects of CMs, technology adoption is added to the formalization stage. Once a CM reaches the institutionalization stage, its technology has reached the diffusion stage in organizations and/or society. The FSM has reached the institutionalization stage and its technology is becoming more and more prevalent in businesses and society. For example, the free software Unix-like operating system, Linux, is quite popular in businesses and is known for its high quality and reliability (Dedrick & West, Chapter 16, this volume).

The ultimate utopian vision of Richard M. Stallman (RMS) is to replace proprietary software with free software all over the world. This vision is a driving force for many volunteers who design, create, test, and maintain free software on the many F/OSS development projects posted on Web sites. The FSF promotes the notion of freedom by posting many articles by RMS. In "Why Software Should Not Have Owners" (www.gnu.org/philosophy/why-free.html) he states:

> Society also needs freedom. When a program has an owner, the users lose freedom to control part of their own lives. And above all society needs to encourage the spirit of voluntary cooperation in its citizens. When software owners tell us that helping our neighbors in a natural way is "piracy," they pollute our society's civic spirit. This is why we say that free software is a matter of freedom, not price.

Elliott shows in her chapter that the success of the FSM in institutionalizing the field of F/OSS around the world is largely due to the strong belief system in freedom and free software that members share. In addition, the pervasiveness of being able to communicate and contribute to F/OSS development any time, anywhere in the ubiquitous computing era has contributed to the resounding success of F/OSS projects. However, even though the number of F/OSS projects registered on the SourceForge Web site (sourceforge.net) has almost reached 1 million, there is a gap in the FSM vision and reality. Many people depend on and trust software vendors to maintain software, offer technical support, and customize the software for a fee as the customer requests. While many organizations have adopted F/OSS (especially the Unix-like operating system Linux), the goal of replacing all proprietary software with free software is far-fetched and too difficult to achieve. Consequently, the FSM will most likely proliferate and continue to draw advocates to its cause for many years to come, thereby continually adding to the diffusion of F/OSS technology.

Although ubiquitous computing software development environments are in their nascent stages, some are now being used and promoted by F/OSS developers. For example, the MIT Project Oxygen has a vision of computation that centers on people, not machines. Several technical challenges await, such as the requirement that Oxygen systems must be "pervasive," "embedded," and "nomadic." A nomadic environment refers to the ability of users and computations to move around freely, according to their needs. Software systems will adapt with minimal user intervention and without interruption to services they provide (www.oxygen.lcs.mit.edu/Overview.html).

F/OSS programmers who use the Linux operating system can now easily move from one location to the next by using the Knoppix Linux distribution. While not standard practice in all F/OSS projects, the Knoppix CD paves the way for ubiquitous computing in F/OSS development. The Knoppix distribution CD is a free/open source real-time Linux CD that boots and runs completely from CD. It includes recent Linux software and desktop environments, with several F/OSS programs such as OpenOffice.org and Mozilla as well as hundreds of other F/OSS programs. Users of Knoppix can work on software development on any hardware platform that accepts Linux. This gives F/OSS developers the ability to contribute to F/OSS projects "anytime, anywhere." We now discuss the ubiquitous computing dominant frame and how the vision of "seamless computing anytime, anywhere" does not match up with reality in a study of professional executives using mobile devices.

Ubiquitous Computing

The fifth frame that has more recently evolved and is ongoing in its conceptualization is ubiquitous computing anytime, anywhere. Mark Weiser coined the term "ubiquitous computing" in 1988 at the Computer Science lab at Xerox PARC, Palo Alto, California. He envisioned future computing devices that would become invisible and fade into the background of people's lives (Weiser, 1991). During the period 1988–1994, Xerox PARC built several experimental devices to support this vision in the form of "tabs," "pads," and "boards." Tabs are inch-scale machines that resemble active Post-It notes—the pads are foot-scale ones that are similar to a sheet of paper (or a book or a magazine) and the boards (which are now commercial products) are yard-scale displays that are the equivalent of a blackboard or bulletin board. This research inspired the creation of many ubiquitous computing workshops and conferences.

The ubiquitous computing era promotes a utopian vision and dominant frame that people will be able to connect to other people and computers "anytime, anywhere." The social and the technical aspects of organizational and social life are melded together such that the technology purportedly will disappear into the background of our social lives (Sørensen & Gibson, Chapter 17, this volume). The CM outcomes of this vision are increased global access to information and increased awareness of freedom and information rights such as privacy. The ubiquitous computing movement emphasizes how the acquisition of technology enables one to connect "anytime, anywhere" to business associates, friends, or family with such technology as PDAs (Allen, Chapter 4, this volume) and mobile phones (Sørensen & Gibson, Chapter 17, this volume) but at the same time results in sensitivity to information rights such as privacy.

Researchers, vendors, and magazine writers portray utopian visions of the advantages of being connected all the time, including the elimination of desktop PCs. Futurists predict that people will use "wearable computing," with devices becoming part of clothing connecting people to each other via wireless technology. In the U.S. and Europe, mobile phones have become increasingly popular, providing access to the Internet, IM, digital cameras, computer games, video clips, and execution of Java programs (Mattern, 2002). Handheld BlackBerry devices (www.rim.com) are becoming popular with business executives and university professors for constant e-mail access (Sørensen & Gibson, Chapter 17, this volume). As with other CMs, the vision of the ubiquitous computing CM does not always match up to reality in organizations, as shown in the study of business executives' use of mobile devices in (Sørensen & Gibson, Chapter 17, this volume).

Connecting "Anytime, Anywhere": An Opaque Reality for Business Executives

In Chapter 17, Carsten Sørensen and David Gibson investigate the extent to which the vision of ubiquitous computing is a reality for a group of sixteen professionals who use mainly mobile ICTs on a routine basis as an integral part of their work. Their study showed that all the core ICTs did not in fact disappear as in Weiser's original ubiquitous computing vision but instead proved a stable and important aspect of working life, such as the mobile phone. Geographical mobility was a significant aspect of the daily existence of most of those interviewed.

The interviewees were highly skilled and educated professionals, selected as a representative sample of modern work life with advanced use of ICTs. Other indications that the participants were part of a networked society were that some had broadband Internet access at home, some were globally mobile, and others spent 80 percent of their time working in clients' offices (increasing the demands for ICTs). The theme of the interviews was based on the day-to-day activities and use of ICT, how the ICT supported their work, and their opinions regarding acceptance of mobile and ubiquitous support. The questions generally focused on workplace technologies such as e-mails, workflows, database systems, desktop computers, laptops, enterprise resource planning computer-based systems, PDAs, mobile phones, pagers, etc.

The authors' results showed that the two main barriers for widespread mobile and ubiquitous support were bandwidth and battery lifetime. For example, two interviewees were from financial institutions that require broadband networked PCs in order to work at real-time speeds. Others complained about low battery life times and that depending on mobile devices required constant concern for adequate battery power. For example, a pediatric surgeon spoke about the importance of her pager's battery power: "The battery runs out when you're in the middle of some emergency and they can't get to you." The empirical data from this study clearly suggest that the disappearance of ubiquitous computing devices into the background as smooth seamless support is not happening yet in professional executive environments.

The surprising conclusion was that the PDA was presented by the interviewees as a topic of failed adoption due to issues such as infrastructure standardization and poor usability because of short battery life. They concluded that one of the most promising technologies is the wireless e-mail client, like BlackBerry (www.rim.com), which allows busy professionals to check and send e-mail while on the move. The basic conclusion from this study is that the ubiquitous computing vision of "computing anytime, anywhere" is still an opaque reality.

Conclusions

As the foregoing review of the dominant frames underlying CMs has shown, CMs are an important part of the real-world diffusion of computing innovations. They seem to be necessary to motivate diffusion and use because computer-based systems have historically been complex and difficult to use. We have shown that utopian visions appear in the ideology surrounding all CMs. These visions may not be realized even though the technology may become diffused. Alternatively, visions may become reformulated even though the underlying technology is similar. Subsequent movements may develop more refined visions that appeal to different audiences and also take advantage of newer technologies that overcome the limits and failures of earlier technologies.

By studying the emerging ubiquitous computing technologies from the CM perspective, one can explore the power of the utopian predictions and the true impact of ubiquitous computing devices on the melding of social and work life. Weiser (1991) suggested that ubiquitous computing devices should "disappear" into the background and become invisible in such a way that the work of everyday life can become indistinguishable from them. As these devices "disappear," people can focus on true organizational goals. However, researchers have shown that this vision is not yet a reality (Sørensen & Gibson, Chapter 17, this volume). In the final chapter in this book we will consider the lessons learned from earlier CMs, plus the emerging lessons from new CMs related to early technologies of the ubiquitous computing era to develop generalizations about the likely diffusion, dominant frames, and outcomes of the ubiquitous computing era.

Endnotes

1. Psion PLC was founded in Britain in the early 1980s as a software company, but shifted its focus in the late 1980s to pocket-sized computers for business executives. In 1991, it released the Series 3 pocket-sized computer, which was a success.
2. Palm Computing was founded in 1992 and its first products were application software for PDA handwriting recognition and desktop connectivity. However, its software business did not flourish so it decided to develop its own version of a PDA in 1996. The PalmPilot became one of the fastest-selling computing products of all time.

References

Benford, R. D., & Snow, D. A. (2000). Framing process and social movements: An overview and assessment. *Annual Review of Sociology*, 26, 611–39.

Blumer, H. (1969). Social movements. In B. McLaughlin (Ed.), *Studies in social movements: A social psychological perspective* (pp. 8–29). New York: Free Press.

Boh, W. F., Ren, Y., Kiesler, S., & Bussjaeger, R. (2005). Expertise utilization in the geographically dispersed organization. Working Paper. Pittsburgh, PA: CMU.

Dasgupta, S., Granger, M., & McGarry, N. (2002). User acceptance of e-collaboration technology: An extension of the technology acceptance model. *Group Decision and Negotiation*, 11, 87–100.

Davis, F. D. (1989). Perceived usefulness, perceived ease of use, and user acceptance of information technology. *MIS Quarterly*, 13(3), 319–339.

DiBona, C., Ockman, S., & Stone, M. (Eds.). (1999). *Open sources: Voices from the open source revolution*. Sebastopol, CA: O'Reilly & Associates Inc.

Dutton, W. H., & Guthrie, K. (1991). An ecology of games: The political construction of Santa Monica's public electronic network. *Informatization and the Public Sector*, 1(4), 1–24.

Elliott, M., & Scacchi, W. (forthcoming). Mobilization of software developers: The free software movement. *Information, Technology, and People*.

Fountain, J. E. (2001). *Building the virtual state: Information technology and institutional change*. Washington, DC: Brookings Institution Press.

Gao, P. (2005). Using actor-network theory to analyse strategy formulation. *Information Systems Journal*, 15, 255–275.

Goffman, E. (1974). *Frame Analysis: An Essay on the Organization of the Experience*. New York: Harper Colophon.

Iacono, S., & Kling, R. (1996). Computerization movements and tales of technological utopianism. In R. Kling (Ed.), *Computerization and controversy: Value conflicts and social change* (2nd ed., pp. 85–105). San Diego, CA: Academic Press.

Iacono, S., & Kling, R. (2001). Computerization movements: The rise of the Internet and distant forms of work. In J. Yates & J. Van Maanen (Eds.), *Information technology and organizational transformation: History, rhetoric, and practice* (pp. 93–136). Thousand Oaks, CA: Sage Publications.

Jones, T. Y. (2005, June 23). Teens Get The Message. *Los Angeles Times*, p. A1.

Kiesler, S., Siegel, J., & McGuire, T. M. (1984). Social psychological aspects of computer-mediated communication. *American Psychologist*, 39(10), 1123–1134.

King, J. L, Kraemer, K. L., Gurbaxani, V., McFarland, F. W., Raman, K. S., & Yap, C. S. (1994). Institutional factors in information technology innovation. *Information Systems Research*, 5(2), 39–169.

Kling, R., & Iacono, S. (1988). The mobilization of support for computerization: The role of computerization movements. *Social Problems*, 35(3), 226–242.

Kling, R., & Iacono, S. (1995). Computerization movements and the mobilization of support for computerization. In S. L. Star (Ed.), *Ecologies of knowledge: Work and politics in science and technology* (pp. 119–153). Albany, NY: State University of New York Press.

Kling, R., & Scacchi, W. (1982). The web of computing: Computer technology as social organization. *Advances in Computers*, 21, 1–90.

Kraemer, K. L., & King, J. L. (1982). Telecommunications/transportation substitution and energy conservation. *Telecommunications Policy*, Part I, 6(1), 39–59 and Part II, 6(2), 87–99.

Lamb, R., & Kling, R. (2003). Reconceptualizing users as social actors in information systems research. *MIS Quarterly*, 27(2), 197–235.

Mander, J. (1991). *In the absence of the sacred: The failure of technology and the survival of the Indian nations*. San Francisco: Sierra Club Books.

Mattern, F. (2002). Ubiquitous computing: Scenarios for an informatized world. Working Paper. Zurich: ETH.

McCarthy, J., & Zald, M. (1977). Resource mobilization and social movements: A partial theory. *American Journal of Sociology*, 82(6), 1212–1241.

Nilles, J. (1983). *Micros and modems: Telecommunicating with personal computers*. Upper Saddle River, NJ: Prentice Hall.

Nilles, J. (1998). *Managing telework: Strategies for managing the virtual workforce*. New York: John Wiley & Sons.

Nilles, J., Carlson, F. R., Jr., Gray, P., & Hanneman, G. J. (1976). The *telecommunications-transportation tradeoff: Options for tomorrow*. New York: John Wiley & Sons.

Orlikowski, W. J. (1992). The duality of technology: Rethinking the concept of technology in organizations. *Organization Science*, 3(3), 398–427.

Orlikowski, W. J. (2000). Using technology and constituting structures: A practice lens for studying technology in organizations. *Organization Science*, 11(4), 404–428.

Orlikowski, W. J., & Gash, D. (1994). Technological frames: Making sense of information technology in organizations. *ACM Transactions on Information Systems*, 12, 174–207.

Rogers, E. (2005). *Diffusion of Innovations*. (5th ed.). New York: The Free Press.

Schuler, D. (1996). New community networks, wired for change. Retrieved December 5, 2005, from www.scn.org/ncn

Snow, D. A., & Benford, R. O. (1988). Ideology, frame resonance, and participant mobilization. *International Social Movement Research*, 1, 197–218.

Snow, D. A., & Benford, R. O. (1992). Master frames and cycles of protest. In A. D. Morris & C. M. Mueller (Eds.), *Frontiers in social movement theory* (pp. 133–135). New Haven, CT: Yale University Press.

Snow, D. A., Rochford, E. B., Worden, S. K., and Benford, R. O. (1986). Frame alignment processes, micromobilization, and movement participation. *American Sociological Review*, 51, 464–481.

Sproul, L., & Kiesler, S. (1991). *Connections: New ways of working in the networked organization*. Cambridge, MA: MIT Press.

Thompson, V. A. (1965). Bureaucracy and innovation. *Administrative Science Quarterly*, 10(1), 1–20.

Tornatzky, L. G., & Fleischer, M. (1990). *The processes of technological innovation*. Lexington, MA: Lexington Books.

Townsend, A. M., DeMarie, S. M., & Hendrickson, A. R. (1998). Virtual teams: Technology and the workplace of the future. *The Academy of Management Executive*, 12(3), 17–29.

Useem, B., & Zald, M. (1982). From pressure group to social movement: Organizational dilemmas of the effort to promote nuclear power. *Social Problems*, 30(2), 144–156.

Venkatesh, A., Chen, S., & Gonzalez, V. M. (2003). A study of a Southern California wired community: Where technology meets social utopianism. Working Paper. Irvine, CA: Center for Research on Information Technology and Organizations, UC Irvine.

Venkatesh, V. (2000). Determinants of perceived ease of use: Integrating control, intrinsic motivation, and emotion into the technology acceptance model. *Information Systems Research*, 11(4), 42–365.

Venkatesh, V., & Morris, M. G. (2003). User acceptance of information technology: Toward a unified view. *MIS Quarterly*, 27(3), 425–478.

Weiser, M. (1991, September). The computer for the 21st century. *Scientific American*, 94–104.

West, D. M. (2004). State and federal e-government in the United States. Providence, RI: Center for Public Policy, Brown University. Retrieved from www.insidepolitics.org

Westin, A. (1967). *Privacy and freedom*. New York: Atheneum.

Westin, A., & Baker, M. A. (1972). *Databanks in a free society: Computers, record keeping and privacy.* New York: Times Books.

Williams, S. (2002). *Free as in freedom: Richard Stallman's crusade for free software*. Sebastopol, CA: O'Reilly & Associates.

Zhu, K., Kraemer, K. L., & Xu, S. (2006). The process of assimilation by firms in different countries: A technology diffusion perspective. *Management Science*, 52(10), 1557–1576.

Chapter 2

Reprints of Seminal Research Papers on Computerization Movements

*Paper #1: Computerization Movements and the Mobilization of Support for Computerization**

Rob Kling
University of California, Irvine

Suzanne Iacono
University of California, Irvine

Reprint from *Social Problems*, 35(3) (June 1988): 226–243 as "The Mobilization of Support for Computerization: The Role of Computerization Movements."

*Mark Poster helped clarify some of our ideas about ideologies, and Kenneth Kraemer helped explore the relationships between utopian computing ideologies and ideologies of utopian urban developments. Leigh Star and Karen Wieckert helped us clarify the overall analysis. This research was supported under NSF Grants DCS 81-17719 and IRI8709613.

Abstract

This chapter describes how computerization is the byproduct of loosely organized movements rather than simply an industry selling products to an eager market. We briefly examine five "computerization movements"—urban information systems, artificial intelligence, office automation, instructional computing, and personal computing. These computerization movements share key ideological beliefs, which we also characterize. The main alternative normative analyses of appropriate computerization come from counter movements whose interests intersect with some special form of computerization: in workplaces, around intrusions on personal privacy, and on consumer rights. These counter movements articulate how computing should be balanced with competing values such as good jobs, fair information practices, and consumer control. We argue that these counter movement views do not add up to a coherent alternative humanistic vision for appropriate computerization.

Introduction

There is a major mobilization for computerization in many institutional sectors in the United States. Computerization is a social process for providing access to and support for computer equipment to be used in diverse activities such as teaching, accounting, writing, and designing circuits. Computerization entails social choices about the levels of appropriate investment and control over equipment and expertise, as well as choices of equipment. Many organizations are adopting computing equipment rapidly, while their understanding of how to organize positive forms of social life around it develops more slowly. However, the most fervent advocates of computerization see the actual pace of computerization in schools, offices, factories, and homes is too slow (Papert, 1980; Feigenbaum & McCorduck, 1983; Yourdon, 1986; also see Kaplan, 1983).

Why is the United States rapidly computerizing? One common answer is that computer-based technologies are adopted only because they are efficient economic substitutes for labor or other technologies (Simon, 1977). Rapid computerization is simply a byproduct of cost-effective computing technologies. A variant of this answer views computerization as an efficient tool through which monopoly capitalists control their suppliers and markets, and by which managers tighten their control over workers and the labor process (Braverman, 1975; Mowshowitz, 1976; Shaiken, 1985).

A second answer focuses on major epochal social transformations and argues that the United States is shifting from a society where industrial activity dominates to one in which information processing dominates (Bell, 1979). Computer-based technologies are simply "power tools" for "information workers" or "knowledge workers" as drill presses are power tools for machinists (Strassman, 1985).

The market assumptions of these common answers have also shaped the majority of social studies of computerization (for a detailed review of the empirical studies of computerization, see Kling, 1980, 1987). These studies focus on computerization in particular social settings that range in scale from small groups and workplaces (Shaiken, 1986) through single organizations (Kling, 1978; Kling & Iacono, 1984) to comparative multi-organizational studies (Laudon, 1974, 1986). These studies of computerization usually ignore the ways that participants in the settings under study develop beliefs about what computing technologies are good for and how they should organize and use them (see, for example, Attewell & Rule, 1984).

During the last 15 years we have conducted systematic studies of computerization in diverse organizations: banks (Kling, 1978; Kling, 1983), engineering firms and insurance companies (Kling & Scacchi, 1982), manufacturing firms (Kling & Iacono, 1984), public agencies (Kling, 1978), and schools (Kling, 1983, 1986). We have also been participant observers of four specific computerization movements: artificial intelligence (1966–1974), computer-based education (1974–1988), office automation (1975–1988), and personal computing (1983–1988). And we have also observed several computerization efforts at our home university as participants, first-hand observers, or coordinators of an assessment team.

On the basis of this research and experience, we believe computerization in the United States is not simply a product of economic forces directed toward progress and efficiency. A wide variety of noneconomic factors must be considered to fully understand the process of rapid computerization that has occurred in Western industrialized societies. The adoption, acquisition, installation, and operation of computer-based systems is often much more socially charged than the adoption and operation of other equipment, like telephone systems, photocopiers, air conditioners, or elevators. We have observed that participants are often highly mobilized to adopt and adapt to particular computing arrangements through collective activities. We have recently begun to see that these collective activities take place both outside and within computerizing organizations, and they share important similarities with various other social, professional, intellectual, and scientific movements. We have observed that strongly committed advocates often drive computerization projects. They develop and encourage ideologies that interpret what computing is good for and how people in these projects should manage and organize access to computing. They usually import these ideologies from discourses about computerization external to the computerizing organization (Kling & Iacono, 1984).

In this paper, we examine how specialized “computerization movements” (CMs) advance computerization in ways that go beyond the effects of promotion by the industries that produce and sell computer-based technologies and services. Our main thesis is that computerization movements communicate key ideological beliefs about the links between computerization and a preferred social order which help legitimize computerization for many potential adopters. These ideologies also set adopters’ expectations about what they should use computing for and how they should organize access to it. In this paper we focus our attention primarily upon the character of the computerization movements and their organizing ideologies.

We describe five specific computing technologies as the focus of computerization movements: urban information systems, artificial intelligence, computer-based education, office automation, and personal computing. These specific CMs, along with movements organized around other computing technologies, form a general computerization movement. There is a core ideology that supports the general CM and there are groups whose world views balance the pursuit of the most advanced computing technologies with alternative social values. Computerization is a process deeply embedded in social worlds that extend beyond the microrealities of any particular organization or setting. In this paper we examine the character of CMs in the hope that our analysis will stimulate new lines of inquiry and more complete analyses.

Computerization Movements

Sociologists have used the concept "movement" to study many different kinds of collective phenomena. The most common term found in this literature is "social movement," often used in a generic way to refer to movements in general. But sociologists also have written about professional movements (Bucher & Strauss, 1961), artistic movements, and scientific movements (Aronson, 1984; Star, forthcoming). From the diverse ways sociologists have used the concept, we found Blumer's (1969:8) general definition most helpful for our analysis: Social movements are "collective enterprises to establish a new order of life." This is an inclusive definition that allows us to consider elements relevant to computerization that other, narrower conceptions would rule out. We also found the work of Zald and his colleagues (McCarthy & Zald, 1977; Zald & Berger, 1978) helpful in that it allows us to consider social forms that are both highly and loosely organized as part of computerization movements.

Computerization movements (CMs) are a kind of movement whose advocates focus on computer-based systems as instruments to bring about a new social order. The mobilizing ideologies of computerization counter-movements (CCMs) oppose certain modes of computerization, which their advocates view as bringing about an inappropriate social order. We will examine five CMs, some CCMs, and their mobilizing ideologies in the next sections. Various scholars who write about movements emphasize the potential importance of activist entrepreneurs who also help drive movements through books, speeches, and other actions. Such activists, who write for broad national audiences, but who do not belong to a particular movement organization, play an important part in the computerization movements we describe here.

"Movements" serves as theoretical constructs. Our descriptions that "people join movements," "people speak for movements," "movements hold a particular ideology," or "one movement is a wing of a second, general movement," and similar attributions are conveniently concise ways of describing much more complicated and varied collective actions.

We also find two distinctions made by Blumer (1969) especially helpful for our analysis. First, Blumer distinguished between "reform" and "revolutionary" movements. The ideologies of revolutionary movements emphasize changing key social relations throughout a social order, whereas reform movements focus on changing a restricted set of social relations. Blumer also distinguished between "specific" and "general" movements. Specific movements are the various wings or submovements of a broader, general movement. Many movements, like those that advance feminism, Eastern religions, civil rights, quantification in the sciences, or computerization, are heterogeneous. The distinction between specific movements and general movements helps us characterize the relationships between distinct wings of a larger movement.

One theme in our discussion of computerization and the specific movements that help produce it is the importance of seeing how local practices and concerns, that is, in the workplace, school, or corporation, are linked to these external developments. By using Blumer's concepts of general and specific movements, we want to draw attention to how similar conceptions about modes of computerization found across many organizations or social settings might be understood.

Few social analyses of computing have examined the mobilizing ideologies that local advocates employ. Few studies suggest that local advocates develop approaches to computerization through participating in CMs that extend outside of their home organizations (see literature reviews by Kling, 1980, and by Attewell & Rule, 1984). People become aware of modes of computerization through the activities and byproducts of CMs: advocates, public speeches and written works, popular stories, television shows, and magazine articles (*Time* magazine became an agent for a CM when it named the computer the "Machine of the Year" for 1982).

Computerization movements are based upon collaborations of participants with diverse interests. In the case of computer-based education, for example, the mass media, parents, and teachers play critical roles in mobilizing support for the spread of computers in classrooms. Instructional computing researchers also stimulate interest in the potentials of new technologies (Taylor, 1980). Local organizations such as school boards and PTAs discuss policies and the practical implications of obtaining resources to implement such concepts as "computer literacy" in the curriculum. Moreover, the ways in which the promises of computer-based education are characterized are similar in many schools. Expert advocates, such as Seymour Papert (1979), have advanced influential analyses that portray "powerful computer systems" in schools as an equality-producing technology, sure to be successful where other technologies and other educational reform strategies have failed.

We (Kling & Iacono, 1984) examined how some managers mobilized support for a complex inventory control system by having employees attend indoctrination sessions sponsored by a professional association. Kaplan (1983) examined the ways that arguments about a "lag" in the rate of adoption and sophistication of medical computing technologies permeated the professional medical computing literature between 1950 and 1980. Laudon's (1974) analysis of computerization in police and social service agencies linked those efforts to professional reform movements of the Progressive era, a link he himself did not pursue in subsequent research (Laudon, 1986).

Some CM participants represent themselves, while others represent their organizations. For example, computer scientists and researchers develop careers as "experts" in a certain computer-based technology and become associated with specific CMs. Other participants, such as consultants and computer users, may have temporary job assignments that attach them to a particular computer-based technology.

Some participants' groups may belong to only one or two CMs. For instance, parents and teachers may participate in the computer-based education CM; materials specialists who are interested in automated inventory control systems may participate in a special "Material Requirements Planning movement" (Kling & Iacono, 1984); urban planners interested in quantitative simulations may participate in the urban information systems movement. Participants in each of these CMs may care little about other modes of computerization. Journalists and news reporters, on the other hand, have become central to the mobilization of computing in general as collaborators providing public exposure to CM advocates. Public forums, trade shows, school board meetings, and similar events enhance interactions among participant groups.

Both specific CMs and the general CM have grown as a result of these interactions. The most active participants in a CM advocate computerization in addition to using computer-based systems. The most active CM participants try to persuade mass audiences and whole professions to computerize in a particular way. CM activists may not identify with the computer industry, as was true for the first personal computer hobbyists (Levy, 1984). By the mid-1980s, CM activists could be found in many institutional sectors of North American economies. They were predominantly middle and upper class professionals.

The main alternative to CMs as explanations of sources of beliefs about computerization and support for adopting new technologies is an "industrial model," which focuses upon the actions of manufacturers and vendors in the computer industry to stimulate sales through advertising and other means. Consumers (including computer-using organizations) buy and use computer hardware and software. Computerization is seen as simply the byproduct of collective actions in markets. The Marxist variant of this market explanation focuses upon the owners and managers of private firms as key agents who adopt systems to increase their profits and control over workers (Noble, 1985). In the next section, we illustrate how five CMs are organized such that they are not merely subsumed within a market. While vendors and various computer users clearly play important roles in stimulating interest in computerization and in shaping the technologies in use, we believe other forms of collective activity—what we call computerization movements (CMs)—also shape expectations and stimulate demand that market analyses ignore.

Five Specific Computerization Movements

Here we describe five specific computerization movements to illustrate how the collective activities of each CM include the development of a mobilizing ideology and organized activity to promote it. These, along with other CMs we do not examine, form a general CM.[1] We examine key ideological elements of these CMs in the next section.

Urban Information Systems

Urban information systems process data about the activities of people in local government jurisdictions, the services they receive, and the internal operations of the local governments. These include systems to support tax collection, police operations, municipal libraries, and urban planning. Support for urban information systems was continuous with progressive reform movements that sought to professionalize local government administration in the early part of the century (Laudon, 1974). Local governments that have pursued these reforms are disproportionately likely to adopt computer-based applications (Danziger, et al., 1982). The urban information systems CM is a relatively low profile movement that forms one segment of a larger professional reform movement to "take politics out of government operations." Its adherents conceive of computerization as fostering government by skilled professionals instead of political appointees and bringing the purported rationality and efficiency of business to governmental operations.

Urban information systems activists have employed associations for local government officials and professionals as movement organizations. Professional organizations for tax assessors, finance officers, and other administrators have been strong supporters of computerization within their areas of expertise. Urban planners, social service professionals, and computer specialists have also found organized support for their computer interests within the Urban and Regional Information Systems Association, which has held annual national conferences since the 1960s. Other professional associations, such as the International City Managers Association, provide information and staff support to foster automation in local governments.

During the 1960s, the federal government stimulated the growth of urban information systems through a wide variety of grants: the U.S. Department of Housing and Urban Development supported planning and social services (Kling, 1978), the Department of Transportation for transportation planning, the Law Enforcement Assistance Administration for police systems, and Housing and Urban Development for several massive demonstration projects (Kraemer & King, 1978). Though federal funding for specific urban projects has been substantially reduced since the late 1960s, urban governments now support their own information systems, which have become embedded in the operations of many departments, especially tax collection, finance, police, welfare, and planning (Danziger et al., 1982). The urban information systems movement is today highly institutionalized.

Artificial Intelligence

The belief that computer-based technologies can be programmed to "think" about complex cognitive tasks is the central tenet held by enthusiasts of artificial intelligence (Turkle, 1984). Early conceptions of artificial intelligence (AI) were framed within an abstract scientific discourse, emphasizing the formal modeling of different domains of knowledge or the study and simulation of human cognitive processes. More recently, some AI enthusiasts have replaced abstract models of universal cognitive processes with the social construct of "expert" systems (Feigenbaum & McCorduck, 1983).

In one of the most enthusiastic accounts, Feigenbaum and McCorduck (1983) assert that almost no meaningful intellectual work will be possible in the "the world of our children" that does not depend upon knowledge-based (e.g., AI) systems. This idea, a controversial one within academic computer science, argues for a vision of the world its proponents hope others will help them construct. Public proselytizing for AI, so conceived, has transformed it from a technological-scientific movement into a CM.

AI spread as a scientific movement within the computer science profession itself. In the 1960s and 1970s interest in AI was focused around the *Artificial Intelligence Journal* and the triennial International Joint AI Conference, originally organized by the secret Artificial Intelligence

Council. More recently, a "special interest group" on Artificial Intelligence (SIGART) within the Association for Computing Machinery and the American Association of Artificial Intelligence (with its monthly publication, *The AI Magazine*) has been established.

Large scale AI research began in the early 1960s under sponsorship of the Advanced Research Projects Agency of the Department of Defense, although other military agencies and the National Science Foundation also supported some of this initial research. This funding was used to create major laboratories at a handful of universities and research institutes. In the late 1970s AI became commercialized as established industrial firms such as Schlumberger and General Motors made substantial investments (Winston & Prendergast, 1984). AI specialty firms emerged along with expert systems and practical natural language processing. In the 1980s artificial intelligence was transformed into a CM as the mainstream business magazines (e.g., *Fortune, Business Week*) began to aggressively promote a fantasy definition of powerful and accessible AI being "here today."

Media accounts usually describe the value of current technologies in terms of their potential capabilities. They often exaggerate their level of development, the quality of product engineering, and the extent to which they have been adopted. They have also exaggerated the attributes of the few commercial applications that do exist. They suggest that these systems "think" like people rather than simply performing the symbolic manipulations on formal representations of the tasks usually performed by people. The American press often promotes AI in sensationalist terms (cf. "Artificial Intelligence," 1984; Applegate & Day, 1984). A recent and representative example appeared on the cover of the February 15, 1988 issue of *Insight on the News*. It heralded its cover story about AI with: "See machines think. Think, machine, think. The world of artificial intelligence." More accurate stories sometimes appear in magazines and newspapers, but they are less common than the sensationalized stories. Despite sensational claims in the press, none of the higher performance AI systems, with the exception of a particular checkers-playing program, has "learned" to modify its behavior, let alone learned the way that humans do.

Computer-Based Education

Computer-based education includes both computer-assisted instruction programs that interact with students in a dialogue and a broader array of educational computer applications such as simulations or instruction in computer programming (see, for example, Taylor, 1980). There is a major national push for extended application of computer-based education at all educational levels. For example, in the mid-1980s several private colleges and universities required all of their freshmen students to buy a specific kind of microcomputer, and others invested heavily in visions of a "wired campus." There was also a major push to establish computer literacy and computer science as required topics in the nation's elementary and secondary schools.

Computer-based education has been promoted with two different underlying ideologies in primary and secondary schools (Kling, 1983). Some educators argue that computer-based instructional approaches can help fulfill the traditional values of progressive education: the stimulation of intellectual curiosity, initiative, and democratic experiences. For example, Cyert (1984) has argued that computerized universities are qualitatively different than traditional universities: college students with microcomputers in their dorm rooms will be more stimulated to learn because they will have easy access to instructional materials and more interesting problems to solve. Papert (1979) argues that in a new computer-based school culture, children will no longer simply be taught mathematics; rather they will learn to be mathematicians. These visions portray an enchanted social order transformed by advanced computing technologies. Other advocates are a bit less romantic, but not less enthusiastic. For example, Cole (1972: 143) argues:

> Because of ... the insatiable desire of students for more and more information at a higher level of complexity and more sophisticated level of utilization ... more effective means of communication must be used ... computers can provide a unique vehicle for this transmission.

Others emphasize a labor-market pragmatism that we label "vocational matching" (Kling, 1983). In this view, people will need computer skills, such as programming, to compete in future labor markets and to participate in a highly automated society; a responsible school will teach some of these skills today. Advocates of computer-based education promote a utopian image of computer-using schools as places where students learn in a cheerful, cooperative setting and where all teachers can be supportive, enthusiastic mentors (Kling, 1986).

The computer-based education movement is not a well-organized national movement. It is far more diffuse and localized than other CMs. In some regions, such as the San Francisco Bay Area, consortia of teachers who are interested in computer-based instruction have formed local movement organizations. At the university level, the Apple Computer Company has formed a consortium of faculty from schools that have adopted Apple computers on a major scale. While this movement organization is linked to a particular vendor, its participants advance a more general vision of computer-based education. Some magazines, such as *The Computer Teacher*, also promote the movement.

Regional conferences usually hosted by schools of education in state universities are held for school teachers and administrators interested in computer-based education.

Academic researchers have been developing instructional courseware for primary and secondary schools since the 1960s. However, such products only became viable when computing equipment costs declined with the advent of microcomputers. By the 1980s, the promotion of computer-based education surged substantially. On one hand, there was growing public belief that public schools were having chronic problems in educating children. On the other, the personal computer industry was reducing the prices of basic equipment and promoting educational applications. Steve Jobs, co-founder of Apple Computer Corporation, lobbied hard and visibly to receive tax advantages by giving a free Apple IIe microcomputer to each public school district.

One microcomputer for a school of 500 students has little educational value, but the industry's marketing efforts and press promotion stimulated public interest in educational computing. Popular literature stresses the capabilities of equipment, ignoring the lack of high quality courseware and inadequate teacher training in computer use (Kling, 1983). Many parents are concerned that their children must be exposed to computers in school though they know little at all about the details of computerized education.

The computer-based education movement received a symbolic boost in the spring of 1983 when the President's Commission on Excellence in Education released an urgent report that recommended that one semester of "computer science" be added to high school graduation requirements. This report is simply one high profile example of many local activities throughout the nation, much as the mobilization for the Equal Rights Amendment was one national level activity that captured the sentiments of many local variants of the woman's movement. In the 1980s there has been continuous ferment at state and local levels with coalitions of administrators, teachers, and parents banding together to lobby for various computer-based education programs in the public schools.

Office Automation

In the 1950s and early 1960s, "office automation" was synonymous with the introduction of computer-based technologies in offices—batch information systems in that period. Today, office automation (OA) is a diffuse term that usually connotes the use of text-oriented computer-based technologies in offices.

OA technologies have two different kinds of roots. Stand-alone word processors evolved from magnetic card and magnetic tape typewriters. The organizational side of these office technologies evolved from kinds of secretarial work and the administrative services departments that commonly controlled organization-wide secretarial pools. The second root is computer systems that tied together text processing and electronic mail along with general-purpose computing capabilities (e.g., workstations). These differences in technology are becoming less significant since specialized word processors are increasingly marketed with a wider array of information-handling functions. However, the social worlds that support these technologies still differ, even though they overlap.

Visionaries of automated offices used the term "office of the future" (Uhlig et al., 1979) as one of their major rallying points. An "office of the future" could never be built since there is no fixed future as a reference point for these technologies. However, a more prosaic conception lies beneath this vision: a terminal on every desk which provides text processing, mail, calendar and file handling, communications, and other computing capabilities with a flexible interface. The scenarios emphasize the deployment of equipment, while OA advocates portray social relations as cheerful, cooperative, relaxed, and efficient—better jobs in better environments (Giuliano, 1982; Strassman, 1985).

These scenarios gloss the realities of worklife in a highly automated office. Some office automation has led to deskilling and highly pressured jobs while work has been upskilled in other offices (Iacono & Kling, 1987). More seriously, the clerical workforce is likely to retain jobs near the bottom of the American occupational structure in terms of pay, prestige, and control of working conditions. This is true even if the content of clerical jobs requires vastly more complex computer-related skills because most clerical jobs specialize in less discretionary delegated work (Iacono & Kling, 1987). The changes in professional work in automated offices are less clear; but it is clear that professionals cannot count on working with ample resources in a cooperative, cheerful environment (Kling, 1987). Computerization is a complex social and technical intervention into the operations of an organization. Conventional CM ideology emphasizes the power of new equipment and downplays the kinds of social choices that can allow powerful equipment to facilitate better jobs. When journalists criticize OA, it is often because the equipment does not deliver the miracles promised by the more enthusiastic advocates (Salerno, 1985).

Several national professional organizations promote OA. Associations of professional administrators and computer specialists have expanded their activities to include OA within their domains while the more specialized Association of Information Systems Professionals has a direct interest in the diffusion of OA. A large number of trade magazines and several academic journals, such as *Office* and *ACM Transactions on Office Information Systems* support the OA movement. A strong office products industry also has developed and promotes OA equipment. This industry includes major vendors of mainframes, microcomputers, and specialized office equipment. Since the late 1970s the American Federation of Information Processing Societies has sponsored an annual trade show and conference of academic and professional OA activists.

Personal Computing

Personal computers (PCs), like video-recorders, have become middle-class luxury appliances of the early 1980s and commonplace in the 1990s. The PC movement began in the early 1970s as groups of hobbyists built their own primitive computers (Levy, 1984). Apple Computer Company and Tandy Corporation grew quickly in the late 1970s by providing two of the first microcomputers for which the purchaser did not have to solder parts and continually fiddle. The PC movement is one of the few CMs that has a distinctly "mass public" audience, although an elite audience of wealthy organizations that have also adopted and institutionalized PCs in some of their operations has developed as well.

Some of the early writings about PCs emphasized personal and social transformations that would accompany widespread PC use (Kay, 1977; Osborne, 1979). Today, the mobilizing ideologies of the PC movement shifted to an instrumental pragmatism based on the capabilities of PCs for professionals. However, many PC enthusiasts believe that "almost everybody" should have a PC. For example, Jim Warren, the founder of a popular computer magazine and a series of immensely popular regional PC fairs, recently commented:

> I continue to feel that computers in the hands of the general public are crucial tools for positive social change. The only hope we have of regaining control over our society and our future is by extracting the information we need to make informed, competent decisions. And that's what computers do. (quoted in Goodwin, 1988: 114)

While PC applications such as word processing, financial analysis, and project scheduling are useful for professionals, "home applications" such as checkbook balancing, recipe storage, and home inventory are perhaps too marginal to justify a PC on instrumental grounds. The assumption that "almost everybody" should have a PC reveals the ideology of the PC movement.

The PC movement is national in scope, and is popularized by high circulation national publications. By the mid 1980s, about 12 PC magazines were widely sold on newsstands in the United States. Many were specialized for audiences who own microcomputers made by particular vendors such as Apple, Tandy, and IBM. Others were specialized for business applications or some particular kind of technology (e.g., programming languages, UNIX). One very popular multi-vendor magazine, *Byte*, circulated approximately 500,000 copies per monthly issue.

The main national level activities are the trade fairs that travel from region to region. The software and hardware vendors in the microcomputer industry now play a major role in these ventures. The PC movement has numerous local movement organizations. The computer clubs in metropolitan areas are usually segmented along the vendor lines (e.g., Apple, IBM, Atari) and are still dominated by hobbyists. In addition, computerized "bulletin boards" are operated by commercial firms and hobbyist amateurs. The two major commercial firms, CompuServe and The Source, serve businesses, professionals, and hobbyists nationwide. The operators of amateur-run bulletin boards are relatively transient and aim their services at computer hobbyists in their metropolitan areas. In the mid-1980s there were over 200 amateur-run bulletin boards in the United States. The PC movement overlaps with the office automation movement and the instructional computing movement since microcomputers have come to play a significant role as focal technologies for each. Some specialized organizations link these movements; for example, in the Los Angeles area, the PC Professional Association holds monthly meetings for PC coordinators who work in business organizations.

The mass media has become a major promoter of the PC movement. Newspapers such as the *Los Angeles Times* run a weekly personal computing column. It is difficult to separate the effects of journalistic promotion from industry advertising. As the PC industry has grown, firms like IBM, Apple, and Commodore, among others, have placed advertisements on prime time television. The PC industry's advertising is significantly enhanced by CM promotion. In the case of the PC movement, the mass media have played a major role. It is relatively rare to find the mass media investigating PC use. Dissatisfaction with the service and support provided by major computer sales chains is commonplace among PC enthusiasts. Journalists are much more apt to write about poor service in auto sales than in home computer sales.

Ideological Elements of CMs

Ideologies of computerization are especially developed in two kinds of writings. Some accounts focus on the coming of an "information society" and treat computerization as one key element in that transformation. In this view, the computerization of America will be an apolitical, bloodless "revolution." All will gain, with the possible exception of a few million workers, such as telephone operators and assemblyline welders, who will be temporarily displaced from "old-technology" jobs. Prophets of a new "information age" like Bell (1979), Toffler (1980), Dizard (1982), Naisbitt (1984), and Strassman (1985) argue that this transformation is an inevitable and straightforward social process. Human intention, pluralities of interest, or large scale conflict play a minor role in these predictions of substantial social transformation.

A second source of computerization ideologies focuses on specific CMs and is of greater interest to us. Few CM activists, including those who publish their arguments, assert their key ideological themes directly. They can be located in books and articles only through a "symptomatic reading" in which the absence of relevant themes is as important or more important than those stated explicitly. For example, if an author argues that every household should have PCs for all family members, she is arguing in effect that families should restructure their budgets such that computing investments are not compromised.

We have identified five key and related ideas from such symptomatic reading. In addition, as students of and participants in several CMs, we have found these ideas recurring in continuing discussion. As a system of beliefs, these themes help advance computerization on many fronts.

Computer-Based Technologies Are Central for a Reformed World

Many CM activists assert (or imply) that computer technology provides an historically unique opportunity for important social changes. For example, Papert (1979: 74) advocates a special mode of computer-based education (e.g., LOGO programming) and strongly criticizes other modes of computer-based education as reinforcing "traditional educational structures and thus play[ing] a reactionary role." Papert clearly articulates the belief that computing is special and different from all other educational innovations of the 1960s in its potential to redress serious widespread social inequities. Papert's analysis is largely individualistic and focuses upon children's cognitive abilities. He makes no attempt to ask whether social inequities are tied to a structured economic system rather than simply to the distribution of skills in society.

Similarly simple assertions about the special role of computing can be found in literature for each of the CMs. In the case of urban information systems, Evans and Knisley (1970) argued that a wide array of pro-social services can be specially supported by urban information systems. Giuliano (1982) suggests that office automation provides a unique historical opportunity to organize offices without tedious clerical work. Hayes-Roth (1984) suggested that AI-based expert systems will radically transform the professions by providing a unique capability in taking over cognitive expertise previously monopolized by people. In each case, these analysts imply that the computer-based technologies they advocate have a historically powerful and unique role.

CM activists often argue that computers are a central medium for creating the world they prefer. This belief gives proposals for computerization a peculiarly technocentric character: computer technologies are central to all socially valuable behavior. This belief is exemplified in characterizations of computer-based education in which any meaningful learning is computer-mediated (e.g., Papert, 1980).

One variant of this argument holds that computing is essential for modern organizations to compete effectively through increased productivity. Productivity, an economic conception, is linked to social progress through economic advance; and computerization, like prayer, will always have this desired result if it is "done properly." In addition, advocates attribute "productivity gains" primarily to new computing technologies, even though other elements, such as work organization and reward systems, play a critical role.

Concerns for productivity are closely linked to concerns for reducing costs. These concerns, and the relatively high cost of "state of the art" computing that helps set expectations, give the practice of computerization a relatively conservative political character. New systems of socially significant scale require the approval of higher level managers who are unlikely to approve arrangements that threaten their own interests (Danziger et al., 1982).

Improved Computer-Based Technologies Can Further Reform Society

Advocates often portray the routine use of ordinary computer equipment as insufficient to reap the hoped-for benefits. Rather, the most advanced equipment is essential. This ideological theme is most clear when CM activists emphasize the continual acquisition of advanced equipment. They give minor attention to how to organize access to it or how to use it for social change. Nationally, the belief is reflected in funding priorities for computing research and development: The overwhelming support is for the development of new equipment. In the organizations we have studied, we have found relatively little money and attention spent on learning how to humanely integrate new computer-based technologies into routine social life.

CM activists often define computing capabilities as those of future technologies, not the limits of presently available technologies. Many promotional accounts for computing reflect this future orientation. For example, Kay (1977) advocates book-sized personal computers that handle graphics, play music, and store vast amounts of data. Hiltz and Turoff (1978) advocate nationwide computer conferencing systems that would connect every household and office, much like telephones. During the last 20 years, computer-based technologies have become substantially cheaper, faster, smaller, and more flexible. Doubtless, computer-based systems will improve technologically during the next two decades similar to the ways in which cars, airplanes, typewriters, and telephones improved between 1910 and 1980. However, CM activists usually dismiss contemporary technologies, except to the extent they foreshadow more interesting future technologies.

In any year, only a few organizations can purchase the state of the art equipment that CM activists recommend. With rapid changes in technological capabilities, today's technological leaders are surpassed by tomorrow's unless they recycle their equipment so rapidly that they never "fall behind." Like people who purchase a new car or stereo with every model change, the heroes of this vision invest heavily and endlessly.

Computer hardware has become faster, cheaper, larger in scale, and more reliable in the last 30 years. Software support systems (like programming languages) have become more powerful and flexible, albeit at a much slower pace. Finally, computer applications have also improved technologically, at a still slower rate. But a focus on future technologies helps deflect attention from the problems of using today's technologies effectively, while offering the hope of salvation soon.

More Computing Is Better than Less, and There Are No Conceptual Limits to the Scope of Appropriate Computerization

This theme goes beyond the previous one that "more computing can help reform society." CM activists usually push hard on two fronts: people and organizations ought to use state-of-the-art computing equipment, and state-of-the-art computing should become universal. In their writing and talks, CM activists usually emphasize the claim that certain groups use the forms of computing they prefer, rather than explaining carefully how people alter their social lives to use or accommodate new technologies. For example, it is common for enthusiasts of computer-based education in schools to report that there are now several hundred thousand micro-computers in use but to spend relatively little time examining how children actually partake in computer-oriented classes.

CM activists imply that there are no limits to meaningful computing by down playing the limits of the relevant technologies and failing to balance computing activity against competing social values. They portray computing technologies as mediating the most meaningful activities: the only real learning, the most important communications, or the most meaningful work, whether now or in the future they prefer. Other media for learning, communicating, or working are treated as less important. Real life is life online (e.g., Feigenbaum & McCorduck, 1983; Papert, 1980; Hiltz & Turoff, 1978).

No One Loses from Computerization

Computer-based technologies are portrayed as inherently apolitical. While they are said to be consistent with any social order, CM advocates usually portray their use in a cheerful, cooperative, flexible, individualistic, and efficient world. This allows computer-based technologies to be shown as consistent with the most cherished social values. Computerization can enable long-term societal goals such as a stronger economy and military for the nation. Any short-term sacrifices that might accompany these goals, such as displaced workers, are portrayed as minor unavoidable consequences.

CM activists rarely acknowledge that systematic conflicts might follow from computerizing major social institutions. Those that are acknowledged are defined as solvable by "rational discourse" and appropriate communication technologies (see for example, Hiltz & Turoff, 1978). Many activists ignore social conflicts in their discussions of computerization and thus imply that computerization will reduce them. Some authors explicitly claim that computerized organizations will be less authoritarian and more cooperative than their less automated counterparts (Simon, 1977). In most of the accounts of office automation, staff are cheerfully efficient and conflicts are minor (see, for example, Strassman, 1985; Giuliano, 1982).

Similarly, in the literature on computer-based education, cheerful students and teachers who are invariably helpful and understanding populate computerized classrooms (see, for example, Taylor, 1980). Spitballs, paper planes, and secret paper messages that pass under the desks do not appear in this literature (Kling, 1983). Teachers who are puzzled by new technologies, concerned with maintaining order in their classrooms, or faced with broken equipment, competitive students, and condescending consultants are also ignored in the published discourse. Occasionally, an advocate of one mode of computer-based education may criticize advocates of others (e.g., Papert, 1979) but these are only sectarian battles within a CM.

Most seriously, the theme that computing fosters cooperation and rationality allows CM activists to gloss deep social and value conflicts that social change can precipitate (Kling, 1983; Kraemer, Dickhoven, Tierney, & King, 1987). In practice, organizational participants can have major battles about what kind of computing equipment to acquire, how to organize access to it, and the standards to regulate its use (Kling & Scacchi, 1982; Kling, 1987).

Uncooperative People Are the Main Barriers to Social Reform Through Computing

In many social settings we have found CM advocates arguing that poorly trained or undisciplined users undermine good technologies

(Kling & Iacono, 1984). Even when they are making their procedures even more complex or automating more exceptions and special contingencies, these advocates argue that the limitations of their coworkers, rather than problems in their strategy of automation, are the major impediments to nearly perfect computer-based systems. Computerization is difficult when compared with the imagery of easy use advanced by CM advocates. In short, people place "unnecessary" limits on the complexity of desirable computer-based technologies and must be properly trained and taught to reorganize their activities and institutions around the new technology.

These central themes of computerization movement ideology emphasize technological progress and deflect competing social values. They are a foundation for social visions that include the extensive use of relatively advanced computer systems. In this vision, computer users should actively seek and acquire "the best" computer technologies and adapt to new technologies that become available, regardless of their cost. In this moral order, the users of the most advanced technologies are the most virtuous. And as in melodramas where the good triumphs in the end (Cawelti, 1976, p. 262), only developers and users of advanced computing technologies find the good life.

These five ideological themes shape public images of computers and computerization. We do not claim that computer systems are "useless" or merely a fad. But these ideological positions help activists to build commitment and mobilize resources for extensive computerization in organizations that adopt computer technologies *beyond the value that mere utility justifies*. It is ironic that activists often employ the imagery of science and objectivity (e.g., "knowledge") to advance their CMs. They deflect attention from what other analysts claim are the social problems raised by computerization—problems of consumer control, protection of personal privacy, quality of jobs, employment, and social equity, among others.

Counter-Computerization Movements

CMs generally advance the interests of richer groups in the society because of the relatively high costs of developing, using, and maintaining computer-based technologies. This pattern leads us to ask whether CMs could advance the interests of poorer groups or whether there are counter-movements that oppose the general CM. Many CM activists bridle at these suggestions. They do not always value "helping the rich." In our fieldwork we have found that CM advocates sometimes see themselves as fighting existing institutional arrangements and working with inadequate resources. We do not suggest that "relative deprivation" triggers CMs. We are suggesting that CM participants can argue that they have non-elite positions even though they work with elite organizations. CM activists often develop coalitions with elite groups that can provide the necessary financial and social resources. The elite orientation of the general CM is sufficiently strong that one might expect some systematic "progressive" alternative to the major CMs.

There is no well-organized opposition or substantial alternative to the general CM. A general counter-computerization movement (CCM) might well be stigmatized as "Luddite." CM activists portray computing simply as a means to reform a limited set of social settings. Therefore, a specific CCM would have to oppose all or most computer-based education developments, or most office automation, or most PC applications, and so on. A successful ideological base for such opposition probably would have to be anchored in an alternate conception of society and the place of technology in it. In practice there is no movement to counter computerization in general, though some writers are clearly hostile to whole modalities of computerization (Braverman, 1975; Mowshowitz, 1976; Reinecke, 1984; Weizenbaum, 1976). These writers differ substantially in their bases of criticism, from Frankfurt School critical theory (Weizenbaum) to Marxism (Mowshowitz, Braverman).

Criticism of computerization and CMs comes from social movements and organizations that focus on specific changes due to computerization, which they see as problematic. For example, civil libertarians are critical of those computing applications that most threaten personal privacy but are mute about other kinds of computing applications (Burnham, 1983). Consumer advocates may be highly critical of strategies of computerization that place consumers at a disadvantage in dealing with supermarkets on pricing or that increase consumers' liability for bank card problems. But neither civil libertarians nor consumer advocates typically focus on problems of computerization in employment. Union spokesmen are especially concerned about how computerization affects the number and quality of jobs (Shaiken, 1985) but are mute about consumer issues. Anti-war activists criticize computer technologies that they think make war more likely but rarely speak to other computerization issues. Consequently, some analysts try to envision computer use that is shaped by other social values—such as consumer control over electronic payments or improvements in working life.

Major policy initiatives in these directions have come from other social movements. For example, consumer groups rather than CMs have been the main advocates of allowing of debit card users protections such as ceilings on liability when cards are stolen, clear procedures for correcting errors, reverse payments, and stop payments (Kling, 1983). Civil liberties groups such as the American Civil Liberties Union (ACLU) have played a stronger role than CMs in pressing for the protection of privacy in automated personal record systems. Labor unions rather than

CMs have been most insistent in exploring the conditions under which work with video display terminals (VDTs) has possible adverse health consequences. Each of these reform movements is relatively weak and specialized. Moreover, each initiative by CCMs to place "humane" constraints on laissez-faire computerization may be met by well funded opposition within parts of the computer industry or computer-using industries. Consequently, the general drift is toward increased and intensive computerization with equipment costs, technological capabilities, and local organizational politics playing major enabling/limiting roles.

Discussion

We have argued that the computerization of many facets of life in the United States has been stimulated by a set of loosely linked CMs guided by mobilizing ideologies offered by CM activists who are not directly employed in the computer and related industries (Kling, 1983). We have characterized CMs by their ideological content, shown how five computer-based technologies are the focus of specific CMs, characterized core beliefs in their ideologies, and examined the fragmentary character of CMs. Our analysis differs from most organizational analyses of computerization by considering CMs that cut across the society as important sources of mobilizing ideologies for computing advocates. Their publications and meetings provide channels of communication for computing enthusiasts outside of the organizations that employ them and which they try to aggressively computerize.

But much more should be done in examining particular CMs. We need to learn in more detail about their participants and social organization and to better understand their relations with computerizing organizations, interest groups, the media, other CMs, and different segments of the computer industry. We hope that this analysis will encourage scholars to examine the CMs in other specific social settings and the activists who push them. These activists play a critical role in setting expectations about what a particular mode of computing is good for, how it can be organized, and how costly or difficult it will be to implement. These expectations can shape participants' attempts to computerize in a specific social setting such as a school, public agency, hospital, or business.

CM activists and participants play a role in trying to persuade their audiences to accept an ideology that favors everybody adopting "state of the art" computer equipment in specific social sectors. There are many ways to computerize, and each emphasizes different social values (Kling, 1983). While computerization is rife with value conflicts, CM activists rarely explain the value and resource commitments that accompany their dreams. And they encourage people and organizations to invest in computer-based equipment rather than paying equal or greater attention to the ways that social life can and should be organized around whatever equipment is acquired. CM activists provide few useful guiding ideas about ways to computerize humanely.

During the last 20 years, CMs have helped set the stage on which the computer industry expanded. As this industry expands, vendor organizations (like IBM) also become powerful participants in persuading people to automate. Some computer vendors and their trade associations can be powerful participants in specific decisions about equipment purchased by a particular company. They also can help weaken legislation that could protect consumers from trade abuses related to computing (Kling, 1983). But vendor actions alone cannot account for the widespread mobilization of computing in the United States. They feed and participate in it; they have not driven it. Part of the drive is economic and part is ideological. The ideological flames have been fanned as much by CM advocates as by marketing specialists from the computer industry. Popular writers like Alvin Toffler and John Naisbitt and academics like Daniel Bell have stimulated enthusiasm for the general computerization movement and provided organizing rationales (e.g., transition to a new "information society") for unbounded computerization. Much of the enthusiasm to computerize is a byproduct of this writing and other ideological themes advanced by CMs.

Most computer-based technologies are purchased by organizations. The advocates of computerization within specific organizations often form coalitions with higher level managers to help gain support and resources for their innovations, which they present as professional reform movements with limited scope. Office automation "only" influences general office practices. Advanced computerized accounting systems "only" influence the finance department and those who manage revenues and expenses. Computer-based inventory control systems "only" influence materials handling in manufacturing firms. In each administrative sector that is professionalized, some related group has taken on the mantle of computerization as a subject of reform. But these professionals do not identify with the computer industry; they identify themselves as accountants, doctors, teachers, or urban planners with an interest in certain computer applications.

By attempting to alter the character of social life across the society, the general computerization movement is basically revolutionary. A few computing promoters exploit a slick "revolutionary" image. As Langdon Winner (1984) aptly observes, Americans have been marketed "revolutionary" toothpastes, home entertainment centers, and plastics. None of these consumer items has revolutionized the social order. According to Winner, the sensible observer would treat claims about a "computer revolution" as marketing hype. We agree with Winner that shallow promotional claims dominate the public "revolutionary" discourse. Moreover, the social changes that one can attribute to computerization are often socially "conservative." But we suspect that the pervasiveness of computerization is having quiet cumulative effects in American life. Certain technologies are relatively plastic and substantially extend people's range of action. Basic technologies for transportation, energy, and communications, such as automobiles, electricity, and telephones, have become central elements of social life in advanced industrial societies. We suspect that computer-based technologies will be as socially important as these other technologies rather than peripheral, like plastics, processed foods, and hair spray.

There is not likely to be a general CCM. More seriously, it is unlikely that humanistic elements will be central in the mobilization of computing in the United States. Central humanistic beliefs are "laid onto" computerization schemes by advocates of other social movements: the labor movement (Shaiken, 1985), the peace movement, the consumer-rights movement (Kling, 1983), and the civil liberties movement (Burnham, 1983). Advocates of the other movements primarily care about the way some schemes for computerization intersect their special social interest. They advocate limited alternatives to particular CMs but no comprehensive, humanistic alternative to the general computerization movement. In its most likely form, our "computer revolution" will be a conservative revolution, which will reinforce the patterns of an elite dominated, stratified society.

Endnotes

1. Other computer technologies, such as electronic funds transfer (Kling, 1978; Kling, 1984), robotics, and supercomputing, are also advanced by CMs. Not all applications of computer technologies, however, are the focus of CMs; for example, payroll systems are not promoted through CMs.

References

Applegate, J., & Day, K. (1984, August 7). Computer firms aim: Artificial intelligence. *Los Angeles Times*, pp. 1, 17.

Aronson, N. (1984). Science as a claims-making activity: Implications for social problems research. In J. Schneider & J. Kitsuse (Eds.), *Studies in the sociology of social problems* (pp. 1–30). Norwood, NJ: Ablex Publishing Co.

Artificial intelligence is here: Computers that mimic human reasoning are already at work (1984, July 9). *Business Week*, 54–57, 60–62.

Attewell, P., & Rule, J. (1984). Computing and organizations: What we know and what we don't know. *Communications of the ACM*, 27(12), 1184–1192.

Bell, D. (1979). The social framework of the information society. In M. Dertouzos & J. Moses (Eds.), *The computer age: A twenty-year view* (pp. 163–211). Cambridge, MA: MIT Press.

Blumer, H. (1969). Social movements. In B. McLaughlin (Ed.), *Studies in social movements: A social psychological perspective* (pp. 8–29). New York: Free Press.

Braverman, H. (1975). *Labor and monopoly capital: The degradation of work in the twentieth century.* New York: Monthly Review Press.

Bucher, R., & Strauss, A. (1961). Professions in process. *American Journal of Sociology*, 66, 325–334.

Burnham, D. (1983). *The rise of the computer state*. New York: Random House.

Cawelti, J. (1976). *Adventure, mystery, and romance: Formula stories as art and popular culture*. Chicago: University of Chicago Press.

Cole, R. I. (1972). Some reflections concerning the future of society, computers and education. In R. L. Chartrand (Ed.), *Computers in the service of society* (pp. 135–145). New York: Pergamon Press.

Cyert, R. (1984). New teacher's pet: The computer. *IEEE Spectrum*, 21(6), 120–122.

Danziger, J. (1977). Computers, local government, and the litany to EDP. *Public Administration Review*, 37(1), 28–37.

Danziger, J., Dutton, W., Kling, R., & Kraemer, K. L. (Eds.). (1982). *Computers and politics: High technology in American local governments*. New York: Columbia University Press.

Dizard, W. (1982). *The coming information age*. New York: Longman's.

Downey, G. (1986). Ideology and the clamshell identity: Organizational dilemmas in the anti-nuclear power movement. *Social Problems*, 33(5), 357–373.

Evans, J. W., & Knisely, R. A. (1970). *Integrated municipal information systems: Some potential impacts*. Washington, DC: U.S. Department of Housing and Urban Development.

Feigenbaum, E., & McCorduck, P. (1983). *Fifth generation: Artificial intelligence and Japan's challenge to the world*. Reading, MA: Addison-Wesley.

Foss, D. A., & Larkin, R. (1986). *Beyond revolution: A new theory of social movements.* South Hadley, MA: Bergen and Garvey Publishers.

Gerson, E. (1983). Scientific work and social worlds. *Knowledge*, 4, 357–377.

Giuliano, V. (1982). The mechanization of office work. *Scientific American*, 247(3), 148–164. (Reprinted in Dunlop and Kling, 1991).

Goodwin, M. (1988). Wild-Man Warren. *PC World*, 6(1), 108–109, 114.

Hayes-Roth, F. (1984). The machine as partner of the new professional. *IEEE Spectrum*, 21(6), 28–31.

Hiltz, S. R., & Turoff, M. (1978). *The network nation: Human communication via computer*. Reading, MA: Addison-Wesley.

Iacono, S., & Kling, R. (1987). Changing office technologies and transformations of clerical work: A historical perspective. In R. Kraut (Ed.), *Technology and the transformation of white collar work* (pp. 53–75). Hillsdale, NJ: Lawrence Erlbaum.

Kaplan, B. (1983). *Computers in medicine, 1950–1980: The relationship between history and policy*. Unpublished Ph.D. dissertation, Department of History, University of Chicago.

Kay, A. (1977). Microelectronics and the personal computer. *Scientific American*, 237(3), 230–244.

Kitsuse, J., & Spector, M. (1977). *Constructing social problems*. Menlo Park, CA: Cummings Publishing Co.

Kling, R. (1978). Automated welfare client-tracking and service integration: The political economy of computing. *Communications of the ACM*, 21(6), 484–493.

Kling, R. (1980). Computer abuse and computer crime as organizational activities. *Computers and Law Journal*, 2(2), 403–427.

Kling, R. (1983). Value conflicts in the deployment of computing applications: Cases in developed and developing countries. *Telecommunications Policy* (March), 12–34.

Kling, R. (1986). The new wave of academic computing in colleges and universities. *Outlook*, 19(1/2), 8–14.

Kling, R. (1987). Defining the boundaries of computing across complex organizations. In R. Boland & R. Hirschheim (Eds.), *Critical issues in information systems* (pp. 307–362). London: John Wiley.

Kling, R. (1990). More information, better jobs? Occupational stratification and labor market segmentation in the United States' information labor force. *The Information Society*, 7(2), 77–107.

Kling, R. (1991). Cooperation, coordination and control in computer-supported work. *Communications of the ACM*, 34(12), 83–88.

Kling, R., & Iacono, S. (1984). The control of information systems development after implementation. *Communications of the ACM*, 27(12), 1218–1226.

Kling, R., & Scacchi, W. (1982). The web of computing: Computer technology as social organization. *Advances in Computers*, 21. New York, Academic Press.

Kraemer, K. L., & King, J. (1978). Requiem for USAC. *Policy Analysis*, 5(3), 313–349.

Kraemer, K. L., Dickhoven, S., Tierney, S. F., & King, J. (Eds.). (1987). *Datawars: The politics of modeling in federal policymaking*. New York: Columbia University Press.

Laudon, K. C. (1974). *Computers and bureaucratic reform*. New York: John Wiley and Sons.

Laudon, K. C. (1986). *Dossier society: Value choices in the design of national information systems*. New York: Columbia University Press.

Levy, S. (1984). *Hackers: Heroes of the computer revolution*. Garden City, New York: Anchor/Doubleday.

Machine of the year. (1928, January 3). *Time*, 13–39.

McCarthy, J., & Zald, M. (1977). Resource mobilization and social movements: A partial theory. *American Journal of Sociology*, 82(6), 1212–1241.

Mowshowitz, A. (1976). *The conquest of will: Information processing in human affairs*. Reading, MA: Addison-Wesley.

Naisbitt, J. (1984). *Megatrends*. New York: Warner Books.

Osborne, A. (1979). *Running wild: The next industrial revolution*. Berkeley, CA: Osborne-McGraw Hill.

Papert, S. (1979). Computers and learning. In M. L. Dertouzos & J. Moses (Eds.), *The computer age: A twenty-year view* (pp. 73–86). Cambridge, MA: MIT Press.

Papert, S. (1980). *Mindstorms: Children, computers and powerful ideas*. New York: Basic Books.

Reinecke, I. (1984). *Electronic illusions*. New York: Penguin Books.

Salerno, L. (1985). Whatever happened to the computer revolution? *Harvard Business Review*, 85(6), 129–138.

Shaiken, H. (1985). *Work transformed: Automation and labor in the computer age*. New York: Holt, Rinehart, and Winston.

Simon, H. (1977). *The new science of management decision*. Englewood Cliffs, NJ: Prentice Hall.

Star, S. L. (1988). Personal communication. February 15. Irvine, California.

Star, S. L. (1989). *Regions of the mind: Brain research and the quest for scientific certainty*. Stanford, CA: Stanford University Press.

Strassman, P. (1985). *Information payoff: The transformation of work in the electronic age*. New York: Free Press.

Taylor, R. (Ed.). (1980). *The computer in the school: Tutor, tutee, tool*. New York: Teachers College Press, Columbia University.

Toffler, A. (1980). *The third wave*. New York: William Morrow.

Turkle, S. (1984). *The second self: Computers and the human spirit*. New York: Simon and Schuster.

Uhlig, R., Farber, D., & Bair, J. (1979). *The office of the future: Communication and computers*. New York: North-Holland.

Weizenbaum, J. (1976). *Computer power and human reason: From judgment to calculation*. San Francisco: W. H. Freeman.

Wilson, J. (1973). *Introduction to social movements*. New York: John Wiley.

Winner, L. (1984). Myth information in the high-tech era. *IEEE Spectrum*, 21(6), 90–96.

Winston, P., & Prendergast, K. (Eds.). (1984). *The AI business: Commercial uses of artificial intelligence*. Cambridge, MA: MIT Press.

Yourdon, E. (1986). *Nations at risk: The impact of the computer revolution*. New York: Yourdon Press.

Zald, M., & Berger, M. (1978). Social movements in organizations: Coup d'etat, insurgency, and mass movements. *American Journal of Sociology*, 83(4), 823–861.

Paper #2: Computerization Movements: The Rise of the Internet and Distant Forms of Work

Suzanne Iacono
National Science Foundation

Rob Kling
Center for Social Informatics
School of Library and Information Science
Indiana University

Reprint from: *Information Technology and Organizational Transformation: History, Rhetoric, and Practice*. Joanne Yates and John Van Maanen (Eds.), pp. 93–136. Thousand Oaks, Ca: Sage Publications, 2001. Publication Draft of July 1998.

Introduction

Recent surveys suggest that about 122 million people worldwide and 70 million people in North America currently use the Internet at home, work, school, libraries, or community centers (NUA LTD, 1998). Since its inception in 1969 as the ARPANET, Internet growth has been explosive. When restrictions against commercial use were lifted in the late 1980s, Internet traffic, defined as data flow on the U.S. Internet backbone, doubled in size roughly each year (Guice, 1998). While numerous surveys have proliferated a wide range of user estimates and considerable controversy about how exactly to measure use, no one disputes the upward curve and fast growth. Public discourse has largely interpreted this phenomenon as the dawning of a new social epoch variously called the Information Age, the Digital Age, or the age of cyber-space and cyber-media (Berghel, 1995). In this age, it is argued almost all forms of social life will be mediated by digital communications, distance will be overcome, a new social order will emerge, and lives will be transformed. The Clinton administration (White House, 1993) has mobilized wide-scale support for this view by promising to further develop the Internet into a national information infrastructure (NII) which will "unleash an information revolution that will change forever the way people live, work and interact with each other."

What is most critical about these assertions of social transformation is not their fidelity (or lack of fidelity) to truth but that they selectively "frame" or provide an "interpretive schema" by which disparate social groups and organizations can understand and interpret the meaning of the Internet for their own social contexts and practices. Such frames are built up in many public debates, not just those about new technologies. For example, public debate about gender and sexuality issues in the U.S. and U.K. military establishments has developed contending frames such as "some institutions/tasks are not for everyone" and "everyone deserves an equal chance" (Fisher, 1997). These frames offer commonsense notions about why things are the way they are or why they should be changed. In practice, they can also be persuasive and mobilize various constituencies to support one side or another.

In public discourse about the Internet, frames have been built up to suggest that organizations will have "faster communications" or "closer relationships with consumers" if they connect to the Internet. Many organizations (e.g., Fortune 1000 firms, government agencies, educational institutions, health organizations, and the like) have resonated with these frames and have been mobilized to get connected. What it means to "be on the 'net" is an ambiguous concept, however. While numerous organizations today have Web sites, some may lack the capability for two-way or multi-way interactions. Others may have both Web sites and interactivity, while still others may have e-mail, but no Web sites. But, increasingly, having some sort of "Internet presence" has become an obligatory part of doing certain kinds of business in the late 1990s.

In this chapter, we argue that the meaning of the Internet is being built up or "framed" in macro-level discourses such as those of the government, the media and scientific disciplines. The spread of these frames across many layers of public discourse mobilizes large-scale support and suggests specific lines of action within micro-social contexts such as organizations restructuring themselves in order to implement and effectively use internetworking technologies in their routine activities. We call these processes computerization movements and suggest that they are similar to other social movements such as the labor movement or the women's movement in the ways that they reject dominant cultural codes and package alternative beliefs, values, and language for new, preferred forms of social life.

In the next section, we present the traditional conceptions of the social processes that have driven the rapid growth of the Internet over the past thirty years, and suggest an alternative social process based on computerization movements (CMs). Then, we describe the ways in which these movements draw on existing ideational materials to frame the key meanings of new technologies and mobilize societal support for them. Framing is a critical part of these processes because it allows ordinary people to gain deeper understandings about how new technologies are used in situations that may be foreign to them. Next, we illustrate computerization movements by focusing on historical shifts in the meaning of a specific movement, computer-based work, and the current set of discourses that have emerged around "new" distant forms of work. Since computerization movements advocate systematic changes in existing organizational arrangements, we should expect that some discourses and activists would emerge to oppose certain modes of computerization, forming a counter-computerization movement. We discuss counter-computerization discourses that have played key roles in defining and altering the meaning of internetworking and computer-based work. Finally, we conclude and suggest ways to incorporate a computerization movement perspective in further study.

Why Are Organizations Rapidly Connecting to the Internet?

The Internet is typically defined as a network of networks or an internetwork. Internetworking means using special-purpose computers or hosts to connect a variety of autonomous networks for transmitting data, files, and messages in text, audio, video, or graphic formats over distances. In 1995, the NSF backbone consisted of almost 51,000 networks (NSF, 1995). According to recent estimates, over 16 million hosts are now connected to those networks (Press, 1997) with 254 million hosts projected by the year 2000 (Matrix Information and Directory Services, 1997). While any number of individuals and organizations routinely track Internet traffic and numerous national surveys have been administered by researchers and media organizations, there are no available statistics on the number of organizations connected to the Internet. Making such an estimate might be difficult, as choices about what counts as an organization would have to be made. For example, IRS tax filings might be used, but then subsidiaries might be overlooked as well as clubs and other nonprofit organizations. We can only surmise from our reading about the Internet that, today, almost all Fortune 1000 firms, major federal and state public agencies, universities and colleges, other nonprofits, and any number of small, entrepreneurial firms are currently connected.

Why are these organizations rapidly connecting to the Internet? One common answer argues that organizations connect to the Internet because of the assumed economic or strategic advantages resulting from changed buyer-supplier relationships. It is suggested that the Internet is a more efficient and effective marketing channel than traditional delivery mechanisms. With the advent of the World Wide Web in 1993–1994, user-friendly browsers available on many desktops, the tremendous growth in the Internet, and the low marginal costs associated with offering products or services to customers, there has been a stampede of businesses to the Net (Rao, Salam, & DosSantos, 1998). Electronic markets should also benefit consumers. By lowering the costs of searching for alternative products, such markets are expected to encourage greater price competition and lower prices (Elofson & Robinson, 1998). Further, use of the Internet opens up new markets by moving organizations closer to their customers (Palmer Griffith, 1998). For example, in education, as the competition for students increases, universities and colleges with small, local markets have expanded their programs to include those who are distant from their campuses. Students who are distant from centers of higher education will also benefit by obtaining degrees from home and by learning from distant experts. From this point of view, the trend for autonomous organizations to get connected is simply a byproduct of the availability of cost-effective telecommunications technologies coupled with benefits assumed through the interconnections. Decisions regarding these connections are based on the resource needs of the organization and expectations of reduced costs and improved capability.

A variant of this answer focuses less on immediate economic gains and more on issues of long-term survival. In this view, connections to the Internet are seen as an essential part of the learning organization. Organizations can no longer learn all they need to know internally (Powell, 1996). New ways of gaining information are essential. For example, marketing information can be gained from electronic communities and online focus groups (Kannan, Chang, & Whinston, 1998). Commercial firms develop partnerships and maintain continuing communication with external parties such as research centers, labs, and even former competitors. Educational institutions and households can also take advantage of the information and services available on the Web. These linkages are both a means of gaining access to new knowledge and a way of exploiting those capabilities for innovation and experimentation. The outcome is long-term economic viability.

A second type of answer focuses on major epochal social transformations and argues that the United States is shifting from a society where industrial activity and modernist systems and infrastructures dominate to one in which information, knowledge, and post-modern systems and infrastructures will dominate (Bell, 1979; Lyotard, 1984). Toffler, a popular writer about these ideas, argues that the Third Wave economy is based on information and that the central event of the past century has been the death of matter (Dyson, Gilder, Keyworth, & Toffler, 1996). He and his colleagues argue for the inexorability of progress, asserting that the Third Wave economy will arrive. As a consequence, everyone should join the "growing millions" in cyberspace. According to this view, Internet connections are nothing less than the first step in the creation of a new civilization.

The first answer depends on organizational or managerial rationalism and has a strong grounding both in conventional economic analysis of information flows along value chains (cf., Porter & Millar, 1985) and in the resource dependence view of organizations in American sociology (cf., Pfeffer, 1987). Connections to the Internet are conceptualized as organizational tools or prosthetic devices that enhance the performativity of an organization in its environment (Poster, 1990). From this point of view, organizations adopt the technologies that are best for them, and they are generally able to implement and use them to their advantage. The second answer depends on technological determinism and an assumed causal relationship between the technological artifacts and methods of an era (e.g., farm implements, factories, and computers) and the economies and societies that emerge. While each of these responses offers insight into internetworking processes, we believe that they ignore some of the broadly non-economic dimensions of sociotechnical change in industrialized countries.

In this paper, we argue for an alternative conception of the rapid growth of the Internet based in a socially constructed process of societal mobilization that we call computerization movements (Iacono & Kling, 1996; Kling & Iacono, 1988). The mobilization of support for the Internet and other internetworking technologies does not mean that these technologies are not useful or valuable for the organizations that adopt them. But, it does mean that there are important macro-social and cultural dimensions that are often neglected in discussions of the rise of these technologies and their implied consequences for organizational change. (See Winter & Taylor, this volume [Yates & Van Maanen, 2001], for a similar discussion of the neglect of macro-social forces in understanding the relationship between new technologies and changes in worklife.)

Our main thesis is that participants in computerization movements build up frames in their public discourses that indicate favorable links between internetworking and a new, preferred social order. These frames help legitimate relatively high levels of investment for many potential adopters and package expectations about how they should use internetworking in their daily routines and how they should envision a future based on internetworking. Within organizations, meaning-making processes are ongoing as members attempt to restructure themselves around these new technologies. The symbolic struggle over these new technologies socially constructs the organizations that adopt them. Organizational change, then, is determined neither by the imperatives of the technology, nor by the planned changes of organizational management (Orlikowski, this volume [Yates & Van Maanen, 2001]. Instead, changes in worklife are shaped (but not determined) by the prevalent discourses informing new technologies and the practices that emerge around them in actual workplaces.

Computerization Movements

Sociologists have used the concept movement to refer to many different kinds of collective action. The most common term found in this literature is social movement, often used in a generic way to refer to movements in general. Lofland (1995, p. 194) defines social movements as "amorphous, sprawling, and far-flung conglomerations of organizations, activists, campaigns, and the like that are construed to share social or personal change goals." But sociologists have also written about professional movements (Bucher & Strauss, 1961), artistic movements, and scientific movements (Aronson, 1984; Star, 1989). What analyses of these movements share is a focus on the rise of loosely organized, insurgent action to displace or overcome the status quo.

Today, the dominant theoretical perspectives for explaining the emergence, recruitment processes, and eventual success or failure of social movements are undergoing a paradigm shift. Structural explanations based in resource mobilization (McCarthy & Zald, 1977) and political process (McAdam, 1982) have been criticized as too mechanistic and limited by their natural science framework (Mueller, 1992). Early social movement theories took seriously the presumed dualism between words and deeds and excluded ideas, beliefs, values, and identity, for example, as critical explanators of collective action.

Recently, however, social movement theory has become more sensitive to the semiotic, meaning sciences and has placed culture at the center of its concerns (c.f., Johnston & Klandermans, 1995; Morris & Mueller, 1992). For example, Snow and colleagues (1986) have focused on the struggle over the production and counter-production of ideas and meanings associated with collective action. From their point of view, social movements are deeply involved, along with the media, local governments, and the state, in the "politics of signification." Within such social intercourse, attributions of blame and transformational goals do not emerge from a void nor are they developed anew each time participants talk to each other, a politician gives a speech or a journalist writes about the movement. Instead, "collective action frames" serve as relatively stable interpretive media by which new members are recruited, the collective meanings of social movements maintained, and oppositional discourses developed (Snow & Benford, 1992).

Similarly, Ann Swidler's (1995) conceptualization of "culture as tool kit" of rituals, symbols, stories, and world-views demonstrates how activists borrow concepts, understandings, language, and values from existing cultural repertoires to construct new understandings, attribute blame for current problems, and prescribe the actions that should be taken to ameliorate them. She argues that during periods of change, old cultural models are rejected and new ones are articulated and constructed from existing ideational materials. Taken together, these views suggest that social movements are socially constructed through the ideational and cultural materials currently available to societal members.

A separate stream of research—on sociotechnical change (Bijker, 1997; Bijker & Law, 1992)—has also focused on the social construction of meaning, but around the development of new technologies. Similar to Snow and Benford's attempts in social movement theory to use "collective action frames" to explain how meanings can be collectively shared and acted upon, Bijker (1997) uses the concept of "technological frames" to describe the ways that social meaning is attributed to technical artifacts—tying together relevant social actors and the particular ways in which they understand a technology as "working." A critical insight in Bijker's conceptualization of frames is that they are built up and "exist" only in discourse. Technological frames are not just cognitive elements—in people's heads—nor do they attain some sort of superstructure status—above people's heads. Instead, technological frames are constituted when interactions among relevant actors begin about a particular artifact.

We base our understanding of computerization movements (CMs) in these larger debates about the role of culture, and specifically discourse and frames, in the mobilization of collective action and the development of meaning around a focal technology. Most research on information technology and organizational change has focused on adoption and change within single organizations. Macro-social and cultural elements are assumed to be unproblematic constants and the issue of why so many organizations at similar points in time attempt to implement the same technologies with varying levels of success is left unexplained. (For some notable exceptions, however, see Orlikowski, 1992; Orlikowski & Gash, 1994; Yates, 1994). The opposite problem can be found in the literature on social and cultural movements. While it focuses on the wide-scale recruitment of constituents for broad social change, it typically fails to examine how organizations are sites for social action and change. Our research brings these bodies of study together.

Our analysis focuses on a process of societal mobilization with three primary elements. The first element is technological action frames. These are multi-dimensional composite understandings—constituted and circulated in language—that legitimate high levels of investment for potential users, and form the core ideas about how a technology works and how a future based on its use should be envisioned. The second element is public discourses. These are the discursive practices—the written and spoken public communications—that develop around a new technology. Public discourse is necessary for particular understandings about new technologies to widely circulate. The third element is organizational practices—the ways in which individuals and organizations put technological action frames and discourses into practice as they implement and use technologies in their micro-social contexts.

These three elements—technological action frames, public discourse, and organizational practices—are related. Technological action frames shape and structure public discourse while public discourse shapes and structures organizational practices. For example, Foucault (1972, p. 168) demonstrates how a shift in medical discourse in the early 1800s during a cholera epidemic "put into operation such a body of rules that a whole domain of medical objects could then be reorganized, that a whole group of methods of recording and notation could be used, that the concept of inflammation could be abandoned and the old theoretical problem of fevers could be resolved definitively." He argues that during this period medical organizations restructured themselves based on these new scientific discourses, altering their traditional practice of medicine and the outcomes for patients (e.g., their chances of actual survival).

These relationships are non-deterministic, however. People's technology practices are usually much more complex than the more restricted public discourses about practices. For many practitioners, there is often a gap between their own discourse and practice. For example, in a recent conversation with a university professor about her class of online students spread across multiple time zones, she enthused about how the class eliminated time and space. But then, she went on to say that she had to be available on Saturdays because many students worked during the week, and she had a rule against e-mail on Sundays to give herself a break. Her course did not eliminate time and space although it did restructure her time and practices. However, she did not know how to talk analytically about these shifts. As a consequence, there was a gap between her discourse about online classrooms and her actual practice.

Relationships among the three elements can also be recursive. People may enrich their discourses and even modify their frames as they struggle to discuss the actual complexity of their practices. As a consequence, practices can generate new discourses and new discourses can build up new technological frames. In addition, various social groups can attribute differential meaning to new technologies, developing contending discourses as they implement and use new technologies in their own organizations. However, influence and change up the levels of analysis—from local practices to public discourse to far-flung understandings of what a technology is good for (its framing)—are more difficult. As with the university professor, private talk about use of a new technology often reflects the dominant public framing—despite the material reality of divergent practices. Much of local practice with new technologies is tacit—at least until users are prompted by an outsider to explain their actions. But even when new understandings become part of local discourse, they often remain local rather than being widely or rapidly circulated across other organizations and social settings. It is for this reason that public discourse about new technologies and the technological frames embedded in them can remain relatively stable and misrepresent actual practice for long periods of time.

Not all technological frames or the discourses in which they are embedded are equally persuasive or mobilizing, however. Computerization movements rise and fall in their influence, and some CMs seem to be much livelier at particular times. Further, computerization movements are not monolithic. Blumer (1969) distinguishes between specific and general social movements. Specific movements are the various wings or submovements of broader, general movements. Many movements, like those that advance feminism, civil rights, systematic management, quantification in the sciences, or computerization, are heterogeneous. These distinctions help us characterize the relationship between a general computerization movement around internetworking, and a specific or distinct wing around its intersection with computer-based work. Next, we discuss in some detail two elements—technological action frames and public discourses—and their role in the emergence of a general computerization movement around the Internet. In a later section on computer-based work, we will focus on the third element—practices—as they are informed by technological frames and discourses and carried out by organizational members.

Technological Action Frames

Theoretical Background

Bijker (1997) suggests that new technologies are interpretively flexible. Different social groups don't see different aspects of a single technology. Instead, they attribute different meanings and constitute different artifacts. For example, the field of cryptography has traditionally received little public attention. Recently, however, debate over a hardware encryption device, the Clipper Chip—now called Skipjack due to a trademark conflict—has become national news. In this debate, the government argues for the widespread use of this device because it would allow them to unencrypt the coded messages of people or organizations that use the Internet for illegal purposes. Computing activists like John Perry Barlow and Mitch Kapor of the Electronic Frontier Foundation, on the other hand, argue that use of this device would increase the government's electronic surveillance capabilities on ordinary citizens and the commercial enterprises that also use the Internet. These activists have framed the device as one that endangers citizen privacy and gives the government a backdoor for electronic eavesdropping (Barlow, 1993). For them, the Clipper Chip is yet another instantiation of Big Brother, whereas for the government, it is a Criminal Catcher.

The opposing meanings about encryption in this example can be conceptualized as "interpretive schemas" or "technological frames" developed by different social groups, in this case, the U.S. government and computer activists, to pinpoint the technology's potential significance to them and to mobilize others to see things their way (Bijker, 1997; Orlikowski & Gash, 1994). Technological frames are useful because they simplify and condense elements of complex technologies and their potential use and thus enable groups of people to interact about what they might mean. Technological frames are conceptual or analytic lenses that are built up within and between social groups as they struggle over the meaning of a technology and constitute it in their discourses. Bijker (1997) lists the major dimensions of technological frames as goals, key problems, problem-solving strategies, requirements to be met by problem solutions, current theories, tacit knowledge, perceived substitution function, user practices, and exemplary artifacts. Taken together, these dimensions constitute the meaning of a particular technology and frame it in specific ways.

Similarly, social movement theorists have articulated dimensions of their related concept, collective action frames. Snow and Benford (1992) suggest that collective action frames serve to punctuate and attribute meaning. Punctuation singles out some existing social condition as intolerable or focuses attention on certain values, such as equality or freedom, which may be at risk. Attributions have two parts: diagnostic, i.e., focusing the blame for current wrongs or problems; and prognostic, i.e., developing beliefs about what should be done to ameliorate a situation and assigning the responsibility for those actions. In our analyses of technological action frames, we will focus primarily on goals, diagnostic and prognostic attributions (including beliefs), current theories, expected user practices, and exemplary artifacts.

Both streams of research—social movements and sociotechnical change—argue that at specific points in time, a particular frame can become dominant. In the development and diffusion of new technologies, dominant frames can stabilize the meaning of technologies for indefinite periods—until they are contested. Social movement theorists suggest that many narrow collective action frames encouraging certain lines of action can surface and co-exist early in a movement's cycle. However, at certain points, within specific social movements, master frames develop in their discourses. For example, Snow and Benford (1992) report that the proposal for a freeze on the development and deployment of nuclear weapons in 1980 energized and renewed peace movement activity that had been dormant for several decades. The idea of a nuclear freeze constituted a new master frame that mobilized previously passive citizens to organize and protest the development of new nuclear weapons. While this new framing may seem to narrow the more expansive peace movement frame, Goffman (1986) suggests that the act of framing does not so much introduce restrictions as it opens up new possibilities. In other words, framing allows for more people and social groups to explicitly target current social problems and understand more clearly what they should do about them. Framing serves to enhance action, not dampen it.

When master frames develop in movement discourse, large-scale social action and mobilizations are more likely. But dominant or master frames can also wither as their meaning becomes less potent to social groups due to the rise of competing, new frames or as cultural conditions change (Snow & Benford, 1992). In our own conceptualization of technological action frames, we will use the terms dominant and master frames to mean the same thing, that is, the rise and relative stabilization of a set of key meanings for a focal technology.

Framing the Internet

A short history. Guice (1998) points out that the common view of the development of the Internet is based in an engineering perspective and straight path between the ARPANET of the late 1960s and today's Internet. He quotes Vinton Cerf, the "father of the Internet" and co-author of the TCP/IP protocol (the Internet's data communication standard), as saying that the Internet is "the direct descendant of strategically-motivated fundamental research begun in the 1960s with federal sponsorship ..." (Cerf, 1995). Guice argues that this account glosses over the many conflicts, twists, and turns that have actually taken place during its development. For example, the ARPANET depended on other protocols for a decade before TCP/IP emerged as an innovation and alternative. Other alternatives still exist. IBM's Systems Network Architecture and OSI (Open-Systems Interconnections) were both developed in the 1970s and the latter has emerged in the 1990s as a European alternative to TCP/IP. Pfaffenberger (1996) makes a similar argument about the development of Usenet, "the poor man's ARPANET," by focusing on its lengthy and often traumatic history as designers and administrators struggled to conceptualize and control the growing network.

But, it is not only the artifacts that have changed over the years. The meaning of internetworking has had similar shifts. Initially, the objective of the ARPANET was to allow for resource sharing. Grand scientific challenges could not be resolved by one government agency, university, or research lab alone. The goal was to harness distributed resources (e.g., knowledgeable people and computers) to solve complex problems faster. Much of the discourse surrounding this frame focused on the power of computation to displace human muscle power from work tasks and extend the reach of the human brain (c.f., Ginzberg, 1982).

But there was a gap between the dominant frame of the technology and its actual use. In practice, electronic mail among distributed colleagues emerged as the key use of the ARPANET. Being on the Net primarily meant having access to e-mail for long-distance communication and collaboration. Many information technology and science-oriented firms were the first private organizations to get connected, primarily so that their scientist and engineering staffs (e.g., in R&D departments) could have access to e-mail. By the early 1990s, many universities, large public agencies, civic organizations, and for-profit technology firms had connected to the Internet. Aside from e-mail, they began to use gopher (an Internet service) to publish documents such as catalogues, white papers, and reports. Being on the Net began to take on other dimensions such as information sharing with external organizations, customers, and the general public.

At about this time, the U.S. government began debating the development of a more extensive, higher bandwidth national information infrastructure (NII) and the various goals and purposes it would serve. Two opposing goals emerged in these policy debates—universal public access versus grand scientific computing (Guice, 1998). With the announcement of the National Research and Engineering Network (NREN) in 1991, it appeared that public spending would support the building of an infrastructure for scientists and engineers—continuing the traditional focus of internetworking—rather than give access to the general public. Between 1991 and 1993, however, the proponents of universal access pushed for their goals as a greater common good and the central idea behind the NII shifted away from the solution of scientific problems toward societal and economic transformations that could potentially benefit everyone.

A number of alternative technological infrastructures were considered for the NII. Proponents and vendors of cable TV and wireless telephony, for example, struggled unsuccessfully to have their infrastructures selected as the model for the NII. While differences between the histories and cultures of these industries and internetworking (e.g., differences in scope, access ethics, economic orientation, and extent of technological development) can partially explain the selection of internetworking (c.f., Press, 1994), Bijker (1997) argues that the stabilization of an artifact is a political process subject to interests and values.

In 1992, the World Wide Web (WWW) was released by CERN, the European Laboratory for Particle Physics. In the next several years, Internet browsers were developed and the WWW became the easiest part of the Internet for ordinary people to use. By 1995 to 1996, many private organizations had created Web sites to advertise their products and, hopefully, sell them to a larger audience. By the late 1990s, for most organizations, being on the Net means having a Web site.

The death of distance. This shift in the goals of internetworking toward universal access not only mobilized more people and organizations to get connected, but it also generated a discourse that assumes societal and global transformation will follow. In particular, geographic distance is said to no longer be relevant. A new dominant technological action frame has emerged—the death of distance: "The world has become a smaller place in the 20th century ... [T]elecommunications technology made terrestrial distances insignificant. The transformation of the world into a global village caused revolutionary changes in the physical and social infrastructure, rivaling those of the industrial revolution" (Adam, Slonim, Wegner, & Yesha, 1997, p. 115).

In this frame, the key problem to achieving full-scale, worldwide integration is distance, and internetworking provides the solution—distance will be "obliterated" (Dyson, 1997). The major scientific theories used to explain these transformations are based in technological determinism. For example, because new information and communications technologies are available at low costs to many people and institutions, Bell has argued for a shift to a post-industrial society whereas Toffler has argued for the emergence of a Third Wave economy. The targeted users of internetworking technologies include everyone, i.e., governments, civil societies, commercial, health, and education institutions; and consumers in general. In practice, these users are expected to get connected to the Internet and extensively use it to communicate and share information. The Internet is envisioned as the major integrating architecture of the world at the end of the 20th century.

This framing of distantiation as central to the meaning of new technologies is not new, however. It has a history that goes back well into the late 18th century. We are not cultural historians and can only indicate a few of the more interesting ways that this frame has been culturally robust over that period. The discourses that embed the death of distance frame typically focus on those technologies that have so vastly increased the speed of travel or communications that the lives and work of people who use them have fundamentally changed. For example, a non-stop jet that allows one to have breakfast in London and dinner in New York on the same day illustrates this idea in a contemporary and prosaic way.

In the late 18th century, the "first victory over time and space" according to Mattelart (1994) was the semaphore telegraph developed in France to establish communication among its armies. Over a period of about 50 years, a network was developed that connected Paris to its provincial cities and consisted of 534 semaphore stations covering 5,000 kilometers. In the U.S., from the late 18th to the 19th centuries, a number of systems were developed: postal, railroad, canal, electricity, and telegraph. With the arrival of each new system, communication was progressively touted as eliminating space and time through increased reach and speed. For example, a journalist writing in the Madison *Daily Tribune* in 1851 heralded the arrival of the railroad to local hog farmers (quoted in Windle & Taylor, 1986, p. 12):

> Before the railroad era it required two weeks and oftener three to drive hogs from Hendricks County to Madison. A drove of hogs loaded on the cars at Bellville on Thursday was landed at North Madison the same afternoon. This is annihilating space and time.

With the arrival of the railroad, distances would no longer be a significant obstacle in the distribution of products to their markets and the east coast of the U.S. could be united with its western boundaries. The mobilization of support for the development of the telegraph was framed in a similar way. Davis (1997, p. 10) reports how a U.S. congressman tried to convince colleagues to give startup money to Morse for the telegraph circa 1847.

The influence of this invention on the political, social, and commercial relations of the people of this widely extended country will of itself amount to a revolution unsurpassed in world range by any discovery that has been made in the arts and sciences. Space will be, to all practical purposes of information, annihilated between the states of the Union and also between the individual citizens thereof.

More recently, Marshall McLuhan (c.f., McLuhan & Powers, 1989) envisioned the growth of broadcasting systems and the ubiquitousness of the television set in households around the globe as a mechanism for the attainment of a "global village." His argument centered on the significance of the medium as an interconnecting mechanism over whatever value specific broadcast content might have for certain groups of people.

Over the past several hundred years, then, enthusiasts and analysts of various new technologies have proclaimed the death of distance and have employed it in their rhetoric about the expected social transformations. Mattelart (1994) argues that a concern with rapid communications and transportation systems grew out of Enlightenment philosophies. Before the Enlightenment, space simply evoked the idea of an empty area. But after Descartes, mathematicians began to appropriate space. They made it part of their domain and invented a variety of different types of spaces (e.g., curved spaces, non-Euclidean space, etc.) (Lefebvre, 1991). Some historians argue that this working out of space through various transportation and communication systems was heightened in North America as part of the Westward expansion of the U.S.—enabling the creation of one national democratic government in a vast continent. Others, including Mattelart, also observe that annihilating distance was not simply a matter of realizing democracy on a grand scale, but was also a product of readily identifiable economic and military interests. In short, the ability to reach across space and time with new technologies has had a strong cultural resonance in many industrial societies.

For the Internet, the significance of the death of distance is typically theorized in two ways. First, space will be structurally transformed and consolidated so that geography, borders, and time zones will become irrelevant (Cairncross, 1997). Rather than pockets of civilization such as industrialized cities and regions being separated or even isolated by vast distance, new spatial forms and practices based on a near frictionless information economy will prevail. A new technological infrastructure based loosely on the current Internet will define this space, open up new markets and information flows, and civilize it into a global, networked society (Castells, 1996).

Second, social relationships will be culturally transformed and democratized. Those on the periphery of society (e.g., in rural areas, workers of night shifts, home workers and schoolers, retired people, etc.) can become more involved and receive the same types of education, medical services and work opportunities that other centrally located actors currently enjoy. Further, people and organizations can directly connect with other people, places, organizations, and real-time world events without the mediating influence of government agents or media organizations. New transnational communities will be forged and institutional power based in geographic centrality and control will be reduced; decentralized social action and perfect information sharing will prevail.

From our research and reading of the discourses associated with internetworking, we have found five recurring beliefs that inform this master frame around internetworking (see sidebar on pp. 84–86, Five Beliefs About Internetworking).

These five recurring beliefs circulate in many discourses and engender the taking of certain lines of action in micro-social contexts, (e.g., individuals subscribing to online services or signing up for online courses, or organizations adopting the newest internetworking equipment). These beliefs are a foundation for social transformations that include the extensive use of internetworking. Technological progress is emphasized and competing beliefs are deflected. In this moral order, the users of the most advanced technologies are the most virtuous. And, as in melodramas where the good triumphs in the end, only developers and users of advanced internetworking technologies will conquer the unknown and achieve the good life.

Five Beliefs About Internetworking

1. Internetworking is central to a new world order. CM activists argue that internetworking is the dominant mechanism for creating and structuring the world that they prefer. Visions of a future, perfect world supplant the imperfect world in which we currently live. The new world will be more participative and democratic, more open and accessible, more diverse and information-intensive because of the central role of internetworking. Use of the Internet will revolutionize the way we do business, educate our young, and conduct our lives. This belief gives proposals for change a peculiarly technocentric character: Internetworking is central to all socially valuable behavior and the panacea for many social problems. Everyone will be closer to everyone else and no one will be excluded.

2. Improved internetworking can further revolutionize the world order. This argument is tied to the notion that the continuous cavalcade of new technologies and the inevitable march toward the future are inextricably linked to the achievement of social progress. Like people who purchase a new car or stereo with every model change, the heroes of this vision invest heavily and endlessly in new computer technologies. When the current social arrangements fail to produce the promised results, rather than be disillusioned or try other alternatives, they place their investment hopes in the next generation of technology. CM activists push hard on two fronts: (1) people and organizations ought to use state-of-the-art internetworking equipment; and (2) state-of-the-art internetworking technologies should be universally available. Beliefs about the importance of state-of-the-art technologies have become so widespread that people are invariably embarrassed by the presence of older equipment or by less than universal access to machines and networks in their own workplaces, schools, and homes. When organizations perceive themselves to be less networked than other similar organizations, they institute planning committees and point to their plans and the progress they have made in achieving more extensive internetworking.

3. Internetworking pushes the conceptual limits of time, space, and the known world. While the first two beliefs focus on the legitimation of aggressive acquisition of internetworking technologies and their central place in a more ideal social world, this belief focuses on the purpose of that investment and what it is good for. Time and space, our own human frailties, and the often-unmanageable aspects of bureaucratic institutions currently limit us. Communications networks and related technologies are said to embody transcendent qualities that will push the limits of the known world. We will no longer be bothered by distance and time differences, all needed information will be available online, and our organizations will become more flexible and nimble and less hierarchical. CM activists imply that there are no limits to meaningful internetworking by downplaying the actual limits of new technologies and the continuing benefits of current technologies. In addition, they fail to balance internetworking activities against competing social values. The Internet mediates the most meaningful activities—the only real learning, the most important communications, or the most meaningful work. Other media for learning, communicating or working are treated as less important. The most important aspects of life occur when online. The physical world is relegated to IRL (in real life) or life off-line (Rheingold, 1993).

4. No one loses from internetworking. The implementation and use of internetworking technologies are portrayed as inherently apolitical activities. CM activists rarely acknowledge that systematic conflicts might follow from the restructuring of major social institutions. Many activists ignore social conflict in their discussions of internetworking or they imply that it will reduce conflict if it already exists. Some authors explicitly claim that connected organizations will be less authoritarian and more cooperative than their less connected counterparts. The belief that internetworking fosters cooperation and collaboration allows CM advocates to gloss over deep social and value conflicts that social change can precipitate. In practice, organizational participants can have major battles about what kind of equipment to acquire, how to organize access to it, and what standards should regulate its use. At the societal level, internetworking is portrayed as consistent with all major societal goals. Conflicts among social groups such as labor, government, and higher education, between workers and their managers, or between teachers and administrators are ignored. Any short-term sacrifices that might accompany the attainment of these goals, such as displaced workers, are portrayed as minor unavoidable consequences.

5. Irrational resistance is the only obstacle to success. The only obstacles to achieving these visions are obsolete regulatory laws and people who "cling irrationally to their old ways" (Lewis, 1998). Examples of stereotypic beliefs about resistant or naive users are not difficult to find in the literature on internetworking. In organizations, MIS staff routinely report that resistant users undermine the implementation of new technologies (Kling & Iacono, 1984). Even when CM activists are advocating increasingly complex technologies, the major impediments to success are technophobic, uncooperative people, and not problems in the computerization strategy or the extent to which activities or organizations must be reorganized to accommodate large-scale changes.

Beyond the rhetoric. While increased access to information, more inclusionary practices and disintermediated relationships may certainly be laudable goals for an internetworking movement, their actual attainment in a purely positive form is hardly certain. In contradiction to the utopian image of a peaceful and inclusive "global village," at the end of the 20th century, various ethnic identities all over the world are fighting for their independence and exclusion from national societies. The rhetoric of time and space elimination is totalizing. It assumes that because internetworking is technically feasible people everywhere will want to get connected and be able to benefit similarly. But, in practice, actual improvements from new technologies are more narrow (e.g., time savings on airplane flights, access to the latest stock transactions) and may only benefit a small elite segment of society. And as Poster (1990, p. 72) has noted, "ruling powers, hegemonic cultural patterns and individual fear" can make it difficult for members of specific groups to interact with each other, let alone with outsiders, regardless of the technology in use. Women in Saudi Arabia and students in the People's Republic of China, for example, have been the focus of their governments' attempts to control their communications.

Further, if global electronic connections displace local interactions and relationships, some geographic regions may suffer. In Bangalore, India, the influx of multi-national software development firms has created regional disparities between the highly skilled people who work for those firms and others still mired in poverty and substandard living conditions (Madon, 1997). As entire segments in the region identify with a cosmopolitan global society, their attention to and identification with local civic issues and needs diminishes and the region suffers. Those in the region not connected risk being seen as irrelevant (Castells, 1996).

Social transformations from global internetworking may have similar disruptive effects on local relationships throughout the world. But even if universal access was available and everyone was connected to this more cosmopolitan network, more comprehensive electronic surveillance becomes increasingly possible. The "gridding of space" (de Certeau, 1984) through global networks makes its occupants and their actions and interactions increasingly available to observation, surveillance, and information gathering. The vision of a global networked society—where everyone knows what everyone else is doing—can also be fearsome. But, today, most people are enthralled with the idea that space and time may be eliminated through internetworking.

Public Discourses

Theoretical Background

Public discourse is essential to the spread of computerization movements. Technological action frames circulate in public discourses and act as a form of currency whose structure and meaning remain relatively constant across a variety of discursive practices. Social agents borrow the technological action frames that they find in public discourse, use them in their own contexts and discourses and, in so doing, often embellish or extend them. As a consequence, the widespread circulation of dominant frames in discourse at macro-levels of analysis (e.g., in that of the government, the media, or professional associations) can influence and shape micro-level discourse and practices—across similarly situated organizations. For example, Foucault (1977), in his research on prisons, discovered connections among macro-level discourse in relevant scientific disciplines, micro-level discourses within the prisons themselves, and the practices of prisons, i.e., the ways in which they restructured themselves. Poster (1990, p. 90) points out that Foucault depended on at least three "layers" of discourse to develop his history of prisons and the motivations for their restructuring: (1) the texts generated in the science of criminology; (2) the tracts of reformers; and (3) the paperwork required for the operation of prisons. Organizational restructuring is often related to the discourses to which that organization pays attention.

Four Layers of Public Discourse

We have uncovered four layers of public discourse that are critical to the campaigns of computerization movement activists: (1) government discourses (Poster, 1990), (2) the discourses of scientific disciplines (Poster, 1990), (3) media discourses (Gamson, 1995), and (4) organizational and professional discourses (Yates, 1999). While we have distinguished these discourses for analytical reasons, they should not be construed as separate in practice. For example, the discourses of governments are widely covered by the media. But media discourse often amplifies and popularizes government discourse. For example, the U.S. government's National Information Infrastructure has become more widely known in the mass media as the "Information Superhighway." The media can also build up contending discourses, for example, by pointing out the "speedbumps" on the Information Superhighway or by covering stories about downsizing and the impacts of new technologies in work organizations. Some combinations of discourse can be powerful. Poster (1990, p. 39) notes that, "When government acts 'technically,' on a 'scientific' basis, to solve a problem its action is automatically legitimate." The combination of government and scientific discourses lends authority, legitimacy, and a rational basis for organizations to take action. To the extent that a master technological action frame about internetworking technologies—the death of distance—is widely circulating, we would expect to find its pervasive use in a variety of public discourses.

Government Discourse

By 1993, internetworking had moved into national discourse and the Clinton White House had published the pivotal text for the internetworking movement, the NII: Agenda for Action (White House, 1993). Since that time, government discourse has been essential in the development of its meaning. From State of the Union and commencement speeches to the formation of new agencies, task forces and programs to the production of reports by the Department of Commerce, the National Science Council, and the White House all incorporate the master technological frame of this computerization movement: Distance is the problem; electronic integration, connections, and internetworking are the solutions; the goals are better education, health services, work environments, and transformed lives; everyone should be a user in many domains of life (e.g., work, learning, leisure, and shopping) and over the course of a life—from childhood to old age. With this document, Bill Clinton and Al Gore promised to link innovation and growth in internetworking with a transformed and reinvigorated society. If developed, the NII "can ameliorate the constraints of geography and economic status, and give all Americans a fair opportunity to go as far as their talents and ambitions will take them." This document established funding for research and development for an NII modeled on the current Internet. By stabilizing the meaning of the NII around a particular set of focal technologies, devices, and transmission protocols—those used in internetworking—and by encouraging the further development of these technologies, the government has, in part, contributed to a major upheaval in the nation's telecommunications infrastructures and industries.

In addition, the NII: Agenda for Action was a strategic reformulation of the meaning of the Internet. With this text and the associated discourses that have since emanated from it, almost all societal organizations are encouraged to connect to the Internet. While the potential benefits of such connections are consistently articulated, the fact that most U.S. organizations may have to painfully restructure themselves in order to actually use and benefit from those connections is rarely mentioned. But government discourse has legitimized this new approach to the organization of businesses, educational institutions, and households throughout the U.S. and many organizations are actively seeking to reorganize themselves around distant forms of social life.

Discourses in Scientific Disciplines

Contrary to the ivy tower stereotype of much academic research and writing, the ideas and findings of many scientific disciplines today are instituted in practice in industry and government agencies (Poster, 1990). Most current discourse about internetworking, even within the hard sciences of engineering and computer science, borrows heavily from sociological conceptualizations of large-scale epochal transformations to explain what these new technologies might mean to the people who use them. While few would label themselves technological determinists, most analyses focus on the accelerated pace of technological innovation as the driving force for societal change (e.g., as costs go down and standards emerge, borders and barriers are broken down) (c.f., Cairncross, 1997).

But the rhetorical strategy of most of these analyses is to stigmatize current infrastructures and systems in terms of the industrial or modern ideas they embed (Dyson et al., 1996) while casting new internetworking infrastructures and systems in utopian terms. Mass media communications systems such as broadcasting and newspaper distribution are characterized by their limitations and current physical infrastructures are vilified. Cities, as centralized hubs of social life, are characterized as decaying systems. While there are no doubt many problems in existing systems, this stigmatization process may actually turn public attention away from finding solutions and then funding them or from carefully reflecting on important social values that may be cast aside (e.g., cities as melting pots and broadcast journalism as a means to synthesize information and frame current events).

Conversely, new communications systems and infrastructures based on internetworking are characterized in utopian terms. They are more direct, participative, democratic, socially engaging and community oriented. These discourses invite public participation in the rejection of the past and uncritical identification with and acceptance of the ideological packaging of internetworking. While some research on electronic communications advances these notions, a growing body of research contends that social interactions over the Internet are not always so utopian. For example, research has found that gender biases can be perpetuated in many electronic groups (c.f., Herring, 1996) and powerful participants can dominate a discussion and use it for their own strategic purposes (c.f., Hert, 1996).

Mass Media Discourses

The symbolic struggle over the meaning of the Internet is carried out daily in general-audience media discourses. In *Business Week*, *Fortune*, and *Wired* magazines as well as on *The News Hour*, *Nightline*, *Frontline*, and CNN, legions of computer scientists, social scientists, entrepreneurs, journalists, and participant observers outline the course of events that is expected to propel U.S. society from its current form into the next millennium. Gamson (1995) suggests that movement activists are media junkies. Internet activists are no different. Many have become mass media stars (e.g., Esther Dyson, Howard Rheingold, and Katie Hafner) with their popular books widely read and cited in many circles. These activists package an ideology about what the Internet means and frame relevant events, beliefs, and actions in ways that make the unfamiliar technology more familiar. Their discourses are often indistinguishable from those of their scientific brethren (and sisters) as they, too, largely borrow from social science theory to attribute blame for current social problems and suggest positive guides based on internetworking to correct them. Their stories about new technologies and what they are good for are not socially neutral, however; they organize in advance how ordinary people and organizations should think about and perform work, engage in learning, and spend their leisure time (de Certeau, 1984).

The media discourses of computerization movement activists are extremely rich. Mainstream magazines as well as cyber-zines portray new social heroes and articulate new models for success. While few today may know the names of the heads of the world's largest banks, everyone knows the names of computer industry luminaries and the places that are the current centers of action (e.g., Silicon Valley, the MIT Media Lab, or CERN). Stories and characters from influential chat rooms, discussion groups, or online communities like the Well or LambdaMOO have become part of popular lore and the foci of much discussion in bars and classrooms alike (c.f., Dibbell, 1996; Hafner, 1997). The passageway to these new cultural and social practices requires the possession of new objects (e.g., Pentium-chip computers, light-weight lap-tops, 56k bps modems, Internet browsers, computer accounts, passwords, and the local phone numbers of Internet Service Providers). Everyday language and activities are transformed as people "surf the net, "log-in," "post" messages, "click on links," and recite "w-w-w dot slash dot com" Web addresses.

Media discourse is a cultural resource from which the general public can borrow to understand the significance of new technologies and the actions they should take to participate. These discourses are not just "out there"; they embed themselves in people's everyday discourse as they repeat common beliefs about these new technologies and struggle over their meaning at work, school, home, or in their informal social networks (Gamson, 1995). One need only examine the extent to which these new words, phrases, people, places, and ideas have seeped into one's own daily conversations with coworkers, friends, and family to understand how these discourses have become embedded in everyday life.

Institutional and Professional Discourses

The last layer of discourse is that which emerges within individual organizational settings and specific professional associations. These discourses add operational specificity to the technological action frames set up by the government, scientific disciplines, and the media. The proponents, champions, and enthusiasts of internetworking within specific organizations and professional associations establish committees to study the new opportunities and their associated costs, deliberate on the meaning of new technologies for their own organizations and professional members, develop and circulate white papers, invite knowledgeable experts to company or professional advancement forums and seminars, and generally educate their members about what these technologies might do for them. They identify current organizational or professional problems and suggest how these new technologies can alleviate those problems while simultaneously transforming them (e.g., allowing them to survive or expand as they enter the next century). In practice, various social groups may develop contending discourses about what these new technologies mean to their organization or profession. For example, Noble (1998) has outlined the struggles at York University in Toronto where faculty went on strike when university administrators forced many untenured faculty to put their courses on video, CD-ROM, or the Internet or lose their jobs. In the end, the faculty retained unambiguous control over all decisions relating to the use of technology as a supplement to their classroom instruction or as a means of instructional delivery.

Within these micro-social contexts, social groups struggle over the meaning of these new technologies as they amplify or contend with the dominant technological action frame to fit their own preferences and goals. In the course of these struggles, organizations are reorganized and professions are redefined. Sometimes, best practices and other testimonials to effective restructuring become public knowledge through stories in trade journals and business publications. But more frequently, discourses about actual practices remain relatively obscure. Organizations may be embarrassed when their adoption of a new technology turns political or their intended results are not quickly obtained. Some of the best accounts of these struggles come from careful historical analyses, ethnographic studies, and case analyses which highlight actual practice and the various sense-making struggles and upheaval that may be associated with organizational restructuring. When these accounts become public, contending discourses can emerge and new technological action frames developed.

Computer-Based Work: On the Road to Distant Forms of Work

Many specific computerization movements have already been spawned by the more general internetworking movement (e.g., electronic commerce, distant learning, telemedicine, etc.). What these specific CMs share is a similar approach for how to organize business, education, and medical practices when geographic distances are no longer considered to be relevant. In this section, we will illustrate our CM perspective by focusing on the rise of distant forms of work. This specific CM intersects and gives new life to a computerization movement that has been influential for some time—computer-based work. We first discuss the technological frames, discourses, and practices related to the earlier computer-based work movement. Then, we discuss its intersection with internetworking and the current discourses around distant forms of work.

Work Automation

Automating the Firm

The use of machines to automate various aspects of office work began in the second half of the 19th century. By the end of the 19th century, typewriters were widely available in many offices (Giuliano, 1982). Fully functional digital computers were developed during World War II. While debates still circulate about whether the first digital computer was the British "Colussus" or the American ENIAC (Edwards, 1996), by the mid-1950s, the Univac, the first commercial computer, was being used for billing and accounting in insurance firms (Yates, 1999). From the 1950s to the mid-1980s, the computerization of work was framed as a work automation activity.

Technological action frames were built up around many work automation technologies, from the earliest organizational accounting systems to computer-based numerical control systems on shop floors to expert systems in professional offices. Managers in many large hierarchical organizations at the time perceived a number of major problems: lack of control over work processes; uncertainty in decision making; and increasing demand for clerical workers to handle the growing volume of business transactions. Their solution was the implementation of work automation systems, i.e., formal, closed-loop, information processing and feedback systems that enabled system-level self-correction and the automation of many work processes and activities through step-by-step procedures. The dominant scientific theories employed to understand how and why organizations should restructure themselves to incorporate work automation systems were cybernetics (Weiner, 1948), systems theory (Churchman, 1971; Dertouzos, 1972; Rapaport, 1986), and theories of organizational information processing (Galbraith, 1974). The primary goals of many organizations that implemented these new systems were increased productivity (including cost reductions) and the reduction of uncertainty.

Scientific discourses about work process automation emerged during the pre-World War II era. At Harvard, Howard Aiken and Wassily Leontif, inspired by Babbage's work in Britain a century before, developed the science of mathematical economy, a formal theory of input-output analysis and a design for an early electromechanical computer (Beniger, 1991). Independently, George Stibitz at Bell Laboratories and John Atanasoff at Iowa State University were developing prototypes of electronic and electro-mechanical automatic digital calculators. Alan Turing, a British mathematician, discovered that machines could carry out mental operations and published a paper called "On Computable Numbers" during the mid-1930s. Later, during the war, Turing worked with a team of scientists at the British Government Code and Cypher School to develop computational devices that could automate and speed up the decryption of encoded German messages (Edwards, 1996).

Yates (1999) reports that in the U.S. during World War II, many mathematically trained actuaries also worked on military projects involving statistics and cryptology and came to learn about new electronic computers through these government discourses and practices. As the war ended and these actuaries went back to work, they were anxious to examine the potential of computers for the insurance industry. At the 1947 meeting of the Society of Actuaries, a committee was formed to study their potential use. The committee worked closely with IBM and Remington Rand's

Univac division to develop technologies that would be explicitly useful to their firms and profession. Their report was distributed to their members in 1952 and helped to spread ideas about how computing could enhance productivity. While initially the committee had wanted to see the development of applications that would specifically help their profession (e.g., in automating mortality studies and financial analyses), these computations represented insufficient volumes of work to justify the expense of the machines. As a consequence, they concluded that the most effective use of new computers would be for routine billing and accounting processes. The efforts of this committee and other similar committees at the Life Office Management Association and Insurance Accounting and Statistical Association initiated sales to a number of insurance companies. These innovations provided models for the evolution of computing in other insurance companies and large firms that routinely handled large volumes of billing and accounting transactions.

During the 1960s, a variety of work automation systems continued to be developed and implemented for use in banks, government agencies, and manufacturing firms. In its most extreme form, organizations expected to be able to increase their productivity through investments in technology and the substitution of machines for labor. In a less extreme form, organizations expected to hire less skilled, lower paid workers who could perform more work with the aid of a machine. In one set of estimates, each word-processing machine was thought to be equal to between one and five typists (Reinecke, 1984) while every robot introduced into an automobile plant could replace two workers (Shaiken, 1985).

Management theorists within academia (c.f., Leavitt and Whisler, 1958; Simon, 1977) saw computerization as a mechanism for enhanced control over decision making in hierarchical organizations. If information from front-line workers could be quickly pushed up the hierarchy and integrated into top-level decision making, managers could recentralize decision authorities, reassert control over work processes, and increase organizational productivity and competitiveness. Top managers in large organizations informed by these new theories and technologies advocated the computerization of their firms. Information became privileged and many management information systems were developed and implemented for use by mid-level managers. An entire new field, Management Information Systems, emerged in academia to develop theories and research programs centered on technological improvements in organizational decision making. Most of these theories and many new technologies such as decision support systems were aimed at enhancing the work of individuals in organizations (e.g., supervisors and mid-level managers). In practice, many organizations had problems developing and implementing these new systems. Gladden (1982) estimated that nearly 75 percent of all systems development projects were either never completed or, if completed, were never used.

Many contending discourses emerged in academia and labor. The early work automation frame reignited the age-old fear that workers have of being replaced by machines (Castells, 1996). In the 1950s, Norbert Weiner (1954) predicted that automation would result in a depression within 25 years that would make the depression of the 1930s seem trivial. A discourse emerged around this idea and maintained this pessimistic position throughout the next several decades (c.f., *The Collapse of Work* [Jenkins & Sherman, 1979] and *Automatic Unemployment* [Hines & Searle, 1979]). From the 1970s through the 1990s, researchers in the field of industrial and labor relations developed a discourse that articulated for a wider audience the process of automation within manufacturing organizations, focusing on de-skilling and computer-mediated work (Adler, 1992; Braverman, 1974; Hirschhorn, 1984; Shaiken, 1985; Zuboff, 1988). Others focused on the impacts of new technologies on clerical and other white-collar workers (Feldberg & Glenn, 1983; Gregory & Nussbaum, 1982; Iacono & Kling, 1987; Mumford, 1983) and on general reductions in the quality of worklife in extensively computerized settings (Attewell & Rule, 1984; Kling & Iacono, 1989). Debates emerged in the discourses of sociology, computer science, and information systems about all of these topics. Many argued, however, that the apparent negative employment effects were overstated due to simplistic notions about the substitution of machines for labor (Hunt & Hunt, 1983). While some occupations, such as telephone operators, clearly have seen reductions in their numbers through the automation of their jobs (Denny & Fuss, 1983), the more or less continuous growth of jobs in the U.S. contradicted the idea that machines could substitute for labor. Moreover, empirical studies on de-skilling, monitoring, and quality of worklife did not find that negative outcomes were necessarily determined by the new technologies—as predicted by the framing of the technology and its associated discourses. Instead, outcomes were non-deterministic and depended on a variety of factors including type of organization, general economic conditions, and the predominant management philosophy.

Automating the Professions and Jobs

By the mid-1980s, the types of computers and applications available in the marketplace had increased significantly. Many professionals and semi-professionals in the workplace were eager to have increased access to these new machines and their related applications to develop their own local systems and manipulate organizational information for their own needs. This type of computer use is often referred to as "end-user computing" (Rockart & Flannery, 1983). However, it was not the ready availability of new machines in the workplace that engendered these changes, but extra-organizational discourse in professional societies promoting the computerization of their members' work. Similar to the Society of Actuaries during the earlier period, national and regional accounting and finance associations advocated the use of PCs and spreadsheets in the early 1980s as part of the professionalization of their members. From the 1970s through the 1980s, material control and production associations pushed for Material Requirements Planning (MRP) systems and, then, Manufacturing Resource Planning (MRP II) systems as ways to rationalize and increase the productivity of manufacturing organizations (Kling & Iacono, 1984). During this same period, several associations, such as the Data Processing Managers Association (DPMA) and the Association of Computing Machinery (ACM), emerged to serve computer specialists and the managers of Data Processing (DP) and Management Information Systems (MIS) departments.

In each administrative sector, some related groups have taken on the mantle of computerization as a subject of professional reform. These professionals do not work for computer vendors; they identify themselves as accountants, production planners, or information systems specialists, for example, with an interest in using certain computer applications in the course of their work in insurance firms, manufacturing companies, or the public sector. In practice, many had to struggle within their organizations to acquire new machines and applications (e.g., PCs and spreadsheet software) (c.f., George, Iacono, & Kling, 1995; Kling & Iacono, 1984, 1989). Many professionals and their managers developed strategies to acquire new machines for their personal use over periods of time, by hiding their purchases in departmental budgets, or by reconstituting cast-off machines (e.g., old test equipment used on the manufacturing floor) for use in their own offices. Since these struggles to gain access to machines and applications constituted grass-roots efforts on the part of various professionals and semi-professionals, there was little discourse that rose to counter the idea of more ubiquitous computing for many types of workers.

Automating the Office and the Distant Worker

By the mid 1980s, most large organizations were already using their own wide-area networks or value-added networks (telecommunications services purchased from outside vendors) to communicate across their distant divisions and workplaces. Many were also implementing local-area networks (within buildings and offices) to enhance work-group computing. Giuliano (1982, p. 150) suggested that in such an "information-age office" people could communicate with one another and with their home offices through "one of a half dozen 'electronic mail' networks now available throughout the U.S." He argued that people would increasingly conduct their work not only in the office, but also while traveling, while on the shop floor, and at home. Not only would they have access to their personal files, but they could also access information from the company's mainframe. The build-up of these technologies in the mid-1980s was the fuel for a number of highly exaggerated and short-lived claims for an "office of the future" where workers could "compute" from home while having real-time access to the critical events and information of a more virtual and paperless workplace (Miles, 1987; Toffler, 1980).

With the decreasing costs of computers and modems, telecommuting, (i.e., remote supervision with a reduction in commuting) as a form of distant work became a viable option (Mokhtarian, 1991). During the mid-1980s, many departments of transportation concerned with increasing traffic jams and air pollution attempted to mobilize many large organizations to experiment with and implement telecommuting programs. They argued that organizations concerned with a shortage of workers or space could expand their work force while still maintaining communications and control through computer networks. For example, workers could respond to customers' telephone calls by utilizing a personal computer and special telephone line at home or at satellite offices. While some companies did implement experimental programs, often to comply with government requirements, most did not move toward telecommuting as a major new form of work.

Much of the empirical research on telecommuting has found that management issues are a factor in preventing its widespread adoption (Staples, Hulland, & Higgins, 1998). Managers report difficulties in managing their workers and dislike their lack of control over work processes. The "Technology and Telecommuting: Issues and Impacts Committee" of the National Science Council (1994) developed a report on the status of telecommuting in the U.S. and found telecommuting to be quite narrow in its traditional conceptualization. We agree and suggest that telecommuting has largely been framed as a work automation technology. It is typically aimed at individual workers who use a computer all day and for whom control over work productivity is paramount. The key management strategies employed to ensure control are either piecework or management by objective. In practice, these workers can be cut off from the discourses of their workplaces and subjected to extensive work monitoring. In the NII: Agenda for Action (White House, 1993), it is argued that people can live anywhere and telecommute to their offices if they are connected to the NII. It is assumed that simply because internetworking technologies are available people will move to less populated areas and land use patterns will change. But most workers are not going to move simply because it is feasible to telecommute.

There are many factors that may cause people to move. Work may be one of them. But, job security is a key worry in U.S. workplaces today and people tend to live where they will have many job opportunities. While the U.S. Department of Transportation estimated that there were about two million telecommuters in 1993 and expected those numbers to grow over this decade, we suggest, however, that over reliance on the technological frame of work automation and the way that it has informed the managerial practices for telecommuting are primary reasons that telecommuting has not been the vast success that was expected—despite its assumed benefits for the public good and the availability of new internetworking technologies.

Work Collaboration

In the late 1980s and early 1990s, disillusionment set in over the lack of productivity gains from the widespread individual use of computers and information systems. Computing and telecommunications systems accounted for half of the capital investments made by private firms while annual rates of productivity growth remained low—especially in the service sector. The wide-scale recognition of this problem was termed the "productivity paradox" (Dunlop & Kling, 1991). A new technological action frame, work collaboration, emerged. Its development depended largely on the earlier counter-discourses about work automation. It was widely argued that workers should be recognized as organizational assets; they should be empowered, not replaced. Environments should be created so that workers can fully contribute to the limits of their ability, instead of being monitored eight hours a day (Creed, Douglas, & Miles, 1996). Since work is a social endeavor, it was argued, technologies should support social communication and collaboration rather than individual work done in seclusion from the ongoing activities of the firm.

Technological frames were built up around many work collaboration technologies (e.g., screen-sharing software, group schedulers, group authoring tools, group support systems, and shared databases). A major problem for management at the time was the lack of evidence of productivity gains from their heavy investments in work automation technologies. The major solution was the use of technologies that would facilitate information sharing and collaboration. Potential users included everyone in an organization. A key belief was that productivity from the new technologies that supported group work had the potential to exceed what had been achieved with PCs used by individuals (Bullen & Bennett, 1991). But, further, it was expected that the use of these technologies would transform organizations into more collaborative places to work. Almost everyone in an organization would have access to organizational information and almost everyone would be empowered to make decisions and innovate as necessary in their jobs. Since the 1950s, the framing of work computerization had come full circle. Computing was originally believed to enable a shift in control and decision authorities to centralized and top management. By the late 1980s and early 1990s, new technologies were expected to decentralize authority and empower lower-level employees and professionals.

Discourses about work collaboration were initially embedded in the software engineering and computer science research labs of commercial firms, such as XeroxPARC, MCC, and SRI, and universities, such as the MIT Laboratory for Computer Science and the University of Arizona GroupSystems research projects. Participants called the technologies they were developing and the forms of work they were espousing computer-supported cooperative (and later, collaborative) work (CSCW). CSCW was coined as a galvanizing catch phrase, and later given more substance through a lively stream of research and the emergence of a community of interest. Conferences identified with the term and participants advanced prototype systems, studies of their use, and key theories about their development and potential impacts. The media promoted this stream of research. But unlike the general internetworking movement that is highly visible in mainstream media, CSCW was discussed primarily in business publications, like the *Wall Street Journal* or *Business Week*, the business sections of daily newspapers, and computer and information science publications (e.g., *Communications of the ACM*). In these discourses, pundits and consultants predicted organizational transformations (e.g., the flattening of organizational hierarchies and the empowering of lower-level workers) through use of these new technologies (c.f., Wilke, 1993).

Researchers examining the early use of CSCW applications in organizational settings found little evidence of transformation, however. Within these sites, there was little discourse about the new technologies (e.g., how to use them, their expected benefits, or their role in the firm). As a consequence, many potential users perceived the new technology in the old work automation frame. Researchers found that they were mainly used as devices for extending the capabilities of individuals (Bullen & Bennett, 1991) or they were not used as originally intended (i.e., for information sharing or collaboration) or at all (Orlikowski, 1993). Further, these researchers argued that the expectation that groupware or CSCW technologies can transform organizations to be more collaborative is based in technological determinism. In practice, many working relationships can be multivalent, and mix elements of cooperation, conflict, conviviality, competition, collaboration, commitment, caution, control, coercion, coordination, and combat (Kling, 1991). But the frames that were built up around collaborative work technologies had come largely from technologists wishing to push their products. Like others before them, they were rejecting the old cultural models of work, and attempting to mobilize support for new ways of doing work. But, managers were slow to buy these technologies.

Distant Forms of Work

During the early 1990s, the themes of many popular management consultants shifted toward more socially rich conceptions of work practices, focusing on cross-functional teams, partnerships, and strategic alliances, for example. Whole literatures emerged heralding new forms of organization—flexible, networked, learning, trust-based governance forms, cluster and virtual. These conceptualizations argued for the importance of lateral forms of communication within and across organizations enabled by new internetworking technologies. The idea of collaborative work was given new life through the intersection of the internetworking CM.

One vision of this new organization argues that large, hierarchical organizations will vertically disintegrate to become small, lean organizations joined in networks and alliances. The apostles of these virtual corporations, like the earlier disciples of other forms of computer-based work, are not shy about pushing their ideas. William Davidow and Michael Malone (1992), who wrote *The Virtual Corporation*, argue that unless the U.S. becomes a leader in forming virtual organizations by the year 2015, it will lose its competitive edge.

While many organizations already had a variety of internal and external networks in place using proprietary protocols and standards, the rise of internetworking stabilized the exemplary artifacts of an emerging and contending technological frame for computer-based work around the Internet and open protocols and standards. Government discourses, which supported the research and development of internetworking technologies, legitimized distant forms of work based on the Internet, the World Wide Web, and other internetworking technologies (despite the narrow conceptualization in the NII of distant work as telecommuting).

Today, the merging of new organizational forms, collaborative work technologies, and the broad internetworking movement has resulted in a new technological action frame with the dominant ideational element of distributed or distant forms of work. Distributed work is defined as: "work that is done in a location different from that of the supervisor, subordinate, or fellow team member" (Technology and Telecommuting Committee, 1994). Technological frames have built up around many new technologies and concepts related to distributed work such as intra- and extra-nets, electronic communities, Web-based conferencing tools, and desktop video-conferencing. Some technologies have been reconstituted from their earlier framing as work collaboration tools. For example, Lotus Notes, a primary work collaboration technology, was initially assumed to enhance work collaboration for anyone and everyone in an organization. Today, it is given to team members and managers who are distributed and who must use electronic communications to accomplish their work. A major problem identified by organizations is that people must work together (e.g., on cross-functional or global teams) while they are often distributed in time and space. For example, many people work on multiple teams, travel to see customers, or are not collocated with their colleagues and teammates. The major solution is internetworking to enable their distributed work. The primary goals of many organizations that choose to adopt distant forms of work are increased communications at all levels within and across relevant social groups of organizations (e.g., the sales force, product repair people, customers, suppliers, buyers, team members, partners, etc.) for real-time or near real-time information sharing and the integration of distributed knowledge.

Not surprisingly, the theoretical basis for this technological frame is forming around the ideas of networks, social networks and knowledge networks (c.f., Sproull & Kiesler, 1991). But the idea of a network is less a theoretical model than a rhetorical tool for researchers to easily discuss the variety of complex and not well understood relationships currently found in organizations today (Guice, 1998). A number of different streams of research have developed around these core ideas. Some studies of virtual organizations, for example, have taken an economic perspective and have focused primarily on buyer-supplier networks rather than worklife (Kraut, Steinfield, Chan, Butler, & Hoag, 1998). Another stream has focused on the technologies used in internetworking and the choices that managers and professionals make about how to communicate with coworkers, not on the work itself or the ways that organizations restructure around these new technologies (c.f., Fulk, Schmitz, Steinfield, 1990; Zack & McKenney, 1995). Studies of computer-mediated communication (c.f., Sproull & Kiesler, 1991) have investigated the use of e-mail and distribution lists in organizations and assert that these technologies can make an organization become networked—as users begin to communicate and form relationships with people that they never would have communicated with otherwise. One study (Hesse, Sproull, Kiesler, & Walsh, 1993), for example, found that oceanographers who are on the periphery of their scientific community benefited more from their use of electronic networks than did those who were more centrally located. In sociology, Powell's (1996) work on trust-based forms of work and Meyerson, et al.'s (1996) work on swift trust have engendered studies of trust in temporary, virtual teams (Iacono & Weisband, 1997; Jarvenpaa & Leidner, 1998). The thread that runs across these various streams is the death of distance—geographic distance is irrelevant. Little attention is paid, however, to the possible social or cultural barriers that may still be present.

But, today, there is a dearth of studies that focus on the practices of distributed work (e.g., how distributed work is accomplished, how people communicate, how monitoring is carried out [or not], how leadership works, how people learn or innovate, or what the impacts of these types of work are on the people who engage in them). One study of distributed work focuses on the long-term communicative practices of the computer scientists and researchers that used the early Internet to develop the Common Lisp programming language (c.f., Orlikowski & Yates, 1995). Other studies are currently being conducted on the use of video-conferencing across distant work sites (Ruhleder & Jordan, 1997) and continuous video-integration of worksites (Graham, 1996). Some discourse about distant forms of work has emerged in reports commissioned by the government (c.f., Technology and Telecommuting Committee, 1994). But this research stream is still very new and few conclusions can be drawn about what the actual practices of distributed workers will be.

While some counter discourse emerged around the early telecommuting technologies (e.g., by pointing out the isolation of telecommuters, their extensive monitoring, and loss of a social office), by and large, distributed workers do not have those problems. Rather than working at home most of the time, they travel with their laptops to see clients or other colleagues. New problems have arisen, however. A white paper on "High Performance Computing and Communications, Information Technology and the Next Generation Internet" reports that there are many logistical and maintenance problems related to internetworking (Kling, 1997). This report expects that these issues will become more salient as the technologies become more sophisticated, the users become less sophisticated and technical support is less available.

Media discourses have also pointed out some of the problems that distributed workers may have: the blurring of home and work, work that encompasses more hours of the day or week, and the extensive learning that has to go on before these technologies can be effectively used. But one of the more ironic twists is the idea that the new "borderless economy," instead of allowing people to live and work anywhere they desire, has created an "elite class of nomads" or the "business homeless" who live nowhere or perhaps even worse live in "mind-numbing" airports much of the time (Iyer, 1998; Rayner, 1998). One unanticipated outcome of distributed work may be that rather than distance becoming irrelevant through new technologies, it may become increasingly relevant as people travel more frequently to accomplish their work. Castells (1996) argues that worldwide networking will exclude entire segments of society—those that are not networked—and result in a highly segmented global society. But given the indeterminacy of the meaning of new and complex technologies, a future based on internetworking can only be discerned at this point with some difficulty.

Summary

In this analysis, we have examined the framing, discourses, and practices of three historical shifts in the computer-based work CM—from work automation (including telecommuting) to work collaboration and distant forms of work. We have seen that with these shifts, new technological action frames were constituted in the discourses of the government (especially for telecommuting), professional associations (especially for work automation), scientific discourses (work automation, work collaboration, and distant forms of work), and the mass media (work collaboration and distant forms of work). While these discourses have mobilized various types of organizations to adopt these technologies, in practice, the goals related to these frames have remained elusive. Productivity gains, especially in the service sector, remained low while work automation was prevalent. Across a variety of work settings with groupware or CSCW applications, collaboration was difficult to achieve. And distant forms of work, rather than integrating distributed people and resources, may actually cause more workers to travel distances. As a consequence, there are continuing gaps between the discourses about these work technologies and actual practices in micro-social contexts. We have also seen that careful scientific studies of the use of these technologies in worklife play a critical role in the development of contending discourses and the further development of new technological action frames. For the most part, the dominant critiques of various modes of computerization have come from the discourses produced by careful scientific research on work practices. These discourses are essential in correcting the many misrepresentations and misunderstandings about the nature of organizational restructuring and how new technologies influence work practices.

Conclusions

We have argued that the rise of the Internet and other internetworking technologies in U.S. organizations has been stimulated by a set of loosely linked computerization movements. We analyzed these movements by investigating how societal mobilization is socially constructed through the interplay of three elements: technological action frames, public discourses, and practices. Technological action frames are built up in public discourses and can be persuasive to broad audiences. They can mobilize similarly situated organizations to reject old cultural models and to identify with new ones, for example, by getting connected to the Internet and restructuring work around these new technologies. Our analysis of organizational change differs from most organizational analyses by considering CMs that cut across society as important sources of interpretations and beliefs about what internetworking is good for and what social actions people should take to secure the future they envision.

Today, a dominant technological frame is being built up around the Internet. A major ideational element is the death of distance. This idea simultaneously attributes blame for societal problems to the distances among distributed people and social institutions and suggests ways to ameliorate the situation—use internetworking to obliterate distance and integrate, connect, or network distributed people and organizations. The media, the government, and scientific disciplines embed these beliefs, goals, and attributions in their own discourses about how internetworking might apply to various sectors of society. Theories derived from scientific disciplines provide organizing rationales (e.g., transition to a networked world, participation in an information society) for unbounded internetworking. Computerization movements play a role in persuading organizations to accept an ideology that favors everybody adopting state-of-the-art internetworking technologies. Their discourses, however, rarely explain the values, resource commitments, and extensive restructuring that accompany their visions. While CMs can generate a rhetoric of transformation, evidence thus far does not point to widespread actual transformations as intended. Actual transformations (or failures to transform) work themselves out in situated practices.

Contending discourses do arise in the mass media, within scientific disciplines, and within organizations as injustices or the loss of valued practices are pointed out for certain groups of people (e.g., the stress of monitoring for clerical workers or the loss of the social office for telecommuters), as critical research findings are made public (e.g., productivity from technology investments is low), or as social conditions change (e.g., more extensive lateral communications are required as many businesses acquire new strategic partners). Contending discourses, by framing technologies in alternative ways, can have powerful effects on the development of new meaning about a set of technologies and can constitute new technological frames. For example, the criticisms of the work automation frame developed into discourses about more collaborative technologies and engendered the development of entire new families of technologies (e.g., groupware and CSCW). Today, there are few contending discourses about distant forms of work. But we have no reason to doubt that as studies of actual practice emerge, the gaps between discourses and practices will be uncovered.

We believe that when one studies the sites where internetworking is being adopted, traces of discourses that have been imported into the adopting organization from other sources will be easy to spot. Members of adopting organizations consult with specialists, belong to professional associations, read professional journals and mass media publications, take courses, are affiliated with government committees, and visit other organizations to examine their practices. To the extent that the framing of a new technology has become dominant, we would expect to find its widespread use in the discourses within and across many organizational sites. And we would also expect to find many gaps between the discourses and the practices as people struggle to understand what a particular technology means and how to apply it in their own work lives. These ideas open up rich lines of empirical research. Much more work needs to be done to examine particular CMs. We need to learn more about the situational and interactional elements of CM activists and the ways in which cultural templates, such as master frames, are developed and translated into practice. We hope that our analysis of the Internet and computer-based work will encourage scholars to examine CMs in other social settings and to analyze their own discourses and practices.

During the last 50 years, CMs have helped set the stage on which the computer industry expanded. As this industry expands, vendor organizations (like Microsoft) also become powerful participants in persuading people to computerize and internetwork. Some computer vendors and their trade associations can be powerful participants in specific decisions about equipment purchased by a particular company or a powerful force behind weakening legislation that could protect consumers from trade abuses related to computing. But their actions alone cannot account for the widespread mobilization of internetworking in the United States. They feed and participate in it; they have not driven it. Despite the lack of evidence for increased productivity in organizations, investment in new computing and telecommunications systems continues to grow at a staggering rate. Part of the drive to internetwork is economic, but part is driven by the efforts of CM advocates in the government, various scientific disciplines, and the popular press who mobilize constituencies. Moreover, the social changes that one can attribute to internetworking can sometimes be disruptive and socially conservative (e.g., loss of attention to regional needs, increased disparity between the "haves" and the "have-nots," more opportunities for government surveillance, etc.), contrary to the positive change portrayed by the internetworking computerization movement. But we suspect that the pervasiveness of internetworking and the new energy infused into the movement through the NII will have a significant cumulative effect on American life.

There is no well-organized opposition or broad-based alternative to the internetworking CM. Even countries like China that have traditionally feared and controlled citizen contact with foreigners have started to develop their own NII's. In the name of "economic informatization," China now allows people to use the Internet, but requires registration with the police. It also blocks certain Web sites and monitors the content accessed by its citizens. A general counter-computerization movement

(CCM) in most countries might well be stigmatized and marginalized as "Luddite." Since CM activists portray internetworking as a means to transform society, a general CCM would have to oppose internetworking in all sectors of society and all institutions, (e.g., in education, work, home, and so on). A successful ideological base for such opposition probably would have to be anchored in an alternative conception of society and the place of technology in it. While there is no active movement to counter internetworking in general, many have joined Senator Exon and others in proclaiming the Internet to be a danger and support the ideas behind his legislation to regulate speech on the Internet (Cannon, 1996). At the same time, organizations such as the Electronic Frontier Foundation and the American Civil Liberties Union continue to struggle to support individual rights to free speech and other civil liberties for Internet users. However, these discourses and counter discourses are highly legalistic and bound up with governmental ideals rather than deeper understandings of actual practices. In their most likely form, the computerization movements of the late 1990s will constitute a conservative transformation reinforcing patterns of an elite-dominated, stratified society.

Acknowledgments

We would like to thank Bryan Pfaffenberger who read an earlier draft and provided insight that helped moved the theoretical ideas in this paper forward. The authors gratefully acknowledge the continuing enthusiasm of Leigh Star for this project and the incredibly detailed and helpful suggestions made by JoAnne Yates, an editor of [the original volume].

References

Adam, N. A., Slonim, A. J., Wegner, P., & Yesha, Y. (1997). Globalizing business, education, culture through the Internet. *Communications of the ACM*, 40(2), 115–121.

Adler, P. S. (1992). *Technology and the future of work*. New York: Oxford University Press.

Aronson, N. (1984). Science as a claims-making activity: Implications for social problems research. In J. Schneider and J. Kitsuse (Eds.), *Studies in the sociology of social problems* (pp. 1–30). Norwood, NJ: Ablex Publishing Co.

Attewell, P., & Rule, J. (1984). Computing and organizations: What we know and what we don't know. *Communications of the ACM*, 27, 1184–1192.

Barlow, J. P. (1993). A plain text on crypto policy. *Communications of the ACM*, 36(11), 21–26.

Bell, D. (1979). The social framework of the information society. In M. Dertouzos & J. Moses (Eds.), *The computer age: A twenty-year view* (pp. 163–211). Cambridge, MA: MIT Press.

Beniger, J. R. (1991). Information society and global science. In C. Dunlop & R. Kling (Eds.), *Computerization and controversy: Value conflicts and social choices* (pp. 383–397). San Diego, CA: Academic Press.

Berghel, H. (1995). Digital village: Maiden voyage. *Communications of the ACM*, 38(11), 25–145.

Bijker, W. E. (1997). *Of Bicycles, bakelites and bulbs: Toward a theory of sociotechnical change*. Cambridge, MA: MIT Press.

Bijker, W. E., & Law, J. (Eds.). (1992). *Shaping technology / building society: Studies in sociotechnical change*. Cambridge, MA: MIT Press.

Blumer, H. (1969). Social movements. In B. McLaughlin (Ed.), *Studies in social movements: A social psychological perspective* (pp. 8–29). New York: Free Press.

Braverman, H. (1974). *Labor and monopoly capital: The degradation of work in the 20th century*. New York: Monthly Review Press.

Bucher, R., & Strauss, A. (1961). Professions in process. *American Journal of Sociology*, 66, 325–334.

Bullen, C., & Bennett, J. L. (1991). Groupware in practice: An interpretation of work experiences. In C. Dunlop & R. Kling (Eds.), *Computerization and controversy: Value conflicts and social choices* (pp. 257–287). San Diego, CA: Academic Press:

Cairncross, F. (1997). *The death of distance*. Boston: Harvard Business School Press.

Cannon, R. (1996). The legislative history of senator Exon's communications decency act: Regulating barbarians on the information superhighway. Retrieved from www.cais.net/cannon/cannon@dc.net

Castells, M. (1996). *The rise of the network society*. Malden, MA: Blackwell Publishers.

Cerf, V. (1995). Computer networking: Global infrastructure for the 21st century. Retrieved from www.cs.washington.edu/homes/lazowska/cra/networks.html

Churchman, C. W. (1971). *The design of inquiring systems: Basic concepts of systems and organizations*. New York: Basic Books.

Creed, W., Douglas E., & Miles, R. E. (1996). Trust in organizations: A conceptual framework linking organizational forms, managerial philosophies, and the opportunity costs of controls. In R. M. Kramer & T. R. Tyler (Eds.), *Trust in organizations* (pp. 16–38). Thousand Oaks, CA: Sage.

Davidow, W. H., & Malone, M. S. (1992). *The virtual corporation*. New York: HarperCollins Publishers, Inc.

Davis, E. (1997). Spiritual telegraphs and the technology of communications: Turning into the electromagnetic imagination. Series on "Watch Your Language" at Public Netbase Media-Space. Retrieved from www.t0.or.at/davis/davislec1.html

de Certeau, M. (1984). *The practice of everyday life*. Berkeley, CA: University of California Press.

Denny, M., & Fuss, M. (1983). The effects of factor prices and technological change on the occupational demand for labor: Evidence from Canadian telecommunications. *Journal of Human Resources*, Spring, 161–176.

Dertouzos, M. (1972). *Systems, networks and computation: Basic concepts*. Huntington, NY: R. E. Krieger Publishing Co.

Dibbell, J. (1996). Taboo, consensus, and the challenge of democracy. In R. Kling (Ed.), *Computerization and controversy: Value conflicts and social choices* (2nd ed., pp. 552–568). San Diego, CA: Academic Press.

Dunlop, C., & Kling, R. (Eds.). (1991). *Computerization and controversy: Value conflicts and social choices*. San Diego, CA: Academic Press.

Dyson, E. (1997). Education and jobs in the digital world. *Communications of the ACM*, 40(2), 35–36.

Dyson, E., Gilder, G., Keyworth, G., & Toffler, A. (1996). Cyberspace and the American dream. *The Information Society*, 12(3), 295–308.

Edwards, P. (1996). *The closed world: Computers and the politics of discourse*. Cambridge, MA: MIT Press.

Elofson, G., & Robinson, W. N. (1998). Creating a custom mass-production channel on the Internet. *Communications of the ACM*, 41(3), 56–62.

Feldberg, R. L., & Glenn, E. N. (1983). New technology and its implications in U. S. clerical work. Office automation: Jekyll or Hyde? Cleveland: Working Women Educational Fund.

Fisher, K. (1997). Locating frames in the discursive universe. *Sociological Research Online*, 2(3). Retrieved from www.socresonline.org.uk/socresonline/2/3/4.html

Foucault, M. (1972). *The archaeology of knowledge and the discourse on language* (A. Sheridan, Trans.). New York: Pantheon Books.

Foucault, M. (1977). *Discipline and punishment* (Alan Sheridan, Trans.). New York: Pantheon Books.

Fulk, J., Schmitz, J. A., & Steinfield, C. W. (1990). A social influence model of technology use. In J. Fulk & C. Steinfield (Eds.), *Organization and communication technology* (pp. 117–142). Newbury Park, CA: Sage.

Galbraith, J. R. (1974). Organization design. *Interfaces*, 4(3), 28–36.

Gamson, W. A. (1995). Constructing social protest. In H. Johnston & B. Klandermans (Eds.), *Social movements and culture* (pp. 85–106). Minneapolis: University of Minnesota Press.

Ginzberg, E. (1982). The mechanization of work. *Scientific American*, 247(3), 67–75.

George, J., Iacono, S., & Kling, R. (1995). Learning in context: Extensively computerized work groups as communities of practice. *Accounting, Management and Information Technology*, 5(3/4), 185–202.

Gladden, G. (1982). Stop the life-cycle, I want to get off. *Software Engineering Notes*, 7(2), 35–39.

Goffman, E. (1986). *Frame analysis*. Boston: Northeastern University Press.

Graham, M. (1996). Changes in information technology, changes in work. *Technology in Society*, 18(3), 373–385.

Gregory, J., & Nussbaum, K. (1982). Race against time: Automation of the office. *Office: Technology and People*, 1, 197–236.

Guice, J. (1998). Looking backward and forward at the Internet. *The Information Society,* 14(3), 201–211.

Hafner, K. (1997). The world's most influential online community (and it's not AOL). *Wired,* 5(05), 98–104, 106–114, 118–122, 124–126, 128, 130, 132, 134, 136, 138, 140, 142.

Herring, S. (1996). Two variants of an electronic message schema. In S. C. Herring (Ed.), *Computer-mediated communication: Linguistic, social and cross-cultural perspectives* (pp. 81–106). Philadelphia: John Benjamins Publishing Company.

Hert, P. (1996). Social dynamics of an on-line scholarly debate. *The Information Society*, 13(4), 329–360.

Hesse, B. W., Sproull, L., Kiesler, S., & Walsh, J. P. (1993). Returns to science: Computer networks in oceanography. *Communications of the ACM*, 36(8), 90–101.

Hines, C., & Searle, G. (1979). *Automatic unemployment*. London: Earth Resources Research.

Hirschhorn, L. (1984). *Beyond mechanization: Work and technology in a postindustrial age*. Cambridge, MA: MIT Press.

Hunt, H. A., & Hunt, T. L. (1983). *Human resource implications of robotics*. Kalamazoo, MI: The W. E. Upjohn Institute for Employment Research.

Iacono, S., & Kling, R. (1996). Computerization movements and tales of technological utopianism. In R. Kling (Ed.), *Computerization and controversy: Value conflicts and social choices* (2nd ed., pp. 85–105). San Diego, CA: Academic Press.

Iacono, S., & Weisband, S. (1997). Developing trust in virtual teams. In *Proceedings of the 30th Hawaii international conference on system sciences, Vol. 2* (pp. 412–420). Maui, HI.

Iyer, P. (1998, March 8). The new business class. *The New York Times Magazine*, 37–40.

Jarvenpaa, S., & Leidner, D. (1998). Communication and trust in global virtual teams. *Journal of Computer-Mediated Communications*, 3(4).

Jenkins, C., & Sherman, B. (1979). *The collapse of work*. London: Eyre Methuen.

Johnston, H., & Klandermans, B. (1995). *Social movements and culture*. Minnesota: University of Minnesota Press.

Kannan, P. K., Chang, A. M., & Whinston, A. B. (1998). Marketing information on the I-Way. *Communications of the ACM*, 41(3), 35–43.

Kling, R. (1991). Cooperation, coordination and control in computer-supported work. *Communications of the ACM*, 34(12), 83–88.

Kling, R. (1997). The NGI as an effective support for professional work and social life. White Paper for Presidential Advisory Committee on High-Performance Computing and Communications, Information Technology and the Next Generation Internet. Retrieved from php.ucs.indiana.edu/~kling

Kling, R., & Iacono, S. (1984). The control of information systems development after implementation. *Communications of the ACM*, 27(12), 1218–1226.

Kling, R., & Iacono, S. (1988). The mobilization of support for computerization: The role of computerization movements. *Social Problems*, 35(3), 226–243.

Kling, R., & Iacono, S. (1989). Desktop computerization and the organization of work. In T. Forester (Ed.), *Computers in the human context: Information, technology, productivity, and people*. Cambridge, MA: MIT Press.

Kraut, R., Steinfield, C., Chan, A., Butler, B., & Hoag, A. (1998). Coordination and virtualization: The role of electronic networks and personal relationships. *Journal of Computer-Mediated Communications*, 3(4).

Leavitt, H. J., & Whisler, T. L. (1958). Management in the 1980s. *Harvard Business Review*, November–December, 41–48.

Lefebvre, H. (1991). *The production of space* (D. N. Smith, Trans.). Cambridge, MA: Blackwell.

Lewis, M. (1998, March 1). The little creepy crawlers who will eat you in the night. *The New York Times Magazine*, 40–46.

Lofland, J. (1995). Charting degrees of movement culture: Tasks of the cultural cartographer. In H. Johnston & B. Klandermans (Eds.), *Social movements and culture* (pp. 188–216). Minneapolis: University of Minnesota Press.

Lyotard, J. F. (1984). *The postmodern condition* (G. Bennington & Brian Massumi, Trans.). Minneapolis: University of Minnesota Press.

Madon, S. (1997). Globalization and development in Bangalore. *The Information Society*, 13(3), 227–243.

Matrix Information and Directory Services. (1997). Internet Growth. Retrieved from www.mids.org

Mattelart, A. (1994). *Mapping world communication* (S. Emanuel, Trans.). Minneapolis: University of Minnesota Press.

McAdam, D. (1982). *Political process and the development of black insurgency, 1930–1970*. Chicago: University of Chicago Press.

McCarthy, J. D., & Zald, M. N. (1977). Resource mobilization and social movements: A partial theory. *American Journal of Sociology*, 82(6), 1212–1241.

McLuhan, M., & Powers, B. R. (1989). *The Global Village*. New York City: Oxford University Press.

Miles, A. (1987). Home informatics: A report to the six countries programme on aspects of government policies toward technical innovation in industry. Delft, Netherlands: Six Countries Programme Secretariat.

Mokhtarian, P. (1991). Defining telecommuting. *Transportation Research Record*, 1305, 273–281.

More, T. (1997). A short history of the Internet. More online at wwwiz.com/issue 14/f01.htm

Morris, A. D., & Mueller, C. M. (Eds.). (1992). *Frontiers in social movement theory*. New Haven: Yale University Press.

Mueller, C. M. (1992). Building social movement theory. In A. D. Morris & C. M. Mueller (Eds.), *Frontiers in social movement theory* (pp. 3–26). New Haven: Yale University Press.

Mumford, E. (1983). *Designing secretaries*. Manchester, U.K.: Manchester Business School.

National Science Foundation (NSF). (1995). History of NSFNET growth by networks. Retrieved from www-static.cc.gatech.edu/fac/Mostafa.Ammar/8113/history.netcount (URL has been updated to working link. Old published URL: nic.merit.edu/nsfnet/statistics/history.netcount).

Noble, D. F. (1998). Digital diploma mills: The automation of higher education. Retrieved from firstmonday.dk/issues/issue3_1/noble/index.html

NUA, Ltd. (1998). How many online? Retrieved June 28, 1998, from www.cs.princeton.edu/courses/archive/fall02/frs129/readings/Digital%20Inequality/estimated%20people%20on%20line%20internat%20may%202002.htm (URL has been updated to working link. Old published URL: www.nua.survey.net/surveys/ about/index.html).

Orlikowski, W. J. (1992). Learning from notes: Organizational issues in groupware implementation. *The Information Society*, 9, 237–250.

Orlikowski, W. J., & Gash, D. (1994). Technological frames: Making sense of information technology in organizations. *ACM Transactions on Information Systems*, 12, 174–207.

Orlikowski, W. J., & Yates, J. (1995). Genre repertoire: The structuring of communicative practices in organizations. *Administrative Science Quarterly*, 39(4), 541–574.

Palmer, J. W., & Griffith, D. A. (1998). An emerging model of Web site design for marketing. *Communications of the ACM*, 41(3), 44–51.

Pfaffenberger, B. (1996). If I want it, it's OK: Usenet and the (outer) limits of free speech. *The Information Society*, 12(4), 365–386.

Pfeffer, J. (1987). A resource dependence perspective on intercorporate relations. In M. Mizruchi & M. Schwartz (Eds.), *Intercorporate relations: The structural analysis of business*. New York: Cambridge University Press.

Porter, M. E., & Millar, V. E. (1985). How information gives you competitive advantage. *Harvard Business Review*, July–August, 149–160.

Poster, M. (1990). *The mode of information*. Chicago: University of Chicago Press.

Powell, W. W. (1996). Trust-based forms of governance. In R. M. Kramer & T. R. Tyler (Eds.), *Trust in organizations* (pp. 51–67). Thousand Oaks, CA: Sage Publications.

Press, L. (1994). National information infrastructures: The Internet and interactive television. Conference on the electronic highway, University of Montreal. Retrieved from som.csudh.edu/fac/lpress/2cult.htm

Press, L. (1997). Tracking the global diffusion of the Internet. *Communications of the ACM*, 40(11), 11–18.

Rao, H. R., Salam, A. F., & DosSantos, B. (1998). Introduction (Marketing and the Internet). *Communications of the ACM*, 41(3), 32–34.

Rapaport, A. (1986). *General systems theory: Essential concepts and applications*. Tunbridge Wells, Kent: Abacus Press.

Rayner, R. (1998, March 8). Nowhere, USA. *The New York Times Magazine*, 42–46.

Reinecke, I. (1984). *Electronic illusions: A skeptic's view of our high tech future*. New York: Penguin.

Rheingold, H. (1993). *The virtual community*. Reading, MA: Addison-Wesley Publishing Company.

Rockart, J. F., & Flannery, L. S. (1983). The management of end-user computing. *Communications of the ACM*, 26(10), 776–784.

Ruhleder, K., & Jordan, B. (1997). Capturing complex, distributed activities: Video-based interaction analysis as a component of workplace ethnography. *Information systems and qualitative research*. IFIP WG 8.2 Working Conference, Philadelphia, PA.

Shaiken, H. (1985). *Work transformed: Automation and labor in the computer age*. New York: Holt, Rinehart, and Winston.

Simon, H. A. (1977). *The new science of management decision-making*. Englewood Cliffs, NJ: Prentice Hall.

Snow, D. A., & Benford, R. D. (1992). Master frames and cycles of protest. In A. D. Morris & C. M. Mueller (Eds.), *Frontiers in social movement Theory* (pp. 133–155). New Haven: Yale University Press.

Snow, D. A., Rochford, B. E. Jr., Worden, S. K., & Benford, R. D. (1986). Frame alignment processes, micromobilization and movement participation. *American Sociological Review*, 51, 464–481.

Sproull, L., & Kiesler, S. (1991). *Connections: New ways of working in the networked organization*. Cambridge, MA: MIT Press.

Staples, D. S., Hulland, J. S., & Higgins, C. A. (1998). A self-efficacy theory explanation for the management of remote workers in virtual organizations. *Journal of Computer-Mediated Communications,* 3(4).

Star, L. (1989). *Regions of the mind: Brain research and the quest for scientific certainty*. Stanford, CA: Stanford University Press.

Swidler, A. (1995). Cultural power and social movements. In H. Johnston & B. Klandermans (Eds.), *Social movements and culture* (pp. 25–40). Minnesota: University of Minnesota Press.

Technology and Telecommuting: Issues and Impacts Committee, National Science Council. (1994). *Research recommendations: To facilitate distributed work.* Washington, DC: National Academy of Sciences.

Toffler, A. (1980). *The third wave.* New York: William Morrow.

Weiner, N. (1948). *Cybernetics.* Cambridge, MA: MIT Press.

Weiner, N. (1954). *The human use of human beings.* New York: Houghton Mifflin.

White House. (1993). The National Information Infrastructure: Agenda for Action. Public domain document.

Wilke, J. (1993, December 9). Computer links erode hierarchical nature of workplace culture. *Wall Street Journal*, pp. A-1, A-7.

Windle, J. T., & Taylor, R. M. (1986). *The early architecture of Madison, Indiana.* Madison and Indianapolis: Indiana Historical Society.

Winner, L. (1996). Who will we be in cyberspace? *The Information Society*, 12(1), 63–72.

Yates, J. (1994). Evolving information use in firms, 1850–1920. In L. Bud-Frierman (Ed.), *Information acumen: The understanding and use of knowledge in modern business* (pp. 26–50). New York: Routledge.

Yates, J. (1999). The structuring of early computer use in life insurance. *Journal of Design History*, 12(1), 5–24.

Zack, M., & McKenney, J. (1995). Social context and interaction in ongoing computer-supported management groups. *Organization Science*, 6(4), 394–422.

Zuboff, S. (1988). *In the age of the smart machine: The future of work and power.* New York: Basic Books.

Part II

Productivity

Chapter 3

The Computerization Movement in the U.S. Home Mortgage Industry: Automated Underwriting from 1980 to 2004

M. Lynne Markus
Bentley College

Andrew Dutta
Department of Organizational Behavior and Human Resources
ICFAI Institute for Management Teachers

Charles W. Steinfield
Department of Telecommunication, Information Studies, and Media
Michigan State University

Rolf T. Wigand
Departments of Information Science and Management,
CyberCollege, University of Arkansas at Little Rock

Abstract

This paper reports on an empirical investigation of a particular computerization movement—the diffusion of automated underwriting in the U.S. home mortgage industry—over a 20-plus year timeframe. This paper demonstrates the influences of technological action frames, particularly the productivity master frame, on automated underwriting use practices. We also show, however, that the link between frames and use patterns is not a simple one. Several framings of automated underwriting emerged over time as a result of interactions among the components of technology ensembles and between technology ensembles and social actors. These interactions can confirm or disconfirm the frames, reinforcing or eroding them and shaping new frames. Today, multiple frames and use patterns exist simultaneously in the industry. These results cannot be understood solely in terms of economic forces. At the same time, they suggest the role of the technology ensemble in technology framing and use practices. These findings enhance our understanding of the dynamics of computerization movements.

Introduction

Kling and Iacono (1988, 1995) inquired "why do organizations adopt new computing technologies?" and challenged us to move beyond simple explanations based on the economics of need. They directed our attention instead to public discourse about computing (see also Iacono & Kling, 2001) and to computerization movement (CM) advocates, such as professional associations, that provide arenas in which people develop technological action frames about what computing is good for and how it can fit into their organizations. They called for careful empirical studies of CMs that focus on the decline of CMs, value conflicts and counter-CMs, and alternative organizational practices of technology use (particularly those that differ from utopian visions).

In response to their call, this paper examines the changing technological action frames and organizational practices in a particular CM as documented in the published discourse of a leading professional association over a 20-plus year time period. Thus, our study brings together the three related elements of Iacono and Kling's (2001) analysis—frames, discourse, and practices. In addition, our study brings in the additional element of *technology ensemble interactions*. Complex information technologies are best thought of as "packages," "webs," "ensembles," or "interaction networks" (Kling, 1980, 1993; Kling, McKim, & King, 2002) in which numerous technical and non-technical components interact with each other and with various social actors. Sometimes, as Kling and Iacono (1988) noted, technology ensembles do not live up to the utopian visions of their proponents, because of setbacks in the course of technology or institutional development. Other times, technology ensembles conflict with established work practices, leading to their rejection. Similarly, successes in technology and institutional development and application can reinforce technology frames and spur widespread diffusion. Thus, we argue that the interactions among the components of the technology ensemble and between the ensemble and social actors and practices should be one of the "social [or socio-technical] processes that drive computerization" (cf. Kling & Iacono, 1995).

Our study examines the diffusion of automated underwriting in the U.S. home mortgage industry. This CM is particularly relevant to the prior work of Kling and Iacono because it directly involves one of the general technologies they examined in 1988—artificial intelligence. In addition, because the electronic exchange of data is a key enabling technology for automated underwriting, our story also touches on the rise of the Internet, the focus of Iacono and Kling's (2001) analysis.

In the next section of this paper we provide theoretical justification for our focus not only on frames, discourse, and practices but also on technology ensemble interactions. Although it is easy enough to separate these elements conceptually, it is more challenging to do so in the analysis of an actual CM. Therefore, after we describe our data sources and analysis procedures and provide some background on the mortgage industry, we present our findings in three sections that, in roughly chronological order, outline a succession of frames and use practices and the intervening processes. We show that the link between frames and use patterns is not a simple one. Several framings of automated underwriting emerged over time as people and organizations reacted to the socio-technical arrangements implied by early frames and as technology ensemble interactions confirmed or disconfirmed the frames. Today, multiple frames and use patterns exist simultaneously in the industry. These results cannot be understood solely in terms of economic forces such as the drive for greater efficiency. At the same time, they suggest that the technology ensemble plays an important role in technology framing and use practices. These findings enhance our understanding of the dynamics of computerization movements.

Theoretical Background

In this section, we discuss two concepts that contribute to the understanding of CM careers: technological action frames and technology ensemble interactions. By "careers" we mean the diffusion of computer-based innovations and related work practices over time. We assume that CMs can exhibit highly variable careers, some succeeding more or less as originally envisioned and fading into taken-for-grantedness, some failing through inability to mobilize supporters, and some radically changing direction as a result of social or technical influences.

Technological Action Frames

Iacono and Kling define technological action frames as "multi-dimensional composite understandings—constituted and circulated in language—that legitimate high levels of investment for potential users, and form the core ideas about how a technology works and how a future based on its use should be envisioned" (Iacono & Kling, 2001). This conception derives from sociological theory on social movements and collective action frames. In that literature, participants in social movements are viewed as "actively engaged in the production and maintenance of meaning for constituents, antagonists, and bystanders or observers" (Benford & Snow, 2000, p. 613). This process of meaning construction is known as "framing." The core tasks of framing are "diagnostic framing" (problem identification and causal attributions), "prognostic framing" (articulation of solutions and action plans), and "motivational framing" (a "call to arms" or rationale for engaging in collective action to solve the problem, including the construction of vocabularies of severity, urgency, efficacy, and propriety) (Benford & Snow, 2000). Frame construction occurs by means of three sets of overlapping processes: discursive processes in the form of talk and written communications, strategic processes in the form of rational analysis and goal-directed thinking, and contested processes in which responses to challenges are formulated (Benford & Snow, 2000).

Much recent research on social movement "frame-work" focuses on the *sources* of collective action frames. For example, action frames are said to arise in cultural conditions, political conditions, and organizational ideology (Reese & Newcombe, 2003) or in the mobilizing structure of the social movement or the larger political opportunity structure (Joachim, 2003). This research occasionally emphasizes the tendency of social movement activists or "entrepreneurs" to "seize opportunities" presented by external conditions and events (Joachim, 2003) to shape the content of their action frames.

The consequences of collective action framework are also interesting. In the social movements tradition, research has focused mainly on the "intended effects" and near-term consequences of framing processes for the emergence and mobilization of social movements; much less work has addressed the longer-term outcomes and consequences of social movements (Giugni, 1998). In institutionalization theory, however, a concept closely related to that of frame-work—theorization—has been proposed as essential for the ultimate success of a certain type of social movement—the diffusion of innovations (Greenwood, Hinings, & Suddaby, 2002). Greenwood et al. built upon work by Strang and Meyer (1993) and Tolbert and Zucker (1996) to argue that, in order for innovations to diffuse widely, they must first be "theorized," a process in which industry associations can play a major role. According to Tolbert and Zucker, theorizing involves two major steps—specification of a major organizational failing and justification of possible solutions to the problem. These two steps are very similar to the diagnostic, prognostic, and motivational tasks of collective action framing of Benford and Snow

(2000). Perhaps the most intriguing observation made by Greenwood et al. (2002) about theorizing (or framing) is that successful theorizing apparently requires the innovation to be framed as a response to a problem experienced by potential adopters, rather than as an opportunity of which they could avail themselves. This observation fits empirical data about the diffusion of administrative reforms, but whether it also applies to technological innovations is an open question. Swanson and Ramiller (1997) argued in support of the notion that a "business problematic" is an essential part of "organizing vision" of information systems innovations. Like theorizing, the organizing vision concept seems nearly identical to that of technological action frames.

Greenwood et al. (2002) also noted that part of the theorizing process involves creating moral or pragmatic legitimacy for the innovation. This observation accords with Benford and Snow's (2000) "vocabularies of severity, urgency, efficacy, and propriety." In addition, it links the process of framing or theorizing with the management and information systems (IS) literatures on organizational legitimacy (Suchman, 1995) and management discourse (Green, 2004; Heracleous & Barrett, 2001; Ramiller & Swanson, 2003; Swanson & Ramiller, 1997). For example, Suchman (1995) discussed three types of legitimacy that organizations can claim for their actions: pragmatic legitimacy, resting on the self-interested calculations of stakeholders; moral legitimacy, employing "prosocial logic" about the public good or action as "the right thing to do"; and cognitive legitimacy, arguments about necessity or inevitability of the action. Green (2004) theorized about the role of justifications in the diffusion of managerial practices and argued that justifications would fall off as diffusion increases and the innovation becomes taken for granted. He also discussed three types of justification—pathos (relating to emotions such as fear and greed), logos (relating to rational calculation), and ethos (relating to norms of appropriateness); he posited that a sequence of justifications starting with pathos, moving to logos, and ending with ethos would produce the most successful diffusion pattern. Heracleous and Barrett (2001) longitudinally analyzed discourse about the implementation of electronic trading in the London insurance market in terms of stakeholders' "arguments-in-use," which contain the framing or theorizing elements of goals, causal attributions, and justifications for actions. They concluded that, although often incomplete, arguments-in-use of conflicting stakeholders exhibit a deep structure that is relatively stable over time and guides stakeholders' interpretations and actions, thus contributing to implementation success or failure. Ramiller and Swanson (2003) and Swanson and Ramiller (1997) analyzed discourse about ("organizing visions" of) IS and technology innovations in terms of the claims' interpretability, plausibility, importance, and discontinuity. Again, these dimensions are reminiscent of Benford and Snow's "vocabularies."

In short, the framing or theorizing of IT innovations is believed to be a factor in their successful or unsuccessful diffusion. Framing or theorizing is a process that unfolds over time. It involves identifying problems; proposing solutions; creating causal arguments linking problems, solutions, and actions proposed to implement solutions; justifying solutions; and rhetorically countering arguments put forth by opponents. Justifications involve claims to various types of legitimacy and appeals to participants' emotions; innovation entrepreneurs may frame their justifications around important contemporary external circumstances and events. The need for justifications is expected to decline as diffusion progresses; they may fade away altogether as an innovation comes to be taken for granted. Certain sequences or types of justifications may promote diffusion better than others.

Technology Ensemble Interactions

Another factor that could be consequential in the diffusion of technological innovations is the innovation itself. Much of the vast literature on the diffusion of innovations is predicated on the empirical observation that some innovations diffuse faster than others. That observation spawned the "... central notion in the study of innovation ... that technologies possess attributes or characteristics and that these characteristics have systematic effects on diffusion ... " (Fichman, 2000, p. 111).

Many theorists have objected to technological characteristics as an explanation of innovation diffusion on the grounds that "choice-theoretic models are 'overrationalized,' treating the merits of an innovation as accessible to [potential adopters'] calculation" (Strang & Macy, 2001, p. 153). By contrast, some researchers argue, "... it is difficult for an organization to determine the reliability, capacity, and precision of a new technology, and whether a newer technology will soon appear to make it obsolete" (Tingling & Parent, 2002, p. 119). "Self-interested actors who might eventually use an innovation worry not only about the current performance of the innovation, but also about future changes in performance. They want to know if the advantage gained by adoption can be sustained" (King et al., 1994, p. 144). Consequently, many organizations defer adoption until more information becomes available, and others may adopt early, not on the basis of rational calculations about the innovation's merits, but by imitating the decisions of early adopting peers (Tingling & Parent, 2002).

The problem with diffusion explanations based solely on social influences such as mimicry, fads, and fashions is that they are "underrationalized." They contend that managers pay close attention to what others do, while lacking interest in what happens when they do it. But business discourse focuses intently on performance ... , not popularity ..." (Strang & Macy, 2001, p. 153). Therefore, *because* managers are unable to assess innovations confidently using rational calculation, they will "seek to learn from the coincidence of innovative strategies and subsequent outcomes" (p. 155). In other words, they are likely to base their adoption decision on "success stories" that publish the results early adopters claim to have received from using the technology. Later, organizations that based their adoption decisions on other adopters' success stories may abandon the technology if it *disconfirms* their expectations. This process of adopting based on stories about technology performance and abandoning on the basis of direct experience is posited as an alternative explanation to mimicry for innovation fads and fashions (Strang & Macy, 2001).

The observation that the experience of disconfirming results can lead to diffusion failure also has echoes in the social movements literature. Social movements have limited ability to account for "discrepancies between ideology [or frames] and experience [of adopters]" (Babb, 1996, p. 1033). Therefore, "some collective action frames are ultimately disconfirmed empirically" (p. 1033). The implication is that "technologies at some points may constrain and obstruct the building of an organizing vision [or technological action frame]. In particular, turbulence, shifts, and setbacks in the core technology's development may jeopardize an associated organizing vision" (Swanson & Ramiller, 1997, p. 467).

A related argument can be found in the literature on dominant technology designs—a single technology architecture that establishes dominance in a technology product class (Anderson & Tushman, 1990). The dominant design may arise from de facto competition in the marketplace; it may reflect the market power of a dominant technology producer (Anderson & Tushman, 1990). It might also emerge from standardization efforts by a national body or an industry association. There is no guarantee that the (rationally) best technology will emerge from these social and political processes. However, when it emerges, a dominant design ends the "period of ferment" in which technology producers try different solutions. Therefore, the emergence of a dominant design is often signaled by a shakeout among technology producers. Furthermore, the emergence of a dominant design ends potential adopters' uncertainty about the merits of the technology and likelihood that it will be rendered obsolete by later technologies. Consequently, "the emergence of a standard [dominant design] is a prerequisite to mass adoption ..." (Anderson & Tushman, 1990, p. 615).

The point here is that technological action frames, theorizations, or organizing visions are neither the same as, nor completely independent of, the technologies to which they relate. Of course, a key issue here is how "technology" is understood. And here again, Rob Kling provided seminal insights. Complex information technologies are often best understood, not as discrete entities or tools, but rather as "packages," "webs," "ensembles," or "interaction networks" (Kling, 1980; Kling, 1993; Kling et al., 2002) of social, technical, and economic components, including specifications of how the components are to be combined in practice. These components interact with each other and with social actors and established practices. In interaction, some technical (Hughes, 1987) or non-technical (Takeishi & Lee, 2005) components may fail to perform as expected, becoming what Hughes called "reverse salients." Information about technology ensemble problems or setbacks or the non-emergence of a dominant design is likely to hinder diffusion, regardless of the attractiveness of the technology's action frame. Conversely, early successes diffused through stories in the press and told at conferences can reinforce the frames and influence diffusion of the new socio-technical practices. In addition, the patterns of socio-technical arrangements implied by frames can mesh with, or conflict with, established practices and the interests of social actors, spurring adoption or rejection. Thus, the interactions among the components of a technology ensemble and between the ensemble and actors and established practices can intervene in the process by which technology frames influence diffusion of practices involving a technology ensemble.

Recap

The foregoing discussion suggests that two interrelated factors influence the careers of CMs, as indicated by the widespread diffusion of particular technologies and their associated use practices. The first is technological action frames, also called innovation theorizing or IS organizing visions, which are reflected in discourse about the innovation. An additional factor is information, both positive and negative, about interactions with the technology ensemble and among its components, such as success stories that present the reactions of and results achieved by earlier adopters, reports of technology setbacks or problems, or evidence of the emergence of a technology standard, also called a dominant design. We argue that technology ensemble interactions represent an important link between the technology frames that shape discourse about a technology ensemble and the ways that the ensemble diffuses in practice. Thus, technology ensemble interactions are an important factor in the careers of CMs.

Methods

We investigate the roles played by technological action frames and technology ensemble interactions in one CM in the U.S. home mortgage industry—the diffusion and use of automated underwriting. The U.S.

home mortgage industry is particularly interesting for an analysis of CMs, because computerization began later in this industry than in many other "information-intensive" financial services such as consumer banking and credit card lending (Lebowitz, 2001). As a result, CMs in the mortgage lending industry are more easily accessible for examination than those that occurred a decade or more earlier. In addition, CMs in the U.S. home mortgage industry are likely to be able to draw on ideologies (Kling & Iacono, 1988) and framing choices (Reese & Newcombe, 2003) that were already well developed in earlier CMs. Automated underwriting is a particularly interesting innovation for our research purposes, because it diffused very rapidly (Jacobides, 2001; Straka, 2000); one would expect that framing in a successful CM would be particularly clear and galvanizing for industry participants.

Our research approach is an analysis of articles about computerization in *Mortgage Banking* magazine (www.mortgagebankingmagazine.com) from 1980 to today. *Mortgage Banking* is a publication of the Mortgage Bankers Association, the leading association for firms in that industry. The publication includes feature articles, company profiles, and a calendar of industry events, as well as news about legislation, economic changes, and technology. Thus, it is an excellent source of historical data on the concepts of interest in this study: automated underwriting action frames, computerization performance, and automated underwriting diffusion. *Mortgage Banking* magazine is indexed in ABI Inform/Proquest from 1977, with full-text availability from 1987.

We first sought to obtain all articles in *Mortgage Banking* that dealt substantively with topics related to general and specific CMs. The terms used to describe computerization have changed over time. "Automation" was the term commonly used in the 1980s; in the 1990s, the terms "technology" and "information technology" came into vogue. The specific technological innovation of interest in this paper was referred to as automated underwriting, credit scoring, or loan origination technology, among other ways. To make sure that we would capture all relevant articles, we conducted Proquest searches with 12 different search terms, which were selected on the basis of trial and error as likely to return the largest number of relevant articles. Eliminating duplicates left a corpus of 632 articles for the period 1982 to 2004 with no relevant articles from 1980–1981.

Two researchers read all articles in the corpus noting the specific technology described, if any, and general themes related to the goals of this research. We then selected the articles related to automated underwriting and closely related concepts (e.g., credit scoring, mortgage scoring, risk-based pricing, underwriters, and enabling technologies such as EDI and standards) for finer analysis. In the second phase of coding, we independently coded each of the remaining 214 articles using the concepts outlined in the theoretical background section. The article within a specific year was the unit of analysis. Data analysis proceeded in several stages. As recommended by Miles and Huberman (1994), we constructed time-ordered matrices, with rows for each article in sequence by date and columns for each of the concepts. We analyzed first within concept to see how, for example, the computerization action frames changed over time. Then we compared across the columns to examine interdependencies among action frames, technology performance, and diffusion outcomes.

Background: The Mortgage Industry and the Automated Underwriting Computerization Movement

In this section we provide important contextual background on the industry and on the technology ensemble we studied. We provide evidence to show that automated underwriting (AU) represents a rapidly successful CM; after about a decade of development, it was introduced in 1994 and declared an "essential" part of the mortgage lending process in 2003. Over the course of this CM, major changes were attributed to AU by industry experts, including a 50 percent reduction in the cost of loan origination and industry structure changes (Wigand, Steinfield, & Markus, 2005). Over the same period, the way in which the technology was framed changed substantially, as did AU use practices.

Background on the Mortgage Industry

Historically, the entire mortgage lending process in the U.S.—assessing borrowers' credit worthiness, evaluating property value, collecting mortgage payments, etc.—was handled by one type of organization—local savings and loan banks. To increase the flow of funds available for mortgage lending, the U.S. government chartered certain private corporations to buy and securitize mortgages. In conjunction with other environmental changes, the growth of two government-sponsored enterprises (GSEs)—Fannie Mae and Freddie Mac—resulted in massive changes in U.S. mortgage industry structure. Although some mortgage lenders continue to hold the mortgages they underwrite in their own portfolios, more than half of all mortgages are sold to investors (Van Order, 2000), thus splitting mortgage lending into two segments—"primary," where borrowers obtain loans from originators, and "secondary," where mortgages are sold by originators and bought by investors (Cummings & DiPasquale, 1997).

Today, the primary mortgage market (representing loan origination, the major focus of this study) is both vertically disintegrated (Jacobides, 2001) and fragmented. There are many specialized organizational types, including mortgage bankers, mortgage brokers, credit reporting companies, mortgage insurers, title companies, escrow companies, and other service providers. Within each of these segments (except mortgage insurance, which is concentrated), there are many providers. However, there are signs of rapid consolidation: It is estimated that the top five lenders currently originate more than 50 percent of residential mortgage loans and that the top ten firms service more than 50 percent of such loans. There is also some evidence of reintegration, at least at the top end of the size spectrum (Van Order, 2000).

By contrast, the secondary market can, for most intents and purposes, be considered a duopsony. The GSEs, Fannie Mae and Freddie Mac, have grown rapidly into dominant players: Roughly 50 percent of the $6.3 trillion (2003 figure) in outstanding U.S. mortgage debt for single family residences is either held in portfolio by the GSEs or is held by investors in the form of mortgage-backed securities guaranteed by the GSEs (Cummings & DiPasquale, 1997). Because they purchase such a large amount of the loan production of the primary market, they act as de facto regulators of the primary market. They cannot only influence primary market underwriting behavior by publishing the guidelines by which they will assess loans for purchase, they can also, to some extent, influence primary market technology adoption by specifying the formats in which they will accept loan documentation.

Another key institutional player in the industry is the Mortgage Bankers Association (MBA) www.mbaa.org. Founded in 1914, MBA is the leading industry association for companies in the real estate finance business, the largest segment of the U.S. capital market. Its approximately 2,800 members cover all industry segments, including mortgage lenders, mortgage brokers, thrifts, insurance companies, etc. MBA represents the industry's legislative and regulatory interests and conducts educational activities and research for its members. As will be discussed more fully later, the MBA, working closely with the GSEs, has been a major force in computerization movements in the mortgage lending industry.

The Automated Mortgage Underwriting Computerization Movement

Mortgage lending was historically viewed as less readily automatable than other types of credit decisions. Until the mid-1990s, the mortgage process was largely manual and decentralized: Tens of thousands of underwriters employed by thousands of mortgage lenders subjectively reviewed borrowers' credit reports and voluminous documentation against their own underwriting guidelines as well as those of conduits and investors (such as the GSEs) (Straka, 2000).

Following serious problems with mortgage defaults in the 1980s, the GSEs and mortgage insurance companies sought to increase their ability to predict defaults and to make AU decisions based on their predictions. Empirical research in the late 1980s and the early 1990s suggested that borrowers' negative equity (owing more than the property was worth) was the greatest risk of default, and the importance of a borrower's credit history was poorly understood. Part of the problem lay in the lack of availability of sufficient credit data, which was distributed across many sources and reported in nonstandard ways. In the early 1990s, "virtually no institution was storing credit records on mortgage loans in an easily accessible medium" (Straka, 2000, p. 213). Motivated by the success of credit scoring techniques in predicting default in other financial services (e.g., credit cards), the GSEs and mortgage insurers began exploring the applicability of that technique in mortgage lending. In 1992, Freddie Mac completed a study using generic credit scores (FICO scores, after Fair, Isaac and Company) and concluded that they were a significant predictor of mortgage default and thus should be a component of computer-based mortgage scoring models.

In 1994, Freddie Mac announced successful pilots of its AU system, Loan Prospector. Shortly thereafter, Fannie Mae introduced its system, called Desktop Underwriter. These AU systems (AUS) were more than just combinations of hardware and software. They were complex technology "packages" or infrastructures or ensembles (Kling, 1980; Kling, 1993) that also included: credit data collected by and from a variety of organizations, computed credit scores, data on properties and loan terms, statistical models, electronic data interchange technology and standards, technical skills, support personnel, and specifications for combining these elements.

Use of AU started slowly. Use of *credit data and scores* took off rapidly after Freddie Mac issued an industry letter in 1995 promoting their value in reducing default risk (*Mortgage Banking*, 1996, Vol. 56, Issue 9, p. 38).[1] However, despite considerable inducements by the GSEs, the use of the GSEs' AU software in combination with electronic data interchange was used for barely a quarter of submissions to the GSEs in 1997. Then, starting around 1998, use of AU expanded rapidly. However, as we show below, AU diffusion involved several different technology ensembles. In 2002, a freelance writer quipped: "If there is a [lender] left on the planet not using Internet technology to lock loans or an automated underwriting system to deliver decisions in minutes, we didn't find it" (2002, Vol. 63, Issue 2, p. 30). Fannie's Desktop Underwriter was referred to as an industry "standard" (2002, Vol. 63, Issue 1, p. 144).

"The most firmly entrenched lending technology by far is AU. Today, AUS technology is virtually essential to the mortgage lending process" (2003, Vol. 64, Issue 1, p. 143).

In early 2006, the results of an industry survey were reported as showing that: "More than 90 percent of lenders have implemented an automated underwriting system (AUS). An estimated 75 percent of new [loan] production is being underwritten with an AUS" (2006, Vol. 66, Issue 4, p. 86).

Although the rapid diffusion of AU post-1998 appears to suggest a straightforward efficiency-driven outcome, our closer examination here shows that technology action frames played a significant role in shaping AU use practices. At the same time, the AU action frames changed sharply over time, influenced in turn by the vagaries of technology ensemble interactions. The framing of AU is described in three major episodes. Table 3.1 summarizes and explains the technologies referred to in the next section.

Findings: The Framing of Automated Underwriting

For the most part, discourse about AU has invoked the productivity master frame. Within this dominant frame, many specific issues have been raised. AU was described as a tool for reducing loan delinquencies and defaults; thereby contributing to lending profitability. AU was argued to reduce the elapsed time and labor cost of underwriting loans, thereby allowing lenders to grow profits and cope with cyclical booms driven by changes in interest rates, while at the same time curtailing underwriter employment or changing the nature of the underwriter's job. AU was claimed to offer opportunities to develop new loan products and to price mortgage loans differently, thus enhancing revenues and expanding markets.

Two other master frames were present in the discourse on AU, but they were subordinated to the productivity frame. With respect to the democratization master frame, AU was argued to improve consumers' access to loans and to enable new business opportunities for brokers and small lenders. Automated credit scoring was claimed to be "fairer" and more "objective" than manual underwriting, thereby reducing discrimination and allowing more people to obtain mortgage loans. Critics countered, however, that human judgment was still required to avoid discriminatory outcomes. And, when AU became more standardized, available in the form of commercial software packages, and supported by the Internet, AU was said to have changed industry structure, eliminating the "technology gap" between large and small companies, and leveling the playing field for small companies and new entrants. With respect to the anytime-anywhere master frame,

Table 3.1 Glossary of Mortgage Industry Technology Terms

Technology	Description	Explanation
Fair, Isaac and Company (FICO) scores	Technique used to assess borrowers' credit-worthiness; scores computed by assigning points to indicators of good/poor creditworthiness.	Successful in predicting borrower default in personal lending (e.g., credit cards), low FICO scores were shown in 1992 to be a significant predictor of mortgage default. It was concluded that credit information should be used in mortgage underwriting decisions and hence should be incorporated into automated underwriting systems.
Automated underwriting (AU) systems (AUS), such as *Loan Prospector* (Freddie Mac) and *Desktop Underwriter* (Fannie Mae)	"Expert" systems, usually built around discriminant models, driven by data about borrower credit worthiness and mortgage characteristics (e.g., appraised property values and loan terms), that result in decisions about whether borrowers qualify for particular loan products and the prices (e.g., interest rates and points) they should be charged.	Development began in the mid 1980s among large mortgage lenders and the GSEs. The GSEs' launching and promotion of AUS in the mid-1990s initiated the widespread diffusion of AUS use.
Electronic Data Interchange (EDI) and proprietary Value Added Networks (e.g., Freddie Mac's *Goldworks*)	Mainframe-era approach to the electronic exchange of data; EDI refers to data and document standards (e.g., X12 standards); VAN refers to the fee-charging network operator that provides high-speed data transmission capability.	Agreed-upon data formats and networking technologies are essential for the successful electronic transmission of data in a form that does not require rekeying (as is the case with fax). Dial-up telephone transmission can substitute for the use of VANs at much lower cost (and lower speed, reliability, etc.). Today, EDI data and document standards are being replaced by XML data and document standards (e.g., MISMO standards) and VANs are being replaced by high-speed Internet transmission. When the GSEs introduced their AUS in 1994/1995, they laid out their own data standards and made available their proprietary VANs for data transmission. Use of the GSEs' data standards was mandatory for use of the GSEs' AUS; use of their VANs was not.
Electronic Partner Networks (EPN)	Extension of the VAN concept to include, not just the GSEs and lenders, but also the service providers with which the lenders did business (e.g., credit agencies, brokers, appraisers).	Originally implemented on the GSEs' proprietary VANs, the GSEs' EPNs were eventually migrated to the Internet. Large lenders also developed their own EPNs.

the Internet was claimed to have brought AU to the "point of sale" and put AU into the hands of consumers.

Although much of the discourse on AU reflects the master frame of productivity, we observed significant differences in how AU was framed over time, particularly with respect to who would control the technology or benefit from its productivity improvements. Chronologically, the first framing was of AU as a productivity tool for the GSEs, not surprising in light of the GSEs' major roles in developing and championing this technology. Over time, AU also came to be seen as a productivity tool for (large) mortgage lenders. And eventually, AU was described as a productivity tool for everyone: small lenders, mortgage brokers, new entrants, and even the consumer.

These different framings undoubtedly influenced the extent of AU adoption and shaped the ways in which organizations used the technology. However, we argue that AU frames did not stand alone in contributing to AU use practices. Technology ensemble interactions also played a role. Specifically, the various framings of AU suggested or implied a pattern of AU use—a set of socio-technical arrangements that might be called a "behavioral script" (Barley & Tolbert, 1997). When organizations evaluated what those scripts meant for them or attempted to put them into practice, they had experiences of various sorts. When these experiences were shared with others, often through stories told in the press and at conferences, technological action frames were either reinforced or eroded, giving rise to new ones. In some cases, AU technology "resisted" the uses to which people try to put it (Pickering, 1995), when a component of the technology ensemble proved to be unworkable technically, socially, or economically. In other cases, organizations refused to make technology investments they believed would alter existing work practices in ways that might disadvantage them. In either circumstance, the ability of AU frames to influence the diffusion and pattern of organizational AU use practices was subject to reinforcement or to disconfirmation and redefinition by technology ensemble interactions—a pattern we observed to repeat several times before AU frames and use practices in the industry started to stabilize and become taken-for-granted parts of the institutional landscape.

In the sections that follow, we describe the three major AU framings we observed over the 20-plus year timeframe of our study. The time periods of each framing are approximate, because frames often emerge well before they become prominent, and because multiple frames can co-exist at any one time. For each frame we discuss its implied socio-technical arrangements, technology ensemble interactions, how the interactions either confirmed or disconfirmed the frame, and the resulting widespread use practices, specifically the extent of AU diffusion in the industry and the nature of its use. Our analysis is summarized in Table 3.2.

AU as a Productivity Tool for the GSEs

By 1991, Freddie Mac had progressed with the development of a statistical approach to AU to the point where the GSE was convinced that the technology could be used on a large scale. There was only one fly in

Table 3.2 The Dynamics of AU Framing and Diffusion

Socio-Technical Package	Technology Ensemble Interactions	Framing Confirmation/ Disconfirmation	Diffusion and Use Practices
AU Framed as a Productivity Tool for GSEs (Emerged circa 1985)			
Lenders were to submit, via EDI, credit information in GSE-specific data formats to GSE(s) for automated underwriting via the GSEs' AUS for a fee.	• Evidence presented that use of credit scoring substantially reduced default risk. • EDI costs were high and automation for brokers and credit reporters was limited. • Lenders faced additional costs from lack of GSE data standards. • Direct access to AUS by brokers could allow brokers to bypass lenders, leading to their disintermediation. • Lenders could lose control over their data, their ability to set prices, their profitability, and possibly their market to the GSEs.	Framing of AU as a productivity tool for GSEs was both reinforced by the success of AUS and eroded by non-acceptance of EDI by brokers and service providers.	• Lenders' use of credit scoring "skyrocketed." • Brokers and service providers continued to use fax or dial-up to transmit data to lenders. • Lender submissions to GSEs via AUS were low.
AU Framed as a Productivity Tool for Large Lenders (Emerged circa 1992)			
(Pre-1999) Lenders were to "prequalify" loans with in-house AUS then transmit data electronically to one or both GSEs in different formats for automated underwriting using the GSEs' AUS. (Post-1999) After certifying lenders' AUS, GSEs would accept the underwriting decisions generated by large lenders' AUS.	• GSEs' AUS developed the capability to handle many new borrower categories and loan types. • Large lenders successfully developed their own AUS. • AUS was shown to reduce lending costs and provide other productivity and consumer benefits. • Commercial AUS packages became available, lowering lenders' adoption costs. • GSEs offered proprietary "electronic partner networks" to connect lenders with their brokers and service providers. • Lenders protested GSE's AUS pricing policies and unwillingness to accept common data standards.	Framing of AU as a productivity tool for GSEs was reinforced by continued AUS success; weakened by the emergence and successes of lenders' AUS, which reinforced the framing of AUS as a productivity tool for large lenders.	• GSEs' AUS were the most used AU systems. • Less than 25% of lender submissions to GSEs used AUS as of 1997. • Some large lenders used their own AUS as prescreening tools in conjunction with use of GSEs' AUS. • Some large lenders used their own AUS for nearly 100% of their loan production by 1999.
AU (via the Internet) Framed as a Productivity Tool for All (Emerged circa 1999)			
AU capability was to be made available to brokers or consumers (by the GSEs, large lenders, small lenders, or new entrants) at the point of sale.	• GSEs moved their electronic partner networks and AU systems to the Internet and provided brokers with direct Internet access to AUS. • Smaller lenders and startups developed their own AU systems. • "Internet-only" businesses began offering AUS online; some technology-savvy new entrants were able to grow into industry leaders. • Lenders extended their AUS to brokers and to consumers via the Internet. • Growth in revenues attributed to online AUS. • Time required for consumers to receive loan approval or loan funding dropped to minutes or hours from days or weeks.	Framing of AU as a tool for GSEs and as a tool for large lenders was significantly eroded by successful uses of AU by brokers, small lenders, and new entrants, giving rise to a new framing of AU as a tool for all and as "essential" to mortgage lending.	• Brokers began demanding access to AUS. • By 2003, AUS viewed as "essential" to the mortgage lending process. • By 2005, 90% of lenders had implemented AUS; AUS were used for an estimated 75% of loan production.

the ointment. The technology ensemble required large amounts of credit data, and the need to key enter data was a serious bottleneck.

> After an 18-month pilot project, the corporation could get good results, as long as it fed the program massive amounts of information. But it was almost more expensive to take the massive underwriting files, extract that data and key it in and let the system underwrite it, than it was to have an underwriter do it. (1991, Vol. 51, Issue 6, p. 17)

The solution to the problem was clear (to the GSEs): For AU to work on a large scale, *mortgage lenders* would have to supply credit data electronically when they submitted their loans for underwriting.

Anticipating this requirement, the MBA had earlier begun working to introduce electronic data interchange (EDI) standards into the loan origination process. In 1988, the MBA launched an initiative to streamline mortgage lending with standardized forms like the Uniform Residential Loan Application and to develop EDI standards for the exchange of credit data (1988, Vol. 48, Issue 12, p. 12). This proactive move reflected the lenders' dissatisfaction with their already considerable experience of using EDI with the GSEs for delivering closed loan packages (the secondary market). The GSEs had different data requirements and transmission standards, forcing lenders to maintain duplicate business processes and technology interfaces.

> [W]hile both systems require much of the same data, a mortgage banker must do a significant amount of manual work before transmitting to either system. In addition, if a lender changes delivery agency, the work must be re-done *because the two systems are not uniform*. (1988, Vol. 48, Issue 6, p. 36, added emphasis)

Lenders were concerned that using EDI-enabled AU would involve extra work for them if the GSEs did not relax their information and documentation requirements (1990, Vol. 50, Issue 7, p. 11). Consequently, the lenders argued that, in order for the electronic exchange of loan origination data to be a success, the GSEs would have to agree to common EDI transmission and data standards:

> [MBA] conference participants agreed that ... if electronic data exchange was to be a success, ... the industry [read: lenders] must broadly support the idea of exchanging data. This broad level of support would only come from a universally recognized data transmission standard, a standard ... *that would not*

> *allow any competitive advantage to a vendor, organization [read: GSE] or company*. (1988, Vol. 48, Issue 6, p. 36, added emphasis)

Despite some progress toward standardization through MBA initiatives, the GSEs persisted in their proprietary technology development paths.

On a "red letter day" in 1993, a highly publicized EDI transaction pilot—a request for payment of a mortgage insurance claim coupled with payment via an automated clearinghouse—was described as foretelling "a technological revolution" (1993, Vol. 53, Issue 8, p. 87). And, in 1994, when the GSEs announced the 1995 availability of their AU services, they also announced their fee-based offerings of value-added network (VAN) services for EDI transmission (1994, Vol. 55, Issue 2, p. 10; 1994, Vol. 55, Issue 2, p. 64).

> Firms need to establish EDI connections *before implementing automated underwriting*, so that information from credit bureaus, mortgage insurance companies, and others can be fed into the electronic underwriting system. (1994, Vol. 55, Issue 2, p. 10, added emphasis)

The lenders expressed numerous concerns about these proposed sociotechnical arrangements. First, EDI standards were not fully developed, leading to fears about having to maintain thousands of different interfaces with brokers and service providers (1994, Vol. 55, Issue 2, p. 10). EDI was further problematic because of its high connect-time charges that put it out of the reach of many small lenders (1995, Vol. 55, Issue 3, p. 38) and of the lenders' business partners, compromising the lenders' ability to fully automate their processes. For example, although many lenders were able to *request* credit reports from reporting agencies electronically, they usually *received* credit reports via fax. Similarly, fax was used by "more sophisticated" lenders (less sophisticated ones relied on mail and courier) to communicate with their brokers. Thus, unless the lenders were to underwrite the costs of operating EDI links with all their partners and of reengineering "the whole process" themselves (1994, Vol. 55, Issue 2, p. 10), *the lenders* might have had to re-key vast amounts of data to comply with the GSEs' requirements. Furthermore, industry participants worried about a "growing 'sophistication gap' in the application of technology between thrifts and mortgage banks and between small competitors and large" (1993, Vol. 53, Issue 4, p. 50). Finally, lenders also worried about the possibility that GSEs would provide AU capability directly to real estate brokers or to the mortgage brokers that originated loans for lenders, fearing that they (the lenders) would be bypassed or disintermediated (Jacobides, 2001).

The GSEs tried to allay these concerns in various ways. First, they waived "reps and warrantees" for lenders who used their AUS. This promise reduced requirements for paper documentation and, in effect, guaranteed lenders that they would not be required to repurchase the loans from the GSEs in the case of underwriting errors. Second, the GSEs assured lenders that they would not make their AUS available for use by brokers or real estate agents. However, the *lenders* could do so. This provision enabled lenders to capture data at the point of sale (the interface between the borrower and the broker or real estate agent) and also enabled the *underwriting decision to be made at the point of sale* (the implications of this opportunity are discussed later). Third, the GSEs never required the lenders to use their VANs (with the attendant fees) to submit loans for underwriting.

> Interestingly, Freddie Mac currently supports direct-dial capabilities for its pilot automated underwriting system, set to debut nationwide early in 1995. The use of GoldWorks—its VAN—is not required. (1995, Vol. 55, Issue 3, p. 38)

Despite the GSEs' protestations that AU would benefit borrowers and "empower" lenders (1994, Vol. 55, Issue 2, p. 10), lenders were slow to adopt AU, and EDI use never became widespread in the industry. In 1995, the MBA proclaimed the "adoption and *real production use* of the established X12 [EDI] standards [its] top priority in 1996" (1994, Vol. 55, Issue 2, p. 10, added emphasis). The MBA was confident that EDI transmission standards would put "such interfacing nightmares ... to rest ... regardless of the disparity with their internal data structures [in other words, regardless of the GSEs' differing data formats]." In spite of the MBA's efforts, less than a quarter of all lender submissions to the GSEs used AU in 1997, two years after the introduction of AU. Furthermore, most brokers and other service providers continued to rely on fax or dial-up (instead of EDI) for several more years, when the Internet became widely available (1996, Vol. 57, Issue 1, p. 136; 2000, Vol. 60, Issue 7, p. 42).

The GSEs' insistence on proprietary data formats reflects their framing of AU as *their* productivity tool, a weapon in their fierce competition with each other. As framed by the GSEs, the AU system (together with EDI) was an electronic hierarchy that would tie lenders and their sources of supply more tightly to the GSEs, thus locking the lenders in. Unfortunately, neither EDI technology nor the lenders cooperated fully with the socio-technical arrangements implied in the GSEs' framing of AU, and other frames emerged, leading to different AU use practices.

AU as a Productivity Tool for Large Lenders

Lenders framed AU differently than the GSEs did. Lenders' experimentation with AU dated as far back as that of the GSEs. In 1986, AU was described as a tool to help mortgage *lenders* reduce delinquencies. Lenders that embraced AU were expected to weather the coming shake-out in the mortgage industry, unlike non-adopters (1986, Vol. 46, Issue 7, p. 18). A mortgage lender reported in 1987 the successful development and use of an AU system based on an analysis of the GSEs' published underwriting guidelines and a statistical sample of the lender's loan data (1987, Vol. 47, Issue 7, p. 64). In 1992, the large lender Countrywide announced its rollout of an AI-based AU system and its discussions with the GSEs about electronic data transmission and potential GSE acceptance of Countrywide's automated lending decisions. In 1993, a group of west coast lenders collaborated with vendors to develop a commercial AU system for lenders "on a budget" (1993, Vol. 54, Issue 3, p. 79).

Lenders' development and use of AUS was a logical step from several points of view. First, some lenders retained some or all of the loans they made in their own portfolios (not selling them to the GSEs) or sold loans directly to investors (without using the GSEs as conduits). There would be little point in paying the GSEs fees for underwriting these loans. Second, until the late 1990s, the GSEs only purchased conventional conforming loans—loans of less than a certain dollar amount that met stringent underwriting criteria. Many lenders sought to serve borrowers with low documentation, impaired credit, or borrowing needs exceeding GSE guidelines. Early on, the GSEs' systems could not handle such loans. Therefore, some lenders saw the need for their own AU tools.

By 1997, however, the GSEs' systems (first widely available in 1995) had evolved to the point where they were able to underwrite government loans, subprime loans, and jumbo loans.

> Manual guideline underwriting worked around univariate 'knockout rules' (such as no loans above a 36 percent debt ratio). Exceptions and risk layering (e.g., poor credit plus debt higher than 36 percent) were allowed (case-by-case or in policy) with little or no risk quantification and feedback. In contrast, scoring tools and AU have allowed the tradeoffs between risk factors to be more precisely quantified, giving the industry greater confidence in 'pushing the envelope' of acceptable expected default rates. (Straka, 2000, p. 217)

It was this "pushing of the envelope" that allowed the GSEs to extend their loan purchases into new loan and borrower categories, which some lenders undoubtedly perceived as strategic encroachment.

Through the use of multivariate analysis, the GSEs' AUS had become "black boxes" and it was no longer possible for the GSEs to publish their lending guidelines in entirety (1997, Vol. 58, Issue 3, p. 46; 2001, Vol. 62, Issue 3, p. 38). This opacity reduced the ability of lenders to estimate whether and at what price one GSE would purchase a loan without running the loan through that GSE's AUS. In combination with strong incentives to use the GSEs' systems (waived "reps and warrantees"), fees charged for using the GSEs' systems, and the GSEs' refusal to accept automated decisions from other AU engines, the lack of transparency in the GSEs' AU systems reduced the lenders' traditional ability to play the GSEs off against each other in search of the best deal (1997, Vol. 57, Issue 8, p. 10). Since the advent of AU, if a lender wanted to compare the agencies' pricing *before* deciding where to sell the loan, the lender had to use both AU engines, incurring higher costs that could amount to several million dollars a year (1997, Vol. 57, Issue 8, p. 10).

Under these circumstances, use of an "independent" AU system "as a prescreening tool in conjunction with the agencies' automated systems" began to seem like a good idea even for lenders that had not already developed their own underwriting systems (1997, Vol. 57, Issue 8, p. 10). The downside was, however, that using multiple systems "further complicate[d] the efficiency problem by layering on the additional cost of using multiple automated underwriting systems in different phases of the origination process" (1997, Vol. 57, Issue 8, p. 10).

The efficiency problem stemmed from lenders' desire to deploy AU at "the point of sale," where a borrower interfaced with the broker or a lender's retail loan officer. The traditional lending process involved a borrower "prequalification" step; prequalification decisions occasionally had to be changed as a result of a GSE's subsequent underwriting decision, leading to borrower dissatisfaction. If lenders could shift the GSE decision to the point of sale, they could improve customer satisfaction, reap significant efficiency benefits from business process reengineering, and possibly gain competitive advantage relative to less sophisticated peers. In the lenders' ideal world, they would be able to run a loan simultaneously through *several* AUS (including their own) and pay the GSEs underwriting fees *only* for the loans the GSEs actually purchased (1997, Vol. 57, Issue 8, p. 10). In this way, lenders could hope to regain some of the pricing leverage over the GSEs that they had lost because of the lack of transparency in AUS. Understandably, the GSEs were not amenable to this suggestion. Nevertheless, the issue did not go away, but resurfaced in 2004.

In this environment of conflict over the GSEs' AU policies, lenders' adoption of AU lagged. In 1997, despite the GSEs having emerged as "dominant providers" of AU services, only 20 to 25 percent of eligible loans went through the GSEs' AU systems (1997, Vol. 57, Issue 8, p. 10).

Most lender participants in an annual mortgage production survey reported that they did not make full use of AUS (i.e., use AU at the point of sale) owing in part to lack of integration with back-end systems (1997, Vol. 58, Issue 1, p. 152). Such integration was hindered by the GSEs' ongoing refusal to accept common data standards—a condition that endured until 2001. Lenders' concerns about AU and their dissatisfaction with GSE policies led to the formation in 1996 of an MBA task force on AU and in 1997 of an MBA task force to promote "interagency cooperation" (1997, Vol. 57, Issue 8, p. 10; 1997, Vol. 57, Issue 7, p. 24).

Despite these MBA initiatives, the GSEs persisted in their technology-based competition. However, by 1999, it was apparent to some observers that Freddie had lost its technology race with Fannie. Freddie quietly began purchasing loans that had been underwritten with Fannie's system. And, "in a landmark agreement," Freddie agreed to purchase mortgages underwritten by lender Norwest's AU system (Marlin, 1999). Under the deal, Norwest began selling nearly all its loan production to Freddie. A short time later, BankAmerica made a similar deal with Freddie, and Countrywide announced a similar deal with Fannie. Recall that Countrywide had first initiated talks about such an arrangement in 1992. Interestingly, despite the "hierarchical" nature of these arrangements, which appear to lock the lenders in to a single large customer, they were hailed as a victory for *lenders*.

> The deal between Freddie Mac and Norwest is a very important deal because it may force Fannie to lower its fees, or shift its business model to compete for business with Freddie Mac.
>
> To other mortgage participants, it's an important deal because it returns to the lender control over the origination event, and may usher in a period of reduced fees for those using [GSEs'] automated underwriting. But it's also an agreement that spotlights the acute dissatisfaction with automated underwriting. (Hochstein, 1999)

Mortgage lenders were dissatisfied with the GSEs' AU policies, because they believed that, like the rest of the technology industry at that time, the GSEs should "give their technology away in order to increase their volumes ... attracting as many users to automated underwriting as possible" (Hochstein, 1999).

Whether or not these deals were a victory for lenders, they fueled lenders' adoption of AU, as did the growing number of widely publicized technology success stories. Research conducted by Fannie, Freddie, and independent entities began reporting substantial benefits to AU adopters around the year 2000. An independent study concluded:

> A large contributor to reducing costs has been the implementation of automated underwriting systems (AUS) and the associated process changes. ... Total underwriting costs were almost one-third lower for those companies that use AUS on more than 60 percent of the loans they originate. (2000, Vol. 60, Issue 6, p. 66)

A Freddie Mac report similarly hailed the successes of AU. "In a 1996 report, Freddie Mac made big claims for its nascent AU service: It's been five years and millions of mortgage originations later. Has Loan Prospector lived up to its billing?" Freddie concluded the answer was yes: Loan Prospector had increased accuracy, enabled faster processing, lowered costs, increased lending fairness, and expanded homeownership opportunities (2001, Vol. 61, Issue 6, p. 70). And a survey conducted by Fannie Mae announced that AU (in conjunction with seamless IT integration) was the most important factor contributing to the superior performance of top performing mortgage lenders (2002, Vol. 62, Issue 6, p. 94).

These and other success stories stimulated extremely rapid diffusion of AU. Used for less than 25 percent of the loans sold to GSEs in 1997, AU use accounted for 100 percent of some lenders' loan production in 1999. By 2001, AU use was "deeply embedded into the business environment" (Jacobides, 2001). By 2003, AU was used by nearly 100 percent of all lenders for at least some portion of the loan volume (2003, Vol. 64, Issue 1, p. 82). Thus, AU was no longer framed as a productivity tool *for the GSEs*. Large lenders had clearly made AU into a productivity tool of their own.

AU as a Productivity Tool for All

In the meantime, experience with AU technology had increased, and commercial packages had become available, allowing smaller lenders and startups to acquire AU engines. For example, Impac, a medium-sized "alt A"[2] lender, decided to develop its own AU system after reviewing the custom software developed by IndyMac, its much larger competitor. In 2001, Impac automatically made decisions on 100 percent of its loans through its AU system, which cost the company $1.5 million to build (Grant, 2001). Interestingly, IndyMac, already a large lender in 2001, was founded in 1993, around the time that AU first became technically viable. IndyMac grew to prominence in the mortgage industry in large part because of its IT prowess (Krogh, El Sawy, & Gray, 2005). Other technology-savvy startups followed its lead.

Quietly at first, but then quite noticeably, the Internet had become integral to the mortgage lending business. The first mentioned successful uses of AU on the Internet occurred in 1999—Finet's iQualify.com (1999, Vol. 59, Issue 6, 26) and Mortgage.com (1999, Vol. 59, Issue 6, p. 19), later purchased by ABN AMRO. Just one month later, *Mortgage Banking*'s editor-in-chief opined that "lenders must regard the Internet as a new medium for originating [loans], not just an advertising or information medium" (1999, Vol. 259, Issue 7, p. 15). In other words, the point of sale had started to shift to the Internet, and that meant that AU had to be available on the Internet for consumers to use.

It also meant that brokers, suppliers of loans to large lenders, had to begin using AU online. Although brokers were by now accustomed to AUS, few submitted their information to AU systems directly. Instead, they used fax to send information to lenders who rekeyed the data into their systems. This was obviously inefficient and contributed to processing errors. At the height of the 1999 refinancing boom, Fannie began offering its AU system to brokers as a service to the industry, reneging on its 1995 promise to lenders that it would not make such access available. At first, there was little response from brokers. Then Fannie embedded Desk Originator into a loan origination software package that many lenders and brokers were using (2000, Vol. 60, Issue 7, p. 42), and brokers' direct use of AU began to increase sharply.

Despite the fact that direct broker access to AUS increased lenders' productivity, lenders vigorously protested against *the GSEs* providing this access to brokers. Lenders were concerned that:

> the brokers would be able to shop around among different wholesalers for the best rate. *GSEs have been aggressively lobbied by the mortgage banking industry to not provide their AU directly to brokers*, potentially disintermediating mortgage banks in the process. (Jacobides, 2001, added emphasis)

Instead, lenders wanted to control brokers' access to AUS (either their own or the GSEs'), because that way they could prevent brokers from "shopping" the loans around to other lenders to get better terms.

Moody's opined that "the mortgage banking industry is in a phase of substantial transformation as a result of the combined impact of technology and the GSEs (2000, Vol. 60, Issue 8, p. 14).

> The value added of [large lenders] is suffering as a result of the democratization of technology. The fact that a broker can now get a mortgage preapproved by Fannie Mae and Freddie Mac is an example of this process at work and represents a major evolution. (2000, Vol. 60, Issue 8, p. 14)

As one article put it, in an IT-related context: "Some lenders are squawking, 'when GSEs compete, we lose'"[3] (Kersnar, 2002).

Large lenders were also squeezed by smaller lenders that did not implement their own AUS but simply used the GSEs' systems to price their loans appropriately, hence competing effectively with larger lenders (Jacobides, 2001). "As a result, pricing competition between mortgage banks has increased" (2000, Vol. 60, Issue 8, p. 14). Ironically, the lenders' earlier concerns (1994 timeframe) that smaller "technology have-not" lenders would suffer from automation were also laid to rest (2003, Vol. 63, Issue 9, p. 99).

Large lenders responded to the increased competition by developing and promoting their own "electronic partner networks," putting their AU capabilities in the hands of their brokers:

> No other area of technology creates the stir that automated underwriting (AU) does. ... [M]uch more important is the way automated underwriting puts investors [read: the GSEs] ahead of wholesale lenders in the mortgage food chain and in direct contact with brokers for the first time. ... Most brokers currently use [either of the GSEs' AU systems offline] as part of their origination routines—consequently, many lenders feel a loss of control over the process. In response, the newest AU options available to brokers are a result of *lenders deciding they need to get back in between the broker and the investor*. These options—almost all private wholesale [lender] Web sites where brokers can submit loans for AU, and in some cases lock the loans as well—include Countrywide's CWBC, InterFirst's MOAI and Indy Mac's e-MITS. (2000, Vol. 60, Issue 7, p. 42, added emphasis)

In addition, large lenders increasingly enabled consumer access to AU on the Internet. By 2002, InterFirst's MOAI online system was "capable of underwriting, locking, closing and funding [loans] online in less than four hours, from start to finish" (2002, Vol. 62, Issue 6, p. 22). Internet-only DeepGreen Bank of Cleveland developed a "lights-out" (fully automated) Internet-based mortgage lending operation with integrated AU decision making (Grant, 2003). Through efforts such as these, the lenders reflected their growing belief that, although there would always be a place for brokers in mortgage lending, arming brokers with technology "misses the boat completely." The new goal was to put technology in the hands of the *borrowers*[4] (2001, Vol. 61, Issue 7, p. 34). AU was now seen as a productivity tool for everyone in the mortgage lending value chain.

Future Framings of AU

Although AU had come to be viewed as an essential part of the mortgage lending process by 2003, it is likely that AU framing and use practices will continue to evolve. Ongoing standardization efforts may contribute to such changes. After the MBA's major EDI thrusts of the late 1988s through mid-1990s, the standardization effort seemed to lose direction, and the GSEs continued to hold to their proprietary data formatting requirements. In 1999, the mortgage industry turned to the promise of Extensible Markup Language (XML) to bring seamless integration between the primary (origination) and secondary (securitization and sale) sides of the mortgage market. Co-opting other EDI and XML standards development groups, the MBA secured the active participation of the GSEs in a data standardization effort, called Mortgage Industry Standards Maintenance Organizations (MISMO). In what a MISMO spokesperson later referred to as MISMO's greatest achievement to date, the GSEs agreed in 2001 to accept common data standards for underwriting. Recall that industry participants had been calling for such standards since 1988.

Not content with this outcome, mortgage lenders took the high ground and appealed to moral legitimacy (borrower benefit) as they renewed their unsuccessful 1997 demand for single-fee access to both GSEs' AUS.

> For the benefit of the consumer, I think it's important that we allow multiple AUSes to review each and every loan. From a technology standpoint, this is an easy accomplishment, and existing technology can more than handle such a feat. ... There are some potential hurdles, of course. The developers of the AUSes must be willing to work in an openly competitive environment. They must also accept industry standards such as those developed by MISMO. ... For this to occur, the industry would need to rally together to advocate for such a solution. (2004, Vol. 64, Issue 10, p. 101)

The results of this emergent reframing of AU and the socio-technical arrangements it implies remain to be seen.

Discussion and Conclusion

After a slow start, AU diffused rapidly in the U.S. home mortgage industry. Tremendous productivity benefits have been attributed to its widespread use. Industry experts estimate that the cost to originate a mortgage loan today is half what it was 10 years ago and that future productivity improvements can still be expected.

But the rapid and widespread diffusion of AU is not a simple story of the economics of need. The AU use practices observed today cannot be adequately explained solely in terms of a drive for greater efficiency. Instead, the history of AU is better understood as a successful computerization movement in which technology use practices were shaped by technology action frames conveyed by means of public discourse about the innovation.

At the same time, there's more to the story of AU than a simple link between frames and practices. As dominant as the productivity master frame is in business and institutional settings (Colomy, 1998; Strang & Macy, 2001), the initial framing of AU as a productivity tool (for GSEs) was hotly contested by large lenders and disconfirmed by interactions with and among the components of the technology ensemble of the day. Use practices corresponded more closely to the results of these interactions than they did to the initial framing of AU. And as a result, a new frame emerged—AU as a productivity tool for lenders. The cycle repeated itself once more as information about the AU technology ensemble continued to accumulate. Partly reinforced by success stories and partly disconfirmed as cheaper and more standardized technology became available, the second framing of AU yielded some ground to a third framing—AU as a productivity tool for all members of the mortgage industry value chain, including small lenders, new entrants, brokers, and consumers. It further appears that the framing and reframing of AU has not yet ended, even though AU has now diffused throughout the mortgage industry and become a taken-for-granted feature of the institutional landscape. As experience with AU continues to evolve—as elements of the technology ensemble continue to interact with each other and with established practices, confirming and disconfirming prior frames—new use practices and new frames are likely to emerge.

Although the early AU frames were partly disconfirmed by technology ensemble interactions, they were never completely displaced. As a result, the use practices implied by early frames continue to endure, albeit in modified form. Thus, today we observe a variety of simultaneous AU use practices in the mortgage industry. We see large lenders and small lenders, new entrants, brokers, and service providers using the GSEs' AU systems (via the Internet instead of EDI). But we also see large and small lenders and new entrants using "their own" AU systems, whether these are home-grown systems or commercial software products and services. In addition, we see consumers with direct access via the Internet to either the GSEs' systems or the systems of various lenders.

We conclude that computerization movements are not monolithic phenomena. As with other social movements, they can fragment into multiple movements that may drift in subtly different directions or actively contend with each other for attention and resources. As these dynamics play themselves out, technology ensembles—not just people and organizations—have a say in what the technological action frames and technology use practices will be.

The career of the AU CM owes not a little to technology ensemble interactions. Had EDI been less expensive or more standardized, had the socio-technical arrangements of the GSEs' AU not conflicted with lenders' established work practices, early opposition to the use of AU might not have materialized, and the alternative AU use practices enacted by lenders might never have taken root. The advent of underwriting data standards may yet enable new practices that are currently unforeseen. Thus, although Kling and Iacono's groundbreaking work reminds us not to privilege economic accounts of the diffusion of new technologies over social ones, our study also reminds us not to forget the dynamic interactions among components of technology ensembles and between technology ensembles and various social actors.

Acknowledgments

This research was funded in part by the National Science Foundation's Digital Society and Technology Program (Award Numbers: 0233634, 0231584, and 0323961). We acknowledge helpful comments and suggestions from Ping Wang.

Endnotes

1. The numbers following the years in these citations refer to the volume, issue, and starting page of the articles we collected and analyzed from *Mortgage Banking* magazine.
2. "Alt A" loans are made to prime credit borrowers who do not supply extensive loan documentation. At that time, GSEs did not purchase many alt A loans. Today, the GSEs' AUS have been extended to enable their underwriting of Alt A and many other types of alternative loans.
3. This is a pun on the marketing slogan of Internet-only LendingTree: "when lenders compete, you win."
4. This was not a game the GSEs could play. They are prohibited by federal charter from originating loans.

References

Anderson, P., & Tushman, M. L. (1990). Technological discontinuities and dominant designs: A cyclical model of technological change. *Administrative Science Quarterly*, 35(4), 604–633.

Babb, S. (1996). A true American system of finance: Frame resonance in the U.S. labor movement, 1866 to 1886. *American Sociological Review*, 61(6), 1033–1052.

Barley, S. R., & Tolbert, P. S. (1997). Institutionalization and structuration: Studying the links between action and institution. *Organization Studies*, 18(1), 93–118.

Benford, R. D., & Snow, D. A. (2000). Framing processes and social movements: An overview and assessment. *Annual Review of Sociology*, 26, 611–639.

Colomy, P. (1998). Neofunctionalism and neoinstitutionalism: Human agency and interest in institutional change. *Sociological Forum*, 13(2), 265–300.

Cummings, J., & DiPasquale, D. (1997). *A primer on the secondary mortgage market.* Boston, MA: City Research.

Fichman, R. G. (2000). The diffusion and assimilation of information technology innovations. In R. W. Zmud (Ed.), *Framing the domains of IT research: Glimpsing the future through the past* (pp. 105–127). Cincinnati, OH: Pinnaflex Educational Resources, Inc.

Giugni, M. G. (1998). Was it worth the effort? The outcomes and consequences of social movements. *Annual Review of Sociology*, 24, 371–393.

Grant, R. (2001). Putting itself into a new league by going to the expense of developing its own automated underwriting system, Impac positioned itself to score big in the future. *Mortgage Technology*, 8, 44–48.

Grant, R. (2003). Deep in the online green: It started with hard choices and a definite focus; it ended up a success story. *Mortgage Technology*, 10, 30.

Green Jr., S. E. (2004). A rhetorical theory of diffusion. *Academy of Management Review*, 29(4), 653–669.

Greenwood, R., Hinings, C. R., & Suddaby, R. (2002). Theorizing change: The role of professional associations in the transformation of institutionalized fields. *Academy of Management Journal*, 45(1), 58–80.

Heracleous, L., & Barrett, M. (2001). Organizational change as discourse: Communicative actions and deep structures in the context of information technology implementation. *Academy of Management Journal*, 44(4), 753–778.

Hochstein, M. (1999). Countrywide in deal that helps Fannie stay No. 1. *American Banker*, 164, 1.

Hughes, T. P. (1987). The evolution of large technical systems. In W. E. Bijker, T. P. Hughes, & T. Pinch (Eds.), *The social construction of technological systems* (pp. 51–82). Cambridge, MA: MIT Press.

Iacono, S., & Kling, R. (2001). Computerization movements: The rise of the Internet and distant forms of work. In J. Yates & J. Van Maanen (Eds.), *Information technology and organizational transformation: History, rhetoric, and practice* (pp. 93–136). Thousand Oaks, CA: Sage Publications.

Jacobides, M. G. (2001). Technology with a vengeance: The new economics of mortgaging. *Mortgage Banking*, 62(1), 118–131.

Joachim, J. (2003). Framing issues and seizing opportunities: The UN, NGOs, and women's rights. *International Studies Quarterly*, 47, 247–274.

Kersnar, S. (2002). LendingTree and LP forge a link: Some lenders are squawking, "When GSEs compete, we lose." *Mortgage Technology*, 9, 28–32.

King, J. L., Gurbaxani, V., Kraemer, K. L., McFarlan, F. W., Raman, K. S., & Yap, C. S. (1994). Institutional factors in information technology innovation. *Information Systems Research*, 5(2), 139–169.

Kling, R. (1980). Social analyses of computing: Theoretical perspectives in recent empirical research. *Computing Surveys*, 12(1), 61–110.

Kling, R. (1993). *Behind the terminal: The critical role of computing infrastructure in effective information systems development and use.* Irvine, California: University of California, Irvine, Center for Research on Information Technology and Organizations.

Kling, R., & Iacono, S. (1988). The mobilization of support for computerization: The role of computerization movements. *Social Problems*, 35(3), 226–242.

Kling, R., & Iacono, S. (1995). Computerization movements and the mobilization of support for computerization. In S. L. Starr (Ed.), *Ecologies of knowledge: Work and politics in science and technology* (pp. 119–153). Albany, NY: State University of New York Press.

Kling, R., McKim, G., & King, A. (2002). A bit more to it: Scholarly communication forums as socio-technical interaction networks. *Journal of the American Society for Information Science and Technology*, 54(1), 47–67.

Krogh, E., El Sawy, O. A., & Gray, P. (2005). Managing online in perpetual perfect storms: Insights from IndyMac Bank. *MIS Quarterly Executive*, 4(4), 425–442.

Lebowitz, J. (2001). An industry of slow adopters. *Mortgage Banking*, 61(7), 72–29.

Marlin, S. (1999). Norwest, Freddie Mac set precedent. *Bank Systems & Technology*, 36, 10.

Miles, M. B., & Huberman, A. M. (1994). *Qualitative data analysis: An expanded sourcebook* (2nd ed.). Thousand Oaks, CA: Sage Publications.

Pickering, A. (1995). *The mangle of practice: Time, agency, and science*. Chicago: University of Chicago Press.

Ramiller, N. C., & Swanson, E. B. (2003). Organizing visions for information technology and the information systems executive response. *Journal of Management Information Systems*, 20(1), 13–50.

Reese, E., & Newcombe, G. (2003). Income rights, mothers' rights, or workers' rights? Collective action frames, organizational ideologies, and the American welfare rights movement. *Social Problems*, 50(2), 294–318.

Straka, J. W. (2000). A shift in the mortgage landscape: The 1990s move to automated credit evaluations. *Journal of Housing Research*, 11(2), 207–232.

Strang, D., & Macy, M. W. (2001). In search of excellence: Fads, success stories, and adaptive emulation. *American Journal of Sociology*, 107(1), 147–182.

Strang, D., & Meyer, J. W. (1993). Institutional conditions for diffusion. *Theory and Society*, 22, 487–511.

Suchman, M. C. (1995). Managing legitimacy: Strategic and institutional approaches. *Academy of Management Review*, 20(3), 571–610.

Swanson, E. B., & Ramiller, N. C. (1997). The organizing vision in information systems innovation. *Organization Science*, 8(5), 458–474.

Takeishi, A., & Lee, K.-J. (2005). Mobile music business in Japan and Korea: Copyright management institutions as a reverse salient. *Journal of Strategic Information Systems*, 14, 291–306.

Tingling, P., & Parent, M. (2002). Mimetic isomorphism and technology evaluation: Does imitation transcend judgment? *Journal of the Association for Information Systems*, 3, 113–143.

Tolbert, P. S., & Zucker, L. G. (1996). Institutionalization of institutionalization theory. In S. Clegg, C. Hardy, & W. Nord (Eds.), *The handbook of organization studies* (pp. 175–190). Thousand Oaks, CA: Sage Publications.

Van Order, R. (2000). The U.S. mortgage market: A model of dueling charters. *Journal of Housing Research*, 11(2), 233–255.

Wigand, R. T., Steinfield, C. W., & Markus, M. L. (2005). IT standards choices and industry structure outcomes: The case of the United States home mortgage industry. *Journal of Management Information Systems*, 22(2), 65–191.

Chapter 4

Visions of the Next Big Thing: Computerization Movements and the Mobilization of Support for New Technologies

Jonathan P. Allen
School of Business and Management
University of San Francisco

Abstract

This chapter examines the public arguments used to legitimize investments in the personal digital assistant industry over a 10-year period. The analysis of three distinct rhetorical processes (promoting the Next Big Thing, rationalizing the failure of the Next Big Thing, and resistance to the Next Big Thing) helps explain how personal digital assistants attracted significant investments from major PC, telecom, and consumer electronics companies, only to have most of these vendors quickly leave the personal digital assistant market. The public arguments surrounding personal digital assistants were found to include aspects of computerization movement ideology, but incorporated elements of a positive social vision within the language of technology and business decision making.

Introduction

In their original paper on computerization movements (CMs), Kling and Iacono (1988) argued that it was essential to understand "the key ideological beliefs about the favorable links between computerization and a preferred social order" and how these ideological beliefs legitimize large investments in computerization. Mobilizing support for a new, unproven technology is a particularly daunting task. It requires large investments, of course, but it also requires much more. An emerging technology must establish itself as a legitimate and important opportunity for a broad spectrum of producers, consumers, and intermediaries. A new technology must progress from a general concept to a specific set of features and support services that can work in particular situations, preserving the support of many different actors and groups along the way. It may be that holding these shifting coalitions of support together requires something like a CM, which draws upon ideological beliefs that lie outside of the normal institutional structures of technology vendors and computer-using organizations.

In this chapter, we examine the public arguments used to legitimize substantial investments in the personal digital assistant (PDA) industry over a 10-year period. While it is often claimed that established technology companies are overly conservative because they do not have enough incentives to pursue emerging technologies (e.g., Christensen's "Innovator's Dilemma," 1997), the information technology (IT) industry has a reputation for enthusiastically pursuing unproven ideas in the race for the next breakthrough computing concept. They even have a name for it: the Next Big Thing. We analyze these public arguments by separating them into three distinct processes: promoting the Next Big Thing, rationalizing the failure of the Next Big Thing, and resistance to the Next Big Thing.

We argue in this chapter that justifying massive investments in unproven PDA technology is an equally massive rhetorical task, in which public arguments take specific forms. We claim that: (a) rhetorical analysis is useful for explaining how the PDA attracted massive investments (as measured by released PDA products) from the major companies in personal computing, telecommunications, and consumer electronics, only to see most of these vendors quickly leave the market; (b) the public rhetoric of the PDA overlaps with the ideology of CMs, but tries to incorporate elements of a social vision within the language of technology and business decision making; and (c) investment patterns (as measured by released PDA products) are consistent with the idea of CMs being influential in specific industries, leading to herding behavior by all but a few companies, which are able to "resist" the prevailing rhetoric of the Next Big Thing.

Rhetoric and CMs

Kling and Iacono (1988) argued that all CMs provide an ideology that helps legitimize relatively high levels of IT investment. These ideologies share five basic assumptions:

1. Computer-based technologies are central for a reformed world.

2. Improved computer-based technologies can further reform society.

3. More computing is better than less, and there are no conceptual limits to the scope of appropriate computerization.

4. No one loses from computerization.

5. Uncooperative people are the main barriers to social reform through computing.

We develop and critique this definition of CM ideology by comparing it with the public arguments for PDA investment over a 10-year period. Particularly when the technology does not yet exist as a marketable product, that is "when a prospective technical order is not yet an established reality" (Guice, 1999), producers and investors play a major role in sustaining technological visions. If producer firms remain within their normal institutional belief systems of maximizing profitability and servicing existing customers, then established players should be very conservative with emerging technologies (as predicted by Christensen, 1997). Instead, computer vendors have pursued many different emerging technologies with, if anything, too much enthusiasm, such as during the Internet bubble (Perkins & Perkins, 2001).

We define rhetoric as "discourse aimed at an audience to gain either intellectual or active adherence" (Perelman, 1982). In the sociology of technology, rhetoric is now seen as a fundamental process in the establishment of new technological forms (e.g., Bijker, 1995). Information systems (IS) researchers now investigate bandwagon effects and explicitly seek out the organizing visions that drive computerization (e.g., Swanson & Ramiller, 2004). An academic community dedicated to the rhetoric of technology has emerged (e.g., Bazerman, 1998). Even the research on social movements in general has experienced a recent "cultural turn" that has focused on the ways that movements have used symbols and language to mobilize and motivate actors (Williams, 2004).

We divide our analysis of PDA rhetoric into three separate processes: promoting the Next Big Thing, rationalizing the failure of the Next Big Thing, and resistance to the Next Big Thing. Rhetoric is obviously involved in promoting new IT concepts, but it is also central to two other persuasive activities in emerging IT industries. Rhetoric is deployed to convince stakeholders that a new IT concept is definitely not the Next Big Thing—some participants are able to persuade themselves that the "conventional wisdom" is incorrect. And, as an experience base develops with an emerging IT, rhetoric plays a role in deciding what lessons to draw from this early experience.

Rhetoric and Emerging Information Technology

Research on the rhetoric of technology has its roots in the study of scientific controversies, though rhetorical analysis was found to be especially relevant for technology because of its focus on human problem solving, and its diverse constituencies. "Technology has always been part of the rhetorical barnyard, part of commerce and finances, customers and vendors, partnerships and corporations, suppliers and production, lawyers and courts … technology, as a human-made object, has always been part of human needs, desires, values, and evaluation, articulated in language and at the very heart of rhetoric" (Bazerman, 1998). Technology design in particular is seen as a process of consensus building among participants with diverse interests (Ornatowski, 1998).

For these researchers, the rhetoric of technology is "the rhetoric that makes the technology fit into the world and makes the world fit with technology … there is a dialectic between rhetoric and the material design as the technology is made to fit the imaginably useful and valuable, to fit into people's understanding of the world" (Bazerman, 1998). Rhetorical studies have investigated many aspects of this fitting and articulation process. Debates are held over the proper role of a new technology, its main purpose, its proper comparison points, and its success criteria (Wickliff, 1998). Visions and expectations for the future are defined (Guice, 1999), often drawing from widespread cultural symbols for legitimacy (Helmreich, 2000; Lambright, 1994). Sponsors are convinced to support new technologies by arguments ranging from financial and political (Lambright, 1994) to nationalistic (Wickliff, 1998), as are potential customers (Ornatowski, 1998). Arguments are used to establish familiar comparison points with already successful technologies (Wickliff, 1998), and to differentiate from undesirable technologies (Mody, 2000). Persuasive language is used to smooth over the inevitable uncertainties that arise in specification and testing (Ornatowski, 1998), and to decide which developmental problems are truly relevant (Mody, 2000). Commitments to negatively perceived technologies are preserved by changing the definition of a new technology, providing it with a new role and purpose (Godin, 1997; B. Kaplan, 1995). Even the fight against new technologies is organized around rhetorical arguments, visions, and symbols (Blume, 1997).

IT would appear to be a particularly good candidate for rhetorical analysis. IT industries are highly interdependent, where many relationships are negotiated rather than dictated through a vertical hierarchy. Technological "winners" become entrenched, and difficult to overthrow. In these conditions, a "culture of new trends" arises because "the apparent inevitability of a trend is necessary for participants in a field to feel confident that their specialized research or engineering efforts will be widely accepted by others in the field" (Guice, 1999).

A few studies of the rhetoric of IT have been done, though published mostly outside of information systems (IS) research venues. Rhetorical forms have been used to identify the "deep structures" that guide interpretations and actions in the London insurance markets (Heracleous & Barrett, 2001). Rhetoric has been used to describe online interaction strategies (Herring, 1999), and to explain "contradictions" between empowerment and controlling strategies in computer-supported cooperative work implementation (Hayes & Walsham, 2000). Researchers have tried to identify the cultural source of symbols that guide IT choices and give them legitimacy, such as the biological metaphors used in computer security (Helmreich, 2000) and the revolutionary metaphors of business process reengineering (Case, 1999). In other studies, rhetoric has been used in a negative sense, as "myths" that need to be exposed or deconstructed (e.g., Pozzebon, 2001). Though studies of the rhetoric of IT sometimes refer to rhetorical theorists such as Aristotle (1984) or Perelman (1982), they often do not draw upon the substantial literature on the rhetoric of technology.

Research Design

The research objective of this study was to analyze the rhetorical arguments used to create a consensus about the potential of the PDA, and compare these arguments to the ideology of CMs as defined by Kling and Iacono. The PDA industry was analyzed over a 10-year period (1988–1997), roughly corresponding to the period between the first commercially released handheld computers intended for a mass market (the Psion Organiser/Organiser II) and the establishment of the Palm Pilot as the first widely adopted product in the PDA industry.

The data for the rhetorical analysis were a collection of trade press articles from the ABI/Inform Global database. A search for articles on "personal digital assistant," "PDA," "handheld," "hand-held," "palmtop," "pen-based," and "pen based" revealed 2,528 articles. After manual inspection to remove irrelevant articles, and product announcements with no accompanying text, 425 articles remained, which included some commentary, evaluation, or statements about the PDA industry or particular PDAs. The articles can be divided into general articles on the PDA industry and articles on specific PDA producers, as shown in Tables 4.1 and 4.2.

Data analysis of the articles involved an interpretation of the forms of rhetoric used in the PDA industry, as manifested in these public documents. In classical rhetoric, going back to the time of Aristotle, generic lines of argument are defined as enthymemes (Aristotle, 1984). Enthymemes are similar to syllogisms in logic, in the sense that they consist of premises, followed by a conclusion. Unlike syllogisms,

Table 4.1 General Articles on the PDA Industry

Year	Articles
Pre-1990	3
1990	5
1991	13
1992	29
1993	41
1994	44
1995	32
1996	28
1997	19
Total	**214**

Table 4.2 Articles on Specific PDA Producers

PDA Producers	Articles
Apple	33
HP	7
Microsoft	26
Motorola	8
Palm	20
Psion	15
Sharp	8
Others	94
Total	**211**

enthymemes are incompletely stated. In an enthymeme, some common premises are assumed to be held by the audience rather than made explicit. "In contrast to syllogisms in logic, enthymemes are usually not fully expressed, with one or more of their premises being taken for granted" (Heracleous & Barrett, 2001).

Heracleous and Barrett (2001) offer both a notation for expressing enthymemes and a description of the process of identifying enthymemes. Enthymemes are expressed as a set of premises and a conclusion that is drawn from these premises. The process of identifying enthymemes is an iterative, interpretive process that moves between two tasks. The first task is to explore individual texts for central themes of argument, and generate enthymemes for individual texts. The second task is to search for common patterns across the entirety of the texts, and examine commonalities and differences between different enthymeme patterns. Both of these tasks use the ethnographic understanding of the researcher(s) as an interpretive aid and as an explicit check (or "triangulation" point) on the interpretations. The ethnographic understanding of the researcher in this study was built up both in formal interviews (17 interviews with industry participants, averaging fifty minutes each, and focusing on the arguments used in the early PDA industry) and during informal interactions. The standard qualitative analysis techniques of constant comparison and searches for negative instances (Strauss, 1987) were also used as an aid to the process.

Background: Persuasion in the PDA Industry

The first observation to make about the PDA industry from 1988 to 1997 is that the PDA truly was considered as a potential Next Big Thing technology by not just one but three separate industries: personal computers (PCs), telecommunications, and consumer electronics. Thirty-four different producers released 71 consumer-oriented PDAs in North America and Europe during this 10-year period (Allen, 2004). The list of companies making substantial PDA investments included major players of the time such as IBM, Compaq, HP, Tandy, Sony, Sharp, Casio, Atari, Fujitsu, and Motorola, in addition to Microsoft (as an operating systems provider) and many start-ups. Though many of these companies soon abandoned the PDA industry, all of them were somehow persuaded to invest heavily in this new and unproven computing technology.

By the mid 1990s, PDAs were beginning to be discussed in public as a commercially disappointing, overly hyped technology. Much of the popular derision focused on one product, the Apple Newton, and the perceived inadequacies of its handwriting recognition. While Apple invested hundreds of millions of dollars in its high-profile commercial disappointment, it was not alone. A consortium led by AT&T released the EO Personal Communicator, a "smart phone" that weighed almost four pounds, to lackluster consumer response. By 1994, interest in PDAs began to drop, as measured by the number of articles in the ABI/Inform database.

The pattern of PDA product releases is summarized in Tables 4.3 and 4.4. The 71 released PDAs are divided into four different types, based on the categories used by participants in the interviews and articles: "palmtops," "pen-based computers," "personal communicators," and "connected organizers." Each of these categories can be seen as a *technological action frame*, providing a composite understanding that supports high levels of investment in a technology and forms the core ideas about how a technology works and how it could be used (Elliott &

Kraemer, Chapter 1, this volume). The key technological features of each category are listed in Table 4.3. The number of released PDA products in each category over time is shown in Table 4.4.

A second key observation to make about the PDA industry is that different technological action frames predominate in different time periods, with many producers converging on similar conceptions of PDAs during key moments. Groups of producers tended to follow a herd, even when there was little or no evidence that a particular PDA vision would be a commercial success. Who were these groups? The first major PDA concept, the "palmtop," attracted the investments of the second-tier PC companies at the time. Later, the "pen computer" concept attracted the largest PC producers, while the "communicator" concept was persuasive mostly to telecommunications device manufacturers. The "connected

Table 4.3 PDA Product Categories

PDA Category	Key Features
Palmtop	Clamshell form factor, PC operating system
Pen-based computers	Pen-based input, handwriting recognition
Personal communicator	Built-in modem, tablet form factor
Connected organizer	PC connectivity, PIM applications (e.g., calendar, address book)

Table 4.4 Released PDA Products, by Category and Vendor

1988–1992	
8 palmtop	Atari, Fujitsu (Poqet), HP, Bicom, Sharp, Olivetti, Zeos
1 pen computer	Momenta
4 others	Psion, Cambridge, Microwriter, Amstrad
1993–1996	
15 pen computer	IBM, Compaq, Mitac, Apple, Sharp, Motorola, Casio, Tandy, AST, HP
8 communicator	BellSouth, Motorola, Sony, AT&T (EO), Nokia
4 palmtop	HP, Gateway
2 connected organizer	Palm, Compaq
3 others	Psion
1997	
19 connected organizer	Casio, NEC, Philips, Ericsson, HP, Sharp, Hitachi, LG, Palm, IBM, TI
2 pen computer	Apple
1 palmtop	Toshiba
2 others	Psion, GeoFox

organizer" concept kept the attention of a few PC companies, but was most persuasive for the consumer electronics companies.

The overall level of investment in this unproven, and largely unsuccessful, technology—along with the shifting herds of producers attracted to a particular PDA definition—is consistent with the argument that there is some kind of persuasive rhetorical argument taking place outside of the normal internal decision-making processes in these companies. Our analysis sought to describe the public discourse about PDA technology during this time.

The specific public arguments used to justify PDA investments are summarized in Table 4.5. Our analysis identified five prominent arguments for promoting PDAs as a potential Next Big Thing technology, labeled as 1S through 5S. After early experience with PDAs, industry players faced the rhetorical task of explaining why the "Next Big Thing" had not yet arrived, and deciding how to proceed on the basis of their explanation (i.e., to disassociate themselves from the PDA concept, or continue to develop it). Our analysis also identified five prominent arguments for rationalizing the failure of an emerging IT, labeled as 1F

Table 4.5 Rhetorical Strategies for Justifying Investment in Emerging IT

Promoting	**Rationalizing**
New mass markets (1S) New concept suitable for large markets left out of previous advances	*Stuck in the niche* (1F) New concept suitable only for established niche markets
Killer feature (2S) Single, dramatic technological improvement will drive acceptance	*Ahead of its time* (2F) Technology feature is not quite ready
Inevitable progression (3S) The logical next step in a long-term trend	*Immature concept* (3F) Still inevitable, but excessively "hyped" and will arrive later than predicted
Bundle together (4S) New concept is combined with other "similar," successful technologies	*Others improve* (4F) "Similar" technologies improve, reducing advantage of new concept
Horse race (5S) Most important question: Which player will win the race to dominate this new market?	*Confused by competing standards* (5F) Too many different players in the market, not allowing standards to emerge

through 5F. These forms of rhetorical argument are discussed in detail in the next two sections.

Promoting the Next Big Thing

The first rhetorical process analyzed was the promotion of PDAs as the next breakthrough concept in the personal computing world. The rhetorical analysis yielded five important forms of argument that received widespread public circulation in the industry: *new mass markets*, *killer feature*, *inevitable progression*, *bundle together*, and *horse race*. The public arguments use a mix of social vision, technology promise, and business urgency to make the case for massive new investments in an unproven technology. The first two arguments, *new mass markets* and *killer feature*, make the most explicit connections between new technology and a better social order. The enthymemes used for each of these forms of argument are summarized in Figure 4.1 and described in more detail later.

New Mass Markets (1S)

The rhetoric of a new technology, as part of the process of making it "fit into the world" (Bazerman, 1998), establishes a vision of the future (Guice, 1999), often drawing from widespread cultural symbols for legitimacy (Lambright, 1994). To build support for a new technology in a

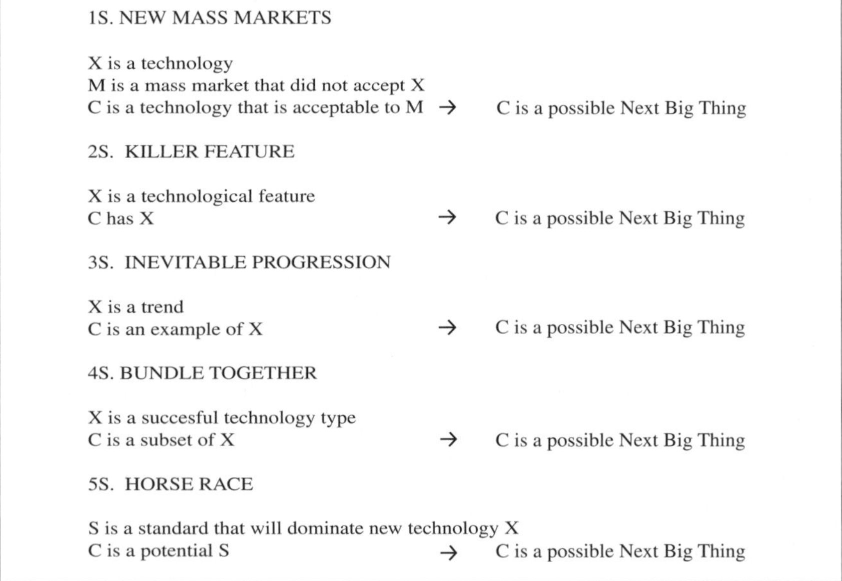

1S. NEW MASS MARKETS
X is a technology
M is a mass market that did not accept X
C is a technology that is acceptable to M → C is a possible Next Big Thing
2S. KILLER FEATURE
X is a technological feature
C has X → C is a possible Next Big Thing
3S. INEVITABLE PROGRESSION
X is a trend
C is an example of X → C is a possible Next Big Thing
4S. BUNDLE TOGETHER
X is a succesful technology type
C is a subset of X → C is a possible Next Big Thing
5S. HORSE RACE
S is a standard that will dominate new technology X
C is a potential S → C is a possible Next Big Thing

Figure 4.1 Enthymemes used in promotion arguments

commercial environment, the *new mass markets* argument identifies a large and lucrative new market that has not been addressed by a previously successful technology.

PDA investments were justified by tying the technology to the dominant computing frame of productivity (Elliott & Kraemer, Chapter 1, this volume), especially a mass market for personal productivity tools. These new mass markets were tied to popular images of modern life, such as mobility and increased time pressures. For the PDA, a number of mass markets were identified that had not been adequately addressed by the PCs of the day. These new mass markets included: consumers intimidated by PCs, white-collar executives, mobile professionals who work from home or client locations, and blue-collar field workers.

Pen-based computers, because of their potential ease of use and lower training costs, were argued to "shatter the glass ceiling that prevents new users from coming into the [PC] industry," with the result that "pen-based computing could be the next mass market for the computer industry" (Keefe, 1991). For those users afraid of keyboards and other PC complexities, the pen-based PDA offered a solution: "If the Macintosh was the computer for the rest of us, the pen is the computer for all of us" (Fitzgerald, 1991). The new mass markets arguments drew upon popular images of white-collar executives who were "afraid of standard personal computers" (Francis, 1991) as well as more positive images of "today's mobile and fast-paced society and the increasing need to keep in touch with business associates, colleagues, family, and others" (Hawkins, 1993). As the emphasis in PDAs began to shift from pen input to mobile communications, the idea of tens of millions of mobile workers was employed to support a vision of "anytime, anywhere communications. The premise is that wireless digital networks, feeding information to powerful handheld phone-fax-computer hybrids, will alter the way people live and work" (Ziegler, 1993).

For players in the PC industry, establishing a link to a new mass market offered the potential riches of "the computer industry's next billion dollar market" (Rebello, 1991) but also addressed the problem of stagnation in the spread of existing technology, as "the new pen-based PCs still represent a refreshing growth opportunity in the troubled PC industry" (Rebello, 1992). The new mass markets argument offers the potential of enrolling a whole new set of supporters for a new technology, including producers, investors, and consumers. The suggested needs of the new mass market then impose themselves on the new technology definition, establishing new problems to be solved and new solution requirements. For example, as long as pen-based input was argued to be the key to serving a mass market of technophobes, no PDA could afford to be without functioning handwriting recognition. As long as mobile communications was the key to serving a new mobile world, wireless communications could not be left out of a PDA product.

Killer Feature (2S)

Early in the life of a new technology, debates are held over its proper role and success criteria (Wickliff, 1998). In a *killer feature* argument, the presence of a single, dramatically improved technological feature makes a new technology a candidate Next Big Thing. For the PDA, pen input was the first proposed killer feature. Following the early commercial setbacks of pen-based computers, other killer features were proposed, most prominently wireless communications. The proposed essential features of PDAs were as varied as intelligent agents, the ability to run Lotus 1-2-3, voice recognition, "social" interfaces such as the Magic Cap virtual mall, Internet access, digital tablets, and the ability to communicate with office equipment.

The first killer feature argument focused on pen input and freeform handwriting recognition, as implied in the name "pen-based computers" given to many early PDA products. "The pen-based computer, which looks something like an Etch A Sketch, may be the most promising development in computing since the Macintosh and the mouse" (Shaffer, 1991). A review in *BYTE* magazine argued that "the pen-input system is one of the most exciting recent developments in computing technology" (Baran, 1992). After the commercial problems of the Apple Newton and other pen-based PDAs, attention focused on wireless communications: "The next trend will no doubt be wireless transmission" (Mandell, 1991). Wireless was argued to be the key feature that would save the troubled PDA industry and therefore should be the focus of future development (Brodsky, 1994). A killer feature argument strongly suggests a distinctive and one-dimensional success criterion for a new technology.

Inevitable Progression (3S) and Bundle Together (4S)

Arguments for investing in a new technology must tie a vision of a better tomorrow to a belief that a specific technology is promising enough to make that vision a reality. We refer to this rhetorical task as establishing technological legitimacy. Both the *inevitable progression* and *bundle together* arguments try to establish technological legitimacy.

A common strategy in the PDA industry was to argue that a PDA vision was simply part of an inevitable trend. In the highly interdependent, standards-driven world of IT, establishing "the apparent inevitability of a trend" (Guice, 1999) is an important rhetorical task. While the inevitability of a particular emerging IT is assumed by most promotion attempts, it is made explicit in the inevitable progression arguments. In this form of argument, a trend is identified in an established technology that explains its continued success. A candidate Next Big Thing technology is argued to be an example of this trend.

For the PDA, the most important trend was size reduction in computers. The PDA trend was "merely a continuation of what has been happening to PCs in general since the early 1980s, with units getting smaller, more powerful, and less expensive" (Taylor, 1991). PC evolution was described as progressing from the desktop, to the laptop, and now the palmtop. "The essence of mobile computing is the notion that a computer will someday be as small as a wallet or a cigarette pack. ... PDAs probably come closest to this paradigm" (Terdoslavich, 1995). To fully take advantage of this argument, the solution requirements of a potential new technology need to include the dimension implied by the inevitable trend.

Another strategy was to argue that the PDA was already a success by linking it to an established winner. For a new and unproven technology, arguments are used to establish familiar comparison points with technologies already perceived to be successful (Wickliff, 1998). In a bundle together argument, an emerging IT is combined with other successful technologies into a single category. A candidate Next Big Thing technology is declared to be a subset of this category.

The PDA was bundled together with other portable or mobile computing devices, with optimistic predictions made for the entire category. "The market for notebook and palmtop computers continues to grow; U.S. shipments of notebooks are predicted to reach nearly $2 billion in 1995" (Remich, 1992). For *CIO* magazine, one of the top ten IT ideas of 1992 was "notebook, laptop, or handheld PCs instead of desktops" (Isaacson, 1992). *Computer Reseller News* described the growth of mobile computing as including notebooks, subnotebooks, and PDAs (Hwang, 1994). While notebook computers were the preferred target of the bundling argument, links were attempted to other successful consumer electronics devices. "The potential exists for PDAs to be as fertile as the calculator" (Delmonico & Gerstein, 1994).

Making a rhetorical link to other established technologies encourages the inclusion of elements from a previously successful technology in a newer vision. For example, the earliest PDAs were defined as "palmtops" and incorporated many elements of standard PCs in their definition.

Horse Race (5S)

A final rhetorical task is to establish a sense of business urgency—a technology may legitimately be promising, and it might bring about an important change in work or leisure, but why should a business make PDAs an investment priority right now? In the IT industry, a widely understood interpretation of any attempt to establish a new technology is to see it as a standards battle: as Microsoft vs. Apple in the operating systems wars, or Microsoft vs. Netscape in the browser wars. In a *horse race* argument, the rhetoric of new technology is framed in terms of a race between competing players or alliances to establish a new standard. The argument assumes that a single standard will dominate technology adoption, and that the proposed technology concept may become this standard.

In the early stages of the PDA industry, arguments were waged over who would win the battle to create a PDA standard operating system. The initial candidates were Microsoft and Go, a start-up company backed by IBM and later AT&T (J. Kaplan, 1994). The debate over the Next Big Thing technology in horse race arguments tends to focus on which potential standard has the most allies and is supported by the most investors and large consumers. Later operating systems such as Magic Cap pointed to its many partner companies to argue that it would become the Next Big Thing. Horse race arguments can modify a proposed technology vision by changing the technology's purpose to include the strategic needs of influential producer and investor partners, in addition to the perceived needs of end consumers. In the case of Go, an early definition of PDAs as pen-based computers shifted to personal communications in an attempt to persuade AT&T to support the technology.

Rationalizing the Failure of the Next Big Thing

The second rhetorical process analyzed was the explanation of the perceived "failure" of early PDA products. Interpreting early experience with a new technology is subject to the limitations of "evidential context": "the meaning of some experimental finding, or test outcome, can seem positive or negative depending upon the problem that the finding is taken to address" (Collins & Pinch, 1998). The perceived success or failure of specific PDA products depended on a definition of the problem that was itself subject to debate: Which markets was the PDA meant to serve? Which features must it include, and at what level of performance? Or was it meant to forward the goal of being first in a horse race, even at the cost of short-term commercial failure? Was the "failure" of the Apple Newton to be interpreted as the death of the PDA concept, an occasion for redefining it, or the inevitable teething problems of a still promising technology?

While a failure to live up to expectations can fuel the creation of a counter-rhetoric, or contending discourse, in the case of the PDA much of the rhetoric sought to preserve the PDA as a potential Next Big Thing technology. Negative early experiences were mainly interpreted as problems with a still promising new technology, taking the form of rationalizing the failure of the Next Big Thing. The rhetorical analysis yielded five important lines of argument that received widespread circulation in the industry: *stuck in the niche*, *ahead of its time*, *immature concept*, *others improve*, and *confused by competing standards*. The enthymemes used for each of these forms of argument are summarized in Figure 4.2. The enthymemes share some of the premises of earlier promotion arguments.

Stuck in the Niche (1F)

The rhetoric of a new technology helps establish a vision of the future that argues for either widespread use, as in the new mass markets argument, or for more limited use. A *stuck in the niche* argument identifies a mass market whose needs have not been addressed by a previously successful technology. It also identifies a candidate Next Big Thing technology that will service the needs of this mass market in the future but as of today is still suitable only for a much smaller market, willing to put up with different levels of performance and cost.

The PDA industry debated the merits of targeting a widespread versus a limited market, using the terms "horizontal" (the mass market) and "vertical" (targeted niche markets). Reacting to the perceived failure

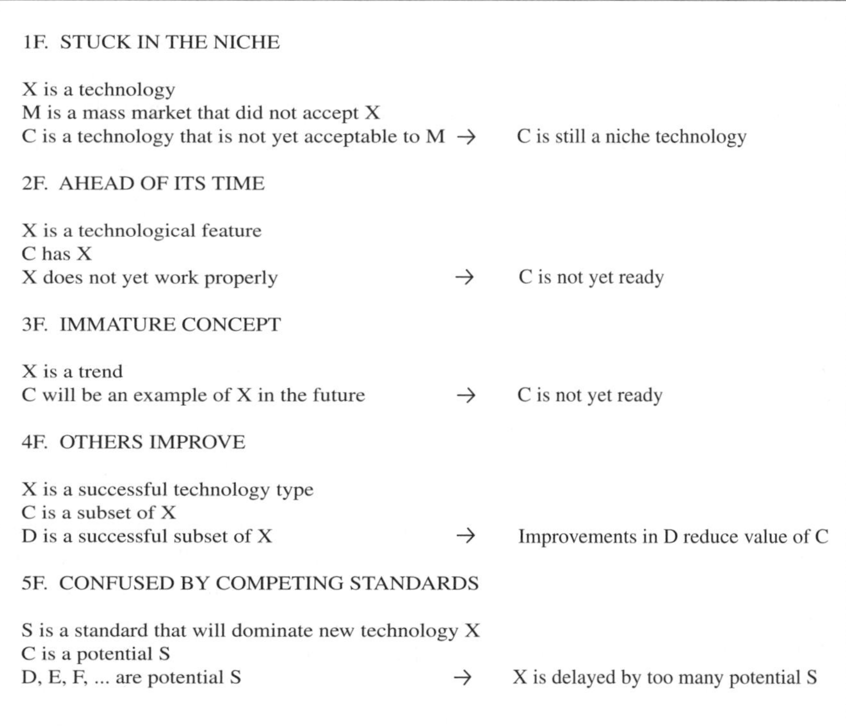

1F. STUCK IN THE NICHE

X is a technology
M is a mass market that did not accept X
C is a technology that is not yet acceptable to M → C is still a niche technology

2F. AHEAD OF ITS TIME

X is a technological feature
C has X
X does not yet work properly → C is not yet ready

3F. IMMATURE CONCEPT

X is a trend
C will be an example of X in the future → C is not yet ready

4F. OTHERS IMPROVE

X is a successful technology type
C is a subset of X
D is a successful subset of X → Improvements in D reduce value of C

5F. CONFUSED BY COMPETING STANDARDS

S is a standard that will dominate new technology X
C is a potential S
D, E, F, ... are potential S → X is delayed by too many potential S

Figure 4.2 Enthymemes used in rationalization arguments

of early pen-based PDAs, "a new focus on vertical markets to augment [Apple's] floundering consumer campaign" (Greenberg, 1994) was argued to be a sensible holding strategy. A "new consensus ... to focus on developing a corporate market" (Yamada, 1995) identified vertical markets such as healthcare, financial services, and agriculture as the most promising short-term directions for PDA development. "It was unrealistic for the PDA guys to jump right into the consumer market ... after the first two or three years of adoption, when the prices come down, it can become more consumer oriented" (Perkins, 1994). The stuck in the niche rationalization preserves faith in the candidate Next Big Thing technology, at the expense of shifting its definition toward near-term survival over longer-term vision.

Ahead of Its Time (2F)

Much like a killer feature argument, the *ahead of its time* argument resolves uncertainty about solution requirements by arguing for a single technological feature as the main goal of a candidate Next Big Thing technology. While the ahead of its time rationalization defines success in terms of a single feature, it further argues that because the feature does not work properly at the moment, the candidate Next Big Thing has yet to prove itself.

Pen-input technology, especially pen-based handwriting recognition, was one of the first features used in ahead of its time arguments. Interpreting the commercial failure of the Apple Newton, a typical reaction was to claim that "[pen technology] does continue to have potential, but ... the handwriting recognition is not there yet" (Bradbury, 1995). In some cases, the definition of handwriting recognition as a PDA solution requirement was preserved: "Although critics complain about problems such as the unit's slow and inaccurate handwriting recognition, market researchers seem convinced that PDAs are here to stay" (Edwards, 1993). For others, the ahead of its time argument led directly to a switch in solution requirements. "Keyboard based-handheld computers ... have risen from the ashes of failed pen-based computers" (Infoworld, 1997).

As the "personal communicator" PDAs also struggled to find mass-market success, ahead of its time arguments claimed that the failure of PDAs was due to inadequate wireless communications technology. According to trade press articles in 1994, "the lack of a solid wireless communications infrastructure in the first generation of PDAs has soured many to its uses" (Fitzgerald, 1994). "Sales to executives will not take off until 1998 when wireless data transmission is easier and more reliable" (Wilson, 1994). Other technology features used in ahead of its time arguments included Internet connections, intelligent agents, voice recognition, and even seamless connection to office equipment. While an ahead of its time argument preserves the rationale for the initial enthusiasm for a particular technological feature, it allows for a redefinition of solution requirements if the technology is "too far ahead" of its time.

Immature Concept (3F) and Others Improve (4F)

A new technology is in danger of losing its technological legitimacy if it fails to live up to early expectations. If a technological trend is claimed to be inevitable, yet a candidate Next Big Thing technology has yet to "succeed" in the eyes of many, one explanation is a misunderstanding of the timing of the trend rather than the trend itself. An *immature concept* argument identifies a successful trend in previous technologies, and claims that a new technology will successfully take advantage of this trend not now but in the future. The potential Next Big Thing technology takes time to "mature," and this development process is seen as inevitable in new technology industries. For example: "Just as the Apple Lisa became our cherished Macintosh and as Windows 1.0 became Chicago, today's PDAs will become tomorrow's treasures" (Isaacson, 1994). The early review of PDAs in *BYTE* magazine argued that "like the PCs of 10 years ago, these machines represent the first generation. In the next few years we'll see great improvements in many of their features" (Baran, 1992).

Because the trend is argued to be inevitable, the explanation for why players supported a candidate Next Big Thing technology too "early" in its development is attributed to expectations management—the technology was excessively "hyped." Much of this rationalization activity focused on the Apple Newton PDA after its problematic debut: The "hype" around the Newton "raised expectations to a level that were never going to be achievable in the short term. ... Newton has hurt the whole market. I don't know why anyone would expect 500,000 of these to be sold the first year out" (Southwick, 1994). The "grand promises" (Bennahum, 1995) made for the new technology, and then broken, become part of the rationalization for why the Next Big Thing has yet to appear.

A familiar comparison point with a previous technology may also help establish the definition of a new technology, but it can encourage competition between the two. In the *others improve* argument, the candidate Next Big Thing technology is bundled together with other successful technologies into a single promising category. However, improvements in the other technologies can then reduce the unique value of the candidate Next Big Thing technology, explaining its lack of success.

In the PDA industry, PDAs were most often bundled together with notebook and laptop computers into a single, promising "mobile computing" category. Improvements in notebook computers, particularly smaller sizes and lower prices, were argued to make the PDA less appealing. "The arrival in 1994 of lightweight notebooks was particularly unfortunate for

PDAs, as power users flocked to light portables that ran established operating systems and had large color displays" (Piven, 1996).

If the others improve rationalization argument becomes widely accepted, then the other competing technologies may in turn affect the definition of problems and solutions for the candidate Next Big Thing. As a new category of "subnotebooks" emerged, attempts were made to define a PDA as a replacement for a small notebook computer. "The days of lugging around heavy-duty equipment on the road could be over thanks to a proliferation of handheld computers" (Infoworld, 1997). Producers such as Apple responded by "trying to reposition the Newton from a high-priced organizer to a platform that offers a lower-priced alternative to notebooks" (Gambon, 1996).

Confused by Competing Standards (5F)

The confused by competing standards argument assumes that a single standard will dominate technology adoption, and that the proposed Next Big Thing might become the standard. However, while the horse race argument manages to rhetorically separate the candidate Next Big Thing from competitor technologies, the confused by competing standards argument complicates the situation by reintroducing a variety of other technologies competing to become the new standard. The fact that so many competing candidate standards exist implies a confusion in the marketplace, explaining why the Next Big Thing technology has yet to emerge.

For PDAs, arguments about standards competition focused on PDA-specific operating systems. The PDA would not develop, it was argued, until "the market determines which pen operating system will become the standard" (Semich, 1993). The uncertainty around standards, and a refusal for industry players to rally around a single standard, is used as the rationalization for the failure of the PDA concept. A confused by competing standards argument can be used to preserve the technical definition of a candidate Next Big Thing technology, while focusing the problem on the standards setting process.

Resisting the Next Big Thing

The third rhetorical process analyzed was resistance to the rhetoric of the Next Big Thing. Though most investments in PDAs tended to cluster into sets of "conventional wisdom," as indicated in Table 4.4 with 15 pen-based PDAs released from 1993 to 1996, there are a few examples of technology vendors that were able to persuade themselves that the "conventional wisdom" was incorrect. Certain parts of the PDA CM were able to form pockets of contending discourse that led them down different technology paths.

The purpose of this section is to briefly present two cases of resistance: Psion and Palm. In the first case, Psion was able to create PDAs with a combination of features that did not fit neatly within any established technology frame. Psion resisted both the temptation to focus on pen-based input and the subsequent industry focus on wireless communications. In the second case, the well-known story of Palm is used to show how a new PDA definition, the "connected organizer," successfully resisted the "conventional wisdom" about PDAs at the time.

While these short cases illustrate that resistance, though relatively unusual, is possible, they cannot answer the more interesting question of why Psion and Palm were able to resist prevailing Next Big Thing rhetoric. Of the many possible explanations, our previous work has focused on how senior managers at Psion and Palm participated in different professional worlds outside of normal PDA industry circles (Allen, 2004). In the language of the social construction of technology literature (Bijker, 1995), senior managers at Psion and Palm had a high degree of inclusion within technological frames than were unfamiliar to established PC, telecommunications, and consumer electronics companies.

The Psion Case

Psion PLC was founded in Britain in the early 1980s as a PC applications software company. By the mid 1980s, Psion had shifted its focus to pocket-sized computers for business executives, creating products such as the Organiser and the Organiser II. Psion released a profitable line of industrial pocket computers (the HC range) and a not-so-profitable notebook-sized device (the MC) before finding its first mass market success in 1991 with the Series 3.

The original Series 3 was similar to the prevailing concept of PDAs as "palmtops" in some ways, but radically different in others. The Series 3 accepted the solution requirement of a clamshell form factor and a keyboard from the "palmtop" definition of PDAs, as opposed to the tablet form used in "pen-based computers." The Series 3, however, redefined the key problem to be solved by PDAs away from the "palmtop" notion of a very small computer running PC software. The Series 3 instead adopted the concept of a computing device that was easy for business executives to use away from their desks. Psion developed a new operating system for the Series 3 that fulfilled the new solution requirements of booting up instantly, quickly switching between different application programs, and preserving battery power. The problem-solving strategies Psion used were partly those familiar to the PC industry, such as computer hardware and software development, but also included strategies more familiar to the consumer electronics industries, such as subcontracting with leading industrial design firms, and extensive user field testing.

As the commercially successful Series 3 matured into the Series 3a (1993) and the Series 3c (1996), promotion rhetoric in the PDA industry shifted dramatically toward the idea of the "pen-based computer" as the Next Big Thing. Debates about the appropriate solution requirements for PDAs changed from PC compatibility to the newer technologies of pen-based input and handwriting recognition. Psion successfully resisted these public arguments, staying with a keyboard-based interface. Psion's Series 3 PDAs revealed a resistance to the bundle together arguments, as Psion never defined its PDAs as competitors for notebook or subnotebook computers after its experience with the MC. Psion also resisted the new mass market argument of "pen-based computer" PDAs, which claimed that handwriting recognition was necessary to service a new mass market of computer-phobic novices. Psion continued to define the PDA in terms of executives who were comfortable enough with PC-like features such as keyboards, application programs, and file systems. The company also resisted the horse race arguments that claimed a new PDA would be successful only if it enrolled big partners to establish a new operating system platform. Psion resisted alliances with companies such as Apple, AT&T, Motorola, and Microsoft, choosing to design and build its own hardware, applications, and operating system.

As the commercial failure of the first "pen-based computer" PDAs became evident, rationalization rhetoric began to interpret this experience in a way that would preserve the promise of PDAs as a Next Big Thing technology. While stuck in the niche rhetoric argued that pen-based PDAs would be acceptable only to industrial niche markets because of their high cost and poor handwriting recognition, Psion continued to refine its Series 3 line for a broader consumer market of business executives. As the troublesome handwriting recognition technology became the focus of ahead of its time arguments, wireless communications emerged as one of the new killer features. When the shift to a "personal communicator" PDA attracted a new round of attention from telecommunications producers, Psion resisted the temptation to define wireless as the most important solution requirement for its consumer Series 3 PDAs, while still incorporating wireless as an option for its industrial HC range. During times of turmoil, Psion preserved its belief in its original PDA definition, in the face of substantial conflicting rhetoric in the industry at large.

The Palm Case

Palm Computing was founded in 1992 as a handheld computer applications software company (Butter & Pogue, 2002). Palm's first products were application software for PDA handwriting recognition (Graffiti) and desktop connectivity (PalmConnect). Palm provided much of the applications software for the Tandy/Casio Zoomer in 1993, a "pen-based computer" PDA that failed commercially around the same time as the Apple Newton. Unable to find a suitable PDA hardware platform for its software in the wake of the Newton debacle, Palm famously decided to develop its own PDA. The PalmPilot was released in 1996. After the commercial failures of the "pen-based computer" and "personal communicator" PDAs, the industry was more than a little surprised to see the PalmPilot become one of the fastest-selling computing products of all time.

The rapid adoption of the PalmPilot, and its follow-on products, established a new technological vision for PDA, the "connected organizer." Because the "connected organizer" is now an established definition for PDAs, it is difficult to remember how counterintuitive this concept was in the mid 1990s. The two most prominent PDA concepts being promoted at the time, "pen-based computers" and "personal communicators," defined the key solution requirements as technological features such as a tablet form factor, pen input, and wireless communications. The PalmPilot instead defined the key solution requirements as seamless connectivity with a PC, and easy-to-use personal information management applications such as calendars and address books. The PalmPilot operating system was designed from the ground up to synchronize easily with, and be dependent on, a PC. In contrast, a key problem to be solved by "pen-based computers" and "personal communicators" was to liberate their users from being tied to PCs that were too difficult for mass market consumers to use.

As the design of the PalmPilot shows, Palm successfully resisted the promotion rhetoric in the PDA industry. The new mass market arguments of the day claimed that people who were uncomfortable with, or afraid of, conventional PCs were the target audience for PDAs. Palm designed PDAs to be a companion device to PCs. Instead of bundling together the PDA with computer-like devices, Palm instead took pencil and paper as the main comparison point and its main competitor technology (Butter & Pogue, 2002). The calendar and address book were tested against paper diaries for speed and ease of use. Palm successfully resisted the killer feature argument that freeform handwriting recognition was the key solution requirement. The PalmPilot accepted pen input one character at a time, using a specially modified alphabet. Palm also resisted the claims of the horse race advocates, choosing to develop the entire hardware and software platform on its own instead of in partnership with a large coalition of companies.

As Palm decided to develop and build a new PDA entirely on its own, rationalization rhetoric in the industry was used to interpret the disappointment with both "pen-based computer" PDAs and "personal communicator" PDAs. Palm resisted the stuck in the niche rationalization by holding on to the vision of a relatively inexpensive mass market product rather than shifting to industrial markets. As industry players argued that all pen input was ahead of its time, as shown by the commercial difficulties of the Apple Newton and Tandy/Casio Zoomer, Palm kept pen input as a solution requirement while modifying the form of the handwriting recognition technology. Finally, the company resisted rationalization arguments that the PDA market was simply confused by competing standards. Instead of waiting for a dominant PDA operating system to emerge, Palm created its own.

The Palm case shows that creating a new technological vision is possible with limited resources, even in the face of promotion and rationalization rhetoric that contradicts the new vision's basic assumptions.

Discussion: The Rhetoric of CMs

Research in the rhetoric of technology has identified many of the different specific tasks involved in legitimizing significant technology investments. These tasks include the definition of a proper role, a vision, and the success criteria for a new technology. They also include establishing boundaries between a technology and other competitor technologies, and establishing the relevance of different problems and problem-solving strategies.

The power of rhetoric can be seen in the ability of unproven technological concepts to attract massive investment. During different time periods in the early PDA industry, particular visions of the Next Big Thing tended to dominate the thinking of PDA producers, as seen in the released PDA products over the decade (see Table 4.4). That the PDA managed to engage the interest of almost every major PC company, consumer electronics company, and many telecommunications equipment companies is testimony to the power of Next Big Thing rhetoric.

Despite its persuasive power, the rhetoric of promotion has limits. These limits can be seen precisely in the examples of PDA producers who released products that, in some way, conflicted with prevailing promotion or rationalization rhetoric. While both Psion and Palm were forced to develop the hardware and software for their path-breaking PDAs almost entirely alone, they both succeeded in resisting the specific rhetorical arguments for the pure "palmtop," "pen-based computer," or "personal communicator" concepts of PDAs.

In this section, we compare our findings on the rhetoric of the Next Big Thing to the definition of CM ideology provided by Kling and Iacono (1995). We argue that the public PDA rhetoric overlaps with the ideology of CMs but tries to incorporate elements of a social vision within the language of technology and business decision making. The *bundle together*, *new mass markets*, and *killer feature* arguments frame elements of a social vision in the language of technical and market viability. The *horse race* arguments are meant to convey more of a sense of business urgency than positive social vision, but have their own strong ideological components. Our analysis identifies a partial, but not complete, overlap with CM ideology, with visions of a positive social order remaining largely, but not completely, implicit.

In their original definition of CMs, Kling and Iacono (1995) identify five key ideological beliefs that help promote positive social visions of technology use. How do our findings in the PDA industry compare? We comment on the five pairs of rhetorical devices found in PDA promotion and resistance rhetoric: new mass markets/stuck in the niche, killer feature/ahead of its time, inevitable progression/immature concept, bundle together/others improve, and horse race/confused by competing standards.

New Mass Markets/Stuck in the Niche (1S/1F)

The new mass markets argument is the rhetoric that most strongly resembles the CM ideology identified by Kling and Iacono. New mass markets rhetoric openly ties the PDA to a positive social vision, such as the idea that PDAs will lift up all those left behind by the complexity of PCs and keyboards into the digital future. PDAs were seen as a new market opportunity for vendors, but just as importantly they served a deep and widespread societal need. This Next Big Thing is argued to be central to a reformed world, can improve society, and no one loses from this kind of computerization. Its ideological power comes from the potent combination of a positive social vision and its compatibility with the language of venture capitalists, marketers, and pundits who desire a large potential new market.

Killer Feature/Ahead of Its Time (2S/2F)

Killer feature rhetoric implicitly argues that not just a technology but a specific technological feature is central to positive change. Because a killer feature argument is more specific about a proposed technological future than other enthymemes, it is more easily challenged by experience and therefore more volatile. For PDAs, the specific killer feature changed drastically over the 10-year period. Visions that defined PDAs as "pen-based computers" or "personal communicators" were obvious attempts to build a constituency within particular investor or producer communities first, with relatively less focus on a positive vision for technology users.

Inevitable Progression/Immature Concept (3S/3F)

The inevitability of the PDA, one of the most powerful and widely used arguments for its potential Next Big Thing status, makes a set of strong but largely implicit assumptions about the social value of the

PDA. If a PDA vision is inevitable (even if slightly immature), then, in the long run, uncooperative people are the main barrier to acceptance.

Bundle Together/Others Improve (4S/4F)

The bundle together argument tries to increase the legitimacy of an unproven technology by linking it to a technology already perceived as successful. The main rhetorical objective is to build credibility for a technology vision, though elements of an existing social vision are likely to carry over to the new technology as well. For "palmtop" PDAs, for example, the revolutionary potential of PCs for personal growth carried over to PDAs, along with the PC's key technical performance criteria.

Horse Race/Confused by Competing Standards (5S/5F)

The horse race argument is the type of PDA industry rhetoric that has the least connection with CM ideology. This metaphor is a rhetorical device intended to build a sense of business urgency—not only that this technology is the Next Big Thing, but that investment needs to happen before others beat us to the finish line. At the same time, the horse race argument implicitly reinforces the idea that the vision of the technology is already well defined, certain, and widely agreed upon in the industry.

Conclusion

The concept of a CM highlights the role of outside analysts, professional organizations, and activists in the computerization process. This chapter identified the public arguments used by outsiders to legitimize substantial investments in PDA technology. We also compared our findings on the rhetoric of the Next Big Thing to the ideology of CMs.

The pattern of (over)investment and herding behavior in the PDA industry argues strongly for some analysis of the persuasive arguments that take place outside of individual companies—this is where the concept of a CM can be useful. This study shows one way of trying to trace the content of a CM empirically, through a catalog of public enthymemes over a substantial period. We used released products as an indicator of whether producer companies had been persuaded by the overall rhetoric of the PDA, and by specific definitions of what a PDA should be.

The emergence of the PDA industry over a 10-year period was analyzed as three rhetorical processes: promoting the Next Big Thing, rationalizing the failure of the Next Big Thing, and resistance to the Next Big Thing. This study identified some of the prominent arguments, or more precisely enthymemes, deployed to promote an emerging technology as the Next Big Thing. These enthymemes included inevitable progression, bundle together, new mass markets, killer feature, and horse race. This study also identified the main enthymemes used to rationalize belief in the PDA as the Next Big Thing, even in the face of apparent setbacks: immature concept, others improve, stuck in the niche, ahead of its time, and confused by competing standards. The examples of Psion and Palm showed the possibility of resisting the prevailing Next Big Thing rhetoric, demonstrating that while potential Next Big Thing arguments can be extremely persuasive, there are distinct limits to their persuasive power.

This study has also conceptualized technology development and adoption as infused with rhetoric and counter-rhetoric. This PDA study has opened up the possibility, however, that serious counterarguments can arise from an industry's attempts to interpret early experiences with a new technology that does not live up to expectations. Contradictory arguments may come from exactly the same kinds of actors over time, or even in some cases the very same analysts. The examples of Psion and Palm demonstrate the usefulness of looking at resistance to the dominant rhetoric as a third rhetorical process—we should not assume that a CM ideology is equally influential across an entire industry or user community.

As we look to the future, the PDA is being discussed in terms of new visions such as "smart phones." If the past is any guide, we should not expect any attempts to define a vision in terms of a single killer feature to remain unchallenged for long. We would do well to examine the rhetoric outside of specific companies that ties PDA capabilities either to a productivity frame (e.g., seamless collaboration with existing systems), a ubiquitous computing frame (e.g., the liberations anytime, anyplace communications), or some other larger vision yet unspecified that melds together social benefit, technological legitimacy, and business urgency. At the same time, we should keep our eyes on the companies that resist the dominant rhetoric, and travel in new directions that challenge a view of PDAs as simply a phone add-on, such as the BlackBerry, or the innovative subscription and billing model of i-mode.

Finally, we should not assume that the ideology of a CM will necessarily provide a social vision that is easily separable from the institutionalized concerns of those being asked to invest in these new forms of computerization. The social vision of the PDA was incorporated within the language of technical and business legitimacy, for example, by linking a technical feature (pen-based interface) with a new mass market (frustrated keyboarders), and with a positive social vision of freely mobile professionals. This is truly "the rhetoric that makes the technology fit into the world and makes the world fit with technology" (Bazerman, 1998).

Acknowledgments

We would like to thank seminar participants at Indiana University, Bloomington, the University of Washington, Seattle, and Microsoft Research for their comments, in addition to the PDA industry professionals who participated in the research. We gratefully acknowledge the support of the ESRC Virtual Society Programme.

References

Allen, J. P. (2004). Redefining the network: Enrollment strategies in the PDA industry. *Information Technology & People*, 17(2).

Aristotle (1984). *The rhetoric and poetics of Aristotle*. New York: The Modern Library.

Baran, N. (1992, April). Rough gems: First pen systems show promise, lack refinement. *BYTE*, 212–222.

Bazerman, C. (1998). The production of technology and the production of human meaning. *Journal of Business & Technical Communication*, 12(3), 381–387.

Bennahum, D. (1995). The return of the PDA. *Marketing Computers*, 15(2), 34–40.

Bijker, W. (1995). *Of bicycles, bakelite, and bulbs: Towards a theory of sociotechnical change*. Cambridge, MA: MIT Press.

Blume, S. (1997). The rhetoric and counter-rhetoric of a 'Bionic' technology. *Science Technology & Human Values*, 22(1), 31–56.

Bradbury, D. (1995). The writing on the wall: Pen-based computing. *Computer Weekly*, 19, 64–65.

Brodsky, I. (1994). PDAs will usher in the next net revolution. *Network World*, 11(45), 49–51.

Butter, A., & Pogue, D. (2002). *Piloting palm: The inside story of palm, handspring, and the birth of the billion-dollar handheld industry*. New York: John Wiley & Sons.

Case, P. (1999). Remember re-engineering? The rhetorical appeal of a managerial salvation device. *Journal of Management Studies*, 36(4), 419–441.

Christensen, C. (1997). *The innovator's dilemma: When new technologies cause great firms to fail*. Boston: Harvard Business School Press.

Collins, H., & Pinch, T. (1998). *The golem at large: What you should know about technology*. Cambridge, UK: Cambridge University Press.

Delmonico, D., & Gerstein, D. (1994). Personal devices: Dream vs. reality. *Computer Reseller News*, 3, 91–94.

Edwards, J. (1993). Waves of the future. *CIO*, 7(6), 58–61.

Fitzgerald, M. (1991). Pen-based future looks bright. *Computerworld*, 3, 48.

Fitzgerald, M. (1994). PDAs face skeptical corporate reception. *Computerworld*, 28(24), 46.

Francis, B. (1991). Pen-based notebooks find their niche. *Datamation*, 37(19), 44–46.

Gambon, J. (1996). PDAs in the palm of your hand. *Informationweek*, 22, 44–46.

Godin, B. (1997). The rhetoric of a health technology: The microprocessor patient card. *Social Studies of Science*, 27(6), 865–902.

Greenberg, I. (1994). New software may put PDAs back in the game. *Infoworld*, 5, 34.

Guice, J. (1999). Designing the future: The culture of new trends in science and technology. *Research Policy*, 28(1), 81–98.

Hawkins, D. (1993). Have you seen your first PDA yet? *Online*, 17(2), 81–85.

Hayes, N., & Walsham, G. (2000). Competing interpretations of computer-supported cooperative work in organizational contexts. *Organization*, 7(1), 49–67.

Helmreich, S. (2000). Flexible infections: Computer viruses, human bodies, nation-states, evolutionary capitalism. *Science Technology & Human Values*, 25(4), 472–491.

Heracleous, L., & Barrett, M. (2001). Organizational change as discourse: Communicative actions and deep structures in the context of information technology. *Academy of Management Journal*, 44(4), 755–778.

Herring, S. (1999). The rhetorical dynamics of gender harassment on-line. *The Information Society*, 15(3), 151–167.

Hwang, D. (1994). Takeout computing takes off. *Computer Reseller News*, 21.

Infoworld (1997). Whole world in your hand? *Infoworld*, 24, 86–94.

Isaacson, P. (1992, December). That wonderful year: A few good ideas. *CIO*, 68–70.

Isaacson, P. (1994). Will 1994 turn out to be the year of the PDA-market boom or bust? *Computer Reseller News*, 24.

Kaplan, B. (1995). The computer prescription: Medical computing, public policy, and views of history. *Science Technology & Human Values*, 20(1), 5–38.

Kaplan, J. (1994). *StartUp: A Silicon Valley adventure*. New York: Warner Books.

Keefe, P. (1991). Pen-based PCs poised for breakthrough. *Computerworld*, 3, 111–117.

Kling, R., & Iacono, S. (1988). The mobilization of support for computerization. The role of computerization movements. *Social Problems*, 35(3), 226–243.

Kling, R., & Iacono, S. (1995). Computerization movements and the mobilization of support for computerization. In S. L. Star (Ed.), *Ecologies of knowledge: Work and politics in science and technology* (pp. 119–153). Albany, NY: State University of New York Press.

Lambright, W. (1994). The political construction of space satellite technology. *Science Technology & Human Values*, 19(1), 47–69.

Mandell, M. (1991). Hardware, from lap-size to hand-size. *Computerworld*, 8, 61.

Mody, C. (2000). A new way of flying: Difference, rhetoric, and the autogiro in inter-war aviation. *Social Studies of Science*, 30(4), 513–543.

Ornatowski, C. (1998). 2+2=5 if 2 is large enough: Rhetorical spaces of technology development in aerospace engine testing. *Journal of Business & Technical Communication*, 12(3), 316–342.

Perelman, C. (1982). *The realm of rhetoric*. South Bend, IN: University of Notre Dame Press.

Perkins, A. (1994, September). Riding down that wireless highway. *The Red Herring*.

Perkins, A., & Perkins, M. (2001). *The Internet bubble: The inside story on why it burst—and what you can do to profit now*. New York: Harper Business.

Piven, J. (1996). PDA market is a value-added dream come true. *Computer Technology Review*, 16(9), 18–20.

Pozzebon, M. (2001). Demystifying the rhetorical closure of ERP packages. *Proceedings of the 22nd international conference on information systems*, New Orleans, 329–337.

Rebello, K. (1991, December 23). But can it leap tall buildings? *Business Week*.

Rebello, K. (1992, March 30). The pen-PC market is moving half steam ahead. *Business Week*, 82–83.

Remich, N. (1992, October). Home sweet office. *Appliance Manufacturer*, 81.

Semich, J. (1993). Pen computing: First, pick an OS. *Datamation*, 39(19), 36–37.

Shaffer, R. (1991). Etch-a-sketch computing. *Forbes*, 148(5), 142.

Southwick, K. (1994). You take the high road and I'll take the low road. *Upside*, 6(6), 56–63.

Strauss, A. (1987). *Qualitative analysis for social scientists*. Cambridge, U.K.: Cambridge University Press.

Swanson, E., & Ramiller, N. (2004). Innovating mindfully with information technology. *MIS Quarterly*, 28(4), 553–583.

Taylor, H. (1991, February). The PC evolution: desktop...laptop...palmtop...?top. *Sales & Marketing Management*, 50–61.

Terdoslavich, W. (1995, August 21). PDAs: Mini communicators? *Computer Reseller News*: 81–82.

Wickliff, G. (1998). The daguerreotype and the rhetoric of photographic technology. *Journal of Business & Technical Communication*, 12(4), 413–436.

Williams, R. (2004). The cultural contexts of collective action: Constraints, opportunities, and the symbolic life of social movements. In D. Snow, S. Soule, & H. Kreisi, (Eds.), *The Blackwell companion to social movements* (pp. 91–115). Oxford: Blackwell.

Wilson, L. (1994, November 14). While PDAs crawl towards acceptance. *CommunicationsWeek*, 25–26.

Yamada, K. (1995, February 6). Resellers key to promoting PDAs to corporate markets. *Computer Reseller News*, 65–69.

Ziegler, B. (1993, April 5). Building a wireless future. *Business Week*, 56–60.

Chapter 5

Framing the Photographs: Understanding Digital Photography as a Computerization Movement

Eric T. Meyer
Oxford Internet Institute

Abstract

In this chapter, the author examines a single computerization movement: digital photography. During the period 1991–2004, the technology in digital cameras was being refined by manufacturers and the advantages and limitations of digital cameras were discussed widely in the popular and trade-oriented media. The author explores this period of technological change using the concept of computerization movements, particularly drawing on how computerization movements use technological action frames, which reflect composite understandings of a technology's function and use that are built up in the language about a technology. Content analysis data of major media sources shows a storyline developing alongside technology developments: The earliest digital cameras were widely hyped as potentially revolutionary but seriously limited in capability, and during the late 1990s concern was expressed regarding a perceived lack of sufficient technological progress toward acceptable quality technology. Once the technological limitations were overcome, widespread adoption was viewed as inevitable, even while concerns about such issues as digital manipulation remained. This simple story, however, does not reflect the more complex tensions experienced in many domains that rely heavily on photography. To explore this more complex story, the chapter also includes a more detailed look at a specialized domain, police and legal photography, where the adoption of digital photography followed a rockier course than the popular media accounts would suggest.

Introduction

Digital cameras, camera phones, and online photo sharing Web sites are growing ubiquitous in the developed world. In 2003, sales of digital cameras surpassed those of film cameras and, in 2004, consumers purchased 48 percent more digital cameras (15.7 million) than film cameras (10.6 million) (Gleeson, 2004). By 2006, the major camera and film manufacturers including Kodak, Fuji, Nikon, Canon, Minolta, and others had essentially abandoned film as they discontinued the manufacturing of most types of film and film cameras (Fackler, 2006). "Citizen journalists" have started sharing their digital camera and cell-phone photos with news organizations when events such as Hurricane Katrina or the London subway bombings occurred (BBC News, 2005; Outing, 2005); photoblogging is also increasing on the Web (Cohen, 2005; Meyer, Rosenbaum, & Hara, 2005). The story being told about digital photography from these perspectives is a positive one: Digital cameras are increasing in popularity because they are cheap, fast, easy to use and fun, and as a result, enable people to take photographs at any time and quickly share them with others.

On the other hand, some individuals and companies who are heavily invested in traditional photography technology are losing out as a result of the digital photography revolution. The business press frequently reports on the economic displacement related to the replacement of traditional film photography with digital photography. For instance, Polaroid declared bankruptcy in October 2001, when the company was hard hit as commercial users such as real estate agents and insurance adjusters switched to digital cameras; as much as 40 to 50 percent of the company's instant film sales were to these sorts of commercial users (Dillon, 2001). Specialty camera stores have struggled to stay in business when faced with purchasing expensive new equipment to print digital photographs, and both mom-and-pop and professional film processing labs have gone out of business (Braga, 2003). People making photographs are choosing to print fewer of their images (approximately 15 percent of digital images are printed—compare that to the double-prints era of the 1980s–1990s), plus small shops and labs have to compete with the self-service kiosks that are becoming ubiquitous at Wal-Mart, CVS, Walgreens, and other mass market stores. Even the powerhouse Eastman Kodak has laid off 15,000 employees, seen its stock price halved, and has struggled to re-shape itself into a digital photography company while seeing its film products, which provided the company with hefty margins, decline from 70 percent of revenue during the 1990s to what the company predicted would be less than 40 percent in 2006 (Gleeson, 2004).

From 2005 to 2007, Kodak began transforming its business from a traditional film company to a digital camera and services company by shutting down film factories, laying off 27,000 people, and expanding its digital division. Kodak's stock was in the red for most of 2005–2006. On January 31, 2007, Kodak reported a quarterly profit (after eight quarters of loss) due to the increases in revenue from the digital division, which earned $323 million gross profit, a 31 percent increase in revenue from the fourth quarter in 2005 versus a $243 million profit from the traditional film group, a 27 percent increase in revenue in the traditional film group (*Business Week*, September 14, 2007).

This chapter will examine the digital photography phenomenon to understand its broader social significance as a computerization movement (CM), particularly as a representative example of the productivity frame identified in this volume. The data in this chapter indicates how the proponents of the digital photography 'revolution' established a CM using the dominant frame of increasing productivity to encourage widespread adoption of digital cameras, both among the general public and within more specialized domains of photographers, and to what extent a counter-computerization movement (CCM) also formed.

Technological Action Frames and CMs

Rob Kling was a leading proponent of studying the relationship between CMs and social change. In his writing on this topic, he distinguished the perspective that he would later call social informatics (Kling, 1999) from other alternative perspectives such as those of sociologists or computer scientists in a number of ways. In examining how using computer-based systems could transform the social order, Kling focused on patterns of adoption, use, and social shaping of technology instead of the more traditional focus on patterns of design and production of technology (Kling, 1991). By focusing solely on how technology is designed and implemented and on its technological possibilities, Kling cautions that one runs the risk both of technological determinism and of falling prey to the hype of computer/information revolutions. A common thread in many of these technology-centric accounts (e.g., Dyson, 1997; Negroponte, 1995; Rushkoff, 1996; and other similar popular 'guru' writings) is the assumption that the inherent properties of a given computer-based system will result in positive and predictable types of changes in social behavior. Kling argues to the contrary that:

> [N]o one has tried to make a careful case—indicating what kinds of social relations have been transformed, at what level

> of social activity, under what conditions, and what has not changed. ... As we know from studies of other social revolutions, such as the industrial revolution and the transition from feudalism to capitalism, major social transformations differ in their timing and depth in different places and social sectors. (Kling, 1991, pp. 346–47)

Kling argues that "what is 'done by computing' is usually affected by a sociotechnical 'system.'...Usually, there is an interplay of multiple interacting influences" (Kling, 1992, p. 352). To better understand the multiple interacting influences, Kling and Iacono (1988) introduced the concept of CMs to examine:

> [H]ow specialized "computerization movements" (CMs) advance computerization in ways that go beyond the effects of promotion by the industries that produce and sell computer-based technologies and services. Our main thesis is that computerization movements communicate key ideological beliefs about the links between computerization and a preferred social order which help legitimize computerization for many potential adopters. These ideologies also set adopters' expectations about what they should use computing for and how they should organize access to it. (Kling & Iacono, 1988, p. 227)

Iacono and Kling (2001) later developed this idea when discussing how the meanings of technological artifacts are framed at a macro-level in their discussion of technological action frames. Iacono and Kling's technological action frames are similar to the concept of technological frames that has been developed in Social Construction of Technology (SCOT) theory to understand the interactions among the actors of a relevant social group. Technological frames, for SCOT theorists, are built up around technological artifacts as interactions among members of relevant social groups converge and move in a similar direction (Bijker, 1995). Bijker argues that technological frames are somewhat similar to Kuhn's (1962) "paradigms." In determining the elements of a technological frame, an analyst needs to consider how members of a relevant social group attribute meanings to artifacts and how the artifacts themselves are constituted. Among the elements Bijker identifies are goals, key problems, problem-solving strategies, system requirements, theories, tacit knowledge, procedures, methods, practice, perceived function, and exemplary artifacts (Bijker, 2001). The importance of the concept of a technological frame is that it allows analysts to incorporate both social and technological elements, and reconcile aspects of purely social constructivist views and technological determinist views of technology:

> A technological frame describes the actions and interactions of actors, explaining how they socially construct a technology. But since a technological frame is built up around an artifact and thus incorporates the characteristics of that technology, it also explains the influence of the technical on the social. (Bijker, 2001, p. 15526)

Iacono and Kling (2001) argue that what they call technological action frames are composite understandings of a technology's function and use built up in the language about the technology; these "core ideas" provide users with a legitimating logic for high levels of investment. Iacono and Kling also identify two additional elements in understanding CMs: public discourses and organizational practices. Public discourses are the language—written and spoken public communications—being used to communicate these key ideological beliefs about the technology around which a dominant technological action frame is being constructed to the target audiences of technology users. Kling and Iacono (1988) argue that to understand computerization movements, one needs to understand not only the participants and their social organization but also needs to understand their relations with, among other things, the media. Kling (1992) also argues that the optimistic claims made about technology in the popular press and within organizations can be partially understood as an understandable effort to garner scarce resources for technology acquisition. Finally, organizational practices are "the ways in which individuals and organizations put technological action frames and discourses into practice as they implement and use technologies in their micro-social contexts" (Iacono & Kling, 2001, p. 100). This stress on organizations has long been integral to Kling's work.

Traditional Photography as Revolutionary

Traditional film-based photography has long been discussed as a revolutionary force for social change in the world. While not a CM, since no computers were involved, it is certainly a technology with strong information-related aspects; an analogy could be made to CMs by calling photography a 'mechanization movement' that was both widely influential and highly successful. Many historians of photography and photojournalism have argued that photography has been a revolutionary instrument for social change in the world. Regarding even photography's earliest days, Marien writes that "one of the earliest indications of the conversion of photography from an invention to an active agent in the social world was the patenting of both the calotype and daguerreotype processes [in 1839]" (Marien, 2002, p. 25). An essential element of photography's revolutionary nature was that it automated the artistic process in ways that painting or sculpture could never hope to:

> By this process, without any idea of drawing, without any knowledge of chemistry and physics, it will be possible to take in a few minutes the most detailed views, the most picturesque scenery, for the manipulation is simple and does not demand any special knowledge. (Daguerre, 1839/1980, p. 12)

Szarkowski argues that this "mechanical and mindless process" was a "radically new picture-making process ... based not on synthesis but on selection" (Szarkowski, 1966/2003, p. 97). The notion that photography is a potentially revolutionary and radical force for social change recurs again and again among photography's leading critics. Freund writes that "the camera has become an instrument of major significance to our society" (Freund, 1980, p. 4), while Sontag adds that "photography has become almost as widely practiced an amusement as sex and dancing ... it is mainly a social rite, a defense against anxiety, and a tool of power" (Sontag, 1977, p. 8). The social impact of photography can be discussed on multiple levels: from the social changes associated with the easy production of family snapshots used to record personal histories to the social impact felt by influential photographs that have documented the range of human suffering in the world. From Matthew Brady's Civil War photographs, to the Works Progress Administration (WPA) photographers who documented America in the depths of depression, to Vietnam-era images of war and protest, to digital photographs of torture in Iraqi prisons, photographs have influenced public perception of events and molded public reaction to public policy (Berger, 1980/2003; Eco, 1986/2003; Marien, 2002; Sontag, 2003). An in-depth study of this topic would require much more space than is available here, but it is useful to touch upon this to help put digital photography in perspective. Keep in mind the language used about photography; in examining how digital photography has been framed, there will be echoes of this 'mechanization movement' in digital photography's CM. Daguerre's references to speed and simplicity, Szarkowski's reference to the ease of using the technology, and the recurring references to the social impact of photography on society will be echoed in the dominant frame being built around digital photography.

The Digital Revolution: Popular Discourses About Digital Photography

A frequent reference in the popular and professional press discourse on digital photography is that it is part of the "digital revolution." Ritchin, for instance, argues that "moving from chemically processed grain to discrete electronic pixels ... [may make digital photography] as distinct from its predecessor ... as the automobile was from the horse-drawn carriage" (1999, p. xii). Much of the popular discourse about the impact of digital photography tends to focus on the embedded features in the technology itself (for some examples in the popular press, see Hull, 2003; M. Rogers, 2003; and Williams, 2003). This techno-centric perspective emphasizes the extent to which new technologies can alter the processes of photography, such as allowing arbitrary image manipulation or the rapid access to vast digital corpuses. This techno-centric perspective focuses on the features of the technology, on the technical skills required to use the technology, and on the changes that individuals may have to make in order to incorporate the new technology into their routines. This individualistic and technologically centered perspective is an essential part of digital photography's dominant technological action frame. By emphasizing the features that lower the perceived barrier to participation in this CM, digital photography proponents legitimate the relatively costly entry to participation. Who were the proponents of digital photography involved in creating digital photography's technological action frames?

> Many players have been involved in popularizing digital photography. Some were unlikely new entrants, among them printer and PC manufacturers; the makers of software for editing, creating, organizing, and storing images online; broadband communications companies; and the manufacturers of cellular handsets. None of these players dominated the industry, as Kodak had [for film]; each had only limited influence. (Chakravorti, 2004, p. 61)

It is easy to argue that these proponents of digital photography have been remarkably successful: in 2003, sales of digital cameras surpassed those of film cameras, and in 2004, consumers purchased 48 percent more digital cameras (15.7 million) than film cameras (10.6 million) (Gleeson, 2004). Clearly, a great many people have been able to, as Kling and Iacono suggested, legitimate their investment in digital camera equipment.

Digital Photography Discourses and the General Public

To gauge the extent to which the popular press has participated in a discourse on digital photography as a CM, this study first examined the frequency of articles on digital cameras or digital photography in several popular news sources available on Nexis: *New York Times* (owned by The New York Times company), *USA Today* (owned by Gannet Co.), and *Newsweek* magazine (owned by the Washington Post company). These choices represent a prestigious national paper that enjoys an agenda-setting role in society (*New York Times*), a national chain newspaper (*USA Today*), and a weekly newsmagazine (*Newsweek*). These media outlets represent a broad readership among the general public. Of course, other media outlets (such as hobbyist magazines and digital photography Web sites) could also be studied if one were interested mainly in how digital photography has been framed among serious hobbyists and practitioners, but for our purposes media targeting a broader audience will tell us more about how digital photography became so widespread among the general public in such a relatively short period of time.

Figure 5.1 and Table 5.1 show the frequency of articles on digital photography[1] in the media sampled for this research; in these data, three distinct time periods become apparent. The first period is from 1991 to 1995, when 88 total articles appeared in the three sources. During this time, all three sources had little to no writing on digital photography, which is not terribly surprising since the earliest digital cameras for sale in 1991 cost approximately $20,000 and few people were using them even in the professional community. Nevertheless, many of the themes that would become widespread in the public discourse developed during this early period. The second period is from 1996 to 1999, which shows a distinct increase in articles (total $N = 541$), with *Newsweek* lagging the other two publications by one year and not really seeing an increase until 1997. The latest period, from 2000 to 2004, sees a large increase in popular writing on digital photography (total $N = 2{,}120$), again with *Newsweek* lagging the *New York Times* and *USA Today* by one year and not seeing an increase until 2001.

It does not appear that this increase in articles on digital photography diminished the frequency with which regular non-digital photography was mentioned in these sources. A Nexis search[2] for articles about non-digital photography showed an average annual frequency of articles from all three sources of 522 in 1991–1995, 628 in 1996–1999, and 616 in 2000–2004; this is not a statistically significant change in any of the individual sources or time periods ($\chi^2 = 6.6$, $p = .16$). This gives some indication that digital photography is considered to be a different topic than non-digital photography, since these new articles are not replacing articles on photography. Instead, they represent a new set of articles on

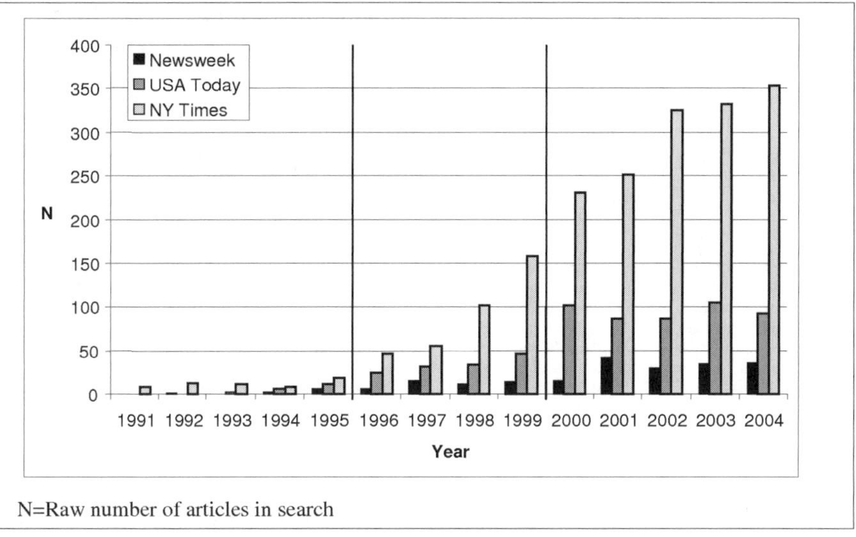

N=Raw number of articles in search

Figure 5.1 Nexis digital photography news articles

a variety of themes (discussed later) that are linked to this new technology of digital photography rather than to discussions of photography as an artistic and documentary process.

Technological action frames, remember, include the core ideas, or what this chapter refers to as themes, about a technology built up in the language about the technology. To determine the themes in the dominant technological action frame for digital photography, the next step involved doing conceptual analysis on this dataset and developing an interactive set of concepts from the literature. Since this research is exploratory in nature, using pre-defined content analysis categories would be problematic. Rather than confirming a hypothesis about the discourse on digital photography, this research seeks to understand the dominant technological action frame built up around digital photography, thus the themes were not known in advance of the research. Each article was coded for its major themes and minor themes (see Table 5.2 for a list of the themes). Any given instance of a minor theme would also be associated with a major theme of a more encompassing nature. If an article discussed the value of digital photography because digital photographs did not cause users to wait for processing (the minor theme of "speed") and also talked about how easy digital cameras are to use ("ease of use"), both of these minor themes represent instances of the major theme, "value of digital photography."

To determine the frequency of reference to themes about digital photography in these media sources, a sample was selected from each of the

Table 5.1 Number of Articles and Sample Size in *New York Times*, *USA Today*, and *Newsweek*

Year	Total n	Sample n	Sample proportion	Total theme instances coded	Themes per article	Total themes	
						Major	Minor
1991–1995	88	60	100% *	117	1.33	7	45
1996–1999	541	107	20%	172	1.61	9	43
2000–2004	2120	107	5%	165	1.54	9	69

*Although the 1991–1995 sample was 100%, it does not equal the total number of articles in the search because 28 articles were not coded after determining that they were only included in the search term for a non-substantive reason, such as a photo credit for an illustration or a weekend event listing with a gallery event included. For the second and third time period, however, when articles of this nature were found, the next article in the sequence replaced it (e.g., for 2000–2004, every 20th article was sampled, and if article 140 was determined to not be an article with any content relating to this study, article 141 would replace it). These re-samples totaled 18 (17%) in the 1996–1999 period and 23 (21%) in the 2000–2004 period; this level of re-sampling required can be explained by the increasing frequency of digital photo credits and digital photography-related arts events in the media sampled.

time periods. For the first period, from 1991–1995, all the articles retrieved in the search were coded for themes (see Table 5.1 note). The entire relevant sample was selected for the first group for two reasons: the total *n* was small (60 cases) and less than Rea and Parker's (1992) rule of thumb to sample a minimum of 100 individuals in any major subgroup of a larger sample, and the themes from this complete survey could then be used as a starting point for the larger samples in the later periods. The themes in the media discourse for the remaining two time periods in the query were determined using a representative random sample of 20 percent and 5 percent, respectively, of the articles in each time period. The results are reported in Table 5.2, and selected themes are summarized in Figure 5.2.

In the 1991–1995 sample, the media examined had several major foci: the value of digital photography for both professionals and consumers in terms of high speed, low cost of consumables, ease of use, ease of manipulation, and convenience. The most commonly recurring theme other than reports of straightforward technical features of new cameras was the high speed of digital photography. Language such as "instantaneously," "at the touch of a button," "minutes after they were taken," and references to "moments," "minutes," and "instantly" all were common in articles using this theme. Another theme that became more prevalent later in this time period was the low-cost of digital photography, although by today's standards the "bargains" were anything but: "The pictures aren't 35-mm caliber, but what's important is that they are very good for a $749 electronic camera." A counter-theme that also appeared stressed the extremely high cost of professional equipment, with six articles quoting prices in the $10,000–$40,000 range for professionals. Interestingly, these high prices were often presented not as a reason to

Table 5.2 Major and Minor Themes* in Digital Photography (DP) Articles in *New York Times*, *USA Today*, and *Newsweek*, 1991–2004

1991–1995 (N=60)		1996–1999 (N=107)		2000–2004 (N=107)	
n=117	**Major themes** (i=7) Minor themes (j=45)	n=172	**Major themes** (i=9) *(new themes)* Minor themes (j=43) *(in italics)*	n=165	**Major themes** (i=9) *(new themes)* Minor themes (j=69) *(in italics)*
43	**Value of DP**	**62**	**Value of DP**	**52**	**Technological features**
12	High speed	11	High speed	49	New products and features
9	Low cost	11	*CCM: Poor quality of photos*	**44**	**Value of DP**
5	Ease of use	9	*CCM: High cost of consumer equipment*	9	Low cost
4	Ease of manipulation	7	Ease of use	5	High speed
4	Convenience	6	Trendiness	3	Trendiness
2	CCM: Problems due to manipulation	5	Low cost	3	Ease of use
2	CCM: Complexity/hard to use	4	Fun	3	CCM: Poor quality of photos
2	Limitations	2	CCM: Complexity / hard to use	2	CCM: High cost of consumer equipment
26	**Technological features**	2	CCM: Problems due to manipulation	2	CCM: Complexity / hard to use
20	New products and features	**32**	**Non-traditional applications**	2	Fun
2	Technological limitations	22	Web applications	**15**	**Social changes**
2	Revolutionary technology	10	Other new applications	3	Social connectedness
15	**Social changes**	**29**	**Technological features**	2	Surveillance
5	Revolutionary	28	New products and features	2	Ubiquity of technology
2	Transformation	**24**	**Business/Economic Issues**	2	New social applications
2	CCM: Negative transformations	9	Business growth	**13**	**Business/Economic Issues**
11	**Professional photographers**	9	Consumption patterns	5	Business growth
9	High cost of pro equipment	5	CCM: Business troubles	3	Consumption patterns
9	**Business/Economic issues**	**11**	**Professional photographers**	2	CCM: Business troubles
4	Business growth	4	Art	**11**	**Non-traditional applications**
2	CCM: Business troubles	**10**	**Social changes**	4	Other new applications
4	**Non-traditional applications**	2	Social connectedness	3	Web applications
4	Web applications	3	Ubiquity of technology	**8**	**Professional Photographers**
3	**Politics and government**	**3**	**Photojournalists**	3	Art
2	Enabling political communication	**2**	**Politics and government**	2	Documentary
26	Other themes (single instance each)	**2**	**How-to articles**	**6**	**How-to articles**
		25	Other themes (single instance each)	5	Choosing features and models
				4	**Photojournalists**
				2	Photojournalism ethics
				4	***Work***
				4	New applications
				46	Other themes (single instance each)

CCM = counter computerization movement theme, i.e., one calling into question the move toward computerization of photography
N = total sample size; n = number of instances in articles containing theme.
i,j = total number of different major and minor themes, respectively, identified in period, including single occurrence themes.
* Only major and minor themes with more than a single occurrence are reported. The number of themes represented in the articles adds up to more than the total number of articles since a single article could contain more than one major theme and minor theme. Repetitions of the same minor theme within an article, however, were only coded once.

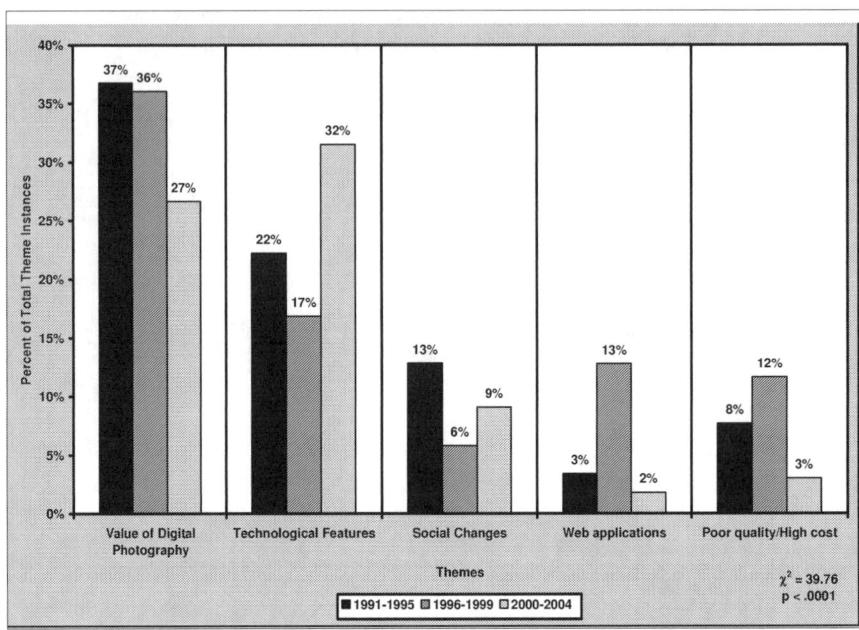

Figure 5.2 Frequency of selected themes in digital photography articles from Table 5.2

believe that digital photography was inaccessible, but appeared to be trying to make consumers feel that the costs in the $1,000 range that they faced were reasonable by comparison. These themes are contributing to a dominant technological action frame that is linking digital photography to a better social order, one where photographers have all the listed advantages, and at a bargain compared to what the professionals are required to spend.

In this early period of media coverage of digital photography, the possibility of the new technology playing a role in social changes, and particularly a revolutionary role, were common. Calling digital photography a "revolution that is now a real threat to conventional photography" or stating that "art is being irrevocably transformed" directly claim a revolutionary role for digital photography, at least in the lives of its practitioners. At this point, there did not appear to be claims, however, that there would be broader social implications beyond the photography world.

There are also early indications of a counter-computerization movement (CCM) developing. This will be discussed in more depth later, but it should be noted that there were 12 instances of claims for negative impacts either already occurring or foreseen by the writer as a possibility. These concerns are among those raised by articles coded in the dataset: "New processes threaten to transform the medium's function in society," "can be changed at will to alter the image," and "gives rise to ethical questions." A common theme of these CCM-type claims in this early period is that most were warnings of potential for trouble, not reports of evidence of trouble other than reports of financial difficulties at some film manufacturing corporations.

During the 1996–1999 period, the articles in the media sampled took a decidedly different track. This was the period of the Internet boom, and the national obsession with all things Web-related is also reflected in the discussions of digital photography. The most notable increase is in articles discussing Web-related applications of digital photography, which jump from 3 percent of instances of themes in articles for 1991–1995 to 13 percent of instances of themes in articles for 1996–1999. Articles included discussions of Web cams, aides on campaigns carrying digital cameras to immediately post pictures of every stop to the Web, a taxi driver posting photos of passengers to a Web site for sale, and digital photos being posted to the Web by adventurers, including someone sailing around the world and an article on mountain climbers and desert runners carrying digital cameras to post images to the Web. It is not surprising that this theme was used by those pushing digital cameras. Wellman (2004) has pointed out that particularly in the early years of the Internet (ca. 1995), many pundits and analysts alike saw it as a "technological marvel, thought to be bringing a new Enlightenment to transform the world" (p. 124).

Other trends to note in Table 5.2 and Figure 5.2 include the drop in the discussion of technological features of digital photography (to 17 percent of instances), including announcements and reviews of new products, features, and accessories. This is coupled with a relatively strong representation (12 percent) of CCM themes criticizing digital photography for being expensive and having low quality, particularly in terms of the available resolution of the printed or viewed output. Some sample language includes: "Think of images from digital cameras as peanut butter sandwiches without enough peanut butter," "inexpensive digital cameras still have a long way to go before they can rival the picture quality of film," and "I may not want a digital camera after all—or at least not yet." In 1997, the *New York Times* in an annual review in the sample gave digital cameras the "Overreaching and Underachievement Award," clearly a counter-computerization theme questioning investments in digital photography. Mentions of new applications tended toward the frivolous: department store Santas, children's toys, and part of the arsenal installed in the "road warrior's" automobile.

There is a statistically significant decline in the discourse on the social impacts of digital photography, dropping from 13 percent of theme instances in 1991–1995 to only 6 percent in 1996–1999. This drop in the discourse may have been caused by the fact that some of the early promise had faded slightly as users were faced with the technological limitations of the equipment that still made images that were inferior in all ways (most notably resolution, speed, and price). In 1996, for instance, Canon announced their Powershot 600, which featured a 0.5 megapixel sensor, a maximum resolution of 832 x 608, and an included capacity of only 18 images, all at a cost of $950. Even by 2000, the 2 megapixel Sony Mavica MVC-CD1000, which burned images onto CD-R media, was a hefty $2,999. With this lackluster performance and elite price tag, the revolutionary promise of the early years seemed to be fading.

The third period, from 2000–2004, saw technological changes that influenced the dominant frame of digital photography as evidenced by the themes, or core ideas being communicated in the media. Most influentially, digital photograph quality improved dramatically at the same time as prices steadily fell. By the end of 2004, four and five megapixel cameras could be bought for $200–300, and even entry-level SLR cameras such as the 6.3 megapixel Canon Digital Rebel were being sold for well under $1,000. In Figure 5.2, the articles touting the value of digital photography in terms of quality, speed, cost, and so on decline steadily throughout the three periods, from 37 percent of instances of themes in articles in 1991–1995 to 27 percent in 2000–2004. Likewise, the articles with a CCM theme about the poor quality and high cost of digital cameras dropped from 12 percent to only 3 percent of theme instances in the 2000–2004 period. This suggests that once the available cameras actually began to meet the promises made about them for the previous decade, namely that they would be able to produce high-quality photographs quickly and cheaply, it was less important to talk about either their potential advantages (now largely realized) or about their actual shortcomings. It became, perhaps, in some people's minds a given that digital cameras could produce acceptable quality output at a reasonable cost, particularly when the reduced cost of consumables was factored into the equation. Instead of discussions of qualities like speed and cost, articles during this time frame discussed things like the freedom digital photography offers ("digital cameras free everyone up … you get a loose quality") and how digital cameras can be used as trendy fashion accessories ("with men there's always this desire to have cool things" and "the hottest way to accessorize"). At the same time, there was a marked increase in the proportion of articles discussing new products and features available to consumers, with this theme surpassing the "value of digital photography" theme for the first time as the most common theme in the sampled articles. These relatively straightforward articles are less concerned with selling the idea of digital photography and more concerned with selling specific cameras. The sales pitch about the inherent value of digital photography had ended successfully for digital photography advocates, and companies were able to get down to the business of selling large numbers of cameras. U.S. sales for digital cameras were 6.5 million units in 2001 and had increased to 15.7 million units by 2004 (Gleeson, 2004; Maidment, 2002).

With the bust following the Internet boom, discussion of Web-related uses of digital cameras dropped sharply. Instances of Internet themes in articles dropped from a high of 13 percent in 1996–1999 to only 2 percent in 2000–2004, and the other new applications of digital photography tended toward the serious rather than the frivolous examples discussed earlier: capturing scientific data, automating astronomical observance, and the restoration of damaged art works. The underlying theme of these examples is that digital photography is not just fun and exciting new technology, but also useful to society by contributing to scientific advances. Work-related uses of digital cameras also made an appearance in print, with descriptions of how they are being used by architects and construction managers on building projects, and how troops in war are using them for communication and identification.

One interesting trend noted in the most recent period is the increasing treatment of digital cameras as simply mundane—often mentioned in passing but without particular note. This shift from framing digital photography as a revolutionary force in society to a mundane and ubiquitous element of society indicates that those within the CM may be signaling their own victory. Why call for revolution if you have already won? However, the fact that it is mentioned that a "digital camera was used to take this picture" implies that the "digital" modifier is noteworthy at some level and either deserves to be mentioned, or perhaps demands to be mentioned in case some might consider the resulting photo suspect (possibly due to fears it may have been digitally altered).

Social aspects make a reappearance in the 2000–2004 sample, increasing to 9 percent of theme instances, although this still is below the 13 percent seen in the first time period. The social changes here tend less toward sweeping statements of how revolutionary digital photography can be and more toward examples of specific domains where social relationships have been altered once digital cameras are introduced. In articles coded in the dataset, discussions of providing students on field trips with digital cameras both to document their experience and to allow their families to see where they have gone ("It's almost like you're taking the trip with them") and articles examining cameras used for police surveillance and industrial espionage are part of the range of topics. Community building also makes an appearance in an article about using digital cameras to build ties among street vendors: "They just love to see pictures of themselves. ... They like being a part of something. Vendors are often alone on foot. There never was much of a community of vendors."

Uneasiness with the Revolution: Digital Photography CCMs

As with any CM, not all discourse about the digital revolution in photography focuses on the utopian aspects. Kling and Iacono (1988) identify what they call counter-computerization movements (CCMs): social movements that focus on key problematic or dystopian aspects of a CM. Kling and Iacono argue that calling for widespread rejection of a popular technology (or at least one that has been successfully framed) would have a low likelihood of success, so the technology's critics instead criticize the aspects the CCM finds most troubling. The following is an example:

> Their unconventional channels of distribution conspire to make [digital images] very difficult to pin down. ... There is an erosion of traditional boundaries between artist or photographer, editor, archivist, publisher, republisher, or viewer. And digital images do not necessarily come embedded in manufactured material substrates. (Mitchell, 2001, p. 53)

Concerns about the easy manipulation of digital images are infrequent (n=2) in the 1991–1995 sample, yet worth noting for the specificity of their concerns. "Any of the numbers can be changed at will to alter the image" comments one, and another remarks that one can "rearrange elements in pictures and create hybrids in which photographs are combined with other kinds of images—all with remarkable ease." These articles go on to frame these as concerns, not advantages: "Technology has taught the camera to lie elaborately" and the "flexibility of the editing process gives rise to ethical questions." In the 1996–1999 sample, as mentioned, concerns about image quality and hardware cost dominated the CCM themes, with 12 percent of the instances of themes in the articles falling into these categories. By the time of the 2000–2004 sample, issues such as the complexity of using digital cameras (n=2) were notable: "The process is so confusing," "I can't do the whole digital camera computer thing yet," and "It seems everyone knows more about digital cameras than I do." Throughout all three periods, there is a steady stream of articles discussing business displacements (combined n=9), particularly with regard to Kodak's ongoing struggles to re-make itself as a digital camera company rather than a film company (see the discussion later of how a variety of companies were affected by digital photography's CM). The CCM-themed articles, while comparatively infrequent, were generally very clear and specific about the concerns about digital photography. This can be compared to many of the pro-adoption articles that often relied on less quantifiable themes geared toward a potential digital photographer's emotions, arguing digital cameras are fun, fast, easy, trendy, and convenient.

Examination of recent literature about digital photography (outside of the media sample) exhibited further evidence of a digital photography CCM. One key CCM theme appearing in popular news reports about digital photojournalism, for instance, is that the ease of deleting images that seem undesirable at the time from a digital camera may result in a loss of images that later would prove to be of interest. Bishop (2004), for instance, argues for the risks of losing images that seemed unimportant at the time they were made:

> The widely reprinted shot of President Bill Clinton embracing Monica Lewinsky at a campaign fund-raiser in 1996 was retrieved by *Time* magazine photographer Dirck Halstead after the scandal surfaced a year later. Halstead had used film and combed through his negatives, according to the Center for American History at the University of Texas in Austin. Colleagues who had used digital cameras had deleted the seemingly innocuous image. (Bishop, 2004, p. 1D)

Even though hobbyists and snapshot photographers may see increases in the number of photographs they take and store, other professional sources agree that photographers edit themselves in ways not possible with strips of film that must be sent to labs. A recent news article (Puente, 2005) estimates that 23 percent of all captured digital camera images are deleted (still leaving an estimated 28 billion images captured). War photographer Peter Howe says, "The problem with digital cameras is, I think, they will radically reduce the amount of images available. If these field commanders are allowed to censor images before they're transmitted, and they don't like a particular image, they can just say, 'Delete it'" (Baker, 2003, p. 7).

Digital manipulation by members of the press is a prominent CCM theme in the media. With the advent of software such as Photoshop that allows relatively easy manipulation of digital images, many photojournalists interpret easily manipulated photographs as a potential threat to their credibility with the reading public. The National Press Photographers Association, for instance, includes the following in their code of ethics: "As journalists, we believe that credibility is our greatest asset. In documentary photojournalism, it is wrong to alter the content of a photograph in any way (electronically or in the darkroom) that deceives the public" (National Press Photographers Association, 1991). However, there are photojournalists who view digital manipulation as a readily available way to correct a photograph that otherwise may not be published. One does not need to ascribe nefarious goals to this social group of "photographic manipulators;" in many cases, they may be making simple changes that, in their opinion, better reflect their vision of reality than the image captured by their camera. *Los Angeles Times* reporter Brian Walski, for instance, was fired after admitting that his front page image of an American soldier in Iraq in front of a group of refugees was actually a montage of two images taken right after each other, but facing in opposite directions. In an interview after his firing, Walski said:

> When I saw it, I probably just said, no one is going to know. I don't know. I've tweaked pictures before—taken out a phone pole. It's not a common practice, but you can do it. I can't speak for anyone else, but I imagine they've done it here and there. This was going overboard—taking pictures and putting them together. I think it's just that I wanted a better image. Then when I did it, I didn't even think about it. (Kyes, 2003)

Digital photographic manipulation in photojournalism has probably not reached closure at this point. The Walski example and others (Meyer & Kling, 2003) demonstrate that while the official organizations have a clear and definitive position on digital manipulation, individual photographers in the "digital manipulators" group continue to manipulate their photographs, even at the potential of risk to their careers.

Digital photography may also have negative consequences for existing film-based photography groups. A recent *New York Times* article (Collins, 2004) argued that digital photography is having a negative social impact by eliminating darkrooms and their oftentimes club-like nature. In large cities like New York, communal darkrooms have long been where many professional and hobbyist photographers both worked and socialized with others in their profession.[3] The social interconnection meant as much as the service" (p. 4) at the recently closed Latent Image Workshop.

It appears that certain CCM themes are both active in the literature and will likely remain so for some time. However, there is little evidence that these CCM themes will have much effect on the continuing displacement of traditional film cameras by digital cameras among the general public. Indeed, few of the examples cited here have much impact on the general population, instead primarily affecting those in special situations (e.g., journalists, hobbyists, and people working in film manufacturing).

Digital Photography in the Legal System

While the general public discourses on digital photography help us to understand the technological action frames involved in establishing digital photography as a CM, to understand how this particular CM has influenced organizational practices and how organizational practices in specific domains have influenced this CM's technological action frames and discourse, it is instructive to examine a more specialized organizational domain. Within the digital photography movement, a number of specialized domains can be identified. The more clearly organizationally oriented domains are in the professional realm, involving either professional photographers or other sorts of professionals using photographic equipment in their jobs. Photojournalism, medicine, astronomy, scientific photography, police and the courts, advertising, and public relations all have segments deeply invested in using photography. While these specialized domains are influenced by the more general public discourse discussed earlier, they also have discourses unique to their own concerns. Since the discourse in these specialized domains takes place in likewise specialized outlets, it is less possible to define a clear randomized sample as was done here. Instead, we can examine one of these domains to show how the relatively simple story told in the public discourse outlined here becomes much more complex when the activities of people using digital photography in complex organizations are considered. The domain of the legal system merits further research; the following discussion will draw on academic and popular sources to discuss themes in the technological action frames in this domain.

Digital photography as a CM has had impacts on many areas in the legal process. From cell phone cameras used to record crimes in progress, to issues surrounding how evidence technicians collect crime scene evidence, to the process used in prosecutions to maintain information flow and a chain of custody for evidence, to rules and procedures in the courtroom, digital photography has altered social relationships, behaviors, and organizational practices. A great deal of literature dealing with these issues has established elements of the dominant technological action frame around digital photography and the law. Relatively little of this literature is written for the general public; most is aimed at practitioners such as police officers, forensic photographers, lawyers, and judges. This section will examine the themes developing in this literature and the practical implications of these themes within the legal system. In particular, by looking at how digital photography adoption is causing tensions within the legal community, we will see that there is a gap between utopian visions of digital photography and the ways digital photography is being put into regular use.

The Police: Crime Scene Issues and Admissibility of Evidence

Police forces are key players in the legal system. Police have been adopting digital cameras for forensic photography of crime scenes, and police have had to develop procedures for dealing with digital photographs generated in the course of their work, as well as those received from others as evidence of potential crimes. Forensic photography is somewhat unique among types of photography because its practices are so thoroughly documented. Unlike many photography professions where individualistic practices are accepted or even encouraged in the name of artistic freedom, practices in forensic crime scene photography must be able to be clearly documented in order for judges to accept photographs into evidence in a trial. The International Association for Identification (1997) has passed a resolution endorsing the use of digital cameras for evidence collection: "electronic/digital imaging is a scientifically valid and proven technology for recording, enhancing, and printing images ... [and] it is accepted ... by the evidence community." Organizations such as the Institute for Forensic Imaging in Indianapolis offer extensive training to crime scene technicians on proper procedures for using digital techniques and maintaining the admissibility of evidence.

The reason for the care given to collection techniques is to help ensure the admissibility of the evidence collected. In general, digital evidence has been allowed by the courts. Hayden (*State of Washington v. Eric H. Hayden*, 1998) affirmed the admissibility of digitally enhanced evidence in the courts and Swinton (*Connecticut v. Swinton*, 2004) established the method for laying the proper foundation for submitting digital evidence. The standard for both film photographs and digital photographs is whether they are a "fair and reasonably accurate representation" of what the photographers observed with their eyes (Parke, 2003). Regarding admissibility, "a photo will be deemed relevant if it tends to prove or disprove a material element of the charge" (Levy-Sachs & Sullivan, 2004).

Although the frame element for evidence collection and admissibility is presented in much of the literature aimed at practitioners as relatively straightforward and requiring little more than usual care for meticulous procedures that is advocated in all evidence collection (Parke, 2003), "some people who train law enforcement agencies in photography estimate that only 25 to 30 percent of U.S. police departments have gone digital" due to concerns about skeptical juries and aggressive defense attorneys winning acquittals by successfully calling digital evidence into question (CNN.com, 2004, February 10). Thus, while the overall dominant frame within the profession of forensic photographers is strongly in favor of computerizing their work, counter computerization themes regarding uneasiness with manipulation of images have been successfully inserted into the dominant frame in the mind of the general public to the extent that these themes alter behavior and slow the adoption of digital techniques within this specialized domain.

The Prosecution: Information Flow and Chains of Custody

The *New York Times* reported in 2002 that the adoption of digital photography is allowing New York police to more aggressively prosecute abuse cases, even when the victim refuses to testify against her abuser (Kershaw, 2002). In the past, blurry snapshots took weeks to be transferred to the courts, and cases had often been dismissed and perpetrators released due to the refusal to press charges. As discussed earlier and as indicated in Table 5.2 (with "poor quality" dropping from n=11 in 1996–1999 to n=3 in 2000–2004), digital camera manufacturers had essentially eliminated digital photography's perceived quality problems in the early 21st century, and digital cameras offered higher quality than 35 mm film or Polaroid cameras that had been used by the police. Now, clear and detailed digital photographs of bruises, scars, etc. are sent immediately to judges and prosecutors who can use the evidence to prosecute abuse cases, with or without the victim's consent, resulting in an increase in convictions. In Queens, New York, prosecutions increased from 51.7 percent of cases to 60.9 percent of cases in the first six months that digital photographs were used. This theme is similar to the victim empowerment theme mentioned earlier, but in this case the victims are being avenged even if they have, for whatever reason, chosen not to cooperate with the prosecution themselves. This is an important social change that also potentially increases an already common tension in the legal system: the reluctance of victims to participate in the prosecution of their abusers. Prosecutors present it as a tool to protect fragile victims against their abusers. According to a New York district attorney, "The use of digital photography has had a critical impact. ... This makes it impossible for the defendant to deny the seriousness of the crime" (Kershaw, 2002). Several studies, however, point out that ignoring victims' wishes can also be problematic for victims' rights as well as potentially for their safety (Ford & Breall, 2000). Other research argues that the perception that victims withdraw from legal proceedings due to their fragility or to a commitment to their abusers has little empirical support in research; instead, victims have found the legal system unreliable, over burdensome, and unresponsive to their needs (Worden, 2000). If this is the case, then thinking that a simple technological solution such as digital cameras will make victims see the legal system more positively is to invest far too much faith in the power of technology.

A key issue for criminal evidence, digital or otherwise, is maintaining the chain of custody for evidence. Berg (2000) points out "If a defendant alleges an image has been altered, or could have been altered, the burden of proof falls upon the state to prove otherwise. ... In many cases, the success of the argument will hinge upon the procedures used to safeguard the security of the images" (p. 5). The chain of custody begins with the first responders to a crime scene and continues through the investigation process, prosecutorial preparation, introduction into trial, and deliberation. During the investigation process, investigators are responsible for preparation, preservation, collection, examination, analysis, and presentation of evidence (Carrier & Spafford, 2003). It is here that another tension arises:

> Law enforcement digital evidence examiners … try to adhere to a general practice of functioning as evidence specialists to avoid the certain pitfalls associated with declaring themselves to be "technology experts." We do not yet have a generation of forensic investigators, examiners, and members of the legal profession who are equally adept at conducting sound, objective thorough investigations and positioning findings in the form of sound litigation in matters involving digital evidence. (Talleur, 2002)

Thus, technology that has been framed in terms of its advantages in practice raises tensions as practitioners try to balance proven investigative techniques with the changes demanded by the application of new technologies. Since there is a suspicion of digital evidence based on a perception of easy manipulation, the chain of custody for digital images or any other digital evidence needs to be strengthened beyond what was expected of traditional evidence in anticipation of needing to overcome potential objections. Traditional photographs only require a witness with personal knowledge of the subject depicted for admission into evidence; the actual photographer need not lay a foundation, nor is there any requirement for expert testimony showing the film's chain of custody (McEntee, 2001). However, with the advent of digital photography, debates have arisen in the legal community over whether digital photographs should be treated differently from film (Berg, 2000; McCarvel, 1995; Shaw, 2002), and there have been suggestions to amend the Federal Rules of Evidence to more clearly account for digital photographs (Bianchini & Bass, 1998).

This chapter has only briefly touched on the issues in specialized professional photographic domains. The issues raised here merit further research. A logical next step is to do more in-depth research in these and other domains using digital photography extensively to discover the extent to which these tensions have influenced social behavior, how the domains have been restructured to lessen these tensions, and how the technology has been socially shaped to meet the needs of these professionals.

Conclusion

This chapter's main purpose was to examine digital photography using a CM framework, particularly with regard to technological action frames as a component of CMs. Technological action frames are the composite understandings of a technology's function and use built up in the language about a technology. The core ideas, or themes, used in the public discourse about the technology are an essential element of the dominant technological action frame, as are the practices of organizations involved in the CM. This chapter used conceptual analysis to generate a set of themes used in the popular media when writing about digital photography during the 1991–2004 time period. While this method has limitations, particularly in terms of mapping elements of the discourse in the media to measurable behavior, it does provide a useful and accessible starting point for beginning to understand how digital photography's technological action frames have been constructed as a CM, and how CCM themes have been expressed. The chapter also examined how digital photography has been framed in the specialized professional domain of police/legal photography. The research found a number of tensions when digital photography has been introduced to this professional setting that were either minimally represented or non-existent in the themes of the general technological action frames. Further research would benefit from more in-depth analysis of how these general themes are reflected in the social systems where digital photography has been considered or adopted.

Digital photography as a CM can be understood at multiple levels of abstraction. First, by looking at the themes or core ideas used to build the technological action frames supporting the CM in the general media discourse, a relatively simple and straightforward story was revealed. The main storyline as laid out in Table 5.2 and Figure 5.2 is that when digital cameras were introduced, they suffered from technological limitations and high cost but offered great potential advantages in terms of both the technology and in terms of potential social application. As digital cameras developed, there was some frustration about their slow progress toward fulfilling their potential, but finally they reached a point where their quality and cost made them an inevitable success. At this point, the industry could focus on adding small features designed to appeal to the widest variety of potential users. Even though minor concerns have been raised about manipulation and economic displacements, the overall story is one of technological success. This story has the advantage of being clear and elegant in its simplicity.

A more detailed examination, however, reveals a much more complex storyline. By looking at how digital photography is being used in specialized settings, a wide variety of social tensions and struggles related to the adoption of digital photography become apparent. The story here is one of workers, particularly those with considerable investments in successful existing systems, faced with new rules, standards, expectations, and relationships. These ongoing tensions arise throughout the system and are still being resolved in a variety of ways.

The digital photography CM has been a very successful one. Professionals and amateurs alike have switched from film to digital photography, and most new technological advances in photography are in the digital realm. However, the unforeseen consequences of this shift are not yet clear. Will camera purchasers become more like computer purchasers, regularly replacing equipment as new models and features are introduced? What are the long-term archival issues as file formats and media standards change? What new uses for photography will be found? What former uses will disappear? These and many other questions await future research.

Endnotes

1. Search term: digital w/2 camera or photograph or photography.
2. Search term: photography AND NOT digital AND NOT video AND NOT "cultural desk" AND NOT "weekend desk."
3. This may seem counter-intuitive to non-photographers who may picture darkrooms as dark, solitary places. Anyone who has spent time in larger communal darkrooms can attest to the high degree of social interaction, both in the lab and in the outer areas where photographers gather to wait for film and prints to dry, run through color processing machines, or just take a break. During my years as a photography student in college in the 1980s, countless hours were spent both in social interaction and in collaborative learning in the college's communal darkrooms. When I think back to that time and compare it to how I use Photoshop (alone at my computer), the differences are striking.

References

Baker, J. (2003, March 21). War photographer warns of censorship, challenges. *The Oregonian*, 7.

BBC News. (2005). Ethics issue for citizen snappers. *BBC News Online*. Retrieved August 28, 2005 from news.bbc.co.uk/2/hi/technology/4746633.stm

Berg, E. C. (2000). Legal ramifications of digital imaging in law enforcement. *Forensic Science Communications*, 2(4).

Berger, J. (1980/2003). Photographs of agony. In L. Wells (Ed.), *The photography reader* (pp. 288–290). New York: Routledge.

Bianchini, V. E., & Bass, H. (1998). A paradigm for the authentication of photographic evidence in the digital age. *Thomas Jefferson Law Review*, 20, 303.

Bijker, W. E. (1995). *Of bicycles, bakelites, and bulbs: Toward a theory of sociotechnical change*. Cambridge, MA: MIT Press.

Bijker, W. E. (2001). Social construction of technology. In N. J. Smelser & P. B. Baltes (Eds.), *International encyclopedia of the social & behavioral sciences* (Vol. 23, pp. 15522–15527). Oxford: Elsevier Science Ltd.

Bishop, T. (2004, July 18). Digital revolution. *The Baltimore Sun*, 1D.

Braga, M. (2003, June 2). Snapping to attention: The impact of the digital age on the photography world has been huge and the effects continue to play out. *Sarasota Herald-Tribune*, 12.

Business Week. (2007). Kodak: Mistakes made on the road to innovation. Retrieved September 14, 2007, from www.businessweek.com/mediacenter/podcasts/thebusinessweek/thebusinessweek_09_14_07.htm

Carrier, B., & Spafford, E. H. (2003). Getting physical with the digital investigation process. *International Journal of Digital Evidence*, 2(2), 1–20.

Chakravorti, B. (2004). The new rules for bringing innovations to market. *Harvard Business Review*, 82(3), 58–67.

CNN.com. (2004). Digital evidence raises doubts. Retrieved February 26, 2005, from www.cnn.com/2004/TECH/ptech/02/10/digital.evidence.ap

Cohen, K. (2005). What does the photoblog want? *Media, Culture and Society*, 27, 883–901.

Collins, G. (2004, June 19). In a digital era, the darkroom is fading as a photographic hub. *New York Times*, B-4.

Connecticut v. Swinton, 268 781 (Conn. 2004).

Daguerre, L. J. M. (1839/1980). Daguerreotype. In A. Trachtenberg (Ed.), *Classic essays on photography* (pp. 11–13). New Haven, CT: Leete's Island Books.

Dillon, N. (2001, October 13). Last shot for Polaroid, victim of the digital revolution. *Daily News*, 51.

Dyson, E. (1997). *Release 2.0: A design for living in the digital age*. New York: Broadway Books.

Eco, U. (1986/2003). A photograph. In L. Wells (Ed.), *The photography reader* (pp. 126–129). New York: Routledge.

Fackler, M. (2006, January 12). Nikon plans to stop making most cameras that use film. *New York Times*.

Ford, D. A., & Breall, S. (2000). Violence against women: Synthesis of research for prosecutors. Retrieved February 26, 2005, from www.ncjrs.org/pdffiles1/nij/grants/199660.pdf

Freund, G. (1980). *Photography & society*. Boston: David R. Godine.

Gleeson, J. (2004, October 18). The picture is clear: Struggling Kodak shifts focus to digital imaging as film industry fades. *The Journal News*, 1D.

Hull, L. (2003, September 27). Digital success 'the end for photographic film.' *Daily Mail*, 43.

Iacono, S., & Kling, R. (2001). Computerization movements: The rise of the Internet and distant forms of work. In J. A. Yates & J. Van Maanen (Eds.), *Information technology and organizational transformation: History, rhetoric and practice* (pp. 93–136). Thousand Oaks, CA: Sage Publications.

International Association for Identification. (1997). Resolution 97-9. Retrieved February 26, 2005, from www.theiai.org/pdf/res97_9.pdf

Kershaw, S. (2002, September 3). Digital photos give the police a new edge in abuse cases. *New York Times*.

Kling, R. (1991). Computerization and social transformations. *Science, Technology, and Human Values*, 16(3), 342–367.

Kling, R. (1992). Audiences, narratives, and human values in social studies of technology. *Science, Technology, and Human Values*, 17(3), 349–365.

Kling, R. (1999). What is Social Informatics and why does it matter? *D-Lib Magazine*, 5(1).

Kling, R., & Iacono, S. (1988). The mobilization of support for computerization: The role of computerization movements. *Social Problems*, 35(3), 226–243.

Kling, R., & Iacono, S. (1995). Computerization movements and the mobilization of support for computerization. In S. L. Starr (Ed.), *Ecologies of knowledge: Work and politics in science and technology* (pp. 119–153). Albany, NY: State University of New York Press.

Kuhn, T. (1962). *The structure of scientific revolutions*. Chicago: University of Chicago Press.

Kyes, Z. (2003). Interview with Brian Walski about the Iraq war and photographic manipulation. Retrieved September 20, 2003, from www.betablog.com/archives/cat_photography.html

Levy-Sachs, R., & Sullivan, M. (2004). Using digital photographs in the courtroom: Considerations for admissibility. Retrieved February 26, 2005, from www.dri.org/dri/pdf/feature_August2004.pdf

Maidment, P. (2002). Forbes.com: Traditional photography needs flash. Retrieved February 22, 2005, from www.forbes.com/technology/2002/09/30/0930photokina.html

Marien, M. W. (2002). *Photography: A cultural history*. New York: Harry N. Abrams, Inc.

McCarvel, R. T. (1995). You won't believe your eyes: Digital photography as legal evidence. Retrieved February 26, 2005, from www.seanet.com/~rod/digiphot.html

McEntee, J. P. (2001, November 01). Evidentiary issues involving digital photographs. *Nassau Lawyer*.

Meyer, E. T., & Kling, R. (2003). *To Photoshop or not to Photoshop: Digital manipulation and the STIN framework*. Paper presented at the Association of Internet Researchers Annual Conference, Toronto, Ontario.

Meyer, E. T., Rosenbaum, H., & Hara, N. (2005). *How photobloggers are framing a new computerization movement*. Paper presented at the Association of Internet Researchers (AoIR) Annual Meeting, Chicago, IL.

Mitchell, W. J. (2001). *The reconfigured eye: Visual truth in the post-photographic era*. Cambridge, MA: MIT Press.

National Press Photographers Association. (1991). Digital Manipulation Code of Ethics: NPPA Statement of Principle. Retrieved September 29, 2004, from www.nppa.org/professional_development/business_practices/digitalethics.html

Negroponte, N. (1995). *Being digital*. New York: Alfred A. Knopf.

Outing, S. (2005). The 11 layers of citizen journalism. Poynter Online. Retrieved May 25, 2006, from www.poynter.org/content/content_view.asp?id=83126

Parke, R. L. (2003). Basic evidence photography (and my case for "going digital"). Retrieved September 15, 2003, from www.nalionline.org/docs/Parke_Evidence_Photography.pdf

Puente, M. (2005). USAToday.com: Memories gone in a snap. Retrieved January 22, 2005, from www.usatoday.com/life/lifestyle/2005-01-20-digital-memories_x.htm

Rea, L., & Parker, R. (1992). *Designing and conducting survey research: A comprehensive guide*. San Francisco: Jossey-Bass.

Ritchin, F. (1999). *In our own image: The coming revolution in photography*. New York: Aperture Foundation.

Rogers, M. (2003, July 22). Practical futurist: What's next for digital photography. *Newsweek*.

Rushkoff, D. (1996). *Playing the future*. New York: HarperCollins Publishers.

Shaw, C. (2002). Admissibility of digital photographic evidence: Should it be any different than traditional photography? *Newsletter of the American Prosecutors Research Institute*, 15(10).

Sontag, S. (1977). *On photography*. New York: Picador.

Sontag, S. (2003). *Regarding the pain of others*. New York: Picador.

State of Washington v. Eric H. Hayden, 90 100 (Wash. App. I 1998).

Szarkowski, J. (1966/2003). Introduction to "The photographer's eye". In L. Wells (Ed.), *The photography reader* (pp. 96–103). New York: Routledge.

Talleur, T. (2002). Digital evidence: The moral challenge. *International Journal of Digital Evidence*, 1(1).

Wellman, B. (2004). The three ages of Internet studies: Ten, five and zero years ago. *New Media & Society*, 6(1), 123–129.

Williams, S. (2003, July 9). Can celluloid survive? The venerable roll of 35-mm film hardly stands a chance against a soaring digital photography market. *Newsday*, B08.

Worden, A. P. (2000). Violence against women: Synthesis of research for judges. Retrieved February 26, 2005, from www.ncjrs.org/pdffiles1/nij/grants/199911.pdf

Part III

Democratization

Chapter 6

From the Computerization Movement to Computerization: Communication Networks in a High-Tech Organization

Anabel Quan-Haase
The University of Western Ontario

Barry Wellman
NetLab, Department of Sociology
University of Toronto

Abstract

We find mixed results when assessing how the expectations of the internetworking computerization movement hold with our case study of a high-tech organization. In the organization, "internetworking technologies" are the main local—as well as global—means of communication. The organization is a *local virtuality*, with e-mail and instant messaging primarily supporting local, within-department connectivity. *Hyperconnectivity* fosters collaboration, community of practice, and commitment to the organization. Despite extensive networking and Internet-fostered democratization, the organization remains hierarchical.

Introduction

The rapidly expanding Internet and its related "internetworking technologies"—as Rob Kling and associates have called it—such as e-mail, instant messaging (IM), and discussion lists, have infiltrated North American life. About 70 percent of the North American population is online to some extent (Miniwatts, 2006), e-commerce is growing, and both the mass and the scholarly media are fascinated with the technological and social wiring of society.

The diffusion of internetworking technologies has been widely evident in organizations. However, the factors motivating organizations to adopt new computing technologies remain unclear. Traditional theories emphasize the economic gains organizations can attain from adopting internetworking technologies because of reduced costs and improved capability.

By contrast, Iacono and Kling (2001) provided an alternative theory—"computerization movements" (CMs)—that emphasizes macro-social and cultural dimensions in the diffusion of internetworking technologies. Central to Iacono and Kling's theory of CMs is the development of *technological action frames* that legitimate in public discourses the adoption and use of internetworking technologies through the establishment of favorable links between internetworking and a new, utopian social order (Iacono and Kling, 2001; see also the overview in Chapter 1, this volume). Moreover, these technological action frames contain "expectations [for adopters and users] about how they should use internetworking in their daily routines and how they should envision a future based on internetworking" (Iacono & Kling, 2001, p. 97).

For Iacono and Kling (2001), social change in an organization is complex due to the implementation of internetworking technologies, and such change can be understood neither in terms of technological imperatives nor by planned changes of organizational management (Markus & Robey, 1988; Orlikowski, 1992; Zack & McKenney, 1995). Instead, their CM theory advocates the integrated analysis of technological features, managerial visions, and "technological action frames"—the latter emerging in discourses about computerization. They argue that "changes in worklife are shaped (but not determined) by the prevalent discourses informing new technologies and the practices that emerge around them in actual workplaces" (Iacono & Kling, 2001, p. 97). For Iacono and Kling, meaning-making processes occur as people adapt to new technologies and embed them in their daily routines and practices.

In this chapter, we use Iacono and Kling's seminal work to examine the routines and practices that emerge around the use of computer mediated communication (CMC) in everyday worklife: internetworking tools that support one-to-one and one-to-many communication, synchronously and asynchronously. Our study investigates the two most prevalent forms of CMC in organizations: e-mail and IM. We use a case study of communication in a medium-size, high-tech firm to investigate how communities of practice in this firm operate online and offline (see also Brown & Duguid, 1991; Wenger, 1998).

Instead of focusing only on changes resulting from technology adoption, we examine gaps between utopian visions and actual work practices. Rather than analytically isolating CMC, we study it in the context of how it is embedded in the ways in which workers actually communicate, including face-to-face (FTF) and telephone communication. We show how CMC has become routinized and integrated in this organization, using ubiquitous multiple communication to maintain *hyperconnected* and *local virtualities* (two coined terms we define later). We analyze how the characteristics of specific CMCs afford somewhat different communication possibilities. For example, the store and forward nature of e-mail supports asynchronous exchanges where sender and receiver do not have to be online simultaneously. By contrast, IM demands simultaneous presence for successful communication.

We focus on four issues central to Iacono and Kling's analytical framework (Iacono & Kling, 2001):

- How do the employees of this high-tech organization use CMC?
- What work practices emerge around CMC?
- Does CMC function separately from the more traditional forms of communication: FTF and telephone?
- Has a networked organization developed, with computerization fostering democratization in organizations?

Technological Action Frames

Iacono and Kling's (2001) analysis of computer ideologies showed how people create meanings around technology that influence adoption and use. To describe this process of adaptation to technology, they introduced the term "technological action frame." The term "frame" had been used earlier in sociology by Erving Goffman, where it describes how groups develop shared understandings that legitimate collective action. Closely linked to the "technological action frame" is the "collective action frame" term used in social movements theory. A collective action frame describes how participants in a social movement collectively create meaning for others, including constituents and observers (Benford & Snow, 2000). Technological action frames focus explicitly on the expectations and hopes associated with technological change. Iacono and Kling (2001) define technological action frames as a group's multi-dimensional shared understandings that support large investments by users in new technology. Technological action frames not only provide explanations about why a technology should be adopted, they also encompass beliefs about how technology works and the outcomes expected from its use.

Technological action frames play an important role in CMs because they make implicit assumptions explicit about the adoption and use of technology. Organizations constantly engage in meaning-making processes as employees integrate technologies into their work practices. Previous CM research has identified several technological action frames associated with specific CMs: productivity, democratization, death of distance, freedom/information rights, and ubiquitous computing (Iacono & Kling, 2001; Elliott & Kraemer, Chapter 1, this volume). Our chapter focuses on the democratization frame in one high-tech organization (see Quan-Haase & Wellman, 2006, for analysis of the death of distance frame in this organization).

Democratization Technological Action Frame

From the standpoint of Iacono and Kling's concept of the "democratization technological action frame" (2001), internetworking technologies can affect the locus of power in organizations, by leading to equalizing effects and vertical forms of communication that might enable workers (rather than management) to be at the center of information exchanges. For example, the cue-reduced nature of text-based digital communication can lead to less salience of such attributes as race, age, and status, which in turn, might foster democratization and equalization in organizations (Short, Williams, & Christie, 1976; Sproull & Kiesler, 1991).

Internetworking technologies could also encourage democratization in organizations by speeding up the exchange of messages, enhancing employees' ability to access many information sources from their desktops, and facilitating communication with a variety of experts (Culnan & Markus, 1987; Rice & Bair, 1984; Sproull & Kiesler, 1991). Such analyses suggest that through internetworking technologies, traditional hierarchical bureaucracies would be short-circuited by employees who have direct access to all, and hierarchical divisions of labor would no longer influence communication patterns. Consequently, decision making would be decentralized, engaging employees at all levels and creating collaborative work settings (Castells, 2000; Leavitt & Whisler, 1958).

Despite early enthusiasm, the results are mixed about the effects of internetworking technologies on organizational structures (Attewell & Rule, 1984; Markus & Robey, 1988; Robey, 1981). On the one hand, studies of organizational communication have shown that CMC can increase the spread, volume, and speed of information flow (Culnan & Markus, 1987; Quan-Haase & Wellman, 2006; Rice & Bair, 1984; Sproull & Kiesler, 1991). On the other hand, some analysts have found that CMC has both centralized and decentralized decision-making (Blau, 1975; Blau, Falbe, McKinley, & Tracy, 1976; Foster & Flynn, 1984), while others have found that CMC has little effect on organizational structure

(Franz, Roby, & Koeblitz, 1986; Robey, 1981; Roehrs, 1998; Zack & McKenney, 1995).

The democratization technological action frame points toward potential positive structural change in organizations resulting from the implementation of internetworking technologies (Iacono & Kling, 1996, 2001). Such technologies can affect the speed of information flow, the quantity of messages exchanged, and the efficiency of work. However, the frame does not take into account the complexity of organizations: Internetworking technologies alone cannot change the structure of an organization because many contextual factors affect the adoption and use of technology (Markus & Robey, 1988; Orlikowski, 1992; Zack & McKenney, 1995). For example, Orlikowski's (1996) study of how an information system is implemented showed that the effect of technology depends to a large extent on the culture of the organization.

Analysts have not come to grips with how people in CMC-intensive organizations actually work and network—online and offline:

> There is no coherent research program ... that seeks to account for the potential or likely effects of major changes in information processing on the bureaucracy. This silence is curious given that during the past two decades, in popular writing and in political practice, many actors have been engaged in "breaking down," "abolishing," and "bashing" bureaucracy. (Fountain, 2001, p. 118)

The utopian visions of the democratization frame should be examined through case studies with rich contextual information about how internetworking technologies are used in actual work processes (Creswell, 1998; Lee, 1999). The combination of multiple sources of information and data collection methods often found in case studies make them a good approach to capture the complexities of the social and institutional contexts in which CMC is used and work practices emerge (Kling, Rosenbaum, & Hert, 1998). Analysts can use such case studies to identify key contextual factors influencing the adoption and use of technologies in organizations, thereby closing the gap between utopian visions of democratization and realistic work practices (e.g., Clement & Halonen, 1998; Zack & McKenney, 1995).

KME: The Organization

Knowledge Media Enterprises (KME)—a pseudonym—is an 80-employee high-tech corporation located in a major North American city. KME was founded in 1997 and expanded during the technology boom. It operates in a highly competitive, rapidly changing environment. To remain innovative, the company relies on collaboration among its technologically savvy employees using e-mail and IM. KME's involvement in knowledge-intensive activity and its high reliance on internetworking technologies make it a good place to study the gap between utopian visions of computerization and the way technology is actually used in everyday practices and routines.

KME offers knowledge-based services and software to clients. Its principal business is hosting and facilitating the online collaborative communities of other organizations. Besides hosting and facilitating business-to-business online communities, KME also supports business-to-consumer online communities, where a community focuses on a specific product or service.

Description of Two KME Departments

We compare work roles and social networks in two main KME departments: *software development* and *client services*. Each is located on a separate floor of the same building. Software developers work in a large open space, a layout adopted to help them to collaborate. By contrast, client services workers are in cubicles, with middle managers having a large common area, and the two upper managers sharing a private office. The different layouts reflect—and reinforce—different communication patterns.

The 12-person software development department creates software packages that customers use in combination with services from the client services department. The primary task of the software development department is to write code. The corporation expects the department to develop and implement new functionalities quickly. Often, there is no predetermined work schedule. In the run-up to a release date, employees work at least 50 to 60 hours per week. They actively assist each other in programming, have frequent impromptu meetings, and socialize often by going out for lunch or coffee. A high level of communication and exchange among developers is necessary because of the interdependence of all components of a project that affects the operability of the software.

The 16-person client services department plans and supports for outside clients online communities of practice and information exchange. Some of their clients are units of large, world-famous organizations. The department creates "virtual localities": online places where participants log in, come to know their electronic neighbors, and share best practices. The tasks of a client service worker (called a "community manager" within KME) include organizing relevant information for the site, keeping the site up-to-date, and monitoring exchanges among community members. While the tasks of client service workers are similar in all online communities, the nature of these communities varies considerably. Some are focused on a product (e.g., car, computer, or food brand), while others revolve around common interests (e.g., soap operas or movies).

The client services department does not operate under the same time, innovation, and collaborative pressures as the software development department. For the client services department, customer satisfaction is the most important measure of success, while performance measures of profit and market share are more important for the software development department. By contrast to software developers, client service workers do not need to coordinate with each other. Instead, they communicate and coordinate with their outside clients and with KME managers. Although most client service workers do similar work, their work does not contribute to a single effort: The success of one account is independent of the success of others. Thus, client service workers differ from software developers by not sharing a common goal and not feeling part of a team.

Research Methods

We collected data in 2002 through a Web survey, interviews, and in-office observations. A detailed self-administered survey gathered information about communication and social networks at each of three organizational distances: within the department, with other colleagues elsewhere in KME, and with people outside KME. Participants reported how frequently they used three types of media at each distance: FTF or telephone, e-mail, and IM.

Out of 28 departmental employees, 27 (96 percent) participated in the survey: 11 in the software development department (including three women) and 16 in the client services department (including five women). Survey participants had worked for KME an average of 28 months (range: 5–48 months). Six had a high school diploma or less, 12 had completed an undergraduate degree, and eight had a graduate degree. Survey participants included three upper managers, five middle managers, and 19 other department members. Middle and upper managers are grouped together in this analysis.

To obtain more information about participants' work practices, we complemented the survey with interviews and observations. Five employees from each department—occupying a range of positions and roles—participated in Quan-Haase's interviews and observations. The two-hour, semi-structured interviews provided flexibility to follow important leads. To guarantee the confidentiality of interviewees, pseudonyms are used throughout our research reports.

People often cannot report accurately on their own behavior, even in interviews. Hence, Quan-Haase also observed everyday work practices in each department to learn about how employees used CMC to exchange information and collaborate. She observed each of the 10 interview participants for one work day, observing all FTF, telephone, and online interactions.

We present here qualitative information, based on the interviews and observations. For more detailed analysis including information from the survey, see Quan-Haase (2004) and Quan-Haase & Wellman (2004, 2006).

KME: A Local Virtuality

The internetworking CM, as discussed by Iacono and Kling, with its "death of distance" technological action frame, predicted that CMC would enhance organizational communication by spanning spatial, temporal, and social distances (Kiesler, Siegel, & McGuire, 1984; Sproull & Kiesler, 1991). From this viewpoint, CMC is a technological driver that creates and maintains global electronic networks that constantly exchange information. While there is no doubt that CMC has changed the nature of communication with its speed, instantaneity, and flexibility, we need to know more how employees use CMC for boundary-spanning communication and how contextual factors affect CMC use in everyday work life (Quan-Haase & Wellman, 2004). Moreover, it remains unclear how employees use CMC in relation to traditional media, such as FTF and the telephone.

Our research shows that computerization at KME has not altered the way that group membership structures communication. Several contextual factors influence the use of CMC in everyday work practice. For example, locality as a physical place to meet and interact is a key dimension for the formation of collaborative community. However, the effects of locality change in the digital era where employees integrate CMC and traditional forms of communication, to create a hyperconnected work environment that simultaneously operates in real and electronic space. At the same time, distance no longer necessarily impedes communication because employees use the Internet to span departmental and organizational boundaries.

Distance and Communication at KME

A large proportion of KME communication is local with other departmental colleagues. This is because the departments heavily structure communication, and they are each physically contiguous on single floors. In both departments, boundary-spanning communication is less frequent than within-department communication. The local focus of communication is more pronounced in the software development department than in the client services department.

Even though both departments show about the same frequency of communication with colleagues elsewhere in the organization, the client services department communicates much more frequently outside of their department than the software development department. A closer examination of the tasks performed by the two departments sheds some light as to why the client services department is outwardly oriented while the software development department is inwardly oriented. The two departments perform different types of tasks, and these tasks have different levels of interdependence. The primary task of the software development department is to write code. Even though all departmental members know how to program, each person is responsible for specific components of the software that require specialized expertise. The interdependent responsibilities for software development among departmental members create strong needs for programmers to consult and coordinate with one another. Charlie, one of the managers, explains:

> The engineers need to talk to their partner about the module that they are working on, and "documentation" needs to know about every single module. "Testing" needs to know about every single module. "Design" needs to know about every single module.

This is not a milieu that supports open source, interorganizational creation of software (Raymond, 2001). Departmental members seek information outside the department only when they do not have the necessary expertise to solve a crucial problem. If necessary, they use online communities of practice to get help from programmers worldwide (see also Brown & Duguid, 1991). However, they usually find answers to their problems within the department or organization. They also respect organizational boundaries because they are producing proprietary code that KME wants to keep confidential for competitive advantage.

The software department has no meaningful contact with KME's customers. They rely on intermediaries—the client services department and the marketing and sales units—to obtain information about users and their requirements.

By contrast, the client services department consists of experts in community management who have an outward orientation. Employees in the client services department work on separate accounts doing tasks that require little information sharing and coordination. Andy, a client services worker, describes:

> We don't meet and we don't talk about stuff. So, it may not occur to the other community managers that anything that occurs with their clients may have any relevance to my client

> and vice versa. I think we need to be more aware of what each other's clients are like.

The independence of tasks in the client services department leads to an individualistic work culture. Still, Andy's statement suggests that client service workers could benefit from sharing best practices, but their vertical division of labor neither necessitates nor fosters collaborative community.

Employees of the client services department do need to be in contact with clients outside of KME. The tasks of a client service worker include organizing relevant information for the site, keeping the site up-to-date, and monitoring exchanges between community members. These exchanges can occur asynchronously (i.e., on bulletin boards) or synchronously (i.e., in real-time chat rooms). If clients post inappropriate material to a site, the client service worker is responsible for removing it. When people behave inappropriately (flaming, swearing, etc.), the offending individuals are banned from the community. Employees engage in frequent discussions with clients about content development, tracking and monitoring, and the evaluation of a Web site. For example, Lori, a client service worker, describes her close relationship with a client: "We communicate so often through e-mail and IM that once the conference call comes around, there is really not much else to talk about."

The physical layout of the two departments contributes to the disparities in communication patterns. Studies of the role of physical configurations for collaboration show that geographical proximity combined with open space increases communication (Allen & Cohen, 1969; Hillier, 1996). The software development department is located in a large open space, with a washroom and a small kitchen next to the meeting room, adopted to help programmers collaborate. Although the department manager has a closed office separate from the common working space, he keeps his office door open most of the time, so that people can walk in.

The client services department has more people and occupies a much larger space that is adjacent to KME's marketing, sales, and head office departments. Community facilitators are in separate cubicles, with supervisors having a large common area, and the two senior departmental managers sharing a private office. Low visibility and the spread of employees over a large space reduce possibilities for sharing information. In addition, because of a fear of interrupting colleagues, the dense workspace discourages impromptu exchanges, as Andy explains:

> Every time I say, "Hey, blah blah blah." They don't need to know about it and it is just an interruption to them. Lori and

> I don't talk as much as we used to during the day because we are too close to other people who are not doing the same stuff and we just get distracted.

The only exception is at meals. To encourage mingling, there is a kitchen, with a large table where employees gather for breakfast or lunch. The company also supplies free breakfasts.

The Reviving of Distance with the Rise of Local Virtuality

Software developers rarely communicate outside of KME, even though they rely heavily on CMC for communication within KME. When expertise is required that is not available within KME, programmers send information requests to other programmers via electronic group discussion lists. CMC thus provides a means to access a community of practice of programmers when information is needed (Brown & Duguid, 1991; Lesser & Prusak, 2000; Wenger, 1998). While this rarely happens, the programmers consider their communities of practice to be important sources of information.

Differences in work practices between the software development and client services department foster distinct communication patterns and uses of internetworking technologies. Much of the work of the client services department consists of interacting with users and customers. CMC is the primary communication mode to keep in contact with customers, supplemented with annual or bi-annual in-person meetings. In-person meetings are rare because many customers are located either elsewhere in the U.S. or on other continents, and CMC has replaced telephone contact.

Local virtuality, the use of CMC for local communication, is endemic in this high-tech organization, where each employee has a computer terminal. Even though people work in physical proximity, they rely on CMC for most of their communication. After all, they are already at their computers and staring at their screens. The time spent writing an e-mail or an IM generally is shorter than the time it takes to have an FTF or telephone conversation. Therefore, CMC allows KME employees to communicate with a large number of people and to communicate with each of them frequently.

The utopian visions of the internetworking CM did not foresee the local virtualities that the routine and habitual use of CMC has created at KME. People are communicating by e-mail and IM with those sitting next to them. E-mail and IM have properties that make local communication flexible and convenient.

The Intermingling of Computerization and Democratization

KME employees are *hyperconnected*, switching between CMC, FTF, and the telephone to communicate in their rapidly changing, technology intensive work. Despite the limitations of text-only CMC, technological savviness, coordination, and task interdependence (in software development) foster high rates of CMC use.

To what extent is horizontal communication occurring at KME? Are employees at the same hierarchical level talking to each other, or are communications hierarchical and centralized in nature? Patterns of connectivity—both online and offline—differ in the two departments.

FTF/Telephone Networks

In the software development department, the FTF/telephone networks show high levels of horizontal connectivity. No software developer is isolated, and the level of connectivity does not vary greatly between software developers. The small workspace encourages frequent informal FTF interactions, in which both work-related and social exchanges occur. Programmers meet frequently FTF in pairs: in the kitchen or at each other's desks. FTF interactions are more frequent than telephone conversations because colleagues are located in the same workspace, minimizing the need to call. FTF exchanges are important for discussing changes in the software and seeking help with complex problems requiring others' expertise. James, a programmer, explains:

> If there is any complexity to it, I use the phone sometimes too. Since some of us sometimes work at home, face-to-face is impossible, but the phone and face-to-face: it is kind of similar in that if it is at all complex, I want it that way just to have it back and forth.

The software development department also meets frequently in formal FTF meetings to discuss developments and problems with the code. Impromptu meetings also take place if a pressing issue arises that requires input from all members of the department.

E-mail Networks

The software developers value e-mail because it gives programmers more time than FTF and IM to think about a message and edit it if necessary. The asynchronous nature of e-mail also conveniently lets people respond at times that are suitable for them. Moreover, the developers feel more comfortable e-mailing someone about less urgent matters because e-mail is less intrusive than IM, FTF, or telephone. As Linda says:

> E-mail, if it is something that I do not need immediate response to. Using e-mail because I can develop a well-thought through thought, and the other person can respond to it at a different time.

The e-mail network in the client services department is sparse, reflecting the independence of tasks. Client service workers can complete their work without requiring coordination with other departmental members. Therefore, even though e-mail is available for quick and convenient information sharing among departmental members, they use it less often than do the programmers because it does not fit with their work tasks.

IM Networks

With IM being always on and departmental members communicating often with each other, we expected the IM network to be denser than the FTF/telephone and e-mail networks. To some extent, this is true in software development, where programmers report an average IM use of 344 days per year within the department—much more than the frequency for FTF/telephone or e-mail contact. The software developers use IM differently than e-mail: They IM more frequently, but with a smaller number of people. They do not feel comfortable sending IMs to colleagues whom they are not close with because IMs are more intrusive than e-mail. When people receive IMs, their computers flash to alert them of an incoming message. Through this flashing, IM draws people's attention to the message and interrupts their workflow. Therefore, IMs are only sent to those colleagues with whom one has a close relationship and feels comfortable interrupting. They are sent mainly when the request is urgent and a prompt reply is required, as Linda, a software developer, explains:

> Instant messaging exists for immediate things, for quick exchanges, where you don't care about archiving. ... I use IM a lot. IM is great if you have one question that you just need an answer to. When you need to explain something in detail, an outline, kind of a business case for doing something, or for getting somebody to take action, e-mail is the best.

Thus, IM promotes horizontal communication more than e-mail because it is used primarily with close colleagues rather than with managers. Employees feel less comfortable interrupting their managers than they do interrupting their colleagues. They use IM when they want a quick response to a brief question, but they use e-mail for complex interactions and for exchanges of computer code. They also use e-mail when they want to archive a message for future reference and to comply with U.S. government regulations (under the Sarbanes-Oxley law) for retention of corporate communications.

The client services department has a less densely knit network than the software development department. On the one hand, FTF meetings bring people and relationships together; on the other hand, it takes less time and effort to write an IM than to hold an FTF/telephone conversation. Moreover, FTF/telephone conversations often require coordination for simultaneous availability while people can flexibly send e-mail at any time.

The IM network of client service workers has more horizontal communication than their FTF/telephone network, with departmental members often exchanging messages. Unlike the software developers who often need an e-mail record of their code and software problems, the client services workers are more apt to use the less formal IM medium.

Conclusions: The Normalization and Routinization of the Computerization Movement

CMs provide a useful framework to examine utopian visions of technological adoption and use. Our study of two departments in a high-tech firm has investigated the extent to which the utopian vision in the democratization technological action frame is played out. We have found that the utopian visions that have driven the implementation of CMC do not fit the reality of how CMC is embedded in work practices and daily routines (see also Quan-Haase, 2004; Quan-Haase & Wellman, 2006). Rather, our study reveals a complex picture of CMC use and social structure that depends on contextual factors.

CMC use at KME is multimodal—e-mail and IM—with three key characteristics:

1. *Hyperconnectivity* – The availability of people for communication anywhere and anytime.

2. *Local Virtuality* – The pervasive use of CMC for interaction with physically proximate people.

3. *Networked Hierarchical Organization* – CMC has not realized the utopian visions of flattened bureaucracies. On the one hand, KME employees are communicating widely in flexible networks; on the other hand, traditional hierarchical bureaucratic structures organize their work and communication.

CMC itself does not create hyperconnectivity, local virtuality, and a networked hierarchical organization. Technologies themselves do not determine work practices and organizational structures, but rather provide possibilities, opportunities, and constraints for social change—what Bradner, Kellogg, and Erickson (1999) have called "social affordances" (see also Bradner, 2001). Moreover, many changes that occur within organizations are complex and depend on contextual factors that can greatly vary from one organization to another (Kling, 1996, 1999; Kling & Saachi, 1982; Markus & Robey, 1988; Orlikowski, 1992, 1996; Orlikowski, Yates, Okamura, & Fujimoto, 1995; Zack & McKenney, 1995).

Hyperconnectivity

KME is hyperconnected. The adding on of CMC to FTF and telephone contact has created hyperconnectivity where community members—at work or elsewhere—are always connected to CMC and available for communication. Employees can easily send an e-mail or IM to any other member of the organization, regardless of status or role (Sproull & Kiesler, 1991). Hyperconnectivity affords new forms of collaboration, such as instant availability of contact and constant monitoring of IMs (Quan-Haase, Cothrel, & Wellman, 2005). Hyperconnectivity combines the traditional availability (and surveillance) of all-to-all contact that was characteristic of pre-industrial villages and work places with the flexible connectivity to socially and physically dispersed others that is characteristic of networked societies (Castells, 2000; Wellman, 1997, 2001). It fosters employee independence and interdependence.

In this hyperconnected organization, and perhaps in many others, pervasive CMC has become the routine means for communicating and sharing information with people within and outside workgroups, departments, and organizations. We may be observing a change in the use of CMC and traditional media in firms where work consists of sitting at desks. Organizations that have multiple technologies available for communication may prefer to rely on CMC for communication. CMC is simply the *modus operandi* of the organization, with organizational norms outweighing the limited social presence of text-only e-mail and IM (Haythornthwaite & Wellman, 1998).

Colleagues do not need to be in FTF contact to trust one another. There are so many frequent shorthand IM conversations that we have marveled at how KME employees withstood their apparent intrusiveness. E-mail is also frequent, but these afford more time for thought, allow the attachment of documents, and provide archives and paper trails. IMs and e-mails are supplemented by FTF encounters, both formal meetings and casual conversations. It is clear that FTF contact is not the only trustworthy form of communication.

In a milieu with much individual networking and little direct supervision, it is hyperconnected CMC that fosters collaborative community within and between departments (see also Heckscher & Adler, 2006). Yet, not all is bliss: The high velocity of CMC can mean overload and distraction.

Local Virtuality

CMC-fostered hyperconnectivity means that KME is a *local virtuality,* despite the physical proximity of fellow employees. Most local communication is by CMC, both e-mail and IM. People go online to exchange e-mails and IMs with colleagues who are sitting next to them. They not only communicate by CMC with fellow department members on the same floor, but also use CMC as their predominant means of communication with people outside of their department and outside of KME. Rather than the utopian dream of the "death of distance" making community independent of geography (Cairncross, 1997), CMC has become a routine way to communicate, locally as well as globally.

Technology does not determine communication behavior at KME. Rather, technology creates possibilities and constraints for behavior. Norms and social structures of interdependence affect media use. For example, software developers use IM more than e-mail, while client service employees rely more on e-mail. The needs of the two departments differ: There is close collaboration among the software developers and a culture that favors rapid IM exchanges. By contrast, client service people—more oriented to having relationships outside of the organization—use e-mail.

A Networked Hierarchical Organization

How does the heavy reliance on CMC affect organizational structures? The internetworking CM asserts that CMC can promote greater use of functional networks with flexible membership—and less use of stable groups—in organizations, diminishing the role of hierarchy in decision making and information flows (Iacono & Kling, 2001; Sproull & Kiesler, 1991; Wellman, 2001). "Democratization" is also a key technological action frame of the internetworking CM. The utopian vision of democratization holds that CMC can transform the social structure of organizations and societies into more egalitarian and collaborative institutions by facilitating bottom up, interactive, two-way, peer-to-peer communication (Kling et al., 1998; Iacono & Kling, 1996, 2001; also see Elliott & Kraemer, Chapter 1, this volume). For organizations, the internetworking CM and the democratization technological action frame should mean the weakening of bureaucracy and the emergence of networked organizations where status, roles, and departmental divisions no longer restrict information flows (Fulk & DeSanctis, 1999; Hinds & Kiesler, 1999, 2002).

When we began studying KME, we expected to find a networked, post-bureaucratic organization where people worked in shifting teams with multiple others, with little structured departmentalization and hierarchy. Instead, we learned that KME started as a bureaucratic, hierarchical organization. Bureaucracy is not a relic of the past, and formal management structure and practices continue to influence communication. Yet KME is a hybrid organization—an "enabling bureaucracy" (Adler & Borys, 1996)—where rules about work and the horizontal and vertical divisions of labor exist along with high levels of trust and community cohesion.

How does a high-tech, hyperconnected organization such as KME reconcile the tension between collaborative, networked community and hierarchy? KME has an explicit hierarchy that relates people and functions. The hierarchy provides a way of organizing individuals around work tasks as well as structuring coordination and communication. KME has formal roles and statuses, with titles such as "Manager." People know what their role is, to whom they report, and what their relationship is. Decision making takes place at the top and is then communicated to employees.

Yet, KME is also an enabling bureaucracy. Rules about work and vertical and horizontal divisions of labor co-exist along with high levels of trust and community cohesion. Employees enjoy sufficient freedom to perform their jobs without reporting constantly to their managers and asking for permission. Their meta-awareness of the reporting structure—combined with hyperconnectivity, trust, expertise, and experience—allows employees to work largely independently while connected to a larger departmental and organizational enterprise.

Moreover, the type of work done by these high-tech employees has reached such complexity that managers often cannot give much input for dealing with technical problems. Such circumstances preclude direct hierarchical-bureaucratic supervision. To function, KME management must trust and rely on their employees to make decisions. For example, although hierarchy is explicit in the software development department, employees communicate by e-mail and IM with those who have the expertise they need, regardless of their status. Yet, employees remain aware of status differences. Although their interactions within the department do not reflect this—people socialize and trust each other—awareness of hierarchy affects employees' interactions with the organization's management. Thus, CMC supports communication with all employees within the department but does not remove hierarchical barriers.

Hierarchical position has more influence in the client services department on who talks with whom. A person's status within the hierarchy plays a key role in how messages are replied to. Lower status employees feel compelled to reply to messages of higher status employees because the receivers of messages know that senders are aware that they have received the message. Thus, awareness of others' availability and status leads to expectations in senders about how long it should take recipients to reply (Erickson & Kellogg, 2000).

For example, Brian, an upper manager in the client services department, received two IMs during our interview. Each time, when the message popped up on the screen, Brian glanced at his screen and quickly scanned it. Both times, he excused himself and spent two or three minutes replying. When asked what had happened, Brian replied, "I usually do not answer messages while I am engaged in a face-to-face meeting unless they are short questions or are urgent."

Yet he answered these messages, because they were from his superior. With IM, the status of the communicator and the urgency of the message can be more compelling than the physical presence of someone FTF.

Implications for the Internetworking Computerization Movement

It would be fatuous to state that KME is the epitome of computerization. Yet KME is a company that lives by, for, and on computer networks. Employees spent most of their times in front of desktops interacting with colleagues within their departments, in the organization, and outside the organization. For these high-tech workers, the computer screen is as much of their work environment as the physical space in which they work. Even employees who sit next to one another often use CMC to interact.

All in all, the internetworking CM has much to celebrate at highly computerized KME. There is collaboration and communities of practice (Brown & Duguid, 1991; Lesser & Prusak, 2000; Wenger, 1998). Although we do not have a comparison case of a non-computerized organization, our survey, interviews, and observations all show the impact of hyperconnectivity, with e-mail and IM always on and always attended to.

The KME evidence only partially supports the internetworking CM's technological action frame that there is connectivity without spatial constraints. Although the great majority of KME's long distance communication uses the Internet, local within-department communication still comprises the bulk of communication—online as well as offline. CM's advocates, mesmerized by the McLuhanesque dream of the global village (McLuhan, 1964; McLuhan & Powers, 1989), need to remember the many reasons that employees have for using the Internet to communicate locally. We caution, though, that because all the members of each department studied worked cheek-by-desktop on one floor, we cannot distinguish between locality and work organization in fostering this local virtuality.

With respect to the gap between the internetworking CM vision of democratization and the reality in an organization, KME does not reflect a full-fledged networked organization (Heckscher, 1994; Heydebrand, 1989; Jarvenpaa & Ives, 1994). Computerization does not have magically transformative powers. A hierarchy—with employees and middle and higher managers—remains in place with clear reporting relationships. Yet, within this hierarchy, computerization enables the professionals at KME to obtain help easily from peers, managers, and subordinates.

Acknowledgments

Support for our research has been provided by BMO (the Bank of Montreal), Communication and Information Technology Ontario, the Institute of Knowledge Management (IKM), Mitel Networks, and the Social Science and Humanities Research Council of Canada. The first author acknowledges assistance from the Alumni Research Awards Program, Faculty of Social Science, the University of Western Ontario. We thank Paul Adler, Manuel Castells, Rob Cross, Margaret Elliott, Charles Heckscher, Lynne Howarth, Kenneth Kraemer, Richard Livesley, Larry Prusak, Beverly Wellman, and the spirit of Rob Kling for their advice, and Jessica Collins, Julie Wang, and Natalie Zinko for their editorial assistance. We particularly thank Joseph Cothrel for facilitating our research and for his thoughtful comments on an earlier draft. We especially want to thank all those employees at KME who completed the survey, and even more so, those who gave generously of their time with interviews and observations.

References

Adler, P. S., & Borys, B. (1996). Two types of bureaucracy: Enabling and coercive. *Administrative Science Quarterly*, 41(1), 61–89.

Allen, T. J., & Cohen, S. (1969). Information flow in research and development laboratories. *Administrative Science Quarterly*, 14(1), 12–19.

Attewell, P., & Rule, J. (1984). Computing and organizations: What we know and what we don't know. *Communications of the ACM*, 27, 1184–1192.

Benford, R. D., & Snow, D. A. (2000). Framing processes and social movements: An overview and assessment. *Annual Review of Sociology*, 26, 611–639.

Blau, P. M. (1975). Structural constraints of status complements. In L. A. Coser (Ed.), *The idea of social structure: Papers in honor of Robert K. Merton* (pp. 117–138). New York: Harcourt Brace Jovanovich.

Blau, P. M., Falbe, C. M., McKinley, W., & Tracy, P. K. (1976). Technology and organization in manufacturing. *Administrative Science Quarterly*, 21, 20–40.

Bradner, E. (2001). *Social factors in the design and use of computer-mediated communication technology.* Unpublished doctoral dissertation, University of California, Irvine.

Bradner, E., Kellogg, W. A., & Erickson, T. (1999). Social affordances of Babble: A field study of chat in the workplace. Proceedings of the Sixth European Conference on Computer Supported Cooperative Work, ECCSW '99, Copenhagen, September.

Brown, J. S., & Duguid, P. (1991). Organizational learning and communities-of-practice: Toward a unified view of working, learning, and innovation. *Organization Science*, 2(1), 40–57.

Cairncross, F. (1997). *The death of distance: How the communications revolution will change our lives*. Boston: Harvard Business School Press.

Castells, M. (2000). *The rise of the network society* (2nd ed.). Oxford: Blackwell.

Clement, A., & Halonen, C. (1998). Collaboration and conflict in the development of a computerized dispatch facility. *Journal of the American Society of Information Science*, 49(12), 1090–1100.

Creswell, J. W. (1998). *Qualitative inquiry and research design: Choosing among five traditions*. Thousand Oaks, CA: Sage.

Culnan, M. J., & Markus, M. L. (1987). Information technologies. In F. M. Jablin, L. L. Putnam, K. H. Roberts, & L. W. Porter (Eds.), *Handbook of organizational communication: An interdisciplinary perspective* (pp. 420–443). Beverly Hills, CA: Sage.

Erickson, T., & Kellogg, W. A. (2000). Social translucence: An approach to designing systems that support social processes. *ACM Transactions on Computer-Human Interaction*, 7(1), 59–83.

Foster, L. W., & Flynn, D. M. (1984). Management information technology: Its effects on organizational form and function. *MIS Quarterly*, 8, 229–236.

Fountain, J. (2001). Toward a theory of federal bureaucracy for the 21st century. In E. C. Kamarck & J. S. Nye (Eds.), *Governance.com: Democracy in the information age* (2nd ed., pp. 117–139). Washington: Brookings Institution Press.

Franz, C. R., Roby, D., & Koeblitz, R. R. (1986). User response to an online information system: A field experiment. *MIS Quarterly*, 10, 29–42.

Fulk, J., & DeSanctis, G. (1999). Articulation of communication technology and organizational form. In G. DeSanctis & J. Fulk (Eds.), *Shaping organization form: Communication, connection, and community* (pp. 5–32). Thousand Oaks, CA: Sage.

Goffman, E. (1986). *Frame analysis*. Boston: Northeastern University Press.

Haythornthwaite, C., & Wellman, B. (1998). Work, friendship and media use for information exchange in a networked organization. *Journal of the American Society for Information Science*, 49(12), 1101–1114.

Heckscher, C. (1994). Defining the post-bureaucratic type. In C. Heckscher & A. Donnellon (Eds.), *The post-bureaucratic organization: New perspectives on organizational change* (pp. 14–62). London: Sage.

Heckscher, C., & Adler, P. (Eds.). (2006). *The firm as a collaborative community: Reconstructing trust in the knowledge economy*. London: Oxford University Press.

Heydebrand, W. V. (1989). New organizational forms. *Work and Occupations*, 16, 323–357.

Hillier, B. (1996). *Space is the machine: A configurational theory of architecture*. Cambridge: Cambridge University Press.

Hinds, P., & Kiesler, S. (1999). Communication across boundaries: Work, structure, and use of communication technologies in a large organization. In G. DeSanctis & J. Fulk (Eds.), *Shaping organization form: Communication, connection, and community* (pp. 211–246). Thousand Oaks, CA: Sage.

Hinds, P., & Kiesler, S. (2002). *Distributed work*. Cambridge, MA: MIT Press.

Iacono, S., & Kling, R. (1996). Computerization movements and tales of technological utopianism. In R. Kling (Ed.), *Computerization and controversy: Value conflicts and social change* (2nd ed., pp. 85–105). San Diego: Academic Press.

Iacono, S., & Kling, R. (2001). Computerization movements: The rise of the Internet and distant forms of work. In J. van Maanen (Ed.), *Information technology and organizational transformation: History, rhetoric, and practice* (pp. 93–136). Thousand Oaks, CA: Sage.

Jarvenpaa, S. L., & Ives, B. (1994). The global network organization of the future: Information management opportunities and challenges. *Journal of Management Information Systems*, 10(4), 25–57.

Kiesler, S. B., Siegel, J., & McGuire, T. W. (1984). Social psychological aspects of computer-mediated communication. *American Psychologist*, 39(10), 1123–1134.

Kling, R. (1996). *Computerization and controversy: Value conflicts and social choices* (2nd ed.). San Diego: Academic Press.

Kling, R. (1999). Learning about information technologies and social change: The contribution of social informatics. *The Information Society*, 16, 217–232.

Kling, R., Rosenbaum, H., & Hert, C. (1998). Social informatics in information science: An introduction. *Journal of the American Society of Information Science*, 49(12), 1047–1052.

Kling, R., & Scaachi, W. (1982). The web of computing: Computer technology as social organization. *Advances in Computers*, 21, 1–90.

Leavitt, H. J., & Whisler, T. L. (1958). Management in the 1980s. *Harvard Business Review*, 36, 41–48.

Lee, T. W. (1999). *Using qualitative methods in organizational research*. Thousand Oaks, CA: Sage.

Lesser, E. L., & Prusak, L. (2000). Communities of practice, social capital, and organizational knowledge. In E. L. Lesser, M. A. Fontaine, & J. A. Slusher (Eds.), *Knowledge and communities: Resources for the knowledge-based economy* (pp. 3–20). Woburn, MA: Butterworth-Heinemann.

Markus, M. L., & Robey, D. (1988). Information technology and organizational change: Causal structure in theory and research. *Management Science*, 34(5), 583–598.

McLuhan, M. (1964). *Understanding media: The extension of man*. New York: McGraw-Hill.

McLuhan, M., & Powers, B. (1989). *The global village: Transformations in world life and media in the 21st Century*. Oxford: Oxford University Press.

Miniwatts Marketing Group. (2006, March 31). *Internet usage statistics for the Americas*. Retrieved July 4, 2006, from www.internetworldstats.com/stats2.htm

Orlikowski, W. J. (1992). The duality of technology: Rethinking the concept of technology in organizations. *Organization Science*, 3(3), 398–427.

Orlikowski, W. J. (1996). Learning from notes: Organizational issues in groupware implementation. In R. Kling (Ed.), *Computerization and controversy: Value conflicts and social choices* (2nd ed., pp. 173–189). San Diego: Academic Press.

Orlikowski, W. J., Yates, J., Okamura, K., & Fujimoto, M. (1995). Shaping electronic communication: The metastructuring of technology in the context of use. *Organization Science*, 6(4), 423–444.

Quan-Haase, A. (2004). *Information brokering and technology use: A case study of a high-tech firm*. Unpublished doctoral thesis, University of Toronto.

Quan-Haase, A., Cothrel, J., & Wellman, B. (2005). Instant messaging for collaboration: A case study of a high-tech firm. *Journal of Computer-Mediated Communication*, 10(4).

Quan-Haase, A., & Wellman, B. (2004). Networks of distance and media: A case study of a high-tech firm. *Analyse und kritik*, 28, 241–257.

Quan-Haase, A., & Wellman, B. (2006). Hyperconnected net work: Computer mediated community in a high-tech organization. In C. Heckscher & P. Adler (Eds.), *Collaborative community in business and society* (pp. 281–333). New York: Oxford University Press.

Raymond, E. S. (2001). *The cathedral and the bazaar: Musings on linux and open source by an accidental revolutionary*. Sebastopol, CA: O'Reilly.

Rice, R. E., & Bair, J. H. (1984). New organizational media and productivity. In R. E. Rice (Ed.), *The New Media* (pp. 185–215). Newbury Park, CA: Sage.

Robey, D. (1981). Computer information systems and organization structure. *Communications of the ACM,* 24, 679–687.

Roehrs, J. (1998). *A study of social organization in science in the age of computer-mediated communication*. Unpublished doctoral thesis, Nova Southeastern University.

Short, J., Williams, E., & Christie, B. (1976). *The social psychology of telecommunications*. London: Wiley.

Sproull, L. S., & Kiesler, S. B. (1991). *Connections: New ways of working in the networked organization*. Cambridge, MA: MIT Press.

Wellman, B. (1997). An electronic group is virtually a social network. In S. Kiesler (Ed.), *Culture of the Internet* (pp. 179–205). Mahwah, NJ: Lawrence Erlbaum.

Wellman, B. (2001). Physical place and cyberspace: The rise of personalized networks. *International urban and regional research*, 25(2), 227–252.

Wenger, E. (1998). *Communities of practice: Learning, meaning, and identity*. Cambridge, U.K.: Cambridge University Press.

Zack, M. H., & McKenney, J. L. (1995). Social context and interaction in ongoing computer-supported management groups. *Organization Science*, 6(4), 394–422.

Chapter 7

Internetworking in the Small

John M. Carroll
College of Information Sciences and Technology
Pennsylvania State University

Abstract

Iacono and Kling (2001) discussed internetworking as an example of a computerization movement. This paper considers community networking as internetworking in the small. Community networking is a computerization movement, in the sense of purveying a particular techno-utopian vision, but it also provides balance and perspective for the far more pervasive computerization movement of internetworking.

Introduction

The computerization movements (CMs) that have helped to construct contemporary understandings of the Internet emphasize broader access to information, discussion, and resources, and the transformation of work and other activity through relaxing physical constraints of time and space. Iacono and Kling's (2001) discussion of internetworking is a case in point. These movements tend to articulate sweeping institutional and societal effects of the Internet: remote collaboration, instant access to people and information from anywhere at anytime, telecommuting, virtual organizations and e-commerce, computer literacy and the information technology (IT) workforce, democratic participation, and global culture. This is a vision of the Internet in the large.

The Internet can be socially constructed at other, more intimate levels of analysis such as one's closest community of practice, home town, local community, neighborhood, or immediate family. This is the Internet in the small. These latter frames of analysis can provide useful contrast and perspective on wider-scope institutional and societal effects. For example, neighborhood-oriented use of the Internet is orthogonal to the debate about whether the Internet does or can entail the "death of distance" vis-à-vis telecommuting, virtual organizations, and e-commerce. On the weekend, the telecommuter may be a scout-master using e-mail to announce the delay of a hike due to a morning shower.

In this paper, I review and reflect upon recent studies of the social impacts and utilization of community networking with respect to social constructions of the Internet. Community-oriented computing has entrained its own utopian vision of the Internet, that of "grassroots" participatory democracy, but it has also served to better frame and balance the techno-utopian vision of internetworking through its emphasis on the integration of the Internet with face-to-face social networks. I focus on the example of the Blacksburg Electronic Village (BEV) (Carroll & Rosson, 1996; Cohill & Kavanaugh, 2000).

Community Networks and the Blacksburg Electronic Village

The roots of community networking are in the activism of the early 1970s—jobs, housing, and veterans' issues in the Berkeley Community Memory, community health in the Cleveland Free Net, and problems of the homeless in the Santa Monica Public Electronic Network. Education was also a formative focus. For example, Big Sky Telegraph supported teachers in rural Montana, linking one- and two-room schools with regional libraries, and providing computer support for the literary and artistic projects of Native Americans. The project was implemented on obsolete computer equipment refurbished by a local women's resource center. It connected a remote and quite dispersed community to the world, for example, giving students access via electronic bulletin boards to professors at the Massachusetts Institute of Technology.

The core of the community networking movement is probably best articulated in Doug Schuler's 1996 manifesto and how-to manual, *Wired For Change* (Schuler, 1996). The title clearly suggests one of the central ideas of a CM, in the sense of Kling and Iacono, namely that applications of IT can catalyze societal reform. A transliteration of Kling and Iacono's (1988) statement of the five ideological touchstones of CMs yields the following:

1. Community networks are central for a reformed world.
2. Improved community networks can further reform society.
3. There are no conceptual limits to the scope of appropriate community networking.

4. No one loses from community networking.
5. Uncooperative people are the main barrier to social reform through community networking.

To be fair to Schuler and others in the community networking movement, it is not clear that anyone ever held all five of these beliefs as such. Indeed, Schuler emphasizes specific limits to the scope and style of appropriate and effective community networking, and acknowledges that some people can lose from community networking.

In the addendum to the 1994 version of their 1988 paper, Kling and Iacono (1995) acknowledge that the five bullets may have been over-specified, and emphasize that the essential point is that CMs embrace technological utopianism, casting some technology as a key enabler of a utopian vision. They acknowledge groups like the Electronic Frontier Foundation and Computer Professionals for Social Responsibility, which they credit with articulating "socially responsible" perspectives on CMs. And, indeed, these groups were directly involved with the development of the community networking movement.

In the early 1990s, as the community networking movement was being consolidated in works like Schuler (1996), computer networking itself was transformed by the emergence of the World Wide Web. In the public sphere of computing this had major effects. First, the community networking movement was rapidly overtaken by competing visions of the Internet. The dominant contemporary understanding of the Internet is less that of a tool to facilitate democracy in a local community context, and more a matter of global access to collaborators and work activity, products and services, information and education, etc. These latter themes are the technological action frames Iacono and Kling emphasized in their 2001 characterization of what they call the "internetworking" CM. This movement also incorporates many relatively anonymous interactions pertaining to shopping and entertainment.

A second effect in the public sphere of computing was within the community networking movement. The World Wide Web rapidly accelerated the development of new community networks, but this second-wave of community networks embraced a broader ideology. Community networks in the 1990s were still about facilitating participation in local community groups and activities, about enhancing neighbor-to-neighbor interactions, about access to and involvement in local government, etc.; they were still motivated in the technological action frame of democratization. But they were also explicitly motivated in the technological action frame of economic development—new paradigms for work, education, and leisure, new opportunities for commerce and tourism, etc. This Internet-in-the-large vision was sometimes called "digital cities"—especially in Europe and Japan, where there had not been much of a first-wave of community networking. In the United States, digital cities and first-wave community networks were often conflated.

The BEV was established in 1993, a bit late from the standpoint of the first-wave movement of local activism (Internet-in-the-small), but early from the standpoint of the global economy (Internet-in-the-large movement). The BEV was created and initially developed largely top-down as a partnership among the town of Blacksburg, the local telecommunications operating company, and Virginia Tech. It attracted state and federal support by characterizing itself as a model project for the Clinton Administration's National Information Infrastructure (NII) initiative, and as a technology response to the Japanese Fifth Generation initiative.

In retrospect, this was just a bit far-fetched, though the BEV arguably did produce regional economic benefits. It evoked many small Internet-oriented businesses, attracted a pioneering group of distance workers, and generated a huge amount of publicity for Blacksburg. Another benefit for the town and the surrounding area was the infrastructure created by the BEV, which included T1 Ethernet connections to all of the county's public schools (quite unusual for a rural county in 1994), extensive how-to-install-and-log-on educational outreach programs run by Virginia Tech, and pervasive community discussions about how and why to use the Internet and what it all might mean for the town and the region. Despite all the hype, the BEV connected neighbors in Blacksburg, facilitated the activities of community groups, provided a channel for the town government to gather and disseminate information, and rather pervasively changed programs and expectations in the Montgomery County public school system.

Thus, despite itself, to an extent, the BEV is an example of an Internet-in-the-small community network, and one that also incorporated an aggressive and successful technology adoption component. By the early 2000s, adoption and use of the Internet was widespread in Blacksburg. For example, in 1999, the BEV community had among the highest per capita use of the Internet in the world; more than 87 percent of residents and 75 percent of businesses were online. At that same time, more than 60 percent of the BEV community had access to broadband at home and/or at work. (See Carroll, 2005, for a more detailed critical history of the BEV project.)

Evaluating the BEV

During the latter 1990s, my colleagues and I participated in a series of participatory action research projects, exploring models for facilitating the ambitions and achievements of community institutions and groups.

For example, we helped the Blacksburg Seniors construct a Nostalgia archive of narratives and images describing what the town was like in the 1960s (that is to say, within living memory; see Carroll, et al., 1999). We worked with a group of science teachers in the county schools to create a virtual laboratory to support collaboration and resource sharing among middle and high school students from four dispersed school sites (Isenhour, Carroll, Neale, Rosson, & Dunlap, 2000).

In 2000, with support from the National Science Foundation (NSF) Information Technology Research (ITR) program, we designed an evaluation project to investigate effects of the adoption of technology—and of the visions and self-perceptions that come with the technology—on the people of Blacksburg and Montgomery County. We carried out a panel study involving a stratified sample of 100 households, representing actual population demographics. We started with a random sample of 1,250 Montgomery county residential addresses purchased from Survey Sample, Inc. in September 2000. The sample was generated randomly by ZIP code, using telephone directory records, post office records, and Department of Motor Vehicles data. The sample was readily available, and was also pre-filtered: 380 invalid addresses had been found and removed prior to our use of the list.

We recruited from the 870 households in the random sample using a 10-item survey that allowed us to classify households with respect to location (residing within the Town of Blacksburg or elsewhere in Montgomery County), user type (access to the Internet from home only, from work only, from home and work, or no access), and education level of head of household (elementary school, high school, 1-3 years of college, 4+ years of college). We recruited households into the study sample to represent these 3 stratification variables in proportion to the actual population of Montgomery County (Kavanaugh, Carroll, Rosson, Reese, & Zin, 2005a; Kavanaugh, Reese, Carroll, & Rosson, 2005b).

Our study involved administering two versions of a lengthy questionnaire to all members of the panel households, spaced about one year apart. A sub-sample of the panel households was also interviewed four times throughout the 18 months of data collection (Dunlap, Schafer, Carroll, & Reese, 2003). Another sub-sample of households had their home use of the Internet logged remotely, for a period of 12 months each, through server proxies for browser and e-mail clients (Carroll, et al., 2006). The study is schematized in Figure 7.1. This study produced a wide range of insights into the effects of the Internet on a range of community capacities, experiences, and achievements. In this discussion, I will focus on a few key results pertaining to local activism and feelings of belonging.

We found that people in the Blacksburg/Montgomery County community who make use of the Internet for civic purposes (for example, people

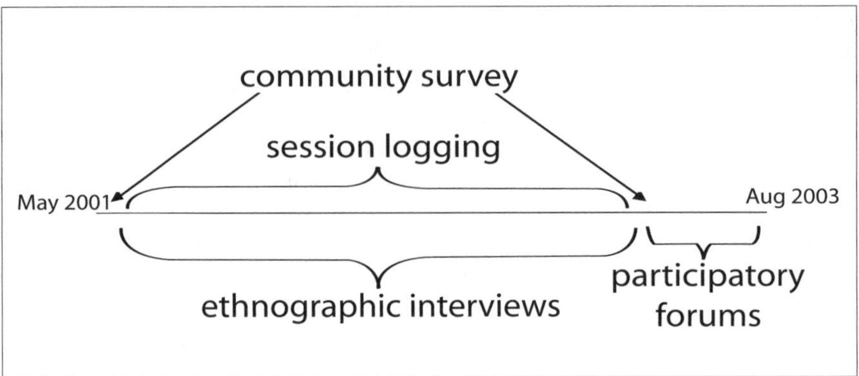

Figure 7.1 Overall research design of the study

who say they look for news online, or participate in local online groups) tend to be activists in the community (they feel they have ideas to improve the local community, they say they work with others to solve community problems, and so on). These results are summarized in the path model (Pedhazur, 1997) in Figure 7.2.

We created this model by regressing the exogenous variables of age, education, and extroversion (the latter measured by a standard scale) on

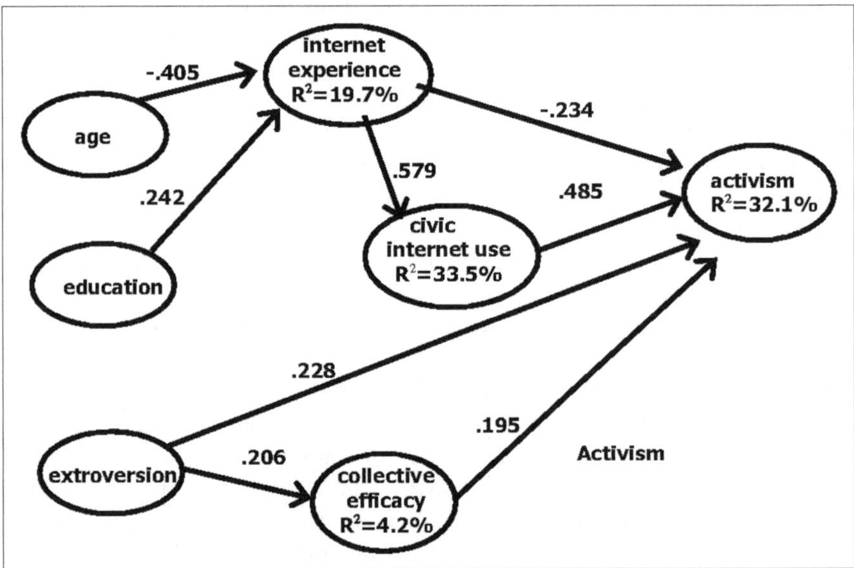

Figure 7.2 Path model from first wave of survey data. People who make use of the Internet for civic purposes tend to be activists; people who (merely) make use of the Internet tend not to be activists.

a set of community-oriented attitudes and the Internet usage constructs (Internet experience, civic use of the Internet, and collective efficacy). (Community collective efficacy is the belief that the community is capable of achieving specific goals as a community; the construct is derived from Bandura [1997], and operationalized by a Likert scale we developed [Carroll & Reese, 2003].) We then regressed the resulting ensembles on community involvement and attachment constructs (in this case, activism).

It is not surprising that younger and better educated people tend to be more experienced and regular users of the Internet, or that extroverts tend to experience greater community collective efficacy. Of more interest are the relations between Internet use and community attitudes and behaviors. In Figure 7.2, it is interesting that although people who use the Internet for civic purposes tend to be more active in the community, Internet experience is a *negative* predictor of activism when unmediated by civic use of the Internet. This suggests a two-population interpretation: some experienced Internet users have recruited the Internet for their civic behaviors, and these individuals tend to be active within their communities. In contrast, another population of experienced users may be using the Internet for other goals; these users report themselves as relatively inactive within their community.

As summarized in Figure 7.3, we also found that people who make use of the Internet for social purposes (e-mailing friends and family) reported a greater sense of community belonging (they help neighbors in need, spend time with friends, and so on). In this model, extroversion is a significant predictor of social Internet use, although it does not predict Internet experience in general, or the use of the Internet for civic purposes. Belonging is directly and positively predicted by the degree of social support people experience (how much they report spending time with friends, sharing worries, getting advice for family problems, being invited to do things, being able to get help, and companionship). Although we do not see a direct negative relationship between Internet experience and community attachment (feelings of belonging to the community), we still see in this model that to the extent that there is a positive relationship between Internet experience and feeling of belonging, it is mediated by social use of the Internet.

These are provocative results. They suggest that people are incorporating the Internet into their lives within local communities, and that they are able to use the Internet effectively to carry out community-oriented behaviors and develop social capital. The Internet does not make people feel civic engagement or behave as better people or citizens. However, it can ease the expression of dispositions toward civic engagement in their behavior. Our results suggest how new technological tools and resources, in this case the Internet, provide new opportunities to

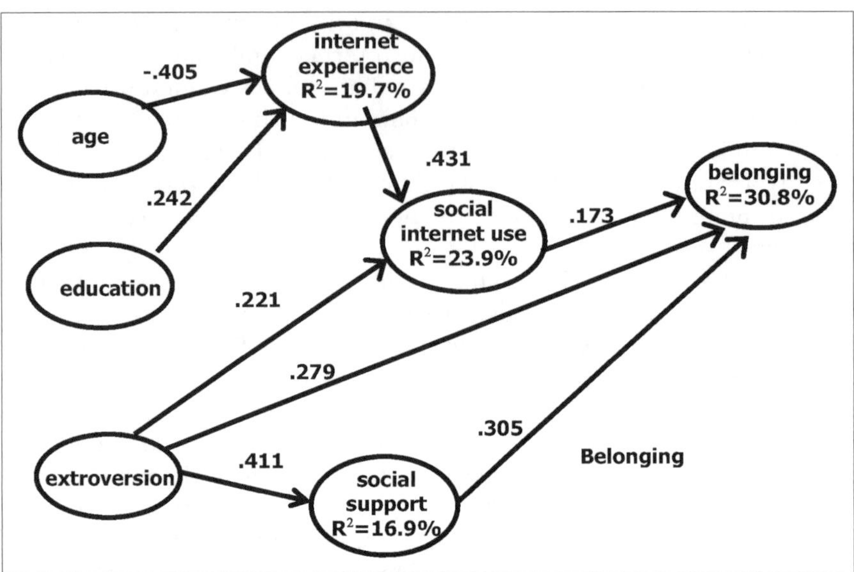

Figure 7.3 Path model from first wave of survey data. People who make use of the Internet for social purposes report a greater sense of community belonging

cultivate and express civic behaviors. (For further details, see Carroll, et al., 2006; Carroll, Rosson, & Zhou, 2005.)

In our survey we asked people what community groups they belonged to, including churches and other places of worship, sports groups, political groups, labor organizations (e.g., unions), school service groups, hobby groups (e.g., garden or chess clubs), local advocacy/interest groups (e.g., with respect to environmental and development issues), residents' groups or homeowners associations, and local chapters of groups like Kiwanis, YMCA, Rotary, etc. For further analysis, we divided our subject population into "bridges" (people who belong to two or more such community groups) and "non-bridges" (people who belong to one or no community group).

Based on prior research, we had reason to think that bridges might be important nodes in the community's social network. Thus, the existence of bridges is a prerequisite for the development of bridging social capital in the community, enhancing the opportunity for people to connect with others in the community who are different from themselves (Putnam, 2000). By spanning groups, bridges facilitate the formation of weak ties across the community, creating new social and economic opportunities (Granovetter, 1973). Bridges enhance the reachability of nodes in the community's social network, minimizing structural holes in the network, which promotes social integration throughout the community (Newton, 1997).

We found that bridges tend to be more extroverted, more informed about what is going on in the community, more trusting of fellow community members, more civic-minded, more socially and politically engaged, and more attached to the community. They tend to have more education and a higher household income, and to feel more community collective efficacy (that is, to believe that the community is capable of achieving specific goals as a community).

We found that community attachment and community involvement outcomes for bridges were facilitated by their use of the Internet. In our survey, relative to non-bridges, bridges responded that since beginning to use the Internet they (1) felt more involved with the local community and local issues, (2) had increased feelings of connectedness with fellow community members, and (3) were more likely to attend local meetings and events. This is interesting because bridges—by definition, and irrespective of their use of the Internet—are already high relative to their peers with respect to community attachment and community involvement. When they make use of the Internet—and presumably for civic and social purposes—it helps them to intensify these feelings.

This is also suggested by secondary patterns of interaction with respect to *how much* people use the Internet. Bridges and non-bridges who are *light* users of the Internet (meaning 1.5 hours per day or less) rate their use of the Internet for social purposes about the same. Bridges are just slightly higher. However, among *heavy* users of the Internet, bridges make substantially greater use of the Internet for social purposes than do non-bridges.

Similarly, bridges who are *heavy* users of the Internet (more than 1.5 hours per day) report attending *more* local meetings and events since going online, than do bridges who are light users of the Internet. This is reversed for non-bridges: Non-bridge, heavy users of the Internet report attending *fewer* local meetings and events than do light users.

Increasing use of the Internet affects bridges (people who are relatively more involved in community life) differently than it does non-bridges (people who are less involved). Bridges report making more use of the Internet for social purposes and attending more local meetings as they use the Internet more. Non-bridges report making less use of the Internet for social purposes and attending fewer local meeting as they use the Internet more. All this suggests that community members who are more involved in the community are now using the Internet to mediate even greater community involvement. (For further discussion of bridges and the differences between bridged and non-bridge, see Kavanaugh, Reese, Carroll, & Rosson, 2005b.)

It is important to acknowledge that all these results and interpretations pertain to the panel of households we studied and to the Blacksburg community they represent. It remains to be established that Blacksburg is a good model of the use and impacts of the Internet in American communities more generally (or for that matter of communities *tout court*).

Discussion

The BEV as realized in the Blacksburg and Montgomery County community is not the BEV that was on the drawing boards in 1993. The BEV certainly did not provide technology capabilities or application models with a scale, scope, or impact to counter the Japanese Fifth Generation (though one could argue that the Fifth Generation was a far more striking failure of a CM to fulfill expectations). The BEV did provide a technology boost to the community, at a variety of levels, and one must concede that Blacksburg is still a relatively privileged community with respect to telecommunications infrastructure, to an extent that it was not prior to the BEV.

Many of the specific elements envisioned in the NII were in fact implemented through the BEV initiative: The schools were networked and the network was widely used by teachers. Local government information, and even some services, were made available through the network. A small but visible group of telecommuters moved into the community. Local doctors posted health information, local businesses posted commercial information, and civic groups—notably the BEV Seniors—posted their information, carried out their business, and facilitated one another through the network.

On the other hand, the civic and social impacts of the BEV—the ones we measured in our evaluation study—were only indirectly caused by this boost in raw technology. The impacts of the BEV that we measured are more directly interpretable as community members appropriating a technology infrastructure to facilitate their pre-existing civic and social objectives with respect to the community in which they live. These effects, which were more central in the first wave of the community networking movement and were placed somewhat in the background in the BEV and other second-wave projects, are perhaps manifestly the core of community networking.

Of course, skepticism about the community networking CM—the vision of the Internet in the small—was in good supply. The internetworking CM (Iacono & Kling, 2001) became dominant, if not pervasive. Even Internet research and development directed to supporting civic activity tended to articulate the civic discourse in a national or international frame (for example, publicagenda.org, rockthevote.com, amnesty.org, homeless.org), and not as locally situated and directly participatory.

Nevertheless, I regard the community networking movement as a counterbalance to the internetworking CM specifically with respect to community formation and development. Our research illustrates how networking support for physical communities can enhance community attachment and community involvement. In Blacksburg, there are specific indications that it is salutary.

The communities we live in are socially rich relative to internetworking communities. The social networks of the communities we live in link members in multiple dimensions. Mike's mom is manager of Wegman's Deli, a member of the Presbyterian Choir, and co-chair of the local watershed protection group. This week she is a letter-writer to the local newspaper. And so on. The extent of this bridging, which our studies of Blacksburg suggest enhances community social capital, is far beyond what one sees in virtual groups, however romantically the internetworking CM may characterize such social structures.

Members of the communities we live in share and collectively manage a highly tangible resource, namely a piece of the earth, and the many layers of infrastructure that are entailed by this—zoning and development, schools and hospitals, public transportation, emergency management, water and sewage systems, recreational facilities, and so on. They share in this ipso facto; it does not require any additional commitment. The fate of the local community matters to its members in a manner unlike other memberships. Whether this is as basic as having a warm hearth in the winter, or as symbolic as maintaining inflated property values, the stakes are high for the members. Relative to this, internetworking communities of practice, communities of interest, communities of belief, and so forth seem rather thin.

The sweeping institutional and societal effects of the Internet embodied in the internetworking CM have inspired and mobilized a wide array of action and reaction. We may have only seen the beginnings. However, people are physical beings and live in the physical world. They may pervasively supplement their lives with online interactions for work, education, shopping, and leisure, but no one can live his or her life in the Internet. We will all continue to have neighbors, to live in physical communities, to share place-based concerns, and to play various roles in community life.

Neighborhood-oriented use of the Internet can extend and strengthen local social networks by facilitating the roles we play and by reinforcing a community's sense of place. As a CM, community networking emphasizes local action and bottom-up control, as a complement to sweeping effects and top-down forces of internetworking. It raises many complementary questions about the Internet, such as how software can more specifically support locally oriented interactions, how community networks can sustain or challenge the status quo with respect to power and social inclusion, and how they facilitate or mitigate parochial aspects of community, like not-in-my-backyard attitudes.

The relationship of these two, somewhat complementary, CMs—community networking and internetworking—provides an interesting direction for elaborating Kling and Iacono's (1988; Iacono & Kling, 2001) analysis of CMs (see also Clement & Hurrell, Chapter 12, this volume). Thus, it may be more generally useful to try to simultaneously articulate complementary CMs, as alternative visions provide mutual perspective on expectations, and perhaps facilitate more action-oriented skepticism. This is related to what Kling and Iacono (1995) called counter-computerization movements (CCMs), but is different in that CCMs are characterized as techno-dystopian, whereas the community networking and internetworking CMs are both techno-utopian, but in quite different ways.

Acknowledgments

This project was partially supported from the Hitachi Foundation, the U.S. Office of Naval Research (under award N00014-00-1-0549 to Virginia Tech), and from the U.S. NSF (under awards EIA-0081102, IIS-0080864, IIS-0113264, REC-9554206, and REC-0106552 to Virginia Tech, and IIS-0353097, IIS-0342547, IIS-0353075, and REC-0353101 to Penn State). I am grateful to Cecelia Merkel and the workshop organizers for comments and suggestions on an earlier draft.

References

Bandura, A. (1997). *Self-efficacy: The exercise of control*. New York: W. H. Freeman and Company.

Carroll, J. M. (2005, in press). The Blacksburg Electronic Village: A study in community computing. In P. van den Besselaar & S. Kiozumi (Eds.), *Digital cities 3: Information technologies for social capital* (pp. 43–65). Lecture Notes in Computer Science, Volume 3081. New York: Springer-Verlag.

Carroll, J. M., & Reese, D. D. (2003). Community collective efficacy: Structure and consequences of perceived capacities in the Blacksburg Electronic Village. *Proceedings of HICSS-36: Hawaii international conference on system sciences,* January 6–9, Kona, p. 222a. Los Alamitos, CA: IEEE Computer Society.

Carroll, J. M., & Rosson, M. B. (1996). Developing the Blacksburg electronic village. *Communications of the ACM,* 39(12), 69–74. Special section on computing at home.

Carroll, J. M., Rosson, M. B., Kavanaugh, A., Dunlap, D., Schafer, W., Snook, J., & Isenhour, P. (2006). Social and civic participation in a community network. In R. Kraut, M. Brynin, & S. Kiesler. (Eds.), *Domesticating information technologies*. New York: Oxford University Press.

Carroll, J. M., Rosson, M. B., VanMetre, C. A., Kengeri, R., Kelso, J., & Darshani, M. (1999). Blacksburg nostalgia: A community history archive. In M. A. Sasse & C. Johnson (Eds.), *Proceedings of seventh IFIP conference on human-computer interaction INTERACT 99* (pp. 637–647). Edinburgh, August 30–September 3. Amsterdam: IOS Press/International Federation for Information Processing (IFIP).

Carroll, J. M., Rosson, M. B., & Zhou, J. (2005). Collective efficacy as a measure of community. *Proceedings of CHI 2005: Human factors in computing systems,* Portland, OR, April 2–7, 1–10.

Cohill, A., & Kavanaugh, A. (Eds.). (2000). *Community networks: Lessons from Blacksburg, Virginia* (2nd ed.). Norwood, MA: Artech House.

Dunlap, D., Schafer, W., Carroll, J. M., & Reese, D. D. (2003). Delving deeper into access: Marginal Internet usage in a local community. *Proceedings of HOIT 2003: Home oriented informatics and telematics, the networked home and the home of the future.* Retrieved from www.crito.uci.edu/noah/HOIT/2003papers.htm

Granovetter, M. (1973). The strength of weak ties. *American Journal of Sociology,* 78(6), 1360–1380.

Iacono, S., & Kling, R. (2001). Computerization movements: The rise of the Internet and distant forms of work. In J. Yates & J. Van Maanen (Eds.), *Information technology and organizational transformation: History, rhetoric, and practice* (pp. 93–136). Thousand Oaks, CA: Sage.

Isenhour, P. L., Carroll, J. M., Neale, D. C., Rosson, M. B., & Dunlap, D. R. (2000). The virtual school: An integrated collaborative environment for the classroom. *Educational Technology and Society*, 3(3), 74–86.

Kavanaugh, A. L., Carroll, J. M., Rosson, M. B., Reese, D. D., & Zin, T. T. (2005a). Participating in civil society: The case of networked communities. *Interacting with Computers*, 17(1), 9–33.

Kavanaugh, A., Reese, D. D., Carroll, J. M., & Rosson, M. B. (2005b). Weak ties in networked communities. *The Information Society*, 21(2), 119–131.

Kling, R., & Iacono, S. (1988). The mobilization of support for computerization: The role of computerization movements. *Social Problems*, 35(3), 226–242.

Kling, R., & Iacono, S. (1995). Computerization movements and the mobilization of support for computerization. In S. L. Starr (Ed.), *Ecologies of knowledge: Work and politics in science and technology* (pp. 119–153). Albany, NY: State University of New York Press.

Newton, K. (1997). Social capital and democracy. *American Behavioral Scientist,* 40(5), 575–586.

Pedhazur, E. J. (1997). *Multiple regression in behavioral research.* New York: Harcourt Brace College Publishers.

Putnam, R. D. (2000). *Bowling alone: The collapse and revival of American community.* New York: Simon & Schuster.

Schuler, D. (1996). *Wired for change: The new community networks.* New York: ACM Press.

Chapter 8

Online Communities: Infrastructure, Relational Cohesion, and Sustainability

Mary J. Culnan
Bentley College

Abstract

Online communities are social networks of geographically distributed volunteers who engage in collective action. They represent a current example of a micro-computerization movement enabled by the Internet computerization movement. This chapter proposes a conceptual model for understanding how online communities evolve over time based on the concepts of infrastructure and relational cohesion. Here, infrastructure is hypothesized to include four elements encompassing both technology and social relations: a critical mass of members, shared content, social control, and information technology. The chapter argues that the infrastructure provides the basis for outcomes that lead to relational cohesion at the individual level and social capital at the level of the social unit. Relational cohesion is necessary to generate commitment behaviors that enable the community to sustain itself over time. The model is illustrated with a case study of the Backstreets Ticket Exchange online community of www.backstreets.com. The success of the Backstreets Ticket Exchange is attributed in a large part to a consensus around democratization that helps maintain a critical mass of members who supply content and also provides a basis for social engagement by the members.

Introduction

The Internet working computerization movement (CM) is a general CM that has spawned a number of specific CMs related to distant forms of work—electronic commerce, distance learning, telemedicine, etc.—and to social transformation through the "death of distance" (Iacono & Kling, 2001). More specifically, it provides a basis for new, democratized social relations by allowing individuals to connect directly with one another independent of geographic location. The result is the formation of new transnational communities (Iacono & Kling, 2001).

Online communities (OCs) are a type of social network that brings together geographically distributed individuals around a common interest. They are the focus of the OC CM, a specific CM related to the more general internetworking CM (Iacono & Kling, 2001). Typically, OCs are self-organizing and consist of individuals who participate voluntarily (Wasko & Faraj, 2005). Examples of OCs include communities of practice typically organized around a professional interest (e.g., Elliott & Scacchi, forthcoming; Fayard & DeSanctis, 2005; Quan-Haase & Wellman, Chapter 6, this volume; Wasko, Faraj,& Teigland 2004), brand communities organized around a product (Muniz & O'Guinn, 2001; Watson, 1997), support groups (Cummings, Sproull, & Kiesler, 2002; Galegher, Sproull, & Kiesler, 1998), and other communities of interest such as sports (Blanchard & Markus, 2004) or chess fans (Ginsburg & Weisband, 2002). A Pew Internet and American Life Project (2001) found that 84 percent of Internet users say they have used the Internet to contact or get information from a group, and 79 percent of these "Cyber Groupies" identify at least one particular group with which they stay in regular contact.

OCs are not new. The Usenet discussion group system was founded as an experiment in 1979 and exists today as Google Groups. The WELL was founded in 1985 as a dial-up bulletin board system and currently has approximately 4,000 members. Today, new Internet communities continue to proliferate. Prominent examples include MySpace and Facebook, which are popular with college and high school students as well as other young adults.

Public discourse about OCs has reflected the "death of distance" master frame for the Internet whereby social relationships are fundamentally transformed and democratized as time and space become irrelevant (Iacono & Kling, 2001). More specifically, proponents of OCs argue that these online groups promote social engagement and exhibit characteristics of physical community including social interactions, reciprocity, shared beliefs, a sense of belonging and community identity, standards of conduct for members, and an ability to take collective action (Papadakis, 2003; Wellman, Quan-Haase, Witte, & Hampton, 2001).

Critics of OCs are skeptical that the social capital and social engagement found in physical communities can be created online among geographically distributed participants (Putnam, 1995; Putnam & Feldstein, 2003). They further argue that OCs exist possibly at the expense of physical communities and raise the potential for physical isolation (Putnam,

1995). An emerging third frame is that relationships formed online lead to new forms of community and larger social networks with a mix of weak ties, often characterized by both online and offline interactions (Nohria & Eccles, 1992; Putnam & Feldstein, 2003; Quan-Haase & Wellman, 2004; Wellman, et al., 2001). While advocates and scholars focus on the positive outcomes of OCs, it is important to note that these same electronic communities also serve the needs of geographically distributed individuals engaged in criminal activities or interested in promoting hate speech.

Much of the early research attempted to establish the concept of OCs as a form of community and to understand outcomes in existing OCs such as collective action, as well as the factors that lead people to contribute to these voluntary social structures given the potential for free riding (Butler, 2001; Constant, Sproull, & Kiesler, 1996; Fulk, Flanigan, Kalman, Monge, & Ryan, 1996; Ginsburg & Weisband, 2002; Gu & Jarvenpaa, 2003; Rafaeli & LaRose; 1993, Wasko & Faraj, 2000; Wasko, Faraj, & Teigland, 2004; Wellman, et al., 2001). Factors that have been hypothesized or shown to be associated with participation or sustainability include size (Butler, 2001; Fulk, et al., 1996), shared information (Fulk, et al., 1996), social controls (Wasko, et al., 2004), and relational or social capital (Wasko & Faraj, 2005). Lacking in this research is an integrative theory that explains the success of OCs. How do they form and evolve over time? What is the relationship between the features of the technology and the adoption context (Elliott & Kraemer, Chapter 1, this volume)? What differentiates a thriving, sustainable OC from others?

This chapter proposes a conceptual model for understanding how OCs evolve over time, based on the concepts of infrastructure and relational cohesion. Figure 8.1 shows the proposed model. Based on theory from organizational communication (e.g., Fulk, et al., 1996), infrastructure is hypothesized to include four elements comprising both technology and social relations: size or critical mass, content, social control, and information technology, including the choices made by the forum administrator or moderator in implementing the technology.

Drawing on social exchange theory (e.g., Lawler, 2001; Wasko, et al., 2004), this chapter proposes that communities emerge when sufficient relational cohesion is created. Relational cohesion results from exchanges that lead to trust (uncertainty reduction) and positive emotions (Kollock, 1994; Lawler, 2001; Lawler & Yoon, 1996). It leads to behavioral commitment to the social unit, as reflected by staying behavior in the face of alternatives, giving of token gifts, and contributing to new endeavors (Lawler, 2001). Each of these elements will be discussed in turn. A case study from one OC, the Backstreets Ticket Exchange (BTX)[1] discussion forums of www.backstreets.com, will be used to illustrate the model in practice.

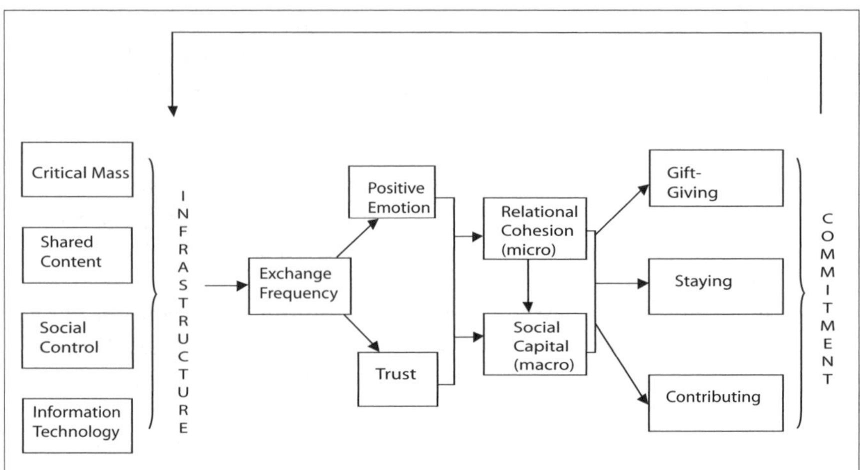

Figure 8.1 Theoretical model of online community sustainability

OC Infrastructure

Star and Ruhleder (1996) characterize infrastructure as a relational concept that emerges with regard to organized practices by people, connected to structures and activities. It consists of articulated components of the system under examination, here an OC. Infrastructure has a number of dimensions, including the fact that it is transparent in use, it reaches beyond a single event, it is learned as part of membership in a community, and it becomes visible upon breakdown. It both shapes and is shaped by the practices of a community (Poole & DeSanctis, 1990; Star & Ruhleder, 1996). For an OC, this chapter hypothesizes that the infrastructure consists of four components, which have been previously identified in the communications literature, as necessary conditions for the collective action that generates public goods necessary to sustain community: a critical mass of participants, a body of shared content, social controls, and information technology (Fulk, et al., 1996).

Critical Mass and Content

Sustainability results from the provision of adequate benefits (Butler, 2001). At a minimum, OCs require a critical mass of members who contribute sufficient content to engage the community. Therefore, critical mass and content are the first two elements of infrastructure. Fulk and her colleagues (1996) draw on the work of Markus (1990) and Connolly and Thorn (1990) to argue that in interactive communication systems, communication and information are the public goods that the systems can offer. Both provide for a variety of generalized exchanges where individuals may both contribute information to and receive information from third parties rather than from the recipient. These exchanges, then, are characterized by generalized reciprocity. The result, given critical mass, is an extensive network of weak ties between each individual and the network as a whole (Granovetter, 1973; Wasko, et al., 2004). Without such a network, there is no community.

There is a strong link between members and content. Members are the key providers of the resources that create the benefits that attract and retain members. Current members need to contribute adequate resources or the social structure will be unable to provide the benefits necessary to retain current members and to attract new members (Butler, 2001). Content is a resource that provides one reason for sufficient numbers of people to join and remain in the network. However, greater volume and diversity of contributions enhances sustainability only if the number of members attracted and retained exceeds the number of members lost due to the increased costs resulting from filtering and noise (Butler, 2001).

Social Controls

Social controls are the third element of infrastructure. As most people participate in OCs anonymously using screen names, there is enormous potential for exposure to flaming and other forms of negative behavior. For example, Wellman et al. (2001) found a strong negative association between the extent of Internet use and commitment to OC. They argued that unpleasant exposure to people who act more disagreeably online than if they were face-to-face accounts for the finding. Social controls including community norms concerning online behavior along with sanctions for people who violate these norms can help minimize negative experiences and maximize positive experiences that promote commitment to the community (Lawler, 2001).

Technology

Technology is the fourth and final element of infrastructure. As with its use in traditional organizations, technology shapes and is shaped by the organization (see Markus, 2005 for a review of this literature). In addition, an OC by definition could not exist without the technology. Resnick (2001) identified six categories of features that can influence community formation, including removing barriers to interaction among dispersed communication partners, expanding interaction networks, the use of access controls to restrict information flows, managing dependencies, maintaining history, and naming conventions.[2]

Salient features that help sustain community include those that allow members to quote a previous post in their reply and to include images or emoticons in postings to help incorporate affect into postings.

Private messages allow members to build relationships with other individual members or to address issues away from public scrutiny. Features that maintain history (e.g., when a registered member joined, how many times they have posted, and the ability to review all of their postings) allow members to assess the reputation and potential trustworthiness of other members. The ability to search and bump a discussion topic or thread makes it possible to revisit or reinforce issues within the community. Finally, the choices made by the forum administrator, such as the number of forums and censorship or moderation policies, are also likely to impact how a particular OC evolves.

Infrastructure as a Basis for Commitment and Social Capital

Infrastructure provides a basis for two outcomes that are hallmarks of successful communities: relational commitment and social capital. The affect theory of social exchange provides an explanation of how individuals develop commitment to exchange relations within a social unit (Lawler, 2001). The core idea of this theory is that structural interdependencies among exchange participants produce joint activities that subsequently generate positive or negative emotions. When positive emotions are attributed to a social unit, the strength of these ties determines collectively oriented behavior. Negative feelings should promote affective detachment if the relationship is perceived to be a stable source of negative feelings, beyond the control of the individual (Lawler, 2001).

Social capital is a related concept that has been defined in interrelated ways by various disciplines such as sociology, organizational science, and political science as features that are embedded in social organizations that are accessed or mobilized to facilitate coordination and communication for mutual benefit such as norms of reciprocity, mutual assistance, and trustworthiness (Putnam, 1995; Quan-Haase & Wellman, 2004; Wasko & Faraj, 2005). While social capital can be used to explain pro-social behaviors by community members including collective action or the degree to which people become involved in their community (Quan-Haase & Wellman, 2004; Wasko & Faraj, 2005), it is a macro concept; the existence of social capital has been used to explain outcomes for a social unit. Relational commitment, however, applies to individuals and explains why an individual becomes attached to a larger social unit, subsequently engaging in pro-social behaviors on behalf of the group. These actions produce social capital.

Theory suggests that frequent exchanges with positive outcomes result both in positive affect and in a reduction in uncertainty about future exchanges (Kollock, 1994; Lawler, 2001; Lawler & Yoon, 1996). Positive affect and trust lead individuals to develop commitment to the community and increase the community's store of social capital. Commitment causes individuals to subsequently engage in pro-social behaviors, thereby strengthening the community's infrastructure as pro-social behaviors create benefits (Cummings, et al., 2002). Members stay in the community rather than defecting and new members are attracted to join; they use the technology to engage and to contribute new content, while existing norms are reinforced. A case study of the BTX community at www.backstreets.com will now be used to illustrate the model.

Backstreets.com

Backstreets.com is the Web site affiliated with *Backstreets* magazine, a Bruce Springsteen fanzine. The magazine, founded in 1980, has no official relationship with the artist or his record label, Sony, which maintains a separate Web site (www.brucespringsteen.net). The *Backstreets* Web site was created in 1995 and includes sections for news, tour schedules, an archive of concert set lists, information about the magazine, a store selling Springsteen merchandise, and the BTX section consisting of three forums for fans to sell or exchange concert tickets with other fans. In late April 2003, a fourth forum, "Loose Ends," was added to BTX for chat with the description "General Boss-related conversation." Community members referred to the community as "BTX" and to themselves as "BTXers" (rather than "Loose Enders"). In summer 2005, Loose Ends was split into four forums:

1. Loose Ends ("The BTX community has a lot on their minds, and it ain't all Bruce")
2. The Promised Land ("This is the forum for all Bruce/E Street-related posts. It can be fun, it can be serious, but it's gotta be Boss")
3. The Vineyard ("Music sharing at Backstreets")
4. Political World ("Red, blue, or purple, take your political debate, discussions and diatribes here")

BTX is an example of a brand community. Brand communities have been defined as a geographically distributed community of admirers of a brand who participate in a structured set of social relationships (Muniz & O'Guinn, 2001). Online brand communities provide an opportunity for companies and their customers to interact and to build new and deeper relationships with a brand (Armstrong & Hagel, 1996; McWilliam, 2000). Brand communities are also one type of community of interest as they bring together people who share a common interest such as sports (Blanchard & Markus, 2004) or chess (Ginsburg & Weisband, 2002). With brand communities, however, the interest is more specific, such as a particular artist (here Bruce Springsteen) rather than rock music in general.

Brand communities for musical artists are a widespread phenomenon. Sony Music, for example, hosts more than 100 discussion forums for its artists. In addition, a wide variety of artist communities may be found on livedaily.com (hosted by Ticketmaster). There are also brand communities organized by fans (Watson, 1997). Yahoo!, for example, lists nearly 35,000 groups for musical artists, and artist discussion groups may be found on Usenet (e.g., rec.music.artists). Independent of sponsorship, all of these communities reinforce support for artists among their fans. Artists, their management, and their labels can also benefit from monitoring these discussions in the same way that other companies benefit from monitoring online discussions about their products (Armstrong & Hagel, 1996; Muniz & O'Guinn, 2001).

Following Blanchard and Markus (2004) and Papadakis (2003), BTX exhibits the characteristics associated with community. These include: (1) a shared identity with boundaries, (2) its own culture, norms, and expectations with deception treated as a community offense, and (3) status and hierarchy as part of its infrastructure. Members display feelings of belonging to this versus other Springsteen communities, even if they participate in more than one of these discussion groups.[3]

BTX Infrastructure: Members and Content

As of Spring 2006, BTX had nearly 20,000 registered members with total posts accumulated since April 2003 across all forums ranging from none to more than 27,000. Approximately 21 percent had registered but never posted, while more than 2 percent of the members had accumulated a total of more than 1,000 posts across all seven forums, suggesting the existence of a critical mass of members despite the likelihood that some registered only to use the ticket exchange forums and never participated in any discussions. It was not clear how people learned about BTX. The discussion forums received no publicity in *Backstreets* magazine. However, a link to the Web site appeared in the first page of results from a Google search for "Bruce Springsteen" and it is also likely that word of mouth drove traffic to the site. Periodic informal surveys conducted on the board indicated that members ranged in age from late teens to their 50s, represented a variety of occupations, and were geographically dispersed, with a large percentage in the northeastern United States, particularly New Jersey and New York City. However, BTX also counted members from Canada, New Zealand, and several European countries.

BTX is a rich source of content ranging from discussions about Springsteen and his music to opinions about sports and current events of all types. Table 8.1 illustrates the range of discussion topics. Of particular

Table 8.1 Sample Discussion Topics

Topic	Description and Examples
Information related to concerts	• Information about ticket sales and ticket drops • Q&A about seat locations and general admission procedures
Setlist watches and concert reviews	• Member attending concert would phone another member at home who would post the song titles as they were performed. Others would post comments about the concert. • Following concerts, members would post reviews and photos, and identify any BTXers they had seen at the concert.
Bootleg trading (generally done in exchange for blank CDs and return postage [B&P])	• Take 1/Leave 1 where member would post their collection. The next person would select one from the list and post their own list for the next person. • Trees for bootlegs where one person would burn copies for 3–5 other individuals in exchange for B&P. Sometimes copies were provided as a freebie.
Technical advice	• How to burn a CD, how to download concerts as bitstream, how to post pictures in a signature file, etc.
Springsteen gossip	• Springsteen sightings, press reports, rumors of a new CD, other rumors, etc. • For the ladies—get a look at this (Springsteen photos)
Bruce Sent Me	• Individual contributions to hunger and other charitable organizations with the designation "Bruce Sent Me" • Sorting food at the NY City food bank • Habitat for Humanity
Offline social events	• Tailgate parties or happy hour before concerts • Spring softball game • Trips (e.g., winter ski trip, Las Vegas trip)
Altruism for BTX members	• Christmas tree decorating party for Molsonboy's children the year his wife died • Ticket Fairies (for people who couldn't buy tickets to a sold-out concert) • BTX Secret Santa • Freebies
"Xk Watch"	• Thread started when some members are approaching a milestone for number of posts (e.g., 1,000, 5,000, 10,000). When the milestone is reached, the member typically posts their reflections on their experiences in the community and other members offer congratulations.
Ongoing miscellaneous games	• Let's have a sing-along (each person posts a line from a Springsteen song in order, when song is finished, a new one is started) • Word association (post a word or phrase triggered by previous posting) • Sheep (as in counting sheep, each person posts the next number or posts a picture with the number)
Non-Springsteen ongoing threads	• BTX Starbucks • BTX Pub • Threadkiller thread • Girls being chatty … and friends • For the guys—this will help those post-tour blues (female celebrity photos)
Miscellaneous	• Politics • Sports • Other (e.g., "my kid got accepted in college," "what are you having for dinner?" "worst Halloween candy," "need advice about X")

*Note: Ticket selling/exchange among members was done in other Backstreets forums.

interest are long-running, ongoing threads. For example, in December 2003, one member started the "Am I a thread killer?" thread by posting, "I don't know, it just seems that whenever I post a reply, that particular thread dies out ... I'm starting to develop a complex..." The thread remains active today, with more than 66,000 postings, and has emerged as an element of the content infrastructure for general conversation, with regular posters identifying themselves as "TKs."

BTX Infrastructure: Social Controls

BTX has strong democratic norms including "all are welcome here," reciprocity, fairness, civility, and altruism. While trading "Brucelegs"—amateur recordings of Springsteen concerts—was an ongoing activity on the board, there were also strong norms against buying and selling of bootlegs and against making copies of any music or videos that were commercially available. On rare occasions where a member had betrayed another member (e.g., reneging on a promise to buy tickets from another member or being a "bad trader"), these individuals were "called out" in public and effectively banned from the board by shunning, but only as a last resort after efforts to resolve the issue privately. It was also made clear that if the offender made restitution, he or she would be welcomed back. While the individual in question could re-register with a new identity, the individual lost whatever status he or she had previously accrued because the post count was reset to zero with the new identity. Most policing was done by the community, with people being urged to ignore inflammatory posts. Only in the case of the most flagrant abuses did members ask the BTX administrator to remove someone from the board.

Interestingly, there were no norms about appropriate content, that is, people could post on any topic as long as other norms (e.g., civility) were followed. Inflammatory posts, generally expressing political views, were tolerated, but flaming in the form of political or personal attacks directed toward an individual were not and could result in being removed from the board by the BTX administrator.

BTX Infrastructure: Technology

BTX runs on a version of phpBB, an open source bulletin board software package. As described earlier, discussions are organized into four general content areas. Table 8.2 provides an overview of the technology features of BTX. Perhaps the features that maintain history are the most critical in helping to sustain this community. For example, it is possible to learn when a registered member joined, how many times they have posted, and review all of their postings. These features help members assess the reputation and potential trustworthiness of an anonymous

Table 8.2 BTX Technology Features

Feature	Description
Search	Search prior posts by keyword or author.
Message formatting	Ability to modify font size, quoting, images, URL linking, emoticons. Ability to edit posts. Ability to easily create a poll/survey.
Permissions	All can view, only registered members can post.
Private messages	Ability to communicate privately with another registered user, one recipient at a time.
Member profiles	Post counts and date joined displayed for all members. User at his/her discretion can create a personal profile (e.g., location, e-mail address, occupation, URL for Web page). Ability to display ascending or descending list of members by date joined or number of posts.
Forum organization	Originally a single forum for all discussions. Currently four discussion forums organized by subject.
Forum administration	Ability to ban by e-mail address, username, single or multiple IP addresses, or host name. Ability for IP tracking of posts and posters. Ability to delete posts and censor screen names and posts by keyword.

Source: www.phpbb.com

individual. The ability to search and bump a thread makes it possible to revisit or reinforce issues within the community.

All four BTX discussion forums are administered by the *Backstreets* publisher, Christopher Phillips, who rarely intervenes, typically only in response to serious complaints from members (e.g., ticket scalping or abusive posts).[4] Registration with a valid e-mail address is required to post in any of the forums or to send a private message to another member, but no registration is required to view postings. However, individuals can register and post under multiple identities and some do.

Building Relational Cohesion at BTX

The Loose Ends forum began in April 2003 in the midst of the tour for Springsteen's *The Rising* CD. Initial exchanges revolved around sharing information about the tour itself such as availability of tickets or information about venues as well as discussions about specific shows such as "setlist watch" threads. The members also organized tailgate parties at a number of Springsteen concerts, which were open to the BTX community and provided an opportunity for members to actually meet. When the tour ended in October 2003, the discussions switched from concerts to exchanging bootlegs of concert performances, and ultimately as people became acquainted, to more general discussions unrelated either to Springsteen or to music more generally.

These exchanges created positive affect and helped build trust, leading to relational cohesion on the part of individual BTX members, and created social capital. With few exceptions, longtime members have not defected, they give token gifts often by offering to burn CDs for others or by providing "freebies"—copies of concerts—with nothing expected in return, and they continue to contribute content to the community.

A posting by a BTX member with the screen name of Killmo illustrates how the BTX infrastructure has helped create the relational cohesion and social capital that make BTX sustainable:

> I am not a techie nor do I profess to have a degree in ABMS,[5] lyrical prowess, Bruce history or anything else in this genre. I joined this board originally for information. For months I pretty much existed here without notoriety. Discussing Bruce, the concerts, drops, boots were all discussions that kept me coming back. But, at some point it seems that 24/7 Bruce is not going to keep a board alive. The droughts between concert tours leave little of Bruce left to discuss.
>
> But, the board has evolved into something much more than a music board. It has become a small virtual community, that in spite of its division at times, remains truly alive ... not just 10 posts made in a day by 10 different people. We joke, we laugh, we cry, we share, we donate ... pretty much illustrative of Bruce's philosophy. That is truly what keeps most of us coming back.

Creating Sustainable OCs

One of the key questions around the concept of CMs is what makes a particular CM successful? Here, infrastructure is hypothesized as the basis for adoption of this particular technology because it creates commitment to the community by its members. Given this theoretical background, which types of community activities are most likely to result in the emotional attributions that help sustain the community? Lawler (2001) hypothesized that joint tasks promote positive affect toward the social unit. Joint tasks are those characterized by non-separability, meaning none of the actors can complete the task alone, creating interdependence, such as a software development project in an open source community. As a result, it is difficult for members to take total credit for positive feelings resulting from a successful task (Lawler, 2001). Lawler argues that joint tasks are also likely to generate a sense of socially mediated self-efficacy, leading to such perceptions as the group can make things happen that individuals cannot accomplish on their own.

Self-efficacy is also a source of positive emotions (Lawler, 2001). Three examples from BTX illustrate the importance of joint tasks in building relational cohesion in this community.

"Karyn's Show"

First, the BTX community collectively defined itself by a single event which demonstrated for the first time that the community perceived it could engage in collective action beyond what any individual could accomplish on their own (Lawler, 2001).

On July 1, 2003, a person with the username "Molsonboy" made his first post:

> My wife and I were supposed to go to the Springsteen Concert in Philadelphia on August 8th. Unfortunately, she recently lost her battle to cancer a week and a half ago. She was only 34. ... I promised her that I would try my best to try and get a song dedicated to her at the concert. I have no idea how I can even get a request in to possible [sic] even to do that ... I know it is a HUGE, HUGE longshot but I am trying everything. Does anyone have ANY IDEA—No matter how silly it may seem—as to possible [sic] request this???

Many people responded with condolences and a wide range of suggestions, such as sending a letter to the concert venue including instructions for writing the letter or providing the mailing addresses for the management companies for Springsteen or members of his band. The morning after the concert, another BTXer posted the following:

> Incredible. Bruce did the dedication. God bless Karyn [Molsonboy's wife].

The bootleg for this concert was subsequently designated as "Karyn's Show." This thread remained active and was bumped to the top periodically with posts similar to this one reminding readers that "this is what we are all about":

> Because newbies should know, and oldies should be reminded.[6]

"Bruce Sent Me"

Second, the BTX community has also engaged in a number of organized efforts to support charitable causes including hunger organizations,

Habitat for Humanity, and Toys for Tots in the name of "Bruce Sent Me." Springsteen had a long history of social activism (Marsh, 2004). For example, during his tours he invited local hunger or other charitable organizations into the concert hall and made an announcement toward the end of each show encouraging his fans to contribute on the way out of the hall, and to get involved in their local community and make a difference. Inspired by his example, a BTXer with the screen name "Jersey Soul" posted the following on October 2, 2003 under the heading "Important End-of-Tour Update ("Bruce Sent Me")":

> As the tour ends, emotions—and credit card bills—are running high. We are excited about the Shea [final] shows, but we are sad that by this time next week the Rising Tour will be a memory. ... We cherish the sense of kinship we have found with Bruce friends old and new, while our spouses and bosses and friends and children have rolled their eyes at us for fourteen months. It's sad but true. ...
>
> So it is fitting that we do something in honor of this momentous occasion, to give back a little and to show that we have learned something along the ride ... this is one thing we can agree on: it is our job as part of a greater community to take care of those less fortunate, and let's face it, if you made it to even one show on this tour, then there are many less fortunate than you, and not just because they have never seen a sea of hands go up in the air during "Lonesome Day."
>
> Over the last year and change in the Bruce fan community, there have been so many acts of kindness that we'd need a separate board just to list them. It's time for one last round of generosity folks. ... What we are asking is that anyone who has been to ANY show(s) on this tour consider making a donation over the next few days in appreciation for the music and to prove that WITH THESE HANDS we are making a difference.
>
> There are many BTXers gathering on Saturday to celebrate/mourn the end of the tour. The tireless organizers of the party at the Metro Club will be conducting raffles and Springsteen quizzes, and collecting donations to benefit World Hunger Year and the Food Bank of NYC. If you are planning to attend the party and contribute there, great. But even if you are not, please consider doing the following.
>
> Go to [URLs] and go to their donations page. Make a contribution of whatever size you care to, and in the "comments" field of the donation form, tell them "Bruce sent me." ... The

idea is to demonstrate in a tangible way what a difference the music we love can make in the world.

In a subsequent post on October 7, 2003, Jersey Soul reported that the effort had raised over $5,500. Subsequently, "Bruce Sent Me" raised nearly $6,000 for the Community Food Bank of New Jersey, which had lost its only refrigerated truck and the contents just prior to Thanksgiving (Strauss, 2003). Commenting on an article in the *New York Times* about the donation, a BTX member with the screen name of Achtungsuz posted on November 23, 2003, "... a group of strangers, essentially leader-free, rallied and raised 1,000s of dollars via the Internet—and they all happen to be Springsteen fans."

"Bruce Sent Me" remains an ongoing part of the community's infrastructure (see www.brucesentme.com for more information). The community continues to be engaged in organized efforts to support a wide range of charitable causes in the form of virtual and non-virtual fundraisers and has raised in excess of $50,000 in addition to supporting other charitable causes (Culnan, 2005).

"Brucelegs" and Trading Trees

Third, a number of ongoing activities also illustrate the role of joint tasks in promoting sustainability. At BTX, physical exchanges among members of "Brucelegs" (CDs of concerts) are an important activity within the community and represent an ongoing joint exchange task. In particular, trading trees, where one member provides a copy of a concert and organizes a structure where the concert will be distributed to branches—other members who have volunteered to burn CDs for "leaves" on the tree—represent an activity that cannot be completed by a single individual. To successfully complete these exchanges, one individual needs to contact another through a private message to arrange the exchange (e.g., provide a mailing address). These exchanges create both positive affect and trust as members depend on other members to uphold their end of the trade, independent of any offline reinforcement. They are also an opportunity for trading partners to develop relationships with other members beyond simply responding to posts. Trading, then, increases positive feelings about the community as well as boosting interpersonal communication between members and involvement in the community itself (Lawler & Yoon, 1996; Quan-Haase & Wellman, 2004).

The Role of Offline Activities in Sustaining OCs

In addition to joint tasks, a factor that has helped sustain the BTX community is the ability of some BTX members to meet offline. Nohria and Eccles (1992), for example, argue that networked organizations require some level of face-to-face interaction to function successfully. In their case study of craigslist.org, Putnam and Feldstein (2003) argue that the local nature of the sites has contributed to building the relationships of trust and reciprocity that are central to social capital. There are similarities between BTX and Craigslist in that BTX is locally rooted to some extent.

While the members of BTX are geographically distributed, the community has a strong presence in New Jersey and metropolitan New York City, making it possible for relationships initiated online to be reinforced offline. Further, many Springsteen fans travel to see their hero and an organized BTX social event precedes many concerts. BTXers report having met each other offline at these events, as well as socializing offline with other members informally. It is interesting to note that another CM, e-commerce, has made it possible for geographically distributed members to participate in offline events because people can purchase tickets online from Ticketmaster.com as well as exchanging tickets with individuals using BTX or eBay, independent of where they live or the location of any given concert.

Conclusion

The BTX community serves as an interesting example of a specific OC CM under the general internetworking CM (Iacono & Kling, 2001). While much research has focused on the adoption of networking technologies within existing organizations, OCs form because the technology creates a "space" for the community independent of any existing formal organization, and the "death of distance" allows people to connect directly independent of geographic location. Even where the space for the community is provided by a company, here *Backstreets* magazine, the community is essentially an autonomous entity. This is in contrast to the case study presented by Quan-Haase and Wellman (Chapter 6, this volume) where a community of practice was created within an existing organization.

It is relatively simple to create the space for an OC. However, merely creating a space does not ensure that a viable community will form and sustain itself. The theory developed in this chapter provides a basis for understanding how technology and social context interact to result in thriving communities such as BTX, or conversely, why some communities fail.

However, it is the adoption of the democratization frame as the utopian vision by BTXers that also helps to explain the success of BTX at a more macro level. An informal scan of the discussion threads indicates that a wide range of members post, albeit with varying frequencies. New posters are welcomed online and invitations to the offline events are extended to all members. Differing points of view are largely tolerated. The public discourse around these norms contributes to retaining existing members and attracting new members. While the initial vision of a place for like-minded fans to congregate helped launch the community, it is this consensus around democratization, then, that helps maintain both a critical mass of members and the fresh content necessary to sustain the community, and provides a basis for social engagement by the members.

OCs offer many opportunities for interesting research. First, much of the existing research is cross-sectional. To understand how communities form and evolve over time, there is clearly a need for longitudinal research. For example, Fayard and DeSanctis (2005) analyzed postings from a knowledge management online discussion forum to understand how this particular OC evolved over the first 15 months of its existence. Longitudinal research is also needed to develop an understanding of how OCs as a CM are framed as the fit between the utopian vision and actual technology use evolves over time (Elliott & Kraemer, Chapter 1, this volume).

Second, research on OCs, like much other research in information systems or technology adoption, has treated the underlying technology as a black box (Markus, 2005; Orlikowski & Iacono, 2001). The OCs that have been the focus of research run on a variety of technology platforms. While the technology provides opportunities and constraints for the formation and maintenance of OCs, the specific features of the technology will influence adoption (Elliott & Kraemer, Chapter 1, this volume; Quan-Haase & Wellman, Chapter 6, this volume). To what extent do the features of these different technology platforms and the choices made by the site administrator who implemented the technology and the moderators who manage the community interactions enhance or inhibit the sustainability of the community? There is a need to identify a set of technology features that can be applied across technology platforms and to then investigate how different features and implementation choices enable or constrain the development of community. Currently there are several well-established Springsteen communities that run on different technology platforms and reflect different choices in terms of how each forum is administered. Their existence provides an opportunity to pursue such a research agenda.

Third, BTXers have engaged in altruistic behavior beyond the community itself such as contributing to charitable causes. Springsteen's fans were well aware of his social conscience from his lyrics, his commitment to community, and his support of various causes beginning with the Vietnam Veterans of America in the early 1980s (Marsh, 2004) and continuing to the present. Clearly Springsteen himself was one influence on the community, as the initial post about "Bruce Sent Me" illustrated. However, it is unlikely that Springsteen alone was responsible for these outcomes. Nonetheless, the collective activities of BTXers demonstrate that social engagement based on loosely coupled activity in large groups is possible and merits further investigation. What other factors serve as catalysts for these types of joint tasks and to what extent members of other OCs participate in similar pro-social activities beyond the community itself are empirical questions.

Finally, this research has focused primarily on community-level outcomes. Other research has investigated why individuals participate in OCs. For example, Wasko and Faraj (2005) investigated how individual motivations and individual social capital were related to knowledge contribution in a community of practice. Other researchers (e.g., Fayard & DeSanctis, 2005; Gu & Jarvenpaa, 2003; or Ma, 2004) have looked at social identity in OCs. As OCs exist only because of participation by individuals, further research on the roles individuals play in creating and sustaining OCs is also needed.

Acknowledgments

The author acknowledges the helpful comments of Margaret Elliott, Kenneth L. Kraemer, and the anonymous reviewers on earlier versions of this chapter. The chapter also benefited from discussions with John King.

Endnotes

1. BTX was originally set up as a trading area for fans to exchange tickets, and has since expanded into an online community. BTX now consists of six forums: three ticket forums; "The Promised Land" for talk about Bruce Springsteen; "The Vineyard" for nonprofit music sharing; and "Loose Ends" for everything else.
2. Resnick (2001) argues for a new construct, "sociotechnical capital," to refer to the productive combination of social relations with information and communication technologies. He goes on to argue that resources are purely social if they are accumulated as a side effect of prior interactions. They constitute capital if they enable people to accomplish more as a group, or improve the exchange of information or resources, or the ability to mobilize for collective action. Resources are sociotechnical if their production or use requires a combination of social relationships and technology.
3. Other Springsteen discussion forums include greasylake.org, josse.org, and the Springsteen section of livedaily.com. References in postings to these other communities and their members as distinct from BTX are another indication of community boundaries.
4. As of May 2006, Phillips had posted only 118 times as btxadmin, generally about site-related issues. It is not known whether he also participates using a separate identity. His 100th post was celebrated on Loose Ends.

5. ABMS is alt.binary.music.springsteen where bitstream versions of concerts could be downloaded. Killmo's post was in response to a post by someone complaining about the range of topics discussed on the board and advocating that discussions be limited to Springsteen.
6. On May 21, 2004, a member with the screen name "MDDave" made a post with the title "Mystery Solved? MDDave lives in a Small World." He wrote that his chiropractor, who had Nils Lofgren, one of the band members, as his patient, had made the connection with the Springsteen organization about the dedication. He stated that another BTXer had provided the doctor with an e-mail about the original posting, the doctor contacted Lofgren's manager who provided a fax number for Jon Landau, Springsteen's manager. The doctor then faxed the e-mail to Landau.

References

Armstrong, A., & Hagel III, J. (1996, May–June). The real value of on-line communities. *Harvard Business Review*, 134–141.

Blanchard, A. L., & Markus, M. L. (2004). The experienced "Sense" of a virtual community: Characteristics and processes. *The Data Base for Advances in Information Systems*, 35(1), 65–79.

Butler, B. S. (2001). Membership size, communication activity, and sustainability: A resource-based model of online social structures. *Information Systems Research*, 12(4), 346–362.

Connolly, T., & Thorn, B. K. (1990). Discretionary databases: Theory, data, and implications. In J. Fulk & C. Steinfeld (Eds.), *Organizations and communication technology* (pp. 219–233). Thousand Oaks, CA: Sage Publications.

Constant, D., Sproull, L. & Kiesler, S. (1996). The kindness of strangers: The usefulness of electronic weak ties for technical advice. *Organization Science*, 7(2), 119–135.

Culnan, M. J. (2005). The pro-social behavior of Springsteen fans: A case study of the BTX online community. Paper presented at Glory Days: A Bruce Springsteen Symposium, Monmouth University, September 9–11.

Cummings, J. N., Sproull, L. & Kiesler, S. B. (2002). Beyond hearing: Where real-world and online support meet. *Group dynamics: Theory, research and practice*, 6(1), 78–88.

Elliott, M. S., & Scacchi, W. (forthcoming). Mobilization of software developers: The free software movement. *Information, Technology and People*.

Fayard, A.-L., & DeSanctis, G. (2005). Evolution of an online forum for knowledge management professionals: A language game analysis. *Journal of Computer-Mediated Communication,* 10(4).

Fulk, J., Flanigan, A. J., Kalman, M. E., Monge, P. R., & Ryan, T. (1996). Connective and communal public goods in interactive communication systems. *Communication Theory*, 6(1), 80–87.

Galegher, J., Sproull, L., & Kiesler, S. (1998). Legitimacy, authority and community in electronic support groups. *Written Communication*, 15(4), 493–550.

Ginsburg, M., & Weisband, S. (2002). Social capital and volunteerism in virtual communities: The case of the Internet chess club. *Proceedings of the 35th Hawaii International Conference on System Sciences*, Hawaii, 1–10.

Granovetter, M. S. (1973). The strength of weak ties. *American Journal of Sociology*, 78(6), 1360–1380.

Gu, B., & Jarvenpaa, S. (2003). Online discussion boards for technical support: The effect of token recognition on customer contributions. *Proceedings of the 24th International Conference on Information Systems*, 110–120.

Iacono, S., & Kling, R. (2001). Computerization movements: The rise of the Internet and distant forms of work. In. J. Yates and J. Van Maanen (Eds.), *Information technology and organizational transformation: History, rhetoric and practice* (pp. 93–136). Thousand Oaks, CA: Sage Publications.

Kling, R., & Iacono, S. (1995). Computerization movements and the mobilization of support for computerization. In S. L. Starr (Ed.), *Ecologies of knowledge: Work and politics in science and technology* (pp. 119–153). Albany, NY: State University of New York Press.

Kollock, P. (1994). The emergence of exchange structures: An experimental study of uncertainty commitment and trust. *American Journal of Sociology*, 100(2), 313–345.

Lawler, E. J. (2001). An affect theory of social exchange. *American Journal of Sociology*, 107(2), 321–352.

Lawler, E. J. & Yoon, J. (1996). Commitment in exchange relations: Test of a theory of relational cohesion. *American Sociological Review*, 61(1), 89–108.

Ma, M. (Jessie). (2004). An identity-based theory of information technology design for sustaining virtual communities. *Proceedings of the Twenty-Fifth International Conference on Information Systems*, 559–570.

Markus, M. L. (1990). Toward a 'critical mass' theory of interactive media. In J. Fulk and C. Steinfeld (Eds.), *Organizations and communication technology* (pp. 194–218). Thousand Oaks, CA: Sage Publications.

Markus, M. L. (2005). The technology shaping effects of e-collaboration technologies—bugs and features. *International Journal of e-Collaboration*, 1(1), 1–23.

Marsh, D. (2004). *Bruce Springsteen: Two hearts, the definitive biography, 1972–2003*. New York: Routledge.

McWilliam, G. (2000). Building stronger brands through online communities. *Sloan Management Review*, 41(3), 43–54.

Muniz, A. M., & O'Guinn, T. C. (2001). Brand community. *Journal of Consumer Research*, 27, 412–432.

Nohria, N., & Eccles, R. G. (1992). Face-to-face: Making network organizations work. In N. Nohria & R. G. Eccles (Eds.), *Networks and organizations: Structure, form and action* (pp. 288–308). Boston: Harvard Business School Press.

Orlikowski, W. J., & Iacono, S. (2001). Research commentary: Desperately seeking the "IT" in IT research—a call to theorizing the IT artifact. *Information Systems Research*, 12(2), 121–134.

Papadakis, M. C. (2003). *People can create a sense of community in cyberspace.* Arlington, VA: SRI International.

Pew Internet and American Life Project (2001). *Online communities: Networks that nurture long-distance relationships and local ties*. Washington, DC: Pew Internet & American Life Project.

Poole, M. S., & DeSanctis, G. (1990). Understanding the use of group decision support systems: The theory of adaptive structuration. In. J. Fulk & C. Steinfeld (Eds.),

Organizations and communication technology (pp. 173–193). Thousand Oaks, CA: Sage Publications.

Putnam, R. D. (1995). Bowling alone: America's declining social capital. *Journal of Democracy*, 6(1), 65–78.

Putnam, R. D., & Feldstein, L. M. (2003). *Better together: Restoring the American community*. New York: Simon & Schuster.

Quan-Haase, A., & Wellman, B. (2004). How does the Internet affect social capital? In M. Huysman & V. Wulf (Eds.), *Social capital and information technology* (pp. 113–132). Cambridge: MIT Press.

Rafaeli, S., & LaRose, R. J. (1993). Electronic bulletin boards and "public goods" explanations of collaborative mass media. *Communication Research*, 20(2), 277–297.

Resnick, P. (2001). Beyond bowling together: Socio technical capital. In J. M. Carroll (Ed.), *HCI in the new millennium* (pp. 247–272). Reading, MA: Addison-Wesley.

Star, S. L., & Ruhleder, K. (1996). Steps toward an ecology of infrastructure design and access for large information spaces. *Information Systems Research*, 7(1), 111–134.

Strauss, R. (2003, November 23). When the feathers flew, Springsteen fans dug deep. *New York Times*, Section 14NJ, p. 3.

Wasko, M. M., & Faraj, S. (2000). "It is what one does": Why people participate and help others in electronic communities of practice. *Journal of Strategic Information Systems*, 9, 155–173.

Wasko, M. M., & Faraj, S. (2005). Why should I share? Examining social capital and knowledge contributions in electronic networks of practice. *MISQ Quarterly*, 29(1), 35–57.

Wasko, M. M., Faraj, S., & Teigland, R. (2004). Collective action and knowledge contribution in electronic networks of practice. *Journal of the Association for Information Systems*, 5(11), 493–513.

Watson, N. (1997). Why we argue about virtual community: A case study of the Phish.Net fan Community. In. S. Jones (Ed.), *Virtual culture: Identity and communication in cybersociety* (pp. 102–132). London: Sage Publications.

Wellman, B., Quan-Haase, A., Witte, J., & Hampton, K. (2001). Does the Internet increase, decrease or supplement social capital?: Social networks, participation and community commitment. *The American Behavioral Scientist*, 45(3), 436–455.

Part IV

Death of Distance

Chapter 9

Virtual Teams: High-Tech Rhetoric and Low-Tech Experience

Sara Kiesler
Carnegie Mellon University

Wai Fong Boh
Nanyang Technological University

Yuqing Ren
Carnegie Mellon University

Suzanne Weisband
University of Arizona

Abstract

Advances in telecommunications and computer technology have nourished visions of ideal technology use. One such vision is the concept of virtual teams. The rhetoric of virtual teams, like the rhetoric of other computerization movements, makes claims to greater efficiency, a better organization, and happier people. With virtual teams, managers reach across the geographically dispersed organization to staff project teams with the best experts at least cost. Employees enjoy working at a distance seamlessly, supported by technology. We describe the experiences of a professional, geographically dispersed organization that had to work across sites and might have nurtured virtual teams. Instead, the rhetoric of collaboration, not technology, inspired top management. Project managers did not create virtual teams, believing them to incur severe coordination costs. To foster collaboration, the company changed incentives, reorganized, and moved offices closer together. The company adopted networking technologies slowly and reluctantly. This low-tech company adapted successfully in an environment of high-tech advice and a cultural value for technology. The rhetoric of virtual teams seems to have shifted significantly in the last decade, perhaps in the face of such low-tech experiences.

Introduction

Recent advancement in computer and collaborative technologies has promoted growing interest in distributed work (Hinds & Kiesler, 2002). More and more organizations are becoming virtual and operate with businesses and employees dispersed in multiple geographic locations. As a result, project teams are increasingly composed of members who are spread across geographic and organizational boundaries. These dispersed project teams play a vital role in bringing together an optimal mix of expertise to accomplish joint objectives, to solve complicated problems, or to develop innovative solutions.

Although there are many ways of structuring distributed work (Grinter, Herbsleb, & Perry, 1999), the notion of distributed work from the 1980s to the present has been represented by concepts such as "virtual teams." Virtual teams are temporary work groups whose members are geographically separated rather than collocated but who work together using networked technologies to communicate and to share resources. The popular literature began to emerge in 1993, although the first book with the concept in the title was *Virtual Teams* by Jessica Lipnack and Jeffrey Stamps, published in 1997. A sizeable popular literature then followed. The literature included extravagant claims, for example, that virtual teams make companies more flexible (Townsend, DeMarie, & Hendrickson, 1998) and overcome the constraints of distance (Cairncross, 1997).

The concept of virtual teams has roots in the rhetoric of the internetworking computerization movement (CM) (Iacono & Kling, 2001) in which the meaning of the Internet has been built up or "framed" in macro-level discourses of the government, media, and scientific disciplines. These frames have mobilized large-scale support suggesting specific ways to use the technology within micro-social contexts such as in organizations. Iacono and Kling (2001) characterized the internetworking CM as a general CM spawning specific CMs such as "virtual teams" or "collaborative work."

During the early days of the virtual teams CM, organizations in practice gradually bought into the rhetoric and began adopting collaborative technologies in the hope of reducing time to market, minimizing costs, fostering innovation, and increasing organizational flexibility. As technologies become more and more diversified and sophisticated, organizations face the challenge of simultaneously understanding the role and impact of collaborative technologies while struggling to integrate these technologies into their organizational practices. Employees working in these organizations, likewise, strive to adapt to the technologies as they learn about their social and technical usage (Knoll & Jarvenpaa, 1995).

These observations led us to consider three sets of questions. First, who was responsible for the rhetoric of virtual teams, who adopted it, and how did this rhetoric change over time? Second, what kind of role does advanced technology play in enabling and facilitating virtual team arrangements? Third, to what extent did the rhetoric of the virtual teams CM motivate action in organizations and how did managers and professionals appropriate virtual team ideas into organizational practices? To answer these questions, we first examined the virtual teams rhetoric and traced the changes in the rhetoric across time by doing a content analysis of eighty-one popular books and magazine articles on the topic of virtual teams. We then conducted a case study examining the use of virtual teams in a professional service organization, to illustrate how rhetoric actually motivates action and gets transformed into organizational practices with or without the assistance of advanced technologies, and to highlight the gaps existing between rhetoric and reality.

In this chapter we first discuss the historical trajectory of the rhetoric behind the virtual teams CM. Next, we present our case study results of how an organization engaged the use of virtual teams, and instead of following the visions of the virtual teams rhetoric, adopted low technology solutions to virtual teaming.

Virtual Teams as Rhetoric

The concept of virtual teams has roots in the rhetoric of the internetworking CM of the late twentieth century, particularly in two ideas or "frames" of the internetworking CM: groups aided by technology, and death of distance. Iacono and Kling (2001) identified four layers of public discourse in which technological action frames are circulated: government, scientific disciplines, media, and organizational and professional discourses. Technological action frames that are promoted in the discourse of government and scientific disciplines are later adopted by individual organizational settings and specific professional groups (Iacono & Kling, 2001) and this adds operational specificity to the CM rhetoric. In this section we show how the virtual teams rhetoric spread in management consulting and academic literature, later influencing the development and use of virtual teams technology by technology developers and technology companies.

Early visions of groups aided by technology are represented in terms like "groupware" and "group decision support systems," that is, computer technology to help groups make expert decisions and share leadership (Grudin, 1994). Group decision support systems were first developed in the late 1960s and 1970s at military installations; 1980s versions were developed at Southern Methodist University, the University of Arizona, and the University of Minnesota. In 1989, IBM marketed TeamFocus as a product. It was used mainly to support collocated meetings for brainstorming.

Early visions of working across distance were represented in public discourse using terms like "information highway," "telecommuting," and "distant work" as technological action frames that promoted people and organizations to invest in collaborative technologies (Iacono & Kling, 2001). The virtual teams rhetoric circulating in early versions of public discourse particularly emphasized the organizational uses of e-mail and distribution lists, which would transform organizations and free employees to work at any location.

After 1995, with the dissemination and technical advances of the Internet, these early vocabularies gave way to terms like "computer-supported cooperative work" (CSCW), "virtual teams," and "online communities," each encompassing forms of geographically distributed collaboration. The idea of distributed collaboration harked back to the early days of networking, when Roxanne Hiltz and Murray Turoff published *The Network Nation: Human Communication Via Computer* in 1978, about group collaborative work at a distance.[1] "Virtual teams" neatly captured the idea of collaboration over distance in groups using technology. The virtual teams discourse as a topic in technology development circles started cropping up in academic conferences such as the International Conference on Information Systems (ICIS) and CSCW in the 1980s. The first three CSCW conferences were attended primarily by technologists from software product development companies (almost 40 percent) and technology researchers at universities (30 percent); a minority were from the telecommunications sector, social sciences, and business (5–10 percent) (Grudin, 1994, p. 21). In several of the ensuing years, panels on the CSCW program discussed the failures of CSCW to support real or virtual teams, but invariably panelists argued that when technology improved, CSCW would be a success. From the mid-1990s to the present, technology companies and entrepreneurs marketed many new technology ideas within the framework of virtual teams, and management consultants and the media picked up the idea as well.

The public discourse on the virtual teams CM in the form of management consulting literature on virtual teams, and the media that disseminated this literature, took off seriously in the 1990s as employees got easier access to the Internet, and work organizations incorporated networking and online facilities into routine office communications. The management consulting rhetoric surrounding virtual teams appears to have closely resembled rhetoric surrounding management fads and fashions, such as process reengineering, self-organizing teams, quality circles, management by objectives, and total quality management (e.g., Abrahamson, 1996; Hackman & Wageman, 1995; Zbaracki, 1998). That rhetoric has two important attributes: (1) statement of a serious business problem, and (2) excessive claims (including success stories) that the new approach solves this problem.

An example follows. According to the Wikipedia, the online community encyclopedia, virtual teams help organizations overcome geographic distance and allow them to hire and retain the best people regardless of location. More specifically, companies need virtual teams for the following reasons:

- Best employees may be located anywhere in the world.
- Workers demand personal flexibility.
- Workers demand increasing technological sophistication.
- A flexible organization is more competitive and responsive to the marketplace.
- Workers tend to be more productive, i.e., they spend less time on commuting and travel.
- The increasing globalization of trade and corporate activity.
- The global workday is 24 vs. 8 hours.
- The emergence of environments that require inter-organizational cooperation as well as competition.
- Changes in workers' expectations of organizational participation.
- A continued shift from production to service/knowledge work environments.
- Increasing horizontal organization structures characterized by structurally and geographically distributed human resources.

This problem statement implies that organizations need to adapt to major changes in the nature of the firm and the needs of "the best" employees. Virtual teams are a solution in three ways: The organization will be more efficient, employees will be empowered and more effective, and business processes will be transformed to create a more successful organization. Thus: "The virtual team will enable organizations to become more flexible by providing the impressive productivity of team-based designs in environments where teamwork would have once been impossible" (Townsend, et al., 1998).

Communities Adopting Virtual Teams Rhetoric

Several communities beyond that of management consultants adopted the rhetoric of virtual teams. An important community was that of technology developers and technology companies. The rhetoric of virtual teams helped developers and companies sell themselves on investments in new virtual teams technology, and helped these same companies sell technology-based support and consulting services to businesses. Thus, by 2000, a good number of large companies were installing centralized services (and hiring consultants) for "knowledge management," including intranets, shared task management software, shared calendars, discussion databases, intelligent document repositories offering library services, and virtual workspaces. Software products to support virtual teams included IBM's Lotus Notes, Microsoft's NetMeeting, Livelink, OpenText, Intraspect, Documentum, eRoom, and NetGroove, the latter created in 1997 by Ray Ozzie, a creator of Lotus Notes. "It's all you need to get your files, projects, meetings, and data all in one place so your team can get on the same page" (from NetGroove's Web page, www.groove.net).

In the technology community, the rhetoric of virtual teams expanded over time to embrace newer technologies, including those loosely tied to the assumptions underlying original arguments for virtual teams (see Zbaracki, 1998). For example, mobile, wireless devices would aid workers "on the go," implicitly acknowledging the continuing role of travel in collaboration. (Virtual teams were supposed to reduce travel.) All of the books and articles we examined advocated adopting the latest computer-based technologies and applications, ranging from instant messaging to palm-top devices.

Virtual teams rhetoric also was embraced and adapted by policymakers in the science and technology arena. An idea closely related to that of virtual teams is "collaboratory." A collaboratory is an organization and online system for supporting collaborative science. In the late 1980s, technologists and technology analysts such as Tom Malone (Olson, Malone, & Smith, 2001) (the economic value of cooperative decentralized systems) and William Wulf (Kouzes, Myers, & Wulf, 1996) (collaboratories for science) had published policy papers on collaboratories. Several federal initiatives followed, such as the Department of Energy's Collaborative Laboratories (www.doecollaboratory.org/history.html).[2] Elite technology industry executives, computer scientists, and scientists such as Nobel prize winner Josh Lederberg (Lederberg & Uncapher, 1989), issued reports to the President (e.g., President's Information Technology Advisory Committee (PITAC)) and to Congress, advocating much higher federal investments in computing and collaborative research programs. NSF's Knowledge and Distributed Intelligence and Information Technology Research research programs are among many that followed, supporting collaborative interdisciplinary research teams. The virtual teams concept gained credibility within this milieu. Thus, the PITAC report of February 14, 1999, "Information Technology Research: Investing in Our Future," said:

> Vision: Research is conducted in virtual laboratories in which scientists and engineers can routinely perform their work without regard to physical location—interacting with colleagues, accessing instrumentation, sharing data and computational resources, and accessing information in digital libraries. All scientific and technical journals are available on-line, allowing readers to download equations and databases and manipulate variables to interactively explore the published research.[3]

Another community that connected with virtual teams rhetoric was the academic community in the fields of organization science, information systems, and computer science. A number of scholars studied virtual teams and the innovations and behaviors surrounding distributed work (e.g., Iacono & Weisband, 1997; Jarvenpaa & Leidner, 1999). Although much of this work described the problems involved in dispersed projects and distributed work, the discourse in scientific disciplines added credence to the value of virtual teams. Thus, academic case studies and discussion of improvements in team process supported by technology probably legitimized virtual teams rhetoric.

In addition, theoretical developments in organization science gave implicit support to an ideal of virtual teams. The most prominent example of such theory is the knowledge-based view of the firm, which argues that the organization's most valuable resource and core competence is its ability to create, store, and apply knowledge to produce goods and services (Grant, 1996a, 1996b). Virtual teams are a natural corollary to the knowledge-based view. Utilizing expertise to deliver services to clients often requires bringing together specialized experts on a team (Demsetz, 1991). Hence the organization's competence is reflected not only in the quality and quantity of its individual experts but also in the integration of its knowledge resources through its deployment of people in project teams to create, respond to, and execute business opportunities (Grant 1996a, 1996b; Teece, 1998). Nordhaug and Gronhaug (1994) advocated a portfolio of competence—a collaborative blending of experts who, together, would perform better than competitors (see also Maister, 1993). Customers would value teams in which high expertise was matched to project requirements (Miner, Crane, & Vandenberg, 1994). Such teams also would have a broad social network that would bring in other resources (Cummings, 2004) and buffer the firm from price competition (Podolny, 1993). In short, knowledge-based theory suggests that if managers create teams with members drawn from across the organization, with an optimal mix of expertise matched to customers' requirements, then the organization's competitive advantage will be improved. Within this framework, the virtual team, linked through technology, offers an unprecedented opportunity to combine knowledge resources effectively and for competitive advantage across time and space.

Virtual Teams Rhetoric Over Time

To investigate changes over time in the rhetoric of the virtual teams CM, we performed a content analysis of the main themes of 81 popular books and magazine articles whose topic was virtual teams. We searched Web sites, newspaper and magazine databases (e.g., ABI/INFORM, Lexis-Nexis), bibliographies, and both online and offline bookstores. Our keywords were "virtual teams," "global teams," "distant teams," "virtual collaboration," and "distributed work." We selected public discourse in the form of newspapers, trade magazines, and popular books that touted the benefits of virtual teams. We excluded book reviews and interviews with book authors, and any software application that would help virtual teams (e.g., videoconferencing) or that focused on technology as a product announcement, telecommuting, or distant education. Finally, because there were so many Web sites associated with management consultants on virtual teams and collaboration, we excluded them in order not to bias our sample.

In our analysis, we coded each book and article's main themes, then grouped these themes into four categories: efficiency, effectiveness, people, and challenge. Figure 9.1[4] shows our results. The efficiency theme, emphasizing claims for saving money, spanning distance, reducing travel, cost savings, or time savings, was a major theme of 27 percent of the books and articles throughout the period of our sample, 1993 to 2004.

We coded claims of positive qualitative change either as "effectiveness" (transforming collaborations, doing new kinds of work) or "people" (recruiting better people, finding the best experts, empowering employees). Our data indicate that these claims peaked in the dot.com era, 1998–2001, and thereafter declined. By 2002, only 25 percent of the books and articles used effectiveness as a major theme and 10 percent used people. Also, we saw an increase in a major theme we call "challenge." In this category, we coded the books and articles that had as a major theme that virtual teams posed some difficulties, and proposed

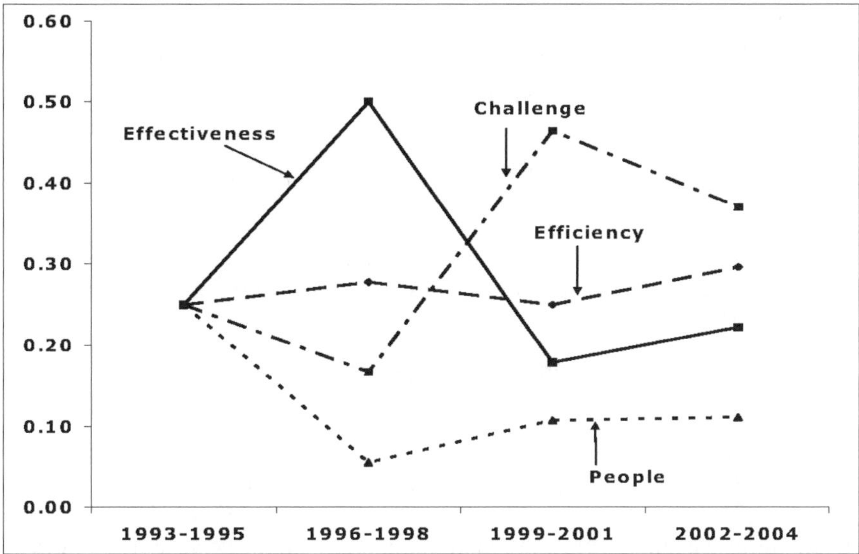

Figure 9.1 Major themes of 81 trade books and magazine articles about virtual teams

approaches for creating and managing successful teams. For instance, the Wikipedia entry cited earlier lists the "critical success factors of virtual teams" as:

- The existence of availability standards.
- Ample resources to buy and support state-of-the-art reliable communication and collaboration tools for all team members.
- The existence of corporate memory systems such as lessons learned databases.
- The existence of written goals, objectives, project specifications, and performance metrics; results orientation.
- Managers and team members with a better-than-average ability to accurately estimate.
- A lower-than-normal ratio of pushed to pulled information.
- Team communication is prioritized by the sender.
- Human resource policies, reward/recognition systems as well as career development systems address the unique needs of virtual workers.
- Good access to technical training and information on how to work across cultures.

- Training methods accommodate continual and just-in-time learning.
- There are standard and agreed-on technical and "soft" team processes.
- A "high trust" culture; teamwork and collaboration are the norm.
- Leaders set high performance expectations; model behaviors such as working across boundaries and using technology effectively.
- Team leaders and members exhibit competence in working in virtual environments.

Exhortations like these acknowledge numerous boundary conditions for virtual team success. Nonetheless, rhetorical excess is still evident in the use of buzz phrases such as "high trust" and "model behaviors," and in the implication that problems are caused by factors extrinsic to the virtual teams approach itself. For example, in the list just given, managers are required to provide adequate training, adequate technology investment, and proper organizational incentives. Employees must have good motivation. Companies must have the right culture. The rhetoric of virtual teams continues while acknowledging difficulties of implementation.

Virtual Teams Case Study

While the rhetoric of virtual teams has moderated over time to acknowledge difficulties in ensuring virtual team success, the evidence from case studies suggests that some companies, particularly those involved in the invention or manufacturing of advanced technology, took arguments about virtual teams seriously (e.g., Boeing: Majchrzak, Malhotra, Stamps, & Lipnack, 2004). Nonetheless, our knowledge about how the arguments led or did not lead organizations to organize around virtual teams is still limited. Institutional theory suggests that symbolism can replace action in organizations (Meyer & Rowan, 1977). Previous studies of management-related rhetoric have shown how using rhetoric to gain legitimacy can support managerial practices that stay essentially the same (Zbaracki, 1998). If so, the rhetoric of virtual teams would have left behavior in organizations fundamentally untouched. We do not know whether few, some, or most organizations that adopted the rhetoric of virtual teams actually organized around virtual teams. We particularly do not know much about "low-tech" organizations, such as professional organizations not in the business of selling technology. To fill this gap, we traced and examined the impact of the virtual teams concept in a low-tech professional organization.

Research Setting

The organization we studied was American Institutes for Research (AIR). Founded in 1946, AIR is a successful, nonprofit organization that carries out applied research, consulting, and technical services. Business in AIR typically is conducted through team projects or engagements. Before AIR can do project work, it must sell its expertise to its customers within a highly competitive business environment. Its competitors include RAND, Educational Testing Service, SAS Inc., Research Triangle Institute, and Westat, among many others. Its customers include U.S. federal agencies such as the Department of Education and the Census Bureau, state governments, private and public companies, and foreign governments. From 1996 to 2002, AIR employed more than 1,000 employees at seven major locations and a number of minor locations. Its ability to win projects depends on pulling together project teams whose members have the expertise customers want for their projects.

Most of the data about AIR are drawn from a study of how managers decided to create dispersed projects from 1996 through 2000 (Boh, Ren, Kiesler, & Bussjaeger, 2005). We also conducted a follow-up analysis of dispersed projects in the organization in the first 10 months of 2002. Finally, from 1996 through 2002, we monitored and documented top management decisions that were meant to effect collaboration across sites. These decisions included changes in the incentive structure for collaboration, a major reorganization of the firm, geographic relocation of offices, and various modest investments in technology. We also interviewed managers and professionals about their experience of managing and working in dispersed project teams. In total, we interviewed five site directors and nine project managers for the period 1996–2000, and we conducted follow-up interviews with the CIO and four other project managers in 2002.

Rhetorical Influence

Around 1996, the Chief Operating Officer (COO) of AIR, at the behest of an AIR Board member, read a book on professional organizations by the management consultant David Maister (1993). The book articulated many ideas that surround the idea of virtual teams—company-wide utilization of expertise, collaboration, and teamwork. AIR had recently expanded through mergers and acquisitions from its original three major sites to six. Maister's book, and the support of some Board members, led the COO to recognize a problem the organization now faced: how to utilize expertise across the growing firm. The COO liked Maister's book so much he ordered copies for all senior managers in the firm and all Board members. With Board encouragement, AIR's top management set a goal of increasing collaboration and joint projects across the organization's sites. A few years later, the COO became the CEO of the company and the driving force for collaboration across geographic locations.

Obstacles to Collaboration

At AIR, because projects were managed locally at each site, collaboration would require managers at different sites to draw on employees from other sites for their projects, or to give employees' time to a different site to work on a distant project. Professionals at AIR typically would not relocate to serve on a project team run by another site; they would work on the project at a distance. Thus, to improve collaboration, AIR managers would have to form dispersed projects in the mold of virtual teams.

Figure 9.2[5] provides a snapshot of dispersed project work across sites in the six main AIR sites in 1996. Arrows pointing to one site from another site represent the number of dispersed projects at a focal site that drew on at least one professional employed by a source site. As the figure shows, dispersed projects were not part of normal business at AIR; in fact, they were rare—only 3 percent of all projects included anyone from another site and only 9 percent of employees worked on a project managed at another site.

Coordination Costs

Managers said they objected to dispersed projects because they carried high coordination costs, which included significant search and team assignment costs because managers did not have an intimate knowledge

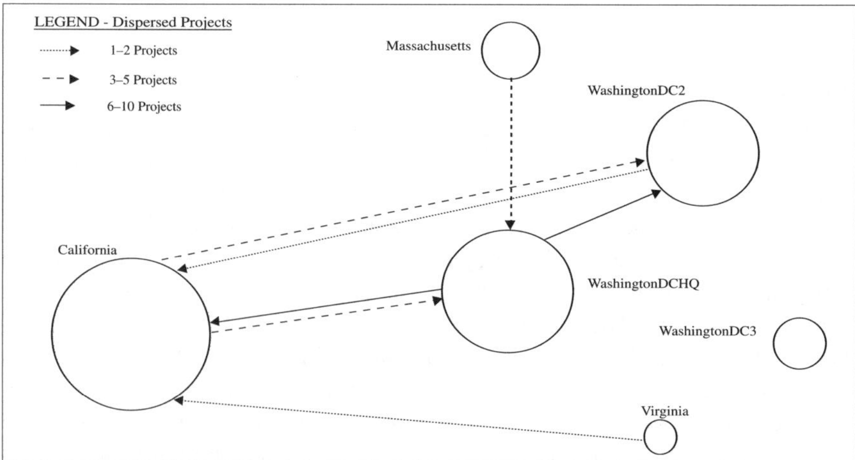

Figure 9.2 Collaboration across sites, 1996 (N = 241 projects, 6 sites)

of employees at distant sites (Finholt, 1993). Coordination costs also were involved in the management of interdependent but dispersed project work. Contrary to what is claimed in the virtual teams rhetoric, members of dispersed project teams spent more rather than less time traveling.

> One [factor] is cost and collaborating across sites increases your costs significantly. ... [O]ne of the major people on this project lives in [city 2,800 miles away] so she has to fly in so we can all meet. That's really expensive. Phone calls, videoconferences, I mean they all add up, the amount of time you have to spend I think really talking through things where you could walk down the hall and have these communications. [Project Manager B]

The assumption, implied here, that talking is essential to project coordination, permeated all of our study interviews. Any financial or physical factor that delayed conversation or inhibited people from talking and sharing information was considered to be a significant cost, given that projects had to be completed within the constraints of the contracted work, on time, and within budget.

> There are few hours in a day overlapping between our normal hours. ... It is not a big deal as long as you are not under immediate pressure to get information ... as long as you are not under crunch, say you need information within the next twelve hours, then that time can be too problematic. [Project Manager C]

Another source of coordination cost in dispersed projects was a perceived lack of direct awareness and control. Awareness and control were possible in local projects because project members and the project manager could observe project activity directly. In dispersed projects, managers could not directly oversee what was happening at other sites.

> [Dispersed project work] can be difficult because when things start to go wrong, you catch it a lot later than you would if it was going wrong in your own office. It's harder to see things going on and when you do, it's harder to figure out exactly where the problem is and where to fix it. ... So for me one of the biggest disadvantages is the cost that [dispersed project work] adds to the project. [Project Manager D]

We thought some employees might be attracted to work at a distance because of the autonomy and flexibility it would permit. But interviewees said that few employees were eager to work on distant projects and nobody especially liked working with distant co-workers. The only advantage of distant work articulated in interviews was that it could offer an opportunity to enter a hot area or improve one's skills, reflected in this comment: "People get exposed to projects they wouldn't in the local office. It helps people's expertise and professional development" [Project Manager A].

Incentive Structure

Perhaps an even more serious obstacle to collaboration was the incentive structure at AIR. Although project and site managers rarely discussed these incentives openly, they were evident in annual reports of each site, which before 1997 never mentioned collaboration or AIR as a whole, and always discussed work at the site. The company, like many professional and technical organizations, was organized as distributed businesses, whereby each office (a site in a different geographic location) grew its own customer base and managed its own costs. The compensation and bonuses for site and project managers were tied to their site's revenue growth, the size of its net earnings (profit), and limiting its indirect costs. Because of the way staff time was counted in calculating growth, revenues, profit, and costs, collaborating with other sites had negative implications for managers. Labor costs, the main portion of revenues and profits, were assigned to the site managing each project. If a site created a virtual team project, bringing in employees from another site, the focal site would have the credit for the hours spent on the project by these team members whereas the source site, the home office of these team members, would lose these hours. Likewise, if a site was asked to send an employee to work on a distant project, that employee would be unavailable locally and the source site would not get credit for that employee's contributions to project revenues.

Managers' bias to staff projects at their own sites, because of the incentive structure of the company, also had ripple effects on the structure of work and expertise in the organization. Each site hired and developed the expertise needed most frequently to staff projects locally. As local work increased, local forms of expertise became each site's most frequently used type of expertise, well suited to existing customers. For example, sites with most of their customers from the education domain developed an expertise in this domain and hired experts with this domain in mind. By 1996 when we started the study, AIR's distribution of expertise across sites was tuned to local expertise and nonrandomly distributed. Each site specialized in one or two types of expertise (mainly a domain expertise) and formed local projects that employed this frequently used expertise (see Boh et al., 2005).

Changing Incentives for Collaboration

When it became clear to management that the site-level reward structure undermined managers' motivation to collaborate across sites and failed to offset perceived coordination costs of dispersed projects, top management tried to change site directors' incentives. If a staff member worked on a project at a distant site, the earnings of that employee would accrue to the site that "owned" this employee. This change in the incentive structure lowered the barriers to collaboration and led to a noticeable increase in the number of dispersed projects and some encouraging project outcomes.

Figure 9.3 shows how the number of dispersed projects had increased by the year 2000. The company had created more collaborative dispersed projects, although these remained a minority of the overall work. The CEO's and other top managers' attitudes about collaboration had become increasingly positive as well. One reason for this attitude change was their experience with atypically high revenues and profits of dispersed projects. In other words, some collaborations were paying off (Boh et al., 2005). This fortuitous outcome occurred for two reasons. First, site and project managers self-selected to create and bid dispersed projects when the value and visibility of the projects were expected to be unusually high; otherwise they would not be willing to incur and bear the higher coordination costs associated with these projects. The opportunity to win

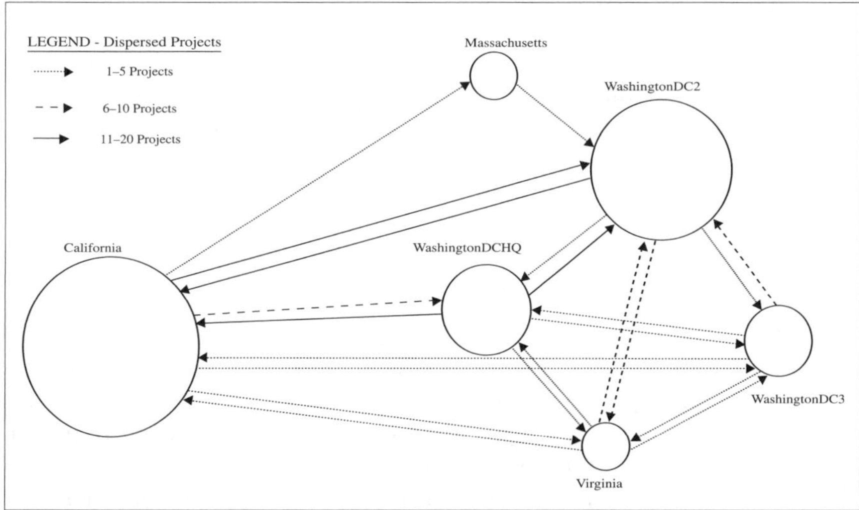

Figure 9.3 Collaboration across sites, 2000 (N = 289 projects, 6 sites)

a bid for a large, profitable, and visible project increased the likelihood that managers would overcome their reluctance to collaborate with other sites, either by enlisting other sites' staff members on the project to obtain desirable expertise, or by releasing a valued staff member to work on a project employed at another site. Second, managers were motivated to create dispersed projects when they could not satisfy customers using local frequently used expertise. In such cases, where a potential customer required scarce expertise unavailable locally, site and project managers, often with pressure from upper management, solicited these scarce experts from other sites. Such projects tended to attract high revenues and fees because, in customizing to the needs of the customer, the company was more competitive and price insensitive, and because the experts involved were highly paid professionals, which would have increased revenues as well.

> I think the most useful thing [about dispersed project work] is the availability of expertise that you don't necessarily have in our office. [Project Manager C]

Interviewees said that management's view of the value of the bid could be a determining factor in whether the project obtained the most valuable staff, even considering additional costs that might be incurred.

> A manager may see a business opportunity, and decide the organization should put a bid in on it, and the site manager agrees, and they put the bid in ... and that manager can pick from anybody in the whole [organization]—the best people to staff that piece of work. [Project Manager H]

> [It's] largely dependent on the sort of profile and attention the project is getting. I think [with] a higher profile, more important project, I have better access to some people [at other sites] ... [compared with a] small, low profile project. [Project Manager G]

Changing Structure

In 2001, the CEO reorganized the company to create a structure that would better support cross-site collaboration. The new organization did away completely with geographic site-level directors and with financial record keeping by geographic categories, except as required by government contracting requirements. (The CEO reported to one of the authors: "As long as we were keeping track of site-level revenues, nothing fundamental was changing. We had to do away with [these records].") The new organization consisted of two major divisions that crossed geographic locations, headed up by two division chiefs, and programs (comprised of domain-related projects) within each division. The reorganization acknowledged management's goal of fostering collaboration regardless of geography. The CEO announced that all measurements of geographically based financial performance at the site level would cease.

The CEO decided to move three sites in Washington, DC into one building to create closer physical ties in the organization. In doing so, he recognized the value of collocation. Indeed, he would have moved the Maryland office as well if an existing lease had not precluded such a move. The CEO also gave notice that collaboration would be the new way of doing normal business. These pronouncements were meant to ensure more collaboration across locations, although managers reported that California and Massachusetts still had "different cultures." The CEO encouraged the new division directors to make many trips to California. These directors and managers of programs that spanned Washington and California held monthly and sometimes weekly planning meetings across sites.

By 2002, collaboration across sites had increased to almost 30 percent of all projects run by the six original sites in our study. Figure 9.4, covering just 10 months of 2002, shows how these collaborations were patterned. Collaboration increased in Washington across the three (former) offices. California continued to collaborate with Washington but was more likely to send people out than bring them in. This trend may reflect the fact that business in Washington grew (in two sites, especially) more than it did in California, putting more pressure on staff in the former to fill positions. Figure 9.5 shows collaboration across the original sites plus new domestic sites. These sites reflect acquisitions, business in new areas, and the hiring of experts who could not relocate. Overall collaboration across sites (including former sites now collocated in the same building) was more dense, almost 40 percent of all projects, even as the organization was adding sites in different states and branching out into more domain areas. These data suggest that collaboration had become better accepted and integrated into the normal business of the company. The original idea of virtual teams had evolved into workable arrangements for distributed work.

Role of Technology

AIR achieved a goal of collaboration without much assistance from technology, contradictory to what is suggested in the virtual teams rhetoric. AIR, as compared with companies such as Microsoft, Sun, IBM, and other technology firms, was a latecomer to networking technology and slow to invest in the technology resources needed to support virtual

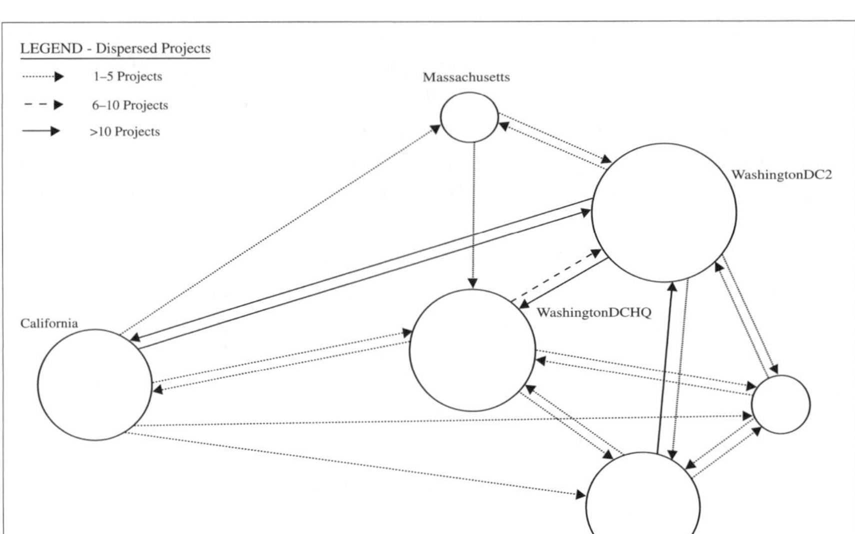

Figure 9.4 Collaboration across sites, 2002 (N = 222 projects [10 months], 6 sites)

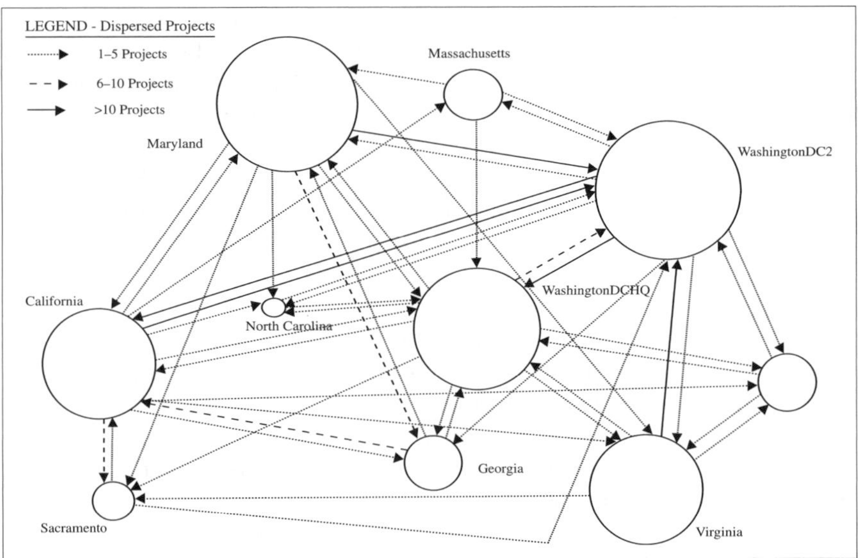

Figure 9.5 New domestic sites and collaboration across all sites, 2002 (N = 273 projects [10 months], 10 sites)

teams. AIR staff did not resist technology, but were not enthusiastic about it either. The company's California office implemented a local area network (LAN) in the 1980s, and the New England office was an industry leader in usability engineering. Upper management did not consider technology and technology integration to be a solution to organizational issues or to contribute significantly to business. The company did not appoint a CIO until 2000 and rather than conducting a national search, management moved a former site director with an interest in technology into the position. Despite reporting directly to the CEO, this person lacked power and influence.

Even by 2003, resources for sharing files and collaborative work spaces were "primitive" (from interview with CIO, July 2003). While the use of videoconferencing increased after the restructuring in 2002, most of the other technologies were still in an early stage of development. For instance, a shared calendar of events was put on the intranet only in 2003, and in the same year a shared database for obtaining information about professional staff experience and expertise was still incomplete. Virtual teams continued to depend predominantly on e-mails, telephone calls, and audioconferencing for distributed work. There were no sophisticated technologies such as team rooms or application sharing for cross-site collaboration. In 2003, each site was still on a different LAN; hence shared folders existed for employees only within the same site.

Organization structure for technology development and support also grew piecemeal. By the 1980s, AIR had an information technology (IT) department for computer support and programming, especially support for statistical work. In the mid 1990s, a separate telecommunications department was established. Finally, AIR appointed a small group to work on the intranet. Development and control of the intranet, staffed by Web site developers, were separate from the IT department, staffed by support personnel, and both were separate from telecommunications. Thus, AIR did not treat shared information, voice, and data communication as interrelated resources.

Throughout the period of our observations, managers did not see a strong connection between investments in technology and collaboration. Thus, as compared with the rhetoric of virtual teams, at AIR, technology and technology support were given a far lower priority. The CEO authorized investments in technology only as they could be demonstrated to support business operations. Because dispersed project collaborations were comparatively rare, the firm's major work did not require advanced technology, and the link to business success was not evident, the company avoided major investments in collaborative technology.

Discussion of the Case Study

Our study of AIR revealed a low-tech organization that embraced some key arguments of virtual teams rhetoric but without the technology dimension. Namely, management and employees, over time, adopted the belief that their geographically dispersed company would need to collaborate across sites and that dispersed team projects would utilize expertise effectively. Collaboration over distance did increase, as shown in Table 9.1.

Table 9.1 Distributed Collaboration Over Time

	Number of dispersed projects	Percentage of dispersed projects	Number of distant members	Percentage of distant members
1996	8	3%	80	9%
2000	38	13%	158	11%
2002 (10 months)	67	30%	571	22%

However, AIR never bought into the technology-laden elements of virtual teams rhetoric. From 1996 through the first 10 months of 2002, when we stopped collecting data, AIR had not created any truly virtual teams, that is, teams where many members were dispersed through the organization and communicated mainly using technology. The number of dispersed team projects involving at least one member from another site did increase significantly over time, but collaboration involved considerable face-to-face interaction and comparatively modest technology, "primitive" as the belatedly appointed CIO reported.

We speculate, with some justification in the literature, that AIR's experience was not unique. First, we guess that many, if not most, companies experienced coordination costs in the pursuit of virtual teams (Iacono & Kling, 2001). Studies have shown that many virtual teams fail or get bogged down with delays (Herbsleb & Mockus, 2003), misunderstandings among project members (Cramton, 2001), site rivalries (Armstrong & Cole, 2002), free riding (Weisband, 2002), distraction from the work due to local site priorities (Mark, Chapter 10, this volume; Mark, Grudin, & Poltrock, 1999), inconsistent procedures across sites (Curtis, Krasner, & Iscoe, 1988), and inability to share information and address conflict (Hinds & Mortensen, 2005; Hinds & Zolin, 2004). This gap between the vision of a CM and actual consequences of organizational use of the CM technology can result in contending discourse in which altered use of the technology is reported (Iacono & Kling, 2001). Thus, AIR managers would not have been alone in believing that virtual teams relying mainly on technology are a difficult and risky business. AIR is also not unique in its low dependence on technology for supporting virtual teamwork. A recent survey of 344 organizations in the United States, Australia, and Hong Kong examining the adoption and use of collaboration information technologies (CITs) found that only two CITs, e-mail and audio teleconferencing, have been widely adopted in these organizations (Bajwa, Lewis, Pervan, & Lai, 2005). Similar results have been found in Jarman's (2005) study of dot-com companies where virtual teams made use of only e-mail, telephone, and audioconferencing to support virtual teamwork, and in Im, Yates, and Orlikowski's study (Im, Yates, & Orlikowski, 2005) of a start-up organization where members relied on phone meetings to coordinate their distributed software development.

We also speculate that AIR's low tech approach—that is, its restructuring of its incentive system, reorganization, and physical relocations to foster collaboration—is not unique either. Some companies are now considering collocation as the best way to support collaboration in teams (Olson, Teasley, Covi, & Olson, 2002). If these speculations are correct, perhaps the rhetoric of the virtual teams CM will result in contending discourse with moderated or changed visions.

Concluding Remarks

Our analysis indicates that there are at least two worlds of virtual teams, one in high-tech rhetoric and one in the low-tech organization we studied. In the high tech rhetoric, virtual teams instantiate the virtues of collaboration across distance, enabled by technology. The idealized vision has changed over time, presumably adjusting to organizations' experience, but remains fundamentally a CM. That is, virtual teams could not operate without the "state of the art technology" mentioned in the Wikipedia list. By contrast, the world view of virtual teams in the low tech world we studied also instantiates the virtues of collaboration over distance, but without the dependence on technology. Indeed, there are no teams connected only by networked communications. There are no state-of-the-art collaboration and communication tools (though there are old, reliable ones). In this low-tech world, what matters are managers who know they must collaborate to compete.

Where might this end? We think rhetoric of the virtual teams CM will continue to evolve and to motivate technology development. As a matter of fact, technology companies and developers have never wavered in their confidence over advanced collaborative technologies as an ultimate solution to challenges faced by virtual teams (Hildreth, 2005). The academic community, nonetheless, has adopted a more realistic view of virtual teams. Acknowledging the complexity and challenges inherent in distributed collaboration, organizational scholars, for instance, have shifted their focus to understanding organizational conditions or processes that might have resulted in these challenges, and to exploring possible ways of addressing the challenges. Recent studies on subgroup dynamics (Mortensen & O'Leary, 2005), leadership at a distance (Weisband, forthcoming), and cultural diversity in internationally distributed teams (Cramton & Hinds, 2005) have provided new theoretical insights and managerial implications in creating and managing successful virtual teams.

We have also observed changes in the rhetoric to "global online communities" rather than "virtual teams" per se. As organizations acknowledge the difficulties of using technology to bring about tight coordination across virtual teams, rhetoric is beginning to shift toward advocating the use of technology to support knowledge sharing across communities. Such communities may have little work interdependency and may span organizational or national boundaries, but can leverage on technology to serve as intra- or inter-organizational memories and to create channels of communication across individuals who are in the same practice so as to support the sharing of knowledge.

As arrangements for collaborating across distance continue to evolve, distributed work arrangements will look somewhat different from what we see today. Experiments in new work arrangements seem to be teaching companies about the costs and benefits of collaboration at a distance, and as technology becomes more ubiquitous, former experiments will probably adapt and become routine work. For instance, rarely do teams communicate with all members at once, as was once envisioned in early writings about virtual teams. Employees are working in dispersed and local teams with multiple people (see Mark, Chapter 10, this volume, for a case study of large-scale collaboration across distances in the aerospace industry). If rhetoric in public discourse on the virtual teams CM has motivated investments in technology, these investments ultimately have made it possible for employees to use a variety of both synchronous and asynchronous technologies to conduct group work. In this way, the rhetoric of CMs indirectly influences distributed work arrangements even in companies, like the one we studied, that do not think technology is very important. Nevertheless, we will still detect the influence of utopian visions from the early virtual teams CM discourse, as reflected by the continuous push toward technological improvements to facilitate collaboration across distances.

Acknowledgments

Preparation of this essay was supported by NSF grant ITR IIS-0325047.

Endnotes

1. The Wikipedia (as of 2/23/05) says: "A virtual team does not always mean teleworker. Teleworkers are defined as individuals who work from home. Many virtual teams in today's organizations consist of employees both working at home and small groups in the office but in different geographic locations."
2. A Ph.D. dissertation on collaboratory rhetoric may be found at www.intertwining.org/dissertation
3. www.itrd.gov/pitac/report
4. Notes for Figure 9.1: Efficiency = claims that virtual teams bring higher productivity, spanning distance, lower costs, less time wasted, and less travel. Effectiveness = claims that virtual teams bring higher quality work, more innovativeness, projects that could not have been done, and new alliances and collaborations. People = claims that virtual teams help recruit the best employees, bring the best experts onto a team, and improve employees' skills and capabilities. Challenge = recognition of problems and difficulties in virtual work, how to make virtual teams successful, how to manage virtual teams, and how to get better technology to support virtual teams.
5. Note for Figures 9.2–9.5: The size of each circle reflects the comparative total number of employees at each site that year. Each arrow to a focal site from a source site represents the number of dispersed projects owned by the focal site that drew on at least one professional employed by the source site.

References

Abrahamson, E. (1996). Management fashion. *Academy of Management Review*, 21, 254–285.

Armstrong, D. J., & Cole, P. (2002). Managing distances and differences in geographically distributed work groups. In P. Hinds & S. Kiesler, (Eds.), *Distributed work* (pp. 167–186). Cambridge, MA: MIT Press.

Bajwa, D. S., Lewis, L. F., Pervan, G., & Lai, V. S. (2005). The adoption and use of collaboration information technologies: International comparisons. *Journal of Information Technology*, 20(2), 130–140.

Boh, W. F., Ren, Y., Kiesler, S., & Bussjaeger, R. (2005). Expertise utilization in the geographically dispersed organization. Working paper. Pittsburgh, PA: CMU.

Cairncross, F. (1997). *The death of distance: How the communications revolution will change our lives*. Cambridge, MA: Harvard Business School.

Cramton, C. D. (2001). The mutual knowledge problem and its consequences in geographically dispersed teams. *Organization Science*, 12(3), 346–371.

Cramton, C. D., & Hinds, P. (2005). Subgroup dynamics in internationally distributed teams: Ethnocentrism or cross-national learning? *Research in Organizational Behavior*, 26, 231–263.

Cummings, J. (2004). Work groups, structural diversity, and knowledge sharing in a global organization. *Management Science*, 50(3), 352–364.

Curtis, B., Krasner, H. & Iscoe, N. (1988). A field study of the software design process for large systems. *Communications of the ACM*, 31(11), 1268–1287.

Demsetz, H. (1991). The theory of the firm revisited. In O. E. Williamson & S. G. Winter (Eds.), *The Nature of the Firm* (pp. 159–178). New York: Oxford University Press.

Finholt, T. A. (1993). *Outsiders on the inside: Sharing information through a computer archive*. Published Doctoral Dissertation. Pittsburgh, PA: Carnegie Mellon University, AAG9412093.

Grant, R. M. (1996a). Prospering in dynamically-competitive environments: Organizational capability as knowledge integration. *Organization Science*, 7(4), 375–387.

Grant, R. M. (1996b). Toward a knowledge-based theory of the firm. *Strategic Management Journal*, 17, 109–122.

Grinter, R. E., Herbsleb, J. D., & Perry, D. W. (1999). The geography of coordination: Dealing with distance in R&D work. In *Proceedings of the SIGGROUP Conference on Supporting Group Work, GROUP '99*, Phoenix, AZ (pp. 306–315). New York: ACM.

Grudin, J. (1994). Computer-supported cooperative work: Its history and participation. *IEEE Computer*, 27(5), 19–26.

Hackman, J. R., & Wageman, R. (1995). Total quality management: Empirical, conceptual, and practical issues. *Administrative Science Quarterly*, 40, 309–342.

Herbsleb, J. D., & Mockus, A. (2003). An empirical study of speed and communication in globally-distributed software development. *IEEE Transactions on Software Engineering*, 29(3), 1–14.

Hildreth, S. (2005, December 19). Come together carefully. *Computerworld*, 39, 23–25.

Hiltz, S. R., & Turoff, M. (1978). *The network nation: Human communication via computer*. Reading: Addison-Wesley.

Hinds, P. J., & Kiesler, S. (2002). *Distributed work*. Cambridge, MA: MIT Press.

Hinds, P., & Mortensen, M. (2005). Understanding conflict in geographically distributed teams: An empirical investigation. *Organization Science*, 16(3), 290–307.

Hinds, P., & Zolin, R. (2004). Trust in context: The development of interpersonal trust in geographically distributed work. In R. M. Kramer & K. S. Cook (Eds.), *Trust and distrust within organizational contexts* (pp. 214–238). New York: Russell Sage Foundation.

Iacono, S., & Kling, R. (2001). Computerization movements: The rise of the Internet and distant forms of work. In J. Yates & J. Van Maanen (Eds.), *Information technology and organizational transformation: History, rhetoric, and practice* (pp. 93–16). Thousand Oaks, CA: Sage Publications.

Iacono, S., & Weisband, S. (1997). Developing trust in virtual teams. *Proceedings of the 30th Annual Hawaii International Conference System Sciences*, Maui, Hawaii, 412–420.

Im, H. G., Yates, J., & Orlikowski, W. (2005). Temporal coordination through communication: Using genres in a virtual start-up organization. *Information Technology & People*, 18(2), 89–119.

Jarman, R. (2005). When Success Isn't Everything—Case Studies of Two Virtual Teams. *Group Decision and Negotiation*, 14(4), 333–354.

Jarvenpaa, S. L., & Leidner, D. E. (1999). Communication and trust in global virtual teams. *Organization Science*, 10(6), 791–815.

Knoll, K., & Jarvenpaa, S. L. (1995). Learning to work in distributed global teams. *Proceedings of the 28th Annual Hawaii International Conference on System Sciences*, 92.

Kouzes, R. T., Myers, J. D., & Wulf, W. A. (1996). Collaboratories—Doing Science on the Internet. *IEEE Computer*, 29(8), 40–46.

Lederberg, J., & Uncapher, K. (1989). Towards a national collaboratory: Report of an invitational workshop at the Rockefeller University, March 17–18, 1989.

Lipnack, J., & Stamps, J. (1997). *Virtual teams: Reaching across space, time, and organizations with technology*. New York: John Wiley & Sons.

Maister, D. H. (1993). *Managing the professional service firm*. New York: Free Press.

Majchrzak, A., Malhotra, A., Stamps, J., & Lipnack, J. (2004). Can absence make a team grow stronger? *Harvard Business Review*, 82(5), 131–155.

Mark, G., Grudin, J., & Poltrock, S. E. (1999). Meeting at the desktop: An empirical study of virtually collocated teams. In *Proceedings of the sixth European conference on computer supported cooperative work ECSCW '99*, Dordrecht, Netherlands.

Meyer, J. W. & Rowan, B. (1977). Institutionalized organizations: Formal structure as myth and ceremony. *American Journal of Sociology*, 83, 340–363.

Miner, J. B., Crane, D. P., & Vandenberg, R. J. (1994). Congruence and fit in professional role motivation theory. *Organization Science*, 5(1), 86–87.

Mortensen, M., & O'Leary, M. (2005, August 5–10). *Subgroups with attitude: Imbalance and isolation in geographically dispersed teams.* Paper presented at the Academy of Management, Honolulu, HI.

Nordhaug, O., & Gronhaug, K. (1994). Competences as resources in firms. *International Journal of Human Resources Management,* 5(1), 89–106.

Olson, G. M., Malone, T. W., & Smith, J. B. (2001). *Coordination theory and collaboration technology*. Mahwah, NJ: Erlbaum.

Olson, J. S., Teasley, S., Covi, L., & Olson, G. (2002). The (currently) unique advantages of collocated work. In P. Hinds & S. Kiesler (Eds.), *Distributed work* (pp. 113–135). Cambridge, MA: MIT Press.

Podolny, J. (1993). A status-based model of market competition. *American Journal of Sociology*, 98(4), 829–872.

Teece, D. J. (1998). Capturing value from knowledge assets: The new economy, markets for know-how and intangible assets. *California Management Review*, 40(3), 55–79.

Townsend, A. M., DeMarie, S. M., & Hendrickson, A. R. (1998). Virtual teams: Technology and the workplace of the future. *Academy Management Executive*, 12(3), 17–29.

Weisband, S. (2002). Maintaining awareness in distributed team collaboration: Implications for leadership and performance. In P. Hinds & S. Kiesler (Eds.), *Distributed work* (pp. 311–334). Cambridge, MA: MIT Press.

Weisband, S. (forthcoming). *Leadership at a distance: Interdisciplinary perspectives.* Mahwah, NJ: Lawrence Erlbaum Associates.

Zbaracki, M. J. (1998). The rhetoric and reality of total quality management. *Administrative Science Quarterly*, 43, 602–626.

Chapter 10

Large-Scale Distributed Collaboration: Tension in a New Interaction Order

Gloria Mark
Department of Informatics
University of California, Irvine

Abstract

Large-scale collaboration is an emerging computerization movement. The development of new technologies and infrastructures to enable such large-scale collaboration is occurring at a fast rate. An example of such an infrastructure is the Cyberinfrastructure program and the Access Grid designed to provide high capacity networks to aid science and engineering collaborations. However, despite the technological enabling of such large-scale collaborations, they are faced with major social and organizational challenges. In this paper, I describe some challenges through a case study of a large-scale engineering design team composed of collocated teams distributed at different sites. The study shows how teams face an inherent tension balancing demands in their collocated environments with distributed teams. These tensions are manifest in the teams' abilities to develop and adopt common terms and methodologies, to overcome misattributions, and in establishing appropriate social networks across distance. I discuss the implications of these tensions between collocated and distributed demands in affecting the trajectory of the large-scale collaboration computerization movement.

Introduction

Computer networking has always been understood through varied interpretive schema. The birth of the Internet grew out of engineering visions by the Advanced Research Projects Agency (ARPA) to achieve technological superiority over the Soviet Union in the 1960s (Castells, 2003). The Internet was originally conceived of as a decentralized network for military computers, and early technologists involved with its development later conceived of it to enable resource sharing. Yet another significant frame surrounding the Internet has evolved: a network that eradicates distance among people (Iacono & Kling, 2001).

As the infrastructure of the Internet developed, so did a range of applications and tools: at first e-mail, and then later sophisticated synchronous and asynchronous networked technologies for enabling distributed work. Today, a wide range is available. In early discussions about the role of networked technologies, scientific and business circles expected that technologies enabling collaboration would lead to organizational transformations such as flattening of hierarchies (Iacono & Kling, 2001; Malone & Rockart, 1991). However, at the time there was also equal skepticism about whether organizational transformations had actually occurred as a result of networking. Some of this skepticism was raised by researchers who observed the widespread failure of organizations to adopt collaborative technologies (Grudin, 1988; Markus, 1983; Orlikowski, 1993; Rogers, 1994).

There was clearly a change, however, for organizations to become more distributed (Castells, 1996). For example, in 1997 Boeing grew immensely both in size and geographical diversity through its mergers with McDonnell Douglas and some business units of Rockwell International. After the mergers, Boeing changed from having 80 percent to only 40 percent of its employees located in the greater Seattle area; the rest were distributed across the United States and other continents. The successful company-wide adoption of data conferencing to support a range of geographically dispersed design teams, enterprise teams, software developers, technical computer support, and ad hoc interactions is a testament to the reliance of the organization on distributed, collaborative work (Mark & Poltrock, 2004). In the mid 1990s, a survey of teams in U.S. companies revealed that 66 percent had at least one member who was geographically distant from the rest of the team (Kinney & Panko, 1996). The Intel Corporation enacted a personnel policy to hire the best person for the position irrespective of the geographic location from where they would work.

Distributed collaboration rose, helped by the rhetoric that such teams could enable people to work together independently of their geographic location. These arguments claimed that organizations would transform and become more flexible (Kiesler, Boh, Ren, & Weisband, Chapter 9, this volume). However, as distributed collaboration began to increase, a concurrent interest arose, especially among scientists and technologists to enable collaboration on a much larger scale. This large-scale computerization movement (CM) was driven by several main impetuses.

The first was the realization that scientific problems were becoming more complex. Several terms encapsulated this idea. In 1961, Weinberg (1961) introduced the notion of "big science." The visionary idea of "collaboratory" was proposed by Wulf (1993) where scientists would collaborate in a global laboratory across distance to share data, resources, and information. "Grand Challenge" problems were identified by the Nobel Laureate Ken Wilson in 1988 as requiring large teams of scientists and computing power to solve, and existed in fields such as astrophysics, computational biology, and climate modeling (Wilson, 1988). Later, the term "distributed intelligence" was used to describe the advantages of combining scientific knowledge from many scientists (Zare, 1997). The interest in solving "Grand Challenge problems and forming collaboratories gave an impetus for large-scale collaboration teams to form and required high performance computing to solve" (Tapia & Lanius, 2001). A number of large collaboratory projects exist in fields ranging from atmospheric science to medicine (c.f. Finholt, 2003).

A second type of impetus was the realization by management of complex organizations that in very complex work, expertise resides not just in individuals but in clusters of individuals, or teams. The Boeing 777 airplane design involved complex task interdependencies within large teams located across the U.S. with corresponding interdependent expertise among individuals (Sabbagh, 1996). The notion of the "network-centric" organization was also introduced, referring to how in such organizational structures the network serves as the primary communication and coordination mechanism for the entire organization (c.f. Ahuja & Carley, 1999). Connecting teams across distance via technology was based on the reasoning that it is not economically feasible to transport entire teams to meet face-to-face. Thus, organizations began to experiment with and invest in scalable technologies and infrastructures where large teams could interact across distance. One such experiment was the World Jam at IBM in which more than 50,000 managers globally participated in fora on the company intranet (Millen & Fontaine, 2003).

A third impetus came from technologists who had visions to create large-scale global networks. One manifestation of this vision was the Access Grid designed as a distributing computing infrastructure to support large-scale collaborative endeavors such as e-science or e-learning. The first large-scale Grid testbed was the i-Way, tested at the Supercomputing Conference in 1995 with 17 sites (Berman, Fox, & Hey, 2002). Soon after, the Grid forum was formed, and subsequently the Global Grid Forum, which worked on developing standards. Numerous research laboratories and universities around the world have developed

Access nodes. These nodes, linked together, use basic audio, video, and data-sharing capabilities to collaborate. Today there have been more than 20,000 certificates issued to users who span 56 countries (Access Grid, 2006).

Along with visions of large-scale networks also came the realization that technologies for use in these networks needed to be reconceived in order to support large-scale collaboration. The limitations of the desktop computing environment in supporting large-scale collaboration soon became apparent. As the size of distributed teams increased, the desktop environment proved inadequate for scaling up. Desktop-based communication and data-sharing technologies such as audio conferencing, application sharing, and small Webcams used for videoconferencing imposed a limit on how many could collaborate at each node. Even three people sitting around a desktop appeared crowded and in conference rooms, cameras imposed a tradeoff of depth (faces) versus breadth (room overview), which did not display faces and gestures well. Furthermore, these technologies were not designed well to provide social cues about group interaction (Ackerman, Hindus, Mainwaring, & Starr, 1997; Mark, Grudin, & Poltrock, 1999; O'Connail, Whittaker, & Wilbur, 1993; Ruhleder & Jordan 1999). Also important is that the desktop environment restricted people's movements. Group members were confined to sitting at a desk individually or at most in groups of two or three, as opposed to being actively engaged in designing or reconfiguring in small groups as scientific teams in a natural collocated setting might do. Desktop computing was not adequate to support multiple scientific team collaboration. Technology needed to change. Thus, the inadequacies of conducting science from the desktop led technologists to reconceptualize how technology could change from supporting distributed virtual teams to supporting virtual organizations composed of many teams.

With visions of nodes now consisting of groups instead of individuals, computer scientists believed that it was important to design technology that would facilitate the development of group social processes across distance. One means to do this was to design technology that could create a strong sense of presence of groups that were at a distance. The large virtual room metaphor grew out of this effort. But the room needed to be equipped. Whereas technologies to support virtual teams commonly consisted of combinations of e-mail, application sharing, and shared workspaces, technologies for large-scale collaboration were envisioned to create a sense of "presence" of groups across distance. The design rationale for immersive projection displays is that multi-projector systems will create immersive environments for large group-to-group collaborations so that they will be able to convey natural audio and visual cues across distance, i.e. that exist during group interaction (Childers, Disz, Olson, Papka, Stevens, & Udeshi, 2000). The goal of wall-size, life-size, high-density TV video conferencing was to use wide-angle high-resolution video cameras that could capture a wide field of view of a room in which groups were dynamically interacting. The high resolution and wall-size was envisioned to create a "window" into another conference room across distance (Mark & DeFlorio, 2001). Thus, the metaphors used in the development of these technologies—"presence" and "the global meeting room"—became part of the discourse surrounding (and marketing) these technologies.

Still a fourth impetus for large-scale collaboration came from governmental funding agencies. Large funding initiatives for "big science" came from the National Science Foundation (NSF) in the U.S., the *e-science* program in the U.K., and the European Union. The *e-science* program in the U.K. was a major funding effort of more than 200 million dollars, which was first budgeted in 2001 to integrate scientific laboratories across different university campuses. The vision of the e-science program was grand: "These moves within science are likely to lead to a paradigm shift in information technology over the next decade, as large as the one which accompanied the adoption of the World Wide Web" (National Environment Research Council). The European Union's Sixth Framework program funding level was also high: 300 Million Euros for cyberinfrastructure related projects (European Commission, 2006).

Funding for development of cyberinfrastructure and related technologies has been especially strong in the U.S. In 2003 the NSF released its report from a Blue Ribbon Panel that recommended funding for cyberinfrastructure development and projects in the amount of more than one billion per year. The report emphasized the value of sharing scientific results and knowledge: "We envision an environment in which raw data and recent results are easily shared, not just within a research group or institution but also between scientific disciplines and locations. There is an exciting opportunity to share insights, software, and knowledge, to reduce wasteful re-creation and repetition" (National Science Foundation, 2003, Chapter 2, p. 4). Thus, the notion of sharing discoveries, data, and knowledge became used freely in the discourses of cyberinfrastructure. Currently, the number of technology projects that fall under the umbrella term cyberinfrastructure continue to grow, funded by the Department of Energy (DOE), NSF, Defense Advanced Research Projects Agency (DARPA), and National Aeronautics and Space Administration (NASA). The role of social science in cyberinfrastructure has not been left out of the discourse. It also has begun to receive recognition, sparked by the recommendation of the NSF Blue Ribbon Panel to include social scientists in the cyberinfrastructure development. Examples showing this interest include the SBE/CISE Workshop on Cyberinfrastructure for the Social Sciences held in 2005 and the information-gathering Commission on Cyberinfrastructure for the Humanities and Social Sciences held in 2004.

Different Technological Frames and Discourse

Iacono and Kling (2001) discuss the importance of public discourse in promoting CMs. The notions of "big science," the Grid, cyberinfrastructure, and large-scale collaboration take on different meanings depending on whether it is used in a scientific, business, government, or the popular domain.

The case of the Grid illustrates the different perspectives among the different stakeholders. In the popular press, the meaning has been vague, encompassing a range of ideas from networking infrastructures to artificial intelligence (Foster, Kesselman, & Tuecke, 2001). Among computer scientists and others in scientific circles, the Grid is very specific, referring to an advanced technical infrastructure that could support large-scale resource sharing. Intended to be an extensible, open architecture, it is sometimes referred to as the *Grid problem* (Foster, et al., 2001) to denote the immensity of the challenge.

To technologists, the underlying notion of the Grid is the sharing of data. This concept means not only supporting communication and data exchange, but also providing access to remote resources such as computers. The Grid is intended to provide an integrated solution for connecting multiple sites across different organizations, for computing, sharing, and managing data and supporting communication. This involves developing not only tools and infrastructure, but also developing protocols for exchanging data.

As Foster et al. (2001) describe the vision: "It is our belief that VOs [virtual organizations] have the potential to change dramatically the way we use computers to solve problems, much as the Web has changed how we exchange information" (p. 3). Fran Berman, the director of the National Partnership for Advanced Computational Infrastructure (NPACI) and the San Diego Supercomputing Center (SDSC) describes its potential as, "The Grid is the computing and data management infrastructure that will provide the electronic underpinning for a global society in business, government, research, science and entertainment. ... The Grid is transforming science, business, health and society" (Berman, et al., 2002, p. 9). Thus, the vision of the Grid for scientists and technologists is not only to increase the scale of collaboration, but also to provide global access to instruments and computing devices. It would enable rich and poor labs to operate on an even playing field through sharing data and resources. This idea was underscored by the NSF Blue Ribbon Panel recommendation which wrote that the technology would enable people to work across institutional rank and barriers "with colleagues at distant institutions, even ones that are not traditionally considered research universities, and with junior scientists and students as genuine peers, despite differences in age, experience, race, or physical limitations" (National Science Foundation, 2003).

To technologists, the Grid holds many promises of revolutionizing the technological landscape. As Larry Smarr wrote, "the effects of computational grids are going to change the world so quickly that mankind will struggle to react and change in the face of the challenges and issues they present" (Foster & Kesselman, 1999).

For business, grid computing represents a different view. Global businesses such as IBM, Hewlett Packard, and Sun have formed a consortium, and to this, the Grid represents a way to increase the computing capability similar to that of the energy grid. The consortium's idea of the Grid is to develop software that could combine numerous computing resources to increase computing power. The consortium's goal is to focus on commercial uses such as oil exploration (Lohr, 2005). Thus, the grid vision for business is to provide access to equipment globally for commercial potential. Similar to how the Internet began, the grid idea emigrated out of government and university laboratories into mainstream business applications.

From Virtual Teams to Virtual Organizations

Thus, the view of distributed collaboration has shifted from a view of supporting small-scale teams to a utopian view of supporting it on a global large-scale. Large-scale group-to-group collaboration is fundamentally distinct from what is commonly considered "virtual teams," which describe a single team connected through an electronic network, with one or a few individuals residing at each node (e.g., Kiesler, Boh, Ren, & Weisband, Chapter 9, this volume; Mark, et al., 1999; Olson & Olson, 2000). There are three main differences that distinguish large-scale collaboration from "virtual teams." The first is the level of funding. The second difference is the scale and nature of the technologies and infrastructure used. The third is that the social issues are different. In synchronous communication, rather than a single communication network existing for a virtual team (e.g., as in audio conferencing), in large-scale group-to-group collaboration there may be multiple networks within and across sites interacting in parallel. It is rather a virtual "team" of "teams."

Despite the utopian visions of the Grid and cyberinfrastructure by technologists, there exists a gap between these visions and the realities of the social consequences that accompany this development. Networks will continue to proliferate, as will the development of applications and middleware, resulting in more access available to instruments and data. However, what is missing in this vision is the attention to the user in coordinating and communicating in such large-scale collaborations. This direction is lagging far behind the impetus pushing the technology.

To the technologists, the Access Grid and associated applications and services represent a way to connect the world globally enabling the sharing of resources from medical, scientific, educational, and other domains. To commercial enterprises, the Grid represents a means to combine resources to increase earning power. To managers, such as those who led the IBM World Jam effort, large-scale networks and technologies mean increased access to knowledge. Yet, for the most part, the users are left out of this discourse.

Creating vast high-speed networks to facilitate e-science is akin to creating a large global laboratory where scientists have access to instruments and data independent of their geographic location. For businesses, it is akin to creating a large global conference room where managers can meet. For engineering, it is akin to creating a global design room where engineers can metaphorically move and interact across space in dynamic configurations. The technology is developing at a rapid pace, but are the users ready? That is, can the users work in such an environment where time and space are removed from different organizational cultures? More to the point, can people work in a large-scale global environment in the way that the technologists envisioned that the environments should function? Are people able to adapt to the new organizational form that the technology brings about?

Iacono and Kling (2001) recognized that though technological breakthroughs such as networked room environments are lauded, at the same time, the social and cultural dimensions of their consequences are often ignored. In this paper I present some of the social consequences involved in configuring large-scale group-to-group distributed collaborations. As I will discuss, some of the problems are quite basic and must be addressed before we can expect that the visions of technology for large-scale collaboration will change the way that science and business are conducted.

Large-Scale Collaboration: A New Interaction Order

Large-scale group-to-group collaboration introduces a new kind of interaction order. In this collaborative setting, people are interacting in multiple social worlds simultaneously: They interact in a collocated team, while at the same time they are also interacting within a larger, distributed team, networked electronically across distance. This notion of duality of collaborative contexts has so far not received attention. More typically, the focus of collaboration studies has been on one particular mode of interaction, i.e. either collocated or distributed, but not both simultaneously. Issues such as fleeting trust (Jarvenpaa & Leidner, 1998), not knowing identity (Ackerman, et al., 1997; Mark, et al., 1999), and lack of collaboration readiness (Olson & Olson, 2000) have been identified as factors affecting distributed team interaction, as contrasted with collocated interaction. However, in a group-to-group collaboration context, we need to address the issues that individuals and teams face as they manage *both* collocated and distributed interactions. Managing interactions in both types of social worlds creates a tension, as I will discuss.

Interacting in Collocated and Distributed Social Worlds

In this paper I present an ethnographic investigation of a large-scale, group-to-group collaboration that illustrates a notion of tension. The object of study is a large distributed technology organization that researches, designs, and develops space-based scientific technologies and missions. A design team was observed from this organization, comprised of four engineering groups distributed around the U.S. The largest team at Site 1 had 24 team members, a second team had 12 members, a third team had 9 members, and a single person participated from another site. Most of the people on teams 1, 2, and 3 had previously worked together within their teams but had never worked with the other teams in the past. The purpose of collaborating was to combine different specializations to work on a conceptual design for an actual space mission. Each site had one or two facilitators. The entire team, composed of the people at all four sites, will be referred to as the distributed Design Team.

The distributed Design Team relied on a number of technologies to collaborate. They used data conferencing, a tool that linked workstations and shared data, a video-teleconferencing (VTC) service, which shared the audio/video of all four sites, and multiple large wall-sized public displays that showed the video and the shared applications. Distributed small group discussions, or sidebars, were managed by a tool that enabled the sharing of multiple voice streams by telephone. More commonplace technologies, such as e-mail and fax, were also available. Within the timeframe of meeting for nine hours, over three days within a week, the team was able to complete a conceptual design for a real space mission. Five team meetings were observed over a period of two years by researchers who were positioned at each site during the meetings. More details of the methodology are reported in Mark, Abrams, and Nassif (2003) and Mark and Abrams (2005).

Whereas one might think of space mission design as an orderly process, it is in fact, messy. To an outsider, the environment within Site 1, the largest, is usually noisy and appears chaotic, with many people talking at once, moving around the room, speaking in small groups, or shouting across the room. The design involves calculating a vast array of different parameters, e.g. choice of technology to employ, trip time, weight, power type, as well as graphically designing the spacecraft configuration. Parameters begin with initial estimates and are constantly refined in an iterative process. The work is highly interdependent, e.g. the power engineer needs information from the mission's design and instruments expert to calculate their work. The interdependencies lead to much interaction to negotiate values or discuss design tradeoffs. The facilitator from each site dominated the public contributions from their respective sites. Team members listened to the VTC most of the time and talked the rest of the time either locally (by muting their VTC microphone) or publicly over the VTC.

Whereas the cyberinfrastructure visions imply an "even playing field" for global sites, the different sites had different meeting room environments. Site 1 engineers worked in an electronic meeting room dedicated to their collocated collaboration. The room had three large public displays visible to all in the room, and one display showed a video image of the remote engineers at the other sites. In contrast, the other two site environments were general purpose conference rooms that were not dedicated to either collocated or remote collaboration, but were rather "cobbled" together with video monitors, projector screens, and workstations.

Tension Between Collocated and Distributed Collaborations

The cyberinfrastructure vision considers that the network will enable the global sharing of data. However, the technologists' visions do not consider the social challenges for distributed scientists to collaborate. The members of the Design Team experienced tension in their participation in the collaboration. Though they were accustomed to collaborating with others at their home site, it was a new experience for most of the team members to be part of a large distributed team. For most members, meeting the requirements of their collocated team took precedence over meeting the requirements of the Design Team. As a result, there were many instances of conflict that arose in the Design Team.

Networks Within and Across Sites

In conceptual space mission design, a central aspect of the work involves negotiations of parameters and design tradeoffs. Sidebars are small group discussions where these types of issues are often discussed while the main meeting is progressing. Sidebars might cover simple questions to seek clarification or to seek specific information (e.g., "what is the surface temperature of Mars?") to challenging assumptions to lengthy and complex design tradeoff discussions, such as how to reduce mass on the spacecraft. Sidebars are in many ways the heart of design work, as it is in these small group discussions where critical decisions are made and design rationale is discussed. Sidebars occur within each site but also technology was provided (a tool that enabled sharing multiple voice streams by telephone) so that the engineers could easily speak in sidebar discussions with other engineers located at other sites. In the collocated teams, team members constantly move between their individual calculations, listening to public conversations, and engaging in sidebar discussions, which are mostly spontaneous. The team members described that they always monitored their local environment, listening for keywords in the surrounding discussions that had relevance for them. When a conversation was considered relevant, the team member would spontaneously join the sidebar.

Nearly all the collocated sidebars were self-organized. Rarely did the facilitator organize a sidebar and only then in response to a request from a remote site. In contrast, sidebars in the larger distributed design team were always delegated by facilitators who announced publicly over the VTC who would join them. Usually no more than four participants were in a distributed sidebar, from up to three different sites. Though any team member could initiate a sidebar, of the 24 distributed sidebars that occurred, only three were self-organized.

Whereas quick clarifications or information-seeking occurred in collocated sidebars, these never occurred in distributed sidebar interactions. Distributed sidebar interaction was formal and challenges of assumptions or design values seldom occurred. It would have been advantageous for the distributed design team, if, for example, through a sidebar the Power engineer at Site 1 clarified or challenged a value with the Power engineer at Site 2. Examples were identified when team members should have initiated sidebars with other engineers across sites to discuss problems with design parameters. Yet they did not do so.

Articulation[1] and coordination should constitute a significant part of distributed interaction, especially in large-scale interaction. Yet only 9 percent of the discussion in distributed sidebars was coded as primarily used for articulation purposes; 91 percent was primarily used for discussing design content. In contrast, 34 percent of the discussion in collocated sidebars was primarily used for articulation and coordination purposes, and 62 percent was primarily used for discussing design content. It was also not the case that much articulation was conducted over the public VTC channel, as only 28 percent of the discussion concerned articulation.

Thus, a pattern of behavior never emerged where distributed team members would spontaneously contact their colleagues to challenge assumptions or values, to clarify ambiguities, or to seek information. Distributed sidebars were formal, far fewer, and delegated by facilitators. In contrast, collocated sidebars at Site 1 could be spontaneously joined. Thus, the Design Team failed to establish a pattern of interaction where people would consult distributed partners for their expertise when needed. Though the technology was available for distributed interaction, the fact that distributed sidebars were rarely self-organized suggests social limitations in working in the large-scale environment.

Discrepant Methodologies Across Distance

Though the cyberinfrastructure vision is to provide an infrastructure to connect people across distance for data-sharing and communication, this notion does not address the reality that different organizational sites often have different policies, guidelines, and work practices. Though nominally the same organization, in reality, each organizational site in this study had its own models for subsystems of the space mission design. The different organizational sites invested considerable resources and personnel in developing models and algorithms for computing different aspects of the space mission, such as propulsion or trip time. For the Design Team to function effectively, common agreement needed to be reached on the models and methodologies used for designing the space mission. However, during the design session, the different sites used discrepant terms to refer to the same concepts. At times each site also used unique methodologies and design processes.

In one case, different sites used different approaches to calculate a mass contingency factor. The mass of the various system components in a mission design must be estimated and they are iteratively refined as the design progresses. Site 1 used a single scaling factor for mass contingency based on their site guidelines. Site 2 used a "bottom-up" approach for mass contingency based on estimating values for each component. A sidebar with participants from Sites 1, 2, and 3 negotiated a hybrid methodology, which corresponded with an organization-wide default value. A new term, "validity," emerged, common for the entire design team. However, the facilitator at Site 1 resisted the solution and a second hybrid solution was reached, in which Sites 1 and 2 would each apply their methodologies for that part of the design for which they were responsible. Yet Site 1 again resisted this solution and wanted another sidebar to reconcile the issue. Thus, though the distributed design team was able to negotiate common methodologies and terms, the proposed solutions were not adopted. Other examples occurred with calculating the mission trajectory and power mode, which are critical parts of the design.

Though the distributed design team could intellectually negotiate new hybrid terms and methodologies, these solutions were not adopted by them. The distributed design team did not retain the solutions that it came up with and did not incorporate it into its process. Distance was surely a factor in the lack of adoption. Adopting a new term or methodology meant overriding what was common practice at their own site. Here the tension faced by teams in adopting a new methodology means going against the work of local colleagues who have laid out the basis for the models that are being used. The question for such a group-to-group collaborative setting becomes whose models should a local team follow—those developed by their local colleagues, or those new ones negotiated so that the distributed teams could have a common basis for collaboration.

Misattributions Using Technology

A third source of tension is due to how the networked technologies influenced perceptions and interactions among the entire team. Several misattributions of interaction could be identified during the design activity that could be traced to a misunderstanding of the technology capabilities.

Users generally form models and expectations about the technologies they use (Norman, 1988). In this paper a user's trust in technology will be defined as the user's belief that the technology will deliver what he/she expects it to deliver, e.g. formed through the history of previous interaction with the specific technology or through training. However, expectation of a technology's capability can occasionally stretch beyond what the technology is capable of delivering. When this happens, "blind trust" occurs with the technology use.

In the Design Team, misattributions occurred when team members acted as if they believed the technology was conveying the same sense of the interaction across distance as it would be perceived locally. Team members developed a blind trust that the collaborative tools that they used to interact and share data across distance were "delivering" the information they intended. The actors extended their assumptions of face-to-face interaction to mediated interaction across distance. They behaved as though their distributed partners would understand their behaviors and work practices as their collocated colleagues would.

One type of misattribution observed was that team members often behaved in the distributed interaction as though "what I say is what you hear." However, there were 24 instances, spread approximately equally over all sites, where team members did not put in the requisite effort in the main meeting conversations to make themselves heard at the other sites. The speaker either forgot to unmute the microphone or spoke too far away from the VTC microphone to be heard remotely. Sometimes remote team members were in sidebars that were not visible to the speaker over the video, and the speaker assumed they were not present. The actors blindly trusted that the technology was "delivering" their voice to the remote sites without needing to adapt their behavior to a large-scale distributed context.

Another misattribution observed occurred when the design team participants had the false belief that the other teams always had access to the same data that they had, believing "what I see is what you see." This led to tensions when discrepancies in data were discovered. Still, another type of misattribution was when team members acted in the distributed interaction as if "what I understand about the data is what you understand about the data." There was not a common understanding across sites when a value in the spreadsheet was considered final. Engineers expected to see particular data values on the large display, but tensions arose when they often revealed surprise to see a different value.

A fourth type of misattribution was when team members behaved as though "what data I can access is what you can access" across distance. They expected that once values were entered into the spreadsheets, they were immediately propagated and accessible to the other remote sites. However, as observed, this linking of data in spreadsheets did not always occur, or sometimes did so only with delays or errors. Again, this created a source of tension between collocated and distributed sites. For example, toward the end of the design session, the design team discovered that an important piece of information—upon which Site 2 based its design—was known to Site 1, yet was never shared electronically with Site 2. Statements were made at the local sites such as "First time I've heard of anything from the trajectory in two days." Site 1 blindly trusted that their value for a specific impulse was received by Site 2; Site 2 had blind trust in the procedure: "Electronically, it says on the sheet 'If [specific impulse] is zero or not available, use [your] own estimate from [your] trajectory run', so I did so."

These examples show that the team members did not appropriately adapt to the large-scale distributed group-to-group context. While interaction is visible within a collocated site, it was not always clear to team members that they needed to invest extra effort to understand the remote members' behaviors and work practices with the technology. Further, for most team members, they were using new and unfamiliar technologies. The actors did not have the opportunity to develop appropriate expectations of the capabilities of the technology. These misattributions of others' interactions led to tensions between collocated and distributed interaction.

Discussion

A gap exists between the utopian visions of the CM of technologies and infrastructures for large-scale collaboration and the social realities of interacting in the environment that these technologies enable. One of the social consequences of the CM of large-scale collaboration is that it connects multiple social worlds across distance. Tensions can often arise unexpectedly between demands from local and distributed worlds.

Conflict is often an inherent part of different social worlds in an organization (Kling, 1980). Such tension in connecting social worlds across organizations is not surprising if we look at the sovereignty-federalism issue as an analogy. Calhoun's theory of nullification at the beginning of the nineteenth century argued that states had a right to declare federal rule void, therefore exercising sovereign powers (Wilson & DiIulio, 1995). Similarly, in distributed organizations, local sites can refuse to obey overall organizational policies, instead following local rules and guidelines. Or, in collaboration across different organizations, no overall policy would exist. Loyalty to the local organizational home is not to be unexpected; organizational sites invest time and effort in developing guidelines that suit the local environment. Employees are generally rewarded by their local managers at their home site and not for participation in a large distributed collaboration, as was the case with the Design Team. Similarly, each of the sites of the Design Team invested a great deal of resources and time in developing algorithms and methodologies for the particular aspect of the space mission for which they had expertise. It is understandable why an organizational site would be reluctant to give up their own methodologies and adopt that of another team or site, or even that created by the large, distributed team. Teams involved in large-scale group-to-group collaboration face a number of tradeoff decisions. Should individuals in distributed collaborations owe their allegiances, in terms of the methodologies they apply and assumptions they use, to their home site organizations or to their distributed teams? Can distributed large-scale teams create their own policies that relate to their new work practices or should team members instead apply their home site policies to the large-scale collaboration? Would following policies that benefit a large-scale team result in the greater good of the overall team as opposed to providing benefits for local sites? What happens when home site and distributed team policies conflict? This study showed that when policies and work practices conflict, teams resort to those developed and used at their local sites.

The utopian visions surrounding large-scale collaboration also do not consider that scientists must reconcile, and in some cases, adopt and create new methodologies. The methodologies used by each site were not readily visible to the other sites across distance. Thus, different groups solving collaborative scientific problems must face a complex social problem. They must first articulate their methodologies and terms, and then find a way to reconcile them. Though hybrid solutions were achieved as a result of articulation, the local teams failed to adopt them. Team processes are deeply embedded (e.g., in the case of Site 1 of the Design Team they were local site design guidelines) and may not readily change even though a common solution across different groups is nominally agreed upon. Group-centric views, found in intergroup collaboration

(Ancona & Caldwell, 1992), can inhibit the adoption of methods from outside the group. Gerson and Star (1986) proposed that a conceptual basis for the design of computer systems must be based on an understanding of articulation. The design of large-scale group-to-group collaborative technologies must enable the visibility of team methodologies and processes so that they can be articulated.

Thus, a source of tension for distributed teams is due to the nonuniform adoption of standard methodologies across organizational sites. The case study showed that it is difficult for teams at different sites to achieve common aligned methods. Bechky (2003) describes that knowledge is contextual in different organizational communities. Decontextualization occurs as different groups use different words and concepts to refer to the same concept. Recontextualization occurs when individuals use methods (e.g., providing a tangible definition) to arrive at a common understanding. Design methodologies and processes were developed in different organizational contexts resulting in deep differences between the teams. In a distributed organization it is challenging for any single standard to hold company-wide. Standards are infused with political and social influences (Bowker & Star, 1997) and are not easily changed. This case study underscores how scientific models used in space mission design constructed by engineers in the same engineering disciplines are subject to social beliefs concerning their validity. Thus, the utopian vision of sharing data and results across different laboratories is not so easily achieved.

The work for teams involved in global collaboration efforts begins before the teams meet. Management at the technology organization in this study tried to achieve common ground by having key actors in the collaboration (e.g., facilitators and some engineers) meet prior to the full Design Team meeting. However, despite these meetings, differences in methodologies and terms never arose in these discussions. There is a need as part of the large-scale CM for social scientists to work together with technologists to overcome group-centric views to adopt common practices for a larger-scale collaboration.

One of the utopian visions for large-scale technology infrastructures is to enable people to collaborate globally to share expertise. Yet people in the Design Team often neglected to seek expertise across distance for clarifications and design tradeoffs. Collocated engineers at Site 1 intentionally spoke keywords that they knew would signal certain others to join their sidebar. Yet these reciprocal expectations did not exist across distance. Challenges to assumptions, or seeking necessary information, was not done in sidebars across distance though the technology enabled this. This suggests that attitudes about distributed interactions were the limiting factor in interactions, and not the technology.

Utopian visions of large-scale technologies also do not consider how users might understand the technology's use. Misattributions of behavior due to people's misunderstanding of technology capabilities can also introduce tension in a distributed interaction. Blind trust in a technology can be engendered by any of the following: lack of training or familiarity with the technology, false understanding of the technology model, or lack of consideration of the technology complexities or capabilities. As an example of the latter, users get frustrated when a videoconferencing image is delayed (due to limited bandwidth). Users often do not generally consider the limits on correctness in computers and the inevitability of design and implementation errors (Smith, 1996). The savvy technology user perhaps has developed realistic expectations of technology's capabilities from experience. But what if the user has not had the opportunity to develop realistic expectations due to the lack of experience with the technology? People form expectations of the technology through experience, training and instruction (Norman, 1988). Without enough experience with a technology, users may not develop the appropriate expectations for the capabilities of a technology.

With the rise of the CM of large-scale collaboration, people are confronted with using new technologies that enable very new forms of interaction. In the Design Team, though all team members were highly experienced with using technologies for conducting their local work, or for work in smaller virtual teams (e.g., e-mail, telephone, fax, perhaps data-conferencing), nearly all Design Team members were unfamiliar with the new combinations of technologies (multiple wall-size displays, video-teleconferencing channel, publishing results on spreadsheets across distance) to connect their team with other teams. Further, nearly all were unfamiliar with the large collaborative setting. Though people may be accustomed to collaborating with others with whom they are collocated, or with individuals across distance, the phenomenon of being part of a team that is collaborating with other large remote teams was a totally new experience for most of the people in the Design Team. Therefore, they may not have had a realistic expectation of the limitations inherent in such systems. They did not realize that they needed to invest extra effort to make the interactions work across distance.

The Design Team met in five sessions, each over the course of a week, over a period of two years. Meeting intermittently was not sufficient for the engineers to learn appropriate expectations about the technology. Yet to what extent is this experience commonplace among users of cyberinfrastructure or the Grid? Studies of other large-scale collaboration efforts suggest that meeting intermittently is common practice (e.g., Lee, Dourish, & Mark, 2006; Star & Ruhleder, 1996).

Another aspect of the technologists' vision of large-scale collaboration is that it ignores the difference in resources that may exist in different scientific labs. Adopting a technology involves utilizing resources: the cost of the technology, the cost of providing technical support, and possibly using limited network resources. Unequal resources at different organizational sites can prevent all members of a distributed team from adopting the same technology, or using it to the same degree. Whereas Site 1 had a dedicated electronic meeting room for the distributed collaboration, the other sites used conference rooms that were not equipped specifically for the distributed collaboration. The management at Sites 2 and 3 did not have the resources (or priorities) for equipping a meeting room dedicated to collaboration. As a result, the different sites had different views of the video images of the other teams and of the public spreadsheets that displayed the parameters. A social consequence of large-scale collaboration is that management may focus on the good of their local organizational site at the risk of missing the benefit for the entire collaborative effort. This myopic view is contradictory to the technologists' vision, yet is a social reality. For entire teams to be connected across distance, a costly suite of room-sized displays, scalable data-sharing capabilities, and/or high quality audio and video is often required to display large numbers of people and information to other sites. As Star and Ruhleder (1996) discovered, the differential resources across research labs affects the uniformity of the equipment and infrastructure that exists and consequently leads to a number of differences in perspectives on the collaboration.

Inequitable reward structures can also promote tension between collocated and distributed social worlds. Distributed team members are often rewarded by local managers for their local work and not for their participation on distributed teams. In the Design Team, a new reward structure was not enacted for people's contribution to the large-scale distributed team. It is not surprising then that the team members did not put in the requisite effort that they needed for the collaboration. The results of this study lead to the broader question of how large-scale collaboration efforts can motivate and reward people to contribute data and expertise? The utopian visions do not address such questions.

Conclusions

While collocated team size is constrained by physical conference room space, the main constraint on distributed team size is the scalability of the collaboration technology used by the team. As scalability limitations become less of a factor, as evidenced by large-scale fora where thousands can participate (Millen & Fontaine, 2003), then the virtual conference room can expand at least in theory toward a nearly "infinite" space. But is the social adaptability to these technologies keeping up with the advances in technology development?

This is exactly the warning that Iacono and Kling made us aware of in their discussions of CMs. The deployment of technologies and infrastructures, such as the Access Grid, to support large-scale collaboration also involves major social and organizational transformations. One of the most important types of transformations is managing the tension that exists between collocated and distributed interactions.

Though technology capabilities exist currently to create a large "virtual conference room" connecting teams across distance, the social adaptability for this new CM is not in step with the technological development. In this paper I have discussed how inherent tensions exist between team members in their management of local and distributed interactions. Though technology can now easily connect large teams across distance to create new collaborative configurations, the basic tensions that exist between collocated and distributed work need to be addressed and brought out as public discourse in this CM. As the Access Grid and cyberinfrastructure continue in their technical development and deployment, more case studies are needed to better understand how such work practices enabled by the technology can succeed. Fran Berman argues that a human infrastructure is integral to the development of a cyberinfrastructure, and calls for interdisciplinary cooperation of social scientists as well as technologists to successfully realize the technology's goals (Berman, 2003). Users themselves have begun to undertake the task to understand and address these social issues, as for example with a research agenda for bio-diversity and eco-systems that has outlined the importance of studying the social and cultural effects of large-scale collaborations (Cushing, et al., 2003).

Tension arises when the requirements and constraints of multiple social worlds conflict. Tension exists in a distributed team when organizational policies and requirements at local sites hinder the adoption of uniform work practices. In large-scale distributed collaboration, a new technological frame must be developed by the users as well as management so that their interaction in this distributed environment constitutes a new and evolving social world.

Acknowledgments

This material is based upon work supported by the National Science Foundation Grant No. 0093496 and JPL/NASA Contract No. 1240133.

Endnotes

1. Following Gerson and Star (1986), we defined articulation as "all the tasks involved in assembling, scheduling, monitoring, and coordinating all of the steps necessary to complete a production task" (p. 260).

References

Access Grid. (2006). Retrieved from www.accessgrid.org

Ackerman, M. S., Hindus, D., Mainwaring, S. D., & Starr, B. (1997). Hanging on the wire: A field study of an audio-only media space. *ACM Transactions on Computer-Human Interaction*, 4(1), 39–66.

Ahuja, M. K., & Carley, K. M. (1999). Network structure in virtual organizations. *Organization Science*, 10(6), 741–747.

Ancona, D. G., & Caldwell, D. F. (1992). Bridging the boundary: External activity and performance in organizational teams. *Admininstrative Science Quarterly*, 37(4), 634–665.

Bechky, B. (2003). Sharing meaning across occupational communities: The transformation of understanding on a production floor. *Organization Science*, 143, 312–330.

Berman, F. (2003). Building a successful cyberinfrastructure. *Envision*, 19(1).

Berman, F., Fox, G., & Hey, T. (2002). The Grid: Past, present, future. In F. Berman, G. Fox, & T. Hey (Eds.), *Grid computing: Making the global infrastructure a reality* (pp. 9–50). New York: John Wiley & Sons, Ltd.

Bowker, G. C., & Star, S. L. (1997). How things (actor-net) work: Classification, magic and the ubiquity of standards. *Philosophia*, 25(3/4), 195–220.

Castells, M. (1996). *The rise of the network society*. Oxford: Blackwell.

Castells, M. (2003). *The Internet galaxy: Reflections on the Internet, business, and society*. Oxford: Oxford University Press.

Childers, L., Disz, T., Olson, R., Papka, M. E., Stevens, R., & Udeshi, T. (2000). Access grid: Immersive group-to-group collaborative visualization. *Proceedings of the 4th International Conference on Immersive Projection Technology*.

Commission on Cyberinfrastructure for the Humanities & Social Sciences. (2004). Retrieved from www.acls.org/cyberinfrastructure/cyber.htm

Cushing, J., Beard-Tisdale, K., Bergen, K., Clark, J., Henebry, G., Landis, E., Maier, D., Schnase, J., & Stevenson, R. (2003). Research agenda for biodiversity & ecosystem informatics. Retrieved from dgrc.org/dgo2004/disc/posters/tuesposters/rp_cushing.pdf

European Commission. (2006). Sixth Framework Programme 2002–2006. Retrieved from ec.europa.eu/research/fp6/index_en.cfm?p=0

Finholt, T. A. (2003). Collaboratories as a new form of scientific organization. *Economics of Innovation and New Technologies*, 12, 5–25.

Foster, I., & Kesselman, C. (Eds.). (1999). *The grid: Blueprint for a future computing infrastructure*. San Francisco, CA: Morgan Kaufmann Publishers.

Foster, I., Kesselman, C., & Tuecke, S. (2001). The anatomy of the grid: Enabling scalable virtual organizations. *International Journal of High Performance Computing Applications*, 15(3), 200–222.

Gerson, E. M., & Star, S. L. (1986). Analyzing due process in the workplace. *ACM Transactions on Office Information Systems*, 4(3), 257–270.

Grudin, J. (1988). Why CSCW applications fail: Problems in the design and evaluation of organizational interfaces. *Proceedings of the Computer-Supported Cooperative Work Conference, CSCW '88*, 85–93.

Iacono, S., & Kling, R. (2001). Computerization movements: The rise of the Internet and distant forms of work. In J. Yates and J. Van Maanen (Eds.), *Information technology and organizational transformation: History, rhetoric, and practice* (pp. 93–136). Thousand Oaks, CA: Sage Publications.

Jarvenpaa, S. L., & Leidner, D. E. (1998). Communication and trust in global virtual teams. *Journal of Computer-Mediated Communication*, 3(4).

Kinney, S., & Panko, R. (1996). Project teams: Profiles and member perceptions. *Proceedings of the Annual Hawaii International Conference on Systems Sciences*, HICSS-29, Hawaii.

Kling, R. (1980). Social analyses of computing: Theoretical perspectives in recent empirical research. *ACM Computing Surveys*, 12(1), 61–110.

Lee, C., Dourish, P., & Mark, G. (2006). The human infrastructure of cyberinfrastructure. *Proceedings of CSCW'06*, Calgary, Canada, 483–492.

Lohr, Steve. (2005, January 24). New group will promote grid computing for business. *New York Times*, p. C7.

Malone, T. W., & Rockart, J. F. (1991). Computers, networks, and the corporation. *Scientific American*, 265(3), 128–136.

Mark, G., & Abrams, S. (2005). Differential interaction and attribution in collocated and distributed large-scale collaboration. *Proceedings of the Annual Hawaii International Conference on Systems Sciences,* HICSS-38, Hawaii.

Mark, G., Abrams, S., & Nassif, N. (2003). Group-to-group distance collaboration: Examining the "space between." *Proceedings of the 8th European Conference on Computer-Supported Cooperative Work, ECSCW '03,* Helsinki, Finland, 159–178.

Mark, G., & DeFlorio, P. (2001): An experiment using life-size HDTV. *Proceedings of the IEEE Workshop on Advanced Collaborative Environments*, San Francisco, CA.

Mark, G., Grudin, J., & Poltrock, S. (1999). Meeting at the desktop: An empirical study of virtually collocated teams. *Proceedings of the 6th European Conference on Computer-Supported Cooperative Work, ECSCW '99,* 159–178.

Mark, G., & Poltrock, S. (2004). Groupware adoption in a distributed organization: Transporting and transforming technology through social worlds. *Information and Organization*, 14(4), 297–232.

Markus, M. L. (1983). Power, politics, and MIS implementation. *Communications of the ACM*, 26(6), 430–444.

Millen, D. R., & Fontaine, M. A. (2003). Multi-team facilitation of very large-scale distributed meetings. *Proceedings of the 8th European Conference on Computer-Supported Cooperative Work, ECSCW '03,* Helsinki, Finland.

National Environment Research Council. Retrieved from www.nerc.ac.uk/funding/escience

National Science Foundation. (2003). Revolutionizing science and engineering through cyberinfrastructure. Report of the National Science Foundation Blue-Ribbon Advisory Panel on Cyberinfrastructure. Retrieved from www.nsf.gov/od/oci/reports/toc.jsp

Norman, D. A. (1988). *The psychology of everyday things*. New York: Basic Books.

O'Conaill, B., Whittaker, S., & Wilbur, S. (1993). Conversations over video conferences: An evaluation of the spoken aspects of video-mediated communication. *Human-Computer Interaction*, 8, 389–428.

Olson, G. M., & Olson, J. S. (2000). Distance matters. *Human-Computer Interaction*, 15(2/3), 139–178.

Orlikowski, W. J. (1993). Learning from notes: Organizational issues in groupware implementation. *The Information Society*, 9(3), 237–250.

Rogers, Y. (1994). Exploring obstacles: Integrating CSCW in evolving organizations. *Proceedings CSCW'94*, 67–78.

Ruhleder, K., & Jordan, B. (1999). Meaning-making across remote sites: How delays in transmission affect interaction. *Proceedings of the 6th European Conference on Computer-Supported Cooperative Work,* September 12–16, 1999, Copenhagen, 411–429.

Sabbagh, K. (1996). *Twenty-first-century jet: The making and marketing of the Boeing 777*. New York: Scribner.

SBE/CISE Workshop on Cyberinfrastructure for the Social Sciences. (2005). Retrieved from vis.sdsc.edu/sbe

Smith, B. C. (1996). Limits of correctness in computers. In R. Kling (Ed.), *Computerization and controversy: Value conflicts and social choices* (2nd ed.). San Diego, CA: Academic Press.

Star, S. L., & Ruhleder, K. (1996). Steps toward an ecology of infrastructure: Design and access for large information spaces. *Information Systems Research*, 7(1), 111–134.

Tapia, R., & Lanius, C. (2001). Computational science: Tools for a changing world. Retrieved from ceee.rice.edu/publications.html

Weinberg, A. (1961). Impact of large-scale science on the United States. *Science*, 134, 161–164.

Wilson, J. Q., & DiIulio Jr., J. J. (1995). *American government: The essentials.* Lexington, MA: D.C. Heath and Co.

Wilson, K. G. (1988). Grand challenges to computational science. *Proceedings of the AIP Conference,* 169(1), 158–169.

Wulf, W. A. (1993). The collaboratory opportunity. *Science*, 261(5123), 854–855.

Zare, R. N. (1997). Knowledge and distributed intelligence. *Science*, 275, 1047.

Chapter 11

Examining the Proliferation of Intranets

Roberta Lamb[1]
University of California, Irvine

Mark Poster
University of California, Irvine

Abstract

In this chapter, we critically examine the confluence of interests that characterized the rapid, widespread adoption of intranets (1996–2002). We reflect on the notion that when a new technology clearly has both emancipatory and control applications, and is easily appropriated at the grass roots level and the organizational level, its diffusion can be rapid and pervasive. There is some theoretical support for and explanatory value to be gained from considering the intranet movement as a specific movement within more general computerization movements, but our more comprehensive understanding engages the convergence discourse—the rhetoric about a new wave of technological capabilities that has bundled computing and communication advances with work and lifestyle changes.

Our discussion draws upon the concepts of social-constructionists, post-industrialists, and social actor theorists to examine the intranet movement. We revisit notions about technologies as "neutral" that precipitate around computing technologies that are used to enhance both freedom and control. Our inquiry positions notions of technological determinism in computerization movement discourse in light of constructionist and post-structuralist concepts and, based on empirical analysis of intranet study data, it explores the value of examining computerization movements as shifts in the mode of information when social actors develop new cultural language/practices.

Defining Movements

In keeping with the theme of this book, we will examine intranets as a specific movement within the general computerization movement (CM) and the internetworking CM discussed in Iacono and Kling (2001). Iacono and Kling focused their studies on the *who* and the *what* of CMs, as well as the detailed histories of agency and institution within particular computerizing organizations. Their work advanced an understanding of sociotechnical CM frameworks that can quickly characterize specific CMs, such as the intranet movement (IM), in terms of a general CM milieu, allowing us to examine intranets more carefully as a mode of information by tracing the development of this new cultural language/practice. In this chapter, we will do just that—but first we want to review some key concepts about CMs as they relate to intranets.

A CM Primer for Intranets

Like Poster (1990) and other information society analysts, Iacono and Kling (1996) have taken issue with the technologically utopian discourse of CM participants, who, "along with the media and the state, emphasize technological progress and deflect competing beliefs, laying a foundation for social visions that include the extensive use of advanced computer systems" (p. 90). Despite such criticism, utopian discourse was in ample supply during the early phase of the intranet movement, when intranet adoption was expected to parallel the exponential curve of Internet adoption, and organizational intranet return on investments (ROIs) were expected to mimic early reports and estimates of 1000 percent or more. According to a 1996 Forrester industry report, 40 percent of the firms surveyed had already implemented intranets, 25 percent were in the intranet planning stage, and 24 percent had begun to consider implementing one (Pincince, Goodtree, & Barth, 1996). In the U.S., Forrester estimated intranet growth to be 60 percent annually, spurred by the nearly unlimited possibilities for applications of this highly configurable information and communication technology (ICT) and by promises of 'jackpot' ROIs.

Iacono and Kling (1996), like Forrester, have critically examined CM organizations (CMOs) that advocate for more intensive and pervasive computing in various social, economic, and political domains. These groups use technological utopianism as a key framing device to amplify current problems, interpret events, and emphasize the advantages of a transformed social order, where computerization and networking are central, over the current arrangements—and *as a CMO recruiting device*

(Iacono & Kling, 1996, p. 92 paraphrased). "A primary resource for all movements are members, leaders, and communications networks ..." and CMOs recruit their new members with the rhetoric of technological utopianism (p. 101). One group that actively embraced intranet rhetoric as a framing and recruiting device was the library community—particularly special librarians, who were looking for a way to better display their value in downsizing organizations and were willing to retool and redefine themselves as "information architects" (Dillon, 2001).

The discourse of specific CMs, like intranets, personal computing, office automation, artificial intelligence, computer-based education, and urban information systems (IS), typically comprises a set of five ideological elements (Kling and Iacono, 1995):

1. Computer-based technologies are central for a reformed world.
2. Improved computer-based technologies can further reform society.
3. More computing is better than less, and there are no conceptual limits to the scope of appropriate computerization.
4. No one loses from computerization.
5. Uncooperative people are the main barriers to social reform through computing.

Using this list of elements, we can quickly and accurately characterize the IM discourse through rhetorical substitution:

1. Intranet technologies are central for a learning organization.
2. Improved intranet-based technologies can further organizational learning through knowledge sharing.
3. More intranet integration is better than less, and there are no conceptual limits to the scope of appropriate knowledge sharing.
4. No one loses from enterprise-wide intranets.
5. Uncooperative people are the main barriers to knowledge sharing through intranets.

Iacono and Kling's (1996) analyses also help us position IM participants within the social network of a general CM. These social actors extend links from the list of CMOs that Iacono and Kling have described into their professional and work organizations where they connect members of functional work groups and other communities of practice. For example, one assemblage of intranet enthusiasts that pre-dated the movement had commonly gathered in the United States at annual National Online Meetings (circa 1980 through the mid to late 1990s).

Prominent participant groups included librarians, educators, and vendors of online information from the pre-Web era (e.g., DIALOG, Westlaw, LexisNexis). They sponsored the first Intranets '99 conference (April 26–28, 1999, www.onlineinc.com/intranets, now defunct URL), which attracted the traditional "online" crowd and also some new constituents: Web services consultants, and information/Web site usability researchers, as well as content/quality/knowledge managers. This last group has come to dominate the discourse of recent intranet conferences and, beginning in 2004, renamed the gathering KMWorld & Intranets (see the latest conference announcement at www.kmworld.com/kmw06).

Among the early IM participants were industry advocates who held themselves up as national exemplars of innovative intranet design and effective intranet use (e.g. the Perkins-Coie law firm, a Washington, DC law librarians association at www.llrx.com, and the MITRE Corporation). These groups put up Web sites and gave keynote speeches and related presentations at intranet conferences to share their acquired expertise. The MITRE Corporation saw this dissemination of information and technological know-how as part of its charter. The law firms considered this activity as an extension of the *pro bono* work tradition.[2] Librarians and library and information science (LIS) academics were particularly active in the intranets movement. During the same period, many LIS schools were being merged with other information technology (IT) schools on campus, while special librarians in industry were under attack by corporate downsizers. For all librarians, then, the new "teched-up" identity of "information architect" seemed attractive and the IM was seen as a vehicle for transporting that new identity into the next millennium. Throughout many commercial organizations, like Manufacturing Conglomerate (see the section "From Home Page to Portal" later in this chapter), Chief Executive Officers (CEOs) put out a call to find innovative uses of Internet-related technologies, which spread the interest in intranets to marketing teams and product development teams in a wide variety of industries. And so, prior to the dot-com bust, the list of IM organizations (IMOs) had grown to include the special libraries association, library educators, industry trade and professional associations, new product managers, human resources staff, project teams, quality control managers, online information providers, and various other hardware and software producers.

By building on Kling and Iacono's framework in this way, we can sketch the who and what of an IM in the U.S., and can begin to more carefully examine IM dynamics. Iacono and Kling (1996) noted that "CMs generally advance the interests of elite groups" because, although "CM advocates more frequently see themselves as fighting existing institutional arrangements ... they must develop coalitions with elite groups ..." (p. 99). For intranets, this observation rings particularly true, because intranets are, by definition, deployed within an organization or a network of cooperating organizations, and are not designed to be otherwise publicly available. We also note that, as with the general CM, "there is no well-organized opposition or substantial alternative ..." (Iacono & Kling, 1996, p. 99) to the IM.

This concordance with Kling and Iacono's reflections might lead us to similarly conclude that the rise of intranets "will lead to conservative social arrangements, reinforcing the patterns of an elite-dominated, stratified society" (Iacono & Kling, 1996, p. 102). However, we find that the cultural language/practices that are enacting IM dynamics have the potential to profoundly reshape social arrangements, rewrite the A-list of elites, and seismically shift the social strata of an Internet-based culture. In the balance of this chapter, we will critically examine CM and IM discourse, then use these insights to analyze two IM dynamics with data from a four-year study of U.S. intranets (Lamb, 2003, 2006). Our discussion will draw on theoretical analyses of post-industrial society developed over the past two decades (Poster, 1990, 1995, 2001, 2004).

Words in Action: Discourse Dynamics

Iacono and Kling (1996, p. 89) "argue that the rise of computer technologies and networking is due to collective action similar to that of other social movements, such as the environmental movement, the anti-tobacco movement, the movement against drinking and driving, or the women's movement, for example." Although Iacono and Kling do not explicitly reference his work, their observations about CMs resonate strongly with Touraine's (1988) concepts about other social movements.

Social Actors and Modes of Information

According to Touraine (1988, p. 63), "it is impossible to define an object called 'social movements' without first selecting a general mode of analysis of social life on the basis of which a category of facts called social movements can be constituted." His definition relies on a mode of analysis that understands social order as the result of conflicts and transactions, and collective behavior as conflictual actions or struggles to defend, reconstruct, and/or adapt an element of the social system: "When conflictual actions seek to transform the relations of social domination that are applied to the principal cultural resources (production, knowledge, ethical rules), they will be called social movements" (Touraine, 1988, p. 64). Although he refers to social movements like CMs or IMs as 'collective actors' (cf. p. 158), the nature of the collective has changed from earlier times when "one could speak not only of nationally defined societies, but also of nationally defined social actors (organized labor or the entrepreneurs, for example). This is no longer true: A great many social actors defend their interests in markets or in competitive, or even conflictual, arenas that are more likely defined by a technology or an economic conjuncture, by strategic conflicts or cultural trends of international scope, than by an overall national reality" (p. 67).

Touraine (1988, p. 74) concludes that "we are entering into a new mode of production, which by giving rise to new conflicts, will give birth to new social movements, extending and diversifying social space but also perhaps extending forms of domination and of social control that will reach deeper and be even more adept at manipulation." Iacono and Kling have examined some of the conflicts of CMs, and in so doing they have highlighted the importance of discourse in shaping social space. For this discussion, we want to hold up for further inspection these two aspects of social movements, conflict and discourse, as key to a new mode of production: the mode of information. As we have argued extensively, "in the mode of information a new set of language/practice is imposed on existing ones, those in face-to-face and print contexts. ... The means of communication are removed from the community of speakers and are abstracted from their material base in the mode of production. ... The new language/practice is a cultural creation" (Poster, 1990, p. 67). The rhetorical devices that we see deployed by CMOs and IMOs to recruit members and to shape intranet discourse are essentially new sets "of structures of domination that are linguistically based" (Poster, 1990, p. 22).

Utopian Vision and Convergence Discourse

If we define the general CM as a social movement, and the IM as a specific CM that privileges a mode of information, we can better understand the rapid proliferation of intranets from 1996–2002, because this framing trains our attention on conflict and discourse. At first glance, we notice that the "convergence" discourse, which commonly explains the rapid uptake of intranets by diverse groups in a wide range of organizational settings, is heavily laden with technological determinism. Advocates commonly suggested that, due to their highly configurable and interoperable technologies, intranets could be used as groupware, as local area network replacements, as local digital libraries, as document management systems, as Internet firewalls, and as Web IS (Castelluccio, 1996; Gibbs, 1997; Hills, 1997; Michel, 1997; Stahl, 1996). And because these technologies are nearly identical to those that power the Web, a similar adoption rate could be expected. A 1998 Internet survey found that 79 percent of firms had a Web site presence (up from 59 percent in 1997) and that for international firms that number rose to 86 percent (up from 69 percent in 1997) (CRITO, 1998). Our own preliminary screening of U.S. Midwest firms showed that in 1998, about 40 percent of the companies we contacted had intranets "up and running" or were just implementing them. Some IS analysts at the time had begun to express concern that intranets might be misused or underutilized (Chellappa, Barua, & Whinston, 1996; O'Hern, 1997). Their concerns extended from firms that did not use intranets at all to firms that were using intranets simply as file servers or as corporate Web servers—not taking advantage of their potential (i.e., technologically determined) capabilities.

The IM discourse about convergence draws strength from general CM logic that supports the related technological action frames of productivity, death-of-distance, and ubiquitous computing (see Elliott & Kraemer, Chapter 1, this volume). Intranet productivity claims center on two main themes. First, maintaining and disseminating critical documents online via a single repository would reduce the physical labor of producing and distributing them on paper or by e-mail, and it would reduce the mental uncertainty of working with versioned document copies—the intranet would be the *only* authorized source. Second, the intranet would remove barriers to knowledge sharing so that information could flow freely into every corner of the organization—effectively removing the communication bottlenecks that cause costly delays. Intranet death-of-distance claims focus on the potential for all members of organizational and inter-organizational work teams to coordinate their efforts via intranet exchanges—"the intranet" would become a single virtual workspace where people and their ideas could come together. Intranet ubiquitous computing claims rest on the global adoption of interoperable Internet protocols across a wide variety of computing and telecommunication devices that could be linked to intranets—anywhere, anytime, any way connectivity could provide continuous intranet access.

In summary, the utopian vision of convergence has been expressed as the coming together of people, documents, and technologies into a seamless oneness—one work group, one information source, one always-accessible technical platform. It borrows concepts from general CM technological action frames to create a specific IM technological action frame of convergence, alignment, and control.

Emancipation and Control

Interestingly, IM discussions that originally focused primarily on the technology (e.g., Intranets '99) have come to include a focus on managerial action (e.g., Knowledge Management & Intranets 2004–2006). Although such shifts in movement discourse seemingly display a convergence of interests, they often mask underlying conflict. The conflict becomes apparent in the contending discourses about intranets that also draw on general CM framing concepts, like democratization, self-expression, and the free flow of information. Intranet democratization claims extend from organizational experiences with

ICTs that have allowed organization members to communicate more directly with each other. Faster, more honest feedback in intranet discussion forums could lead to better decision making at all levels; intranet sites that provide greater awareness of organizational goals and procedures could improve coordination of distributed units; innovation could be spurred by knowledge sharing among work groups via intranets; and more egalitarian working conditions could be encouraged by a resultant sense of shared motivations and interlinked intranets. This specific IM contending discourse of diversity, autonomy, and emancipation is no less utopian, but its focus is on increasing the degrees of freedom for organization members with technology rather than constraining them within one mode.

New Language/Practices

The conflicts about intranets, therefore, center not on whether they *should* be created and used, but on *how* and *by whom* that should be accomplished. When a new technology, like intranets, clearly has both emancipatory and control applications, and is easily appropriated at the grass roots level and the organizational level, its diffusion can be rapid and pervasive. This can level the playing field in some ways by reducing barriers to adoption, but it can present formidable challenges to resolving conflict through technological consensus, as multiple intranets take shape throughout the organization. When intranet interests come into conflict, the contests often foster either new uses of technology that resolve conflict around key practices, or new rhetorical devices that mask unresolved conflict. Both outcomes are marked by noticeable shifts in the discourse, and our data show that such IM discourse shifts are interesting moments of innovation and negotiated order (see the following section on IM dynamics).

These new language/practices about intranets are productions of a mode of information that defines the information age—they are configurations of information exchange. Poster has argued that new configurations of communication can "alter significantly the network of social relations, [and] restructure those relations and the subjects they constitute" (Poster, 1990, p. 8). In *The Second Media Age*, he described how "electronically mediated communication (what [he calls] 'the mode of information') both challenges and reinforces systems of domination that are emerging in a postmodern society and culture. [His] general thesis is that the mode of information enacts a radical reconfiguration of language, one which constitutes subjects outside the pattern of the rational, autonomous individual. This familiar modern subject is displaced by one that is multiplied, disseminated and decentered, continuously interpellated as an unstable identity" (Poster, 1995, p. 57).

When we bring together Poster's concept of a mode of information with Touraine's description of a social actor, we can examine general CM, and IM specifically, as the development of new cultural language/practices for electronically mediated exchange by social actors. From this perspective, we can begin to see how the IM preference for convergence discourse underlines Touraine's (1988, pp. 124–125) point that "we are entering into a type of society that can no longer 'have' conflicts: Either these are repressed within the framework of authoritarian order, or the society acknowledges itself as conflict, indeed is conflict, because it is nothing more than the struggle of opposed interests for the control of the capacity to act upon itself." We can also see how this way of thinking anchors CM characterizations made by Iacono and Kling to sociological and historical frameworks. For example, in a society that can no longer have conflicts, intranet technology is likely to be portrayed as *neutral*—where no one loses.

In the next section we will analyze the intranet movement and its convergence discourse by examining two IM dynamics that highlight the contradictory propensity of intranets for emancipation and control:

- Hegemony and *différance*[3] – degrees of integration
- Monitoring and self-monitoring – degrees of autonomy

Our analysis will revisit notions about technologies as *neutral* that precipitate around computing technologies that are used to enhance both freedom and control.

Intranet Movement Dynamics

The examples presented for discussion in this chapter have come from Lamb's multi-year, multi-industry study of intranet development and use in mid-western U.S. organizations (1998–2003). Surveys and case studies were conducted among manufacturing firms, law firms, healthcare organizations, commercial and residential real estate firms, and restaurant organizations. Preliminary data collection was conducted through face-to-face and telecom interviews with operational employees, IT staff, managers, and organization members whose responsibilities spanned the traditional boundaries of these roles. Interview protocols were iteratively refined by theoretical sampling (Strauss & Corbin, 1990) and by concurrent analysis of preceding interviews. Supporting materials pertaining to intranet design and use were also collected and analyzed over the course of the larger study.

Data collection and analysis were guided throughout the study by key concepts about the social construction of technology (Bijker, 1995) as well as theoretical insights about organizational isomorphism drawn from institutionalist theory (Scott, 1995). This sociotechnical focus highlighted several aspects of intranet development and use, particularly intranet enrollment in efforts of quality control and regulatory compliance, the "ensemble" quality of "systems in use," and the need for resultant intranets to accommodate multiple uses and multiple stakeholders. Bijker's (1995) concepts about the interpretive flexibility of technological artifacts, and the role of relevant social groups in the often very quick stabilization of the technology, were central to the study in its early years; while understandings of "drift" (Ciborra, 2000) have helped to focus follow-on data collection at the case study firms and to guide analysis of the larger intranet movement. Although we had originally envisioned that the organization would be a proper unit of analysis for intranet study, we found that a focus on "an intranet and its community of practice (COP)" provided a more cohesive unit for theorizing about intranet adoption and use.[4]

In the following discussion, we draw upon prior publications about this research that extensively analyze the study data, but not through a CM perspective. Here, we refocus our analyses on conflict and discourse in IM, paying particular attention to the micro-level processes that shape macro-level IM and CM dynamics. Because the concepts that inform these analyses may be new to some readers, we have divided each subsection into two parts: a conceptual overview and a condensed reanalysis of our published intranet study findings.

Degrees of Integration

One important moment in the intranet movement was marked by a rhetorical shift in the discourse from concerns about intranet "home pages" to intranet "portals." Our IM reanalysis of this shift critically interprets social constructionist concepts to frame it as an ongoing conflict between hegemony and *différance* that attends the integration of organizational intranets.

Social Constructionism

CM analysis concepts relate to macro-level phenomena. As Elliott and Kraemer note in Chapter 1 of this volume: "They work at the macro-social level in motivating people to join a CM. Individuals and organizations then appropriate these frames into their micro-social contexts. These frames circulate in public discourses designed to mobilize membership in a particular CM." When studying intranets with a smaller unit of analysis (i.e., the intranet and its COP) and then reanalyzing that data in macro-level analysis, it is helpful to enlist concepts that can relate macro-level IM phenomena to micro-level processes around intranet use, such as social constructionist perspectives.

For example, in our intranet studies "The Intranet" does not exist. In its place we find many loosely connected "intranet islands," each one of which may serve a particular work group or community of practice within the firm. Social constructionists view these work groups as social actors who can shape organizational structures through their iterative everyday practices, and who can initiate change through these very processes (Berger & Luckman, 1967). Social actors interact with variously constituted "others" to form the basis of social institutions and identities (Goffman, 1959, 1974). Technological artifacts, like intranets, are integral to these interactions and so shape identity and institutions. In use, technologies like intranets are part of a sociotechnical system—an extension of practice and also a part of structure—having dual effects and creating unintended outcomes. The technological action frames that have formed in the public discourse around intranets strongly influence how they are used within organizational units and other communities of practice (Bijker, 1995; Orlikowski & Gash, 1994; Wenger & Snyder, 2000).

According to Bijker (1995), relevant social groups shape sociotechnical systems in broadly predictable ways, and his SCOT (social construction of technology) theory suggests how a particular ICT may evolve:

- New technological artifacts have *interpretive flexibility*. Whether artifacts "work" or "don't work" depends entirely on who uses them and how they use them.
- In the early stages, an artifact may *develop multi-dimensionally*. The artifact may assume more than one basic form.
- *Relevant social groups* interpret and redefine the artifact as they adapt it to their purposes and apply their understandings of what it is.
- The form and interpretation of the artifact will *stabilize* as relevant social groups reach consensus about the form, or as one group's interpretation dominates.
- Once an artifact has stabilized, it is difficult to change. *Interpretive flexibility is significantly reduced.*

Bijker's concepts about the interpretive flexibility of technological artifacts, and the role of relevant social groups in the often very quick stabilization of the technology, extend and augment general constructionist theory concepts. They share a common theoretical heritage with technological action frame arguments (Orlikowski & Gash, 1994), and they are frequently used in tandem with another important line of theorizing, Wenger's work on COPs, to examine collective activities and intranet-supported organizational interactions (cf. Wenger & Snyder, 2000).

From Home Page to Portal

A shift in the intranet discourse from "home pages" to "portals" emerged from concerted efforts by corporate IT groups to integrate intranets under one enterprise-wide technical framework, and also to usurp intranet format and content control from small, local (functional) groups in order to implant it more firmly within larger corporate COPs.

Proponents of intranet portal integration campaigns often attempted to make grass roots intranets available and accessible at a corporate level, believing that wider sharing of intranet content with those not local to the content development would benefit the firm as a whole, but also hoping that by imposing some standards, the integration would lessen demands on thinly stretched IT resources. Many integrations were fraught with conflict, as local groups vied with corporate IT groups to gain or retain control of resources (and jobs) in a "dot-com boom and bust" environment. Most intranet integration efforts were look-and-feel oriented to provide a standard interface so that "outsiders" within the firm could more easily find what they sought. In practice, however, outsiders made very little use of grass roots intranets since they were by definition outside the project team, the formal work group, or the community of practice. Pragmatically, many companies' IT departments tempered their attempts to achieve full integration, electing instead to pursue integration at the intranet hardware and software level (i.e., tcp/ip networking, basic internet technology applications—ftp, http, smtp—and a basic but expandable client desktop) and to leave intranet content and intent in the control of local business units. Despite a noticeable (and actually beneficial) lack of deep integration, the local "home page" rhetoric has disappeared and the "portal" rhetoric has won out. This terminology shift signifies corporate dominion over the organizational grass roots intranets—that goal alignment and convergence have been achieved, that conflict has been resolved, and that the organization is sharing knowledge and leveraging expertise.

Constructivist concepts can describe how relevant social groups construct sociotechnical reality—and they should lead researchers to expect rhetorical constructions of reality. Similarly, the strength of a technological action frame centered on the imperatives of productivity can help to explain the zeal of intranet integration campaigns. However, a key observation in this study is that, regardless of the degree of intranet integration sought or claimed, the integration is very often measurably absent. The portal becomes a simulacrum of integration—and that is actually a good thing.

For example, Manufacturing Conglomerate (a pseudonym) is a Fortune 500 company with headquarters in the midwestern U.S. This organization has grown over the last decade, through a series of acquisitions and mergers, into a firm with two very different areas of manufacturing expertise (MC1 and MC2). At the beginning of this study (1998), more than 15 intranets were in use within the company. Most were linked and protected by a common firewall. However, a few of the more recently merged MC2 firms were still operating on different networks and their intranets were not accessible by others in the larger organization, due to difficulties in reconfiguring firewalls and perceived restrictions on sharing intranet information. Some of the fully accessible intranets served MC1, others served MC2, but none had been designed for a corporate-wide audience. To help ease the growing pains, Manufacturing Conglomerate's new CEO wanted to communicate a strong message throughout the firm: "We are one company!" He envisioned that a corporate intranet would be an effective mechanism for sending his message, and in 1998 a corporate-wide committee was convened to develop an intranet integration plan. The goal was to create a corporate intranet portal that would eventually replace the disparate intranet islands throughout the firm.

Soon afterward, yet another merger was announced. The "one company" discourse continued, and the corporate portal remained a CEO priority, but only superficial progress was made toward merging the various intranets. They continued to serve their local constituents, albeit with a slightly different look and feel to the Web-based interface.

In early 2001, MC1 (at one time the main focus of the company) was sold to a private investment firm and those business units lost access to all but the data on their local intranet servers. There was no longer a need to communicate the "we are one company" message across two very different manufacturing divisions, because Manufacturing Conglomerate was now two companies. As a result, the "new" corporate intranet was abandoned. However, for both MC1 and MC2, the local intranets are just as important as ever to local processing, and the divisional intranet of MC1 has become an important vehicle for globally communicating across the divested unit locations. Interestingly, people within the firm had long "suspected" that something like the split would happen.

At many firms like this one, intranet-enabled knowledge sharing is more apparent than real from an enterprise-wide structural standpoint. Meanwhile, the superficially integrated focal intranets effectively support the COPs and project teams that they were created to serve as a nexus of sharing. Even when weeded out by corporate IT integrators seeking hegemony, we found that grass roots intranets have a tendency to grow back in support of the *différance* of the social actors who would use them. This resistance to hegemony has proven particularly helpful when firms exercise their agility in rapidly changing industries, allowing key functional groups and inter-organizational COPs to keep operating as their corporate structures are shuffled or eliminated.

In IS journals, there are as yet no Feyerabends crying out "against integration," but there is clearly a need for a theoretical perspective around systems integration that includes non-transactional types of integration, and that also incorporates the notion that integration must be reversible or deconstructable at critical junctures to support a common range of inter-organizational interactions. Little research attention has been given to disintegration, reverse integration, or the unpacking of integrated systems—there is not even a good term for them. The need often coincides with divestiture or decentralization, but these terms do not adequately incorporate the complexities of extracting embedded information infrastructures in ways that support autonomy and/or new integration opportunities.

In our research, we found that organization members recognize the contradictions in their words and actions. Local intranet owners speak to corporate management in terms of "portals" and "integration" when they fight for control over these resources and the freedom to expand and develop their intranets as need demands and opportunity allows. Neither the IM discourse nor the IS literature give them a good vocabulary for making their arguments. Our empirical insights suggest that better approaches to ICT integration need to explicitly accommodate collectivities other than "the organization" and inter-organizational interactions other than "the transaction." For many non-transactional integrations, it would seem that a "project-based" approach could be appropriate (Lamb, 2003). Hardt and Negri (2000) have situated the crises of modern authority at precisely this juncture in the struggles for emancipation and control, and they have identified new forms of organizing (e.g., swarming) around collective enterprise (e.g., projects) that will become more prevalent as ICTs (e.g., intranets) proliferate. These projections suggest that discourse may not be able to mask the conflict for long—particularly if Touraine (1988, p. 108) is right and "the growing complexity of programmed society can result only in a decreasing degree of integration."

Degrees of Autonomy[5]

A second interesting moment in the intranet movement that we will discuss begins with a restructuring of professional roles and identities and ends with a shift of control to a new elite for whom CM and IM discourse and technologies have cut both ways—physicians in health maintenance organizations (HMOs). Our discussion centers on the ways in which ICTs like intranets are enlisted by physicians who self-monitor their activities as they struggle for autonomy, even as the same ICTs are used to set up standards and frameworks for convergence.

Self-Monitoring and Professional Identity

Educational background and membership in professional associations shape our sense of who we are, how we should conduct our professional activities, and how others should regard us. The rise of professionalism in modern society has increased and standardized the ways in which people identify themselves and signal their occupational competencies (e.g., the MBA degree for managers, the MD for physicians), and it has also provided codes of conduct for interactions among professionals and those they serve (Larson, 1977). The professional self is just one identity facet of the multiple, decentered modern subject that is continuously interpellated by the technologies of the mode of information (Poster, 1995). ICTs play a role in forming and enacting professional identity by presenting professionals with expanded opportunities for coordination, interaction, and feedback (Finholt, 2002; Olson & Olson, 2000). ICTs, like intranets, can increase the flows of information available to the professional, so that the ongoing narrative of self-identity occurs in an inter-organizational context, negotiated through self-monitoring as well as interactions and relationships with others (Giddens, 1991).

According to psychological theorists, the propensity to self-monitor is a personality trait that ranges from high to low. High self-monitors actively try to shape their social worlds by constructing public selves that they believe will affect the perceptions of others in socially enhancing ways (Snyder & Gangestad, 1986). Foucault (1977) offers another way to understand self-monitoring behavior: as surveillance. He claims that self-monitoring activities primarily serve the controlling principals of society, and only secondarily serve the self-monitoring individuals themselves. Techniques and technologies align individual goals with organizational goals, as prescribed in management control literature (Keen, 1991). Within regimes of disciplinary control (e.g., total institutions, such as the prison), Foucault describes how "architectures" (like Bentham's Panopticon) can be designed to induce people, regardless of their personality traits, to monitor their own behavior in conformance to specific guidelines or norms.

Central to this understanding is the idea that power/knowledge is a unit of operation that can be exercised to exert control over others through dividing practices, scientific classifications, and subjectification. "Power is not something that is acquired, seized or shared, something one holds onto or allows to slip away ..." (Foucault, 1980, p. 94). Power is relational "... it becomes apparent when it is exercised ... [and] is not associated with a particular institution, but with practices, techniques, and procedures" (Townly, 1993, p. 520). Similarly, knowledge does not exist in isolation as independent and detached: "[k]nowledge is the operation of discipline. It delineates an analytical space and ... provides the basis for action and intervention" (Townly, 1993, p. 520). "It is not possible for power to be exercised without knowledge, it is impossible for knowledge not to engender power" (Foucault, 1980, p. 52).

CM discourse challenges organizations to leverage ICTs in order to maximize their human capital by closely monitoring workers and continually improving workers' alignment with organizational goals. Walsham and his colleagues have found that workplace introductions of new ICTs and their associated monitoring practices have played important roles in structuring systems of professional expertise—usually decreasing the discretionary authority of organizational professionals (Barrett, Sahay, & Walsham, 2001; Barrett & Walsham, 1999; Walsham, 1998, 2001). However, in the face of increasing processes of control, other studies show that organizational professionals continually seek techniques and strategies to increase or regain power/knowledge (Townly, 1993; Knights & Wilmott, 1985). One way they do this is through self-observation, often understood as a form of surveillance that may involve computerized monitoring (Knorr-Cetina, 1999). By engaging in such activities, Foucault would note that professionals are, ironically, complicit in their own control. Nevertheless, many prefer self-monitoring to monitoring and are willing (and able) to define the parameters of their own control.

Power/Knowledge Intranets

The organizational structures of the healthcare industry have reshaped the action of 21st-century professionals in profound ways. Like other professionals in law and academia, physicians' roles have become increasingly rationalized around economic and quality concerns (Heinz, Laumann, Nelson, & Michelson, 1998). The primary care physician (PCP) in our intranet study is a professional agent, contracted or employed to provide healthcare services for an HMO. These professional agents differ significantly from the employee agent of classical agency theory—their ICT-enhanced self-monitoring practices enable them to achieve even higher levels of alignment with a set of organizational goals that they continually refine through boundary spanning activities.

ICT systems, including intranets, have been repeatedly put forward in solutions to the problems of healthcare human resource management. "At one extreme, then, is the possibility of recasting the identity of doctors as quasi-managers, with budgets, responsibilities, and delegated powers over their professional colleagues. However, there is also the possibility of an alternative pattern in which the new management information generated by ICT systems is diffused into the peer-based professional discourse of doctors, in the belief that their practices will gradually evolve in directions consistent with the values of the architects of Resource Management. This could be seen as the encouragement of 'self-control' or 'auto-regulation'" (Coombs, Knights, & Wilmott, 1992, p. 67).

In our intranet study, PCPs have sought to maintain some autonomy in this power/knowledge dynamic, and sophisticated (and expensive) ICT systems have become an important part of their self-monitoring strategies (Lamb, 2006). The PCPs we interviewed monitor their own unit's performance based on HMO regional guidelines and using HMO ICT systems, but many of them also challenge these guidelines with their own medical practice experience and research, and develop new systems for their own and related practice monitoring. Self-monitoring is performed by a variety of boundary spanners at several different levels, and intranets are key components of their systems of self-control. For example, at Pure HMO, one of the healthcare organizations in our study:

- Physician/researchers have their own specialty practice and also conduct medical research. Their research may be focused on a particular procedure, using Pure HMO patient outcome data, and new clinical practice guidelines (CPGs) from this research are often immediately put into standard practice by posting them on the intranet and by linking the intranet documents to ICT-based drug prescription protocols.
- Physician/ICT developers have taken it upon themselves to enhance their own practice by developing or purchasing ICT software and related instrumentation, and by developing local intranets for sharing region-specific practice guidelines.
- Physician/managers are focused on improving their own practice, as well as that of their associate physicians. There is a managerial staff at Pure HMO, but physicians actively steer the organization, as has been the tradition among professional practice groups, such as law firms where partners manage the infrastructure and set strategic direction. For national guidelines, Pure HMO has a central unit that issues reports, holds regional seminars, and makes comparative analyses across regions using Pure HMO clinical data. These methods appeal to PCPs' sense of professional excellence and to regional competition to develop motivations for implementing the guidelines.

The interrelated activities of these three types of boundary spanners (physician/researchers, physician/managers, physician/ICT developers) coordinate the development of CPGs and CPG implementation through the design-in-use of existing ICT infrastructure. Boundary spanners are critical to achieving goal alignment at Pure HMO because, motivated by self-monitoring incentives or tendencies, they co-construct expanded roles and organizational structures that incorporate ICTs (like intranets and hospital management IS with automated "active guidelines" alert mechanisms) into their ways of working. Professional autonomy is then negotiated through a set of processes that carefully coordinates compliance and monitoring activities with continuous improvement and self-monitoring activities. Self-monitoring practices can, thereafter, be more easily adopted by other physicians at Pure HMO in ways that foster goal alignment with changing external regulations, as well as internal quality targets. In other words, in an effort to monitor their own practice outcomes, these boundary spanners have extended the organizational infrastructure for monitoring all physicians at Pure HMO and for improving evidence-based clinical practice.

These PCP self-monitoring practices are distinct from, but tightly integrated with, monitoring performed by Pure HMO's internal analytical unit, and the monitoring functions of external groups like HIPAA (Health Insurance Portability and Accountability Act of 1996). Many PCP self-management activities are guided by considerations of cost and quality, as well as professional ethics, and they affect local and national outcomes in ways that benefit the whole organization (i.e., increasing goal alignment, decreasing residual loss) when they result in the development and implementation of new or better clinical practice guidelines. For theorists who focus on social actors, this seems about right: "Since the idea of management has replaced that of organization, it is natural that the theme of self-management should replace that of socialism, that is, the workers' control over the organization of labor" (Touraine, 1988, p. 111).

These findings, and other recent publications (Doolin, 2004; Kohli & Kettinger, 2004), indicate that ICT-enhanced self-monitoring can establish a win-win scenario for principals and professional agents, but only when boundary spanners are able to negotiate the new order by adjusting organizational goals, ICT implementations, and/or outcome measures. This observation may be particularly salient for organizations in sectors such as healthcare that must balance the conflicting goals of low cost and high quality. We have also found that, to remain effective, this flexibility should extend to the ICTs themselves. For example, as the intranet hype of the late 1990s died down, we expected that intranets as an artifact would have begun to stabilize (Bijker, 1995). However, at Pure HMO and other organizations in the study, the shape and content of intranets continued to "drift" (Ciborra, 2000). Moreover, this ability to drift continually seemed crucial to accommodating the conflicting goals of high quality, low cost, and professional autonomy. So while notions of drift generally refer to system dynamics that have become unmanageable and misaligned with higher quality goals, our intranet examples provide a counterpoint—suggesting that systems may drift toward higher quality as well as away from it.

In this example, we have illustrated a critical dynamic of the mode of information and have tried to make some rather abstract concepts more apparent: The interpellation of a "professional" is always incomplete; the subject is always multiple; identity and control are intertwined (Poster, 1990, 1995). At Pure HMO, boundary-spanning PCP roles become redefinitions that engender new power/knowledge relationships. The intranets become a workshop of language/practice constructions. As in Foucault's explanation of the Panopticon that effectively creates the inmate as a subject, the HMO ICT system creates the self-defining PCP. At Pure HMO, constructing a professional identity entails defining the information and the system that will measure and monitor that entity. In this way, self-definition and self-monitoring produce a negotiated order of limited autonomy. When PCPs can define HMO practice, and what it means to be a "good" practitioner, by defining the clinical statistics that are to be measured, as well as the language of CPG definition, measurement, and evaluation, they can retain some autonomy as professionals and, in collective action, become a self-ruling elite. This shift in the IM discourse is at the performative level, rather than at the denotative or connotative level. Rather than masking the underlying conflict, it resolves it through a new cultural language/practice.

Concluding Discussion

In our examination of two key dynamics of the IM, we have used the analyses of Iacono and Kling as a helpful starting point. We have interleaved their analyses with our own understanding of an emergent information society and its manifestations of the mode of information. By critically examining the intranet convergence discourse, we see how these technologies actually do provide new places to form identity; how more online resources and mandated disclosures actually do provide information that empowers professionals to monitor organization-wide activities; and how flexible integration actually is accommodated by an ICT-supported organizational discourse that masks underlying conflict. Such implementations stand in stark contrast to technologically deterministic prescriptions for effective intranet management.

Clearly, the CM and IM entail dynamics that engage the social actor in a new set of cultural language/practices that combine the rhetorical and the real (or the constructed) in ways that mask conflict. ICTs are deeply implicated in these dynamics, making CMs and IMs, as Kling and Iacono have argued, social movements in their own right. However, it would be naive to consider these social movements as principal actors, and to relegate their participants to mere "membership." As Baudrillard

(1981) cautions, the social actor is not the industrial worker of critical theory that "presupposes the naivete and stupidity of the masses" (Baudrillard, 1981, p. 81). In our studies, we find that information age workers are keenly aware of the discrepancies between CM and IM discourse and the reality of everyday conflictual work life, and they purposively contribute to the construction of their sociotechnical worlds.

This understanding of information society actors demands some flexibility in defining the unit of analysis for CM studies and it has raised some methodological concerns among general social movement analysts. "An urgent need exists for developing new research approaches that look directly at social action itself, that study actors not only in their acts but also in the analyses they draw from these acts, and who attempt to bring out, beyond the response behavior imposed by a social order, the questioning behavior through which society produces itself conflictually" (Touraine, 1988, p. 139). In a small way, the data collection and analysis methodology that supports our discussion rises to Touraine's challenge. The social actor approach, which we developed, used, and refined in a series of qualitative studies, helps us reconceptualize people together with their ICTs (Lamb & Kling, 2003). In this instance, the methodology encourages a presentation of the social actor that adds value to an examination of the CM and IM by focusing on sociotechnical networks, boundary spanners, drift, and design-in-use. This approach takes into account the performative aspects of ICTs by considering the social actor in the mode of information to be a unit of analysis that consists of people and their ICTs. When considering IM dynamics, we have conceptualized the social actor unit as, alternatively:

- A professional individual + his/her support staff + ICTs, in their working environment, or
- Variations on project-based work groups using ICT ensembles in organizational settings.

In this way, we have begun to examine the ways that social actors interact—as people and their ICTs collaborating and coming into conflict with other people and their ICTs.

Throughout this chapter we have used this methodology to provide empirical examples that show how the dynamics of the mode of information are fueled by the juxtaposition of two utopian IM visions:

- The convergence/alignment/control technological action frame that draws on general CM promises of productivity, death of distance, and ubiquitous computing to promote particular uses of intranets; and
- The diversity/autonomy/emancipation contending discourse that draws on general CM promises of democratization, and

stands on principles of freedom, to promote wider dissemination of information and more autonomous uses of intranets.

We have linked our data discussions to a set of related theoretical explanations that focus our attention on discourse and conflict so that we can better understand how "convergence" takes shape among competing utopian visions. Our examinations of the shift from home page to portal, and the shift from monitoring to self-monitoring, show that, in the face of conflicting goals such as integration and local variation, or low cost and high quality, there is a need for continuous flexibility and for malleable ICT configurations.

One common theme throughout our intranet study was the expressed need by social actors for lower costs, higher productivity, higher quality, and greater flexibility, as well as the hope that intranets could in some way help them achieve these conflicting objectives simultaneously. Wrapped up in this notion is the idea that, because it affords organization members more degrees of freedom, and also allows them to implement "best practice" standardizations of professional practice, which are often one-dimensional, the intranet is a neutral technology. By coupling the mode of information perspective to CM and IM analyses, we gain an appreciation for the decidedly non-neutral role of intranets in the power/knowledge dynamics of organizations. We see how, among PCPs in HMOs as well as members of flexible manufacturing organizations, "the subject is constituted through practices of subjection or in a more autonomous way, through practices of liberation, of liberty, ... on the basis, of course, of a number of rules, styles, inventions to be found in the cultural environment" (Foucault quoted in Poster, 1995, p. 83). Essentially, our examples illustrate that, like power/knowledge, the emancipation/control fusion is inseparable. Simple conceptualizations of ICTs like intranets and databases that characterize them as sources of emancipation, through freedom of information, fail to account for ICTs' performative aspects—their ability to constitute subjects. In our attempts to reconceptualize social actors who actively develop new intranet language/practices as people and their ICTs, we explicitly recognize these performative aspects, as well as the propensity for convergence discourse to mask CM and IM conflicts.

Acknowledgments

This study was funded by National Science Foundation, Information and Intelligent Systems, Computation and Social Systems Research Grant Awards to Roberta Lamb #98-76879 and #00-96169 (1999–2003). Any opinions, findings, and conclusions or recommendations expressed in this material are those of the authors and do not necessarily reflect the views of the National Science Foundation (NSF).

Endnotes

1. Roberta Lamb passed away in November 2006 during the production of this book. She was an Associate Professor in the Donald Bren School of Information and Computer Sciences at the University of California, Irvine at the time of her death. In her career, Roberta made outstanding contributions to research in information systems and social informatics. She had recently completed a four-year NSF-funded study of the development of organizational intranets and the interorganizational relationships that shape intranet use. She had also recently completed a Fulbright Scholarship at the University of Turku in Finland. She served as deputy editor of *The Information Society*, associate editor of *Information Technology and People*, and social aspects theme editor of the *Journal of Digital Information*. Roberta was also widely recognized as an excellent teacher and mentor to students. We will miss her as a colleague and scholar.
2. In a follow-up study interview, one active firm member explained that he was doing much less intranet expertise sharing in 2003, because he believed that most firms had already come up to speed on these technologies.
3. *Différance* is derived from the French word *différe*, which means "to defer or postpone" and "to differ." Jacques Derrida, a well-known French philosopher, coined the term in the 1960s used in the context of deconstruction. *Différance* suggests that words and signs can never fully reveal what they mean, but can only be defined or explained using more words (www.wikipedia.com).
4. A more detailed description of the intranet study methodology can be found in Lamb (2003).
5. For a detailed discussion of this dynamic, see Lamb (2006).

References

Barrett, M., Sahay, S., & Walsham, G. (2001). Information technology and social transformation: GIS for forestry management in India. *The Information Society*, 17, 5–20.

Barrett, M., & Walsham, G. (1999). Electronic trading and work transformation in the London insurance market. *Information Systems Research*, 10, 1–22.

Baudrillard, J. (1981/1994). *Simulacra and simulation* (Sheila Faria Glaser, Trans.). Ann Arbor: University of Michigan Press.

Berger, P., & Luckman, T. (1967). *The social construction of reality*. Harmondsworth, U.K.: Penguin.

Bijker, W. E. (1995). *Of bicycles, bakelites, and bulbs: Toward a theory of sociotechnical change*. Cambridge, MA: MIT Press.

Castelluccio, M. (1996). Internet/intranet? *Management Accounting*, 78(3), 52–53.

Center for Research on Information Technology and Organization (CRITO). (1998, Winter). Beyond e-mail: Orange County companies' use of Internet grows more sophisticated. *Center for Research on Information Technology and Organization Newsletter*.

Chellappa, R., Barua, A., & Whinston, A. B. (1996). Intranets: Looking beyond internal corporate Web servers. In R. Kalakota & A. B. Whinston (Eds.), *Readings in electronic commerce*. Reading, MA: Addison-Wesley.

Ciborra, C. (Ed.). (2000). *From control to drift—The dynamics of corporate information infrastructures*. Oxford: Oxford University Press.

Coombs, R., Knights, D., & Wilmott, H. C. (1992). Culture, control and competition: Towards a conceptual framework for the study of information technology in organizations. *Organization Studies*, 13(1), 51–72.

Dillon, A. (2001). Practice makes perfect: IA at the end of the beginning? *Bulletin of the American Society for Information Science and Technology*, 27(4), 28–29.

Doolin, B. (2004). Power and resistance in the implementation of a medical management information system. *Information Systems Journal*, 14, 343–362.

Finholt, T. A. (2002). Collaboratories. In B. Cronin (Ed.), *Annual Review of Information Science and Technology*, Vol. 36 (pp. 73–108). Medford, NJ: American Society for Information Science and Technology/Information Today.

Foucault, M. (1977). *Discipline and punish: The birth of the prison*. Harmondsworth, U.K.: Penguin.

Foucault, M. (1980). *Power/knowledge: Selected interviews and other writings 1972–1977*. New York: Pantheon Books.

Gibbs, M. (1997). An intranet is an intranet, but is it also an extranet? *Network World*, 14(4), 66.

Giddens, A. (1991). *Modernity and self-identity*. Cambridge, U.K.: Polity Press.

Goffman, E. (1959). *The presentation of self in everyday life*. New York: Doubleday.

Goffman, E. (1974.) *Frame analysis*. Cambridge, MA: Harvard University Press.

Hardt, M., & Negri, A. (2000). *Empire*. Cambridge, MA: Harvard University Press.

Heinz, J. P., Laumann, E. O., Nelson, R. L., & Michelson, E. (1998). The changing character of lawyers' work: Chicago in 1975 and 1995. *Law & Society Review*, 32(4), 751–776.

Hills, M. (1997). *Intranet as groupware*. New York: John Wiley and Sons.

Iacono, S., & Kling, R. (1996). Computerization movements and tales of technological utopianism. In R. Kling (Ed.), *Computerization and controversy: Value conflicts and social choices* (2nd ed., 85–105). San Diego: Academic Press.

Iacono, S., & Kling, R. (2001). Computerization movements: The rise of the Internet and distant forms of work. In J. Yates & J. Van Maanen (Eds.), *Information technology and organizational transformation: History, rhetoric, and practice* (pp. 93–136). Thousand Oaks, CA: Sage Publications.

Keen, P. G. (1991). *Shaping the future: Business design through information technology*. Boston, MA: Harvard Business School Press.

Kling, R., & Iacono, S. (1995). Computerization movements and the mobilization of support for computerization. In S. L. Starr (Ed.), *Ecologies of knowledge: Work and politics in science and technology* (pp. 119–153). Albany, NY: State University of New York Press.

Knights, D., & Wilmott, H. C. (1985). Power and identity in theory and practice. *Sociological Review*, 33(1), 22–46.

Knorr-Cetina, K. (1999). *Epistemic cultures: How the sciences make knowledge*. Cambridge, MA: Harvard University Press.

Kohli, R., Kettinger, W. J. (2004). Informating the clan: Controlling physicians' costs and outcomes. *MIS Quarterly*, 28(3), 363–394.

Lamb, R. (2003). Intranet boundaries as guidelines for systems integration. *International Journal of Electronic Commerce*, 7(4), 9–35.

Lamb, R. (2006). Healthcare practice ISOlation: Articulating systems that drift toward higher quality. *International Journal of Medical Informatics*, 76(1), S159–S167.

Lamb, R., & Kling, R. (2003). Reconceptualizing users as social actors in information systems research. *MIS Quarterly*, 17(2), 197–235.

Larson, M. S. (1977). *The rise of professionalism: A sociological analysis*. Berkeley: University of California Press.

Michel, R. (1997). Intranet introspective. *Manufacturing Systems*, 15(10), 20–22.

O'Hern, P. (1997). Intranet makeover. *Network World*, 14(12), 122–125.

Olson, G. M., & Olson, J. S. (2000). Distance matters. *Transactions on human computer interaction*, 15, 139–179.

Orlikowski, W. J., & Gash, D. (1994). Technological frames: Making sense of information technology in organizations. *ACM Transactions on Information Systems*, 12, 174–207.

Pincince, T. J., Goodtree, D., & Barth, C. (1996). The Forrester report: Network strategies. Forrester Research, Inc.

Poster, M. (1990). *The mode of information: Poststructuralism and social context*. Chicago: University of Chicago Press.

Poster, M. (1995). *The second media age*. Cambridge, MA: Polity Press.

Poster, M. (2001). *What's the matter with the Internet?* Minneapolis: University of Minnesota Press.

Poster, M. (2004.) The digital unconscious: Identity theft and security, or, what's the use of having an identity. Creative Commons.

Scott, W. R. (1995.) *Institutions and organizations*. Thousand Oaks, CA: Sage Publications.

Snyder, M., & Gangestad, S. (1986). On the nature of self-monitoring: Matters of assessment, matters of validity. *Journal of Personality and Social Psychology*, 51(1), 125–139.

Stahl, S. (1996). Document management arrives on the Web. *Information Week*, 570, 21.

Strauss, A., & Corbin, J. (1990). *Basics of qualitative research: Grounded theory procedures and techniques*. Newbury Park, CA: Sage Publications.

Touraine, A. (1988). *Return of the social actor: Social theory in postindustrial society* (M. Godzich, Trans.). Minneapolis: University of Minnesota Press.

Townly, B. (1993). Foucault, power/knowledge, and its relevance for human resource management. *Academy of Management Review*, 18(3), 518–545.

Walsham, G. (1998). IT and changing professional identity: Micro-studies and macro-theory. *Journal of the American Society for Information Science*, 49(12), 1081–1089.

Walsham, G. (2001). *Making a world of difference: IT in a global context*. Chichester: John Wiley & Sons, Ltd.

Wenger, E. C., & Snyder, W. M. (2000, January–February). Communities of practice: The organizational frontier. *Harvard Business Review*, 139–145.

Part V

Freedom and Information Rights

Chapter 12

Information/Communications Rights as a New Environmentalism? Core Environmental Concepts for Linking Rights-Oriented Computerization Movements

Andrew Clement
University of Toronto

Christie Hurrell
Centre for Health and Environment Research

Abstract

With the growing role that information and communications technologies play in everyday life, a range of advocacy movements has begun to emerge around various "rights" everyone should enjoy in relation to their informational activities—for example, rights to personal privacy, access to information resources and infrastructure, free expression in online fora, control over one's digital creations, etc. While these various rights movements are largely growing up in isolation from each other, these increasingly can and are being seen as varied aspects of a broader "information/communications rights" movement. There are a number of striking parallels between this emergence and interweaving, and the rise of the environmental movement(s) 40 years ago, when a similarly varied range of concerns (e.g., about local degradations, species loss, ozone depletion, toxic emissions, etc.) and their particular advocacy actions developed a more shared sense of the "environment" and the need for coordinated custodianship. Using key features of the growth of the environmental movement as a framework, this chapter analyzes three of the most prominent computerization movements associated with information rights, namely community networking (and information and communications technologies for development), free/open source software, and informational privacy. It examines the core principles and key indicators of movement development, highlighting the linkages and tensions with each other as well as the environmental movement. The chapter concludes that there is good potential for their integration within a broader, nascent information/communications rights movement, and points out some of the challenges in achieving this.

Introduction

While there are many individually identifiable computerization movements (CMs), there is no over-arching CM as such.[1] Nor should we expect to find one, given the disparity of goals and values reflected among them. However, there are plenty of overlaps and potential connections among them that have so far been largely unexplored. The various CMs related to informational rights offer a promising starting point to look for the emergence of a broader, synthetic CM based on alliances between hitherto distinct movements.

A defining characteristic of CMs, according to Kling and Iacono (1988), is their orientation to social reform. Some CMs go so far as to position the pursuit of particular, fundamental rights at the core of their ideologies. Prominent among these information rights-oriented CMs (IRCMs) are these three:

- Community networking (and information and communications technologies [ICTs] for development), which promotes universal access to and effective use of computers and information infrastructures to enhance local community-based economic and social development.
- Free and Open Source Software (F/OSS), which advocates for multiple software "freedoms" (to run, copy, distribute, study, change, and improve the software) and promotes the use of free software over proprietary software.[2]
- Informational privacy, which seeks to protect personal information and promote "informational self-determination."

In each case there are movement advocates, both individuals and organizations, which "focus on computer-based systems as instruments to bring about a new social order (Elliott & Kraemer, Chapter 1, this volume). Among their driving ideological beliefs can be found the central beliefs—about the role and scope of computing in social reform, and the obstacles to its achievement[3]—that characterize CMs (and counter-CMs [CCMs]).[4] Utopian as well as dystopian (and anti-utopian) visions of the future play a visible role in defining goals and identifying adversaries. Activists push these movements, articulating principles and manifestos, recruiting members and allies, establishing advocacy organizations, and tackling opponents. While often experiencing setbacks, they each legitimately claim some notable achievements.

But beyond these commonalities and a shared broad interest in "rights," these CMs currently have remarkably little connection between them, and are isolated from each other in terms of their constituencies, methods, and conceptual underpinnings. This lack of connection risks fragmentation of effort, thereby undermining their effectiveness. Particularly when compared with social movements in other areas, including those similarly oriented to human and civil rights, these three CMs can at best be regarded as fledgling, in the sense that they have not mobilized broad public support nor, consequently, yet achieved a significant reforming influence on social institutions. One social movement that is notably more mature and successful in this respect is the environmental movement. Having coalesced earlier and sharing several striking commonalities with these IRCMs, the environmental movement offers a promising point of comparison and inspiration.

A measure of a CM's maturity is the degree to which its core issues are relevant to the concerns of a diverse public and can offer practical, or at least promising, action strategies. This, in turn, garners popular attention and support, providing the basis for effective mobilization. In the case of the environmental movement, there are many people who over the past few decades have come to understand that such everyday activities as eating, breathing, drinking, cleaning, driving, and so on are intimately and often problematically linked to each other, as well as to wider issues of the quality and sustainability of life on earth. A further achievement is that there is wide recognition of a more or less coherent program of recommended remedies by individuals, cities, corporations, and governments that even if not fully complied with, at least substantively informs debate.

People also conduct their affairs with and within an increasingly complex informational environment, constituted out of a widening range of media, symbol systems, and socio-material practices centuries in the making. Computerization has significantly intensified these interactions and raised (or re-raised) a host of issues that confront people, overtly and subtly, on a daily basis. As millions of individuals now routinely go online, they encounter a web of interrelated challenges, such as expensive devices, inscrutable interfaces, flaky connections, viruses, spam, obnoxious pop-ups, proliferating porn, unreliable and insecure operating systems, impaired identities, inaccessible databases, unresponsive technical support staff, intrusive Internet service providers, dis-information campaigns, corrupted news media, and an onslaught of information often of questionable authenticity and value. It requires skills, effort, and resources to achieve and sustain a smoothly functional information/communication environment for all. The various CMs mentioned here collectively address most of these obstacles while each offers significant insights and distinctive programs directed toward accomplishing the ideal, but from the point of view of the individual users, there is little obvious correlation between the various CM issues and their online experience. If rights-oriented CMs are to engage the popular imagination in the way that the environmental movement has, they need much more than just greater publicity—there must be a clearer articulation of the ways in which these movements' principles are related to each other and to the day-to-day experiences of the average computer user.

The primary aim of this chapter is to investigate the potential for a greater alignment among these CMs, drawing specifically on the core precepts of environmentalism as conventionally understood. It will do this mainly by exploring the similarities, and differences, between the nascent information rights movement, as reflected in the public statements of prominent North American, European, and international IRCM advocacy organizations, and the much more fully developed environmental movement. In keeping with the social informatics ideals, it strives to examine "new social phenomena that emerge as people use ICTs" and thereby achieve a "better understanding of the design, use, configuration, and/or consequences of ICTs such that they are more workable for people in organizations and society" (Kling, 1999).

The chapter is structured as follows. The next section discusses the emergence of the environmental movement as a coming together of many disparate movements, each with distinctive issues and a diversity of popular organizations, mobilizing means, strategies, and targets. It emphasizes the emergence of the unifying conception of the "environment" as a shared commons vital for the sustenance of life, characterized by diverse, interdependent ecologies, and then explores how these concepts could be used by CMs. Each of the three IRCMs is discussed in turn, highlighting their historical, conceptual, and ideological roots, identifying their differences as well as overlaps, and revealing the common threads shared with the environmental movement. The value of this analysis is illustrated by reviewing the online challenges raised here in light of environmental insights. The chapter concludes with a sketch of recent developments toward a synthetic information/communications rights CM and the prospects for further integration.

The Rise of the Environmental Movement

While the roots of the environmental movement can be traced back several centuries, in North America it became popularized only after World War II, amidst an increasingly prosperous, well-educated, and consumer-oriented society. The higher standard of living after the war increased people's access to wilderness areas, and also equipped them with the resources and skills to protect their local environments. Environmental concerns became widespread in North America during the 1960s, and seem to have coalesced into a recognizable "movement" by the 1970s. But this social movement was and continues to be fragmentary, comprised of many groups of disparate composition, ideology, and aims. Despite this, the movement has had success in uniting toward a common cause. Three broad strands of environmental concern are worth noting for their specific contributions to what eventually became known as the environmental movement.

The first of these was the wilderness movement, which came into prominence in the 1950s through the efforts of groups such as the Sierra Club, the Audubon Society, and the National Geographic Society. These groups lobbied to protect remote and spectacularly beautiful areas against industrial encroachment, in order to preserve them for aesthetic and recreational enjoyment. The post-war boom forced wilderness lovers to become more vocal in the defense of remote areas.

The second theme was a concern by communities all over North America to protect areas closer to home, in an effort to conserve community assets. The campaign to protect wetlands is one example of this impulse, which succeeded in mobilizing a diverse range of interests, from scientists to hunters, toward a common cause. Whether they were interested in these lands for aesthetic, recreational, or functional reasons, citizens recognized them as a common good worthy of conserving. Attempts to ward off threats to common environmental assets were also manifested in community actions to halt large-scale intrusions such as dams, highways, and oil refineries. Environmental struggles were characterized as a local resistance to some "outside" force, such as a government agency or corporate industry. While more formal environmental organizations with regional or national agendas often supported these local actions, the sustaining drive of protection campaigns was an "accumulation of local grievances and thwarted hopes" (Hays, 2000, p. 320).

The third theme in the growing environmental movement of post-war North America was a concern with personal and community health. Advances in medicine and public health meant that the threat of bacterial diseases was much diminished, and citizens' perspectives on health began to change, with an emphasis on healthy living, good nutrition, and exercise. As personal and scientific evidence showing the link between environmental factors and human health mounted, individuals and communities began to mistrust industry and government spokespeople who de-emphasized the danger of such environmental threats as toxic waste dumps or chemical fertilizers. The "disconnect" between official explanations of environmental threats and the realities of personal experience resulted in an attitude of frustration among the general public, and a stance of self-reliance in matters of health. The natural food movement, influenced by the counter-cultural atmosphere of the 1960s, was one result of this attitude.

What unites these three broad areas of environmental concern is their grass-roots social and political drive: They were not typically tied to particular power groups or political parties. In addition, the growing movement was deeply influenced by scientific discoveries. The new fields of environmental science and ecology showed how seemingly separate problems (e.g., smog and human illness) could in fact be intimately related, and hugely popular books such as Rachel Carson's *Silent Spring* (1962) created a public dialogue around these issues.[5] The widening diffusion of the television meant that spectacular environmental disasters were delivered in full color to living rooms across North America, eliciting wide support for local struggles and an awareness of environmental threats. Other protest movements of the 1960s and 1970s, especially the peace movement, also shaped the environmental movement. Environmental concerns fit into larger pushes for social justice, and the activist belief that groups of ordinary citizens could and must push for change inspired both established and new environmental groups to adopt fresh strategies in their goal to protect the environmental commons.

Traditional groups such as the Sierra Club adopted new, more aggressive strategies. In 1965, the Sierra Club launched its first lawsuit, and soon after founded the Sierra Club Legal Defense Fund, which continues to use the concept of "environmental rights" to wage high-profile battles against big businesses implicated in wilderness destruction and pollution. Newer groups grew out of a frustration with traditional approaches and the activist political stance borrowed from the anti-war movement. These groups ranged from Greenpeace, which encouraged activists to "bear witness" and engage in nonviolent resistance, to Earth First!, whose followers engaged in civil disobedience and illegal actions such as tree spiking. Although the actions of these protest generation groups often angered more conservative parts of the movement, by the late 1960s the younger group of environmentalists constituted the broad base of support for environmentalism, as well as providing some of its most influential spokespeople (Sale, 1993).

By the mid 1970s, although still fraught with internal tensions and preoccupied with divergent aims, the environmental movement had certainly achieved a much broader scope. Old conservationist concerns about the impact of human society on a particular wilderness area or species had widened to include a concern for the impact human actions had on the environment in general. The 1970s became the "decade of environmental legislation" in North America, seeing laws passed on air pollution, water quality, and species protection. The U.S. Environmental Protection Act of 1969 required all actions undertaken by a governmental agency in the United States to undergo an Environmental Impact Assessment before proceeding. In 1972, the United Nations hosted a conference on the Human Environment, reflecting the realization that environmental issues were global in scope and required collective custodianship. The Stockholm Declaration that was adopted at the conference contains principles of environmental protection and development, as well as practical recommendations for their implementation. These legislative changes, although by no means complete victories, demonstrate the wide influence of the environmental movement and the general acceptance of the notion that the Earth represents a "public good" that deserves protection. The current widespread acceptance and promotion (at least in principle, if not in practice) of environmental values in most sectors of the "developed" world, from individual waste reduction and sorting practices, to municipal recycling programs, to prominent international protocols, are certainly a testament to the movement's force and scope.

Environment

In achieving this degree of coherence and popular appeal, the environmental movement has overcome some formidable obstacles. Notable among these is finding common cause among the wide range of individual movements (such as around wilderness protection, global warming, ozone depletion, endangered species, community composting, and even specific sites or tracts of land). In part, this diversity and fragmentation stemmed from the lack of obvious relationships among these movements. Contributing to their unification was the development of a discourse that helped people see the hitherto hidden interconnections and their implications for everyone. A key element of a unifying discourse is the concept of the "environment" itself—loosely treated as "all the stuff that surrounds us and which we rely on for our basic activities." To say that it is potentially anything and everything of course makes it difficult to pin down its meaning in any particular context, but this very ambiguity likely well served the unifying of the various movements because they could all say they were fundamentally about the same thing that was so consequential for us all. The concept of a unified environment encouraged individuals to see themselves as a part of an environmental community of interdependent parts, and to take a moral responsibility for the health of that community. As early environmentalist Aldo

Leopold (1949) wrote: "The land ethic simply enlarges the boundaries of the community to include soils, waters, plants, and animals, collectively: the land" (p. 203).

The informational/computational analog to the natural environment is most simply termed "information environment," that is, those aspects of the general environment constituted out of the information artifacts and practices that we interact with in conducting our everyday affairs. Within this broad notion, it is useful to focus on a central aspect that has been treated analytically by various authors: the "information infrastructure." Bowker and Star (1999) note of this technical environment: "We hardly know what we have built. No one is in control of infrastructure; no one has the power centrally to change it. To the extent that we live in, on, and around this new infrastructure, it helps form the shape of our moral, scientific and esthetic choices" (p. 319). Clement and Shade (2000) note that the information environment encompasses communications media both old and new, and emphasize that users of information have diverse needs and desires in relation to the information environment. Like the concept of the natural environment, the information infrastructure is a broad concept with broad implications for those who use it. Thus, it makes sense for individuals and communities of computer users to take an interest in, and some responsibility for, the health and development of this complex and always-evolving set of relationships and systems.

Commons

Another concept that has been useful for the mobilization of environmental ideals is the notion of the natural world as a common or public good. Common goods, as defined by economists, are competitive and nonexcludable, while true public goods are both noncompetitive and nonexcludable. Environmentalists have defined most natural resources, such as forests or fish stocks, as common goods, while a smaller number of environmental assets, such as clean air, are seen as public goods. Seeing most of the natural world as a common yet consumable set of resources unites the environmental and the social, and resonates with some of the core values of mainstream environmentalism. The drive to establish national parks, the proliferation of legislation to protect water and air quality, and the signing of international protocols to curb pollution have all been helped along by a general commitment to the idea that air, water, and land are invaluable assets that communities benefit from and are responsible for, and that should not come under private ownership or control. This broad concept of public rights and responsibilities is an accessible entry point into the often complex and impenetrable world of scientific studies and gloomy environmental predictions. It has been used to great effect by environmental groups seeking to effect policy change, because it moves environmental concerns into the same policy arena as common goods such as public health and education, concepts that have long been able to mobilize a broad level of support among citizens.

ICTs, as environmental assets before them, are often described by CMs as common goods or resources. The concept is used by the CMs discussed in this chapter in a number of ways: to ensure participatory and transparent governance of the Internet and other ICTs, to curb commercial intrusion into online 'spaces,' to ensure equitable public access to new technologies, to distribute and use free software, and to preserve a common level of privacy for those who use ICTs. Those trying to curb the commercialization of ICTs stress that the transformative power of the Internet and related technologies can be realized only if they are free from state and market control. The Association for Progressive Communications (APC) states of the development of the Internet: "Today, as governments and businesses become more and more interested in 'controlling' the Internet, we need to defend the Internet as a secure and accessible space for social justice, campaigning and for promoting development" (APC, 2004).

This drive to preserve public space online that will benefit large numbers of people resembles the push in the 1950s to establish national parks and to protect land against commercial development. Online advertising, media conglomeration, and expensive, opaque proprietary software become the virtual equivalents of toxic waste and polluting and greedy corporations. Big corporations are portrayed by CMs as selfish and shortsighted, concerned only with profit and not with the long-term benefit of computer users. The F/OSS movement has been especially vocal in its criticism of large software companies such as Microsoft. But although the concept of an informational commons has motivated activists in CMs, it has not yet mobilized broad public support for the protection of a public digital sphere. While national governments have made policy decisions to support public access to ICTs, ensuring access to meaningful electronic resources and tools free from corporate influence or control has largely been left up to individual efforts. However, each of the CMs discussed in this chapter has something to gain from the commons analogy, and could gain strength for their causes by more explicitly aligning issues of common access and control of ICTs with other common good issues already widely supported by citizens and governments.

Ecology

The concept of an all-encompassing natural environment provided a discourse that helped motivate the nascent environmental movement. The conceptual framework introduced by ecology, however, offered a more precise way to document and understand the interconnections in the natural world. Numerous books on ecology—first scientific and then more popular—have had a huge impact on the environmental movement. The discipline of ecology, being the study of interactions between and among organisms and their environment, has shown that these interactions are ubiquitous and important for the continued health of the planet. Ecologists' discoveries were useful for those working toward progressive environmental change. An ecological approach to the environment resonated with the growing popular awareness that seemingly disparate phenomena, such as pollution and cancer, were in fact inextricably linked. In her influential book *Silent Spring*, Rachel Carson (1962) pointed to the disastrous and unintended effects of insecticides on the larger community of animals and humans, and suggested that these poisons be renamed "biocides" to reflect their universally destructive nature. Ecology gave the environmental movement a new way of conceptualizing the relationships between elements of the natural world, as well as a new language and methodology to express its goals, thus lending to the movement the authority of science.

Since the initial, biological definition of ecology was put forward in the 1950s, the concept has been used to explain human, political, and economic interactions. CMs have also used the ecology model to explain and examine relationships between people and ICTs in "information ecologies." Nardi and O'Day (1999) define information ecologies as systems of "people, practices, values and technologies in a particular local environment" (p. 49). Community networking advocates have framed access to the Internet in an ecological manner, focusing not just on basic connectivity but on "effective use" (Gurstein, 2003), which encompasses the wide range of social and political dimensions of access. The F/OSS movement has stressed that seemingly "invisible" parts of the technological milieu, such as software, actually have a huge impact on people's ability to participate in culture and to exercise their rights to free speech and movement. Unlike proprietary software, F/OSS gives full control of the technology to its users, providing they have the necessary skills to exercise this control. Giving computer users more control over the technological environment is also a preoccupation of the informational privacy movement, which tries to educate users about how personal information is collected and shared online by governments and corporations. The group Privacy International warns: "As consumers engage in routine online transactions, they leave behind a trail of personal details, often without any idea that they are doing so. Much of this information is routinely captured in computer logs" (Privacy International, 2004).

The Electronic Frontier Foundation has launched a "Privacy Now!" campaign to educate computer users to the implications of their online behavior. This campaign is similar to efforts such as recycling or energy-reduction campaigns, which have been successful at educating citizens about the implications of their activities in the natural environment. Just because human bodies are left behind when entering the information environment does not mean that online actions and interactions cannot have very real and serious consequences. The language of ecology has helped CMs to animate and draw attention to the complex systems that underlie computer use. It has also pointed to the intimate connections between the diverse parts of the information environment, from fiber-optic networks to software programs to individual behaviors such as online shopping. This integrative approach could be useful for diverse CMs trying to craft a more cohesive and coherent movement based on areas of mutual and related concern.

Considering these achievements of the environmental movement, and with the themes of environment, ecology, and commons in mind, we turn to exploring the developmental trajectories of three rights-oriented CMs.

Community Networking

Community networking and its closely allied research area of community informatics "encompass the social appropriation of information and communication technologies for local benefit, self determination and social inclusion in decision making" (www.cirn2005.org). With its local geographic orientation, community networking as a movement traces its North American origins to the early 1970s with experiments in public access to online community notice boards via terminals linked to time-sharing mainframe computers (e.g., Community Memory in Berkeley and Vancouver, and Santa Monica's Public Electronic Network). In the 1980s, with the emergence of personal computers, the focus was on dial-up access to locally oriented bulletin board systems, which flourished in the early 1990s as freenets, precursors to commercial Internet service providers (see National Public Telecomputing Network, www.nptn.org). At their peak, these services in aggregate claimed well over 1.5 million users. More recently, as the cost of basic Internet access has dropped in urban centers, freenets have declined and the emphasis has shifted to accessing broadband and wireless fidelity networks, especially in rural and remote areas, and to developing locally relevant community content (see Association for Community Networking, www.afcn.org).

Governments have assisted with community networking, but principally as a way to stimulate electronic commerce and e-government services. In the U.S., the Technology Opportunities Program (TOP) and, in Canada, the Community Assistance Program (CAP) has each invested several hundred million dollars since the mid 1990s, but are now terminated (TOP) or in decline (CAP).

The focus of attention in community networking is widening to include initiatives in the third world, where access to ICTs is actively promoted by a disparate array of advocates (UN agencies, foundations, non-governmental organizations [NGOs]) as a way to enhance greater north–south connection and stimulate local socio-economic development. Among the organizations encouraging this trend are NGOs such as the APC and its member organizations (e.g., SangoNet in South Africa), FEMNET, SIGNIS, Panos, and others. Many are linked through the World Forum on Community Networking. Under the banner of ICT4D (ICTs for Development), these civil society organizations played a visible role in the 2003 and 2005 UN World Summit on the Information Society (WSIS).

The main technological action frame (Iacono & Kling, 2001) that has animated this movement is that of universal access to the information/communication infrastructure and the pool of human knowledge. In part this is regarded as a social justice issue of promoting equity (e.g., bridging "digital divides"), but also it is about building and maintaining an "information commons" or public informational sphere (Schuler, 1996).

Adopting a multi-layered "access rainbow" model for this infrastructure helps conceptualize such universal access as involving much more than basic connectivity and computer facilities to encompass the more social and political dimensions of ICT adoption (Clement & Shade, 2000). Complementing the focus on these broad concepts of interoperable networks and coherent policy frameworks, attention is also paid to the local ecologies of systems implementation and information practices that are essential for achieving effective use (Gurstein, 2003).

While the software deployed in these various initiatives has typically been a varied mix of proprietary, shared, and "homegrown" software, as the sophistication and range of community-oriented applications expand, there is growing interest in standardizing on F/OSS. Surman and Reilly (2003) note that besides the practical advantages to OSS, including the lack of licensing fees and the opportunities for collaborative development, community-minded groups can benefit from the open source culture: "As the values of open source begin to be imagined and implemented beyond software, there is a great opportunity for those within civil society to explore new models of collaboration, resource sharing and political actions. This opportunity should be embraced" (p. 6). This impulse among community groups provides the potential for stronger connections to the next CM we discuss.

Free/Open Source Software

Of the three IRCMs we examine here, F/OSS is the one that most visibly exemplifies a CM.[6] Its central advocacy organization, the Free Software Foundation (FSF), and its founder, Richard Stallman, in particular, promote an ambitious mission of social reform, based on the "development of new free software—and on making that software into a coherent system which can eliminate the need to use proprietary software." Central to their definition of free software is a set of freedoms encoded in the General Public License (GPL) and based explicitly on the ideals of the American Revolution of 1776 (Elliott & Scacchi, 2004, p. 8). The FSF famously defines "free software" as:

> [A] matter of liberty, not price. To understand the concept, you should think of "free" as in "free speech," not as in "free beer." Free software is a matter of the users' freedom to run, copy, distribute, study, change and improve the software. More precisely, it refers to four kinds of freedom, for the users of the software:
>
> The freedom to run the program, for any purpose (freedom 0).
>
> The freedom to study how the program works, and adapt it to your needs (freedom 1). Access to the source code is a precondition for this.
>
> The freedom to redistribute copies so you can help your neighbor (freedom 2).
>
> The freedom to improve the program, and release your improvements to the public, so that the whole community benefits (freedom 3). Access to the source code is a precondition for this.
>
> A program is free software if users have all of these freedoms (www.gnu.org/philosophy/free-sw.html).

In a deliberate and significant way, F/OSS constitutes a software commons from which everyone (with the appropriate skills and technical means) can draw. The vitality of the commons, in terms of the quality and range of the software, relies principally on the community of "hackers" dedicated to F/OSS principles (Elliott & Scacchi, 2004), as well as the legal power of the GPL, a key provision of which requires derivative creations to be similarly licensed under the GPL. Analysis of F/OSS production as a form of social organization suggests that it offers a powerful alternative model to conventional modes of software production (Castells, 2005). As Scacchi points out in his analysis of computer game designers (Scacchi, Chapter 14, this volume), the accessibility of the

F/OSS community has the potential to bring together hitherto unrelated CMs.

An important tension resides within this model, since much of the energy behind building and sustaining the commons comes from the purity and meritocratic elitism of "hacker culture." This tends to exclude those who are not software experts and potentially means that software is less likely to be built for applications where there is little interest or peer encouragement among F/OSS developers (e.g., health, primary education).

However, this has not yet emerged as a major limiting factor in its dramatic growth. In the past few years the F/OSS movement has achieved some remarkable gains, particularly as GNU/Linux is beginning to challenge the dominance of the Microsoft Windows operating system. Its public profile is rising on news stories of its apparent superiority over proprietary software in key performance areas. Major computer industry firms, notably IBM, promote business models built on F/OSS, while a growing number of national and state governments around the world (e.g., Korea, Brazil) are standardizing on F/OSS products or including them in their procurement policies. Penguin Days, intended "to bring together open source developers and technology support staff for nonprofits," contribute to the spread of F/OSS in the civil society sector, where cost factors and ideological commitments favor such alternatives (www.penguinday.org). This public discourse and subsequent implementation of F/OSS systems is helping to solidify this CM's place in mainstream organizational practices.

F/OSS is also providing inspiration to non-software economic production systems based on "peer-production" (Benkler, 2001) as well as broader culturally and politically oriented movements of "free culture" (Lessig, 2004; freeculture.org). The relationship between F/OSS and the community networking movement is so far rather uni-directional. On the one hand, F/OSS generally relies on people already having access to digital technologies and the skills to use them. Relatively little attempt has been made to create interfaces highly accessible to those not already adept, or to develop applications outside the domain of the interests of the F/OSS "inner circle." On the other hand, community networking advocates are increasingly building on F/OSS infrastructures and developing the applications that are oriented to easy and effective use.

In F/OSS, "conspicuous contribution" (Neice, 2000) is celebrated much more than the protection of personal information. It is therefore not surprising that there is currently even less connection between it and the informational privacy movement than between it and community networking groups. It is to the privacy movement that we now turn.

Informational Privacy

The informational privacy movement shares with F/OSS a strong and fundamental commitment to the ideal of personal "freedom." While the frequently cited core conception of privacy as the "right to be left alone" is more than a century old (Warren & Brandeis, 1890), the modern privacy movement dates from the 1960s when advocates brought the growth of massive computerized data banks of personal information to public, policy, and academic attention. Allan Westin's books, *Privacy and Freedom* (1967) and *Databanks in a Free Society* (Westin & Baker, 1972), make this rights ideal explicit and provide the seminal definition of informational privacy as "... the claim of individuals, groups, or institutions to determine for themselves when, how, and to what extent information about them is communicated to others" (Westin, 1967).[7]

In important respects the privacy movement enjoyed an early and resounding success. The five data protection principles in the Code of Fair Information Practices formulated by Westin and others in 1973 were expanded to eight in the Organization for Economic Cooperation and Development's (OECD) "Guidelines on the Protection of Privacy and Transborder Flows of Personal Data" (1980) and now underpin virtually all the national data protection legislation worldwide. Modeled on their environmental forerunners, privacy impact assessments (PIAs) are also becoming required in various jurisdictions (Clarke, 2004).

The privacy movement is also characterized by some quite effective advocacy organizations, mainly at the national level. Most notable are Privacy International, based in London, and the Electronic Privacy Information Centre (EPIC), which grew out of Computer Professionals for Social Responsibility and is now based in Washington, D.C. These two organizations frequently bring media attention to breaking issues of privacy, identity, and surveillance, while annually co-producing one of the most comprehensive and authoritative reports in the field, the Privacy and Human Rights Survey.[8]

A third indication of movement success is the widespread popular recognition in North America and Europe of the importance of personal privacy and the contemporary threats to it. This is shown in the consistently high and growing levels of concern reported in recurring public opinion surveys dating back to the 1970s. This trend continues as people go online, as revealed in the AOL/Roper Starch Worldwide Adult 2000 Cyberstudy (see Figure 12.1).

However, these apparent successes are belied by studies of people's actual practices (Solove, 2001), the growing invasions into personal privacy documented in the annual Privacy and Human Rights reports (EPIC/PI, 2004), and the great difficulty that the advocacy organizations have in mobilizing public support around anything other than dramatic public "scandals."

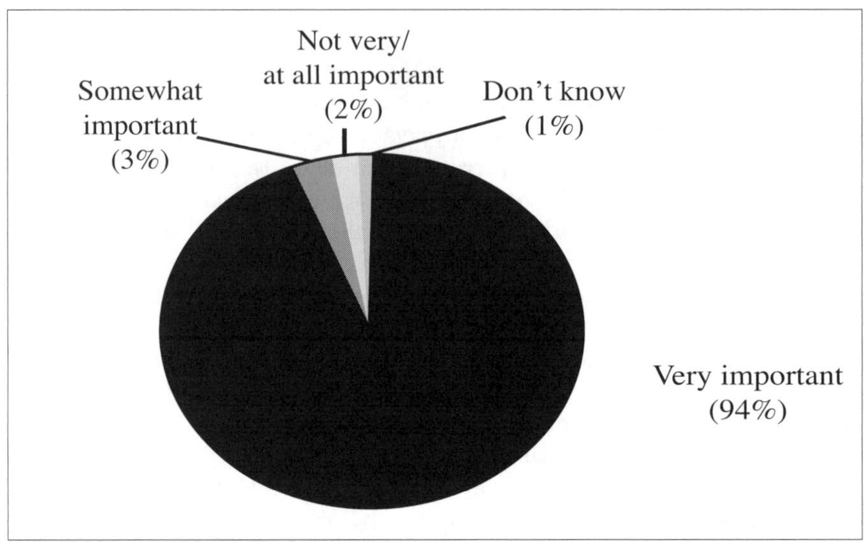

Figure 12.1 How important is it for you to have your security and privacy protected when you are online? (Source: AOL/Roper Starch Worldwide Adult 2000 Cyberstudy)

Part of these difficulties can be attributed to the conception of privacy as principally an individual concern—quite understandable given the explicit language about "personal information" and "the right to be left alone." As Regan (2002) notes, when privacy protection is treated as an individual calculation, "people are less likely to make choices that protect their privacy unless these choices are relatively easy, obvious and low-cost" (p. 401). This leaves data-hungry organizations with a free hand to invade privacy with relative impunity, even when they offer "opt-out" consent provisions. As an alternative technological frame, Regan suggests that "viewing the issue of online privacy as a common pool resource provides a [more helpful] entry point for defining the problem and crafting policy solutions" (p. 402). In keeping with the environmental notion of a shared commons, treating privacy as a public good can point the way out of the mutually mistrustful surveillance cycle. Just as people have accepted the idea that waste and toxins which apparently disappear into the environment come back later to harm us individually and collectively through invisible webs of ecological interaction, so too there is a potential for an informational ecology awareness to develop to the point that people will take personal and political steps to better manage the personal information commons.[9]

A Nascent Over-Arching Information/Communications Rights Social Movement?

Beyond their obvious orientation to computerization, these three CMs all share a focus on human rights issues. However, so far they pursue these in quite disparate ways. In this respect, they are similar to advocacy organizations in the early stages of the environmental movement, working in relative isolation from each other. The underlying issues of these CMs—universal access, intellectual freedom, and privacy, respectively—are, of course, not confined to computerization but are long-standing issues that each has pre-existing movements associated with them. This suggests that one way to enhance their effectiveness would be to make linkages with other, non-computerized human rights movements such as those pursuing civil liberties, community media, and global justice. The spread of the Internet is in turn bringing these previously non-CMs into greater contact with CMs, allowing the two sets of groups to organize around common goals.

One such alliance is the Platform for Communication Rights, which, formed in 1996, is a grouping of NGOs that uses a common strategy relating to communication and democratization to "work for the Right to Communication to be recognized and guaranteed as fundamental to securing Human Rights founded on principles of genuine participation, social justice, plurality and diversity and which reflect gender, cultural and regional perspectives" (CRIS, 2004). In November 2001, the Platform initiated the Communication Rights in the Information Society (CRIS) campaign, whose purpose is to ensure that the issues of communication rights and the democratization of the information infrastructure are kept on the agenda of the WSIS. The CRIS campaign's inclusive goals, which incorporate many of the aspirations of the CMs discussed in this chapter, and the fact that it has been able to mobilize support from a broad range of NGOs, foundations, and individuals all point to the potentially fruitful results of coalitions between CMs and existing human rights/social justice movements.

A complementary approach, and certainly not a mutually exclusive one, is for CMs to draw lessons from the environmental movement. This succeeded in bringing a wide range of disparate advocacy efforts into a more unified force for social reform in part by developing an integrative collective action frame centered on the idea of a shared geo-biological environment that was vital for sustaining life and which needed collective as well as individual custodianship. The inclusiveness of this conceptual frame would offer similar advantages to complementary yet distinct CMs, such as the ones described by Carroll (Chapter 7, this volume): community networks, which focus on micro-level interactions and relationships, and internetworking, which is associated with macro-level processes, can both benefit from the idea of a shared information and communication resource or commons.

The three CMs discussed in this chapter face a similar challenge. The recurrence through each of these CMs of such environmental movement-inspired ideas as the information commons and information ecologies, as well as the broader information environment and "infosphere," strongly suggest that there is a conceptual basis at least for the emergence of an over-arching CM around a shared concern for information and communications rights that can draw from the rich experience of the environmental movement.[10] In order to attract wide support among average computer users, CMs need to clearly show how they are working to address the challenges and problems associated with daily life using ICTs, including expensive software, identity theft, spam, inaccessible databases, intrusive Internet service providers, etc. Currently, community networking, F/OSS, and privacy movements are addressing these issues, but not in a way that unites these diverse concerns and demonstrates that it is necessary to see them as interconnected parts of a larger environment. By focusing on the over-arching issue of information and communication rights within a more widely shared technological action frame, each individual movement might become more aware of how the aims and activities of other fledgling CMs are complementary facets of a stronger and more integrative social movement.

By borrowing key framing concepts of the environmental movement, CMs can more fully illuminate the concept of an information environment, full of interconnected and complex systems of actors. The conceptual and discursive tools offered by the environmental movement can then serve to illuminate the hitherto shadowy corners of the infosphere and bring computerization issues into a broader public arena. For example, creating media spectacles to draw public attention to the interconnectedness and fragility of the environmental commons that we depend on, as environmental groups such as Greenpeace have done so successfully, can suggest similar strategies for information rights organizations tackling informational abuses. Environmental metaphors are especially useful when discussing the information environment, because they put what can often seem a vague and intangible set of virtual actors and systems into a familiar perspective. By framing the infosphere as an embodied ecological environment, CMs can more easily articulate a set of rights and responsibilities for the citizens who operate within it, and can work together to develop and protect an information environment that is widely accessible and responsive to the needs and aspirations of computer users—a challenging prospect, to be sure. As groups concerned with computerization issues start to coalesce into larger advocacy campaigns such as CRIS, and attempt to have an impact on high-level policy discussions such as the WSIS, the environmental movement could provide a fruitful vein of comparison to reflect upon future strategies and aims of CMs.

Endnotes

1. The call for participation for the invitation-only workshop to honor the late Professor Rob Kling—"The Social Informatics Workshop: Extending the Contributions of Professor Rob Kling to the Analysis of Computerization Movements," March 11–12, 2005, University of California, Irvine (cf. www.crito.uci.edu/si)—names 24 CMs (July 15, 2004, p. 5).
2. This brief summary of purpose is taken from the description of the Free Software Movement (FSM) found in Elliott and Scacchi (2004).
3. Kling and Iacono (1988) concluded, from their study of CM discourse, that a system of beliefs containing five themes help advance computerization on many fronts. The fifth belief is relevant to our discussion: "Uncooperative people are the main barriers to social reform through computing." Most of these movements would not regard individuals *per se* as the main barriers, but larger organizations or institutions, with their prominent leaders serving as proxies and symbolic targets (e.g., Bill Gates for Microsoft Corp. and George W. Bush for the U.S. government).
4. It should be noted that informational privacy is probably better characterized as a CCM, as it is mainly oriented to resisting incursions of computerization promoted by others. The promotion of "privacy enhancing technologies (PETs)" is in turn a counter-example of this. It is often (increasingly) the case that movements promoting a particular vision of computerization for social reform (i.e., a CM) are pitted against other CMs promoting different computerization goals or paths (i.e., can be characterized as CCMs). The point is not whether these are CMs or CCMs, but whether they fit the characteristics of social movements.
5. More recently, social scientists, particularly in the technoscience studies tradition, have also contributed by challenging the presumptions of a nature/society dichotomy and pointing out the deeply social character of "environment" (see Latour, 2004).
6. There are some important, and contested, distinctions between the concepts of "free software" and "open source," but except where specifically noted, for the purposes of this chapter they will be treated as a single movement using the term commonly applied—free/open source software (F/OSS). It is also referred to as FLOSS (free/libre open source software), a term that emphasizes the *libre* meaning of the word "free" rather than the "free of charge" or gratis and is less anglocentric (en.wikipedia.org/wiki/FLOSS). On the distinctions between the Free Software and the Open Software movements, from an FSM perspective, see www.gnu.org/philosophy/free-software-for-freedom.html. This paper leans more to the free software side because it reveals its movement characteristics more clearly. There are also clear connections to the Free Speech Movement, founded 20 years earlier. See the Free Speech Movement Archives, www.fsm-a.org.
7. This is now referred to as "informational self-determination," a term first used by the West German Federal Constitutional Court.
8. The 7th annual Privacy and Human Rights Survey, published by Privacy International and the U.S.-based Electronic Privacy Information Center, reviews

the state of privacy in 60 countries and warns that invasions of privacy across the world have increased significantly in the past 12 months. The 800-page report is available free of charge at www.privacyinternational.org/survey/phr2004

9. A very different approach is taken by Brin (1999) in *The Transparent Society*. He contrasts the "reflex response" of many privacy advocates with his preferred concept of "reciprocal transparency." Brin argues that most privacy advocates have a "reflex response" when faced with privacy concerns, where they reactively shut down flows of information. He argues that this solution conflicts fundamentally with human nature, and is an unrealistic response in the face of the inventiveness and amorality of the market. Instead, he advocates for "reciprocal transparency" which opens data flows wider: "For instance, if some company wishes to collect data on consumers across America, let it do so only on condition that the top one hundred officers in the firm must post exactly the same information about themselves and all their family members on an accessible Web site" (1999, p. 81). By giving all members of society equal access to information and the tools of surveillance and control, Brin sketches out a libertarian approach that instead of trying to protect individual privacy, does away with the whole project. In this rather different fashion, he shares with Regan the idea that a collective, commons approach is the way out of the current shortcoming of the privacy debate.
10. Infosphere should be distinguished from the "noosphere," which refers to the "sphere of human thought," but like it, extends and transforms the geosphere and biosphere (en.wikipedia.org/wiki/Noosphere).

References

Association of Progressive Communications. (2004). Retrieved November 30, 2004, from www.apc.org

Benkler, Y. (2001). The battle over institutional ecosystem in the digital environment. *Communications of the ACM*, 44(2), 84–90.

Bowker, G., & Star, S. (1999). *Sorting things out: Classification and its consequences*. Cambridge, MA: MIT Press.

Brin, D. (1999). *The transparent society: Will technology force us to choose between privacy and freedom*? Reading, MA: Addison Wesley.

Carson, R. (1962). *Silent spring*. Boston: Houghton Mifflin.

Castells, M. (2005). Innovation, information technology, and the culture of freedom: The political economy of open source. Retrieved Jan 31, 2005, from www.openflows.org/article.pl?sid=05/01/31/2028221

Clarke, R. (2004). A history of privacy impact assessments. Retrieved September 29, 2004, from www.anu.edu.au/people/Roger.Clarke/DV/PIAHist.html

Clement, A., & Shade, L. R. (2000). The access rainbow: Conceptualizing universal access to the information/communication infrastructure. In M. Gurstein (Ed.), *Community informatics: Enabling communities with information and communications technologies* (Vol. 2005). Hershey, PA: Idea Group Publishing.

Communications Rights in the Information Society (CRIS). Retrieved December 1, 2004, from www.crisinfo.org

Computer Professionals for Social Responsibility. (2004). Retrieved December 1, 2004, from www.cpsr.org

Electronic Privacy Information Center (EPIC). Retrieved December 1, 2004, from www.epic.ca

Electronic Privacy Information Center (EPIC) & Privacy International. (2004). Privacy and Human Rights: An International Survey of Privacy Laws and Developments. Retrieved December 6, 2004 from www.privacyinternational.org/survey/phr2004

Elliott, M., & Scacchi, W. (2004). Mobilization of software developers: The free software movement. Retrieved November 30, 2004, from www.ics.uci.edu/~wscacchi/Papers/New/Elliott-Scacchi-Free-Software-Movement.pdf

FEMNET. Retrieved December 1, 2004, from www.femnet.or.ke

Free Software Foundation. Retrieved December 1, 2004, from www.gnu.org/fsf/fsf.html

Gurstein, M. (2003). Effective use: A community informatics strategy beyond the digital divide. Retrieved December 4, 2005, from firstmonday.org/issues/issue8_12/gurstein

Hays, S. (2000). Environmental politics since 1945. Pittsburgh: University of Pittsburgh Press. ISOC: Internet Society. Retrieved December 1, 2004, from www.isoc.org

Iacono, S., & Kling, R. (2001). Computerization movements: The rise of the Internet and distant forms of work. In J. Yates & J. Van Maanen (Eds.), *Information technology and organizational transformation: History, rhetoric, and practice* (pp. 93–136). Thousand Oaks, CA: Sage Publications.

Kling, R. (1999). What is social informatics and why does it matter? *D-Lib Magazine,* 5(1), 205–220.

Kling, R., & Iacono, S. (1988). The mobilization of support for computerization: The role of computerization movements. *Social Problems*, 35(3), 226–242.

Latour, B. (2004). *Politics of nature: How to bring the sciences into democracy*. Cambridge, MA: Harvard University Press.

Leopold, A. (1949). *A sand county almanac*. New York: Oxford University Press.

Lessig, L. (2004). *Free culture: How big media uses technology and the law to lock down culture and control creativity*. New York: Penguin Press.

Nardi, B., & O'Day, V. (1999). *Information ecologies: Using technology with heart.* Cambridge, MA: MIT Press.

Neice, D. (2000). *Conspicuous contributions: Signs of social esteem on the Internet.* Doctoral dissertation, University of Brighton, Sussex.

Panos London. Retrieved December 1, 2004, from www.panos.org.uk

Privacy International. Retrieved November 30, 2004, from www.privacyinternational.org

Regan, P. M. (2002). Privacy as a common good in the digital world. *Information, Communication and Society*, 5(3), 382–405.

Sale, K. (1993). *The green revolution: The American environmental movement, 1962–1992*. Toronto: Harper Collins Canada.

SANGONeT. Development Information Portal for NGOs in South Africa. Retrieved November 17, 2006 from www.sangonet.org.za

Schuler, D. (1996). *New community networks: Wired for Change*. New York: Addison-Wesley.

SIGNIS. Retrieved November 28, 2004, from signis.net

Solove, D. J. (2001). Privacy and power: Computer databases and metaphors for information privacy. *Stanford Law Review*, 53(6), 1393–1462.

Surman, M., & Reilly, K. (2003). Appropriating the Internet for social change: Towards the strategic use of networked technologies by transitional civil society organizations. Social Science Research Council, November 2003. Retrieved from www.ssrc.org/programs/itic/civ_soc_report

Warren, S., & Brandeis, L. (1890). The right to privacy. *Harvard Law Review*, 4(5), 193–220.

Westin, A. (1967). *Privacy and freedom*. New York: Atheneum.

Westin, A., & Baker, M. A. (1972). *Databanks in a free society: Computers, record keeping and privacy*. New York: Times Books.

World Forum on Community Networking. Retrieved November 29, 2004, from www.globalcn.org

Chapter 13

Examining the Success of Computerization Movements in the Ubiquitous Computing Era: Free and Open Source Software Movements

Margaret S. Elliott
University of California, Irvine

Abstract

Computerization movements are a type of social movement whose advocates focus on computer-based systems as instruments to bring about a new social order. The success of social movements has been defined in various ways: social acceptance, gaining new advantages, creation of new social policies, the implementation of new laws, or a shift in public perception. However, there is a dearth of research in how computerization movements achieve success. In this chapter, I examine the success of the free software movement and the open source movement in mobilizing people and organizations to join their efforts to develop and use free software. Factors contributing to success include strong beliefs in free software, shared opposition to organizations opposing free software, the split of the free software movement into two movements (the free software movement and the open source software movement), ubiquitous access to work, software artifacts, and evangelistic literature.

Introduction

Computerization movements (CMs) are a special type of social movement whose advocates focus on computer-based systems as instruments to alter the existing social order. Research has shown that CMs communicate key ideological beliefs to mobilize movement participation through public speeches, written works, popular stories, television shows, and magazine articles (Iacono & Kling, 1996, 2001; Kling & Iacono, 1988). However, there is a dearth of research into how CMs develop over time into successful movements. This chapter examines the success of a new genre of CM in which large-scale computerization is assumed to have taken place, and information and communication technologies (ICTs) facilitate the mobilization of membership. Specifically, I examine how the free software movement and the open source software movement have achieved success in mobilizing participants through their respective movement organizations, the Free Software Foundation (FSF) (www.fsf.org) and the Open Source Initiative (OSI) (www.opensource.org), to develop, use, and promote "free" software to such an extent that the technology has reached the diffusion stage (Rogers, 2005). In addition, I discuss how technology of the ubiquitous computing era facilitates the success of these movements. Being connected "any time, any place" provides vast opportunities for evangelism of CM ideology and for global access to CM software artifacts.

CMs differ from other types of social movements such as the women's movement or the equal rights movement in that a CM's ideology is centered on the acquisition of *technology* that can alter a social or work world. The success of typical social movements has been defined in various ways: social acceptance, gaining new advantages, creation of new social policies, or the implementation of new laws (Gamson, 1975). Some argue that the most important societal change that can occur is a shift in public perception (Iacono & Kling, 1996). For example, the movement against drinking and driving and affiliated organizations like Mothers Against Drunk Driving (MADD) have changed public perception about drunk drivers. How, then, can the success of specific CMs be characterized? This chapter attempts to answer that question by drawing upon social movement research (Blumer, 1969; Dawson & Gettys, 1935; Zald & Ash, 1969) to show the stages that the free and open source software (F/OSS) movements have gone through in their evolution from inception to continuing success.

Kling and Iacono (1988) distinguished between a general CM, which supports overall computerization of societies worldwide, and specific CMs, which advocate the adoption of specific computer-based systems. In this way Kling and Iacono (1988) drew attention to the similar trends of specific CMs across many organizations or social settings.[1] Specific social movements have well-defined objectives or goals, a movement organization, recognized leadership, and loosely formed alliances. In the early stages, specific social movements have no clear objective and exhibit impulsive behavior (Blumer, 1969). As a social movement develops, this disbursed disorganized behavior becomes organized, solidified, and persistent. One framework offered to characterize this rise from disorganization to organization is the set of four stages (Dawson & Gettys, 1935): social unrest, popular excitement, formalization, and institutionalization.

In this chapter, I use this framework to characterize the success of the F/OSS movements by tracing their development through these four stages resulting in the adoption and diffusion of F/OSS on a global scale. To accommodate the unique characteristics of CMs, the dimension "technology adoption" has been added to the formalization stage and "technology diffusion" to the institutionalization stage. In order for a CM to become institutionalized, the CM technology must have a critical mass (Markus, 1987) of people and/or businesses that believe in the benefits of the technology and are actively engaged in its use.

The following elements of a CM contribute to the successful diffusion of the particular technology being promoted by the CM (Iacono & Kling, 2001):

- Technological action frames – Multi-dimensional composite understandings that serve as a catalyst for people to invest vast amounts of time and money into the acquisition of new technology serving to frame their ideas about how to use the technology.
- Public discourse – Written and spoken rhetoric that develops around the technology found in various discourses: government, scientific organizations, academic institutions, public press, and organizational and professional arenas.
- Organizational practices – Ways that organizations (virtual and real) inculcate the use of technological action frames and discourse into everyday practices that result in the acquisition of CM technology in micro-level settings.

In this chapter, I show how the technological action frames of the F/OSS movements contribute to their success and how they correlate with the four stages: social unrest, popular excitement, formalization, and institutionalization.

The chapter is organized in the following way. First the background literature review for social movements and CMs is presented, followed by a brief description of ubiquitous computing. Next, the movement organizations, the FSF and the OSI, are described, followed by a section on the growth and development of the F/OSS movements through four stages. Finally, I complete the chapter with a discussion and conclusion.

Background

Social movements can be seen as collective enterprises to establish a new order of life (Blumer, 1969). They develop from a sense of unrest. People are motivated to join a movement when they become dissatisfied with some aspect of the social order and hope that the movement will result in a new system or scheme of living. In the beginning, a social movement is amorphous and lacking in form. As the movement takes hold with members, it becomes more organized, with a recognized set of social rules and values, often with a movement organization (Zald & Ash, 1969), and leader(s) who promote the movement through written and oral treatises. As a social movement develops, it tends to become organized, solidified, and persistent. The framework used in this chapter consists of four stages: social unrest, popular excitement, formalization, and institutionalization (Dawson & Gettys, 1935).

Kling and Iacono (1988) argue that computerization of many ways of life in the United States has been influenced by a set of loosely linked CMs, headed by mobilizing ideologies offered by CM activists who are not necessarily direct employees in the computer industry. They distinguish between a general computerization movement in society in which activists proclaim "revolutionary" social changes and specific CMs focused on specific technologies. They compare five specific particular CMs by the ideological content focusing on the following computer-based technologies: urban information systems, artificial intelligence, computer-based education, office automation, and personal computing. Their research differs from previous organizational analyses of computerization because they identify how these CMs cut across society as important sources of mobilizing ideologies for computing activists.

In their study of internetworking, Iacono and Kling (2001) combine the sociological notion of *collective action frames* (Snow & Benford, 2000; Snow, Rochford, Worden, & Benford, 1986) with the concept of *technological frame*s (Orlikowski & Gash, 1994) to coin the term *technological action frames*. Collective action frames are the conscious strategic efforts by groups of people to fashion shared understandings of the world to legitimate and mobilize collective action, whereas technological frames are the notions that people collectively develop about the appropriate use of types of technology. Technological action frames are collective understandings that mobilize people to invest time and money into new technology and form core ideas about how the specific technology works and should or could be used. Such frames work at a macro level to influence micro-social uses in specific settings such as organizations or personal use.

Based on the conceptual model of CMs presented in Chapter 1 in this book (Elliott & Kraemer), the outcomes of CMs are varied: continuation, merging with other CMs, fading out, or the derivation of a counter-computerization movement (CCM). The technological anti-utopianism writings associated with specific CMs often spawn a CCM related to that CM's specific computer-based hardware or software. The anti-utopian views of the CCM advocates usually arise in response to a threat from the use and development of the specific technology promoted by a CM. For example, Microsoft Corporation's efforts to downplay the advantages of free software with anti-utopian views could be characterized as a CCM. There is no evidence of a general CCM forming in response to the general CM (Iacono & Kling, 1996; Kling & Iacono, 1988).

The eventual diffusion of CM technology follows the course of several stages: adoption, use, and widespread implementation into organizations and society. (See Elliott and Kraemer, Chapter 1, this volume, for a detailed account of the varied paths a CM might follow.) In this chapter, I show the correlation between the stages of the social movement and the technological action frames that help the F/OSS technology to become diffused worldwide.

Ubiquitous Computing

Ubiquitous computing refers to ICTs that enable us to connect "any time, any place" to a social or work world (see Elliott & Kraemer, Chapter 20, this volume, for a description and analysis of CMs in the ubiquitous computing era). This field of research has also been known as pervasive computing (Lyytinen & Yoo, 2002), invisible computing, and calm technology (Weiser, 1991). Indeed, ubiquitous computing technology surrounds us from that nagging e-mail we need to read or answer (from work or home) to those missed messages on our cell phones. Increasingly people are working out of home offices using high-speed Internet connections for global communication. Futurists (Mattern, 2002) predict that new technologies of ubiquitous computing will link the real world of objects, products, and supply chain manufacturing items with the virtual world of the Internet or e-commerce—"smart" objects with location sensors will be tracked by businesses and friends and family. The utopian vision of the ubiquitous computing CM paints a picture of excitement and convenience as technology is promoted as melding with our social lives such that we are oblivious to the technology. In fact, this vision does not match with reality, as suggested by Sørensen and Gibson (Chapter 17, this volume) in their study of people using cell phones for professional use. The authors concluded that the two main barriers for widespread mobile and ubiquitous support were "bandwidth and battery life time."

Researchers, vendors, and magazine writers portray utopian visions of the advantages of being connected all the time, including the elimination of desktop PCs. Futurists predict that people will use "wearable computing," with devices becoming part of clothing connecting people to each other via wireless technology. In the U.S. and Europe, mobile phones have become increasingly popular, providing access to the Internet, instant messaging, digital cameras, computer games, video clips, and execution of Java programs (Mattern, 2002). BlackBerry devices (www.rim.com) are becoming popular with business executives and university professors, yet instead of the "calmness" envisioned in ubiquitous computing as predicted by Weiser (1991), research shows that people are becoming addicted to their use (Mazmanian, Orlikowski, & Yates, 2005), and e-mail serves as a constant interruption in everyday routines.

Ubiquitous computing has contributed to the success of the F/OSS movements in providing pervasive computing environments such that people can easily develop and use F/OSS "anytime, any place" while also spreading the word about the advantages of using F/OSS. For example, the GNUe project (Elliott & Scacchi, forthcoming) prefers the use of Internet Relay Chat (IRC) as its primary means of communication, and since its contributors are from all over the world in varying time zones, they hold meetings at various times. Because all volunteers have home computers with high-speed connections, they can "meet" in a chat room to resolve technical issues, to socialize, and to catch up on movement gossip.

Another way that ubiquitous computing has facilitated the success of the F/OSS movements is by enabling the storage and access of downloadable software modules, software development and installation guidelines, and archives of group activity such as recordation of the IRC sessions. Around 1985, the Internet emerged with the Advanced Research Project Agency Network (ARPANET), resulting in online communities exchanging messages on Usenet groups. This was helpful in spreading the word about the FSF and its downloadable software. By the late 1980s, e-mail was beginning to appear in select scientific and government communities, and more and more people were participating in Usenet groups.

In the 1990s, the advent of the Web enabled virtual communities to evolve into social and work worlds. The 2000s brought the use of advanced technologies for "ubiquitous computing" where people can connect to the Web anywhere through personal computers using Web browsers, personal digital assistants (PDAs) (Allen, Chapter 4, this volume), mobile phones (Sørensen & Gibson, Chapter 17, this volume), and BlackBerry devices (for reading e-mail).

Ubiquitous computing development environments enable F/OSS developers to work on their code or design "anytime, any place." F/OSS programmers who use the GNU/Linux operating system (OS) can now easily move from one location to the next by using the Knoppix GNU/Linux distribution. Knoppix is a free/open source real-time Linux CD that boots and runs completely from CD. It includes recent Linux software and desktop environments, with several F/OSS programs such as OpenOffice.org and Mozilla as well as hundreds of other F/OSS programs. Users of Knoppix can work on software development on any hardware platform that accepts Linux and use the Knoppix CD in a remote location for "ubiquitous" software development (www.knoppix.org).

Free Software Foundation and Open Source Initiative

Free software refers to software that is open to anyone to copy, study, modify, and redistribute (Stallman, 1999). The FSF, founded in 1985 by Richard M. Stallman (known as RMS in the F/OSS communities), advocates the use of its GNU General Public License (GPL) as a copyright license that creates and promotes freedom. A popular term heard in the free software community is "Think free speech, not free beer." It is used to emphasize the importance of the defense of freedom, not just the ideal of promoting software that is free of cost. It also serves as a technological action frame that mobilizes people to join the free software movement. The term "open source" software was coined in 1998 when a group of free software movement advocates became concerned that the term "free software" was anathema to businesses.

There was a series of events that led to the formation and success of the OSI. As the free software movement became more visible in the mid-1990s, other literature began appearing on the rationale for developing and using free software. Eric Raymond wrote an essay entitled "The Cathedral and the Bazaar" in 1997 (Raymond, 2001) in which he explicated the reasons why he believed that open source licenses resulted in software that is of higher quality but costs less than typical in-house software development. This essay became very popular in the programming community, highlighting the open source community to a wider audience.

Around the same time, Netscape (www.netscape.com) was in a battle with Microsoft over whose browser would dominate the market—Netscape Navigator or Internet Explorer. After reading Raymond's essay and hearing that Microsoft would release its Explorer as part of Windows, managers at Netscape made the decision to open up Netscape software for Netscape Navigator 5.0 (announced on January 22, 1998). This decision greatly increased the open source community's reputation to the world and to the U.S. business community. In 1998, Eric Raymond, Bruce Perens, and Tim O'Reilly held a meeting and decided that in order to encourage business investment in open source software, the free software people needed to do better marketing.

This meeting was the genesis for the OSI whose mission is to (1) promote the pragmatic benefits to the business community of open source software, and (2) create a certification process for F/OSS licenses that meet the open source definition. The OSI is a nonprofit corporation dedicated to managing and promoting the Open Source Definition for the good of the community. Suddenly, vendors started paying attention and offering support for Linux, including Oracle, IBM, and Corel. Since 1998, other companies such as HP have supported Linux as an alternative to Unix or Windows. In 2000, the Sourceforge Web site (source forge.net) was initiated by VA Linux (now supported by the Open Source Technology Group, a wholly-owned subsidiary of VA Software Corporation) and now includes a Concurrent Versions System (CVS) repository, mailing lists, bug tracking, message forums, task management software, Web site hosting, permanent file archival, full backups, and total Web-based administration. In February 2000, this site hosted 2,370 projects and 15,060 registered users. In 2006, it was estimated that more than 1 million users were registered, with more than 100,000 open source projects listed.

The major difference between the software development processes advocated by the FSF and the OSI is in the licensing requirements. The OSI promotes more liberties with open source licensing than does the FSF. For example, the OSI supports licenses that accept combinations of open source software with proprietary software while the FSF promotes strict adherence to the principles listed in the GPL, which requires software to be redistributed as free software exclusively. The free software movement, through its movement organization, the FSF, has spawned a number of free software projects in which software developers advocate and follow the principle of creating and using free software exclusively. At the time of writing, 5,150 projects are listed on the FSF Web site (www.fsf.org). Both the FSF and the OSI are nonprofit organizations with the purpose of recruiting and educating people to support F/OSS.

Stages of Computerization Movements from Inception to Institutionalization

Over time, social movements go through developmental stages as the social movement organization and its culture is established. One way to examine success of a CM is to trace its growth from inception to its institutionalization when it is embedded in society. For the purposes of this chapter, we have assumed that once a CM has made it to the institutionalization phase, it has reached a level of success that promotes continued membership. Another assumption is that even though a movement is institutionalized, its goals may not have been fully achieved so it is still an active institution. For example, the free software movement has a goal of transforming all source code from closed to free, but since achieving this is highly unlikely, the free software movement will be an institution for quite some time. In this section I analyze the success of the F/OSS movements in terms of four stages of development (Dawson & Gettys, 1935) and discuss five mechanisms (Blumer, 1969) that social movements utilize as they grow through those four stages: (1) agitation, (2) development of *esprit de corps*, (3) development of morale, (4) formation of an ideology, and (5) development of operating tactics. For each stage the corresponding technological action frame that predominated is discussed.

Stage 1: Social Unrest

In the initial stages of a social movement, there may be factors in society making people feel uneasy and restless. This makes people susceptible to appeals and suggestions that fuel their discontent. The role of agitation in this phase is very important in mobilizing people to join a movement. The purpose of agitation is to attempt to loosen people's old attachments or beliefs and replace them with new ideas and impulses. An agitator can be an excitable, restless, aggressive individual, or a calm, quiet, and dignified person stirring people through action, not words—for example, Martin Luther King, Jr. was an agitator for the Civil Rights Movement in the 1960s.

The founder and agitator for the free software movement was clearly RMS who, with a group of hackers in the 1970s, worked in the AI laboratory at the Massachusetts Institute of Technology (MIT). The MIT hackers developed their own operating system (OS) to replace the Digital Equipment Corporation (DEC) OS for its PDP-10 machine (Raymond, 2001; Williams, 2002). Written in the arcane computer language, assembler code, the MIT hackers called it ITS for "Incompatible Time-sharing System." In the early 1980s DEC disbanded the PDP-10, leading the way for RMS to start the GNU project with his own version of a UNIX OS called "HURD," resulting in the many Unix-compatible utilities available today including Emacs, a word processor for Unix. This was in development in parallel with the LINUX kernel OS and formed the basis for the GNU project (cf. www.gnu.org). As chronicled in Stallman's many essays (Stallman, 2002), he was passionate about people's right to alter any source code, and this led to the formation of the FSF in 1985.

The social unrest stage of a CM is not always easily identifiable as in a typical social movement that might be trying to reverse a social injustice such as ethnic prejudice. The goal of a CM is to mobilize people to acquire computerization and may not be seeded in widespread social unrest. However, when looking at the incubation period of the free software movement, one can see that its agitator, RMS, had a clear motive in promoting freedom. The technological action frame, "All software should be free," became RMS's mantra and is evident in the description of the FSF purpose:

> The Free Software Foundation (FSF), founded in 1985, is dedicated to promoting computer users' right to use, study, copy, modify, and redistribute computer programs. The FSF promotes the development and use of free (as in freedom) software—particularly the GNU operating system (used widely today in its GNU/Linux variant)—and free (as in freedom) documentation. The FSF also helps to spread awareness of the ethical and political issues of freedom in the use of software.
>
> Many organizations distribute whatever free software happens to be available. In contrast, the Free Software Foundation concentrates on development of new free software—and on making that software into a coherent system which can eliminate the need to use proprietary (18k characters) software. (www.fsf.org)

In one of RMS's articles, "Free Software Is a Matter of Freedom?" (www.gnu.org), he states:

> Society also needs freedom. When a program has an owner, the users lose freedom to control part of their own lives. And above all society needs to encourage the spirit of voluntary cooperation in its citizens. When software owners tell us that helping our neighbors in a natural way is "piracy," they pollute our society's civic spirit. This is why we say that free software is a matter of freedom, not price.

In the early stages of the free software movement, the discourse regarding the ideological beliefs of the FSF was centered on white papers by members of the FSF and focused on a small cadre of dedicated hackers. With the advent of the Web in the early 1990s, membership in the FSF increased dramatically along with the advent of more and more "free" software projects listed on the GNU Web site. The Web provided RMS with another avenue of reaching more converts to spread the word about the importance of using free software as opposed to proprietary software.

Many other articles by RMS explaining his fervent beliefs in free software can be found on the FSF Web site (www.fsf.org). RMS is clearly an agitator who has established himself as one of the key leaders of the free software movement. He has earned several awards for his leadership in promoting free software:

- 1990 – Richard Stallman was awarded a $240,000 fellowship by the John D. and Catherine T. MacArthur Foundation.
- 2001 – Richard Stallman was awarded $830,000 as a co-winner of the 2001 Takeda Award for Techno-Entrepreneurial Achievement for Social/Economic Well-Being to honor "the origination and the advancement of open development models for system software—open architecture, free software, and open source software."

From 1971 to 1984, the free software movement was localized to RMS and the MIT AI lab hackers who believed in the philosophy of sharing source code with other programmers. Eventually, they parted ways, some hired by proprietary companies to develop software. Finally, in January 1984, RMS resigned from MIT so that he could continue to develop free software without the university laying claims to his software. By 1985, he had developed a substantial portion of the HURD and its accompanying utilities, which later became part of the GNU/Linux package. He then formed the FSF, a tax-exempt charity, to support his software development and that of his collaborators. He personally created a C compiler, debugger, a text editor (the well-known Emacs), and other tools. Once the FSF was founded, the free software movement moved into the next stage of development, popular excitement, where the dominant technological action frame came to be known as "free as in free speech, not free beer."

Stage 2: Popular Excitement

RMS and his collaborators were instrumental in recruiting others to join the FSF during the late 1980s and early 1990s. The stage of popular excitement in a social movement is characterized by people meeting to examine their shared beliefs. The goals of the movement are not as random and aimless but become more focused. There are more clearly defined goals about how social change can occur. Here the leader is likely to be a prophet (as in religious movements) or a reformer. During this period, RMS began organizing the FSF into a movement organization with definite goals. He created the GPL, also known as "copyleft," to ensure that his code would always be freely available and modifiable for others. The GPL specifies that users of the source code can view, change, or add to the code, provided that they make their changes available under the same license as the original code. In the GPL, RMS lists the freedoms that any person should have when using software under the GPL:

- Freedom to run the program for any purpose
- Freedom to study how the program works and adapt it to their needs

- Freedom to redistribute copies of the software at will
- Freedom to improve the OSS program and to distribute the altered version
- Required distribution of the originating license that specifies the freedoms and rights concerning the preceding properties

By 1990, RMS and his team of programmers had created a substantial portion of UNIX utilities and all they needed for a complete free OS was the Unix-like kernel. They started work on the HURD system, an OS based on the MACH microkernel architecture (first developed at Carnegie Mellon). However, at the same time, Linux Torvalds, a graduate student at the University of Helsinki, wrote a Unix-like kernel based on a small Unix clone. Torvalds named it Linux and submitted it to several mailing lists and newsgroups for review. Eventually, other programmers started using the code and submitting changes to Torvalds. Then the Linux kernel was combined with GNU by others to form the GNU/Linux OS, which is used by millions today.

With the advent of GNU/Linux, more people began using and modifying the software. This availability of an *entire* OS to replace Unix created quite a stir in the free software community and inspired people to begin free software projects that could be executed in the free environment of GNU/Linux. In addition, this set the stage for the OSI to promote the open source software movement with its technological action frame centered on encouraging businesses to use GNU/Linux along with their proprietary software. Thus, the F/OSS movements moved into the next stage of movement development, formalization.

Stage 3: Formalization

During the formalization stage, a movement becomes more clearly organized with rules, policies, tactics, and discipline. One way that CMs differ from other types of social movements is that for their movements to be successful, people need to adopt the technology being advocated by the CM organizations. During this stage, a CM becomes more organized and technology adoption must happen with enough people for the next stage to occur—institutionalization. Without the volunteer efforts of programmers to complete the code, the F/OSS movements would not have reached the institutionalization stage. Programmers are the *raison d'être* for the establishment of F/OSS as an institution and their willingness to develop and use the software is essential to the success of the F/OSS movements. Three of the five mechanisms by which a social movement coalesces and becomes organized are relevant to the understanding of the formalization stage of a CM: (1) development of *esprit de corps*, (2) development of morale, and (3) formation of an ideology (Blumer, 1969). These three dimensions are discussed here in detail. During the formalization stage of the free software movement, a new dominant technological action frame emerged: "Businesses can benefit from use of free software." During the period 1995–2000, the free software movement split into two factions with two separate movement organizations: the FSF and the OSI. Whereas the FSF advocates the development and use of free source code without the use of proprietary software, the OSI supports a new technological action frame that allows for the combination of free and proprietary software. This split in ideology resulted in an increase in businesses investing time and money into the ongoing development and diffusion of F/OSS software.

The Development of Esprit de Corps

Once the FSF was established in 1985, it began to grow steadily, with increased participation by advocates in the development and use of free software. The members of the FSF developed a sense of *esprit de corps* and began spreading the word to the rest of the world. *Esprit de corps* can be thought of as the organizing of feelings that were aroused by agitation in the name of the movement. It is important to the success of the movement because it develops feelings of rapport, intimacy, shared experience, and of forming a select group (Blumer, 1969). A common theme in free software communities is the importance of contributing to the free software cause as a means of giving something back to the community. For example, during an interview with a key developer from the GNUenterprise (GNUe) project, when asked about motivation for all of his volunteerism in programming and managing the GNUe project, he replied that individuals' motivations vary. He and a colleague started out with the idea of creating free software and became "hooked" on the movement for ethical reasons.

In the GNUe project, a prime form of communication is the daily IRC where people work as a team to resolve conflicts, create software, and socialize at the same time. They become friends even if some have never met face to face. In addition, when newcomers join the IRC and offer to help work on the project, they are gladly welcomed into the community without need for verification of references or programming reputation (Elliott & Scacchi, forthcoming). Another important aspect of this formalization stage is the development of morale.

The Development of Morale

To succeed, a movement must have a persistent and fixed loyalty. "Morale can be thought of as giving persistency and determination to a movement; its test is whether solidarity can be maintained in the face of adversity. In this sense, morale can be thought of as a group will or an enduring collective purpose" (Blumer, 1969, p. 17). The loyalty of members of the FSF to the creed of the free software movement is evident in the methods used to produce free software. There are three kinds of convictions associated with morale: (1) conviction of the rectitude of the purpose of the movement accompanied by the belief that the goals of the movement will result in a lofty vision of an improved world, (2) faith in the ultimate goal of the movement, and (3) belief in the movement's sacred mission (Blumer, 1969). Morale can be built up as a religious faith in the movement's purpose as members view their leader with saint-like properties. In the following example, there are signs of the strong beliefs in free software that help build morale in the free software movement.

In the GNU case study, my colleague Walt Scacchi and I found examples of two situations where fierce loyalty to RMS and his tenets of free software development were evident (Elliott & Scacchi, 2003a, 2003b). In this example, a programmer refused to use a documentation tool that included a non-free component. The following exchange shows the strength of the convictions people have in using and developing free software. During a two-day chat, one person argued about using non-free software temporarily to read some documentation. He became enraged when no one would agree with his strict adherence and made a reference to RMS by sending a message to the mailing list:

> I think it is extremely **** that a GNU project would require me to install non-free software in order to read and modify the documentation. I mean if I cannot make vrms happy on my debian system them [sic] what good am I as a Free Software developer? Is docbook really this much of a pain? I can build html versions of stuff on my box if this is what we have to do. This just irks me beyond anything. I really shouldn't have to be harping on this issue for a GNU project, but some ppl like to take convenience over freedom and this should not be tolerated.

Then the person who developed the documentation responded with a lengthy e-mail stating at the end that his motivation for doing this work is for the "freedom of my son:"

> By the way, Daniel, using/writing Free software is NOT about making RMS happy or unhappy. He's a great guy and all, but not the center of the free universe, nor the motivating factor in many (most?) of our lives. For me, my motivation to be here is a free future for my son.

The Development of Group Ideology

The ideology of a social movement is an essential element in assuring the persistency and development of a movement. It consists of a body of doctrine, beliefs, and myths (Blumer, 1969). The ideology usually consists of two forms: (1) an erudite and scholarly approach, and (2) a popular appeal to the uneducated and the masses (emotional symbols, phrases, etc.). During the formalization stage of the free software movement, the group ideology was strengthened by RMS's erudite writings and the availability of these articles on the Web site. In addition, during this stage the popular phrase "Think free speech, not free beer" became a symbol of the free movement ideology. The FSF produced pamphlets and members attended Linux conventions to spread their ideology and to promote membership by manning booths.

In 1998, the OSI split from the FSF with the intent to stir interest from businesses for the use and development of free source code. At the same time Web site technology such as Netscape browsers was made available and both the FSF and OSI were able to design Web sites offering FAQs, downloadable software, chat rooms, mailing lists, extensive philosophical literature, and users' manuals. The Sourceforge Web site was formed, creating a centralized location where people can recruit developers to work on free/open source projects. As the two segments recruited more members, their respective Web sites began posting opinion papers on how free and open source are different from one another, even though most open source software projects supported by the OSI use the FSF-recommended "copyleft" license, the GPL (see www.fsf.org for details).

For example, on the FSF Web site, the following illustrates how FSF members view open source:

> Another group has started using the term "open source" to mean something close (but not identical) to "free software." We prefer the term "free software" because, once you have heard it refers to freedom rather than price, it calls to mind freedom.

On the OSI Web site, the following describes its intent:

> The Open Source Initiative is a marketing program for free software. It's a pitch for "free software" on solid pragmatic grounds rather than ideological tub-thumping. The winning substance has not changed, the losing attitude and symbolism have. See the discussion of marketing for hackers for more. So that it is clear what kind of software we are talking about, we publish standards for open-source licenses. We

> have created a certification mark, "OSI Certified," to be applied only to software that is distributed under an open-source license that meets criteria set by the Open Source Initiative as representatives of the open software community. We intend this mark to become a widely recognized and valued symbol, clearly indicating that software does, in fact, have the properties that the community has associated with the descriptive term "open source." (www.opensource.net)

The FSF and OSI have certainly grown over the last 10 years and have established themselves with enough users and contributors to be in the institutionalization stage. The group ideology has spread to international communities.

On the Libervis.com Web site (www.libervis.org), a 20-year-old engineering major from Croatia started a community center for free software. The mission of the site is:

> Libervis.com is an ambitious project of building a free software (aka open source) community center (FOSS center) on the Web by providing a Web infrastructure (forums, blogs, wiki, articles) for seamless communication, discussing and learning about any FOSS related area of interest. This community center welcomes all people interested in free software, whether they are supporters of the pragmatical open source ideology or pure free software ideology, but we take stand on the side of free software movement and want to educate everyone that uses free software and enjoys its benefits about the importance of freedom which stands behind these benefits.

The group ideology for free software has spread around the world and is constantly reaching new people. The free software movement and open source software movement have reached an institutionalization phase where more and more people are aware of the movements through the public discourse readily available on Web sites and circulated at professional conventions.

Stage 4: Institutionalization

Institutions consist of cognitive, normative, and regulative structures and activities that provide stability and meaning to social behavior (Scott, 2001). When a CM reaches the institutionalization stage, the technology being advocated by the CM has reached a diffusion stage (i.e., organizations and society are actively pursuing the use of F/OSS for personal and business applications) as outlined in the conceptual model for a CM in Chapter 1 of this volume.

By the time a social movement has reached the institutionalization stage, it has developed into a fixed organization with dedicated personnel and a business structure to carry out the goals of the movement. Leaders take on the role of administrators during this stage. The role of tactics (Blumer, 1969) is important in this stage of development in cementing the established reputation of the movement and in continuing the recruitment of members. Both the FSF and OSI have myriad sets of documentation available on their respective Web sites. Topics covered include movement philosophy, recommendations for volunteerism, links to related sites for downloading free software, detailed documentation on licensing, variations of the GPL, and contact information for movement personnel such as the board of directors, and potential speakers for hire. The role of tactics is important in this stage to maintain the movement membership and retain the current members. Both the FSF and the OSI have developed sophisticated Web sites to spread their public discourse, drawing in more and more people with links to personal blogs of RMS and wikis among others.

Discussion

This chapter traces the historical development of the free and open source software movements, using a framework with four stages of development for social movements (Dawson & Gettys, 1935): social unrest, popular excitement, formalization, and institutionalization. Both the free software movement and the open source software movement have mobilized people to join their efforts through various forms of public discourse proclaiming their technological action frames. CMs do not develop in the same fashion as other types of social movements due to the need for technology adoption to occur at sufficient levels in order for the movement to sustain itself and attain institutionalization where the technology has reached diffusion in society and industry. Thus, in this analysis, technology adoption was added to the formalization stage and technology diffusion was added to the institutionalization stage. As part of that technology adoption/diffusion process, the belief in free software often cements a programmer's dedication to the proliferation of F/OSS projects through volunteer work. These beliefs form a shared ideology between the free software movement and the open source software movement. In addition to their basic shared history, the F/OSS movements are pulled together by integrating factors that constitute their culture (Gerlach, 2001): shared ideology and shared opposition.

Shared Ideology

Movement ideology serves participants at two levels: (1) a sharing of basic beliefs or core themes, sometimes articulated as slogans (e.g., "Think free speech, not free beer"), and (2) differing interpretations of and emphases on core themes (Gerlach, 2001). Core beliefs can be shared because they are ambiguous and flexible, capable of being changed to fit a particular group's situation.

Beliefs form the core of ideologies, and as such are an important motivation for individuals to work on free software projects. Recent studies of individuals' motivations for contributing to F/OSS development show ideological motivation. Intrinsic motivations such as pleasure in programming and identity with the open source community were found to be primary reasons for people to participate in F/OSS programming (Hars & Ou, 2002; Lakhani & Wolf, 2005). In the survey of 79 free/open source programmers (Hars & Ou, 2002), 16.5 percent of respondents rated high on altruism and 30 percent identified strongly with the open source community or had a kin-like relationship with other open source programmers. In a larger survey of 684 free/open source contributors from 287 projects (Lakhani & Wolf, 2005), 42 percent strongly agreed and 41 percent somewhat agreed that the "hacker"[2] community was their primary source of identity, while 30 percent believed that all source code should be open. A group of altruistic-type programmers (28.6 percent) surveyed were motivated by giving code back to the F/OSS community.

Shared Opposition

The recognition or perception that there is external opposition to their cause helps to draw diverse movement groups together to expand. The split of the FSF and OSI has resulted in participants with a spectrum of beliefs about how to proceed with sharing software—at the one extreme are those who believe all software should be free (i.e., never use non-free) and at the other are those who believe any combination of free and non-free is acceptable (Elliott & Scacchi, 2003a, 2003b, 2004, forthcoming). However, most participants feel that big businesses like Microsoft should be sharing their source code to large-scale programs such as Windows. This shared opposition enables the two groups to work together and serves to reinforce their ideology.

Although the two movements split over ideological differences, they are united in their position that big businesses like Microsoft should share their software. Eric Raymond (2001) posted a series of memos written in October 2001 by a Microsoft executive (www.opensource.org) and given to him by a company insider:

> Open Source Software (OSS) is a development process which promotes rapid creation and deployment of incremental features and bug fixes in an existing code/knowledge base. In recent years, corresponding to the growth of Internet, OSS projects have acquired the depth & complexity traditionally associated with commercial projects such as OSs and mission critical servers. Consequently, OSS poses a direct, short-term revenue and platform threat to ... particularly in server space. Additionally, the intrinsic parallelism and free idea exchange in OSS has benefits that are not replicable with our current licensing model and therefore present a long term developer mindshare threat.

The "Halloween Documents" (named by the free software community because they were written at the end of October) are periodically updated by Raymond whenever he receives more information about Microsoft's opposition to open source.

Conclusions

The ultimate utopian vision of the free software movement is for all source code to be readily available to all individuals, much like books are available in a public library (i.e., companies like Microsoft give away Windows source code so that consumers can fix bugs and create new versions themselves, etc.). That goal may never be achieved because both the United States and other developed countries sell software for a profit, and giving away millions of lines of code for "free" is anathema to the typical business model. However, these CMs have made inroads into how software companies do business. Software and hardware vendors such as HP and Sun are beginning to sell hardware with the open source GNU/Linux OS included. In addition, an occupational community (Van Maanen & Barley, 1984) has emerged from these movements (Elliott & Scacchi, forthcoming) where F/OSS developers are hired as paid consultants to implement and maintain F/OSS applications in businesses. Table 13.1 shows a summary of the factors related to the success of the free software movement and OSI.

The F/OSS movements are a new genre of CM that assumes mass computerization is available. Through centralized movement organizations located on Web sites, these movements have been successful in recruiting individuals either as users or contributors (e.g., programmers, technical writers, or software designers). Their integrated ideology (belief in free software) and integrated opposition (big business trying to block free software) have fueled both of these movements to proliferate. Other factors leading to their success and growth are recognized and respected leaders

Table 13.1 Growth and Success of FSM and OSI

	Factors Related to Success of the FSM and OSI
1	1998 – FSM and OSI split into two organizations. Each develops strong following.
2	Strength in beliefs promoted by agitators.
3	Shared opposition to Microsoft and other large companies who are against free and open source software.
4	Ubiquitous Computing – Facilitates goal achievement.
5	Evangelism – Web access to documentation of movement philosophy.

of the movements (i.e., agitators), development of a strong morale and *esprit de corps*, and technological advancements of ubiquitous computing environments (Sørensen & Yoo, 2005; Sørensen, Yoo, Lyytinen, & DeGross, 2005) that enable connections to work and home any time, anywhere for global access to a work product (i.e., free or open source project). In order to generalize these findings to other CMs of the ubiquitous computing era, future research could include the application of this framework to analyze the success or failure of other CM technology.

Endnotes

1. For an in-depth discussion of previous CM research, see Elliott & Kramer, Chapter 1 in this volume.
2. A slang term for a computer enthusiast, i.e., a person who enjoys learning programming languages and computer systems and can often be considered an expert on the subject(s). Among professional programmers, depending on how it is used, the term can be either complimentary or derogatory, although it is developing an increasingly derogatory connotation. The pejorative sense of *hacker* is becoming more prominent largely because the popular press has co-opted the term to refer to individuals who gain unauthorized access to computer systems for the purpose of stealing and corrupting data. Hackers themselves maintain that the proper term for such individuals is cracker.

References

Blumer, H. (1969). Social movements. In B. McLaughlin (Ed.), *Studies in social movements: A social psychological perspective* (pp. 3–29). New York: Free Press.

Dawson, C. A., & Gettys, W. E. (1935). *Introduction to sociology*. New York: Ronald Press Co.

Elliott, M., & Scacchi, W. (2003a, November 9–12). *Free software developers as an occupational community: Resolving conflicts and fostering collaboration.* Proceedings of GROUP '03, Sanibel Island, Florida.

Elliott, M., & Scacchi, W. (2003b). *Free software: A case study of software development in a virtual organizational culture* (Technical Report No. UCI-ISR-03-6). Irvine, CA: Institute for Software Research, University of California, Irvine.

Elliott, M., & Scacchi, W. (2004). Free software development: Cooperation and conflict in a virtual organizational culture. In S. Koch (Ed.), *Free/open source software development* (pp. 152–172). Hershey, PA: Idea Group Publishing.

Elliott, M., & Scacchi, W. (forthcoming). Mobilization of software developers: The free software movement. *Information Technology and People*.

Gamson, W. A. (1975). *The strategy of social Protest* (2nd ed.). Belmont, CA: Wadsworth Publishing.

Gerlach, L. P. (2001). Structures of social movements: Environmental activism and its opponents. In J. Arquilla and D. F. Ronfeldt, (Eds.), *Networks and netwars: The future of terror, crime, and militancy* (pp. 311–361). Los Angeles, CA: Rand Corporation.

Hars, A., & Ou, S. (2002). Working for free? Motivations for participating in open-source projects. *International Journal of Electronic Commerce*, 6(3), 25–39.

Iacono, S., & Kling, R. (1996). Computerization movements and tales of technological utopianism. In R. Kling (Ed.), *Computerization and controversy: Value conflicts and social change* (2nd ed.). (pp. 85–105). San Diego, CA: Academic Press.

Iacono, S., & Kling, R. (2001). Computerization movements: The rise of the Internet and distant forms of work. In J. A. Yates & J. V. Van Maanen (Eds.), *Information technology and organizational transformation: History, rhetoric and practice* (pp. 93–136), Thousand Oaks, CA: Sage Publications.

Kling, R., & Iacono, S. (1988). The mobilization of support for computerization: The role of computerization movements. *Social Problems*, 35(3), 226–242.

Lakhani, K. R., & Wolf, R. G. (2005). Why hackers do what they do: Understanding motivation and effort in free/open source software projects. In J. R. Feller, S. Fitzgerald, S. Hissam, & R. K. Lakhani (Eds.), *Perspectives on free and open source software* (pp. 3–21). Cambridge, MA: MIT Press.

Lyytinen, K., & Yoo, Y. (2002). The next wave of nomadic computing: A research agenda for information systems research. *Information Systems Research*, 13(4), 377–388.

Markus, M. L. (1987). Toward a "Critical Mass" theory of interactive media. *Communication Research*, 14(5), 491–511.

Mattern, F. (2002). Ubiquitous computing: Scenarios for an informatized world. Retrieved from www.m-lab.ch/pubs/Scenarios.pdf

Mazmanian, M. A., Orlikowski, W. J., & Yates, J. (2005). CRACKBERRIES: The social implications of ubiquitous wireless e-mail devices. In C. Sorensen, Y. Yoo, K. Lyytinen, & J. I. DeGross (Eds.), *Designing ubiquitous information environments: Socio-technical issues and challenges* (pp. 337–344). Cleveland, OH: Springer.

Orlikowski, W., & Gash, D. C. (1994). Technological frames: Making sense of information technology in organizations. *ACM Transactions on Information Systems*, 12, 174–207.

Raymond, E. S. (2001). *The cathedral & the bazaar: Musings on Linux and Open Source by an accidental revolutionary*. Sebastopol, CA: O'Reilly & Associates.

Rogers, E. (2005). *Diffusion of innovations* (5th ed.). New York: The Free Press.

Scott, W. (2001). *Institutions and organizations*. Thousand Oaks, CA: Sage Publications.

Snow, D. A., & Benford, R. O. (2000). Framing processes and social movements: An overview and assessment. *Annual Review of Sociology*, 26, 611–639.

Snow, D. A., Rochford, E. B., Worden, S. K., & Benford, R. O. (1986). Frame alignment processes, micromobilization, and movement participation. *American Sociological Review*, 51, 464–481.

Sørensen, C., & Yoo, Y. (2005). Socio-technical studies of mobility and ubiquity. In C. Sørensen, Y. Yoo, K. Lyytinen, & J. I. DeGross (Eds.), *Designing ubiquitous information environments: Socio-technical issues and challenges* (pp. 1–16). New York: Springer.

Sørensen, C., Yoo, Y., Lyytinen, K., & DeGross, J. I. (2005). *Designing ubiquitous information environments: Socio-technical issues and challenges*. Cleveland, OH: Springer.

Stallman, R. M. (1999). The GNU operating system and the free software movement. In C. DiBona, S. Ockman, & M. Stone (Eds.), *Open sources: Voices from the open source revolution* (pp. 53–70). Sebastopol, CA: O'Reilly & Associates, Inc.

Stallman, R. M. (2002). *Free software, free society: Selected essays of Richard M. Stallman*. Boston: GNU Press.

Van Maanen, J. V., & Barley, S. R. (1984). Occupational communities: Culture and control in organizations. *Research in Organizational Behavior*, 6, 287–365.

Weiser, M. (1991, September). The computer for the 21st century. *Scientific American*, 94–104.

Williams, S. (2002). *Free as in freedom: Richard Stallman's crusade for free software*. Sebastopol, CA: O'Reilly & Associates.

Zald, M. N., & Ash, A. (1969). Social movement organizations: Growth, decay, and change. *Social Forces*, 44(3), 327–340.

Chapter 14

Emerging Patterns of Intersection and Segmentation When Computerization Movements Interact

Walt Scacchi
University of California, Irvine

Abstract

Rob Kling and Suzanne Iacono introduced and investigated computerization movements, counter-computerization movements, and computerization organizations in a series of papers starting in the late 1980s. Their analyses focus on characterizing structural properties, ideologies, and consequences of computerization movements and organizations. This chapter starts from their foundations to investigate a set of three new computerization movements: open source software development, computer games, and grid computing. I focus attention on examining not only structural properties, ideologies, and consequences of these three computerization movements and associated organizations but also structural processes that characterize what happens when computerization movements come together, and consequences that emerge as a result of these intersecting movements. This focus on identifying emerging patterns of intersecting computerization movements, as well as the segmenting of these computerization movements, is the principal contribution of this chapter.

Introduction

This chapter examines three established yet continually emerging worlds of computing. These are the worlds of open source software (OSS) development (Scacchi, 2002), computer games (Scacchi, 2004), and grid computing. Each of these worlds can and has been subject to some of the analytic frameworks that emphasize either ethnographic, empirically grounded theory building or technological rationalization. However, in this chapter, it will be most effective to examine what happens as these computerization movements (CMs) collide or pass through each other in ways that might not be readily predicted from separate studies of each movement or computing sub-world. Subsequently, this study builds on the analytical frameworks of Rob Kling and colleagues (Kling & Iacono, 1988; Iacono & Kling, 2001) over nearly 20 years of research in social analyses of CMs.

The chapter is organized as follows. The next section reviews CMs, social movements, and other related framings of collective action within the computing world. It is followed by an examination of three current CMs: OSS, computer games, and grid computing. Each movement is examined and compared with prior CMs. This reveals trends and structural patterns found in these current movements which differ from those examined in the studies by Kling and Iacono. In particular, attention is focused on how these three current movements intersect each other and the consequences that can result. This is followed by a discussion that presents some ways to advance studies of CMs based on the topics covered in the chapter. In the conclusions that close this chapter, there are recommendations for new research problems to be investigated related to emerging CMs and to the collective actions and social dynamics that animate their evolution.

Understanding CMs

The analyses of Kling and Iacono (1988, 1995; Iacono & Kling, 1996, 2001) and others in this volume build from a foundation of prior theoretical and empirical studies of CMs. Traditionally, these studies have drawn attention to structural patterns arising within a CM, ideological tenets and technological action frames (cf. Orlikowski & Gash, 1994; Iacono & Kling, 2001) that form the rhetorical core of the CM, and organizations that persist and are associated with advancing the CM. A closer look at the social movements literature reveals additional conceptual foundations that can expand and refine what can be examined when studying social movements, and by extension when studying CMs and counter-CMs.

Kling and Iacono also drew on the analysis of Zald and colleagues (Zald & Berger, 1978; Useem & Zald, 1982) to flesh out other properties of social movements that could help characterize CMs. For example, Zald and colleagues observed that social movements can occur within organizations as a participatory strategy for collective action that seeks to affect some organizational reform or major organizational transformation. Such movements may be based on effecting political change within an organization. Alternatively, organizations may emerge whose purpose is to help guide or lead a movement in effecting social change through organized collective action. Finally, such an organization may focus its efforts on mobilizing its movements around certain technologies either in support of or opposition to the entrenched technologies of dominant institutions. Zald and colleagues identify these as technology movements or technology counter-movements, depending on whether the organization guiding the social movement supports or opposes the existing technological order. The CMs characterized by Kling and Iacono employ these notions of the role of key organizations and technological movements and counter-movements.

Many scholars have studied and theorized about social movements, which now also influence how we may view CMs. Gerlach (1971, 2001) and others (e.g., McAdam, McCarthy, & Zald, 1996; Snow, Soule, & Kriesi, 2004) find that social movements are segmentary, polycentric, and networked (SPIN), therefore heterogeneous and cyclic. Segmentary means that movements are composed of many diverse groups that grow, divide, fuse, proliferate, contract, and die. Polycentric means social movements have multiple and sometimes competing leaders or centers of influence, and the persistence of such positions of authority may be short-lived. Networked means movements are integrated through multiple relationships among movement participants, the overlapping and joint activities they engage in, shared communication media, ideals, and opponents. These networks may therefore be recognized as constituting social networks (including organizations), technological networks (including computing systems and networked information infrastructures), and mutually dependent sociotechnical networks which can all therefore exist within technological movements or CMs and counter-movements (cf. Scacchi, 2005; Sproull & Kiesler, 1991).

The structural characteristics of SPIN are useful additions to the Kling and Iacono framing that help flesh out important other structural properties of CMs and counter-movements. For example, if CMs follow a SPIN cycle, then they must be segmentary rather than monolithic, polycentric rather than singular, and networked rather than hierarchical or fully decentralized and disconnected. This implies that no one advocate, group, or organization truly speaks for or leads all the participants associated with a CM. Similarly, it implies that conflicts exist within each movement, as do struggles to wrest control from those currently in positions of movement leadership. Finally, ideological beliefs, values, and norms (cf. Elliott & Scacchi, 2005) reinforce these structural characteristics when employed by movement participants to frame what are core problems, how they are to be addressed or resolved, and how work is to be divided and performed among participants (McAdam et al., 1996; Snow et al., 2004). However, there is no single rhetoric or master narrative that uniquely characterizes such heterogeneous and dynamically evolving social movements, though individual statements, authored works, proclamations appearing in the media, and the like are sometimes treated as defining or characterizing a social movement.

Kling and Gerson (1977, 1978) also introduced the concept of "computing world" as another way to characterize how collective action within the social world of computing is organized and articulated. The computing world combines Strauss's (1978) social world perspective and Zald's technological movements (cf. Zald & Berger, 1978; Useem & Zald, 1982), while a given sub-world of computing or occupational community (cf. Gerson, 1983; Elliott & Scacchi, 2005) is centered around work with distinct kinds of computing systems or technologies. These papers add an interesting new dimension to that of CMs in that they propose to ground and focus on characterizing movement dynamics within the computing world as being driven in part by technological innovation practices and processes (Kling & Gerson, 1977; Kling & Scacchi, 1982; Scacchi, 1981). Broader patterns of technological innovation, resource transactions, computing work trajectories, and occupational careers within and across organizations help articulate patterns of segmentation and intersection within the computing world and sub-worlds (Gerson, 1983; Kling & Gerson, 1978). The patterns of intersection within these worlds reiterate Strauss's foundational notions while segmentation patterns correspond to the SPIN cycle reported by Gerlach (2001). Technological innovation, segmentation, and intersection thus introduce a set of dynamics that animates and provides a motive force for CMs.

Collectively, these studies reveal a sustained intellectual focus of computing, computing world, and CMs as a complex sociotechnical regime of organizational and technological resources arrayed through recurring patterns of negotiation, reallocation, and control that simultaneously enable and constrain what people can accomplish in their work with computing. But computing and computerization continue to evolve and new regimes and movements are emerging which may or may not change the landscape of analytical framings that have appeared, and thus merit study and reapplication so as to re-establish their relevancy and theoretical validity.

Three Emerging CMs

The CM studies of Kling and Iacono initially examined five movements: urban information systems, artificial intelligence (AI), personal computing, office automation, and computer-based education (Kling & Iacono, 1988). They later added two additional CMs, for virtual reality and computer-supported cooperative work (CSCW) (Kling & Iacono, 1995). For the most part, all of these CMs, with the exception of CSCW, have mostly receded in their prominence or aggressive promotion. Why and how they have faded is an open question beyond the scope of this chapter. However, it is fair to say that it may be explained in part by reference to the comparative success or failure of these early CMs to facilitate the broad diffusion of computing innovations that are often the focus of each respective CM (cf. Rogers, 1995). However, none of the studies by Kling and Iacono examined the dynamics that drove these movements, nor whether any of these CMs drove into one another and with what consequence. This is the point of departure in the remainder of the study presented here.

Specifically, it is now possible to examine a new set of CMs, not only in terms of their structural properties and ideological foci as found in previous CM studies but also with regard to some of their dynamics, including attention to where and how different CMs may intersect each other, and to what ends. Accordingly, three CMs now in the limelight can be examined and compared, both as separate movements and as intersecting or overlapping movements. The three CMs for study are those focused on OSS development, networked computer games, and grid computing.

Open Source Software

Structural Patterns of the OSS Movement

The OSS movement (cf. Dedrick & West, Chapter 16, this volume; Elliott, Chapter 13, this volume) is populated with thousands of OSS development projects, each with its own Web site. Whether the OSS movement is better recognized as a counter-movement to the proprietary or closed source world of commercial software development is unclear. For example, executives from proprietary software firms have asserted that (a) OSS is a national security threat to the U.S. (O'Dowd, 2004), or (b) OSS (specifically that covered by the GNU Public License or "GPL") is a cancer that attaches itself to intellectual property (Greene, 2001). However, other business sources seem to clearly disagree with such characterizations and see OSS as an area for strategic investment (Gomes, 2001). Nonetheless, more than 120,000 projects are registered at OSS portals like SourceForge.net, as seen in Figure 14.1, while other OSS portals such as Freshment.org, Savannah.org, and Tigris.org contain thousands more.

The vast majority of these OSS projects at SourceForge appear to be inactive, with fewer than two contributing developers. However, at least a few thousand OSS projects seem to garner most of the attention and community participation, but no one project defines or leads the movement. The Linux Kernel project is perhaps the most widely known, with its celebrity leaders, such as Linus Torvalds. It is also the most studied

Figure 14.1 Home page of the SourceForge.net OSS Web portal, indicating more than 120,000 registered projects and more than 1.3 million registered users (Source: sourceforge.net, accessed June 7, 2006)

OSS project. However, there is no basis to indicate that how things work in this project prescribe or predict what might be found in other successful OSS projects. Thus, the OSS movement is segmented about the boundaries of each OSS project, though some of the larger project communities have emerged as a result of smaller OSS projects coming together. Finally, a small set of empirical studies (cf. Hars & Ou, 2002; Koch, 2005) shows that F/OSS developers often work on more than one project at a time, that upwards of two or three OSS developers contribute to two or more OSS projects, and perhaps as many as 5 percent contribute to ten or more OSS projects. The density and interconnectedness of this social networking characterizes the membership of the OSS movement, but at the same time the multiplicity of projects reflects its segmentation.

Ideological Tenets of the OSS Movement

The OSS movement arose in the 1990s (DiBona, Ockman, & Stone, 1999) from the smaller, more fervent "free software" movement (FSM) (Gay, 2002) started in the mid 1980s. The FSM (Elliott & Scacchi, 2005) was initiated by Richard M. Stallman (Gay, 2002), who is the founder of the FSM, the Free Software Foundation (FSF, www.fsf.org), and the GNU project (www.gnu.org). The FSM members identify their affiliation and commitment by openly developing and sharing their software following the digital civil liberties expressed in the GPL. The GPL is a license agreement that promotes and protects software source code using the GPL copyright to always be available (always assuring a "copy left"), so that the code is open for study, modification, and redistribution, with these rights preserved indefinitely. Furthermore, any software system that incorporates or integrates free software covered by the GPL is asserted henceforth to also be treated as free software. This so-called viral nature of the GPL is seen by some as an "anti-business" position, which is the most commonly cited reason for why other projects have since chosen to identify themselves as strictly OSS (Fink, 2003). However, new/pre-existing software that does not integrate GPL source code is not infected by the GPL, even if both kinds of software co-exist on the same computer or operating system, or access one another through open or standards-based application program interfaces.

Surveys of OSS projects reveal that 50 percent or more (including the Linux Kernel project) employ the GPL, even though there are only a few thousand self-declared free software projects. OSS projects, such as the Apache Web server, KDE user interface package, and Mozilla/Firefox Web browser, have chosen not to use the GPL but to opt for a less restrictive, open source license. In simple terms, free software is always open source, but OSS is not always free software. So the FSM has emerged or has been subsumed as a sub-world within the larger OSS movement. Subsequently, OSS licenses have become the hallmark carrier of the ideological beliefs that help distinguish members of the free software movement from those who share free software beliefs but prefer to be seen as open source or business-friendly developers. They also distinguish those who identify themselves as OSS developers but not practitioners or affiliates of the free software sub-world.

Organizations of the OSS Movement

A variety of organizations, enterprises, and foundations participate in encouraging the advancement and success of OSS (Weber, 2004). Nonprofit foundations have become one of the most prominent organizational forms founded to protect the common property rights of OSS projects. The Open Source Initiative (OSI) (www.opensource.org) is one such foundation that seeks to maintain the definition of what "open source software" is and what software licenses satisfy such a definition. OSI presents its definition of OSS in a manner that is considered business friendly (Fink, 2003), as opposed to "free software," which is cast by its advocates as a social movement that expresses civil liberties through software (e.g., source code as a form of free speech) (Gay, 2002). The OSI's Bruce Perens, who wrote the Open Source Definition (cf. www.opensource.org) and co-founded the OSI, is a prominent figure in the evolution of OSS. He advocates OSS as a viable economic and innovative alternative to proprietary software. The FSM also has an established nonprofit organization that advocates free software—the FSF. Bruce Perens is often compared to the FSF's Richard M. Stallman, who seeks to "put back the free in free enterprise" (Gay, 2002). Beyond this, a sign of success of the largest OSS projects is the establishment of a nonprofit foundation or a not-for-profit consortium that serves as the organizational locus and legal entity, which can engage in contracts and intellectual property rights agreements that benefit the project. A small but growing number of corporations in the information technology (IT), financial services, and other industries have taken on sponsorship of OSS projects, either as an external competitive strategy (e.g., IBM's Eclipse project and SUN's NetBeans project compete against Microsoft .NET products) or as an internal cost-reduction strategy (West & O'Mahony, 2005).

Computer Games

Structural Patterns of the Computer Games Movement

Computer games[1] have become a pervasive element of popular culture. More than 100 million computers have been sold for computer gaming applications, and every personal computer (PC), personal digital assistant (PDA), and cell phone now comes with computer games installed (King, 2002). More than 600 million users have played computer games over the Internet at some time, while hundreds of thousands of users play networked multi-player games each day, as indicated in Figure 14.2. Furthermore, the most popular networked games, such as Half Life: Counter-Strike and World of Warcraft (WoW), have millions of online players, while the most popular single-player games (or game-based synthetic worlds) like The Sims have tens of millions of players.[2] Computer games are, it is safe to say, a global entertainment technology, and one that increasingly defines the leading edge of personal computing technology.[3] However, computer game technology in general, and computer games in particular, have little presence or advocacy within academia, or within computer science research laboratories. This stands in contrast to other CMs such as AI or personal computing, which clearly had a base of support within the academic and research communities when they first appeared.

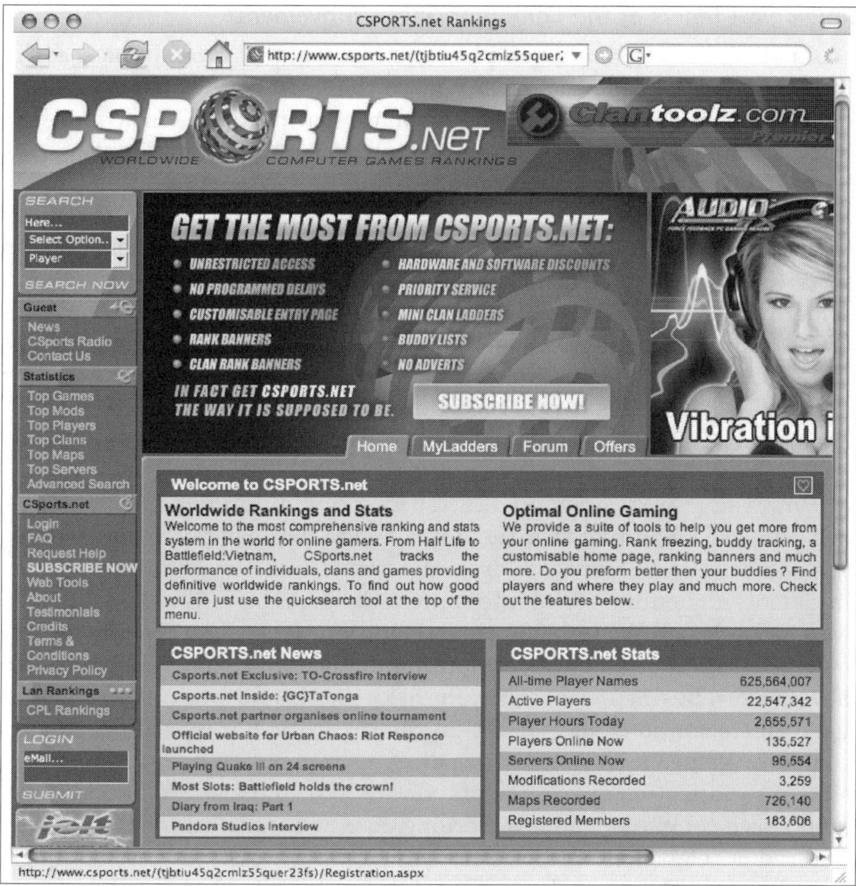

Figure 14.2 Some descriptive statistics characterizing Internet-based use of multi-player computer games, indicating more than 22.5 million active game players (Source: www.csports.net, accessed June 7, 2006)

Similarly, it is a challenge to ascertain whether avid computer game players or game developers identify themselves as part of a revolutionary or reform movement rather than as people who enjoy using computers to play games and have fun. If anything, this makes it seem that if there is a computer game movement, it might be one that seeks to reform the vision of computers as simply instrumental devices that support administrative or technical work tasks to one in which computers can be treated as hedonistic devices that support fun, playful competition, and sustained periods of immersive fantasy and use. The computer games movement might, then, appear to be focused on diffused cultural and technological change rather than sharply targeting organizational or institutional change. But a closer look may reveal more than this.

Ideological Tenets of the Computer Games Movement

As elements of popular culture, computer games would not seem to constitute a social movement any more than some other personal technology (transistor radios, pocket calculators, or portable music players). Further, the popular press associated with computer games, periodicals like *PC Gamer*, *Electronic Gaming World*, and dozens of other similar titles, or even trade titles like *Game Developer*, do not seem to convey that computer games are in some way a social force or mechanism for social change; instead computer games are about fun and play, and something entertaining to play for those who have grown up in the modern computer age. Furthermore, the technology, design, and development practices of commercial game developers seem more strongly aligned (or gender biased) to the interests of young male adults (Cassell & Jenkins, 1999), and such interests would not typically be recognized as a basis for a social movement.

However, there is growing interest from humanists and business pundits who are beginning to articulate a vision that computer games have the potential to be part of a dramatic transformation of culture, entertainment, and online social interaction. For example, Prensky (2001), as well as Beck and Wade (2004), see computer games as a precursor for a new generation of business computing applications that will transform how modern businesses operate. Prensky (2001) and Gee (2003) see similar transformations arising within the institution of education, in that computer games also appear to operate as immersive learning and persistent socialization environments. Gee (2003), and also Wolf and Perron (2003), see computer games emerging as a new cultural medium, much like radio, television, and cinema, which may transform the language, experience, and venues for communication, learning, and social action. Such game-based computing environments or media may therefore represent a new force giving rise to educational reform, as well as to new ways and means for learning on the job or on demand. So it appears that the ideological basis for a social movement centered about computer games is emerging from outside of its industrial centers of development, and from academic interests not typically associated with promoting IT.

Organizations of the Computer Games Movement

The computer game industry already generates larger annual revenues (approximately $10 billion in 2004) than the feature film industry (less than $9 billion in 2004), and computer games (software) are often the leading edge embodiments of game consoles and personal gaming computers (hardware). Large corporations like Electronic Arts, Microsoft, Sony, and Nintendo indicate the international basis of this technology, and countries like Korea probably have the highest per capita penetration of computer games with broadband network connectivity. Small game design studios like Id Software, Epic Games, BioWare, Valve Software, and Sony Online Entertainment in the U.S., and NC Soft in Korea, are responsible for much of the software technology and "game engines" that are the core of computer games. In contrast, popular game titles marketed in retail venues like Best Buy, Circuit City, Amazon.com, and Wal-Mart in the U.S. are distributed by large firms such as Electronic Arts, Ubisoft, Atari, THQ, Microsoft, and others that effectively control the retail channels for computer games, and thus what games become widely available on a regional, national, or international basis. Furthermore, other large IT companies like IBM, SUN, Dell, and HP are all now shipping both PCs and clustered server systems that are preconfigured and packaged to support computer games or game-centered businesses (e.g., online networked game play service providers) for sale to individual or corporate buyers.

Mid-size semiconductor manufacturing firms like NVidia and ATI now dominate the market for devices specialized to support computer game graphics (graphics processing units, GPUs), while these GPUs now represent the most complex digital processors in the computer industry. Small, boutique PC vendors like Alienware, Voodoo, Falcon, and others have emerged and thrive on selling highly customized PCs that are configured and optimized (including "overclocked" central processing units and graphics processing units). Elsewhere, a small but growing number of massively multi-player online games (MMOG) and online role-playing games (MMORPG) like Everquest, Ultima Outline, WoW, and Second Life are making a profit from software game sales and online subscriptions as well. In the case of Everquest, Ultima Outline, and WoW, their parent companies have realized millions of dollars in revenues not only from sales of the games but also from pay-to-play online subscriptions from players who subscribe on a monthly basis. In the case of WoW, the most popular subscription-based MMORPG in the U.S. and other parts of the world, more than 6 million players pay between $11 and $15 a month to play the game and participate in the online experience and community of WoW. Furthermore, these MMORPG have emerged on the international scene offering not only persistent (24/7) online game play worlds but also real-world economic systems that are generating income and wealth comparable in gross domestic product (GDP) terms to developed nations. For example, in the virtual game world of Norrath, virtual players sell and buy virtual artifacts in real U.S. dollars with the goods traded constituting a GNP for Norrath of $135 million, making it the 77th richest country in the world (about the same as Russia) with a per capita GNP of $2,226. This places its economy ahead of the nation of China and just behind that of Russia (cf. Castronova, 2005).[4]

The U.S. Department of Defense is investing heavily in the development and distribution of computer games as interactive media and educational technologies for conveying the modern military (combat) experience, as well as for training troops in small team tactical warfare. The game America's Army (AA), which is available for free download from the Web, has become the most widely distributed networked computer game in history, with more than 20 million copies in circulation and nearly 6 million users registered on its associated Web portal who play on one or more of the 40,000 AA servers accessible over the Internet. However, it is difficult to find examples in other government agencies involved in funding research and development (R&D) (e.g., National Science Foundation [NSF], National Aeronautics and Space Administration [NASA], Department of Energy [DoE], National Institutes of Health [NIH]) that are investing in computer games or game-based applications.

Finally, there are a number of Web portals or Web sites supported by game players. These are generally "virtual organizations" (DeSanctis & Monge, 1999; Kiesler, Boh, & Ren, Chapter 9, this volume; Tuecke, Foster, & Kesselman, 2001) whose primary organizational or teamwork form is based on the use of electronic communication systems and media such as e-mail, Web sites, discussion forums, Weblogs (blogs), and others. However, the game-related virtual organizations are generally not going concerns organized for financial gain or capital growth, but instead are organized as online venues for social, community, and clan interaction around favorite games. Game development companies appreciate the economic and market development value of these online communities and sometimes actively sponsor or host them on their corporate Web servers (cf. Kim, 2000). Three types of virtual organizations for games include fan sites, clan sites, and tournament sites. Fan sites attract and organize the efforts of game players who want to share their game play experiences, results, or creations (e.g., game-related artworks) with other like-minded enthusiasts. Clan sites draw the attention of avid or hardcore game players who want to be identified with a group of like-minded, accomplished players or game modders[5] (Cleveland, 2001) in order to advance their game play or game development skills. Player-based clans seek to subsequently engage in team-oriented (clan versus clan) play within multi-player games. Such multi-team engagements, as well as advanced player versus player engagements, are facilitated through tournament sites, which seek to elicit top-tier game players in professional or near-professional levels of game play. The most popular networked, multiplayer games often have hundreds of fan and clan sites that identify themselves with a particular game or set of related games, while tournament sites are often associated with either a specific game or game vendor (QuakeCon.org for games from Id Software, BlizzCon.com for games from Blizzard Entertainment), or with regional, national, or international game play events,[6] and thus also bring along corporate sponsors to finance the event and to showcase their products to game players.

Grid Computing

Structural Patterns of the Grid Computing Movement

Compared with the other two CMs discussed here, grid computing is a CM whose activities and promoters are much more like the CMs examined in Kling and Iacono's studies. The advocates of grid computing envision a new order for how large-scale enterprise computing should be structured in terms of hardware, software, and networking. Grid computing is envisioned to be based on loosely coupled/distributed computer clusters and shared storage systems (hardware), grid-based middleware services and remote application services (software), and high throughput data networking (Foster, 2003). An enterprise that plans to adopt grid computing is one that must plan to make a major investment in new computing technologies and development services. Ironically, the major reason most commonly cited for such investment is cost reduction and resource flexibility, which are to be realized through migration from monolithic legacy system applications to loosely coupled and incrementally reconfigured applications that are composed from "best of breed" applications services. So grid computing is supposed to realize its benefits through offering an enterprise a new, agile computing application environment, one that might be adapted to meet the ebb and flow of business cycles. In this way, application services can scale up to meet growth demands or can scale down to shrinking demands. However, all of these capabilities are mostly yet to be demonstrated in real-world business settings where agility or adaptability is critical to an enterprise's operations or success.

Ideological Tenets of the Grid Computing Movement

Perhaps the most common message associated with grid computing is that it represents the future of enterprise computing (Foster & Kesselman, 2003). Grid computing is not in general advocated as personal or small group technology; instead, it is intended primarily for large enterprises with substantial IT budgets or investments. For many years, computing grids remained the playthings of researchers, but by 2005 they were said to have finally come of age (Worthington, 2005). The key to grid computing is said to be focused on "federating" existing computing resources, thereby breaking down the technological boundaries that make enterprise computing more expensive and less reliable than it should be (Foster & Kesselman 2003; Worthington, 2005). Similarly, grid computing is about enabling the configuration and reconfiguration of virtual organizations (Tuecke et al., 2001), whereby it becomes possible to configure computing grids that transcend the boundaries of the (physical) organizations where they reside. However, such a capability seems to ignore the long legacy of research into organizations and organization science (e.g., DeSanctis & Monge, 1999; Kiesler, Boh, Ren, & Weisband, Chapter 9, this volume), let alone the politics of organizations, organizational computing, resource fiefdoms, or even science data wars (Hunter, 2003).

Organizations of the Grid Computing Movement

Compared with the other two CMs discussed here, the grid computing movement appears to be smaller in terms of the number of participating organizations, but those that do participate tend to be primarily large enterprises, consortia, or research laboratories. Grid computing is an emerging commercial marketplace in the IT industry, so all the major IT firms like IBM, SUN, Microsoft, HP, Oracle, and others are creating hardware-software-networking product lines that embrace grid computing (or "Web services") technologies. The GRID Forum (www.gridforum.org) is a trade association interested in promoting grid technologies for scientific and commercial computing applications, as well as hosting conferences and trade shows to help promote the commercialization and standardization of these technologies.

Finally, most government agencies involved in funding R&D in the U.S., Europe, and beyond are all investing in R&D projects that seek to stimulate the deployment, growth, and standardization of grid computing technologies, especially in support of large science laboratories or major science research projects (e.g., in areas such as genomics, high energy physics, astrophysics, computational chemistry, and others). However, the large IT consultancies like Accenture, EDS, PricewaterhouseCoopers, and others are yet to provide large-scale service offerings based on grid computing platforms or technologies, compared with their (highly profitable) service offerings based on software technologies like enterprise resource planning (ERP) or customer relationship management (CRM) systems.

Intersecting CMs

Just as people at work participate in multiple social worlds, they might also participate in multiple computing sub-worlds, and thus in multiple CMs, as these computing worlds intersect and segment (cf. Kazmer & Haythornthwaite, 2001). This section explores and characterizes the structural patterns and dynamic processes that arise when otherwise independent CMs intersect one another, as well as the segments that may form and persist as a result of the intersection.

OSS and Computer Games

The world of OSS and computer games is an active area of engagement and collective action (Scacchi, 2004). These two independent CMs clearly intersect each other. Similarly, there are well-established and easy-to-identify segments within these intersecting movements in the form of OSS-based computer games projects found on the Web. For example, on the SourceForge.net Web portal, there are more than 13,000 self-declared OSS-based computer games projects out of the 120,000 OSS projects, as seen in Figure 14.3. However, this sub-world is the second largest community of interest in OSS within SourceForge, representing just over 10 percent of the total of OSS projects at that portal.

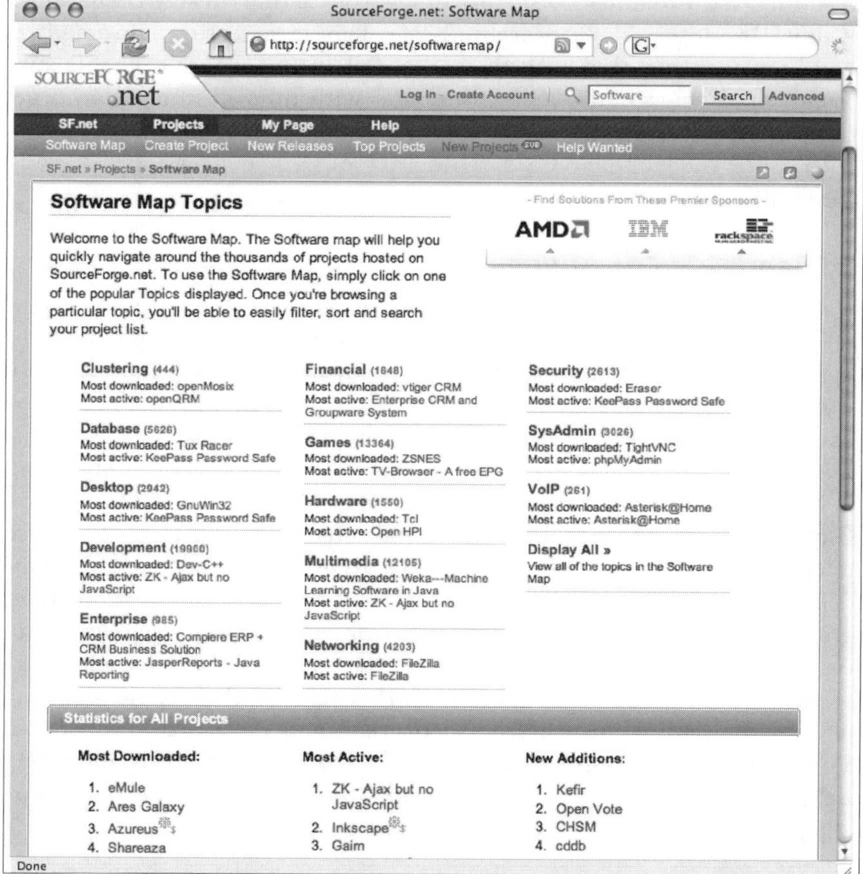

Figure 14.3 Screen display from SourceForge.net, indicating the "Games" OSS project category, which includes more than 13,000 projects, second only to "Development" (Source: sourceforge.net/softwaremap, accessed June 7, 2006)

Nonetheless, the existence of 13,000 OSS computer game development projects points to the emergence of a computing world that apparently conflates the fun and play of computer games with the community participation and technical development work of OSS development. Put differently, if one is working as an OSS developer for personal enrichment, then developing and playing computer games should be fun. It might also be a provocative and non-traditional way to learn about computer science, software development, and computer game design (cf. Gee, 2003; Prensky, 2001), well outside of established educational institutions. But whether it leads to a productive professional career as a commercial software developer or business venture is unclear. However, it can, in fact, provide an entry into the computer game industry, as OSS-based computer game development, through demonstration of "game modding" (Cleveland, 2001) or innovative game design experience (Game Developer, 2006; Scacchi, 2004). This intersecting movement is highly active compared with those that follow. It appears that this sub-world could emerge into a separate CM, with its own innovation practices, ideological beliefs, and internal segmentation and intersection with other independent CMs. These are described in a related study (Scacchi, 2004).

OSS and Grid Computing

OSS and grid computing, most often referred to as "open grid services," are intersecting CMs at a scale smaller than OSS and computer games but larger than computer games and grid computing. It appears that this sub-world will not emerge into a distinct CM but instead will more likely be assimilated back into the world of grid computing. Reasons for why this may occur include the following. First, the software core of grid computing is the middleware technology called Globus (Foster & Kesselman, 2003). Globus has been and remains OSS, as indicated in Figure 14.4. The choice to open source Globus was tied to the desire to have an open standard for defining and integrating grid services (aka Web services), as well as integrating with both new and pre-existing open data communication protocols. Similarly, the nascent effort to establish ad hoc "flash mob computing" services (cf. www.flashmobcomputing.org), which entail the rapid assembly of supercomputing clusters from networked and participant-contributed PCs, seems to have failed to emerge as a sustainable grid-like computing infrastructure, even though many OSS technologies have been marshaled and configured to demonstrate the potential.

Computer Games and Grid Computing

Computer games and grid computing are intersecting CMs at the scale smaller than the preceding two. But traces of their intersection

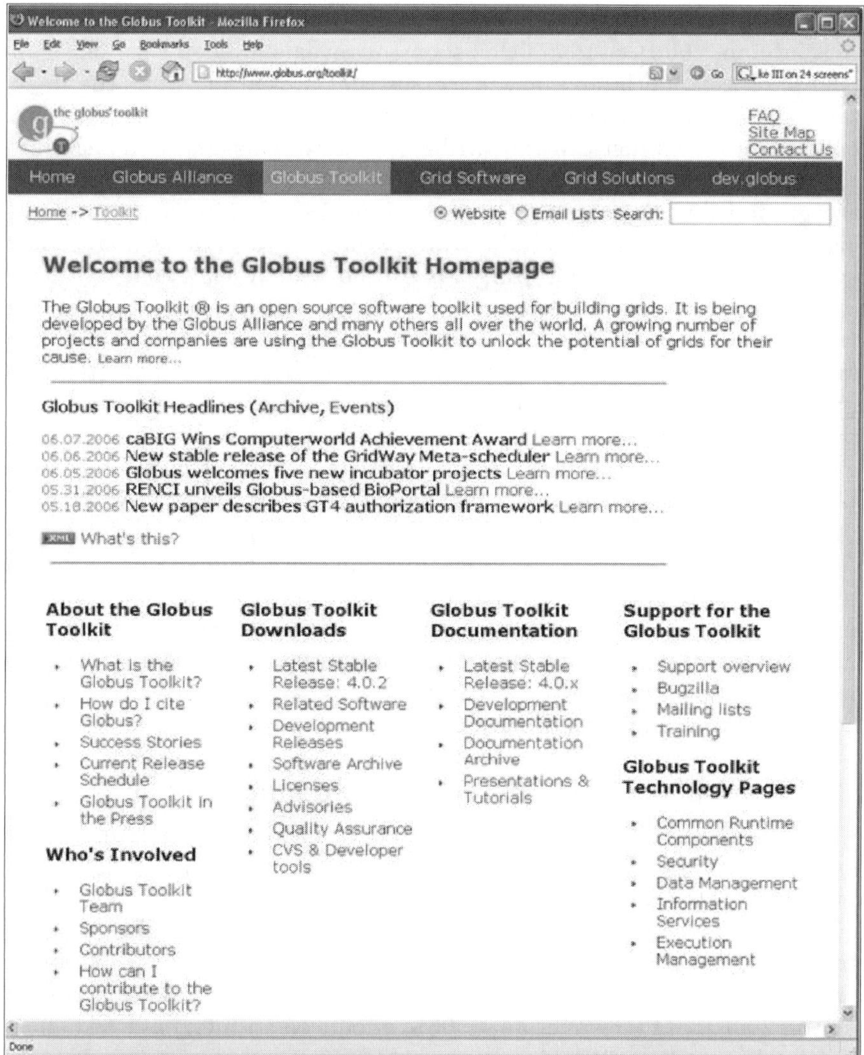

Figure 14.4 Background information on the OSS Globus Toolkit for building computing grid applications (Source: www.globus.org/toolkit, accessed June 7, 2006)

and emerging persistent segments that span and relate the two can be found and examined (Levine & Wirt, 2004). Similarly, the Sony Corporation has announced that its PlayStation3 computer game console[7] is designed to be hardware, software, and network compatible with grid computing (cf. Worthington, 2005). Other companies like Emergent Game Technologies and IBM have also announced interest in offering grid-based middleware services that support continuously scalable

MMOG infrastructure (cf. Deen, Hammer, Bethencourt, Eiron, Thomas, & Kaufman, 2006). Study of this segment reveals a narrow set of recurring practices and innovation processes that appears to limit the near-term growth into a separate CM. It seems that this sub-world may emerge into a distinct CM that will more likely be assimilated back into the world of computer games. Reasons for why this may occur arise from recognition that the market for grid computing remains uncertain outside of scientific research applications, while the revenues generated by the computer game industry already exceed $10 billion a year.

Furthermore, the emergence of the MMOG-based persistent online worlds and external economic systems points to plausible opportunities for marketing and deploying computer game-oriented grid systems to national or international game service providers. At the same time, computer game grids represent a new arena for technical innovation by game developers, as well as an arena for new kinds of computer game play experiences for end-users that may conflate having fun with making money (or not!). Finally, it may represent a bundling of technologies that governmental agencies which fund advance educational research (e.g., NSF) may find to be an appealing venue for exploring new concepts in large-scale game-based learning environments. Such applications may find interest more within the computer science research community, where grid computing research is currently taking place, than in education or humanities programs.

OSS, Computer Games, and Grid Computing

This is the smallest and least populated sub-world of computing that spans each of the three CMs. The fact that there are any identifiable and persisting activities within this segment is noteworthy and significant, since they must interlink three otherwise independent CMs. In 2005, there were no established projects or corporate ventures in this arena, though the idea of their existence seemed to be in circulation. But in spring 2006, IBM (Deen, et al., 2006) announced an internal R&D effort that seeks to support the development of MMOGs that run on grid technologies using OSS game engines. Whether this community can emerge, survive, and achieve the critical mass of social networking that can precipitate reinforcing network externalities is an open question. However, examining how participants in this segment can or might interact collectively and whether there is a common overlapping ideology is of interest. For example, there are many large-scale "LAN parties" where computer game players congregate (i.e., move to a common location) to build truly large-scale local area networks (LANs) and interconnected game servers to play both commercial games and OSS game mods, and then disappear all in a matter of days, much like when the circus comes to town. Figure 14.5 portrays such an example from QuakeCon, one of

Figure 14.5 Overview of a large, informal computing grid for playing commercial computer games and open source game mods, found at the QuakeCon 2005 LAN Party (Source: www.quakecon.org/gallery_byoc.php, accessed June 7, 2006)

the largest annual gaming enclaves and social events, formed around a large-scale LAN-based computing environment similar in capability to a flash mob computing cluster. Subsequently, this nascent sub-world of computerization that intersects OSS, computer games, and grid computing is perhaps most interesting as a boundary case whose future or continuing emergence is unclear, as is its status as a viable CM. Put differently, it may represent a case where the conditions needed to support the emergence of a CM are partially articulated, but whose longer-term success or demise is unclear. This sub-world thus represents an interesting boundary case for further study, so as to determine whether it will in fact emerge as a sustained computerization sub-movement, or whether it lacks some critical structural, ideological, or organizational component to sustain its emergence.

Discussion and Conclusions

This chapter examines CMs surrounding OSS, computer games, and grid computing, none of which had yet been subjected to critical analysis prior to the studies found in this volume. It also adopts an updated perspective on CMs in terms that seek to reveal the segmented, polycentric, and networked dimensions of the social worlds and sub-worlds that constitute these movements. In doing so, it became possible not only to examine each of these CMs on their own, but also to explore whether and how these movements might intersect one another and thus manifest inter-movement conditions and dynamics. This kind of analysis was suggested by early works of Kling and Gerson (1977, 1978) more than 25 years ago, but this analysis strategy still proves viable, as well as a source of new insights into how CMs are animated and evolve. Perhaps this is due to the growing maturity and ubiquity of computing technology and culture, as well as to our ability to critically examine them more closely.

This analysis also helps reveal that CMs and computing worlds are more diverse and of a more complex structure than perhaps may have been seen in prior studies. Also, the outcome of the intersection of different CMs is not uniform and does not necessarily give rise to a new, persistent sub-world of computing, though new sub-worlds do arise, as appears to be the case with the world of OSS for computer games. In fact, just the opposite can happen—one computing sub-world can effectively subsume the intersection of another computing sub-world, resulting in the two former sub-worlds being assimilated back into the dominant computing sub-world. This appears to be the situation resulting from the intersection of the sub-world of OSS and grid computing, as well as grid computing and computer games. Finally, the nascent intersection of these three CMs points to a fledgling sub-world whose sustained existence is sufficiently unclear and ill-defined to determine whether any of the three CMs will likely assimilate it. Subsequently, this homeless sub-world perhaps becomes most interesting from a critical perspective because of how it helps reveal and deconstruct the boundary conditions that arise as computing worlds and marginal social movements intersect one another.

Established groups within a CM can and often will fragment, resulting in either new groups with different members and allies or the departure of the disenfranchised. Consequently, CMs are probably more heterogeneous than homogeneous, though collective action still emerges, and shared beliefs or ideologies are expressed and renewed through communication media shared within a given movement. This revised perspective seeks to avoid or mitigate assumptions that all participants who are identified or associated with some CM or counter-movement myopically subscribe to some master narrative of ideological beliefs or uncritically agree to follow prescribed courses of collective action without reflection, disagreement, consternation, or conflict. Thus, CMs must be examined in ways that highlight their heterogeneity, their segmented social worlds, and the sociotechnical interaction networks that enable these segments to collectively act toward partially articulated and often conflicting goals.

Acknowledgments

The research described in this report was supported by grants #0083075, #0205679, #0205724, #0350754, and #0534771 from the U.S. National Science Foundation. No endorsement implied. Mark Ackerman at University of Michigan, Ann Arbor; Les Gasser at University of Illinois, Urbana-Champaign; John Noll at Santa Clara University; and Margaret Elliott, Chris Jensen, and others at the UCI Institute for Software Research are collaborators on this research effort.

Endnotes

1. Historically, many authors identify computer games as "video games" as if to suggest their significance stems from their video/visual display rather than from their basis as a computer or computing system.
2. It is also worth noting that parlor games like Solitaire, Minesweeper, and Pinball may be even more pervasively deployed, being found on hundreds of millions of PCs and related devices.
3. Consider the fact that the most expensive PCs are those configured for high-performance computer gaming.
4. The market for producing and selling in-game resources, assets, or high-rank game characters can be seen, for example, in postings found on eBay.com, where top-price items for games like Everquest or WoW range from hundreds to thousands of U.S. dollars, even though the end-user license agreements associated with these games may restrict or prohibit such unauthorized trade of copyrighted game properties.
5. A mod or modification is a term used in computer gaming to specify a change (partial or full conversion) to the electronic game that can be a part of a purchased game or a replacement of the entire game. People who create and share the mods are known as game modders.
6. The World Cyber Games (based in Korea) is an example of an international league of national game teams made up of game play enthusiasts who play for cash prizes (up to $50,000 to each winner per game, per event), gaming equipment, and product endorsements.
7. Sony has already sold more than 100 million PlayStation 1 and PlayStation 2 computer game consoles worldwide.

References

Beck, J. C., & Wade, M. (2004). *Got game: How the gamer generation is reshaping business forever*. Cambridge, MA: Harvard Business School Press.

Cassell, J., & Jenkins, H. (Eds.). (1999). *From Barbie to Mortal Kombat: Gender and computer games*. Cambridge, MA: MIT Press.

Castronova, E. (2005). *Synthetic worlds, the business and culture of online games*. Chicago: University of Chicago Press.

Cleveland, C. (2001). The past, present, and future of PC mod development. *Game Developer*, 8(2), 46–49.

Deen, G., Hammer, M., Bethencourt, J., Eiron, I., Thomas, J., & Kaufman, J. H. (2006). Running Quake II on a grid. *IBM Systems Journal*, 45(1), 21–44.

DeSanctis, G., & Monge, P. (1999). Introduction to the special issue: Communication processes in virtual organizations. *Organization Science*, 10(6), 693–703.

DiBona, C., Ockman, S., & Stone, M. (1999). *Open sources: Voices from the open source revolution*. Sebastopol, CA: O'Reilly Press.

Elliott, M. S. & Scacchi, W. (2005). Free software development: Cooperation and conflict in a virtual organizational culture. In S. Koch (Ed.), *Free / open source software development* (pp. 152–172). Hershey, PA: Idea Group Publishing.

Fink, M. (2003). *The business and economics of Linux and Open Source*. Upper Saddle River, NJ: Prentice Hall PTR.

Foster, I. (2003). What is the grid? A three point checklist. White paper, Univa Inc.

Foster, I., & Kesselman, C. (Eds.). (2003). *The GRID 2: Blueprint for a new computing infrastructure*. San Francisco, CA: Morgan Kaufman.

Game Developer. (2006). Retrieved from www.gdmag.com/homepage.htm

Gay, J. (Ed.). (2002). *Free software free society: Selected essays of Richard M. Stallman*. Boston: GNU Press, Free Software Foundation.

Gee, J. (2003). *What videogames have to teach us about learning and literacy*. New York: Palgrave Macmillan.

Gerlach, L. P. (1971). Movements of revolutionary change: Some structural characteristics. *American Behavior Scientist*, 14, 812–836.

Gerlach, L. P. (2001). The structure of social movements: Environmental activism and its opponents. In J. Arquilla & D. Ronfelt (Eds.), *Networks and netwars: The future of terror, crime, and militancy*. Santa Monica, CA: The Rand Corporation.

Gerson, E. M. (1983). Scientific work and social worlds. *Knowledge: Creation, diffusion and utilization*, 4(3), 357–377.

Gomes, L. (2001, June 13). In your face! MS open source attack backfire. *The Wall Street Journal*.

Greene, T. C. (2001, June 2). Ballmer: "Linux is a Cancer." *The Register*. Retrieved from www.theregister.co.uk/2001/06/02/ballmer_linux_is_a_cancer

Hars, A., & Ou, S. (2002). Working for free? Motivations for participating in open source software projects. *International Journal of Electronic Commerce*, 6(3), 25–39.

Hunter, P. (2003). Datawars: Grid computing democratizes proteomics; security concerns limit some efforts. *The Scientist*, 17(8), 53–54.

Iacono, C. S., & Kling, R. (1996). Computerization movements and tales of technological utopianism. In R. Kling (Ed.), *Value conflicts and social change* (2nd. ed.). San Diego, CA: Academic Press.

Iacono, C. S., & Kling, R. (2001). Computerization movements: The rise of the Internet and distant forms of work. In J. A. Yates, & J. Van Maanen (Eds.), *Information technology and organizational transformation: History, rhetoric, and practice* (pp. 93–136). Newbury Park, CA: Sage Publications.

Kazmer, M. M., & Haythornthwaite, C. (2001). Juggling multiple social worlds. *American Behavior Scientist*, 45(3), 510–529.

Kim, A. J. (2000). *Community building on the Web: Secret strategies for successful online communities.* Berkeley, CA: Peachpit Press.

King, L. (Ed.). (2002). *Game on: The history and culture of videogames.* New York: Universe.

Kling, R., & Gerson, E. M., (1977). The social dynamics of technical innovation in the computing world. *Symbolic Interaction*, 1(1), 132–146.

Kling, R., & Gerson, E. M. (1978). Patterns of segmentation and intersection in the computing world. *Symbolic Interaction*, 1(2), 24–43.

Kling, R., & Iacono, C. S. (1988). The mobilization of support for computerization: The role of computerization movements. *Social Problems*, 35(3), 226–242.

Kling, R., & Iacono, S. (1995). Computerization movements and the mobilization of support for computerization. In S. L. Starr (Ed.), *Ecologies of knowledge: Work and politics in science and technology* (pp. 119–153). Albany, NY: State University of New York Press.

Kling, R., & Scacchi, W. (1982). The web of computing: Computer technology as social organization. In M. Yovits (Ed.), *Advances in Computers* (pp. 1–90). New York: Academic Press.

Koch, S. (Ed.). (2005). *Free/open source software development.* Hershey, PA: Idea Group Publishing.

Levine, D., & Wirt, M. (2004). Interactivity with scalability: Infrastructure for multiplayer games. In I. Foster & C. Kesselman (Eds.), *The grid: Blueprint for a new computing infrastructure* (2nd ed.). San Francisco: Morgan Kaufmann.

McAdam, D., McCarthy, J. D., & Zald, M. N. (1996). *Comparative perspectives on social movements: Political opportunities, mobilizing structures, and cultural framings.* Cambridge, U.K.: Cambridge University Press.

O'Dowd, D. (2004, July 19). No defense for Linux: Inadequate security poses national security threat. *Design News.* Retrieved from www.designnews.com/article/CA435615.html

Orlikowski, W. J., & Gash, D. (1994). Technological frames: Making sense of information technology in organizations. *ACM Transactions on Information Systems*, 12, 174–207.

Prensky, M. (2001). *Digital game-based learning.* New York: McGraw-Hill.

Rogers, E. (1995). *The diffusion of innovations* (4th ed.). New York: Free Press.

Scacchi, W. (1981). The process of innovation in computing: A study in the social dynamics of computing. Unpublished Ph.D. dissertation, Information and Computer Science Department, University of California, Irvine, Irvine, CA.

Scacchi, W. (2002). Understanding the requirements for developing open source software systems. *IEE Proceedings—Software*, 149(1), 24–39.

Scacchi, W. (2004). Free/open source software development practices in the computer game community. *IEEE Software*, 21(1), 59–67.

Scacchi, W. (2005). Socio-technical interaction networks in free/open source software development processes. In S. T. Acuña & N. Juristo (Eds.), *Software process modeling* (pp. 1–27). New York: Springer Science+Business Media Inc.

Snow, D. A., Soule, S. A., & Kriesi, H. (2004). *The Blackwell companion to social movements.* Victoria, Australia: Blackwell Publishers Ltd.

Sproull, L., & Kiesler, S. (1991). *Connections: New ways of working in the networked organization.* Cambridge, MA: MIT Press.

Strauss, A., (1978). A social world perspective. *Studies in Symbolic Interaction*, 1, 119–128.

Tuecke, S., Foster, I., & Kesselman, C. (2001). The anatomy of the grid: Enabling scalable virtual organizations. *International Journal of Supercomputing Applications*, 15(3), 2001.

Useem, B., & Zald, M. (1982). From pressure group to social movement: Organizational dilemmas of the effort to promote nuclear power. *Social Problems*, 30(2), 144–156.

Weber, S. (2004). *The success of open source*. Cambridge, MA: Harvard University Press.

West, J., & O'Mahony, S. (2005). Contrasting community building in sponsored and community founded open source projects. *Proceedings of the Annual Hawaii International Conference on Systems Sciences*, HICSS38, Waikola Village, Hawaii.

Wolf, M. J. P., & Perron, B. (2003). *The video game theory reader*. New York: Routledge.

Worthington, D. (2005, February 21). Interview: The future of grid computing. *Beta News*, 21.

Zald, M., & Berger, M. (1978). Social movements in organizations: Coup d'etat, insurgency, and mass movements. *American Journal of Sociology*, 83(4), 823–861.

Chapter 15

Seeking Reliability in Freedom: The Case of F/OSS

Hamid R. Ekbia
Indiana University

Les Gasser
University of Illinois at Urbana-Champaign

Abstract

The risks and hazards involved in computerized environments have turned "reliability" into a major organizing theme in the free software movement. The idealized vision in this computerization movement is that more reliable, secure, and efficient software can be produced under the free/open source software (F/OSS) model than in the alternative proprietary model. The principal public rationales for this vision credit widespread community participation, egalitarian social structures, and open sharing of designs, code, and experience. Interestingly, detractors point to just these elements as reliability risk factors for F/OSS-built products. Both of these visions are frequently based on simplistic accounts of development processes that ignore many of the complexities involved—complexities that cross both social and technical dimensions. This chapter describes and explores the gap between the movement visions, their detractors, and richer outside realities. We report findings from a longitudinal study of Bugzilla—a large-scale, shared, online collaborative issue-tracking and representation system widely used to manage software problems in F/OSS projects, including the well-known products of the Mozilla Foundation. We show how the processes involved in bug-fixing are significantly more convoluted than suggested by the advocates of F/OSS. We also argue that arguments made by F/OSS detractors are biased and dystopian in nature. Both the advocates and detractors base their claims on implicit or explicit assumptions that we analyze here.

Introduction

Risk, hazard, error, and uncertainty are ubiquitous features of modern sociotechnical environments. The dilemmas they pose in computerized settings have been recognized and documented for decades (Kling & Scacchi, 1979; Gasser, 1986). Accordingly, safety, security, and reliability are almost universally recognized goods for the general public, for policymakers, and for technological elites. This widespread interest in reliability characterizes the society's relationship with computer technologies on at least two levels. On the broad social level, the stakes of unreliable computer systems have raised public awareness of the issues involved. From Mars Rovers to electric power grid controllers to online voting schemes, "reliability" is a widely held virtue for software-intensive systems. The crash of space shuttle Columbia in 2003 that was attributed to a feeble simulation program, the problems that surfaced in counting votes in the American Presidential elections of 2000 and 2004 and for electronic voting in general (Celeste, Thornburgh, & Lin, 2005), and the continuing vulnerability of corporate and government computer systems to software worms and viruses are just a few examples of the issues at stake. On a personal level, what people experience on a day-to-day basis is also marked by a kind of unreliability associated with the notorious performance of most commercial software and systems—e-mails disrupted, servers down, files lost, identities stolen, and computers crashing in the middle of unsaved work. Such episodes constitute a key experiential moment of computer use, turning it into a source of frustration and grievance. These broad and personal elements constitute major themes of a public discourse on computer technologies.

While there is intense debate about the social costs and benefits of reliability and about appropriate means of achieving it, an increasingly vivid discourse is organized around F/OSS. The participants in this discourse argue for the efficacy and reliability of F/OSS from the perspective of developers who are involved in the production of software, partisans who do not code/design the systems, or users only—e.g., people using Linux in a for-profit organization who know little about the free software movement (FSM). As in other CMs, this discourse is a major component of the FSM (Elliott & Kraemer, Chapter 1, this volume; Iacono & Kling, 2001).

This chapter studies the role of "reliability" as an organizing theme in the FSM. The FSM involves strong ideological elements organized around the theme of freedom, which plays a key role as a symbolic frame in this movement (Elliott & Kraemer, Chapter 1, this volume). The adoption and expansion of F/OSS in recent years has given rise to well-established results, but futuristic visions about the potentials of the FSM are also at work among its advocates. The other ideal vision in the FSM is, therefore, that software can be produced according to the F/OSS model in a more reliable, secure, and efficient manner than the alternative proprietary model. This vision, which invokes reliability as another organizing theme in the FSM, appeals to a public (frustrated and) fascinated by issues of (un)reliability. However, it is sometimes based on underestimated accounts of the complexities involved in the development of large-scale software. This generates a gap between visions and the outside reality, which we seek to expound and analyze here. One example of this is the idea that bugs in F/OSS can be found and resolved more readily, giving rise to more reliable products. We present our findings from a longitudinal study of Bugzilla that reveals a much more complex and convoluted process than suggested in this idea. In what follows, we discuss the two ideal visions and how they link to reliability as a mobilizing concept in the FSM, examine the vision in the FSM that the F/OSS model of development results in more reliable software, report our findings from a longitudinal study of Bugzilla, and analyze the gap between these findings and the FSM vision.

Free Software Movement: One Movement and Two Visions

In recent years, F/OSS has been the subject of various studies from different perspectives, ranging from the technical and organizational to the legal, socioeconomic, and political. Elliott and Scacchi (forthcoming), for example, have studied F/OSS in the context of the FSM. Building on Kling and Iacono's (1988, 1995) notion of CMs, these authors analyze the FSM as a genre of such movements that attempts "to revolutionize software development practices by advocating that all software be 'free' for access, study, modification, and (re)distribution" (p. 3). Freedom, in these four senses, plays an *abstract* ideological role in the mobilization of participants in the FSM. In addition, however, freedom has a *concrete* practical meaning in the development of F/OSS projects. Participants in these projects "confront, internalize, and develop *concrete* meanings of freedom hinged to legal and technical issues" involved in the development of software (Coleman, 2005, p. 4).

The FSM is driven by two distinct but interrelated visions. One is the utopian vision, advocated by the Free Software Foundation (FSF) that considers the four "freedoms" as the ideological underpinning of a social movement against "software sellers [who] want to divide the users and conquer them" (Stallman, 1985). The other is the ideal vision of the open source movement that seeks to establish F/OSS as an alternative to the proprietary form of software development, capable of producing more "reliable" software. Both of these visions are integral to the FSM. The participants of the FSM proselytize their cause in terms of "freedom" and "reliability" as two key values of the movement. The two visions have a dialectic relationship that reflects their interdependence but it also generates within the FSM an *internal* tension, which has been the subject of broad studies recently (e.g., Berry, 2004; Coleman & Hill, 2004). In addition, there is an *external* tension between the ideal visions, on the one hand, and the practical reality of the production of software. This tension, clearly reflected in heated debates between the partisans of the FSM and their detractors, is the focus of our study in this chapter, but a brief discussion of the internal tension would put things in perspective.

The Two Meanings of Freedom

Kling's view of CM was based on a particular account of social movements, known as *resource mobilization theory* and formulated by Gamson (1975), McCarthy and Zald (1977), McAdam (1982), Tarrow (1994), Tilly (1978), and others. Resource mobilization theory is the dominant account of social movements in North America (Canel, 1995). What makes this view distinct from traditional functionalist accounts such as Marxism is its emphasis on collective action as a mediated process of framing and consensus mobilization. Resource mobilization theorists argue that collective action is not a direct result of structural development; rather it is triggered by cultural symbols that provide collective action *frames*. A frame is an "interpretive schema that simplifies and condenses the 'world out there' by selectively punctuating and encoding objects, situations, events, experiences, and sequences of actions within one's present or past environment" (Snow & Benford, 1992, p. 137). Tarrow argues that, "Movements frame their collective action around cultural symbols that are selectively chosen from a cultural toolset and creatively converted into collective action frames by political entrepreneurs" (Tarrow, 1994, p. 119). Gamson's (1992) notion of an "injustice frame" is a typical item in the toolset. In the FSM, freedom appears as a key item in the toolset, but there are at least two meanings of it—freedom as an abstract ideological symbol, and freedom as a concrete technical idea. The two abstract and concrete meanings of freedom are both elements of a futuristic vision of the FSM. The first meaning casts this vision in sociocultural terms of liberty, sharing, and help, and the second meaning formulates it in more technical and practical terms of openness, accountability, and reliability. These meanings mutually support and enhance each other, and together they constitute key elements of a broader vision of the FSM.

Freedom as a Symbolic Frame

> The philosophy of Free Software is that you are entitled to certain freedoms in using software. Freedom to study what a program really does. To change it—if it doesn't do what you want, to change it so that it does. And to redistribute copies of it, to share knowledge with the rest of humanity. (Stallman, 2002, p. 6)

The first meaning of freedom in the FSM derives from an anarcho-socialist ideology that is critical of the shift in Western societies toward proprietary software in the last three decades (Bradley, 2004). This vision, famously articulated by Richard Stallman, gives priority to the ethical and political aspects of freedom: "To be able to live in an upright way, treating your friends decently, sharing, helping them when they ask you for help. Living as part of a society, instead of a dog-eat-dog jungle" (Stallman, 2002, p. 6). The application of freedom as a cultural symbol in the FSM finds different manifestations in public debates of intellectual property, copyright versus copyleft, various licensing guidelines, and so on. In the latter case, for instance, licensing issues allow developers to negotiate the scope of freedom as it applies to social and legal questions concerning particular licenses (of which there are currently more than five dozen available; Coleman, 2005, p. 56). The oldest example of this is perhaps Stallman's articulation of the first F/OSS license, General Public License (GPL), first formulated in the GNU Manifesto in the following manner (and recently reiterated by him in the excerpt cited earlier).

> I consider that the golden rule requires that if I like a program I must share it with other people who like it. Software sellers want to divide the users and conquer them, making each user agree not to share with others. I refuse to break solidarity with other users in this way. I cannot in good conscience sign a nondisclosure agreement or a software license agreement. (Stallman, 1985)

Freedom as a Technical Principle

> [W]hile coding remains an essentially solitary activity, the really great hacks come from harnessing the attention and brainpower of entire communities. (Raymond, 1998)

Free software is above all a technology, based on the everyday micro-practices of many developers and maintainers. For this group of people, the notion of freedom acquires a practical meaning much more concrete than the ideological meaning articulated by Stallman. These proponents draw upon the notion of "social good," but unlike the ethical principles of FSF, their discourse is technical and neoliberal in nature. Drawing upon the 19th-century anarchist vision of a highly individualistic social order, the proponents of this view believe that collective goods can be produced through the selfish action of individuals (Berry, 2004, p. 80). Technically speaking, the main advantage of F/OSS for these developers is in its capability to be fixed, improved, and reused elsewhere. Various licensing schemes try to capture this advantage in their rules and guidelines. The Debian's Social Contract, for instance, consists of four promises that (partially) read as follows:

- Debian will remain 100 percent free software [...]
- We will give back to the free software community [...]
- We won't hide problems ... we will keep our entire bug-report database open for public view at all times. Reports that users file on-line will immediately become visible in our system.
- Our priorities are our users and free software ... we will provide an integrated system of high-quality, 100 percent free software, with no legal restrictions that would prevent these kinds of use.

To accomplish and deliver this promise of free and high-quality software, the Debian community has developed a set of internal principles (transparency, accessibility, accountability, and non-discrimination), governance mechanisms (democratic rule, a guild-like meritocracy), and an ad hoc process of rough consensus that are followed in a rather strict manner by its leaders and members alike. The Debian Free Software Guidelines codifies these principles to establish correct procedures for technological production, licensing, and social organization. Most notably, "openness and accountability are something these developers expect from code" (Coleman, 2005, p. 18). Openness refers to the GPL's four freedoms (access, use, modification, and distribution), and accountability has to do with the continued responsibility of developers in regard to the quality and reliability of their code. In the practical rationale of F/OSS, these are the flip sides of the same coin. Openness encourages participation, while accountability delineates boundaries on who can contribute on the basis of technical proficiency and prowess. In this fashion, the community forges an attachment between freedom and reliability, turning the latter into a mobilizing theme of the FSM along with the former.

Reliability as an Organizing Theme

The two ideal visions outlined here differ in their ideological sources—one draws upon the anarcho-socialist ideals of sharing and helping, while the other derives its insights from the libertarian principle of maximizing utility through the collective effort of selfish agents. Despite their differences, however, these visions have a lot in common. As Coleman and Hill (2004) have argued, the meaning of freedom articulated by Stallman is "broad enough to allow for its translation into other terms, yet defined enough to allow for a directed and robust social movement." In other words, Stallman's manifesto can at some level be seen as "a business plan in disguise" (Tiemann, 1999). We argue that the theme of reliability, being central to this "business plan," provides an organizing theme that links the two visions. The ideological advocates of the FSM recognize the significance of this link. Stallman, for instance, opposes the philosophy of the open source software, which, in his view, turns freedom into a "purely technical issue ... [that] allows us to develop more powerful software faster" (Stallman, 2002). But he is quick to add, "We in the Free Software movement recognize these practical benefits, and they are nice."

Reliability in Theory

> Given enough eyeballs, all bugs are shallow. (Linus's Law)

For many partisans of F/OSS the best path to reliable, secure software technology is maintaining the transparency and openness of software artifacts and their development processes. Eric Raymond is probably the most outspoken proponent of this idea through what he has dubbed Linus's Law, succinctly stated in the previous assertion (1998, p. 9). Based on this "law," Raymond (1998, 2001) contrasts the standard model of proprietary software development ("the cathedral") and that of the F/OSS model ("the bazaar") mainly in terms of how they view and treat bugs. According to the cathedral-building view of programming, "bugs and development problems are tricky, insidious, deep phenomena," and hence it takes months of scrutiny by a dedicated few to convincingly fix the bugs. On the other hand, in the bazaar view, "you assume that bugs are generally shallow phenomena" (or turn shallow with thousands of eager developers watching them), so you release often in order to get more corrections without a fear of possible bugs being initially undetected. Raymond argues that treating users as co-developers is the "least-hassle route to rapid code development and effective debugging." He takes Linux as an example to argue that the bazaar model "would scale up with number of users and against system complexity."

Essentially, the claim is that openness leads to reliable (bug free) software. This line of argument forms the basis of claims by other partisans of F/OSS. For instance, in a position briefing document, *The Open-Source Software Institute* (OSSI) claims that "Open Source is a highly secure and reliable alternative to single-source technologies," where "it is not unusual to find security flaws corrected within hours of discovery" (OSSI, 2003).

Raymond and other proponents of F/OSS base their claims on lessons derived from their practice as open source developers, maintainers, or users. When unpacked, however, these claims are also based on a number of assumptions, some of which are explicitly articulated by the proponents while others remain implicit and unstated. The key assumptions can be summarized as follows:

- *The Clear-Bug Assumption* – Bugs are clearly delineated entities or processes that can be readily detected and isolated by trained (and even untrained) "eyes."
- *The Quick-Fix Assumption* – Fixes to bugs are also readily discernible and agreeable—once a bug is detected, resolving it follows in a straightforward manner.
- *The Open-Eyes Assumption* – Complexity can be beaten by sheer quantity—there is an inverse relationship between the number of eyes watching source code and the time and effort it takes to fix a bug.
- *The High-Efficacy Assumption* – F/OSS methods are easily scalable—what happens on a small project can be scaled up to larger ones.

Despite their alleged obviousness, all of these assumptions are contestable in practice; they need to be examined through tedious longitudinal studies of real F/OSS projects. This is what we have undertaken in our study, which has led us to many critical issues and questions. For example, is degree of observability the critical factor, or do knowledge organization, essential complexity of the artifacts, and socio-technical structure of the ongoing discourses play central roles? (c.f. Gasser & Ripoche, 2003; Sandusky, Gasser, & Ripoche, 2004). The FSM's distributed software artifacts, distributed collective information representations, and distributed collective practices of development and use are indeed large, multifaceted, and complex. This complexity seriously limits participants' real understanding of software failures and limits their ability to correct such failures. The impacts of complexity are real, F/OSS methods are not magic, and talk about the miracles of F/OSS is cheap.

Conversely, the detractors of F/OSS also make simplistic claims about how and why F/OSS is unreliable, and fail to appreciate the innovative practices of description and debate that underpin F/OSS development, or to articulate what fosters unreliability in these practices (Scacchi, 2003). These claims are, in turn, based on a number of explicit and implicit assumptions, which we shall briefly examine. In sum, the discourses that promote or excoriate F/OSS on reliability grounds are one thing, the real practices, and theoretical/pragmatic limits of achieving reliability are quite another. Each has its complex dynamics, and they interact.

Reliability in Practice

We would like to examine these claims and counter-claims by studying the processes represented in instances of the Bugzilla problem management system. Bugzilla exemplifies a class of "bug-tracking" tools. As an open-source product of the Mozilla Web browser suite project, Bugzilla is one of the most widely used bug-trackers in the F/OSS movement. Mozilla, a successor to the well-known Netscape Communicator, is a modern, open-source Web browser suite containing a standards-based HTML rendering engine, a Web browser, a mail/news reader, an HTML page composer, an IRC Chat tool, and so on. The users and developers in the Mozilla community manage software problems using a (now widely dissemminated) repository tool called "Bugzilla," which itself was built as part of the Mozilla project. Through arrangement with the Mozilla Organization, we procured a sanitized snapshot of the Bugzilla problem database for Mozilla, with security-related problem reports and user passwords removed. All information in our snapshot was also freely available on the Web in the Bugzilla repository at the time our copy was made. This snapshot contains approximately 129,000 problem reports, some 88,000 of which were resolved at the time of this study. The average report contains approximately ten unstructured comments, though some contain as many as 250 or more.

Technically and functionally, Bugzilla is a large, open, persistent Web-based database that captures named, numbered reports on specific problems found by both developers and users of the system whose bugs it tracks. Bugzilla represents information in these reports in two ways. First, Bugzilla captures structured information indicating attributes such as sequential bug number, reporter, date, product in which the problem was found, context for the problem (e.g., hardware and operating system platform, product version number), status of the problem's analysis/resolution, known relationships to other reported problems (e.g., "depends-on" and "blocks"), and tags representing eventual disposition (such as "fixed/verified," "duplicate," "wontfix," etc.). Most structured fields are accompanied by (interface-enforced) controlled vocabularies of allowable terms. In this way, part of the method is rigidly organized via long-term Bugzilla design decisions about what information is represented, in what forms, with what named representations (field names, vocabularies). Occasionally, meta-discussions arise concerning revisions to the terminology and categorization schemes for all reports. These sorts of information organization and index-structuring decisions occur in all collective representation tools, and they have numerous consequences for coordinating activity mediated by those tools (Bowker & Star, 1999).

With this background in mind, we now examine what we have learned from our longitudinal study of Bugzilla against the quadruple assumptions outlined earlier.

Bugs Are Not *Readily Detectable*

The central claim of Linus's Law is that a sufficiently large number of developers is all that is needed to detect bugs. This claim is based on at least two assumptions: one technical and the other psychological. The technical assumption is that a bug simply consists of deviations from specification. This is a simplistic view of bugs on at least two counts. First, despite common intuition, software specifications are not stable and rigid constructs; they constantly change and adapt to the evolving context. This generates a kind of indeterminacy that makes the assessment of deviation from specification difficult, if not impossible. Second, bugs are immanent and contentious objects that cannot be readily detected and agreed upon. The objects of interaction among developers are *not* bugs per se but bug reports, which are representational artifacts with a complex internal structure. As any act of representation is also an act of translation, this turns bug recognition into a mediated process of translation (Latour, 1999).

The psychological assumption behind Linus's Law is best described by Raymond (1998) as follows: "Every good work of software starts by scratching a developer's personal itch."

This assertion is only correct in limited circumstances where, for instance, developers are in close interaction with users or in decision-making positions. Only then might a personal itch *start* software development. Broadly speaking, however, the assertion is not accurate. In most real-world situations, software development is driven by economic or organizational needs and requirements of users and clients. In those situations, personal itches play a minor role, if any. As such, they cannot explain the complex negotiation and sense-making processes that take place in the software development process. This observation holds true across the board. The modes of negotiation and consensus building might differ between proprietary (cathedral) and open source (bazaar) models, but they are negotiations nevertheless.

Example 1 in Appendix 1 (at the end of this chapter) illustrates one instance of negotiation over what categories should be retained in a Bugzilla-based repository used in one F/OSS desktop management system project. This dialog illustrates several complexities in the relationship between categorization and information use over time, including how to establish persistent definitions for terms, interactions between the repository and other critical software, uncertainty about and differential availability of information for decision making, and so on. One clear message of this example concerns the sociotechnical complexity of the (ongoing) process of managing the reliability of categorization, in a system for managing reliability of software.

Fixes Are **Not** *Readily Available*

Similarly, the other assumption behind Linus's Law is that once a phenomenon or behavior acquires the status of a bug, resolving it would be a straightforward matter of figuring out a technical "fix," and the main requisite for this is technical skill and proficiency. This assumption is based on a purely technical view of software development, and it crucially ignores the complex social and organizational processes that are involved in bug-fixing—e.g., varying visions and expectations of what a fix should consist of, the role of reputation and status in making these determinations, power differentials among developers, and so on. In Bugzilla, as in any other collaborative environment, the question of "What is a fix?" cannot be separated from the question of "Who provided the fix?" and, more importantly, "Who accepted the fix?" Therefore, Raymond's dictum—that "You often don't really understand the problem until after the first time you implement a solution"—only makes sense within the bigger context of a consensus building process. That is, if we take into account the role that others play in establishing something as a fix—e.g., by extending Raymond's dictum so as to include what needs to be done to convince others of the validity and viability of a solution.

Each bug report in Bugzilla contains a free-format textual description of the problem it represents. This description is unstructured and often "multi-media." It frequently contains screenshots, traces of program runs or compilations, and quotations from actual source codes or machine-code dumps. From a conventional discourse-analysis standpoint it is very "noisy" and often requires specialized auxiliary tools to access and to analyze, such as image viewers or machine-code interpreters. Over time, the original unstructured description is progressively augmented with comments from developers and users detailing new experiences, debating interpretations, managing work, and establishing conclusions or fixes. Other discourses take place in complementary archived e-mail systems and other persistent computer-mediated channels, and thus another complexity is maintaining informational awareness and coherence across different media and different channels. The complexity of these channels and their interactions, not just sheer numbers of observers, reporters, and analysts, makes the difference (e.g., Eisenstadt, 1997; Lieberman, 1997). Example 2 in Appendix 1 illustrates a process of negotiating a contentious debate over the severity and priority of a particular issue. This issue was originally opened in early 2000. Currently (early 2005) the report contains more than 280 comments, and is still open. One salient feature of this discourse as a sensemaking exercise is the complexity of maintaining and integrating contextual information and establishing its relevance. The discourse in the example section cited occurred in mid-2002, and some arguments rest in part on the need for compatibility with dial-up Internet connections. As fewer people rely on dialups, rationales based on them become less critical, but may still be embedded in decisions that influence reliability-maintaining (bug fixing) actions years later—recall that this bug report is still open.

Complexity Can Be Sometimes, Not *Always, Beaten by Quantity*

Most real-world software artifacts, commercial or F/OSS, are complex systems consisting of millions of lines of code and hundreds of modules produced, coupled, and maintained by teams belonging to different organizations following different procedures in diverse socio-cultural environments. Complex problems can be complex for many reasons, including deep logical complexities that sheer quantitative change in amounts of observation or analysis cannot per se affect. Moreover, as the number and diversity of observations, analyses, observers, and analyzers increases, so does the social and interpretive complexity of the discourses through which the actual work of discovering and explicating problems is carried out. In short, software artifacts are complex systems at various technical, organizational, and social levels. The management of this complexity, therefore, is what software development is crucially about. By the same token, studying these development processes as cases of complexity management might be a useful way of looking at them. Different models of software development—e.g., the standard (proprietary) versus F/OSS—differ partly in this respect.

The standard model of software development for tightly organized (e.g., commercial and industrial) projects seeks to manage complexity by partitioning and linearizing the process. It comprises a set of stages carried out in a basically linear fashion. Each earlier stage sets the context of decisions and actions for the following stage. A typical staged development model includes activities of analysis, specification, design, implementation, testing, release, and use. These stages of activity occur in the order given, with minimal feedback and return to earlier stages. Each stage is supported and enacted using specialized stage-specific tools and infrastructure (e.g., specification languages for capturing specifications, language editors and compilers for implementation, automated test and debugging tools for test phases, etc.). This linear model relies on the ability to fully specify the functionality of software before the software is implemented. With this constraint, specification provides a natural guide for implementation, and implementation can be carried out in a focused (i.e., minimally experimental) way. Similarly, a full functional specification provides a standard against which testing can be done. This model of testing to a preexisting standard provides a more-or-less unambiguous definition of software quality: High quality software is software that meets its specifications. Bugs, in this conception, are simple mismatches between specification and performance.

As mentioned earlier, all software contains "bugs," and to some degree most users find problems putting software to work in their specific contexts of use (Gasser, 1986). However, with the linear development model, two central questions arise: First, are there classes of systems whose functionality cannot be specified before they are implemented and used? Second, (how) can linear models be scaled up to ever-larger, more modular systems, built by widely distributed communities such as F/OSS efforts? Attempts to address these questions have resulted in refined versions of the standard model. A simple model of the process is as follows. Developers use tools to build a version of their artifact, and then deliver it to users. When a user has a problem, one common approach is to make the problem *explicit* by converting the experience of the problem into some communicable form and addressing it to developers. This model can be called a *user-integrated* development process. A key step here is the user's transformation of a problem from an *unrepresented local phenomenological event* into an *explicit representation* that can be communicated—whether that representation be a transient spoken description (e.g., in a telephone call) or a more persistent written or diagrammed document.

In a small-scale user-integrated project, where users may have easy access to developers, feedback on artifact use and problems may be informal, non-persistent, and direct (represented by the small dashed line in Figure 15.1). However, as development processes become larger-scale and as relationships between users and developers become more complex, both users and developers must employ complexity reduction strategies to manage the volume of information and to sustain their relationships. One typical way to do this is to create more formalized, persistent feedback systems to capture and manage information about problems. Such feedback systems typically take the form of a collection, database, or repository of reports on problems and issues, sometimes accompanied by accumulated information and discussion about each issue and what steps are being taken to deal with it (represented by the larger dashed line and repository in Figure 15.1). In practice, communities organize formalized feedback systems in several ways. More *unstructured* repositories use easy-to-capture, searchable information lists supported by widespread technologies such as hypermail archives or newsgroup managers; examples of these repositories include Chandra X-ray software and Apple Computer's problem-management newsgroups. More *structured* repositories employ specialized, less widely available database tools designed specially for problem management; examples of these include Bugzilla (bugzilla.mozilla.org), Scarab (scarab.tigris.org), and many others.

All user-integrated problem-tracking repositories that we have examined contain at least two kinds of information: (1) *informal* information such as descriptions of issues and discussion of workarounds and repair strategies, and (2) some way of capturing and interrelating ongoing streams of comments and activity records relating to the issue. Structured repositories normally also contain formalized, even quantitative information such as statuses and timelines for tracking activities, controlled vocabularies for specifying issue attributes, lists of people involved in an issue, votes for importance, module in which the problem appears, and so on. Figure 15.2 presents a general view of a repository structure. It specifically represents the Bugzilla approach, but the idea is quite general.

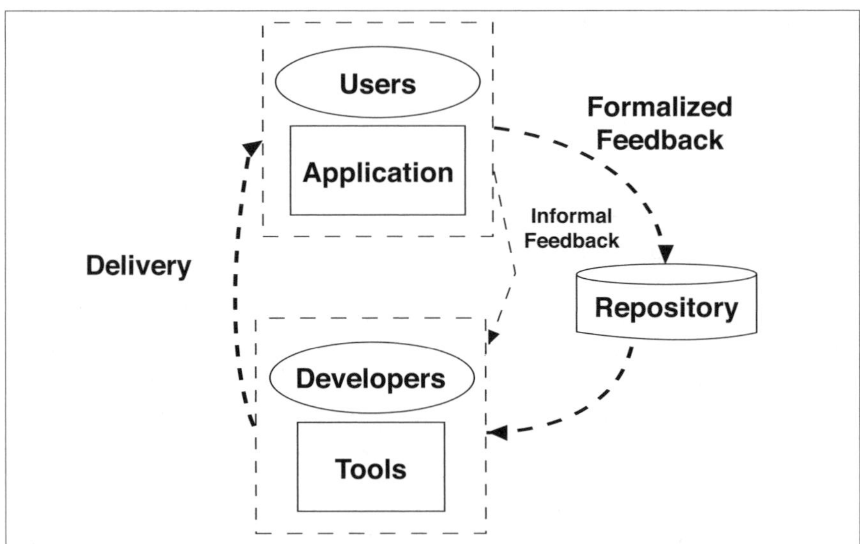

Figure 15.1 Development feedback

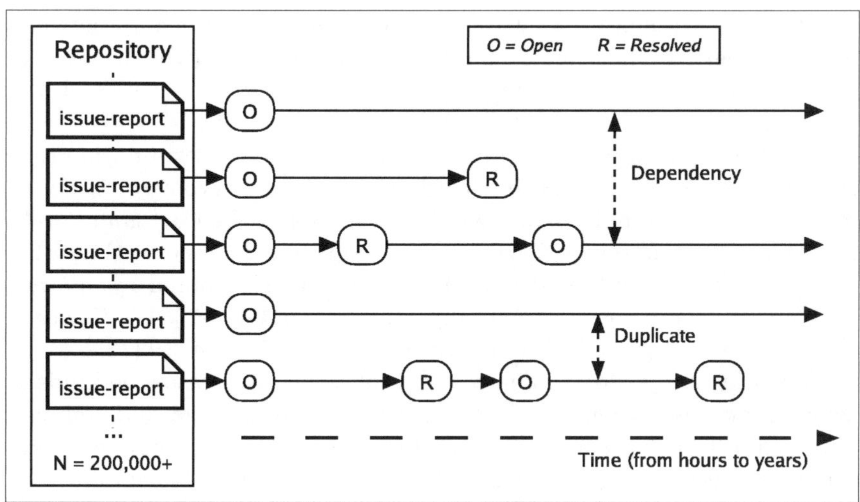

Figure 15.2 Repository structure

To be sure, structures and techniques such as these provide effective means of dealing with complexity in Bugzilla and other similar systems. However, there is a limit to the degree of complexity that they can handle. There are numerous examples of the limitations (e.g., dealing with bug dependencies, duplication, etc.). In one instance, we examined a cluster of six linked reports. The randomly chosen report 12345 is linked to three others. It "depends on" report 15069 and "blocks" both 11091 and 17976 (Report A "depends on" on report B if A can be resolved only after B is resolved; "depends on" and "block" are roughly reciprocal relationships). These in turn are linked to 13449, 19313, and 32442. Conceived as a tree structure, the rough tree of relations is as follows: 15069 is the origin, 12345 and 13449 "depend on" it, 13449 also depends on 19313, which depends on 32442, and finally 11901 depends on 12345. So how does the community manage this complex web of relationships?

Our study shows that report dependencies must be manually recognized and entered. The dependency tree function built into Bugzilla must be intended to help with this task, but all that it does is give the "titles" of the bugs in the tree. Furthermore, there seems to be no explanation of why the bugs are dependent on each other, and the members of the community do not seem to question the relationships once they have been recognized (i.e., if someone has bothered to make the relationship explicit, then the prevailing assumption is that it is a true relationship). The interesting question is whether the occurrence of these relationships starts to fall off as the community gets larger and as the number of reports increases.

Similar questions arise about another kind of relationship between bugs—namely, duplication. This relationship is shown by the presence of "DUPLICATE" in the "Resolution" field of the duplicate record and in a comment in both the duplicate and "locus" reports. How is "duplication" different from "dependency?" Presumably, there is a determination that the problem laid out in both records is the "same" problem, but who makes this determination, and what does it mean to be the "same" problem? For example, record 7176, comment #5 (by "rhp") notes that "this bug is a duplicate of bug 19251." However, this is disputed by another developer in comment #6: "Actually, it's a dup of bug #19313." There is no reply from "rhp" and 7176 is marked as a duplicate of 19313.

This brief study of dependency and duplication illustrates the kinds of issues that arise when a software system becomes large and complex beyond a certain degree. F/OSS communities have developed increasingly sophisticated tracking and analysis tools to deal with this complexity—free-text keyword fields, additional comments, and "meta-bug" reports in Bugzilla are examples of such tools. However, as the data graphed in Figure 15.3 illustrates, the efficacy of these techniques is still challenged by the growing number of bug reports, the complex web of interrelationships among them, and the resulting, dynamic socio-technical complexity (Sandusky, et al., 2004; Ripoche, 2006). Figure 15.3 plots every resolved bug report by number against the amount of days taken to resolve that bug report. The density in the points toward the bottom of the figure illustrates visually that many bug reports are resolved in a relatively short time (e.g., under 100 days, and in many cases in just a few hours via triage or identification of duplicates). In contrast, other issues have remained unresolved for years (e.g., points above 700 days).[1] These data pose a direct challenge to the universality of two of the assumptions in Raymond's arguments—namely, the open-eyes and the high-efficacy assumptions. If the Raymond assumptions are reflected to some extent in actual data (and this remains to be examined fully) it might be for reasons much simpler and less radical than the F/OSS community assumes. While it is clear that many bug reports in our corpus were resolved quickly, it is not evident how much of the quickness resulted from Raymond assumptions. For example, qualitative analysis of a limited sample indicates that in many instances, rapidly resolved issues were very simple and/or subject to highly routinized community procedures such as triage and duplication-marking. Of course, we would expect these factors to play out in non-F/OSS contexts as well. Overall, we'd like to know whether "eyes" and "openness" can also ease the resolution of issues that are socially, informationally, and technically complex, and/or when and how more participants makes them harder (c.f. Brooks, 1995). In short, we need better models of the relationships between dynamic community structures, dynamic information structure, and the dynamics

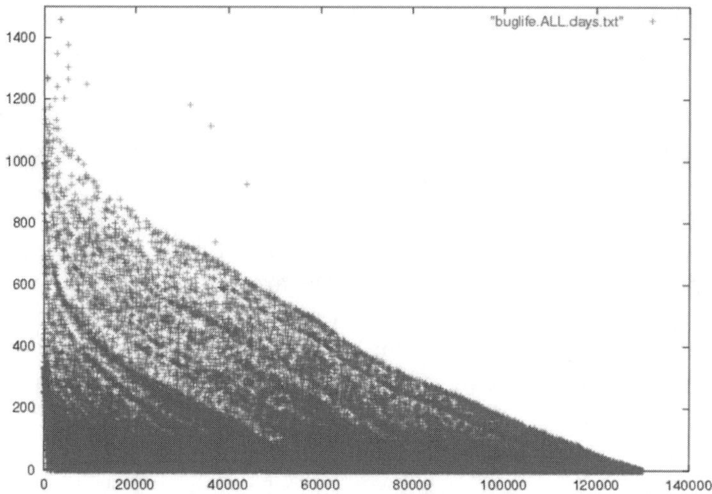

Figure 15.3 Bugs take from hours to years to get resolved (plot of bug report number, *X*, vs. days to resolve, Y, for all resolved reports in the corpus)

of problem definition and resolution, to understand better why certain problems take longer to resolve (Ripoche, 2006).

Conclusion: From Vision to Reality

This discussion demonstrates that some of the basic assumptions behind Linus's Law are not upheld in practice, pointing to a gap that exists in the FSM between vision and reality. Our analysis shows that the vision in FSM that software can be produced on the model of the bazaar that is superior in quality and reliability to the alternatives developed under the proprietary model is a utopian vision that is only partially fulfilled. Not only is the vision based on a narrow view of the character of bugs and their fixes as purely technical processes, it also underestimated the issues of complexity and scaling that bewilders most software development projects of today.

On the other hand, the detractors of the FSM also base their claims on a set of worn-out, and sometimes biased, ideas and assumptions, underestimating the strength of the methods and techniques implemented in F/OSS. Various kinds of arguments are presented by the detractors, but they generally fall into two classes. Some argue that F/OSS is not built on a viable business model that can compete with proprietary software. The adoption in recent years of Linux by IBM and other software development houses provides examples of business strategies that can utilize the benefits of F/OSS in a competitive environment. The second class of arguments points to the vulnerabilities of F/OSS in terms of security, questioning the fundamental reliability claim of the FSM. By raising the possibility of "insider malicious code" of outside competition distributing a hacked version of a F/OSS software, and of other fictitious schemes, the presenters of these arguments exploit the current psychological environment of risk and uncertainty that was mentioned at the outset of this writing.

In sum, both the advocates and detractors of F/OSS base their claims on implicit or explicit assumptions that are not fully borne out in real life. The gap between reality and these utopian (or dystopian) visions may not be bridgeable, but it can be reduced by a close analysis of the underlying assumptions.

Endnotes

1. Note that the visible slope of the longest-duration resolved reports in Figure 15.3 is simply an artifact of the age of the database at the time of the measurement and the bug reporting rate—actually the increase rate for report numbers (which varies slightly over time, hence the curved slope). Clearly no report could be shown with a longer time-to-resolution than the time elapsed since it was reported. This slope is approximately captured by the following equation:

   $y = a - (x * r)$

   where

   y = maximum possible duration of report (age since initially reported)

   a = age of the complete database snapshot in days

   x = bug report number

   r = rate of bug report number increase (i.e., new reports made per day)

References

Berry, D. M. (2004). Contestation of code: A preliminary investigation into the discourse of the free/libre and open source movements. *Critical Discourse Studies*, 1(1), 65–89.

Bowker, G. C., & Star, S. L. (1999). *Sorting things out: Classification and its consequences*. Cambridge, MA: MIT Press.

Bradley, D. (2004). Open source, anarchy, and the utopian impulse: Why I must write GNU. *Media and Culture*, 7(3).

Brooks, F. (1995). *The mythical man-month: Essays on software engineering*. Reading, MA: Addison-Wesley Professional.

Canel, E. (1995). New social movement theory and resource mobilization theory: The need for integration. *International Development Research Center*. Retrieved November 9, 2004, from web.idrc.ca/en/ev-54446-201-1-DO_TOPIC.html

Celeste, R., Thornburgh, D., & Lin, H. (Eds.). (2005). *Asking the right questions about electronic voting*. Washington, DC: National Academies Press.

Coleman, B., & Hill, M. (2004). How free became open and everything else under the sun. *Media and Culture*, 7(3).

Coleman, G. (2005). Three ethical moments in Debian. Dissertation, Department of Anthropology, University of Chicago.

Eisenstadt, M. (1997). My hairiest bug war stories. *Communications of the ACM*, 40(4), 30–37.

Elliott, M. S., & Scacchi, W. (forthcoming). Mobilization of software developers: The free software movement. *Information Technology & People.*

Gamson, W. (1975). *The strategy of social protest (*2nd ed.). Belmont, CA: Wadsworth Publishing.

Gamson, W. A. (1992). The social psychology of collective action. In A. D. Morris & C. M. Mueller (Eds.), *Frontiers in social movement theory*. New Haven, CT: Yale University Press.

Gasser, L. (1986). The integration of computing and routine work. *ACM Transactions on Information Systems*, 4(3), 205–225.

Gasser, L., & Ripoche, G. (2003). Distributed collective practices and F/OSS problem management: Perspective and methods. *Proceedings of the 2003 Conference on Cooperation, Innovation & Technologie* (CITE'03), Université de Technologie de Troyes, France, December 2003.

Iacono, S., & Kling, R. (2001). Computerization movements: The rise of the Internet and distant forms of work. In J. Yates & J. Van Maanen (Eds.), *Information technology and organizational transformation: History, rhetoric, and practice* (pp. 93–136). Thousand Oaks, CA: Sage Publications.

Kling, R., & Iacono, S. (1988). The mobilization of support for computerization: The role of computerization movements. *Social Problems*, 35(3), 226–243.

Kling, R., & Iacono, S. (1995). Computerization movements and the mobilization of support for computerization. In S. L. Star (Ed.), *Ecologies of knowledge: Work and politics in science and technology* (pp. 119–153). Albany, NY: State University of New York Press.

Kling, R., & Scacchi, W. (1979). Recurrent dilemmas of computer use in complex Organizations. *Proceedings of the National Computer Conference*, New York, 48, 107–116.

Latour, B. (1999). *Pandora's hope: Essays on the reality of science studies*. Cambridge, MA: Harvard University Press.

Lieberman, H. (Ed.). (1997). The debugging scandal and what to do about it. Special Issue of *Communications of the ACM*, 40(4).

McAdam, D. (1982). *The political process and the development of black insurgency*. Chicago: University of Chicago Press.

McCarthy, J. D., & Zald, N. (1977). Resource mobilization and social movements: A partial theory. *American Journal of Sociology*, 82, 1212–1241.

OSSI (2003). The Open Source Software Institute. Retrieved April 4, 2004, from www.oss-institute.org

Raymond, E. S. (1998). The cathedral & the bazaar. *First Monday,* 3(3).

Raymond, E. S. (2001). *The cathedral & the bazaar*. New York: O'Reilly.

Ripoche, G. (2006). The mutual shaping of information and social networks in OSS debugging. Working Paper, Graduate School of Library and Information Science, University of Illinois at Urbana-Champaign.

Sandusky, B., Gasser, L., & Ripoche, G. (2004). Bug report networks: Varieties, strategies, and impacts in an OSS development community. *Proceedings of the ICSE MSR Workshop*, Edinburgh, U.K.

Scacchi, W. (2003). When is free/open source software development faster, better, and cheaper than software engineering? Working Paper, *Institute for Software Research*, UC Irvine. Retrieved February 12, 2005, from www.ics.uci.edu/%7Ewscacchi/Papers/New/Scacchi-BookChapter.pdf

Snow, D. A., & Benford, D. B. (1992). Master frames and cycles of protest. In A. D. Morris & C. M. Mueller (Eds.), *Frontiers in social movement theory* (pp. 133–155). New Haven, CT: Yale University Press.

Stallman, R. (1985). The GNU Manifesto. Retrieved May 1, 2005, from www.gnu.org/gnu/manifesto.html

Stallman, R. (2002). Let's share. *Open democracy.* Retrieved March 24, 2006, from www.opendemocracy.net/articles/ViewPopUpArticle.jsp?id=8&articleId=31

Tarrow, S. (1994). *Power in movement: Social movements, collective action and politics.* Cambridge, U.K.: Cambridge University Press.

Tiemann, M. (1999). Future of cygnus solutions: An entrepreneur's account. In C. DiBona, S. Ockman, & M. Stone (Eds.), *Open sources: Voices from the open source revolution*. Sebastopol, CA: O'Reilly & Associates.

Tilly, C. (1978). *From mobilization to revolution.* Reading, MA: Addison-Wesley Publishing Co.

Appendix 1: Examples of Bug Reports

Example 1: Negotiating Descriptive Categories

I'd like to nuke some keywords in the ongoing quest to keep things "clean."

PATCH: we have good patch editing by now. I'm not entirely sure of the status of querying for these, though, so perhaps we need to fix that before we remove PATCH altogether.

BLOCKED_BY_FREEZE: same as above, though we should flame the list about open BLOCKED_BY_FREEZE bugs before deleting it and losing the information.

The only objection I can think of to this would be that sometimes someone submits an entirely new file (documentation or an entirely new source code file or whatever), and thus technically it isn't a "patch" (yeah, I know people *can* submit new files as part of a patch, but some discourage this) and thus appear to fall outside the current mechanisms. Not that this is a good objection (it's a rare use case, so I don't think these keywords would be used in searches and thus would be useless), but it might be worthwhile to somehow indicate to people that anything that is being considered for committing can be marked as a patch whether or not it technically really is.

Hrm. Is there no better way we can handle that?

1.X-PARITY: I don't think we care about GNOME 1.x parity anymore.

DOCS_NEEDED: evidence suggests this is not used ATM.

PATCH_NEEDED: patches are always needed. I hate this keyword. :)

Agreed, nuke em.

HELPWANTED: doesn't make much sense to me, but appears to be more widely used—perhaps someone should review the open ones to see how they are used in the wild?

Any volunteers? (If we do keep it, maybe we should make others more aware of it?)

SCREENSHOT: do we care? why do we need this information?

I have used this a number of times and even added it to bugs I was triaging, but now that you ask about it, I can't imagine anyone doing a search with this keyword and so it appears to be useless.

XIMIAN: hasn't been used in ages.

You would know better than anyone whether this is still needed or can be nuked. ;-)

It has ... historical value. Nothing more.

Others to add to your list:

BUGBUDDY: We are keeping up on this so poorly as to become less than useless. Most of the bugs that appear in bug-buddy are no longer being duplicated at all, and most of the bugs that are being duplicated aren't appearing. We should replace this with the output of something like bugzilla.gnome.org/reports/recent-mostfrequent.cgi; then the list is automatically updated for us.

Agreed. [F], do you recall how bug-buddy is using that list? How easy/hard would it be to create a form of recent-most frequent that worked?

MANDRAKE: This isn't being used. There are a total of two bugs with this keyword, and both were closed well over two years ago.

Hrm, I thought [F] had requested it more recently. We should poke him about it.

PURIFY: Actually, it doesn't really need to be removed, but if it's kept it needs a rename. Unfortunately, the only name I can think of at the moment is valgrind, but it'd be great if we could think of a more general name.

It was actually PURIFY - [J] had access to a copy and was using it on solaris, and requested the keyword for that reason. Don't know if that is still the case. Maybe PURIFY-VALGRIND as the keyword name or something?

Example 2: Negotiating Severity and Management in Techno-Historical Use Contexts

- - - - - Additional Comment #177 From [M] - - - - -

I was wondering why this bug is marked as an enhancement

Because inaccessible pages get an error message dialog. Now, people want it enhanced, as an error *page*. Makes sense, huh?

Please refer to comment 160, and bug 111904, which was major and then duped to this. This bug too should be major, as well as regression, since before last November, modal dialogs were not being popped up due to unreachable embedded elements. Bug 111904 should be unduped and fixed. There should not be an error page displayed due to unreachable elements.

- - - - - Additional Comment #178 From [T] - - - - -

Putting up an error dialog instead of an error page is in no way "major loss of function". Please make comments about how to resolve other bugs in their respective bug reports.

- - - - - Additional Comment #179 From [H] - - - - -

Putting up an error dialog instead of an error page is in no way "major loss of function".

It is if it's modal. I've had problems before with downloads being cancelled, etc, because Mozilla has put up a "Can't connect to..." or "...cannot be found..." dialog for some unrelated page while I've been away from the machine waiting for it to finish. Usually happens when (has little to do with this bug, sadly) the mail client can't poll my mail server, but also happens if I have a auto-reloading frame in another tab, such as the Salon front page.

If I can't download something unattended without closing all other tabs, and if I had mail and news open, exiting the browser completely and restarting, then I'm experiencing "major loss of function." I reckon so, anyway.

- - - - - Additional Comment #180 From [C] - - - - -

Sorry for the extra chatter, but I just filed Bug 149037 as an intermediary step, that might cut down some of the annoyance of this bug.

Chapter 16

Movement Ideology vs. User Pragmatism in the Organizational Adoption of Open Source Software

Jason Dedrick
University of California, Irvine

Joel West
San Jose State University

Abstract

The free and open source software computing movements have argued that free and open source software projects lead to better software, freedom from vendor control, and social benefits by sharing software and its associated source code. While these movements grew out of the interests of programmers to write better software for their own purposes, the open source movement has focused on gaining widespread adoption of free and open source software by businesses and other organizations. This requires acceptance by information technology organizations and professionals, whose views of free and open source software have been largely ignored in prior research. We interviewed 21 information technology professionals in 14 business and public sector organizations to uncover their views on free and open source software and the extent of adoption by their organizations. We found that most users do not value access to source code, and very few have ever modified source code even when they use open source software. Users are much more interested in the low cost of free and open source software, which the movement downplays, and there is no consensus about the relative quality of open source versus closed source software. The main point of agreement is on the importance of control and choice, and the freedom from vendor lock-in that comes with free and open source software. Finally, we found that users are generally agnostic about the ideologies of the free and open source software movements, but that in some cases movement advocates act to encourage adoption within their organizations.

Introduction

The emergence and adoption of new technologies can lead to important social changes. While social change may occur as an unintended by-product of technological change, advocates of new technologies often have promoted them as instruments of positive social change. One example is computer technology, which has been championed by so-called computerization movements (CMs) (Kling & Iacono, 1988).

A CM is defined as "a kind of movement whose advocates focus on computer-based systems as instruments to bring about a new social order" (Kling & Iacono, 1988, p. 227). Members of CMs advocate the adoption of specific computing uses and arrangements such as artificial intelligence, office automation, computer-based education, personal computing, and internetworking (Kling & Iacono, 1988; Iacono & Kling, 2001).

Two CMs that have gained considerable attention in the past decade are the free software and open source software movements, jointly denoted by the acronym F/OSS in research publications. These overlapping (but distinct) movements use a combination of mobilizing rhetoric as part of their public discourse. Some are framed in ideological terms of social transformation, allowing developers to study, improve, and redistribute software freely for the good of the broader community (Stallman, 2002). The movements also employ more utilitarian frames, claiming that F/OSS is a superior approach to software development that produces higher quality code much faster than commercial software projects (Raymond, 2001).

These two movements also have other distinguishing characteristics. Unlike other CMs, the F/OSS movements do not promote computerization but rather a change in the economic relationship of a computer technology to its producers and users. A major goal of the movements is to recruit more F/OSS developers and users (cf. Elliott & Scacchi, forthcoming). These movements are also the latest stage of a broader open software movement that extends back to 1969 with the creation of the Unix operating system.

Finally, these movements require cooperation between two distinct groups—F/OSS developers and adopters. So far, there has been considerable research on the organization and motivation of F/OSS developers

(Lerner & Tirole, 2002; Markus, Manville, & Agres, 2000), but little on the motivations of current or potential users.

In our study, we ask the following research questions:

- What are the ideology, beliefs, and motivations of F/OSS movements?
- Are these beliefs shared by potential organizational adopters of F/OSS?
- What role do members of the F/OSS movements have as change agents in getting information technology (IT) organizations to adopt free or open source software?

We first briefly review the history of the F/OSS and earlier movements. We then describe the results of an empirical field study of professional IT managers and their attitudes toward F/OSS adoption. From this, we draw conclusions about the degree to which adopters of F/OSS technology are influenced by the dominant frames and utopian visions of the two F/OSS movements.

Three Decades of Open Software Movements

West and Dedrick (2001) show how during the 1990s, the technology and business strategies of the F/OSS movements grew directly out of the Unix ecosystem of the 1970s and 1980s, leveraging both its technical design and associated supply of complementary assets. The free software movement (FSM) drew directly from the desires of Richard Stallman and Linus Torvalds to make a free copy of Unix, while key leaders of the open source software movement previously worked to distribute their existing (BSD) Unix.

At the same time, there are important differences in the action frames of the two F/OSS movements, which Stallman (2002) terms "two political camps."[1] There were similar divisions within the earlier Unix movement, particularly with regard to motivating and organizing innovation. As such, the Unix (open systems), free software, and open source software movements represent three distinct but related efforts within a larger movement we collectively label the "open software" movements (see Table 16.1).

Unix: Academic Research and Open Systems

The F/OSS movements are a direct outgrowth of the development of the Unix operating system and its associated movement. The Unix movement established standards and skills essential for future F/OSS developers, resulted in widespread distributions of source code under

Table 16.1 Contrasting the Open Software Movements

Movement	Unix		Free Software	Open Source
Starting date	1969		1984	1998
Sub-movement	BSD	Open Systems		
Leaders	Academic programmers	IT vendors, users	Programmers	Programmers, IT vendors
Leadership orientation	Technical excellence	Business adoption	Technical excellence	Business adoption
Philosophical goals	Academic research	Vendor independence	Software freedom	Pragmatic success
Licenses*	MIT (1985) BSD (1989)	*proprietary*	GPL (1989) LGPL (1991)	MPL (1998) CPL (2001)
Key technologies	V7 (1979) BSD (1977) X11 (1987) Motif (1990) 4.4BSD-Lite (1994)		GNU Emacs (1984) gcc (1987) Gnome (1997)	Apache (1995) MySQL (1995)
Key institutions	IEEE POSIX (1984) X/Open (1984) Open Software Foundation (1988) Unix International (1988) Open Group (1996)		Free Software Foundation (1985) Software Freedom Law Center (2005)	Open Source Initiative (1998) Apache Software Foundation (1999) Open Source Development Labs (2000)
Sponsors	ATT, DARPA, DEC, IBM, Sun		n/a	IBM, HP, Intel
Spokesmen	Bill Joy		Richard Stallman Eben Moglen	Linus Torvalds Eric Raymond

* Licenses conforming to the Open Source Definition and approved by the Open Source Initiative

F/OSS licenses, and fostered goals (notably reduced vendor control) that would later become pillars of the F/OSS movements.

Beginning in 1969, the Unix operating system was developed by AT&T computer science researchers for use by themselves and their peers. AT&T was not in the computer business at the time, so the research project was licensed (in source code form) to users throughout the world. With the source available, sophisticated users made their own changes: By 1976 users had begun to circulate bug fixes and other improvements, some of which were eventually included by AT&T in subsequent releases (Salus, 1994).

Although AT&T restricted distribution and licensing of the Unix source code to individuals or businesses associated with AT&T researchers, the Unix operating system gained a loyal following for two reasons. First, in making good tools for their own software development, the AT&T researchers created a system that appealed to a wide range of computer scientists. Second, almost from the beginning it was designed for portability between hardware systems, the only major operating system to provide such flexibility.

From this, there were two major sub-movements that diffused Unix to non-AT&T users during the 1980s and 1990s. First, led by U.C. Berkeley, Unix became a major basis for computer science research in the U.S. and elsewhere. Second, the portable operating system fueled the vendor-independence goals of the open systems movement.

BSD-Related Academic Research

Of all the research and other improvements to Unix outside AT&T, the largest proportion came from the Computer Science Research Group at the University of California at Berkeley. University programmers began to develop their own supplemental code for Unix, shipping the first Berkeley System Distribution (BSD) in 1977. From 1980–1994, the Berkeley researchers shipped their own BSD-enhanced Unix distribution with source code to sites with a valid AT&T Unix license (Salus, 1994; West & Dedrick, 2001).

But the requirement to hold an AT&T license limited the adoption of BSD, particularly by individuals and smaller businesses. In 1990, Berkeley staffer Keith Bostic began soliciting volunteers via the Advanced Research Project Agency Network (ARPNET) to re-implement the AT&T code.[2] In 1994 Berkeley released 4.4BSD-Lite, the first Unix implementation not encumbered by an AT&T license. This code formed the basis of the NetBSD and FreeBSD open source projects, which were soon available under the BSD license for free download on the Internet (McKusick, 1999; Morin, 1995; West & Dedrick, 2001).

At MIT, researchers used the BSD operating system as the basis for developing a graphical user interface. The result was X11, which was released in source code form and became the basis of nearly all subsequent Unix (and Linux) graphical interfaces. The project was largely funded by cash, equipment, and developers donated by Digital Equipment Corporation and IBM.

Open Systems

The open systems movement was driven by users' desire to reduce IT vendor power associated with control over *de facto* standards and high switching costs. It was supported by IT vendors that had been unsuccessful in establishing their own proprietary *de facto* standards. To allow buyers to easily switch between or integrate systems from competing vendors, the movement pushed for open standards, notably for application software (both internally developed and third party) and computer networking. But unlike the academic research, the openness was manifested by open standards, with software still developed and distributed as proprietary implementations (Gabel, 1987; Grindley, 1995; West, 2003).

An early linchpin of the movement was abstracting the range of Unix implementations to create a formal compatibility standard to increase application portability between operating systems. Beginning in 1984, the Institute of Electrical and Electronics Engineers sponsored the

POSIX (Portable Operating System Interface) standardization effort (Isaak, 2006).

Other key technologies of the open systems movement were based directly on the earlier academic research, including the TCP/IP network code developed for BSD Unix. BSD's most visible leader, Bill Joy, left Berkeley in 1982 to co-found Sun Microsystems, the first large IT vendor to be fully committed to an open systems strategy (Garud & Kumaraswamy, 1993). Sun later played a major role in promulgating Unix adoption and shaping Unix standards. However, rival standards from competing vendor factions limited portability and reduced user adoption (Grindley, 1995).

To summarize, key characteristics of the Unix-related movements included:

- Programmers writing software for their own needs, i.e., for others like them.
- User access to source code, which allowed quick error correction and customization.
- Free (price) distributions (under BSD and MIT licenses) of software developed for research projects.
- Direct vendor sponsorship (as at MIT) of public software research.
- Efforts by users to increase control of IT infrastructure and reduce IT vendor power by reducing the vendor lock-in created through switching costs.

Free Software

Of the related open software movements, the FSM is the most overtly ideological, with its utopian view of a new cooperative economic relationship between software developers, users, and their shared code. As founder Richard Stallman explained:

> Every decision a person makes stems from the person's values and goals. People can have many different goals and values; fame, profit, love, survival, fun, and freedom are just some of the goals that a good person might have. When the goal is to help others as well as oneself, we call that idealism.
>
> My work on free software is motivated by an idealistic goal: spreading freedom and cooperation. I want to encourage free software to spread, replacing proprietary software that forbids cooperation, and thus make our society better. (Stallman, 2002, Ch. 15)

Today Stallman's story is widely known—how he worked as a programmer at MIT, found it increasingly frustrating to be unable to modify (or share modifications of) proprietary software, how he eventually quit in 1984 to start Project GNU (cf. Stallman, 1999, 2002). The next year he founded the Free Software Foundation (FSF), a nonprofit corporation to support his nascent FSM. In his own words, Stallman's ethos was formed by his early career developing academic software:

> Whenever people from another university or company wanted to port and use a program, we gladly let them. If you saw someone using an unfamiliar and interesting program, you could always ask to see the source code, so that you could read it, change it, or cannibalize parts of it to make a new program. (Stallman, 1999, p. 53)

From this he began his campaign for "software freedom," to have "free software" supplant all proprietary software: "'Free software' is a matter of liberty, not price. To understand the concept, you should think of 'free' as in 'free speech,' not as in 'free beer.' Free software is a matter of the users' freedom to run, copy, distribute, study, change and improve the software" (Free Software Foundation, 2005).

To define "free software," Stallman derived four levels of "software freedom," oriented toward the needs of fellow programmers (see Table 16.2). As a practical matter, that meant that Stallman and his FSF allies judged software licenses and business models to indicate which ones conformed to the norms of the movement. The software freedom principles were codified in the GNU General Public License (GPL), which imposes a doctrine of compulsory sharing (also known as "copyleft") in exchange for free use and modification rights for the source code (Rosen, 2004; West, 2005).

The goals of Project GNU were to create an entire free software operating system, which from its earliest days was conceived as an unlicensed Unix clone. The project began by making line-oriented software development tools for other programmers, including the emacs text editor and the gcc compiler.

In 1991, college student Linus Torvalds also wanted a Unix that was cheap to run on his own PC. After being dissatisfied with Minix, he started to write his own, using both Minix and prior Unix standards to write something that would run existing Unix applications. He based the operating system on the GNU tools and after a year licensed Linux under the GPL (Moody, 2001, pp. 31–50). By the time Torvalds was on the cover of *Forbes* magazine (August 1998), Linux had become the success story of the FSM. The success of Project GNU and particularly Linux created visibility for the GPL among sympathetic programmers.

Table 16.2 Basic Principles of the Free and Open Source Software Movements

Free Software Foundation	**Open Source Initiative**
Four Freedoms	*Open Source Definition*
0. The freedom to run the program, for any purpose. 1. The freedom to study how the program works, and adapt it to your needs. Access to the source code is a precondition for this. 2. The freedom to redistribute copies so you can help your neighbor. 3. The freedom to improve the program and release your improvements to the public, so that the whole community benefits. Access to the source code is a precondition for this.	1. Free Redistribution [*without restriction or royalty*] 2. Source Code [*must be included*] 3. Derived Works [*must be allowed and distributable]* 4. Integrity of The Author's Source Code [*may be protected*] 5. No Discrimination Against Persons or Groups 6. No Discrimination Against Fields of Endeavor 7. Distribution of License 8. License Must Not Be Specific to a Product [*so technology can be used in other products*] 9. License Must Not Restrict Other Software [*allowing mixing with proprietary software*] 10. License Must Be Technology-Neutral

Sources: Free Software Foundation (2005), Open Source Initiative (2002)

Thus, as of February 2005, 66.3 percent of the projects on SourceForge.net used the GPL, while the second most popular license was the library version of the GPL with 10.7 percent.

The focus by Stallman and allies on the ideology and purity of the FSM brought both attention and controversy. Like other movements, it sought to redefine language to advance its cause—as when Stallman declared war on terms such as "intellectual property" and "Linux." But Stallman's efforts to rebrand the Torvalds effort as "GNU/Linux" stirred animosity between the two men (as captured by Moore, 2002). More fundamentally, Torvalds explicitly rejected the free software ideology; in one famous exchange, he told a critic: "Quite frankly, I don't *want* people using Linux for ideological reasons ..." (KernelTrap.org, 2002). Thus, in 1998, key Linux supporters began a new movement, one driven by practical rather than ideological goals.

Open Source Software

In January 1998, Netscape announced it would release on the Internet the source code to its Web browser. In response, in February a group of Linux advocates met in Silicon Valley to strategize ways to promote the adoption of Netscape, Linux, and other similar technologies by mainstream businesses (Raymond, 1999). They saw the mobilizing rhetoric of the "free software" movement as a major obstacle:

> [W]e have a problem with the term "free software" itself, not the concept. ... The problem with it is twofold. First, it's confusing; the term "free" is very ambiguous (something the Free Software Foundation's propaganda has to wrestle with

> constantly). Does "free" mean "no money charged?" or does it mean "free to be modified by anyone", or something else?
>
> Second, the term makes a lot of corporate types nervous. While this does not intrinsically bother me in the least, we now have a pragmatic interest in converting these people rather than thumbing our noses at them. There's now a chance we can make serious gains in the mainstream business world without compromising our ideals and commitment to technical excellence—so it's time to reposition. We need a new and better label. (Raymond, 1998)

They proposed the term "open source" to describe their new business-friendly movement, which was immediately endorsed by Linus Torvalds. Later that year, they created a nonprofit organization, the Open Source Initiative (OSI). They also established a set of principles and began to certify licenses that conformed to those principles (Raymond, 1999). The initial licenses fell into two groups: the academic research licenses (BSD, MIT) and licenses of the free software movement such as the GPL and Lesser GPL (Rosen, 2004).

While some of the initial participants shared Stallman's beliefs, the hallmark of the open source movement was its pragmatism.[3] Raymond (1999) outlines key tactics that continue to be used today, including building on the success of Linux, marketing to top corporate decision makers, focusing on the Fortune 500 and mainstream business press. The plan also included using the Open Source Definition and OSI certification of licenses to control the boundaries of the open source movement (Scacchi, Chapter 14, this volume). Today, this OSI certification defines IP policies that are acceptable within the F/OSS movement, although the FSF maintains its own list of approved licenses.

Such pragmatism was vociferously rejected by Stallman as undercutting the moral and ethical foundation of his free software movement:

> The main argument for the term "open source software" is that "free software" makes some people uneasy. ... [Some developers] figured that by keeping quiet about ethics and freedom, and talking only about the immediate practical benefits of certain free software, they might be able to "sell" the software more effectively to certain users, especially business. The term "open source" is offered as a way of doing more of this—a way to be "more acceptable to business." The views and values of the Open Source movement stem from this decision.
>
> This approach has proved effective, in its own terms. Today many people are switching to free software for purely

> practical reasons. ... Sooner or later these users will be invited to switch back to proprietary software for some practical advantage. Countless companies seek to offer such temptation, and why would users decline? Only if they have learned to value the freedom free software gives them, for its own sake. It is up to us to spread this idea—and in order to do that, we have to talk about freedom. (Stallman, 2002)

Comparison of the Open Software Movements

The origins of the F/OSS movements can be traced directly to the Unix expertise of their respective founders. Both Stallman and Torvalds began their development to make a Unix-compatible operating system that fit their requirements. The creators of the OSI and the Apache project all came from a Unix, BSD, or Linux background (DiBona, Ockman, & Stone, 1999; Moore, 2002). Thus, it is not surprising that many of the successes and guiding principles of the F/OSS movements built directly upon prior successes in the Unix movement. Above all, these movements value free access to source code, which began with AT&T's (paid) licenses for Unix source code. This was cemented by Berkeley's campaign to make source code available to the public at no charge, forming the nucleus of open source projects such as FreeBSD. Among technical users in the open standards movement, access to source code was highly valued for the flexibility and control it provides. The same source code also reduces vendor lock-in, which during the open systems movement was achieved through open standards. And the free source (of BSD, Linux, and other F/OSS projects) was enthusiastically sought by students, hobbyists, and other individual users (Moore, 2002).

But there is more to the F/OSS movements than Internet Protocol (IP) policies. As West and O'Mahony (2005) note, F/OSS projects are defined not only by an IP policy but by a virtually dispersed development methodology and a community governance model. As a development approach, the two F/OSS movements are indistinguishable. They share the same development tools and even Web sites such as SourceForge.net. The two movements also share with the earlier BSD movement a technical ethos and pride in technical achievement, in part because many of the authors were writing software for their own use and for approval and adoption by their peers. Often cited is the comment (attributed to Eric Raymond) that open source software is based upon programmers "scratching an itch," but that observation also describes a tradition of programmers building products for themselves and their peers dating back to Ritchie and Thompson's first Unix efforts in 1969.[4]

In many cases, F/OSS packages have succeeded based on good design and implementations by these motivated and knowledgeable developers.

For example, both Linux and BSD offered a low-cost Unix implementation for students, while Apache filled a key gap in the Web server market (Kogut & Metiu, 2001; West & Dedrick, 2001). One key aspect of good design is a modular architecture, which was a major design goal of the Unix operating system (Salus, 1994, p. 53). Such a modular technical design (adopted by BSD, Linux, Apache, and other F/OSS projects) later proved to be an essential prerequisite to decentralized F/OSS development (Baldwin & Clark, 2000, 2003; Kogut & Metiu, 2001). Early proof of this came when the BSD group attracted volunteers to re-implement the Unix operating system (one module at a time), based on only the published interfaces (McKusick, 1999).

Open source advocates argue F/OSS inherently has higher quality due to its collaborative development approach (Ekbia & Gasser, Chapter 15, this volume). The most often cited claim again comes from Raymond (1997), who wrote: "Given enough eyeballs, all bugs are shallow." Other potential technical benefits of F/OSS development include feature improvements through user innovation (Franke & von Hippel, 2003) and enabling high-quality, peer-to-peer support (Lakhani & von Hippel, 2003).

However, there are important differences between the two F/OSS movements. The open source software movement celebrates the freedom of firms or individuals to create new proprietary or F/OSS projects from open source software; the free software movement forbids the former and decries the latter as wasteful "forking."

Other differences come with the rights and responsibilities of IT vendors in their respective communities. IT vendors are willing to invest in developing shared F/OSS for commodity technology that provides little opportunity for differentiation (West & Gallagher, 2006). Projects such as Apache, Mozilla, and Linux (through the Open Source Development Labs (OSDL)) depend heavily on cash and donated labor provided by major IT vendors promoting their own economic interests (such as selling Linux workstations); their respective leaders are pillars of the open source software movement but have only weak ties to the FSM. Most notably, Linux uses a free software license and builds upon many tools developed by Stallman's Project GNU, but is managed by Torvalds and others at OSDL who clearly prefer the ideology (and branding) of the open source software movement.

Some of the OSDL sponsors also backed earlier academic research, such as IBM and Digital Equipment Corporation (DEC) (now HP) sponsoring MIT's X11 development. But otherwise, corporate sponsorship makes the open source software movement seem more like the open systems movement than the BSD/MIT efforts from which it gained valuable technology and IP principles. This cultural divide within the F/OSS movements—between engineering and business goals—is illustrated by their respective artifacts. The BSD project of the 1980s and Stallman's

Project GNU of the 1990s used fanciful animals and T-shirts to appeal to engineers. Meanwhile, the open systems and open source software industries were organized around trade journals and trade shows that provided opportunities for IT vendors to promote their respective wares to potential adopters.

The goal of the open source software movement in particular was to promote widespread adoption by consciously attempting to speak the language of potential adopters in business and other organizations. The question we address is, to what extent has the movement's rhetoric matched the actual interests of users, and to what extent has the movement's rhetoric and mobilization efforts influenced the adoption decisions of potential users?

Research Design

We gathered data on organizational adoption of F/OSS. In designing our study, we identified differences between F/OSS and proprietary software that were likely to be relevant to users. First, adopters have access to the source code due to the nature of the F/OSS licenses and thus can view and modify the code to meet their own needs. At the same time, access to source code and the availability of free distributions of F/OSS on the Internet makes it difficult for vendors to charge high prices for commercial distributions.

Second, the F/OSS is produced by a loosely affiliated virtual community of software developers, both inside firms and outside them. While support services may be sold by third parties, such software lacks the single point of responsibility provided by a package from a major proprietary vendor, potentially increasing the perceived risk of adoption. Thus, when technology adopters compare an open source package to a proprietary one, they are likely to see a very different bundle of costs and benefits, as we found in our field study.

Studying Adoption Motivations

We chose to focus on organizational adoption of the best known F/OSS package, the Linux operating system. We concentrated on its most popular configuration, the Linux on Intel (aka "Lintel") server platform standard, as it competes with Windows, Unix, and other proprietary operating systems.[5]

There were two reasons for this decision. First, IT managers enjoyed a wide range of server alternatives. Unlike on the desktop, where one platform has held more than 90 percent share since 1997, for servers there were three major categories—Unix servers using proprietary RISC-based processors, servers based on Microsoft Windows and Intel-compatible commodity hardware ("Wintel"), and those using Linux (or BSD) using the same commodity hardware.

The server market was also attractive because Lintel server adoption is one of the greatest successes of the F/OSS movements, as measured by both market share and public notice. In 1999, the number of Linux servers passed the number of Unix servers (West & Dedrick, 2001). From 1999 to 2002, IDC estimated that annual shipments of new Linux servers increased from 173,000 to 598,000, while revenue from their sales increased from $749 million to $2 billion (Shankland, 2003). Coming in direct competition with Microsoft, Sun, IBM, and HP, this success has captured a good deal of attention in both the trade and business press.

At the same time, from our respondents we sought to place the Linux attitudes into a broader context of open source attitudes and adoption. As such, we gathered data about additional open source server software, of which the Apache Web server was the most frequently mentioned.

Data Collection

We used a comparative case study approach, which allows researchers to capture the experience and context of actors as they relate to decision makers (Benbasat, Goldstein, & Mead, 1987). We conducted a series of in-depth interviews (mostly in person) with U.S. firms and government agencies from November 2002 through October 2004 (see Table 16.3). The semi-structured interviews were guided by a common protocol and typically lasted 45–90 minutes. Where possible, we talked with both the chief information officer (CIO) (or other senior management information systems [MIS] executive) and an operational staffer such as a system administrator. We hoped that by doing so we could develop a more complete picture, incorporating the view of both top management and those "in the trenches." Also, we could provide a degree of data triangulation (Benbasat, et al., 1987) by comparing the responses of the two interviewees for consistency.

From this data, we used established procedures for generating theory from qualitative data (Dubé & Paré, 2003; Eisenhardt, 1989; Glaser & Strauss, 1967). As recommended by Glaser and Strauss (1967) and Benbasat, et al. (1987), site selection and protocol evolved over time. An initial set of interviews was conducted in four organizations chosen on dimensions of theoretical relevance, particularly size and industry. These interviews were transcribed and coded to look for patterns among responses, and a preliminary set of findings was developed. We then continued to refine the protocol with questions to pursue those findings further and to add organizations to the sample to capture more categories such as technological sophistication and additional industries.

Table 16.3 Characteristics of Sample Firms

Name	Business	Org. (unit) Size†	Primary Platform	Linux Adoption	Informants
Beach Co.	Rec. equipment	80	Windows	Web site only	1
Bio Branch	Pharmaceuticals	560 (150)	Linux	Predominant	1
Biotech	Pharmaceuticals	1,000	Unix	Internet and database applications	2
Dataco	Online data retrieval	2,700 (1,500)	Linux	Phasing out Unix	1
E-store	E-commerce	7,500	Unix	Shifting from Unix to Linux	1
FastFood	Restaurant chain	200,000	Mixed	None	1
FinCo	Financial services	130,000	Mixed	Partial adoption	1
NatLab	Government research lab	(8,000)	Unix	Phasing out Unix	2
ISP	Internet service provider	11	Linux	Since founding	1
NewMedia	Content provider	35	Unix	Partial transition	2
NorthU	Public university professional school	114,000 (325)	Mixed	Replacing Unix with Linux, while keeping Windows	3
Semico	Semiconductor design	2,500	Mixed	Limited; evaluating further use	2
SouthU	Public university professional school	114,000 (300)	Windows	Abandoned previous limited use	2
Travel Service	Travel-related reservations	6,000	Mainframe	Partial adoption	1

Total: 14 companies, 21 informants
† Size of parent organization (unit) in number of employees

Data analysis was flexible and opportunistic (Benbasat, et al., 1987; Eisenhardt, 1989); it included coding interview notes, developing visual displays of the data on white boards, and counting the number of interviewees who mentioned a particular point. Interviews were also studied and tapes listened to in order to distinguish the emphasis placed on different factors and to find quotes that were especially striking in representing a particular point of view.

Users' Perceptions of F/OSS Benefits

After analyzing the findings from the interviews, we contrasted their perceptions of F/OSS benefits with the public discourses of the F/OSS movement activists. In particular, we looked at user perceptions of attributes of F/OSS and potential benefits and costs of adoption.[6] These included the importance of access to source code, the importance of cost in motivating adoption, the importance to users of having control over their destiny, and the perceived quality of F/OSS when contrasted to proprietary software. Finally, we looked at users' perceptions of the movements themselves and the role of the CM advocates as change agents within organizations.

Access to Source Code

A key ideological tenet of both the F/OSS movements is that providing access to source code is critical to enabling users to adapt software to their needs and to share their improvements with the community. This access is undoubtedly vital for those users who want or need to modify the code for their own purposes, or who want to fix bugs that they find. However, our interviews suggest that most IT organizations and professionals are not interested in doing so. Instead, they simply want to install, run, and administer software, and have no need or sometimes even ability to analyze and modify the code. A typical view expressed by one interviewee sums it up: "Our people are not the type to start tweaking source code or doing their own bug fixes."

Perceptions of the utility of access to source code vary from valuable to dangerous. Most favorable was NatLab, which saw access to source code as vital in its efforts to develop systems capable of highly sophisticated scientific analysis. Biobranch's Informatics Director also saw value, saying: "We knew we had to develop a lot of custom tools, and without having access to the open source community and to the source code, it would be really difficult." Biotech's Associate Director of IT Infrastructure saw both benefits and risks: "It's nice to have, but having source code is like having a gun with bullets. You can shoot yourself in the foot." By contrast, for FastFood, such tinkering was something to be avoided completely: "We don't want to have anybody mucking with that. We're trying to use as much off-the-shelf software as possible."

As a measure of the value of source code, we inquired whether or not the organizations ever used the open source code itself. Eleven of the 14 organizations interviewed were using Linux in some capacity (and another used Apache), yet only four actually made any use of source code.

The differences in perception might be explained by several factors. First is user experience and skills. E-Store's central technology officer (CTO) said his company has some of the world's best Linux kernel engineers, who are fully comfortable modifying the source code if needed to achieve the performance required for the company's high volume e-commerce business. By contrast, BeachCo's Vice President of Administration admitted that he could not even administer a Unix system without having a manual nearby, to say nothing of actually looking into the source code.

A second factor is the maturity of the software. Several respondents who did use and even modify source code at times stated that it was not necessary for mature products such as Linux, Sendmail, and Apache. BioBranch's Informatics Director stated: "In the olden days, I've recompiled the Linux kernel and kind of tuned the kernel. But now I don't do any modifying at the kernel level." Biotech's Associate

Director of IT Infrastructure said: "Linux is more mature now and doesn't need modification."

A third factor is that users do not see value in modifying underlying infrastructure programs such as Linux and Apache, but are more likely to modify applications that are directly related to their business and customers. An example is E-store, whose CTO said: "We do participate with the open source movement, not with the operating system itself, but with other pieces we use. We modify code for applications because it's closer to where our customers are. We're not an operating systems company."

Open Source Means Lower Cost

While both F/OSS movements have downplayed the importance of cost as a motivation, for users lower cost is by far the most commonly cited benefit of F/OSS. Everyone who had adopted F/OSS mentioned cost, and in nearly every case cost was the main reason for adopting. For instance, the CTO of E-Store, which has made extensive use of Linux and other F/OSS, stated his views on open source in a way that quite closely matches Stallman's warnings about utility-driven adoption: "That's our open source policy: If it's cheaper, that's what we do. If some proprietary vendor comes to us and says here's a proprietary solution that has lower cost and higher performance and reliability, then we'll go and do that."

The cost calculation of F/OSS versus proprietary software is more complicated than the "free beer" notion would suggest, however. In the case of Linux, a major cost advantage relative to proprietary Unix systems is due to the fact that Linux runs on cheap Intel-based hardware rather than on more expensive proprietary hardware from Sun, HP, or IBM. This is very important for organizations that have committed to running some variant of Unix and could do so more cheaply with Linux, as was the case for ISP, E-Store, BioBranch, NewMedia, and Dataco. When the alternative under consideration was Windows, the hardware issue was not relevant, as Windows runs on the same hardware platform as Linux. At least some users considered the total cost of ownership, including licensing, support, and internal staff costs, in their calculations. In the case of SouthU, this meant that the beer was not free or necessarily even cheap. "It's 'free'—licensed free, but it's not free to use. You guys have heard the saying, 'free as in beer'? It's not free as in beer. ... You have to have the people there to maintain it and develop it and foster it and all those things, and that costs money. And that costs *more* money than the actual licenses for the software."

Still, for some users, the lower direct costs paid for F/OSS were a factor. This was true especially for businesses that have to pay the commercial price for proprietary software, but not so for the universities, which enjoy the educational discount. Some, such as ISP, do not even pay the cost of a commercial Linux distribution, preferring to save money by downloading the free version.

Open Source Means More Control and Choice for Users

Both free software and open source software advocates claim that F/OSS gives users control over their destinies and frees them from the tyranny of commercial software vendors ("don't you *want* to be out from under Microsoft's thumb?"). As one manifesto wrote: "Programming is also about empowerment, what Eric Raymond calls 'scratching an itch.' Most Open Source projects began with frustration: looking for a tool to do a job and finding none, or finding one that was broken or poorly maintained. Eric Raymond began fetchmail this way; Larry Wall began Perl this way; Linus Torvalds began Linux this way. Empowerment, in many ways, is the most important concept underlying Stallman's motivation for starting the GNU project" (DiBona, et al., 1999, pp. 13–14).

This is one issue on which many users agreed with the movement's rhetoric and valued the benefit touted by its advocates. Even SouthU, whose CIO had standardized on Windows and was somewhat uncomfortable about F/OSS in general, adopted the open source Apache and ModPerl applications to host a custom-developed course management program when faced with a major price increase from the vendor of a proprietary version of the Perl programming language. "[The vendor] had originally established an educational price for the support contract, and they abolished that, which essentially made our contract equal to that of any commercial enterprise. It would have been hard for us to pay, but in addition, if [the vendor's program] fails, [our program] is down and we can't fix it because we didn't write [the vendor's program]."

A more direct critique of closed source vendors was lodged by the CIO of Biotech. His belief that standardizing on Windows made organizations vulnerable to "extortion" on the part of Microsoft had been confirmed in his mind by changes in the vendor's licensing policies just prior to the interview. "Microsoft has done such an excellent job of alienating IT people, with their new licensing schemes and their really extortionate attempts to keep their margins up there at historic levels, that everybody's looking for alternatives. Now everyone's feeling the same way because they've been burnt. They've seen what happens when you have a pseudomonopoly situation developing in your company. You shouldn't be surprised when your vendor extracts pseudomonopoly rents."

This view was echoed by NorthU's Associate Director, who said the company had adopted Linux partly because of concerns over Microsoft's control. "There was a lot of disenchantment with Microsoft, the monopoly, and being dictated from Redmond. So we were very interested in alternatives."

Another aspect of the choice/control issue was the concern that a proprietary product would disappear from the market, because the vendor either disappeared or decided to abandon that product line. This was expressed by the CIO of SemiCo, who said: "If the world is moving to a Linux standard, even over a very long time frame, you don't want to be on the wrong path following a proprietary standard."

Open Source Means Better Software and Support

Software reliability is the key discourse of the open source software movement, with proponents claiming that the F/OSS development process inherently leads to more reliable software and critics claiming the opposite (Ekbia & Gasser, Chapter 15, this volume). While we do not empirically measure reliability or other indicators of software quality, we do have strong evidence of users' perceptions of quality, and in our sample there is little support for the idea that F/OSS are necessarily more or less reliable than proprietary software.

Considering Linux in particular, there was a fairly wide range of opinion. Biotech's Associate Director of IT Infrastructure felt it was just as good as, or even better than, the proprietary HP-UX Unix that the company also used. FinCo actually tested Linux against Solaris and AIX on equivalent hardware and said that Linux outperformed the other two. Others such as SemiCo's CIO were ready to move some applications (such as an SAP[7] module) but not others (a critical database) to Linux, due to reliability concerns. FastFood was comfortable using Linux only for print or file servers, not for any enterprise applications. When compared with Windows, several found Linux to be more reliable and secure, but others found Windows to have the advantage in ease of administration thanks to better tools and user interface.

Only one interviewee, NewMedia's CTO, felt that F/OSS were inherently inferior: "The quality of the code is crappy—you get what you pay for. It's all written by college students." He did admit that a program such as Apache was "good enough for what it does. A lot of stuff that we do on the Web isn't like writing shrink-wrap software, and the level of catastrophic failure isn't that catastrophic."

Even E-store, the heaviest Linux user among our respondents, admitted that Linux still is not as reliable as the proprietary Tru64 Unix system, and suggested the F/OSS model might be a barrier to reliability. The CTO said: "There may be some fundamental issues around the open source model. Is there an incentive to create software that's as reliable as the incentive that an HP would have?"

BioBranch offered a contrary opinion. The company's Informatics Director felt that the F/OSS process helped support innovation that benefited his company. "As an end user, I couldn't care less if Linux is open; we're not going to modify that. But if it was closed, changes to it would be a lot slower. Other people are doing advanced things like parallel computing, and if it weren't open, they wouldn't be making the changes we'd like to see."

While opinions vary about the quality, reliability, and speed of innovation in F/OSS, there is no general perception that the F/OSS model inherently leads to better quality software.

Another issue related to the quality of the software itself is the matter of technical support for users. IT organizations are accustomed to having support from vendors for the software they use, either as part of the cost of the software or as a separate contract. Since there is no vendor for F/OSS, users must get support either from the F/OSS community via online forums, from vendors of particular distributions, such as Red Hat or Novell, or from third-party service companies that offer support contracts. The open source software movement argues that the community provides better support than that offered by vendors (whose support teams it considers almost useless) and says that F/OSS needs less support anyhow. In its response to the "myth" that it is hard to get reliable support for open source software, OSI claims that "business users will generally find that mature open-source products are far more reliable to begin with, and that when support is needed it is dramatically cheaper and easier to get than from closed vendors" (OSI, frequently asked questions).

This view is quite different from that of our user respondents. Most of them were uncomfortable relying entirely on the community for support, even though several acknowledged that their experience with the community had been quite positive. For instance, SemiCo's central information officer (CIO) said: "We now have to go through enormous effort to ensure patch compatibility. With Linux you get the latest patches every day." Yet he, along with most others, said that vendor support was either necessary or would greatly increase their comfort level with adopting F/OSS. Of particular importance was support for Linux from a Linux distributor or from a hardware vendor such as HP or IBM. Most critical was support from application vendors, as no one was willing to run an application on a Linux server without certification and support from the application vendor.

In the end, MIS organizations and professionals are quite risk averse, as the easiest way for them to get noticed by their superiors is to have a system fail. In this case, having a support contract means having not only support but also someone else to hold accountable for resolving the problem. As SouthU's CIO said: "I'm nervous about open source. I'm not paying anybody to support it and thus I'm depending largely on goodwill and luck and skill of my own people affecting their own solutions and soliciting solutions from other people for free. That explanation looks amateurish when you offer it to a dean or to a faculty when a production system is down in my opinion."

Views on the Movement and the Role of Advocates

Our interviewees expressed a range of views on the F/OSS movement itself. A few were strong enough advocates to be considered members of the movement. One was the Web Systems Administrator of NorthU, whose interest in open source began as a student at the same university. "When I got my master's in information management, I was working a lot alongside people who do research completely on social issues. I was affected by social impacts of technology coming out of that program. I was concerned about the proprietary software movement versus the open. If I had to say anything, open source fits with my personality. I don't like being subject to the limitations set by someone else."

Others identified themselves as advocates, including respondents at Biotech and FinCo. At the opposite end was the CTO of NewMedia, who claimed he steered clear of hiring "people with GNU disease" and said: "I don't believe that all software should be free, which is the underlying philosophy of these groups."

The prevailing view was pragmatism. Users select the platform or application that best suits their needs, in terms of price, performance, and features. This was summed up by NorthU's CIO, who said: "We're agnostic here. We're not religious about operating system platforms."

Members of a CM are potential change agents within organizations. Depending on their position and power, they could do anything from advocating F/OSS to making organizational policy toward F/OSS. We found that movement believers did attempt to advocate for F/OSS, but did so within the bounds of institutional restraints. For instance, they would support F/OSS options when a new application was being developed or a change of platform was being considered for other reasons, but did not advocate switching existing systems to F/OSS. Also, arguments for F/OSS were made in terms of cost or performance; no advocate would argue that the organization should adopt F/OSS because closed source software is "anti-social" or "tramples on users' freedoms," as suggested by Richard Stallman.

An example of the role of advocacy was Biotech's Associate Director, who stated that he "made sure that we consider Linux whenever an operating decision is made or up for reconsideration." This is confirmed by the company's CIO who pointed to the Associate Director for Infrastructure as having played a role in Biotech's increased use of Linux, and suggested we interview him. A similar role was played by the Web Systems Administrator at NorthU. His supervisor, the Associate Director, said: "I had to be convinced by [the Web Systems Administrator] to bring up [a new application] on Linux." The FinCo advocate said that he and others had pushed Linux use "under the radar" in pilot projects, and later got Linux accepted as a standard within the company. This status was further legitimized by the creation of a formal Linux group within the information systems organization.

The role of F/OSS advocates as change agents is clearly constrained by organizational goals and norms, and by their position within the organization. However, the evidence suggests that such advocates can have an impact in encouraging adoption by their organizations.

Contrasting the Frames of Activists and Beneficiaries

The clearest pattern of our findings was the gap between the dominant frames of the two F/OSS movements and the actual reasons why organizations adopted free or open source software.

While some (e.g., Elliott & Kraemer, Chapter 1, this volume) argue that such contending discourse may eventually resolve to a revised dominant frame, we saw little evidence of resolution of such differences, either within the F/OSS movements or between the movements and adopters. Different populations kept to their distinct visions, discourses, and technological action frames. Both free and open source software developers work side by side in creating code and promoting adoption of that code, while hewing to their respective technological action frames. The frames of the free software movement work to attract other programmers, but held little appeal for corporate IT decision makers, even as they gladly adopted technology such as Linux, gcc, and Gnome. Although the utilitarian framing of the open source software movement anticipated the pragmatic user motivations, even their public discourse was not completely accepted by the organizational adopters.

What were the similarities and differences between the developer and adopter frames? As summarized in Table 16.4, we found the following:

Table 16.4 Perceptions of Movements vs. Users

Frames and Perceptions	Free Software Movement	Open Source Software Movement	Organizational Adopters
Primary goal	"Software freedom"	Widespread adoption	Economic utility
Access to source code	Fundamental	Fundamental	Valued by some, used selectively
Better quality software and support	Not emphasized	Primary benefit of open vs. closed source	Mixed views on quality, want a support contract
Control and choice	Key goal	Key goal	Important to many
Cheap software	"Think free speech, not free beer"	Not emphasized	Key benefit, universally valued
Perceptions of the movement	True believers, purists	Pragmatic evangelists	Agnostic

- The fundamental objectives of organizational users are utilitarian. Our respondents were interested in selecting, deploying, and supporting cost-effective software that satisfied key requirements for features and reliability. This is consistent with the tone of the open source software movement, which claims it merely wants to promote open source software "on solid pragmatic grounds rather than ideological tub-thumping." The free software movement, meanwhile, criticizes the open source software movement for appealing to "narrowly practical values," i.e., the very things that matter to users.
- The lynchpin of both movements—full access to software source code—was surprisingly of mixed value to users, including even some of the more aggressive F/OSS adopters. Some firms valued having source code—usually for rapidly evolving business-driven applications rather than stable infrastructure software. In other cases, the respondents identified the availability of the source code as "nice to have" but said that it had little utility for them. And in a few cases, respondents worried that the ability to modify source code could ruin configuration control efforts, increasing future support costs and overall system risks.
- A key action frame of the open source software movement—that the F/OSS process leads to more reliable software, faster development time, and better support via the online community—was clearly not consistent with the perceptions of users. While there was a range of views, most respondents felt that Linux was somewhat less reliable than proprietary Unix operating systems, while more reliable but harder to use than Windows. And while the support of the F/OSS community was often praised, few users were willing to forego the security of a formal support contract from a reputable IT company.
- One point of agreement between the movements and our respondents was the value placed on having more control over one's destiny and not being at the mercy of proprietary software vendors. Open software is perceived as increasing user choice and control, which have both ideological value to the movements and pragmatic value to users.
- The most important benefit of open software to users is the one that the movements both try to downplay, i.e., low cost. While Stallman commands us to think "free speech, not free beer," and the open source advocates emphasize quality rather than cost, it is clear that organizational users are thinking about cost more than anything else when considering F/OSS. Some users even

saw the utopian F/OSS development process mainly as a way of getting volunteers to develop software at a low cost: as one stated, "we want to be free riders." Others most valued that Linux offered them a way to run a Unix quality operating system on cheap Intel hardware. This may not be surprising, given that IT organizations operate under tight budgets in the post-dot-com era, but it presents a dilemma for the movements: Will top programmers be willing to volunteer their time if their efforts are being touted as mainly a way for user organizations to save money on software?

- Finally, we found that most IT managers were agnostic about open versus closed source software, with no one calling for their organization to refuse to deal with vendors who will not reveal their source code (as both free and open source rhetoric advocates). We did find a few F/OSS movement members operating within the user organizations, and in several cases they appeared to be acting as change agents promoting adoption. Their advocacy was constrained by the goals of the organization, so they tended to argue for F/OSS on utilitarian grounds. As such, the free software movement might regard them as ideologically impure, but in their own way they were actually carrying out the objective of the open source software movement to promote open software for pragmatic rather than ideological reasons.

The lack of support for ideological motivations serves as a reminder that the picture compiled of a CM will depend on when and where it is compiled. As noted by Rogers (1962), the earliest individuals to adopt an innovation are more knowledgeable, information-seeking, and risk-taking than the subsequent early and late majorities of the population. So with any innovation adoption, the earliest adopters are atypical of the eventual mass market—they adopt (or join a movement) based on an idea rather than a fully formed realization of success.

The earliest case studies, advocacy reports, and academic research on F/OSS adoption (e.g., those with data from 1999 or earlier) necessarily focused on the earliest adopters, in this case primarily programmers/hackers and users who bought into the movement's ideology. Meanwhile, our later sample reflects mainstream U.S. organizational users of Linux and Apache, who, not surprisingly, were less interested in movement rhetorics. This view is consistent with "early majority" adopters that Rogers (1962) terms "deliberate" and Moore (1991) refers to as "pragmatists." Future research could contrast user attitudes toward CMs among adopters in such an "early majority" to those in earlier and later populations.

Endnotes

1. With regard to intellectual property (IP) strategies, the term "open source" is a proper superset of "free software," and the respondents in our study treated it as such. Because of the differences in movement goals, in this chapter we use "F/OSS" to refer to free and open source software. European members of the free software movement often include "libre" in the acronym ("FL/OSS"), but we have not found an example where "libre" is not synonymous with "free software" as defined by Stallman (1999, p. 56).
2. One of the rewritten packages that Bostic solicited was a lightweight database that became known as BerkeleyDB. In 1996, to support and eventually commercialize this software, Bostic co-founded the open source company Sleepycat Software (interview, February 4, 2005).
3. Some would argue that the decisions were driven by self-interest: Many of the initial participants were already working for businesses that made money from Linux, and in 1999 Raymond himself would become a director of one of those firms, VA Linux. But in our ongoing research, we have observed both ideology and self-interest motivating leaders of both F/OSS movements.
4. The exact phrase "Every good work of software starts by scratching a developer's personal itch" is found in Raymond's oft-quoted essay, "The Cathedral and the Bazaar" (e.g., Raymond, 1997, 2001, p. 32). However, a 1994 history of Unix attributes to Berkeley programmer (and Sendmail creator) Eric Allman the observation, "One general rule of software design is that you should be writing a program that you want to use" (Salus, 1994, p. 145).
5. "Unix" and "open systems" are often used interchangeably, but we adopt the classification scheme of West (2003), in which proprietary Unix-based reduced instruction set computer (RISC) systems reflect an intermediate point between fully open and fully proprietary systems.
6. Adoption of server software fits the Swanson (1994) definition of a "Type 1" adoption decision, i.e., one that mainly impacts the IT staff. Because such systems are largely invisible to end-users, in our analysis we treat the responses of the IT managers as representing the interests of the users' organization.
7. SAP refers to the largest European software enterprise, with headquarters in Walldorf, Germany. SAP was founded in 1972 as Systemanalyse und Programmentwicklung by five former IBM engineers in Mannheim, Germany and the acronym was later changed to Systeme, Anwendungen und Produkte in der Datenverarbeitung ("Systems, Applications and Products in Data Processing"). In 2005, the company's official name was just SAP AG.

References

Baldwin, C. Y., & Clark, K. B. (2000). *Design rules.* Cambridge, MA: MIT Press.

Baldwin, C. Y., & Clark, K. B. (2003). The architecture of cooperation: How code architecture mitigates free riding in the open source development model. Harvard Business School–MIT Sloan Free/Open Source Software Conference: New Models of Software Development, Cambridge, MA, June. Retrieved from opensource.mit.edu/papers/baldwinclark.pdf

Benbasat, I., Goldstein, D. K., & Mead, M. (1987). The case research strategy in studies of information systems. *MIS Quarterly*, 11(3), 369–386.

DiBona, C., Ockman, S., & Stone, M. (Eds.). (1999). *Open sources: Voices from the open Source revolution*. Sebastopol, CA: O'Reilly.

Dubé, L., & Paré, G. (2003). Rigor in information systems positivist case research: Current practices, trends, and recommendations. *MIS Quarterly*, 27(4), 597–635.

Eisenhardt, K. M. (1989). Building theories from case study research. *Academy of Management Review*, 14(4), 532–550.

Elliott, M., & Scacchi, W. (forthcoming). Mobilization of software developers: The free software movement. *Information, Technology and People.*

Franke, N., & von Hippel, E. (2003). Satisfying heterogeneous user needs via innovation toolkits. *Research Policy*, 32(7), 1199–1215.

Free Software Foundation. (2005). The free software definition. Retrieved May 26, 2006, from www.gnu.org/philosophy/free-sw.html

Gabel, H. L. (1987). Open standards in computers: The case of X/OPEN. In H. L. Gabe (Ed.), *Product standardization and competitive strategy.* Amsterdam: North-Holland.

Garud, R., & Kumaraswamy, A. (1993). Changing competitive dynamics in network industries: An exploration of Sun Microsystems' open systems strategy. *Strategic Management Journal*, 14(5), 351–369.

Glaser, B. G., & Strauss, A. (1967). *The discovery of grounded theory: Strategies of qualitative research*. London: Wiedenfeld and Nicholson.

Grindley, P. (1995). Open computer systems: A standards revolution. In P. Grindley (Ed.), *Standards strategy and policy: Cases and stories* (pp. 156–194). Oxford: Oxford University Press.

Iacono, S., & Kling, R. (2001). Computerization movements: The rise of the Internet and distant forms of work. In J. A. Yates & J. V. Van Maanen (Eds.), *Information technology and organizational transformation: History, rhetoric and practice* (pp. 93–136). Thousand Oaks, CA: Sage Publications.

Isaak, J. (2006). The role of individuals and social capital in POSIX standardization. *International Journal of IT Standards & Standardization Research*, 4(1), 1–23.

KernelTrap.org. (2002). Linux: Open source ideology. Retrieved February 25, 2005, from kerneltrap.org/node/159

Kling, R., & Iacono, S. (1988). The mobilization of support for computerization: The role of computerization movements. *Social Problems*, 35(3), 226–242.

Kogut, B., & Metiu, A. (2001). Open source software development and distributed innovation. *Oxford Review of Economic Policy*, 17(2), 248–264.

Lakhani, K. R., & von Hippel, E. (2003). How open source software works: "Free" user-to-user assistance. *Research Policy*, 32(6), 923–943.

Lerner, J., & Tirole, J. (2002). Some simple economics of open source. *Journal of Industrial Economics*, 52(2), 197–234.

Markus, M. L., Manville, B., & Agres, C. E. (2000). What makes a virtual organization work? *Sloan Management Review*, 42(1), 13–26.

McKusick, M. K. (1999). Twenty years of Berkeley Unix. In C. DiBona, S. Ockman, & M. Stone (Eds.), *Open sources: Voices from the open source revolution* (pp. 31–46). Sebastopol, CA: O'Reilly.

Moody, G. (2001). *Rebel code: Inside Linux and the open source revolution*. Cambridge, MA: Perseus.

Moore, G. A. (1991). *Crossing the chasm: Marketing and selling high-tech products to mainstream customers*. New York: HarperBusiness.

Moore, J. T. S. (2002). *Revolution OS.* Movie.

Morin, R. (1995). BSD-based OS releases, part II. *UNIX Review,* 13(4).

Open Source Initiative. Frequently asked questions. Retrieved February 25, 2005, from www.opensource.org/advocacy/faq.php

Open Source Initiative. The open source definition. Version 1.9, 2002. Retrieved February 25, 2005, from www.opensource.org/docs/definition.php

Raymond, E. S. (1997). *The Cathedral and the Bazaar*. Retrieved February 25, 2005, from hackvan.com/pub/stig/articles/cathedral-paper/cathedral.txt

Raymond, E. S. (1998). Goodbye, "free software"; hello, "open source." Retrieved May 26, 2006, from www.catb.org/~esr/open-source.html

Raymond, E. S. (1999). The revenge of the hackers. In C. DiBona, S. Ockman, & M. Stone (Eds.), *Open sources: Voices from the open source revolution* (pp. 207–219). Sebastopol, CA: O'Reilly.

Raymond, E. S. (2001). *The cathedral and the bazaar: Musings on Linux and Open Source by an accidental revolutionary*. Sebastopol, CA: O'Reilly.

Rogers, E. M. (1962). *Diffusion of innovations*. New York: Free Press.

Rosen, L. (2004). *Open source licensing: Software freedom and intellectual property law.* Upper Saddle River, NJ: Prentice Hall PTR.

Salus, P. H. (1994). *A quarter century of UNIX.* Reading, MA: Addison-Wesley.

Shankland, S. (2003, May 23). IDC: Servers to make mild recovery. CNET News.com. Retrieved from news.com.com/2100-1010_3-1009814.html

Stallman, R. M. (1999). The GNU operating system and the free software movement. In C. DiBona, S. Ockman, & M. Stone (Eds.), *Open sources: Voices from the open source revolution* (pp. 53–70). Sebastopol, CA: O'Reilly.

Stallman, R. M. (2002). *Free software, free society: Selected essays of Richard M. Stallman*. Boston, MA: GNU Press.

Swanson, E. B. (1994). Information systems innovation among organizations. *Management Science*, 40(9), 1069–1092.

West, J. (2003). How open is open enough? Melding proprietary and open source platform strategies. *Research Policy*, 32 (7), 1259–1285.

West, J. (2005). Understanding open source licensing: Three how-to guides. *IEEE Software*, 22(4), 114–116.

West, J., & Dedrick, J. (2001). Proprietary vs. open standards in the network era: An examination of the Linux phenomenon. *Proceedings of the 34th Annual Hawaii International Conference on System Sciences,* Maui, HI.

West, J., & Gallagher, S. (2006). Patterns of open innovation in open source software. In H. Chesbrough, W. Vanhaverbeke, & J. West (Eds.), *Open innovation: Researching a new paradigm* (pp. 82–106). Oxford: Oxford University Press.

West, J., & O'Mahony, S. (2005). Contrasting community building in sponsored and community founded open source projects. *Proceedings of the 38th Annual Hawaii International Conference on System Sciences,* Waikoloa, HI. Retrieved from opensource.mit.edu/papers/westomahony.pdf

Part VI

Ubiquitous Computing

Chapter 17

The Professional's Everyday Struggle with Ubiquitous Computing

Carsten Sørensen
London School of Economics and Political Science

David Gibson
Accenture

Abstract

For the modern professional it is essential to have flexible access to information sources and interaction with clients and colleagues. They adopt and use a variety of information and communication technology to facilitate their daily work practices. Mobile phones, e-mail, pagers, laptops, and personal computers all aim to facilitate the flexibility necessary for conducting their work. The visions of the ubiquitous computing computerization movement, as most famously formulated by Mark Weiser, provide an idealized framework we can project onto the relationship between modern professionals and their technologies. It clearly outlines a technological action frame of invisible computing anytime, anywhere. Ideally, these highly skilled professionals with intense demands on their time should not be *supported* by various information and interaction technologies. Instead, core domesticated technologies should be *embedded* in their work. Their time keeping is not *supported* by a wristwatch, they simply wear one. Ubiquity, in the ubiquitous computing computerization movement discourse, is exclusively associated with positive ether-like characteristics rendering it available and relevant at any time, while at the same time being invisible or at least in the background. This chapter examines how the visions of the ubiquitous computing computerization movement to support professional work meet the harsh realities of work life through interviews with 16 individual professionals from 16 different organizations. The chapter aims to answer the question of the applicability and reality of ubiquitous computing in today's work environment and where technology is in terms of limitations for the professional. The study clearly demonstrates that the joint life of professionals with their technologies of choice is not one best characterized by the technical and the social merging seamlessly. It is instead one burdened by constant attention. More widely, the chapter demonstrates the seemingly unproblematic core assumptions of the ubiquitous computing computerization movement as generally problematic. In fact, we argue that the closer information and communication technologies are coupled with the human body as well as with routines and rituals, the more difficult it is for the technology to disappear.

Introduction

Much of the current and, indeed, past technology discourse on pervasive, mobile, and ubiquitous computing highlights the immense potential of various kinds of technological innovations. These visions are mainly informed by the imagined potentials of technologies, and it is fair to assume that much of the debate focuses on visions rather than realities. Every new generation of mobile, pervasive, or ubiquitous technology comes packaged with the next generation of sparkling vendor-formulated promised lands—this is indeed the core concern of this entire book.

We are sold the vision of 3G mobile telephony, and hope that the technology providers will solve the problems of shifting from 2G to 3G networks with the same handset before we have to use them. Even before these technologies are diffused widely, there are already calls for 3.5G and 4G potentially offering very high-speed data transfer rates. Already, emerging technologies allow relatively transparent shifting between various networks, such as the global system for mobile communication (GSM), the general packet radio service (GPRS), and Wireless Fidelity (WiFi). It can, of course, be expected that the heterogeneous elements in the data and voice infrastructure will converge and, from the point of view of use, become one. Technologies such as Skype and Microsoft Exchange 2007 combine various asynchronous and real-time communication technologies and present integrated interfaces to operate these.

A computerization movement (CM) can be characterized as a social movement emphasizing the inherent social benefit of extensive use of computer hardware, software, and associated technologies. There are, as this book thoroughly discusses, a wide range of such movements concerned with the advantages of computing technology, including productivity, democracy, instant interconnectedness, freedom, and ubiquity. This chapter explores the ubiquitous computing CM. We have recently seen the drive toward equipping everyone with a personal digital assistant (PDA) and, currently, we all seem to have a pressing need to carry tablet personal computers (PCs) and take low-resolution pictures of each other using our new mobile phones. A consortium led by Nicholas Negroponte seeks to populate developing countries with wind-up laptop computers under the slogan "One Laptop per Child" (laptop.org). While providing a laptop to people in developing countries may be beneficial, it is unclear how this computerization capability, in and of itself, can essentially transform lives when it is more important in these countries to provide everyone with a reliable source of clean water.

Iacono and Kling (2001) characterize CMs in terms of:

- Technological Action Frames (TAFs) – Multi-dimensional composite understandings legitimating investment and forming visions about current and future use of the technology.
- Public discourse – Communication within and between government, scientific organizations, mass media, as well as professional and user-organizations concerned with the particular technology
- Organizational practices – How the technological action frames and public discourses are put into practice at a micro-level.

One recent dominant CM is the ubiquitous computing CM. It has been forwarding the compelling vision of ubiquitous computing, where complex technologies of all kinds seamlessly blend into the background and form an invisible fabric of modern life, similar to the way in which the clocks, in general, and wristwatches, in particular, have gradually blended with human practices of time management. This discourse is the underlying fabric of arguments made in favor of mobile technologies, for home entertainment technologies, and for a range of other information technology (IT) innovations, such as RFID technology. The most famous proponent of this discourse is Mark Weiser whose seminal article (Weiser, 1991) outlined the future of computing. This ubiquitous computing discourse is frequently discussed in a range of contexts, including the highly technical professional trade press, in research proposals as rationalization for research funds allocated to computer science research, and in academic journals. The discourse seeks to convince us that the miniaturization of computing equipment and sensor technology, along with widespread networking of this equipment, will bring about a situation where not only are computers everywhere, but these computers will also disappear into the fabric of life and provide unnoticed advantages of automatic connections and support. It is difficult to argue against the hardware vision of a move from one CPU per thousands of people, over to the PC age with one CPU per person in developed countries, to a future scenario with thousands of CPUs per individual around the globe. The main question is to what extent the mere presence of all these CPUs will lead to a ubiquitous utopia, or if it indeed is filled with essential problems and questions (Albrecht & McIntyre, 2006; Mann & Niedzviecki, 2002).

The aim of this chapter is to investigate the organizational practices of translating the visions of the ubiquitous computing CM into everyday work with technology. It presents discussions with highly skilled and highly paid modern professionals on how they use and perceive modern pervasive and mobile technologies. The analysis both contextualizes the ubiquitous computing CM and highlights some of the issues of a more pragmatic nature relating to the intricate relationships between professional work practices and the use of technologies in carrying out these practices. The aim here is to compare the vision of the ubiquitous computing CM with the realities faced every day by a group who most intensely seeks to embrace the vision, namely highly skilled and highly paid modern professionals. This group embraces advanced technology to help overcome temporal and geographical barriers in their detailed information and knowledge work. Whereas the technology-driven CM discourse is obsessed with new gadgetry, the professionals are more concerned with the utility of the technologies and how the technologies can help enhance their productivity. They are concerned with the job at hand, and are not interested in concerning themselves with technology as such. It is interesting that Alan Kay's vision of the Dynabook (en.wikipedia.org/wiki/Dynabook), Steve Mann's vision of wearable computers (wearcam.org), Kevin Warwick's cyborg projects (www.kevinwarwick.com/Cyborg2.htm), and others have a professional interest in ubiquitous computing technology and spend considerable time and effort in breaking new barriers (Mann & Niedzviecki, 2002; Press, 1992; Warwick, 2002). However, for the modern urban professionals, this futuristic technology is simply a means for doing the job at hand.

This chapter critically examines the main issues emerging when the theory of ubiquitous and pervasive computing meets the realities of modern urban professionals' experiences. This is accomplished by combining a theoretical analysis of empirical evidence obtained through interviewing 16 modern professionals about their daily life with mostly mobile information and communication technologies (ICTs). Through these accounts of articulated experiences of technology use, we can investigate to what extent the vision of the ubiquitous computing CM is an experienced reality—to what extent the professionals feel their core technologies disappear in the background.

The study clearly demonstrates that all the core technologies do indeed *not* disappear. Some proved to be a steady and important aspect of working life, such as the invaluable mobile phone. Other technologies were very much present as a constant source of need for attention. Yet again, a technology such as the PDA was mainly present as a topic of failed adoption. The PDA generally disappeared completely out of view and into desk drawers. The main issues raised by these professionals spanned highly complex underlying issues such as infrastructure standardization, as well as quite basic ones such as poor usability due to short battery life of essential technologies. The most promising technology was found to be wireless e-mail clients, such as the BlackBerry (www.rim.com), allowing professionals to check and send e-mail while on the move. This enforces the message that professionals prefer simple services providing flexibility based on complex underlying infrastructures. However, the more this technology disappears into the fabric of everyday life, the more problematic it can turn out to be, as the recent term "Crackberries" indicates (Mazmanian, Orlikowski, & Yates, 2005). We conclude that the successes of mobilizing technologies have not been mirrored by an increase in embedded services and applications. Technologies still occupy a front stage for the users. They are inadequate, intrusive, and a constant area of concern. The ubiquitous vision is still an opaque reality.

The Vision of Ubiquitous Computing

One of the characteristics of many contemporary ICT innovations is the duality of a client application based on a common infrastructure, such as the mobile phone (King & Lyytinen, 2003). Another is that the technologies are shifting from traditionally supporting information management and transactions toward supporting computer-mediated interaction (Braa & Sandahl, 2000). This implies that technologies will increasingly relate directly to the social context in which they are used—for example, the mobile phone storing a list of names and phone numbers, or the workflow management system through coordination mechanisms modeling a collaborative work process (Sørensen, 2003; Sørensen, Kakihara, & Mathiassen, 2002). In this sense, we would argue that one of the persistent developments during the past 20 years is the increasing representation and modeling of the social in the technical. The vision of the ubiquitous computing CM can be viewed as the ultimate convergence of the social and the technical. Here, there is no longer any distinction between the two. The technical has disappeared before our eyes and subsumed itself both in the social and in our understanding of what is in fact technical and what is social. Ubiquitous computing represents the utopian realization of human–computer interaction

(Banavar et al., 2000). As Mark Weiser stated in his 1991 paper: "the most profound technologies are those that disappear ... they weave themselves into the fabric of everyday life until they are indistinguishable from it." He further argues that when technology "disappear[s]" we can focus on the true organizational tasks, "we are freed to use them without thinking and so to focus beyond them on new goals" (Weiser, 1991). Weiser further argues that we will truly realize the practice of ubiquitous computing when machines "fit the human environment instead of forcing humans to enter theirs [which] will make using a computer as refreshing as taking a walk in the woods" (Weiser, 1991). Lyytinen and Yoo (2002) explain the vision in terms of nomadic information environments consisting of infrastructures and services critically relying on the convergence of core technologies, support for mobility, and mass scale diffusion.

Current ICT developments from the corporate mainframe in the 1970s have led us from centralized support via personal desktop and laptop computers, toward a whole range of personalized or person-centric technologies (Kalakota & Robinson, 2002; Sørensen, 2005). Mark Weiser explained developments in terms of the historical development from the mainframe era with many people using one computer, over the PC era characterized by one person using one computer, to ubiquitous computing signaling one person using many computers (Weiser, 1999).

Ubiquitous computing can also be characterized by distinguishing between the degree of mobility of the technology and the degree of embeddedness (Lyytinen, 2003). The terms pervasive and ubiquitous computing are frequently used synonymously, but in this chapter we will separate the two in a distinction between high and low degree of mobility of embedded computing. As illustrated in Figure 17.1, ubiquitous computing is characterized by high degrees of both mobility and embeddedness, whereas mobile computing and pervasive computing have low degrees of embeddedness and pervasiveness, respectively. The extent to which computational capability is embedded is generally related to the extent to which the technology records information about its environment. A standard PC, for example, is a stationary technology, generally unaware of most aspects of its surroundings, such as its place in the world beyond an IP address, and the person operating it, beyond some chosen user name. A laptop is essentially a more mobile variant of the PC. An advanced washing machine that constantly measures the quality of the water, the degree of dirt on the clothes, and interactively chooses the washing program according to certain conditions has a high degree of embeddedness, although it is a stationary technology. The mobile phone is to some extent aware of its surroundings in that it will constantly negotiate access to base stations and therefore have information concerning its location. However, the vision of ubiquitous

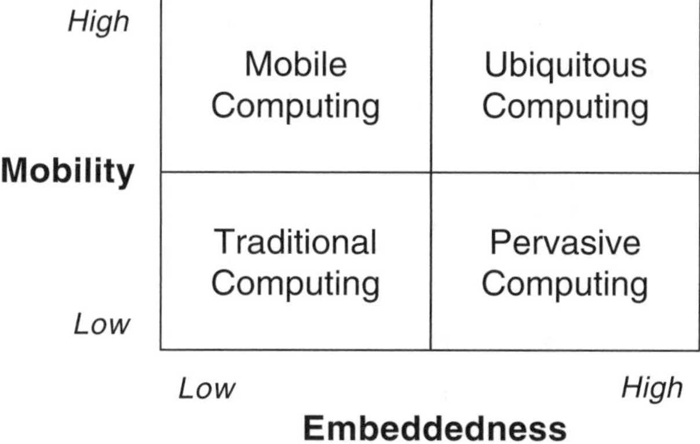

Figure 17.1 Characterizing ubiquitous computing

computing is one where a multitude of environmental aspects are engaged with largely uncertain consequences and where computing can both disappear onto the body, as well as into the physical environment (Albrecht & McIntyre, 2006; Mann & Niedzviecki, 2002; McCollough, 2004; Norman, 1999; Sørensen, Yoo, Lyytinen, & DeGross, 2005).

Ishii and Ullmar (1997) expand on Weiser's vision by observing that the world operates in that of "computation" (bits) and that of the physical (atoms). Ishii and Ullmar's goal is to forge a much stronger relationship between the two, as they set out to describe and design a world in which both atoms and bits meet in unison (Abowd, Mynatt, & Rodden, 2002). Norman (1999) discusses the development from generalized computers to information appliances. Moving into a ubiquitous computing environment calls for an interdisciplinary approach in order to understand and model both the world of digits and the world in which we live and interact (Estrin, Culler, Pister, & Sukhatme, 2002).

A large number of research programs and projects have explored mainly technical challenges in establishing ubiquitous computing. Three of the most prolific people in the field are Alan Kay with his vision of the Dynabook (en.wikipedia.org/wiki/Dynabook), Steve Mann who since the early 1980s has spent considerable time wearing cameras and computers (wearcam.org), and Kevin Warwick who has experimented with the organic merger of humans and computational elements (www.kevinwarwick.com/Cyborg2.htm) (Mann & Niedzviecki, 2002; Press, 1992; Warwick, 2002). The European Union Program *The Disappearing Computer* (www.disappearing-computer.net) has funded projects aimed at creating ubiquitous computing artifacts and studying how these artifacts could interact and support new user experiences.

Since 1999, the ubiquitous computing research community has organized conferences on ubiquitous computing (ubicomp.org) and a number of academic journals. Most of this research is exclusively guided by an engineering or design rationale aimed at pushing the technical limits. Although some of the research employs empirical studies, these will almost always serve the direct purpose of informing the design process. There is little research that aims directly at understanding how the realities of working life with computers relate to the visions of ubiquitous computing.

Professionals in Workplace Interaction

There has generally been a lack of empirical validation and fieldwork that look at professionals' work practices and new technology-mediated styles of interaction (Kakihara & Sørensen, 2004; Nardi, Whittaker, & Schwarz, 2002). Abowd et al. (2002) suggest "there has been surprisingly little research published from an evaluation or end-user perspective in the ubiquitous computing community." This study showed how modern professionals manage their information and interaction, and how they view the role of the ICT they choose to use. There is, in particular, among highly skilled and specialized knowledge workers, a significant element of choice regarding what technologies are adopted and how they are applied (Robertson, Sørensen, & Swan, 2001). Modern professionals must, as members of teams in knowledge-intensive organizations, be able to flexibly make decisions, interact with a large number of people, and often be highly geographically mobile (Kakihara, Sørensen, & Wiberg, 2004). They must be able to work fluidly, buy and sell at real-time speeds, advise, approve, inquire, develop relationships, coordinate, collaborate, communicate, and problem-solve on a daily basis. The adoption of new technologies, especially the widespread adoption of mobile phones and networked information systems, has provided these professionals with the ability to work both away from the office and while traveling, transcending both space and time with respect to device and human action, respectively (Dix, et al., 2000).

Past research of theoretical work focuses on a narrow brand of organizational interpersonal communication such as interactions that are *extended, multiparty, formal, and one-shot* (Egido, Galegher, & Kraut, 1990; Whittaker, Frohlich, & Daly-Jones, 1994; Wiberg & Ljungberg, 2001) instead off those that are ongoing, informal, person-to-person, and flexible (Dahlbom & Ljungberg, 1998; Nardi, et al., 2002). Castells (1996) links the technological development in the 1970s to the culture of freedom, individual innovation, and entrepreneurialism, which grew out of the American university campuses of the 1960s and created the "global village" that led to a dramatic increase in project and team-based cooperation.

Technologies, including desktop video conferencing, mobile phones, collaborative software, PDAs, and Internet/intranet systems, converge to forge the foundation of providing professionals with the tools to respond to the threats of the business environment. This new workplace would be unrestrained by geography, time, and organizational boundaries; it would be a virtual workplace where productivity, flexibility, and collaboration reach unprecedented levels (Townsend, Demarie, & Hendrickson, 1998). While the tools and technological environments used to gain agility lie at the heart of this paper, Weiser (1991) states that a technological device is only a transitional step toward achieving the real potential of IT. He extends this notion by explaining that the devices used by workers cannot be accountable for the true nature of ubiquitous computing. Instead, the nature of ubiquitous computing lies not in the technology itself, but rather in the human psychology of the technology disappearing. Dahlbom and Ljungberg (1998) describe the term flexibility as an ideal scenario, in which professionals can use technology to leverage their ability to conduct work beyond geographical and temporal constraints. In establishing a technologically flexible work environment, the professional gains and creates fluidity of work practices (Schwarz, Nardi, & Whittaker, 1999). However, as argued by several, mobile technologies can result in interaction overload through the inherent asymmetry of interaction (Goffman, 1959; Kakihara, et al., 2004; Nardi & Whittaker, 2000).

In order to better understand state-of-the-art technology use, we conducted a series of 16 interviews with professionals over a three-week period during the months of June and July 2002. The interviews were all recorded in participants' workplaces in London, except one interview conducted by phone to New York. The aim of the interviews was to explore how the professionals utilized ICT for performing their daily tasks. All interviews were tape-recorded and each lasted around one hour. The interviewees were mostly high-level professionals and executives, or knowledge workers (Newell, Robertson, Scarbrough, & Swan, 2002; Robertson, Sørensen, & Swan, 2000). Therefore, the sample is not representative in a broader demographic sense, but is biased toward highly skilled and educated professionals and selected to represent modern professionals experiencing the demands of modern working practices in terms of accelerated pace, a dynamic constellation of professional relationships, and an advanced use of ICT (Schwarz, et al., 1999). See Table 17.1 for an outline of the interviewees.

Professionals' Working Life with Technologies

Our study demonstrates that not only do professionals rely heavily on a range of ICT, but also that professionals must devote time almost on a

Table 17.1 Interviewee Profiles

	Title and Job Nature
1	Managing Director Global Investment Bank
2	European Digital Advertising Director
3	Hedge Fund Manager
4	Pediatric Surgeon
5	Construction Project Manager
6	IT Director
7	IT Entrepreneur
8	Energy Broker
9	Accountant
10	Investment Banker
11	Security Consultant – Information Technology
12	Chief Executive Officer – Interactive Marketing
13	Business Consultant – Information Technology
14	Vice President – ICT solutions provider
15	Christian Chaplain – Religious Work
16	Global Business Development Executive

daily basis to select, configure, tinker with, and reflect upon their core technologies. This immediately produces a tension between the ideal visions generated by the ubiquitous computing CM promising easy and unburdened use of the technology, and the experienced reality where the technology will often be in the way. The research documents crucial encounters between professionals and their technologies of choice or rejection. It shows a rich picture of multiple complex technologies and services that do not effortlessly recede into the background. As argued by the Business Consultant "… all of my devices add some complexity to work." One of the aspects emphasized is that the professionals frequently change context of work and that technology use must be adapted to a given context, as voiced by the Entrepreneur: "It's context-specific, you use different tools in different situations."

We found two main barriers for widespread mobile and ubiquitous support: bandwidth and battery life. In a changing business environment, professionals must be given the tools and resources to respond effectively to those changes. Some business environments change more rapidly than others. Real-time industries such as financial institutions are good examples. The Hedge Fund Manager and the Energy Trader both work in high real-time industries. The current state of technology dictates that they must be positioned at broadband network PC terminals in order to cope at real-time speeds. This implies that they cannot easily rely on personalized mobile and wireless solutions simply due to the lack of bandwidth. The Hedge Fund Manager stated that the only instrument he would require to do his job anywhere would be a broadband connection. The Investment Banker's biggest frustration with the technological environment was that it was slow. Out of the 16 people interviewed, three stated that battery life acted as a limitation of flexibility. As connection bandwidth constantly improves through the roll-out of 3G and WiFi services, in particular, battery life seems to be a major technical challenge (Malone, 2004).

E-mail was used by all 16 professionals. In fact, all but one of the participants used e-mail as the primary communication tool for work practices. The interactive marketing CEO stated that e-mail provided the ability to communicate complex ideas instantaneously. The Vice President emphasized that e-mail only provides data and not always the proper context for interpreting the data into information. The Accountant argued that e-mail is information-rich since he felt that it provided him with a comprehensive source of information. The Advertising Account Director argued that e-mail enabled him to get important points across. The Vice President of the technology company pointed out that:

> E-mail is for CYA. Cover Your Ass, because you need a trail. Unfortunately, too many people are concerned with that so they use a phone. I like the phone to solve problems because the phone is synchronous, so you talk to them and you make them come up with a resolution right then and there, whereas e-mail doesn't provide you with the definitive response.

The complete reliance on e-mail coupled with increased demands for flexible and mobile working can be viewed as key explanations of why several professionals voiced great interest in BlackBerry technology (www.rim.com), which supports instant global access to e-mail from small handheld terminals. It represents a simple client technology offering a highly flexible networking service of providing mobile access to e-mail, but based on a highly complex, underlying infrastructure (Mathiassen & Sørensen, 2002). For the professional, being able to envision the immediate benefits of adopting the technology and investing time in learning how to use it is essential, as clearly demonstrated by Robertson et al. (2001).

Whereas several interviewees mentioned the BlackBerry e-mail client as an interesting and desirable technology, the general PDA was considered far from the preferred work tool. The Advertising Director explained that: "I just realized that hey, this is an extra device, it's not a productivity device, so I sold them all on e-Bay and I'm glad they're gone." The Entrepreneur reaffirmed this sentiment by stating that he had two PDAs but did not use either of them. He had made several attempts to use PDA technology but felt that the usability of the device is still far too low for the technology to be useful. Only one out of all of the interviewees admitted to having an active relationship with a PDA, which was used when traveling and then only for reading downloaded Web articles while commuting on the underground train. Thus, in this study, only one professional found the PDA useful and only in relation to the ability to access the Web. This is quite similar to previous research results with regard to the influence of networking services on the usefulness of mobile phones, instant messaging, and e-mail. Flexible networking services can easily influence users' perceptions that the technology itself is useful, even if the technology involves associated negative consequences such as information and interaction overload (Ljungberg & Sørensen, 2000). In contrast, the lack of flexible networking services in most of the PDAs used by the interviewed professionals led to a relative lack of successful adoption. It represents yet another gadget that takes up time and effort in terms of synchronizing contents while it offers a complex and uncertain set of potential benefits including flexible networking services. The rejection of PDA technology has also been documented by Jonathan Allen in Chapter 4 of this volume discussing the failure from a design perspective. The failure of PDAs supporting learning in the U.K. health sector has also been documented (Wiredu, 2005; Wiredu & Sørensen, 2006).

The phone naturally formed a core technology for professionals. The Investment Banker categorized the phone as a medium used to indicate importance: "If it's important, call me; if it's not, then send me an e-mail." The Global Business Development Executive stated that she decided to use the phone in sensitive cases, since the phone conversation provided contextual information about the other party, with faster and more tailored feedback. The Chief Executive Officer argued that phone calls provided extra details to speed up the processes of a business deal. The Construction Project Manager concurred and stated that the telephone facilitated a quick response to time-sensitive problems. The IT Security Consultant distinguished between functional and more psychological aspects of phone conversations:

> If I have my mobile phone, I know I can be anywhere and not worry about it … the phone is for directness, and you can infer a lot from peoples' tone of voice that you can't get from e-mail. E-mail, I think, is more political, because you're writing it for

a purpose and a point, as opposed to a telephone conversation, which is more interactive.

Whereas the crucial communication technologies such as e-mail and the phone are digital, we found evidence for the continued reliance on the traditional ubiquitous IT: paper. However, the research also points to a progression toward a "paperless" office. Several of the professionals indicated the desire to implement paperless work, an issue contended by research (Sellen & Harper, 2003). The IT Director reported the psychological attachment to paper with some people displaying the "must-print-it-to-feel-it-to-have-it" mentality. The Vice President stated that he printed most documents, as he found it easier to read on print than on screen. Several professionals reported that their organizations were implementing the paperless office to increase efficiency, and in general there was a desire to engage in paperless working. The Construction Project Manager voiced his frustration with a paper-based office in that accessing information via a computer would be easier. The Pediatric Surgeon stated that in hospitals, most of the paper-based information should be digitized, as it would facilitate instant access. Paper, however, displays such a diversity of uses, pervasiveness, and flexibility in use that it is very difficult to replace (Hughes & King, 1993). It can be argued that removing paper from work processes around the world will be incredibly difficult, if not impossible (Sellen & Harper, 2003). The ways in which paper is brought into use may change, but the precise ubiquitous nature of paper-based documents being micro-mobile (Luff & Heath, 1998) carriers of information brings with it a highly standardized storage medium and utilizes a very stable reader technology—humans. In this sense, paper is perhaps one of the primary obstacles for ubiquitous computing since it represents an already established ubiquitous information infrastructure. Living in a world with both paper-based and electronic infrastructures requires scanners and printers acting as gateways between the two.

Instant messaging was seen as one of the most popular and context-rich means of social interaction. The Entrepreneur felt that his MSN Messenger conversations could be quite innovative, in particular when engaging in multi-party conversations where many creative ideas emerged. For him, the global availability of MSN Messenger was important. The Energy Broker dedicated three screens to the Instant Messenger at one of his work-stations and had around 30 of his clients engaging in online discussions with him at any time. He argued that introducing instant messaging technology had reduced phone calls by 50 percent. However, as argued by the Entrepreneur, the de-contextualization (Kallinikos, 2001) of face and body language would easily lead to confrontations and difficult situations.

Videoconferencing garnered negative reactions from the participants. All of the participants who commented about videoconferencing found it to be imperfect. As argued by the Business Development Executive, it was found to be unsuccessful and would need to support an atmosphere similar to that of meetings. The IT Director explained a scenario where a salesperson at his company was advised to avoid a trip to Germany by using videoconferencing, when in fact the clients preferred a face-to-face meeting. He further claimed that the videoconferencing vendors and proponents played down the real differences between co-located meetings and videoconferencing experienced by all users in the organization. The Investment Banker argued that at times, videoconferencing had proven effective when budget or time constraints had made traveling unfeasible, but that bankers mostly prefer face-to-face meetings. The attitudes toward videoconferencing show that the overwhelming favorite means of communication of course was face-to-face meetings. This coincides with the research of Keisler, Boh, Ren, and Weisbrod (Chapter 9, this volume) in which they studied a low-tech company that preferred face-to-face meetngs over virtual distributed work. This supports the stark distinction between the context-rich fluidity of face-to-face communication and the lack of flexibility that current technology provides. The Technology Vice President completely disregarded technology for providing any context for interpreting information. The Entrepreneur expanded that comment by saying that there were limitations to the use of the technology, and that it will never become a replacement for face-to-face interaction. The voiced preference of face-to-face conversations as opposed to video-mediated ones has been widely discussed in the literature (Heath & Luff, 2000; Olson & Olson, 2000).

However, when comparing the advantages of videoconferences over face-to-face meetings, expectations of videoconferences creating a sense of physical presence can probably never be realized. By using certain mediating technologies, we adopt notions of presence over time. We accept telephone presence because we are used to talking to others over the phone. We may perhaps establish a similar, yet distinct, notion of presence when connecting and interacting with others through instant messaging. We may even eventually develop some behavioral patterns accommodating 3G mobile videophone conferencing. However, in neither of these examples would we characterize the un-mediated and the mediated situations as the same.

Infrastructure Issues

The previous section discussed the client technologies used by the interviewees. This section focuses on the underlying issues of infrastructure standardization (Lyytinen, 2003). The infrastructure issues related to problems regarding limitations of standardization can be divided into three groups: standardization of information sources, standardization between devices, and standardization of networks. The vision of the ubiquitous computing CM is essentially hinging upon the widespread availability of standardized and interoperable technologies. The problems associated with early 3G mobile phone systems integrating 2G and 3G technology demonstrated the problems associated with increasingly complex infrastructures. And as ubiquitous computing critically relies on standards, understanding problems of use is an essential part of critically reassessing the visions of this CM.

Regarding information source standardization, the Entrepreneur highlighted lack of real-time file sharing as a major limitation. He further emphasized the practical difficulties in maintaining consistent versions of documents, appointments, and messages across several computers. The Investment Banker, whose organization created a mandate of a "paperless" office, explained that there is no information standardization between the offices in London and Toronto. This attests to the lack of coordination and standardization between the information sources of the two parts of the same organization. The Advertising Account Director explained how he had to extract a file from the server at work and download it onto the hard drive of his laptop. He then proceeded to take the file on his laptop to Paris and amend the update to the file with his client. Once the changes were completed in Paris, he then traveled back to London in order to transfer the file from his laptop back to the server at work. He argued that a real-time standardization of information transfer would greatly save the time and the effort of extracting, changing, and replacing the files. The professionals clearly expressed the need for collaborative services providing a shared workspace, awareness support, and coordination mechanisms (Mathiassen & Sørensen, forthcoming). These collaborative services would, in more substantial ways than networking services, support collaboration across working contexts.

Device standardization relates to the convergence of multiple devices into one, or the provision of easy interoperability of several devices. The IT Security Consultant expressed frustration with the lack of integration between devices. The Business Consultant confirmed this when outlining his ideal technological set-up. He would like a centralization of his important information on a server combined with device-convergence so that instead of four or five devices, he would only need one or two. The devices would ideally be synchronized from the server. Some aspects of this service have been implemented in Apple's iSync (www.apple.com/isync), allowing users to synchronize address book data, bookmarks, and appointments between PC, laptop, PDA, iPod, and mobile phone via a centralized server.

Standardization between devices is closely related to standardization of information sources. This is also an important issue related to the support for flexible working practices as well as enabling a more efficient support infrastructure for this style of collaboration (Al-Taitoon & Sørensen, 2004; Braa & Sandahl, 2000). Device standardization would encompass the mobile phone, the PDA, the Internet, and any other device that is used. Illustrating some of the experienced complications, the Managing Director stated that in order to get his laptop connected to the Internet he would engage in a complex procedure:

> [Y]ou've got your pin numbers, you've got your bank card, your personal stuff, work ID, telephone ID, mobile phone, voice mail, and it's impossible to remember all of the different security codes. So I'm in China and I have to figure out what phone to use and I have to boot it up and I figure out passwords and get all that in, then I got to figure out where I'm dialing in to ... you need some type of standardization otherwise you have different people using different systems; it just doesn't work ... when you're in different countries and you need different adapters for the plugs and the phones and things like that.

Network standardization, or connectivity, was the most heavily criticized problem. As argued by the Managing Director, the technology must work and it must work everywhere. The Advertising Director illustrated network standardization problems with the example of continually logging on and off when moving the laptop from one IP connection to another and thus, changing network addresses. Obviously some of these problems have technical solutions, such as the increasingly popular wireless network connections. The Construction Project Manager voiced frustration with not being able to fulfill others' expectations of being constantly available and in touch. The IT Director pointed out the need for the networking infrastructure to at least function in hotels. As the mobile professional will spend many working hours in the early mornings and evenings in their hotel room, providing easy and flexible network connections here is important. Standardization between networks was a predominant complaint with real-time professionals such as stock traders, brokers, and hedge fund managers, as opposed to project based professionals such as sales people, strategists, and accountants. As argued by the Hedge Fund Manager, "timeliness in everything—anything that is recorded is technically out of date. Information is out of date in an hour or two." This can attest to the fact that the need for coordination and standardization between networks is crucial for the professional's agility. The Energy Broker highlighted this by arguing that flexibility essentially boils down to accessibility, and was supported by the Investment Banker who argued that daily operations consist of constantly emerging decision making and that not being available for half an hour was highly problematic.

As an infrastructure can be characterized as enabling, pervasive, and in the background, then a ubiquitous computing environment can be viewed as an infrastructure. Regarding the standardization of networks, the professionals' comments clearly demonstrate some highly pragmatic obstacles for the much touted "anytime, any where" society (Kleinrock, 1996), such as the complexity of juggling phone and power adapters, along with corporate login procedures and ISP telephone numbers. Most of the highly successful services are networking services where the essential aspect is the infrastructure standardizing the connection (Sørensen, et al., 2002). Standardizing the information infrastructure elements is an ongoing process. For example, the Open Mobile Alliance (www.openmobilealliance.org) is working on the SyncML standard for synchronizing data from mobile wireless clients.

On a more substantial note, the ubiquitous computing CM has essentially hinged its visions on the notion of any time, anywhere access to computing and networking resources. The assumption has simply been that flexible, fluid individual choices are what make up a working day. However, much work is tied by temporal and spatial constraints, and even if that is not the case, the genuine ability to work freely, wherever and whenever desired, in a competitive job market, implies that the choice of where and when to engage in work will be a strategic aspect of work (Cousins & Robey, 2005; Kakihara, et al., 2004; Sørensen, 2004; Wiberg & Ljungberg, 2001).

Ubiquitous Visions—Opaque Realities

Mobile phones, laptops, and mobile e-mail clients may indeed integrate entirely into everyday practices of professionals. Several studies have shown this group's reliance on advanced mobile technologies, such as highly mobile Tokyo professionals (Kakihara, 2003), off-premise foreign exchange traders, global bank executives (Al-Taitoon, 2005), health professionals (Wiredu, 2005), police officers (Pica, 2006), and a range of other roles (Andriessen & Vartiainen, 2005; Krogstie, Kautz, & Allen, 2005; Lattanzi, Korhonen, & Gopalakrishnan, 2006; Sørensen, et al., 2005). Several research efforts have explored how mobile technologies, in general, and the mobile phone, in particular, integrate into everyday life (Brown et al., 2001; Hamill & Lasen, 2005; Harper, Palen, & Taylor, 2005; Katz & Aakhus, 2002; Licoppe, 2004; Ling, 2002; Ling, 2004; Rheingold, 2002). The near future may bring new and sophisticated location and context-based mobile services further supporting remote collaboration (Dix, et al., 2000;

McCollough, 2004; Schiller & Voisard, 2004; Sørensen, 2005). However, the essential role of these technologies and their associated services are governed by the social conditions in which they are functioning—an aspect that is mainly introduced in the ubiquitous computing CM when it serves the purpose of the discourse.

The mere fact that the technology mediates interaction implies that this is not merely an issue of connecting people, but rather recognizing that distance matters (Olson & Olson, 2000). The symmetrical connections between people are not merely connections in a vacuum. The knowledge shared by both parties that a mobile phone call is a personal request from one person to another implies that refusing to answer implicitly can be viewed as a rejection of an offer to connect. As individuals essentially are deeply concerned with others' impression of them, the technology may disappear into the background, but the other people forming part of the interaction will certainly not (Goffman, 1959). This implies that a situation that can be conceived, from a technological perspective, as a fluid work arrangement may indeed, from a social perspective, involve significant issues of unease, disturbances, and discomfort (Kakihara & Sørensen, 2004; Pica & Kakihara, 2003; Whittle, 2005; Wiberg & Whittaker, 2005). Furthermore, from the individual's point of view, the simple negotiation with the technology of settings and preferences, is work in itself—an aspect of the articulation of work (Strauss, Fagerhaugh, Suczek, & Wiener, 1985). Jointly, people engage in processes of articulating work in terms of arranging when and how to coordinate work (Schmidt & Simone, 1996; Wiberg & Whittaker, 2005). The reason there is no need to pay attention to wristwatches and glasses is that these technologies do not support the negotiation of mutual interdependencies with others, nor do they offer symmetrical connections that must be negotiated in asymmetrical social contexts.

As with computer-supported cooperative work technology, it cannot be assumed that the general uptake of advanced ubiquitous computing services will lead to specific and generally agreed-upon outcomes. There may be widely different views of what the technology actually is and also widely different interests concerning its purpose (Karsten, 1995; Orlikowski, 1993; Robertson, et al., 2001). Furthermore, the extent to which ubiquitous technologies offer interpretive flexibility implies that their use will engage complex processes of mutual adjustment and social conditioning in order to become embedded (Ling & Pedersen, 2005). Ubiquitous technologies are social technologies to the extent that they offer rudimentary or complex representations of social action and actors. The closer the proximity of the technologies to the body and mind, the more easily they become coupled and uncoupled (Sørensen & Pica, 2005). Imagine a heads-up display showing the screen of a mobile phone. Such a close connection would make network operator SMS messages urging the user to switch networks much more disruptive than if the phone is in a handbag or pocket. This coupling and uncoupling of the technology is an essential and unavoidable aspect of using personal technology for communication, and we can characterize this in terms of rhythms of interaction (Pica, 2006; Sørensen & Pica, 2005).

So, even if the essential issue of battery life is entirely resolved with fuel cells or other purely technological advances, life with ubiquitous computing will still be very much devoted to engaging with and negotiating the use of technology, rather than one resulting in the technology disappearing in a puff of smoke as though invisible as predicted by Weiser (Weiser, 1991). For one, more advanced networked features connecting heterogeneous technologies may even lead to a growing need for regular reboots of things that previously did not even contain computers such as blenders, toasters, and TVs.

The combined consequences of mass diffusion of converging mobile technologies have enabled dramatic developments where computer technologies have been redefined as both mobile and pervasive. Technological developments have made this possible, but it has also been accomplished based on a demand for computing power in increasingly mobile settings (Norman, 1999; Sørensen, 2003). The current debate distinguishes between the issue of mobility and the issue of embeddedness, where mobile informatics focuses on the socio-technical use of mobile technologies, while the debate over ubiquitous computing focuses more on embedding these mobile technologies so they disappear. When considering successful technologies supporting professionals, there is extensive use of mobile technologies, such as mobile phones and laptops, although much less for PDAs. Mobilizing computing and communication is a significant technical challenge and this study showed how bandwidth problems and lack of standardization caused constant problems. Nonetheless, the respondents generally required extensive mobile technologies enabling them to be connected continuously. However, the study clearly showed that the computing support was by no means embedded and pervasive. It was a constant source of conversation, problems, and negotiation.

When we review much of the research conducted within the fields of mobile and ubiquitous computing, it seems that the mobilization of the technology itself has been much more successful than the widespread growth of pervasive computing power. The vision of the computer disappearing from sight and into walls, cars, appliances, and us is still strong, but the realities of modern working life remain focused on the visible and disruptive, rather than disappearing technologies. Embedding computers into toasters, washing machines, and cars has been a much more successful endeavor than providing pervasive support for working processes. Perhaps we need to redefine the notion of embedding in a human and social context. It could be argued that the extent to which wristwatches and glasses represent ubiquitous technologies in that they are ever-present and glide into the background as essential everyday appliances, then mobile phones may be rapidly assuming the same position.

Most research in ubiquitous computing seems to be concerned with establishing new infrastructures and with building new technical gadgets utilizing these infrastructures. Few empirical studies explore state-of-the-art technology experiences. This could be interpreted as relying extensively on a traditional model for scientific innovation where the research effort drives technology development, which, in turn, increases the general welfare of society. However, the relationship is much more complex (King & Lyytinen, 2003). It can be argued that with flexible platform technologies, the ways in which technologies are used determine their true characteristics. Also, in terms of state-of-the-art technology use, the world of organizational practices may be less technologically advanced than hypothetical technological settings. The mere complexity of real-life technology use will not be captured in small-scale laboratory design projects. Hence, the proper understanding of the technological possibilities for establishing ubiquitous computing environments is only possible in the context of organizational settings. Consequently, research on the design of ubiquitous technologies must be accompanied by proper understanding of the everyday practices of people.

The Internet-era challenge of obliterating distance has been replaced with a much earthier vision of contextual computing and social computing (McCollough, 2004). This particular vision emphasizes the role of places, spaces, contexts, and the specific as opposed to the ubiquitous computing CM where space has no meaning and is obliterated (Cairncross, 1997; Kleinrock, 1996). Visions of proximity-based social software and context-based computing may well be a part of a future CM, one that will deserve to be scrutinized and tested not just on technological merits, but on the realities of social context as well. Recently, there has even been an emerging trend that can be called an anti-computerization movement, headed by Nicholas Carr (2003, 2004). As a response to the crash of the technologically driven visions of the so-called dot-com era, Carr formulates the thesis that in many organizations, ICT should be viewed as a utility along the lines of water, electricity, and gas. Since the mutual interrelationships between business objectives, technology support, and actual actions are highly complex, it is highly unlikely that any given technology will be adopted in the same way across different contexts. What therefore is needed is to engage in critical examination of the assumptions of any CM to investigate its impact and strength.

References

Abowd, G., Mynatt, E., & Rodden, T. (2002). The human experience. *IEEE Pervasive Computing, Mobile and Ubiquitous Systems*, 1, 56.

Al-Taitoon, A. (2005). *Making sense of mobile ICT-enabled trading in fast moving financial markets as volatility-control ambivalence: Case study on the organisation of off-premises foreign exchange at a middle-east bank.* Unpublished Ph.D. Dissertation, London School of Economics, London.

Al-Taitoon, A., & Sørensen, C. (2004). Supporting mobile professionals in global banking: The role of global ICT-support call-centres. *Journal of Computing and Information Technology*, 12(4), 297–308.

Albrecht, K., & McIntyre, L. (2006). *Spychips: How major corporations and government plan to track your every move with RFID.* Nashville, TN: Nelson Current.

Andriessen, J. H. E., & Vartiainen, M. (Eds.). (2005). *Mobile virtual work: A new paradigm?* Berlin: Springer.

Banavar, G., Beck, J., Gluzberg, E., Munson, J., Sussman, J., & Zukowski, D. (2000). *Challenges: An application model for pervasive computing.* Paper presented at the Sixth Annual ACM/IEEE International Conference on Mobile Computing and Networking.

Braa, K., & Sandahl, T. I. (2000). Documents: From paperwork to network. In K. Braa, C. Sørensen, & B. Dahlbom (Eds.), *Planet Internet* (pp. 41–64). Lund, Sweden: Studentliteratur.

Brown, B., Green, N., & Harper, R. (Eds.). (2001). *Wireless world.* London: Springer-Verlag.

Cairncross, F. (1997). *The death of distance: How the communications revolution will change our lives.* Boston: Harvard Business School Press.

Carr, N. G. (2003, May). IT Doesn't Matter. *Harvard Business Review.*

Carr, N. G. (2004). *Does IT Matter? Information technology and the corrosion of competitive advantage.* Boston: Harvard Business School Press.

Castells, M. (1996). *The rise of the network society.* Oxford: Blackwell.

Cousins, K. C., & Robey, D. (2005). Human agency in a wireless world: Patterns of technology use in nomadic computing environments. *Information and Organization*, 15, 151–180.

Dahlbom, B., & Ljungberg, F. (1998). Mobile informatics. *Scandinavian Journal of Information Systems*, 10(1/2), 227–234.

Dix, A., Rodden, T., Davies, N., Trevor, J., Friday, A., & Palfreyman, K. (2000). Exploiting space and location as a design framework for interactive mobile systems. *ACM Transactions on Computer-Human Interaction*, 7(3), 285–321.

Egido, C., Galegher, J. R., & Kraut, R. (1990). *Intellectual teamwork: Social and technological foundations of cooperative work.* Hillsdale, NJ: L. Erlbaum Associates.

Estrin, D., Culler, D., Pister, K., & Sukhatme, G. (2002). Connecting the physical world with pervasive networks. *Pervasive Computing*, 1(1), 59–69.

Goffman, E. (1959). *The presentation of self in everyday life.* New York: Bantam.

Hamill, L., & Lasen, A. (Eds.). (2005). *Mobile world: Past, present and future.* London: Springer.

Harper, R., Palen, L., & Taylor, A. (Eds.). (2005). *The inside text: Social, cultural and design perspectives on SMS.* Dordrecht, The Netherlands: Springer.

Heath, C., & Luff, P. (2000). *Technology in action.* Cambridge, U.K.: Cambridge University Press.

Hughes, J. A., & King, V. (1993). Paperwork. In S. Benford & J. Mariani (Eds.), *COMIC Deliverable 4.1: Requirements and metaphors of shared interaction* (pp. 153–170). Lancaster, U.K.: Lancaster University.

Iacono, S., & Kling, R. (2001). Computerization movements: The rise of the Internet and distant forms of work. In J. A. Yates & J. Van Maanen (Eds.), *Information technology and organizational transformation: History, rhetoric, and practice* (pp. 93–136). Thousand Oaks, CA: Sage Publications.

Ishii, H., & Ullmar, B. (1997). Tangible bits: Towards seamless interfaces between people, bits and atoms. *Proceedings of the ACM Conference on Human Factors in Computing Systems*, CHI' 97, Atlanta, GA.

Kakihara, M. (2003). *Emerging work practices of ICT-enabled mobile professionals.* Unpublished Ph.D. Dissertation, The London School of Economics and Political Science, London.

Kakihara, M., & Sørensen, C. (2004). Practicing mobile professional work: Tales of locational, operational, and interactional mobility. *INFO: The Journal of Policy, Regulation and Strategy for Telecommunication, Information and Media*, 6(3), 180–187.

Kakihara, M., Sørensen, C., & Wiberg, M. (2004). Negotiating the fluidity of mobile work. In M. Wiberg (Ed.), *The interaction society: Practice, theories, & supportive technologies* (Chapter 7), Hershey, PA: Idea Group Inc.

Kalakota, R., & Robinson, M. (2002). *M business: The race to mobility*. New York: McGraw-Hill.

Kallinikos, J. (2001). *Recalcitrant technology: Cross-contextual systems and context-embedded action*. Unpublished manuscript, London.

Karsten, H. (1995). "It's like everyone working around the same desk": Organisational readings of Lotus Notes. *Scandinavian Journal of Information Systems*, 7(1), 3–32.

Katz, J. E., & Aakhus, M. (Eds.). (2002). *Perpetual contact*. Cambridge, U.K.: Cambridge University Press.

King, J., & Lyytinen, K. (2003). When grasp exceeds reach: Will fortifying our theoretical core save the information systems (IS) field? In T. Järvi & P. Reijonen (Eds.), *People and computers: Twenty-one ways of looking at information systems: Festschrift Celebrating Markku Nurminen's 60th Birthday* (Vol. TUCS General Publication No. 26, ISBN 952-12-1178-4, pp. 143–165). Turku, Finland: Turku Centre for Computer Science, Finland.

Kleinrock, L. (1996). Nomadicity: Anytime, anywhere in a disconnected world. *Mobile Networks and Applications*, 1, 351–357.

Krogstie, J., Kautz, K., & Allen, D. (Eds.). (2005). *Mobile information systems II: IFFIP working conference on mobile information.* New York, NY: Springer-Verlag.

Lattanzi, M., Korhonen, A., & Gopalakrishnan, V. (2006). *Work goes mobile: Nokia's lessons from the leading edge*. Chichester, England: John Wiley & Sons.

Licoppe, C. (2004). Connected presence: The emergence of a new repertoire for managing social relationships in a changing communication technoscape. *Environment and Planning D: Society and Space*, 22, 135–156.

Ling, R. (2002). *The social juxtaposition of mobile telephone conversations and public spaces.* Paper presented at the International Conference of the Social Consequences of Mobiles Phones, Chuchon, Korea.

Ling, R. (2004). *The mobile connection: The cell phone's impact on society*. Amsterdam: Morgan Kaufmann.

Ling, R., & Pedersen, P. E. (Eds.). (2005). *Mobile communications: Re-negotiation of the social sphere*. London: Springer.

Ljungberg, F., & Sørensen, C. (2000). Overload: From transaction to interaction. In K. Braa, C. Sørensen, & B. Dahlbom (Eds.), *Planet Internet* (pp. 113–136). Lund, Sweden: Studentlitteratur.

Luff, P., & Heath, C. (1998). *Mobility in collaboration*. Paper presented at the Proceedings of ACM 1998 Conference on Computer Supported Cooperative Work.

Lyytinen, K. (2003). *The next wave of IS research: Design and investigation of ubiquitous computing*. Paper presented at the Panel presentation on "Mobile Interaction and Pervasive Social Technologies" panel at ECIS, Naples, Italy.

Lyytinen, K., & Yoo, Y. (2002). The next wave of nomadic computing: A research agenda for information systems research. *Information Systems Research*, 13(4), 377–388.

Malone, M. S. (2004, April). Moore's Second Law: If we don't do something about increasing battery life, we're toast. *Wired*, 12, 37–38.

Mann, S., & Niedzviecki, H. (2002). *Cyborg: Digital destiny and human possibility in the age of the wearable computer*. Toronto: Doubleday Canada.

Mathiassen, L., & Sørensen, C. (2002). *A task-based theory of information services*. Paper presented at the Information Systems Research Seminar in Scandinavia (IRIS'25), Denmark.

Mathiassen, L., & Sørensen, C. (forthcoming). A theory of organizational information services. Under review for international journal.

Mazmanian, M. A., Orlikowski, W. J., & Yates, J. (2005). Crackberries: The social implications of ubiquitous wireless e-mail devices. In C. Sørensen, Y. Yoo, K. Lyytinen, & J. I. DeGross (Eds.), *Designing ubiquitous information environments: Socio-technical issues and challenges*. New York: Springer.

McCollough, M. (2004). *Digital ground: Architecture, pervasive computing, and environmental knowing*. Cambridge, MA: MIT Press.

Nardi, B., & Whittaker, S. (2000). *Interaction and outeraction*. Paper presented at the Proceedings of Computer Supported Cooperative Work, Philadelphia, PA.

Nardi, B. A., Whittaker, S., & Schwarz, H. (2002). NetWORKers and their activity in intensional networks. *Computer Supported Cooperative Work*, 11, 205–242.

Newell, S., Robertson, M., Scarbrough, H., & Swan, J. (2002). *Managing knowledge work*. New York: Palgrave.

Norman, D. (1999). *The invisible computer: Why good products can fail, the personal computer is so complex, and information appliances are the solution*. Cambridge, MA: MIT Press.

Olson, G. M., & Olson, J. S. (2000). Distance Matters. *Human-computer interaction*, 15, 139–178.

Orlikowski, W. J. (1993). Learning from notes: Organizational issues in groupware implementation. *The information society*, *9*(3), 237–250.

Pica, D. (2006). *The rhythms of interaction with mobile technologies: Tales from the police*. Unpublished Ph.D. Thesis, London School of Economics, London.

Pica, D., & Kakihara, M. (2003). The duality of mobility: Understanding fluid organizations and stable interaction. *Proceedings of the ECIS 2003*, Naples, Italy.

Press, L. (1992). Dynabook revisited—Portable computers past, present and future. *Communications of the ACM*, 35(3), 25–32.

Rheingold, H. (2002). *Smart mobs*. Cambridge, MA: Perseus Books.

Robertson, M., Sørensen, C., & Swan, J. (2000). Managing knowledge with groupware: A case study of a knowledge-intensive firm. *Proceedings of the Annual Hawaii International Conference on System Sciences* (HICSS-33), Maui, Hawaii.

Robertson, M., Sørensen, C., & Swan, J. (2001). Survival of the leanest: Intensive knowledge work and groupware adaptation. *Information Technology & People*, 14(4), 334–353.

Schiller, J., & Voisard, A. (2004). *Location-based services*. San Francisco: Morgan Kaufmann.

Schmidt, K., & Simone, C. (1996). Coordination mechanisms: An approach to CSCW systems design. *Computer Supported Cooperative Work: An International Journal*, 5(2/3), 155–200.

Schwarz, H., Nardi, B., & Whittaker, S. (1999). *The hidden work in virtual work*. Paper presented at the International Conference on Critical Management, July 14–16, Manchester, U.K.

Sellen, A. J., & Harper, R. (2003). *The myth of the paperless office*. Cambridge, MA: MIT Press.

Sørensen, C. (2003). *Research issues in mobile informatics: Classical concerns, pragmatic issues and emerging discourses*. Paper presented at the Workshop on Ubiquitous Working Environment, Weatherhead School of Management, Case Western Reserve University, Cleveland.

Sørensen, C. (2004). *Trust and technology in mobile information work,* Technical Report. London: Microsoft Ltd.

Sørensen, C. (2005). Beyond the transaction perspective for knowledge management software artifacts. In K. C. Desouza (Ed.), *New frontiers in knowledge management* (pp. 117–146). Basingstoke, Hampshire, U.K.: Palgrave Macmillan.

Sørensen, C., Kakihara, M., & Mathiassen, L. (2002). *Mobile services: Functional diversity and overload*. Working Paper No. 118. London: Department of Information Systems, The London School of Economics and Political Science.

Sørensen, C., & Pica, D. (2005). Tales from the police: Mobile technologies and contexts of work. *Information and Organization*, 15(3), 125–149.

Sørensen, C., Yoo, Y., Lyytinen, K., & DeGross, J. I. (Eds.). (2005). *Designing ubiquitous information environments: Socio-technical issues and Challenges. Proceedings of IFIP 8.2*. New York: Springer.

Strauss, A., Fagerhaugh, S., Suczek, B., & Wiener, C. (1985). *Social organization of medical work*. Chicago and London: University of Chicago Press.

Townsend, A., Demarie, S., & Hendrickson, A. (1998). Virtual teams. Technology and the workplace of the future. *The Academy of Management Executive*, 12(3), 17–29.

Warwick, K. (2002). *I, Cyborg*. London: Century.

Weiser, M. (1991, September). The computer for the twenty-first century. *Scientific American*, 94–110.

Weiser, M. (1999). Ubiquitous Computing. Retrived from www.ubiq.com/hypertext/weiser/UbiHome.html

Whittaker, S., Frohlich, D., & Daly-Jones, O. (1994). Informal workplace communication: What is it like and how might we support it? *Proceedings of the ACM 1994 Conference on Human Factors in Computing Systems*, Boston, MA, 131–137.

Whittle, A. (2005). Preaching and practising "flexibility": Implications for theories of subjectivity at work. *Human Relations*, 58(10), 1301–1322.

Wiberg, M., & Ljungberg, F. (2001). Exploring the vision of "Anytime, Anywhere" in the context of mobile work. In Y. Malhotra (Ed.), *Knowledge management and virtual organizations* (pp. 157–169). Hershey, PA: Idea Group Publishing.

Wiberg, M., & Whittaker, S. (2005). Managing availability: Supporting lightweight negotiations to handle interruptions. *ACM Transactions of Computer-Human Interaction*, 12(4), 1–32.

Wiredu, G. (2005). *Mobile computing in work-integrated learning: Problems of remotely distributed activities and technology use.* Unpublished Ph.D. Dissertation, London School of Economics and Political Science.

Wiredu, G., & Sørensen, C. (2006). The dynamics of control and use of mobile technology in distributed activities. *European Journal of Information Systems*, 15(3), 307–319.

Chapter 18

Politics of Design: Next-Generation Computational Environments

Mark S. Ackerman
University of Michigan

Abstract

This paper describes and analyzes two next-generation computational environments and their architectures: the Semantic Web and pervasive computing. Each of these necessarily carries with it political assumptions about how the environments will be used, and these political assumptions are reflected in the accompanying computerization movement's rhetoric. However, unlike "first growth" computerization efforts, both the Semantic Web and pervasive computing will result within a growing infrastructure that does not allow top-down design (or even overall design) but within which new designs must fit. The underlying assumptions for both environments are largely libertarian but with differing modalities of user control. This paper examines the libertarian assumptions, the promise of democratization in one but not the other, and the resulting conceptual tensions surrounding these two second-generation computerization movements.

Introduction

Computerization movements (CMs) carry with them hidden assumptions about the nature of political relationships, as Rob Kling pointed out (Kling, 1991). These assumptions include the nature of power and the political relationships among the major stakeholders in the construction, adoption, and use of the systems involved in the CM. For designers, these assumptions are often implicit and hidden; nonetheless, they are present.

In this paper, I describe and analyze two next-generation computational environments and their architectures:

- The Semantic Web – This is an attempt to add meta-data suitable for automatic inferencing to Web pages. Envisioned services include the automatic purchasing of goods (e.g., "What's the cheapest way to fly to Chicago?") and the linked provision of information (e.g., "Who wrote a good book on Social Informatics?").
- Pervasive Computing – Pervasive or ubiquitous computing presumes a future with hundreds or thousands of computational devices in everyday environments such as offices and homes. Envisioned scenarios include smart buildings, home shopping, sensor networks, and medical monitoring.

Each of these necessarily carries with it political assumptions about how the environments will be used. However, unlike "first growth" computerization efforts, both the Semantic Web and pervasive computing will result within a growing infrastructure that does not allow top-down design (or even overall design) but within which new designs must fit. The underlying assumptions for both environments are largely libertarian but with differing modalities of user control. This chapter, then, examines the libertarian assumptions, the promise of democratization in one but not the other, and the resulting conceptual tensions in the CMs surrounding each.

The chapter examines these two CMs through the writings of Berners-Lee and Weiser, the two founders of the CMs. It does so not to criticize per se, but rather to be critically realistic about the possibilities, issues, and tensions in these two technologies and these two CMs.

Computerization Movements

In a series of papers, Kling and Iacono detailed their view of CMs. For this paper, of particular interest is Kling and Iacono (1995), where they defined a CM as "... a kind of movement whose advocates focus on computer-based systems to bring about a new social order." They saw, as signal indicators of a CM, the following five features:

1. Computer-based technologies are central for a reformed world. "CM activists often argue that computers are a central medium for creating the world they prefer" (Kling & Iacono, 1995). This can include, however, merely productive organizations, leaving open an analysis of what constitutes a "reformed world."

2. Improved computer-based technologies can further reform society. "CM activists often define computing capabilities as those of future technologies, not the limits of presently available technologies" (Kling & Iacono, 1995).

3. More computing is better than less, and there are no conceptual limits to the scope of appropriate computerization. State-of-the-art computing should become widespread.

4. No one loses from computerization. In Kling and Iacono's view, "Computer-based technologies are portrayed as inherently apolitical. While they are said to be consistent with any social order, CM advocates usually portray their use in a cheerful, cooperative, flexible, individualistic and efficient world. ... Any short-term sacrifices ... are portrayed as minor unavoidable consequences" (Kling & Iacono, 1995). While social power is better understood by technical designers, CMs are still often framed without sufficient regard to the issue.

5. Uncooperative people are the main barriers to social reform through computing. "In many social settings, we have found CM advocates arguing that poorly trained or undisciplined users undermined good technologies. ... In short, people place 'unnecessary' limits on the complexity of desirable computer-based technologies" (Kling & Iacono, 1995). Institutional barriers are now better understood by technical designers, but the point generally stands—people, whether by themselves or in collectivities such as organizations, institutions, or government, are the main barriers to reform through computing.

Despite the premise of the fourth feature that CM technologies are portrayed as basically apolitical, Kling and Iacono's analyses of their five specific CMs all suggest that these CMs bring with them a view of the "proper" political relationships among system and stakeholders, technologists, and users, and even workers, management, and society.

Kling and Iacono demonstrate that the new, desired social order inherently conveys a set of political relationships, which the principal designers attempt to inscribe into their technology. Of course, it is not so simple; the path from inscription to use-in-practice is a winding one. People can adopt and adapt the systems as they wish, within some limits. A CM provides a set of "technological action frames" through which to view a technology. The frames structure public discourse, attempting to persuade organizational members to view this technology accordingly and so influence organizational practices. (In later work, Kling expanded organizational practices to societal practices as well.) In Iacono and Kling's view,

> Technological action frames shape and structure public discourse while public discourse shapes and structures organizational practices. ... These relationships are non-deterministic, however. People's technology practices are usually much more complex than the more restricted public discourses about practices. For many practitioners, there is often a gap between their own discourse and practice. (Iacono & Kling, 2001)

It is open how much the inscription of political and social views into a system influences later use (Orlikowski, 2000). In any case, Kling and Iacono's contribution is largely in the explication of the technological action frames and the resulting public discourse, and this contribution is considerable. While CMs can differ widely (Kling and Iacono note mostly the varying maturity of different CMs, but other differences will be explored later), CMs attempt to instill in their participants and in the public a sense of technological utopianism, hiding the political and social realities (Kling & Iacono, 1995). The following analyses examine some current technological action frames and their attempts to structure public discourse.

Implicit in Kling and Iacono is that social movements have general theoretical features. Several issues are important to consider for the following analysis. First, any social movement of a significant size is a hubbub of social activity. There is a range of voices and power arrangements. Accordingly, it is important in understanding any given CM's implications to consider who gets to speak for a CM and who is listened to (and by what group). Second, any social movement is a collection of individuals embedded in a complex social milieu. As with any evangelical social group, a social movement will have a range of adherence and beliefs, goals and motives, as well as durations and trajectories of membership. It will be arranged within a social environment that has power relationships, and within the CM there will be a similar network of power arrangements. That is, a social movement attempts to move a contested terrain toward a specific point of view. In Iacono and Kling's view, "... at certain points, within specific [i.e., within all given] social movements, master frames develop in their discourses" (Iacono & Kling, 2001).

Finally, CMs have trajectories themselves, and these trajectories change over time. Initially, the different groups within a CM (and outside of it perhaps) are attempting to influence others, since technological action frames are not yet codified and organizational practices have not yet become routine. Only later will technological action frames consider the nuances and tradeoffs of use. Here, we will largely consider two kinds of computational systems at the beginnings of their trajectories.

Next I provide an overview and analysis of the Semantic Web project.

The Semantic Web

The Semantic Web is partially a vision of a next-generation Web and partially a set of protocols and technologies that concretely instantiate that vision. I will largely concern myself with the vision here, but it is important to understand the technology and the history of the project.

The earliest conceptions of the Semantic Web are reflected in Tim Berners-Lee's works (1998a, 1998b). As the Web matured and the overwhelmingly furious pace of protocol design and development slowed, Berners-Lee began to define his "what next" project. Taking time from his role as the director of the World Wide Web Consortium (W3C), he began sketching out a system whereby Web-based sites and intelligent agents could communicate about content. Early funding from The Defense Advanced Research Projects Agency (DARPA) was secured, and others began to work on the project as well. Thus, efforts to define a set of protocols and standards to define this communication and content markup lay partially within the W3C staff as a funded research project, partially within a DARPA sponsored program (with many university and defense vendor companies), and partially as a "regular" W3C project (with the usual mix of W3C coordination and industrial-sponsor participation).

The Semantic Web's purpose is to allow a "semantically" rich set of markup capabilities for Web content. This is to allow computers to be able to make inferences about the content and provide users with new, beneficial capabilities. At its simplest level, the Semantic Web might allow retrieval engines to retrieve sites that marked themselves up, for example, as selling airline tickets or particular machine parts. Retrieval engines would be able to distinguish between homonyms, and sites could be more specific about their contents and intent. As the Semantic Web advanced, agents would be able to make inferences on this data. For example, one might be able to ask for the cheapest airline ticket on an airline upon which the user has frequent flyer miles and that leaves after 4 P.M. I will return below to other scenarios, those heavily discussed in the master technological action frames for the Semantic Web.

The technology of the Semantic Web consists of a number of markup languages and protocols. The details are not important here, but it is important to understand how the technology is structured. When the Semantic Web began as a project, Web-based documents were primarily restricted to HTML, the Web's display markup language, and XML, a language allowing a set of generic markup tags. Neither was very structured, allowing too much ambiguity for easy handling by computers. HTML merely marks up whether a paragraph is to be normal, outlined, or numbered, or whether text is bold, plain, and so on. No description of the content itself is easily possible. For example, one cannot say that "This paragraph is the introduction." (This is a step backward from SGML, the early markup language from which HTML was constructed.) XML allows markup of content, but the markup is flat in that no relationships between parts of the document can be specified. Without a centralized and authorized dictionary, both for vocabulary and relationships, it is not possible to automatically infer relationships between two different documents produced in two different places. For example, the same tag might mean different things, and even if they meant exactly the same thing for the two authors, the relationship of that specific content might be very different to other parts of the document.

To correct these problems, a number of new standards were proposed. The first, RDF (Resource Description Framework), allows relationships to be demarked. RDF allows authors to write "ontologies," or precise definitions of the relationships between terms. RDF allows authors to create tuples consisting of a name, relationship, and target URI (or Web identifier). For example, one might create "Mark Ackerman" is "an author of" "this document." RDF depends on XML; or rather, the standard allows XML to be one of the languages in which RDF can be expressed. (There are alternative syntaxes.)

RDF was in progress before the Semantic Web effort started; it was required by digital libraries and other content providers. In addition to RDF are the efforts started within the Semantic Web project. For brevity, I skip RDF-S, which adds capabilities for handling subclassing in ontologies. The next major standard is OWL, or Ontology Web Language. OWL comes in three "sizes," depending on the needs of the Web service. The most minor version of OWL provides the ability to markup descriptions of Web services; the most complete version allows full Artificial Intelligence (AI) ontologies. The middle version, which will be discussed here, is not complete from an AI perspective: Some inferences cannot be done, and reasoning is not guaranteed to finish. It is, however, quick and suitable for most Web requirements. OWL adds additional ontological capabilities, such as cardinality, property typing, class relationships, and so forth. Recently, work has continued with rule-based inferencing.

This analysis depends largely on the *Scientific American* article about the Semantic Web (Berners-Lee, Hendler, & Lassila, 2001). Published in 2001 by Tim Berners-Lee, James Hendler (at the time, the DARPA program manager and a prominent AI researcher), and Ora Lassila (at the time, a W3C staff member with AI training), the article is an explanation and invitation to the informed public. This is supplemented with other published works (Berners-Lee, 1998a, 1998b; Berners-Lee & Miller, 2002).

The *Scientific American* article's initial page is a graphic of a computer monitor with ones and zeros as well as the words "i [sic] know what you mean." The article itself begins with "A new form of Web content that is meaningful to computers will unleash a revolution of new possibilities." Even this phrase is interesting—"new" entices the reader, the promise is "Web content meaningful to computers" (which perhaps hints of the importance of this new form and invokes AI images of smart machines).

It is worth repeating the opening scenario for the *Scientific American* article at some length:

> The entertainment system was belting out the Beatles' "We Can Work It Out" when the phone rang. When Pete answered, ... His sister, Lucy, was on the line from the doctor's office: "Mom needs to see a specialist and then has to have a series of physical therapy sessions. Bi-weekly or something. I'm going to have my agent set up the appointments." Lucy instructed her Semantic Web agent through her handheld Web browser. The agent promptly retrieved information about Mom's prescribed treatment from the doctor's agent, looked up several lists of providers, and checked for the ones in-plan for Mom's insurance within a 20-mile radius of her home and with a rating of excellent or very good on trusted rating services. It then began trying to find a match between available appointment times (supplied by the agents of individual providers through their Websites) and Pete's and Lucy's busy schedules.
>
> ... In a few minutes the agent presented them with a plan. Pete didn't like it—University Hospital was all the way across town from Mom's place, and he'd be driving back in the middle of rush hour. He set his own agent to redo the search with stricter preferences about location and time. Lucy's agent, having complete trust in Pete's agent in the context of the present task, automatically assisted by supplying access certificates and shortcuts to the data it had already sorted through. (Berners-Lee, et al., 2001)

In this scenario, machines automatically and efficiently take care of laborious tasks. This is reminiscent of selling domestic appliances (Cowan, 1983). The words "promptly" and "automatically" indicate the efficiency of the machine, but more importantly, the scenario strongly implies that the machines are themselves trustworthy and capable. The scenario jumps over a number of intermediary steps, such as rating the medical providers and understanding medical requirements. The beginning and end of the scenario, as presented here, implies cooperation and consent. No conflict, glitches, or competition are mentioned.

But, even the possibilities of this scenario are not final. Berners-Lee and Miller suggest:

> The most exciting thing about the Semantic Web is not what we can imagine doing with it, but what we can't yet imagine it will do. Just as global indexes and Google's algorithms were not dreamed of in the early Web days, we cannot imagine now all the new research challenges and exciting product areas which will appear once there is a Web of data to explore.
>
> The Semantic Web starts as a simple circles-and-arrows diagram relating things, which slowly expands and coalesces to become global and vast. The Web of human-readable documents spawned a social revolution. The Semantic Web may in turn spawn a revolution in computing. In neither case did a change occur in the power of one person or one computer, but rather a dramatic change in the role they can play in the world, by being able to find out almost anything virtually immediately. (Berners-Lee & Miller, 2002)

All of this sounds like the CM for Artificial Intelligence (AI) in the 1980s. However, this CM is quick to distance itself from AI. Berners-Lee notes, "The concept of machine-understandable documents does not imply some magical artificial intelligence which allows machines to comprehend human mumblings" (Berners-Lee, 1998b). Indeed, the explanation of the Semantic Web is prosaic in its technicality:

> The Semantic Web addresses this problem in two ways. First, it will enable communities to expose their data so that a program doesn't have to strip the formatting, pictures, and ads from a Web page to guess at the relevant bits of information. Secondly, it will allow people to write (or generate) files which explain—to a machine—the relationship between different sets of data. For example, one will be able to make a "semantic link" between a database with a "zip-code" column and a form with a "zip" field that they actually mean the same thing. This will allow machines to follow links and facilitate the integration of data from many different sources. (Berners-Lee & Miller, 2002)

In the *Scientific American* article, the authors explain:

> Further markup on the page (not displayed by the typical Web browser) uses the ontology's concepts to specify that Hendler received his Ph.D. from the entity described at the URI http://www.brown.edu/—the Web page for Brown. Computers can also find that Hendler is a member of a particular research project, has a particular e-mail address, and

> so on. All that information is readily processed by a computer and could be used to answer queries (such as where Dr. Hendler received his degree) that currently would require a human to sift through the content of various pages turned up by a search engine. (Berners-Lee, et al., 2001, p. 41)

The authors go on:

> In addition, this markup makes it much easier to develop programs that can tackle complicated questions whose answers do not reside on a single Web page. (Berners-Lee, et al., 2001, p. 41)

The authors explain that the Semantic Web is different from AI in two significant ways. First, it is merely a layer above the existing Web. It does not require extensive changes, although it does require additional labor. Second, it is decentralized. As Berners-Lee and Miller explain, "The ability for 'anyone to say anything about anything' is an important characteristic of the current Web and is a fundamental principle of the Semantic Web" (Berners-Lee & Miller, 2002). Earlier AI efforts, such as CYC, were monumental and centralized; the Semantic Web preserves the radical decentralization of the Web in its structure. The Semantic Web allows many ontologies to exist simultaneously, and Semantic Web agents must deal with potentially dissimilar ontologies and rules.

Despite this prosaic description of the technology, visions of the Semantic Web are quick to swing back toward machine intelligence. (One might note that AI itself has largely abandoned its early goal of creating a synthetic human intelligence.) For example, the *Scientific American* article describes simple agents and goes on to say:

> The consumer and producer agents can reach a shared understanding by exchanging ontologies, which provide the vocabulary needed for discussion. Agents can even "bootstrap" new reasoning capabilities when they discover new ontologies. Semantics also makes it easier to take advantage of a service that only partially matches a request.
>
> A typical process will involve the creation of a "value chain" in which subassemblies of information are passed from one agent to another, each one "adding value," to construct the final product requested by the end user. (Berners-Lee, et al., 2001)

Indeed, the article ends with:

> The Semantic Web is not "merely" the tool for conducting individual tasks that we have discussed so far. In addition, if properly designed, the Semantic Web can assist the evolution of human knowledge as a whole. (Berners-Lee, et al., 2001)

and

> The Semantic Web, in naming every concept simply by a URI, lets anyone express new concepts that they invent with minimal effort. Its unifying logical language will enable these concepts to be progressively linked into a universal Web. This structure will open up the knowledge and workings of humankind to meaningful analysis by software agents, providing a new class of tools by which we can live, work and learn together. (Berners-Lee, et al., 2001)

In all fairness, one must realize that to do their job of convincing a reader, the authors must avoid visions of AI, since there are many AI dystopias in the media as well as a popular disappointment in the AI hype and craze of the mid-1980s. At the same time, to mobilize support, the authors must promise the new. It would be interesting to speculate on what drives Americans' fascination with the future and the new (as well as the lingering pervasiveness of technological utopianism and economic greed in predicting the future), but for this paper's purposes, it is merely necessary to note that the authors tap into this never-ending fascination and yet are wary of it.

In any case, the Semantic Web articles are noticeably lacking in any discussion of the social world. The vision is limited to allowing separate language worlds to communicate and assuming they will want to do so. Questions of who controls the ontologies, which relationships are expressed and which are not, and how ontological categories come to be matched are not discussed (Bowker & Star, 2000). Even questions of how ontologies or statements are maintained and supported over time are not discussed. It is assumed that the development of ontologies is open to all, and in fact, many attempts will be made. As with current Web sites, however, it is entirely possible that ontologies or rules will become the province of large corporate or institutional entities with the financial and programming resources to support them. It is also possible that such entities might not want to openly share or cooperate with others.

The Semantic Web offers a vision of radical libertarianism, with all of the political concerns that such libertarianism suggests. Nonetheless, the Semantic Web offers the technology to allow such a libertarianism to succeed. Any given person, organization, group, or society, even in the face of corporate or institutional restrictions, can place its own ontology and rules onto the Web. Just as any entity is free to offer any Web page about any topic and with any slant, the Semantic Web also offers that capability.

I will show next that Pervasive Computing, while arguing for the same libertarian decentralization, does not offer this capability.

Pervasive Computing

Pervasive computing—sometimes called ubiquitous computing or pervasive environments—is often touted as the next generation of computer architectures. The idea is simple: Processors will be so cheap and high-bandwidth networks so available that there will literally be computers everywhere. Sensors will be ubiquitous. A building's rooms may have dozens of embedded computers, a person may have implanted medical systems, and even clothing may have computational or display elements. Hundreds or thousands of computationally based services may be processing data and providing applications. As Weiser's seminal 1991 paper begins:

> The most profound technologies are those that disappear. They weave themselves into the fabric of everyday life until they are indistinguishable from it. (Weiser, 1991)

There are hundreds of pervasive computing papers published every year, as with the Semantic Web. Relatively few still are industrial or marketing articles; the market is still nascent. Here we will consider largely Mark Weiser's papers, as he was the founder of the area. Much of his vision has been kept by researchers in this field, although they have been more mechanical and less concerned with the socio-historical. Again, I do not expound Weiser's point of view to be sharply critical; I merely want to explore the CM's points of view. Weiser set the tone for the entire pervasive (ubiquitous computing) CM; his words were deeply influential on researchers and practitioners alike. While he died unexpectedly in 1999, the field continued on, and as one might expect, over time, numerous voices have tried to influence the CM. Some more recent researchers, especially those influenced by the field of Human–Computer Interaction, have acknowledged some of the problematic issues raised by the technology (Abowd & Mynatt, 2000; Abowd, Mynatt, & Rodden, 2002), discussed the gap between reality of use and visions of mobile technology use (Sørensen & Gibson, Chapter 17, this volume), or acknowledged the social requirements (e.g., Kindberg & Fox, 2002; Langheinrich, 2002). These researchers, nonetheless, are still optimistic about the technology and its possibilities. Others are more instrumental, focusing on the technical problems.

However, many continue the predominant themes of Weiser, perhaps even accentuating the positive (e.g., CMU Project Aura, 2000; Dertouzos, 2001).

Pervasive computing, at its core, attempts to reconcile computers and everyday life by attempting to make the computer as easy to use as any everyday experience:

> Silicon-based information technology, in contrast, is far from having become part of the environment. ... [T]he computer remains largely in a world of its own. It is approachable only through complex jargon that has nothing to do with the tasks for which people actually use computers. The state of the art is perhaps analogous to the period when scribes had to know as much about making ink or baking clay as they did about writing. (Weiser, 1991)

Weiser's work reflects the dominant concerns in PARC, the research center in which he wrote. His reflection of everyday activities echoes ethnomethodologically inspired emphases:

> ... [O]nly when things disappear in this way are we freed to use them without thinking and so to focus beyond them on new goals. (Weiser, 1991)

This is also a criticism of classical AI, less muted than that of the Semantic Web:

> No revolution in artificial intelligence is needed—just the proper imbedding of computers into the everyday world. (Weiser, 1991)

The scenarios Weiser paints are often broad-brush and historical—technologies that have changed over time and become more commonplace. Socio-historical transitions are, at best, minor:

> How do technologies disappear into the background? The vanishing of electric motors may serve as an instructive example: At the turn of the century, a typical workshop or factory contained a single engine that drove dozens or hundreds of different machines through a system of shafts and pulleys. Cheap, small, efficient electric motors made it possible first to give each machine or tool its own source of motive force, then to put many motors into a single machine.

> A glance through the shop manual of a typical automobile, for example, reveals twenty-two motors and twenty-five more solenoids. They start the engine, clean the windshield, lock and unlock the doors, and so on. By paying careful attention it might be possible to know whenever one activated a motor, but there would be no point to it. (Weiser, 1991)

Weiser understood that this would fundamentally change the relationship between humans and computers, as part of this inevitable historical process. Of course, the development of motors (beginning with water and then steam actually) changed the Western world with large-scale factories, urbanization and industrialization, and the resulting significant displacements of artisans and other workers.

Outside of the large-scale vision, changes in computer applications are almost prosaic. Unlike the Semantic Web with its large-scale applications, pervasive computing has very small-scale applications in its usage vision:

> This will ... let people arrange their computer-based projects in the area around their terminals, much as they now arrange paper-based projects in piles on desks and tables. Carrying a project to a different office for discussion is as simple as gathering up its tabs; the associated programs and files can be called up on any terminal. (Weiser, 1991)

In fact, some of the applications envisioned by Weiser have already become commonplace:

> To manipulate the display, users pick up a piece of wireless electronic "chalk" that can work either in contact with the surface or from a distance. Some researchers, using themselves and their colleagues as guinea pigs, can hold electronically mediated meetings or engage in other forms of collaboration around a liveboard. (Weiser, 1991)

Weiser argued against "intelligent agents," arguing instead for small applications with little reasoning. He believed, however, that the final outcome would be similar to AI's general goals:

> In the next revolution, as we learn to make machines that take care of our unconscious details, we might finally have smarter people. (Weiser, 1996)

Weiser argued that such capability would come from many small applications with little reasoning (similar to the later claims of Hutchins, 1995). It should be noted that later advocates of pervasive computing argue for "proactive" agents in the environment, inferencing of context, and location awareness (e.g., Satyanarayanan, 2001; Dey, Salber, & Abowd, 2001; Mynatt, Rowan, Craighill, & Jacobs, 2001; and Sawhney & Schmandt, 1999).

Pervasive advocates note the possibility of social issues, although the social issues do not play a significant role. The social issues are often limited to privacy and trust, occasionally including issues in location and context awareness made possible with sensor networks. Still the outlook is generally held to be positive:

> A well-implemented version of ubiquitous computing could even afford better privacy protection than exists today. ... If anything, the transparent connections that they offer between different locations and times may tend to bring communities closer together. ... Sociologically, ubiquitous computing may mean the decline of the computer addict. (Weiser, 1991)

What is clearly missing is a sense of who gets control over the placement and operation of services, sensors, and data. Clearly in a pervasive environment as envisioned, there will be many computational services getting flows of data from sensors and inferencing services. Even more than today, a "user" may not be aware of those trafficking in his data. Furthermore, in the visions of pervasive computing, many systems with many owners may operate within a single environment, and those systems and their owners will exist within a complex set of relationships (many hidden) with any given user (Ackerman, Darrell, & Weitzner, 2002). The user may lack effective control. Sørensen and Gibson (Chapter 17, this volume) examine the idealized visions of pervasive and ubiquitous technologies, as argued here, against the mundane practicalities that users might face.

In Weiser's vision, there is little centralized infrastructure that ties these hidden and everyday computational devices together. Pervasive computing is also libertarian, in that it assumes that any given device is equivalent and that some user can pick the services, sensors, and data he wishes. In reality, the environments may largely choose which services and sensors are present, and the data will flow automatically. Furthermore, these services and sensors must interoperate to be effective, and if data fusion is profitable (as it may be for tracking purchase decisions), then data flows must also interoperate. A need for interoperationalization leads, without an adequate infrastructure design, to large vendors or institutions controlling significant portions of the infrastructure. In this case, the libertarian bias of pervasive computing will not lead to democratization, but rather to oligarchic arrangements. The democratization that does occur could very well be limited to the mass consumerism.

Conclusions: The Politics of Design

As CMs, the Semantic Web and pervasive computing rely on the CMs that have preceded them. This can be seen even in their names. Earlier CMs like "artificial intelligence," "machine learning," "information highway," or "organizational memory" took their names by concatenating existing, everyday entities ("highway" or "memory") and added to them an abstract, computer-based term on the left (Ackerman, 1994). The names derived some of their symbolic power by arguing that the new CM would be like some natural entity but indeed would be better. "Semantic Web" and "pervasive computing" rely, instead, on their right-hand terms being existing infrastructure ("Web" and "computing"). They add to this a left-hand term that adds even more abstract meaning. In other words, they rely on readers understanding existing computational infrastructure and being able to infer from them; these CMs have been created as second-generation CMs.

Because the Semantic Web and pervasive computing rely on preexisting notions of computerization, they display two common biases. First, they both nominally eschew previous, under-performing CMs, especially AI. In fact, both CMs include and supplement previous AI visions of the future. These AI visions have a deep resonance, I would argue, for Americans and will not lightly vanish. And, these CMs build upon previous CMs' successes.

Second, and more importantly, both CMs are founded on the libertarian-infused infrastructures of the Internet, networking technologies, and distributed computing. As such, these new CMs carry forward a sense that a libertarian sense of control is appropriate; other possibilities for political relationships have largely vanished. I have argued here that this libertarian sense of control, however, brings with it a sharp tension—how will all the disparate parts work together? Over time, who will allow the competing portions of the environment to work together, how will conflicts be reconciled, and the necessary updates and maintenance occur? Neither CM deals extensively with this tension (a problematic aspect of this libertarian bias, but is an easier sell for the CM). But, the Semantic Web, perhaps because of its roots in the Web infrastructure, shows an understanding in its design that interoperationalization is necessary and conflict must be reconciled and managed. This understanding offers some hope for democratization of effort and control, although the current history of the Web argues more heavily for corporate influence. (Indeed, the W3C is largely a corporate consortium.) I have argued, on the other hand, that pervasive computing, as it has grown since Weiser, by ignoring issues of conflict and control, is likely to head toward vendors or other institutions providing islands of interoperationalization and thus maintaining oligarchic control over the infrastructure.

How these new CMs play out is, of course, an empirical question. This discussion argues that Iacono and Kling's viewpoint is likely to be correct:

> In its most likely form, the rise of computer technologies and networks, while promising technological utopias for all, will lead to conservative social arrangements, reinforcing the patterns of an elite-dominated, stratified society. (Iacono & Kling, 1996, p. 102)

Yet, they also argued that:

> The best answers come from a kind of close empirical observation that opens up the real possibilities, limitations, paradoxes, and ironies of computerization situated in very real social settings. (Kling & Iacono, 1991, p. 74)

This is vital to the design of these next-generation environments. The future of people's control over their environments—computational, domestic and organizational, or political—is critical. Influencing the environments' design, and countering the accompanying CMs, requires a constant attention to empirically grounded observation and critical discussion.

Acknowledgments

I am deeply indebted to Rob Kling for his help in understanding computerization and the social world. I began under Rob's informal tutelage as a newly minted MIT PhD. His fierce dedication to empirically grounded studies and critical realism, as well as his unrelenting enthusiasm for social analysis and computer-based technologies, has served as a constant encouragement and a constant call.

I am also indebted to a host of people for the understanding reflected here (however poorly). These include Walt Scacchi, John King, Kenneth Kraemer, Jonathan Grudin, Paul Dourish, Keith Edwards, and Chris Schmandt, as well as debates with many people at MIT's Project Oxygen and the World Wide Web Consortium (W3C), including David Karger, Ralph Swick, Danny Weitzner, and Joseph Reagle.

References

Abowd, G. D., & Mynatt, E. D. (2000). Charting past, present, and future research in ubiquitous computing. *ACM Transactions on Computer–Human Interaction*, 7(1), 29–58.

Abowd, G. D., Mynatt, E. D., & Rodden, T. (2002). The human experience. *IEEE Pervasive Computing*, 1(1), 48–57.

Ackerman, M. S. (1994). Metaphors along the information highway. *Proceedings of the symposium on directions and impacts of advanced computing systems (DIAC 94)*.

Ackerman, M. S., Darrell, T., & Weitzner, D. J. (2002). Privacy in context. *Human–Computer Interaction*, 16(2–4), 167–176.

Berners-Lee, T. (1998a). Semantic Web roadmap. Retrieved from www.w3.org/DesignIssues/Semantic.html

Berners-Lee, T. (1998b). What the Semantic Web is not. Retrieved from www.w3.org/DesignIssues/Semantic.html

Berners-Lee, T., Hendler, J., & Lassila, O. (2001). The semantic web. *Scientific American*, 35–43.

Berners-Lee, T., & Miller, E. (2002). The Semantic Web lifts off. *ERCIM News*, No. 51. Retrieved from www.ercim.org/publication/Ercim_News/enw51/berners-lee.html

Bowker, G. C., & Star, S. L. (2000). *Sorting things out: Classification and its consequences*. Cambridge, MA: MIT Press.

CMU Project Aura. (2000). CMU Project Aura concept video. Retrieved from www.cs.cmu.edu/~aura/auravideo.mpg

Cowan, R. S. (1983). *More work for mother: The ironies of household technology from the open hearth to the microwave*. New York: Basic Books.

Dertouzos, M. L. (2001). *The unfinished revolution: How to make technology work for us—instead of the other way around*. New York: Collins.

Dey, A. K., Salber, D., & Abowd, G. D. (2001). A conceptual framework and a toolkit for supporting the rapid prototyping of context-aware applications. *Human–Computer Interaction*, 16(2–4), 97–166.

Hutchins, E. (1995). *Cognition in the wild*. Cambridge, MA: MIT Press.

Iacono, S., & Kling, R. (1996). Computerization movements and tales of technological utopianism. In R. Kling (Ed.), *Computerization and controversy: Value conflicts and social choices* (2nd ed., pp. 85–105). New York: Academic Press.

Iacono, S., & Kling, R. (2001). Computerization movements: The rise of the Internet and distant forms of work. In J. Yates & J. Van Maanen (Eds.), *Information technology and organizational transformation: History, rhetoric, and practice* (pp. 93–136). Thousand Oaks, CA: Sage Publications.

Kindberg, T., & Fox, A. (2002). System software for ubiquitous computing. *IEEE Pervasive Computing*, 1(1), 70–81.

Kling, R. (1991). Value conflicts in the design and organization of EFT systems. In C. Dunlop & R. Kling (Eds.), *Computerization and controversy: Value conflicts and social choices* (1st ed., pp. 421–435). Boston: Academic Press.

Kling, R., & Iacono, S. (1991). Making a "computer revolution." In C. Dunlop & R. Kling (Eds.), *Computerization and controversy: Value conflicts and social choices* (1st ed., pp. 63–75). Boston: Academic Press.

Kling, R., & Iacono, S. (1995). Computerization movements and the mobilization of support for computerization. In S. L. Starr (Ed.), *Ecologies of knowledge: Work and politics in science and technology* (pp. 119–153). Albany, NY: State University of New York Press.

Langheinrich, M. (2002). A privacy awareness system for ubiquitous computing environments. In *Ubicomp 2002: Ubiquitous computing: 4th International Conference*, Goteborg, Sweden, Sept. 29–Oct. 1 (vol. 2498). Berlin: Springer.

Mynatt, E. D., Rowan, J., Craighill, S., & Jacobs, A. (2001). Digital family portraits: Supporting peace of mind for extended family members. *Proceedings of ACM CHI 2001 Conference on Human Factors in Computing Systems*, 333–340.

Orlikowski, W. (2000). Using technology and constituting structures: A practice lens for studying technology in organizations. *Organization Science*, 11(4), 404–428.

Satyanarayanan, M. (2001). Pervasive computing: Vision and challenges. *IEEE Personal Communications*, 8(4), 10–17.

Sawhney, N., & Schmandt, C. (1999). Nomadic radio: Scaleable and contextual notification for wearable audio messaging. *Proceedings of ACM CHI 99 Conference on Human Factors in Computing System*, 96–103.

Weiser, M. (1991, September). The computer for the twenty-first century. *Scientific American*, 94–110.

Weiser, M. (1996). Open house. *Interactive Telecommunications Program Journal*, 2(0).

Chapter 19

Social Movements Shaping the Internet: The Outcome of an Ecology of Games

William Dutton
University of Oxford

Abstract

The idea that many computing developments, such as the revolution in personal computing, are tied to social movements is a heuristically rich theme developed by Rob Kling and his colleagues, as captured by the concept of a computerization movement. This perspective provides a useful counter to notions of a single inventor or a technologically determined "best way" in relation to broad changes tied to technological innovations, as major developments in computing are often the outcome of complementary or conflicting social movements and their intersections. An important approach to understanding these social dynamics is to examine the unfolding interaction of various actors pursuing a diverse array of goals and objectives. In this chapter, I conceptualize this view as an "ecology of games," explaining how this framework for understanding the forces shaping social transformation through the use of technological innovations can supplement and complement the computerization movement perspective. The issues raised are illustrated by examples relating to the history, present, and future of the Internet, from its invention to the emergence of ubiquitous computing built around its worldwide network of people and technologies.

A New Perspective on Social Movements: The Invention and Governance of the Internet

Improving understanding of the social dynamics that translate a landmark technical innovation into a breakthrough in real-world contexts is key to understanding the history and future of technical change. Rob Kling and his colleagues (e.g., Kling, 1984; Kling & Iacono, 1988, 1995) provided a valuable argument to support this understanding by showing that many innovations in computing, such as those that formed around personal computers (PCs) and the development and use of free/open source software (F/OSS), should be understood as social movements, or what they called "computerization movements." As Kling and Iacono (1995) commented, computerization movements (CMs) "communicate key ideological beliefs about the favorable links between computerization and a preferred social order." Although this ideological position is a characteristic driving force of such CMs (Elliott & Kraemer, Chapter 1, this volume), these movements are also composed of collective activities in their own arenas, within which there can be actors with different perspectives (e.g., between the free software and open source software movements within F/OSS). Those involved in such CMs can also be significant actors in wider arenas, where complementary and competing forces produce outcomes where there may be a gap between the CMs' vision and reality, such as with the F/OSS movement in the wider software marketplace (Elliott & Kraemer, Chapter 1, this volume).

This conception of CMs provides an important advance over a narrow technological focus when examining the social dynamics of technological advances, since no technical innovation will be of major significance unless it is tied to social change. For example, it provides a welcome counter to the notion of the "single inventor" or "single technical breakthrough" behind innovations with wide ramifications. The search for the single inventor is common across many technologies (Williams & Edge, 1996), as indicated by much research and debate around the question of "who invented the Internet" (Cerf, 2005) and about whether a particular technical advance, such as packet switching, or a particular Internet Protocol (IP) led inevitably to the present form of this network of networks. Some of the early pioneers acknowledge various "fathers of the Internet" and "technical turning points" in the Internet's history, which suggests that the Internet's development was determined primarily by a chain of cumulative technical innovations by key inventors (Berners-Lee, 1999; Castells, 2001; Cerf, 2005).

However, a growing literature on the social shaping of technology, to which Kling and his colleagues have made a valuable contribution, demonstrates that technical innovations and their outcomes are crucially shaped by, and are inseparable from, the economic, social, and policy contexts in which the technologies are designed, developed, and used. Many radical or incremental technical inventions fail to generate important social outcomes, while others have widespread impacts. For instance, PCs were initially developed in the late 1970s by "home brewing" do-it-yourself technical entrepreneurs. At first, attempts by managers and professionals to introduce them into the workplace were actively discouraged as being institutionally counter-productive—until the groundswell of grassroots demand based on practical benefits, fuelled by experiences with home-based PCs that seemed more beneficial than corporate systems, led to PCs becoming integral to organizational operations. In contrast, top-down attempts to promote a breakthrough, such as frequent government and industry efforts to encourage use of the video phone, have been rejected by users.

The CM perspective helps to explain how technologies fundamentally reshape the way in which we can do things, and why their successful diffusion is as much a process of social as technical change. The value of this view is reinforced by its relevance to contemporary developments, such as around F/OSS or Weblogs, the so-called "blogging revolution." Major developments in computing, such as the Internet, are the outcome not just of a single social movement—as highlighted by the CM concept, such innovations are tied to both technical inventions and social movements. Outcomes from these social dynamics often emerge from several intersecting movements or through connections to counter-movements, together with a variety of other social factors that shape the development of a technology such as public policy and regulation. For instance, questions about "who invented the Internet" are being eclipsed by issues around "who should govern the Internet," as there is an escalation in the number and diversity of new actors and interests involved in shaping the Net.

This chapter argues that it might be useful to embed these different conceptions of CMs, technical invention, and public policy within a larger framework of action where computerization developments are understood as the outcome of the unfolding interaction of various actors pursuing a diverse array of goals and objectives. This new conceptualization, an "ecology of games," provides the basis for an integrative framework in which to analyze the co-evolution of economic, cultural, organizational, legal, and other intertwined dimensions of social transformations. The chapter describes key features of the ecology of games in supplementing the CM approach, using historical and contemporary examples of how the Internet has been, and will be, shaped. The aim is to demonstrate how this framework can take forward existing conceptions of the dynamics of CMs and technological change into an era of widespread ubiquitous computing (Sørensen & Gibson, Chapter 17, this volume) and other information and communications technologies (ICT)-enabled social and economic change.

Ecology of Games

Definitions

This chapter uses the term "game" to indicate an arena of competition and cooperation structured by a set of rules and assumptions about how to act to achieve a particular set of objectives, and an "ecology of games" is seen as a larger system of action composed of two or more separate but interdependent games (Dutton, 1992a). Defined in this way, the idea of an ecology of games helps to reveal the dynamics of technical, social, and policy choices shaping the development of a technology. Aspects of an ecology of games—games, rules, strategies, and players—offer a "grammar" for describing the system of action shaping technological change. As a framework for analysis, it overcomes major limitations of single-inventor notions and adds new insights to understanding computerization as a social movement.

Background to the Ecology of Games Concept

The concept of an ecology of games was developed far afield from innovation in ICTs. In the 1950s, Norton Long (1958) used the idea to provide a new perspective on pluralist versus elitist debate over who governs local communities. Most such theorists viewed policymaking as one isolated game in which all players seek to shape policy within the rules defined by the political and economic system. While both pluralist and elite perspectives on the policy process can be described as an ecology of games, they represent two quite different ecologies.

Long claimed that, generally, local events are governed neither in rational-comprehensive ways nor by a pluralistic set of elites nor by a more networked economic elite. He argued that these perspectives might oversimplify the system of action governing the course of public affairs. Instead of primarily being concerned with governing the community, as both pluralist and elite theorists assumed, major players were as much—or more—focused on such matters as selling real estate, being elected to the city council, developing land, creating a general plan, and finding a decent home. To understand the behavior of these players, it was therefore useful to think of them as real estate agents, candidates for the council, land developers, planners, and house hunters, rather than people only or even primarily seeking to govern their community.

The development of communities could then be understood as the consequence of an unfolding history of events driven by the often unplanned and unanticipated interactions among individuals playing relatively independent games. Rather than individuals making decisions about the larger community, they most often made decisions as the occupant of a particular role within a specific game. Thus, the evolution of local communities might be viewed as the outcome of a history of separate but interdependent games.

Since Long published these ideas, elite and pluralist debates have been sustained, but have also been overtaken by new perspectives on power and public policy. Elite traditions have encompassed notions of a managerial, bureaucratic, or technocratic elite as well as various formulations of class, neo-Marxist, and structuralist perspectives that focus more on the underlying structure of the economic and political system than on the actions of particular elites. Pluralist traditions have been sustained by a growing body of sector-specific policy studies, which tend to assume a relatively specialized set of actors and decisions, and by a revival of interest in the ways that the state and other institutions contribute to policy outcomes (March & Olsen, 1984).

Nevertheless, the ecology of games continues to offer a viable alternative to prevailing theoretical perspectives, not only on the policy process but also on technological change. I have revisited Long's notion of an ecology of games and developed further elaborations of this concept to provide a heuristically rich and useful framework for understanding the dynamics of decision-making processes in technology and public policy in a wide range of areas (Dutton, 1992a, 1992b, 1999, 2004a; Dutton & Guthrie, 1991; Dutton & Mackinen, 1987; Vedel & Dutton, 1990).

Key Benefits and Characteristics of the Ecology of Games Perspective

The ecology of games as defined here explains how players in a game have "a sense of purpose and a role" and "a set of strategies and tactics" (Long, 1958, p. 252). Within this framework, structural and institutional factors can be linked to the behavior of actors by the manner in which they help to define the goals or rules of particular games. For instance, I have argued that the separation of powers distinguishes the rules of some games shaping communication policy in the U.S. from those in parliamentary democracies like the U.K. (Dutton, 1992a, 1992b). It is in such ways that the ecology of games offers a potential for bridging levels of analysis in the social and policy sciences.

All games share several key attributes. First, every game has a set of goals, purposes, or objectives, and some games have multiple objectives. For example, a bureaucrat within a regulation game might seek to avoid conflict. Second, a game has a set of prizes. These may vary widely, from targeting profits to seeking authority or recognition to achieving greater social equity. The prizes gained during a game are distinct from the objectives of the players. For example, prizes for a bureaucrat associated with resolving conflict over time might be such personal benefits as a higher salary or larger office.

Third, games have rules that govern the strategies or moves open to players. A regulation game is governed in part by administrative law and the rules might need to be made public and be seen to be fair, as they also need to be for games played for amusement. However, the rules need not be public or fair in certain games, such as those played for private interests. The rules may change over time, and there may even be no consensus on the rules of the game and what they mean (Crozier & Friedland, 1980). Finally, a game has a set of players, defined by the fact that they interact—compete or cooperate—with one another in pursuing a game's objectives. A regulatory game not only incorporates bureaucrats, legislators, regulated firms, and industries but could also include the public, courts, and other actors willing and able to become involved.

In an ecology of games, individual games can be interrelated in several ways. Some players might simultaneously participate in different games, while others might transfer from one game to another (Long, 1958). Plays (moves or actions) made in one game can affect the play of others. Also, the outcome of one game might affect the rules or play of another. Players might be able to anticipate a range of strategies open to individuals, organizations, or other actors if they know what roles those actors play in the game(s) most central to them. Conversely, when players' actions appear irrational to an observer, it is likely that the observer does not know the rules and contexts of the games in which players are most centrally involved; the players' moves in one game might actually be constrained by their moves within other games.

Generally, the notion of an "ecology" of games underscores the degree to which not all players in any given "territory"[1] or arena, such as an organization or geographic place, are involved in the same game. The term "ecology" implies that there is an interrelated system of actors, which illuminates the fact that different players within that arena are likely to be involved in a variety of games. As already indicated, those involved in a CM can be players within one or more other games (e.g., those involved in the F/OSS movement can be players in a variety of games, such as the protection of information rights as well as software supply).

Games Shaping the Internet

The ecology framework recommended in this chapter indicates that no one person or group "invented" the Internet in the form it currently takes, and no one "governs" the Internet. Instead, it argues that a complex innovation like the Internet is best viewed as the outcome of an ecology in which specific actors seek to achieve their own goals within one or more separate but interrelated games. The direction of technological change is shaped by the unfolding consequences of strategic choices about matters more directly significant to the actors than those related to specific technical choices, as illustrated in this section through examples in three aspects of the Internet: its invention and early history, a discussion of current developments of broadband infrastructures and services, and efforts to govern the Internet.

Inventing the Internet

Much has been written about the invention of the Internet (e.g., Castells, 2001; Cerf, 2005), weighing the relative contributions of different innovations, groups, organizations, and technical advances. However, informed treatments of this history show that the Internet did not follow a linear path of development. On the contrary, it emerged through the interaction of different advances across different sectors, made by a variety of individuals, groups, and organizations with different aims and objectives. For instance, the rise of the Free Software Movement (Elliott & Scacchi, forthcoming) and the Open Source Initiative as CMs (Dedrick & West, Chapter 16, this volume; Ekbia & Gasser, Chapter 15, this volume; Elliott, Chapter 13, this volume; Scacchi, Chapter 14, this volume) was facilitated by the Internet and Web, particularly their ability to connect developers around the world and the open view of Web page coding. In turn, this movement fueled investment in the Internet. The origins and development of the F/OSS CM were quite separate from efforts to invent the Internet, but became interwoven with and influenced the evolving culture of Internet producers and users (Weber, 2004).

The traditional "single inventor" Internet story started within the U.S. Department of Defense's Advanced Research Project Agency (ARPA), which began in 1958 (Cerf, 2005; Dutton, 1999, p. 89, Box 4.6). It launched a network, the ARPANET, in 1968 to link a few small computers. This was the first computer network to use a "packet switching" technique to offer high resilience in message transmission even if some nodes in the network were not available. Packet switching remains a technical cornerstone of the Internet, into which ARPANET eventually evolved. Vincent Cerf, Robert Kahn, and other important members of the team steering ARPANET developments are frequently seen as "fathers of the Internet."

However, numerous other critical technical developments involved a wide variety of other experts and a variety of organizations in many countries, such as the switch in 1983 to the IP Transmission Control Protocol developed in the U.S. and U.K. However, even among the ARPANET pioneers, key features that subsequently boosted the popularity of the Internet were not initially prioritized. For example, Cerf has recalled (Roop, 2005): "E-mail sort of sneaked up on us in 1971 and surprised everybody with its utility." And he added: "What really triggered a big explosion of information online was the introduction of the World Wide Web."

Significant social movements did develop around the work of Cerf, Kahn, and their colleagues. For example, they founded, and have remained as major figures within, the Internet Society (ISOC). This has become one of the major international associations of people who have championed the Internet, encompassing more than 20,000 members in more than 180 countries. ISOC's Board of Trustees is a virtual "Who's Who" of the Internet world, albeit anchored primarily in the U.S. (www.isoc.org).

The Web made its impact only in the 1990s, emerging from a set of networking projects at the European Laboratory for Particle Physics (CERN) in Switzerland, where Tim Berners-Lee (1999) was one of the Web's driving forces. A prototype he developed in the early 1990s was influenced by Ted Nelson's (1987) visionary work on the Xanadu project, started in 1966 with the aim of creating a commercially viable network that would give you a screen in your home from which you could see the world's hypertext libraries (Nelson, 1974, pp. 56–57). Xanadu, in turn, was inspired by Douglas Engelbart's "oN-Line System" (NLS) at Stanford Research Institute, which aimed to make computers a more useful tool to help people think and work. Engelbart and Nelson, like many other visionaries, did not generate social movements around themselves or their inventions. However, their ideas mattered in the course of developments that shaped the Internet. Similarly, ARPANET's technical innovations can be traced to many earlier innovations created with a variety of goals in computing and telecommunications fields. This further weakens the single inventor hypothesis, but also illustrates the degree to which technical inventions and new ideas matter, even if not always crystallized in significant social movements.

The role of CERN in developing the Web provides a stark illustration of how a vast number of Internet users were highly influential in the shaping of the technology's capabilities and applications. Researchers in academic, business, and government laboratories around the world made especially significant contributions, not only in specific technical innovations but in establishing a culture of open flows of information and trust within and between network communities, reflecting that of the academic research community. This culture influenced the architecture of the Internet. For example, the original design for the Internet had relatively poor levels of inbuilt security but smooth access to diverse information, which later became obstacles to expanding the network into business and domestic life where users require higher levels of protection (Blumenthal & Clark, 2001).

The emergence of the Internet from defense and public policy games as an experimental network linking a few computers to become today's worldwide phenomenon did not happen just because a few people turned bright ideas into practical systems, although many did. It resulted from a huge number of players in intertwined academic, commercial, technical, industrial, and other games making decisions about how specific aspects of the Internet should be designed, developed, used, or governed. Each decision met goals and made sense within different arenas, with the interaction between choices in each game combining to create the 21st-century phenomenon of the Internet, Web, and related ICTs.

Broadband Internet Infrastructures and Services

Overlapping sets of telecommunications, media, and regulatory and policy games have propelled recent rapid innovations in high-speed "broadband" communication technologies, such as optical fibers and direct subscriber line technologies that speed up digital transmission on traditional telephone lines. The creation and rapid growth of "always on" broadband Internet services that can deliver multimedia content to users whenever they want and wherever they are, on the move or stationary, has propelled the Internet to a new dimension of use and potential for enabling social transformations.

The ecology of games affecting broadband Internet outcomes exemplifies the kinds of ecologies that influence the history, present, and future of the Internet and its governance. Table 19.1 illustrates how the many actors, strategies, and movements, shaping the provision and use of broadband Internet developments, form an ecology of games taking place in a variety of arenas at the same time, with outcomes emerging from interactions among the multiplicity of players in the many different games in each arena.

Cultural and policy contexts matter to the outcomes of the kinds of games indicated in Table 19.1. For instance, in some countries an issue like providing a multimedia package that mixes television, telephony, and broadband Internet services would involve a number of regulatory games within and between different institutions responsible for different media; in others, just one regulator covers many old and new media, such as the U.K. Office of Communications, formed in 2003 to cover telecommunication, broadcasting, and print industries. Certain governments have a strong general anti-monopoly agenda with legislative backing, although ICT multimedia convergence makes it harder to define the precise boundaries of ICT and media marketplaces within which one player can be said to be overdominant. Other countries either see these industries as being part of an economic game that is best left to market forces or, conversely, wish to place them under state control.

Table 19.1 Illustrative Games Shaping Outcomes Tied to the Use of the Internet and Related ICTs

Games	Main players	Goals and objectives
Economic development	Governments, public agencies, investors; non-government organizations (NGOs); activists in developing countries	Players build ICT infrastructures to attract business, investment, and jobs to localities; players in disadvantaged area seek to use that infrastructure to close social and economic divides.
Communitarian	Neighborhoods, community groups, Internet enthusiasts	Individuals and groups seek free or low-cost, open access to the Internet, sometimes competing with commercial users or providers.
Copyright/digital rights management	Content providers versus consumers and ICT industries; information rights activists; regulators	Telecommunications firms, media industries, and users compete over interpretations of rights in access to information and services.
Software development and use	F/OSS CM promoting free software versus commercial proprietary software producers and distributors	F/OSS developers seek to achieve greater equity of access to benefits from the use of ICTs; commercial suppliers compete for market share and profits.
Telecommunication regulation, such as network neutrality	Telecommunications firms, regulators, investors, consumers	Regulators umpire moves of competing firms, taking account of conflicting and complementary goals among players.
Broadband access	Traditional telephone companies using DSL technologies, cable TV firms, wireless, and other vendors	Suppliers compete for shares in a market, where frequently DSL and cable vendors have been the main broadband players winning lines into homes and offices.
Content provision	Media giants versus Internet entrepreneurs; media novices versus professionals	Established and emerging producers of Internet content compete to reach audiences.
Consumer protection	Consumers, consumer groups, suppliers, regulators	Legislators and regulators respond to competing views of the consumer's interests in ICT provision.
E-games	Pro/anti e-enablement players in government, business, education, and commerce	Organizations put their vitality at stake through over-/under-investment in online infrastructures and applications.
Implementation	Users, ICT product and service suppliers, consultants	Users struggle to implement and maintain ICTs in order to reap the potential benefits.

Source: Dutton, Gillett, McKnight, and Peltu, 2003, p. 54, Table 4

The goals set for regulators vary according to the particular political and economic policies being pursued.

Market forces, government policy, and telecommunications marketing strategies have generally been the strongest driving forces behind the growth of broadband Internet (Dutton, Gillett, McKnight, & Peltu, 2003). However, there have been social movements of relevance to broadband, such as what might be called the WiFi (wireless fidelity) grassroots communitarian CM that nourished the growth of local wireless-based computer networks, starting in the U.S. and then taken up around the world (Dutton, 2004a). Another is peer-to-peer file sharing, as used in key music distribution services to share tracks and albums held on the computers of users connected to the Internet, rather than via a centrally controlled online music store. A related movement has been developing around ensuring the neutrality of the Internet with regard to the nature of content. This opposes efforts by some Internet service providers (ISPs) to tier their services in order to charge different rates for particular content, such as for the provision of on-demand video entertainment. This network neutrality movement pits civil society advocates and Internet evangelists concerned with open access to information against some telecommunications providers and policymakers who are more focused on the development of new markets.

Of course, as indicated in Table 19.1, broadband Internet is part of the wider Internet ecology of games, within which many CM and other social movements play an active role. For instance, social movements and CMs concerned with using ICTs for economic and social development in disadvantaged regions of the world and social sectors within countries are also important actors in the economic development game. The Blacksburg Electronic Village (Carroll, Chapter 7, this volume), part of the Clinton Administration's National Information Infrastructure vision of the social value of greater Internet use, illustrates how a CM motivated by the creation of a more civic-minded society can play a role in influencing outcomes in the communitarian game. A growing information rights CM (Clement & Hurrell, Chapter 12, this volume), including F/OSS actors, is challenging key traditional perspectives in the copyright/digital rights management game. As already indicated, F/OSS is itself a game whose outcome influences other Internet games, creating a new vision of what can be achieved by actors making certain decisions about their objectives in developing and using software, which has generated innovations in software development and use that have had wider impacts.

Broadband Internet could change the rules of some media games, for instance through outcomes from the continuing attempts to build new forms of integrated multimedia operations by exploiting technical digital convergence, as with IP-enabled services. It can also open up new roles for those who have been communicatively empowered by broadband access, as when media consumers become media producers by setting up Web sites offering their own blogs, online news media, and discussion forums.

Internet Governance

The ecology of games viewpoint is relevant to a growing interest in reassessing and rethinking Internet governance institutions and mechanisms in light of the rapid global expansion of this network of networks.[2] Despite the development of an increasingly well informed debate on this issue, discussion on Internet governance often seems to stumble over the notion that someone or somebody does, or can, govern it. The idea of Internet governance is so controversial that substantive treatments of specific policy issues often do not get beyond an argument about the validity of the concept.

For example, the Internet community, policymakers, and the public at large are divided over the question of whether governments should be involved in regulating the Internet at all. This is illustrated in a 2005 Oxford Internet Survey conducted by the Oxford Internet Institute, which found that Internet users in Britain are not predominantly pro or anti government regulation of the Internet—they are divided. We asked users (Dutton, di Gennaro, & Hargreave, 2005, p. 48): "Some people think the Internet should be regulated, others think government should not regulate the Internet. What do you think?" Most (45 percent) said they did not know or were undecided. Less than one-third (29 percent) thought that governments should regulate, but a nearly equal number of users (27 percent) thought governments should not (see Figure 19.1).

To some involved in Internet development, provision, and use, the word "governance" conjures up the unwelcome notion of governments moving into a thriving arena that has been fostered by seemingly ungoverned entrepreneurial and technical ingenuity. This raises the specter of killing the vitality of the Internet through governmental, administrative, political, industrial, and legal barriers to technical innovation.

Yet there are those who contend that more national and international public oversight and regulation of the Internet is essential because of its growing significance, both in opening up new combinations of ICT-enabled services, such as in providing voice and related IP-based capabilities, and in dealing with spam, viruses, and a growing range of online problems experienced by users. Even some prominent critics of Internet "governance" suggest a term such as "coordination" as an acceptable alternative to solving problems faced by the network's users and providers.

A way forward could be to recognize that, in some form, decisions about Internet governance at international, national, and local levels are inescapable. For example, decisions by government not to regulate the Internet, not to tax Internet-enabled commerce, or to seek to coordinate activities of various stakeholders are decisions that affect Internet governance and regulation. This could be helpful to policy debate to

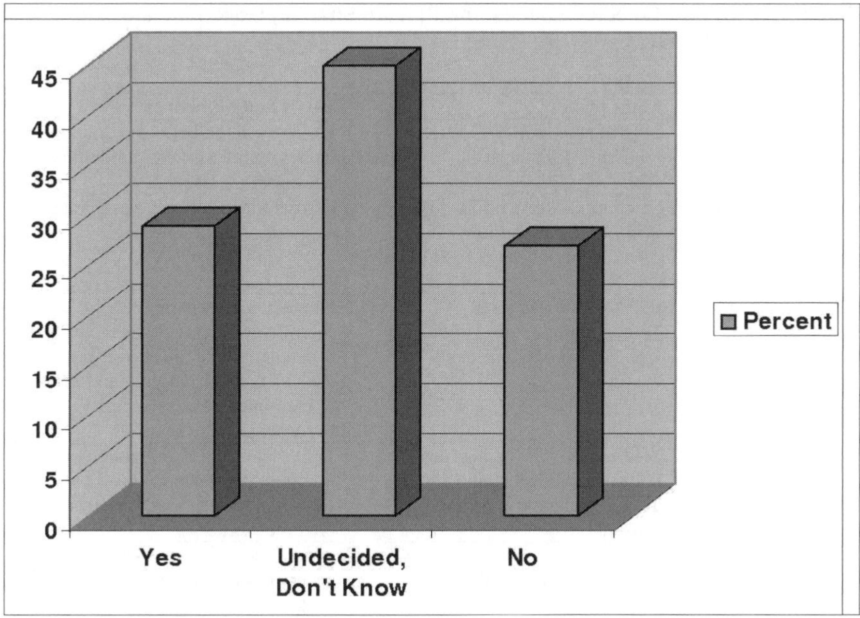

Figure 19.1 **British opinion on Internet regulation: Should government regulate the Internet? (Source: OxIS 2005, number of respondents = 2,185; see Dutton, di Gennaro, & Hargreave, 2005, p. 48)**

emphasize that Internet governance does not imply a specific policy regime. For instance, the U.S. First Amendment is government policy and government is deeply involved in protecting freedom of expression in the U.S. context. Other countries have different approaches to this right. The difficulties of addressing the diverse interests in the Internet governance game are illustrated by the conclusion of the report by the Working Group on Internet Governance (WGIG, 2005), established by the United Nations to investigate and make proposals for action on Internet governance. It recommended a number of options rather than specific solutions, together with advice on the need to improve institutional and stakeholder coordination, for example through the recently created Internet Governance Forum.[3]

Another significant issue is the question of who or what "governs" (or can govern) the Internet *per se*. A more productive view would be to understand the governance of the Internet not as something capable of being in the control of any one set of actors but as the outcome of an ecology of games, as illustrated by just a few of the many Internet governance games shown in Table 19.2. For instance, the management and operation of the Internet are greatly affected by the system of allocating names and numbers in the IP address space, such as Web domain name

Table 19.2 A Few Selected Games and Players Shaping Governance of the Internet

Games	Main players	Goals and objectives
Names and numbers	Individual experts, ICANN, registries, ISPs, users	Obtain, sell, and allocate domain names, addresses, etc. to identify sites, servers, users.
Standards	Standards-setting bodies, World Wide Web Consortium (W3C), Internet Engineering Task Force (IETF)	Efforts to establish and propagate standards for the Internet.
Jurisdictional turf struggles	ICANN, International Telecommunication Union (ITU), UN, national governments	National actors participate in Internet governing bodies to gain or retain national control over policy, such as through filtering and access to encrypted data for security purposes.
Political speech, freedom of expression	Media rights advocates, activists, politicians, news media, governments, writers and artists, censors	Individuals and organizations aim to facilitate or constrain flows of information, political views, and creative works.
Secrecy vs. open government	Governments, citizens, civil society, business and industry	Actors seek to open up or control access to information collected and held by governments, such as through freedom of information provisions or national security legislation.

and e-mail address allocation and management. Key players in this game include the nonprofit Internet Corporation for Assigned Names and Numbers (ICANN), commercial ISPs, registries, and users. Substantial commercial, personal, and national interests and convenience are at stake in these games, so most actors set great store on establishing rules that create a fair playing field without an overdominance by particular vested interests.

Vulnerabilities that threaten the Internet's continuing expansion have stimulated much activity around Internet governance (Dutton & Peltu, 2005). For instance, there is increasing trouble in making core technical changes to Internet protocols and infrastructure (Dutton, 2004b). One reason for this is that it is becoming harder to reach technical agreements because crucial choices about which solution to apply can no longer be determined largely by a relatively small group of public-spirited and mutually trusting experts, as was still possible until the late 1990s, when there existed a relatively simple ecology of Internet-related games. The escalation in the number of players with an interest in the Internet is shown by the holding of meetings with about 2,000 members of the Internet Engineering Task Force (IETF), the international community of network specialists concerned with the evolution and smooth operation of the Internet.

An even greater challenge is that once a technical decision is reached, getting it adopted on the millions of computers linked to the Internet is becoming increasingly difficult. Not only is there a growing range of technical barriers to core innovations, such as firewalls, but decisions in each specialist arena of expertise overlap and intermesh with decisions by actors in other key sectors. For instance, vested interests and competitive pressures make Internet service and product providers reluctant to pioneer changes. Users are also demanding increased protection through firewalls and other controls, while also expecting the Internet to remain open to any use they want, even when it stretches the Internet beyond its limits—as with companies using it for safety-critical controls despite inherent vulnerabilities in the current Internet infrastructure.

From the perspective of an ecology of games, not only does no one govern the Internet in the rational–comprehensive sense, but very few people or organizations are actually seeking to govern it as such. Instead, most actors try to achieve more focused objectives that provide more immediate prizes, for instance developing a market for registering names and numbers, keeping a bank's computer system secure from hackers, avoiding spam e-mails, and so on. Governance of the Internet can then be understood as the outcome of a variety of choices, made by many different players involved in many separate—but interdependent—policy games or areas of activity.

Refocusing debate on the more specific policy games shaping governance of the Internet could move the focus away from controversies over government regulation of the Internet *per se*, and away from attempts to create a rational–comprehensive structure or process for governing the Internet. Both starting points are likely to block international progress in this important area.

It is by decomposing or unpacking this complex ecology of games that policymakers and activists can focus on the objectives, rules, and strategies of specific games that drive particular players, while also recognizing that each game is being played within a much larger system of action in which the play and outcomes of any one game can reshape the play, and thereby the outcomes, of other separate, interdependent games.

However, the creation of games can be a strategic approach to progressing policy debate and decision making. For example, much early debate around Internet governance was focused on whether the U.S. Department of Commerce should continue to exercise control over ICANN. This issue has been contentious, and possibly dysfunctional, by focusing too much attention on a largely symbolic issue when many other aspects surround Internet governance. Therefore, fostering the development of an Internet governance game could help broaden debate. Likewise, debate over Internet governance has tended to become separated from that over the role of ICTs in economic development, when they could be more closely tied together. For instance, the first IGF Forum is entitled "Internet Governance for Development,"[4] indicating a close connection between these two issues. Such tactics can be understood as moves aimed at influencing the larger ecology of games shaping the governance of the Internet.

Ubiquitous Computing: A CM?

Finally, the emergence of ubiquitous computing and communications (Elliott & Kraemer, Chapter 20, this volume; Sørensen & Gibson, Chapter 17, this volume) is seen by some as an ultimate state in the evolution of the information society, as it offers an "any time, anywhere, anyhow" networked digital environment. In this respect, it could be a normative forecast of a future in which computers blend into the background of our lives as the technology advances beyond the PC.[5] This vision of the future is endorsed by a number of individuals, companies, and public officials and thus could form a significant CM in the future.

However, very few people are seeking to pursue the aim of making computers recede into the background of their work and everyday life. Instead, again, they are trying to accomplish far more specific objectives, such as applying technologies like radio frequency identification, electronic tags to monitor inventories, or creating new ICT-based products and services. As one possible outcome of contemporary developments in computing, it might be more useful to view ubiquitous computing as the ultimate outcome or the sum of all games shaping the future of computing. That said, if we view ubiquity as one possible outcome of an ecology of games, the future is open to many other possible outcomes. Ecologies are shaped by the separate but interrelated choices made by a multitude of actors pursuing a variety of objectives within many, shifting arenas of action.

Conclusion

The games perspective described in this chapter can be applied to explain the entwined social, technical, organizational, and other forces that shape the emergence of changes tied to the increasingly ubiquitous use of the Internet and related ICTs. At the same time, it embeds many ideas from the CM concept and reinforces the value of its central illumination of the ways in which the motivations and actions of people and organizations in particular social contexts shape the ultimate design and impacts of the technology and policy in real-world settings. It has illustrated how social movements, such as the CMs whose goals are to promote open source or to employ ICTs for development, are critical to many games shaping the future development, use, and governance of the Internet. And it has placed these movements within a larger system of action to offer a framework for thinking about the highly complex system of interactions shaping outcomes relating to the Internet phenomenon, including a recognition of the significance of many technical inventions and new ideas that may fail to kindle social movements.

This framework emphasizes the potential for unanticipated, unplanned developments, while raising doubts about perspectives on technological change, such as the single inventor thesis, that posit a more governed, isolated, and predictable system of action. In fact, it helps explain why prediction is likely to elude those involved in technology and policy studies who seek to attain it. Although it challenges some traditional tenets of structural and institutional explanations of social and political orders, the ecology of games concept strongly supports the thrust of institutional perspectives, such as those articulated by March and Olsen (1989, p. 9): "… the long-run development of political institutions is less a product of intentions, plans and consistent decisions than incremental adaptation to changing problems with available solutions within gradually evolving structures of meaning" (see also Cohen, March, & Olsen, 1972; Lane, 1990; March & Olsen, 1984.)

Policymakers and many technologists might like to deal with more predictable outcomes but, as indicated by the CM and ecology of games viewpoint, the real world is far more "messy" than simplistic story lines of the inevitable, unfolding predetermined paths toward a future carved out by heroic inventors and their unerring technological swords. In reality, those swords are double-edged, for example, with the Internet delivering software viruses, spyware, spam, and pedophile contacts along with its global treasure trove of information and multiple communication channels. In addition, the actual outcomes are determined by a multitude of heroes and heroines making small and large strategic decisions every day about whether or not to use the Internet or other ICTs.

Major upheavals in industry sectors, the opening of significant new patterns of domestic and working life, and shake-ups in major policy sectors, such as Internet governance and regulation, are often created by developments that few, if any, have predicted well in advance. The examples related to the Internet given in this chapter illustrate the value of the ecology of games in illuminating the dynamics and uncertainties of CMs within larger systems of action. They also show how inventions, new ideas, and myriad choices by consumers and users contribute to such transformations linked to technological change.

Acknowledgments

This chapter is based on a sense that Rob Kling would find it to be a useful contribution to his own thinking. Rob asked me for copies of my work on the ecology of games during the year preceding his untimely death. I had a sense that he found merit in this approach. I hope my ideas have been merged with his own conceptions in a way that he would find worthy of debate.

Endnotes

1. For Long, territories were defined by local communities. However, the territory of an ecology of games as defined in this paper could be a household, a locale, an organization, or a nation. It might even be global, such as the contemporary arena for Internet governance (Sapolsky, Crane, Neuman, and Noam, 1992).
2. This section builds on Dutton (2005).
3. For more information see: www.intgovforum.org
4. See: www.intgovforum.org
5. A illustrative example of this vision is provided at: www.ubiq.com/ubicomp

References

Berners-Lee, T. (1999). *Weaving the Web: The origins and future of the World Wide Web*. London: Orion Books.

Blumenthal, M., & Clark, D. D. (2001). Rethinking the design of the Internet: The end to end arguments vs. the brave new world. *ACM Transactions on Internet Technology*, 1(1), 70–109.

Castells, M. (2001). *The Internet galaxy: Reflections on the Internet, business, and society*. Oxford: Oxford University Press.

Cerf, V. (2005). A brief history of the Internet. Unpublished document. Retrieved from www2.fhs.usyd.edu.au/arow/isd/Resources/History_of_Internet.htm

Cohen, M. D., March, J. G., & Olsen, J. P. (1972). A garbage can model of organizational choice. *Administrative Science Quarterly*, 17, 1–25.

Crozier, M., & Friedland, E. (1980). *Actors and systems.* Chicago: University of Chicago Press.

Dutton, W. H. (1992a). The ecology of games shaping telecommunications policy. *Communications Theory*, 2(4), 303–328.

Dutton, W. H. (1992b). The ecology of games in telecommunication policy. In H. M. Spools, R. J. Crane, W. R. Neuman, & E. M. Noam (Eds.), *The telecommunications revolution* (pp. 65–88). London and New York: Routledge.

Dutton, W. H. (1999). *Society on the line: Information politics in the digital age.* Oxford: Oxford University Press.

Dutton, W. H. (2004a). *Social transformation in an information society: Rethinking access to you and the world.* Paris: UNESCO Publications for the World Summit on the Information Society.

Dutton, W. H. (2004b). Can the Internet survive? Why your decisions matter. Nominet.uk News. Retrieved from www.nominetnews.org.uk/dec04/debate.php

Dutton, W. H. (2005). A new framework for taking forward the Internet governance debate. Position paper for *The struggle over Internet governance: Searching for common ground* Forum, Oxford: Oxford Internet Institute, 5–6 May. Retrieved from www.oii.ox.ac.uk/research/publications.cfm

Dutton, W. H., & Guthrie, K. (1991). An ecology of games: The political construction of Santa Monica's public electronic network. *Informatization and the Public Sector*, 1(4), 1–24.

Dutton, W. H., & Mackinen, H. (1987). The development of telecommunications: The outcome of an ecology of games. *Information & Management*, 13(5), 255–264.

Dutton, W. H., & Peltu, M. (2005). The emerging Internet governance mosaic: Connecting the pieces. *OII Forum Discussion Paper No. 5*. Oxford: Oxford Internet Institute, University of Oxford. Retrieved from www.oii.ox.ac.uk/research/publications.cfm

Dutton, W. H., di Gennaro, C., & Hargreave, A. M. (2005, May). The Internet in Britain: The Oxford Internet Survey (OxIS). Oxford: Oxford Internet Institute, University of Oxford. Retrieved from www.oii.ox.ac.uk/research/publications.cfm

Dutton, W. H., Gillett, S. E., McKnight, L. W., & Peltu, M. (2003). Broadband Internet: The power to reconfigure access. *OII Forum Discussion Paper No. 1*, Oxford: Oxford Internet Institute, University of Oxford. Retrieved from www.oii.ox.ac.uk/research/publications.cfm

Elliott, M. S., & Scacchi, W. (forthcoming). Mobilization of software developers: The free software movement. *Information, Technology and People*.

Kling, R. (1984). Computing as an occasion for social control. *Journal of Social Issues*, 49(1), 77–96.

Kling, R., & Iacono, S. (1988). The mobilization of support for computerization: The role of computerization movements. *Social Problems*, 35(3), 226–242.

Kling, R., & Iacono, S. (1995). Computerization movements and the mobilization of support for computerization. In S. L. Starr (Ed.), *Ecologies of knowledge: Work and politics in science and technology*. (pp. 149–153). Albany, NY: State University of New York Press.

Lane, R. (1990). Concrete theory: An emerging political method. *American Political Science Review*, 84(3), 927–940.

Long, N. E. (1958, November). The local community as an ecology of games. *American Journal of Sociology*, 64, 251–261.

March, J. G., & Olsen, J. P. (1984). The new institutionalism. *American Political Science Review*, 78(3), 734–749.

March, J. G., & Olsen, J. P. (1989). *Rediscovering institutions*. New York: The Free Press.

Nelson, T. (1974). *Dream machines*. Chicago: Hugo's Book Service.

Nelson, T. (1987). *Literary machines*. Swarthmore, PA: Mindful.

Roop, J. (2005, February 16). Net origins. *Style weekly*. Retrieved from styleweekly.com/article.asp?idarticle=9802

Sapolsky, H. M., Crane, R. J., Neuman, W. R., & Noam, E. M. (Eds.). (1992). *The telecommunications revolution*. London and New York: Routledge.

Vedel, T., & Dutton, W. H. (1990). New media politics: Shaping cable television policy in France. *Media, Culture and Society*, 12, 491–552.

Weber, S. (2004). *The success of open source*. Cambridge: Harvard University Press.

WGIG (2005). Working Group on Internet Governance. *Report of the Working Group on Internet Governance*. Retrieved from www.wgig.org

Williams, R., & Edge, D. (1996). The social shaping of technology. In W. H. Dutton (Ed.), *Information and communication technologies: Visions and realities* (pp. 53–67). Oxford: Oxford University Press.

Part VII

Conclusion

Chapter 20

Comparative Perspective on Computerization Movements: Implications for Ubiquitous Computing

Margaret S. Elliott and Kenneth L. Kraemer
University of California, Irvine

Abstract

The collection of papers in this book highlights the importance and impact of computerization movements on individuals, organizations, and society. We have shown how computerization movements, which are driven by utopian visions of a specific technology's use, are generated and modified in response to realities in organizations and society, or move on to the "next big thing." In this final chapter, we draw conclusions from the historical evolution of computerization movements across four eras of computerization: Mainframe, Personal Computer, Internet, and Ubiquitous Computing. We present five generalizations of computerization movements across the four eras based on the chapters in this book. The study of computerization movements is intended to deepen understanding of how a special kind of technological social movement influences people in how they think about computing and communications technology and thereby shape technology decisions in organizations and society.

Introduction

The collection of papers in this book highlights the importance and impact of computerization movements (CMs) on individuals, organizations, and society. We have shown how CMs, which are driven by utopian visions about the technology's use, are generated and change in response to realities on the ground, or move on to the "next big thing." We have also shown that these movements range from those promoting hardware technologies (mainframes, personal computers [PCs], personal digitial assistants [PDAs], digital cameras, or mobile phones) to infrastructures such as the Internet, extranets and intranets, to software applications such as expert systems (e.g., mortgage banking) and to software genres such as free/open source software (F/OSS) (e.g., GNU/Linux).

In this final chapter, we draw conclusions from the historical evolution of CMs across four eras of computerization: Mainframe, PC, Internet, and Ubiquitous Computing. We then present five generalizations gleaned from looking across these eras. They are summarized here and discussed more fully later in the chapter:

- There is a continuing gap between CM visions and the reality of technology use in organizations and society.
- CM rhetoric tends to shift from the utopian to the pragmatic with experience and contending discourse.
- Technologies that require a support infrastructure to be built as part of their implementation take longer to diffuse than those that can use existing infrastructures, resulting in a lower probability that a CM requiring a new infrastructure will lead to successful diffusion.
- The realities of day-to-day use of a CM's promoted technology cannot be predicted precisely in advance, but informed technology assessments can be made by better understanding of similarities and differences of emerging and earlier technologies. Such assessments can improve the success of a CM.
- The social context shapes technology use as much or more than the technology per se. New technology often reinforces existing organizational and social arrangements, rather than disrupting, changing, or transforming them. CMs that leverage the technology-organization linkage will be more successful than those that do not.

We conclude with the contributions of this book and the implications of our generalizations for vendors, managers, users, and scholars.

Comparative Analysis of CMs in Four Computerization Eras

In general, CMs have been instrumental in promoting the diffusion and use of computing innovations since the first mainframe computers were introduced in the 1950s. As new technologies have emerged, new CMs have also emerged to create visions of the technology's use and value that promote their adoption and use. Although the individual technologies have been many, they can be clustered around the four computerization eras associated with key technologies that represent strategic inflection points (Grove, 1996) in the history of computing. We have identified four eras and related CMs: the Mainframe era, PC era, Internet era, and Ubiquitous Computing era. We use these eras to provide a comparative perspective on the creation, maintenance, and outcomes of CMs over time.

Table 20.1 shows the four eras and corresponding time periods. Although several of the eras overlap in time, we show the new technologies that were prevalent during each era (column 1), and how they influenced the emergence of CMs. We then list the key CM activists for the technology (column 2) and the major venues for the CM discourse of the activists during each era (column 3). Next, we show the CM frames and visions (column 4) and, finally, examples of some outcomes of CMs that emerged during each era. In the next four sections, we discuss each of the four eras and elaborate on the key dimensions for each.

The Mainframe Era

Mainframe computers were the first practical application of computer technology for important business functions such as numerical analysis of actuary or mortality studies, fast numerical computations, and military or scientific large-scale applications. During the 1950s and 1960s, large companies started investing in mainframes across a wide range of industries and firms. During the 1950s and 1960s, large-scale calculations such as billing, which previously required many clerks for completion, were being calculated with mainframe computers. Centralized database management systems became common for record keeping and by the 1970s, word processing on mainframes was coming of age in most businesses.

Along with the mainframe paradigm came centralized processing with "dumb" terminals connected from various locations to enter or retrieve information. Since companies were investing vast amounts of money to acquire a mainframe computer, internal departments for maintenance and security of such systems became a requirement. Most organizations were vertically integrated with shared access to the mainframe's vast computing capacity. Many Management Information Systems (MIS) departments formed within organizations to develop and manage the complex computing applications offered by use of a mainframe.

During this period, mainframes were manufactured and advertised by large vendors such as IBM, Burroughs, Honeywell, NCR, Sperry

Table 20.1 Historical Comparison of Computerization Eras and CMs

Era	New Technology (Hardware & Software)	CM Activists Industry and Users	CM Discourse Venues	CM Frames & Visions	Examples of CM Outcomes
Mainframe Era 1950–1970	Mainframes; Distributed processing (Terminals); Calculators **Software:** Programming language compilers: Fortran, Pascal, Cobol, Basic; Database management systems; Business apps.; Scientific apps.	Vendors from IBM, DEC, UNISYS and other major computer vendors; Journalists; User groups; Government and industry users	Papers and speeches in form of: Application briefs; Government sponsored events; Newspapers and magazines; Trade shows and academic conferences	Organizational productivity; Improved learning; Machines can "think" like humans; Computers will reform society, government, education, and businesses and promote productivity and better decision making	AI (limited success); Computer-based education (widespread diffusion); Office automation (ongoing diffusion); Urban IS (Kling & Iacono)
PC Era 1975–1990	PCs; Macintosh; Unix Boxes; Networking; Client-server technology **Software:** PC apps. and compilers for PCs; Windows; E-mail in Orgs	Elite users; PC hobbyists; Apple; Microsoft; HP; SUN and others; PC users and managers in organizations	PC User groups (word of mouth); PC conventions; PC magazines and electronic journals; Professional groups; Mass media (TV, magazines, radio)	Individual productivity both at work and at home; PCs will change the world and improve productivity, promote democratization in organizations (reduce hierarchical management structures); PCs and handheld devices will improve society	Automated Underwriting CM (Markus et al.)—ongoing with some success; PDA—difficult to diffuse to general population (Allen)
Internet Era 1985–2005	Internet; Broadband connections **Software:** Internet-based global e-mail; Web apps.; intranets; Internet games; Videoconferencing; CSCW apps.; Distributed work at a distance; Virtual communities; F/OSS development	Computer-literate public—business and home users (global access); Cicso and others (networking industry activists); Activists for government sponsored initiatives (e.g. NII)	Web sites and white papers by Internet societies and special user groups (e.g., Linux, FSF, OSI); Internet advertisements	Internet connections provide death of distance; Improved democratization on global scale; Internet improves coordination, cooperation of groups across distance; Internet improves government participation	Internetworking CM—No increase in civic involvement (Carroll); no change to hierarchical communication (Wellman); Distributed work CM—difficult to integrate distributed work technology (Kiesler et al.; Mark); FSM—promotion and development of free software ongoing with some success (Elliott; Scacchi); Businesses using Linux (open source) to save

					money, not for ideological purposes (Dedrick & West); Digital Camera CM: success of digital camera (Meyer)
Ubiquitous Computing Era 2000 and beyond	Handheld devices; PDAs w/Web access; Blackberrys; Sensors & wearable computers **Software:** Downloads; Linux on a CD for computing anywhere; E-mail/Web access through handheld devices: Handheld devices for e-mail, PDAs, mobile phones	Almost everyone/ everywhere	Blogs; wikis; Myspace	Work and home life enhanced by being connected "anywhere, any time"; Ubiquitous computing is wave of future to transform home and work lives for the better; Ubicomp will promote "calmness" by computer devices in the background (Weiser vision); Ubicomp devices promote productivity (recent visions)	Mobile phones are "in the way" and unreliable for professionals (Sørensen & Gibson)

Rand, and Digital Equipment Corporation (DEC), to name a few. The hardware itself was very bulky and expensive and the typical customers in the 1950s were large enterprises such as government agencies, aerospace firms, financial institutions, and insurance companies. The software for this technology included compilers for scientific programming languages such as FORTRAN or for business languages such as COBOL. The targeted market for large mainframes was mainly financial executives and engineers. The discourse was highly technical and in the form of advertising, direct-mail brochures, and "team" sales calls (Jabloner, 2006). The dominant frame was that computers could increase speed of scientific and business calculations and thereby make businesses more productive. An interesting example of the utopian writing appears in a 1948 brochure in which the Eckert-Mauchly Computer Corporation (later Sperry-Rand) advertised the benefits of the UNIVAC computer as follows:

> WHAT'S YOUR PROBLEM? Is it the tedious record-keeping and the arduous figure-work of commerce and industry? Or is it the intricate mathematics of science? Perhaps your problem is now considered impossible because of prohibitive costs associated with conventional methods of solution. The UNIVAC SYSTEM has been developed by the Eckert-Mauchly Computer Corporation to solve such problems. Within its

> scope come applications as diverse as air traffic control, census tabulations, market research studies, insurance records, aerodynamic design, oil prospecting, searching chemical literature and economic planning. (cf. www.computerhistory.org/brochures/ for a detailed display of computer brochures of the 1950s–1980s available as a download by the Computer History Museum in Mountain View, California)

During the 1960s, mainframes were more integrated into businesses and the advertisements started showing signs of targeting the business manager for use in MIS (www.computerhistory.org/brochures). The predominant CM that emerged was what Kling and Iacono (1988) called the "general CM" promoting computerization in society and businesses as a way to improve productivity and reform society. Advertisements emphasized the flexibility and versatility of using a computer as well as the advantages of having a machine that can make logical decisions. By the 1970s, the CM activists included vendors as well as business managers and employees who felt there were significant benefits from using computers at work. During this period, the size of the mainframe became smaller with companies such as DEC producing a smaller version of a mainframe at a reduced price. Computer vendors started marketing computers to new groups: managers of departments within large organizations and small scientific and technical organizations.

Computer vendors such as IBM and Digital Equipment Corporation (DEC) formed and supported so-called "user groups" comprised of the computer professionals from their major customers. The vendors promoted concepts for computer use to business and government executives through meetings and publications such as "application briefs," which detailed different organizations' computer applications and success in glowing terms. They also showcased the lead executive, his computing manager, and his organization at user group meetings. In addition, CM activists influenced others to join the computerization bandwagon through CM discourse in user groups formed around software languages such as FORTRAN and COBOL.

The primary motivation for computer use was organizational productivity. For example, Kling and Iacono (1988) analyzed the formation and strength of four CMs of the mainframe era: Urban Information Systems, AI, Computer-Based Education, and Office Automation. They showed that activists for these CMs proclaimed that the use of mainframe computers would enhance productivity in business, government, and education. Other themes espoused by activists were either reformist (computer-based technologies are essential for a reformed society, improved computer-based technologies are needed to carry out reform, greater computerization is required for reform, and there are benefits for everyone from such computer-based reform) or anti-Luddite (the notion that uncooperative people were the main reason for lack of reform through computerization) (Kling & Iacono, 1988). The CM activists essentially tried to persuade business and government organizations to invest vast amounts of money in computer technology in all sectors of society to achieve greater productivity and organizational reform.

The outcomes of the CMs that emerged during this period are varied. The artificial intelligence (AI) CM started with the utopian vision of creating machines that can "think like humans"—a vision not yet achieved today even though IBM's Deep Blue computer with AI software has beaten world class chess players. The office automation and computer-based education CMs began with claims of completely transforming the way people conduct business and the way children learn, but the claims became tempered as people began to realize how difficult it was to do.

However, the utopian visions portrayed in the CM rhetoric of this period did not necessarily meet with the reality of use in society and organizations as evidenced in the case studies of Kling and Iacono (Chapter 2, this volume).

The PC Era

The PC era, which emerged full blown in the 1980s, created a completely new paradigm for computer investment and use in organizations. However, it had earlier roots in the 1972 HP 9830 all-in-one desktop computer; in the 1975 PC kit from Altair and the BASIC programming language that ran on the Altair; and in the early 1980s, the Apple PC. By the 1980s, computer vendors were mass marketing the sale of PCs to business users and to computer hobbyists. The PC Era activists included vendors, department managers in organizations, user group members, and home hobbyists.

The hardware of this period included small-scale PCs for home and office use as well as large-scale versions of PCs called workstations, which were capable of running the UNIX operating system. These larger PCs were later connected with local area networks (LANs) using client-server technology. The software for PCs included programming language compilers, software systems to design graphical user interfaces, graphics design systems, word processors, games, and others. Eventually, in the early 1980s e-mail surfaced on small mainframes called minicomputers, such as the DEC VAX computers, enabling small and large corporations to use e-mail for communication through distributed processing.

But the PC era really began in 1983 when IBM teamed up with Microsoft to create the DOS operating system running on an IBM PC, the forerunner to the WINDOWS operating system. With the advent of DOS, both hobbyists and business users could "program" their computers and easily manage file systems with simple English-like commands. In an effort to promote widespread diffusion, IBM had created an open architecture, which meant that any firm could build and sell PC clones—even using components from suppliers to IBM. The low price and widespread availability of PCs coupled with the proliferation of software systems during this period promoted the purchase and use of PCs for home, office, and education.

In 1984, Apple unveiled its Macintosh computer with its innovative and snazzy graphical user interface (GUI), and by 1985, Microsoft released the Windows operating system for the PC with a similar GUI. By 1985, there were more than 200 firms building and selling computers in the U.S.

Although PCs were sold through the vendor's sales force, they were broadly available in computer stores, electronics stores, department stores, and discount stores. The PC also spawned new user groups for computer applications and particular platforms (Macintosh vs. IBM PC) adding to the growing set of CM activists for this era. Trade shows began featuring large, splashy demonstrations of PC applications by vendors. By the 1990s, home-based computing was increasingly popular both with computer hobbyists and those who work at home.

During this period, the mass media played a major role in the promotion of the PC movement with PC magazines proliferating—at least a dozen PC magazines sprang up during this era serving as a venue for CM discourse. PC columns appeared in major newspapers, as did computer stories in general circulation magazines, including the in-flight magazines of airlines. In 1982, *Time* magazine named the PC its "Machine of the Year" and in 1983 *Business Week* referred to it as the "Office PC." In a 1983 brochure from IBM advertising the PC, the utopian vision is not only that of increased productivity, but anything that one can imagine:

> The IBM Personal Computer is a versatile, reasonably priced computer with many advanced hardware features that have set new industry standards since the computer's introduction. It could increase productivity in business, at home, or wherever it is used. Its true capabilities are a function of your own imagination and creativity. (cf. www.computerhistory.org)

Vendors, retailers, and media represented a large group of activists who, collectively without any intended coordination, led the public discourse about personal computing resulting in a vast distributed CM. One of the most famous mass media advertisements is Apple's "1984" Super Bowl commercial (cf. en.wikipedia.org/wiki/1984_(television_commercial)) in which Apple launched its Macintosh PC during a break in the third quarter of Super Bowl XVIII. The ad showed a young woman running through a futuristic world to throw a sledgehammer at what was implied to represent IBM Corporation as a way to show the demise of mainframe monopoly and the rise of the Macintosh PC. At the end, the following message was displayed referring to the novel *1984* by George Orwell, in which technology is viewed as dystopian with a computer system dubbed "Big Brother" watching peoples' everyday lives: "On January 24th, Apple Computer will introduce Macintosh. And you'll see why 1984 won't be like 1984."

The productivity theme surfaced often in the early writings about the wonders of PCs, but was focused on "personal productivity" with organizational productivity as a by-product. Eventually, the PC became a household item where the number of American households owning a PC went from 8 percent in 1983 to 62 percent in 2003 (55 percent of those households had Internet access). Along with the investments by companies into outfitting their business with PCs came an interest and corresponding surge in the purchase of networking hardware and software. Companies began networking PCs together into client/server LANs. As more and more companies invested in network technology, CM activists began promoting the democratization theme—that work groups and departments would have control over their own computing rather than be subservient to the high priests in the MIS Department, and that as a result of this control over information, they would also gain more power and influence within organizations, leading to the end of hierarchy.

One of the key beliefs regarding organizational productivity during this era was that computer-supported group work had the potential to exceed what had been achieved with PCs used by individuals (Bullen and Bennett, 1991). Researchers and vendors started promoting the use of computer-supported cooperative work (CSCW) systems to facilitate information sharing and collaboration. Furthermore, the democratization frame was emphasized proclaiming that CSCW systems would transform communication in organizations so that almost everyone in an organization would have access to organizational information and be empowered to make decisions. Forecasts were made by researchers that new technologies would decentralize authority, engage employees at all levels of a typical hierarchical organization, and create collaborative work settings (Castells, 2000; Leavitt & Whisler, 1958; Wilke, 1993). While some studies of organizational communication have shown that computer-mediated communication (CMC) can enhance levels of information exchange (Quan-Haase & Wellman, 2006; Sproull & Kiesler, 1991), others have shown it has had little effect on organizational structure (Franz, Robey, & Koeblitz, 1986; Roehrs, 1998; Zack & McKenney, 1995).

The Internet Era

With the advent of e-mail and widespread use of the Internet, media and academic writers began emphasizing the advantages of CMC technologies with the themes of democratization, death of distance, and information rights. Studies by scholars (Mantovani, 1994; Sproul & Kiesler, 1991) on the use of CMC in organizations to engender democracy in managerial-employee relations emphasized the dependence on the social context of CMC and on the rules determining its use. Several specific CMs were activated during this period such as computer games, digital photography, desktop computing, information rights, and community networking, to name a few. When use of the Internet became widely available through Web servers and browsers such as Netscape during the 1990s, PC vendors started including modems and connectors for broadband technology.

During the late 1980s, businesses and universities began taking advantage of the availability of LAN and wide area network (WAN) connections to use e-mail for internal and external communication. Businesses began wiring PCs together for peer-to-peer networks enabling individuals to communicate globally. With the advent of the Web and Internet browsers such as Netscape and Microsoft's Explorer in the early 1990s, many more people could easily access information and exchange data on a trans-global scale. The themes of productivity, democratization, and death of distance were promoted in academic and mass media publications. The Internet with its "network of networks" links over two million host or server computers around the world.

The internetworking CM (Iacono & Kling, 2001) incorporated more activists than previous eras due to the increasingly computer-literate public who serve as activists in businesses and homes. Government sponsored initiatives such as the National Internet Infrastructure (NII) promoted the spread of internetworking use during the 1980s. During the 1990s with the advent of the Web, more and more individuals and businesses created Web sites that also served as venues for CM activists. For example, the Free Software Foundation (FSF) and the Open Source Initiative (OSI) both created Web sites during this period to promote membership in their foundations in support of the F/OSS movements (cf. www.fsf.org and www.opensource.org).

The nonprofit FSF was established and proliferated during this era and continues today to promote the freedom and information rights themes. As a result of the availability of broadband connections, many new CMs emerged during the Internet era, such as distributed work, CSCW, knowledge management, F/OSS, e-business, e-democracy, and e-health, among others. Many of the CMs that emerged during this era are ongoing and their outcome is yet to be determined. Two examples of relative success in terms of diffusion are the F/OSS movements. The

Free Software Movement (FSM) CM is an interesting example of a new genre of CM that emerged during this period (Elliott, Chapter 13, this volume) in which the acquisition of technology is assumed to be readily available and the mobilization for membership in the CM is related to software development of free software (as opposed to purchasing new technology). The utopian vision of eliminating all proprietary software and replacing it with free software is so far-fetched that it will probably never be realized. However, this movement has reached a certain level of diffusion with regard to its software projects. The www.gnu.org Web site now boasts about 43,000 registered GNU projects with about 2,800 registered users, so it has made an impact on the development and use of software systems in our society. Their counterpart, the OSI organization, lists more than 1 million projects with about 100,000 users (www.opensource.org). Since they advocate mixing free and proprietary source code, the OSI's membership has swelled faster than the FSM. The increasing use by businesses of the GNU/Linux operating system is a testament to the successful diffusion of the F/OSS. The study by Dedrick and West (Chapter 16, this volume) illustrates how the ideology of the FSM is not a factor when businesses decide to use open source software as an option. They are more interested in profit savings and reduction of dependence on vendors for software changes. Two papers in this book illustrate the difficulties in implementing distributed work technology for videoconferencing in organizations (Kiesler, Boh, Ren, & Weisband, Chapter 9, this volume; Mark, Chapter 10, this volume). These CMs are discussed in more detail later.

The Emerging Era of Ubiquitous Computing

The "ubiquitous computing" era takes it name from the term coined by Mark Weiser at the Computer Science lab at Xerox PARC. He envisioned future computing devices that would fade into the background of peoples' lives, becoming more or less invisible (Weiser, 1991). During the period of 1988–1994, Xerox PARC built several experimental devices to support this vision in the form of "tabs," "pads," and "boards." Tabs are inch-scale machines that resemble active Post-It notes; the pads are foot-scale ones that are similar to a sheet of paper (or a book or a magazine), and the boards (which are now commercial products) are yard-scale displays that are the electronic equivalent of a blackboard or bulletin board.

Activists of this CM predict that people will use "wearable computing" with devices becoming part of clothing, connecting people to each other via wireless technology. Indeed, wireless technologies such as PDAs and mobile phones have become extremely popular, particularly in Asia and increasingly in Europe and the U.S., for providing access to the Internet, instant messaging, digital cameras, computer games, video clips, and execution of Java programs (Mattern, 2001) and are becoming popular with business executives, professionals, and academics for constant e-mail access (Middleton & Cukier, 2006).

But, the ubiquitous computing CM is not just about hardware devices. So-called "ubiquitous software development environments" are now being promoted by F/OSS developers. For example, the MIT Project Oxygen has a vision of computation focused on the ability of users and accompanying technology to move around freely in a nomadic environment, according to their needs (www.oxygen.csail.mit.edu/Overview.html). Several technical challenges wait, as the requirement for Oxygen systems must be "pervasive," "embedded," and "nomadic." Software systems will adapt with minimal user intervention and without interruption to services they provide. An example of this nomadic-type system is the Knoppix GNU/Linux distribution available on a real-time CD that boots and runs the Linux operating system completely from the CD. Users of Knoppix can work on software development on any hardware platform that accepts Linux, providing F/OSS developers the ability to work on F/OSS projects "anytime, anywhere" in the world.

As this software sub-movement illustrates, the utopian vision created by Weiser (1991) inspired others in industry and academia to follow. It led to the creation of annual workshops and conferences such as the IFIP UBICOMP (Ubiquitous Computing) workshops (Dourish & Friday, 2006) and the IFIP Working Group 8.2 conferences (e.g., "Designing Ubiquitous Information Environments: Socio-Technical Issues and Challenges," Sørensen, Yoo, Lyytinen, & DeGross, 2005). Specialty academic journals have formed such as *IEEE Pervasive Computing*, *Journal of Ubiquitous Computing and Intelligence*, and *Personal and Ubiquitous Computing*. Although the movement has been largely confined to industry and academic circles, it is beginning to have traction in the public media as the wearable Apple iPod has become ubiquitous almost overnight.

The potential for CM activists during this era includes just about everyone everywhere due to the widespread prevalence of Internet connections and handheld devices for instant communication, such as the popular instant messaging (IM), which enables silent messaging using handheld devices. Now CM discourse can be found on blogs, wikis, and special Web sites for communicating personal thoughts to the world at large (cf. www.myspace.com).

The Ubiquitous Computing Era promotes a utopian vision that people will be able to connect to other people and computers "any time, anywhere" and that this will be unambiguously beneficial to individuals, organizations, and society. However, we show in the discussion sections to follow that the realization of being connected "anytime, anywhere" is not always as utopian as CM activists portray it.

Generalizations Concerning CMs

Looking across these eras of computerization, and the material presented in the chapters of this book, we develop six generalizations with implications for the emerging era of ubiquitous computing and for future research and practice.

Gap Between CM Vision and Reality

The case studies show a persistent, and sometimes large gap between the vision and reality of CMs. Examples of this gap range from the use of the Internet to improve democratization in organizations (Quan-Haase & Wellman, Chapter 6, this volume) and communities (Carroll, Chapter 7, this volume) to large-scale implementations of communication technologies to improve collaboration among distributed teams in national and multinational corporations (Kiesler et al., Chapter 9, this volume; and Mark, Chapter 10, this volume).

The gap between the expectations of the "democratization" frame and the reality of use are evident in the organizational case study by Quan-Haase and Wellman (Chapter 6, this volume). The vision of technology creating a more democratized organization did not come to fruition in their study of IM and e-mail in a high-tech organization. Employees of the firm KME used both technologies for local and global communication, but the expectation that this would lead to flattening of the firm's hierarchical management structure did not occur. Workers focused more attention on and responded quicker to IM or e-mail from a superior than from a colleague. Although an increase in egalitarian relationships between management and workers did not occur, there was greater collaboration among co-workers within and between departments. In Carroll's (Chapter 7, this volume) study of Blacksburg, West Virginia, the entire community had been networked with the vision that citizens would become more civic minded and community oriented. However, the technology merely reinforced the civic involvement of people who were already interested in community affairs. Thus, in both the organization and the community cases, there was a considerable gap between the CM vision of "democratization" and the actual use of such technology to "democratize."

There was also a gap between vision and reality with regard to the "death of distance" theme of CMs. Kiesler and colleagues' (Chapter 9, this volume) study of the American Institute for Research (AIR) showed that groupware that had been adopted to enable virtual meetings among distributed teams was used for low-level day-to-day business operations because the technology could not support higher level activities. As a consequence, AIR used face-to-face meetings for decision making and complex coordination and virtual meetings for routine messaging and exchange of information. Mark (Chapter 10, this volume) identified an unanticipated consequence of technology use with distributed teams—one not addressed in CM discourse on the death of distance. She found that a large engineering team located at different sites faced serious tensions between the demands of their collocated, local environments and those from the overall team management. The utopian vision is that the technology enables people to collaborate easily, but its implementation failed to address the need to establish complementary social conventions to deal with the conflict in demands between local and global environments.

As these chapters illustrate, the reformist rhetoric in CM visions of what the technology can do for organizations and society tends to differ from the reality of use. Vendors and other promoters of particular CMs need to recognize that such gaps between utopian visions and the reality of technology use may prevent successful diffusion. Users, in particular, need to be aware of the impending gap between the benefits promoted by CM activists (vendors, technologists, media, academics) for a newly formed CM vision and the actual costs and benefits, including the distribution of costs and benefits. In addition, these chapters suggest that the utopian visions for "anytime, anyplace" ubiquitous computing are likely to be very difficult to achieve. As illustrated in Sørensen and Gibson's chapter (Chapter 17, this volume) on the use of PDAs and cell phones by professionals, there is a need for technical staff to provide ongoing support to ensure integrity and security of organizational information because most users simply cannot do it on their own. Indeed, learning to use and maintain these devices poses challenges that make the device appear as a "disturbing nuisance" rather than a "calming assistant" as claimed by Weiser (1991).

CM Rhetoric Shifts from Utopian to Pragmatic

The cases in the book have shown that as technology is deployed and used, the related CM rhetoric eventually shifts from utopian to pragmatic as described in our conceptual model in Chapter 1. Experience with technology use results in contending discourse that leads to counter-CMs, changes in design or changes in use of the technology and, in turn, to change in the dominant technological frame or vision that promotes its use. This occurs when people develop greater understandings of the technology's use, when they adopt selected aspects of the technology, or when they focus on areas of the technology's greatest benefit to them. This evolution toward pragmatism can lead to a new CM or to modification of the original CM vision that is more suited to realistic work practices.

The digital camera CM illustrated by Meyer (Chapter 5, this volume) is an example of this shift in paradigmatic view in discourse. In the initial stages of the production and sales of digital cameras, the magazine and Web discourse promoted the advantages of digital cameras peppered with utopian predictions of what this type of camera could do for a professional photographer's productivity. The initial costs, which were in the range of $5,000 to $7,000, could be justified by professionals but were beyond the general public's reach. As prices closed on in $1,000, the advantage of using digital cameras by the general public began to appear in public discourse, but grew dramatically when lower priced ($300–$500) digital cameras became available. Visions for the camera's use shifted to everyday rationales related to personal and family use. Digital photograph quality improved dramatically at the same time as prices fell. Thus, by the end of 2004, a high-quality camera with four to five mega pixels could be purchased for $200–$300 and high-end six mega pixel cameras for under $1,000. The shift in the technology and in the vision and rhetoric about the inherent value of digital photography helped to spur digital camera purchases from 6.5 million units in 2001 to 15.7 million units by 2004 (Gleeson, 2004).

Thus, CM rhetoric tends to shift from the utopian to the pragmatic over time, as participants become aware of the actual uses and impacts of new technology. However, the time gap for such information to reach decision makers, organizational users, and the general public can be large. Thus, there is a clear role for social informatics research to speed up feedback about usability and impacts of new technology to designers, user organizations, the media, and the general public.

Diffusion Time Longer for CM Technology with Complex Infrastructures

For those CMs in which the technology and surrounding infrastructure are broad, complex, and multi-faceted, it takes longer than usual for the technology to diffuse. Markus and colleagues' (Chapter 3, this volume) example of automated underwriting in mortgage banking provides an excellent example of how this occurs when user applications rely on large physical infrastructure, which itself underwent repeated change during the twenty-year period of the case (see earlier discussion in this chapter). Elliott (Chapter 13, this volume) and Dedrick and West (Chapter 16, this volume) illustrate how the complexity of the human infrastructure can also slow diffusion. Elliott's analysis of the FSM gives examples of how a free software project—GNUe (www.gnuenterprise.org)—sought to build a business application intended to replace proprietary ERP systems. The project had only one-half the planned modules completed and only 15 companies using them after ten years of work.

Dedrick and West's (Chapter 16, this volume) study of Linux use found that, contrary to the FSM and OSI movements' vision that source code should be free so that users can modify it as they wish, business users were adopting the technology primarily for low cost and freedom from the vendor lock-in that comes with commercial software (e.g., Windows, Unix). They were agnostic about the ideologies of the FSM and OSI movements, but very concerned about the stability and the support infrastructure for Linux-based applications—the chief factor reported as preventing greater diffusion. These examples illustrate that as the Internet has made available a global physical infrastructure, the human infrastructure becomes a more significant factor shaping technology diffusion.

Difficulty in Technology Prediction and CMs

As the foregoing sections illustrate, the realities of day-to-day use of a CM's promoted technology cannot be precisely predicted in advance. Often the outcome of a CM evolves to include unexpected uses of the technology promoted by a CM, and these may swamp the original intended uses. For example, Culnan (Chapter 8, this volume) reports that the Backstreets Ticket Exchange (BTX) online community (www.backstreets.com) for fans of Bruce Springsteen and its chat rooms/bulletin boards were set up for fans to meet online and exchange tickets, but the site has evolved to promote donations to charities recommended by Springsteen. Ekbia and Gasser's (Chapter 15, this volume) analysis of the reliability of F/OSS systems shows that some outcomes are totally unexpected. Their study of the bug reports of F/OSS systems showed that some bugs are inherently difficult to resolve in the F/OSS method of software development because of its decentralized nature. The software proponents of F/OSS promote the CM by proselytizing the benefits as more reliable than typical software systems due to the many "eyes" that view and fix the code (Raymond, 2001). In reality, some bugs might never get resolved. Ekbia and Gasser found 129,000 problem reports listed in the bug reporting system for Mozilla, yet only 88,000 had been resolved over a five-year period. For one particular bug, there were 280 comments over the period, yet the bug remained open. Traditional software development, with a central manager responsible for a project, is much more successful at ensuring bugs are fixed than the decentralized approach touted by the F/OSS movement. As the old adage goes, "when everybody is responsible, nobody is responsible."

Thus, the capabilities of the technology are almost never what is advertised in the vision of the CM by the activists, whether vendors, users, journalists, or academics. This is exacerbated by the promotion rhetoric surrounding technology introduction and use. Vendors have an economic interest in promotion of benefits and downplaying costs and problems. Even if problems are known by the vendors, they have commercial interests in not sharing them with users. Thus, it may take users a long time to find out that the promoted vision does not match reality. It may also take vendors a long time to realize that their vision does not fit the reality of the market and what users want or need (Allen, Chapter 4, this volume). Once they have invested in new technology, users also have an interest in highlighting the positive and downplaying the negative. Journalists can be independent and take a critical stance, but their deadline-driven work tends to prevent follow-up and long-term analysis of new technologies. Only academics are in a position to take the long view and do serious social analysis of the uses, impacts, and interactions of technology and organizations. In the short- to mid-term, however, academics can provide useful assessments and predictions by looking for parallels in the experiences with earlier technologies.

For example, in the book *Computers and Politics* (Danziger, Dutton, Kling, & Kraemer, 1982), the authors argued that although the findings were based on the mainframe era, they applied to subsequent eras (mini-computer and PC) because they were based on fundamental relationships between technology, organizations, and people. The authors argued that the central concern expressed in *Computer and Politics* for greater equality of access to computing resources in governments had not been resolved by the advent of the PC, despite the rhetoric of democratization in the PC era. The continuing concern about democratization in the Internet era in chapters by Quan-Haase and Wellman (Chapter 6, this volume) and Carroll (Chapter 7, this volume) illustrates that neither the democratization of computing, nor of governments had been greatly advanced by any of the technologies although they are increasingly used. The theoretical rationale supporting Danziger and his colleagues' argument was the "reinforcement politics" hypothesis, which posits that computing will always be used to reinforce the existing political and managerial elites in organizations and society.

This example illustrates the need for, and the usefulness of, academic efforts to do long-term technology assessments based on their own and others' research. Rob Kling was often heard to say that technology impact assessments ought to be required for IT projects in the same way that they are required for environmental projects, and that the information and computer sciences would do well to provide students with the tools to do so.

Context Shapes Computing Use and Effects

Perhaps the most fundamental theme in the CM literature is that computing use is shaped by the organizational and institutional context, including the political context. This was illustrated in the work of Markus and colleagues, Quan-Haase and Wellman, Mark, and Lamb and Poster (in their discussion of the politics of information sharing in intranets, Chapter 11, this volume). Dutton (Chapter 19, this volume) also illustrates this point in his chapter on the conceptualization of the Internet emergence and ongoing maintenance as an "ecology of games." The games perspective compliments the CM perspective by helping to explain the intertwined social, technical, organizational, and other forces that shape the emergence of changes tied to the increasingly ubiquitous use of the Internet. In this chapter, Dutton illustrates how social movements, such as the CMs whose goals are to promote open source or to employ ICTs for development, are critical to many games shaping the future development, use, and governance of the Internet.

Mark Ackerman (Chapter 18, this volume) points out that the technology's architecture might carry hidden assumptions about political relationships among the stakeholders who construct, adopt, and use computing. He analyzes two CMs—the Semantic Web and pervasive computing—and shows that the technologies are being built with nontransparent political assumptions about the relationships among the stakeholders. Ackerman argues that neither of these CMs deals sufficiently with the tension of updates and maintenance and who will control competing designs in the future. He suggests that because of its participative roots, the Web might move toward democratic efforts to reconcile differences, but it also could be controlled by corporate concerns, given its historical mixture of F/OSS and corporate-sponsored software and projects. Ackerman's analysis suggests that although many of the CMs described in this book evolve from the libertarian-infused infrastructures of the Internet, networking technologies and distributed computing, how these disparate parts work together in the future to ensure the resolution of conflicts is an empirical question.

Computing technologies and their architectures have political implications about the distribution of costs, benefits, and control, which are seldom apparent to all participants in CMs. These political implications are often buried in CM rhetoric, and therefore it is incumbent upon participants to bring them into the open.

Conclusions

The main focus of this book has been on the question of why organizations adopt computing technologies. The simplistic answer is that organizations can achieve economic benefits from computer use (i.e., improved productivity), but a richer answer can be found in the concept of CMs. We used the CM construct from Kling and Iacono (1998) to characterize adoption decisions as occurring within the broader social context of organizations, where public discourse about computerization in general, and specific technologies in particular, create utopian visions about the benefit of computer use. These visions are created and promoted by futurists, vendors, journalists, academics, and organizational users who play various roles as activists, followers, sideliners, skeptics, and critics; all are participants in a special kind of technological social movement that influences how people think about computing and communications technology and thereby shape technology decisions in organizations and society. These movements tend to have an underlying bias toward computerization, and although occasionally there are counter movements that temporarily halt or redirect things, and although there may be disappointing gaps between the vision and reality of specific movements, the overall effect of CMs is to create a pro-computerization bias "in the air." The study of CMs is intended to deepen understanding of how these movements form, evolve, and have impacts in organizations and society.

Contributions

In their seminal publication on CMs, Kling and Iacono (1988) characterized the effort as "a first step in bringing attention to the evolution of CMs and how they influence organizations and societies." This book is a second step that has sought to extend research into CMs in several ways: (1) bringing together a group of leading researchers in social informatics to address CM theory and concepts in their work, (2) addressing contemporary CMs focused around the Internet, (3) showing how CMs have changed since the earlier research by Kling and Iacono, and (4) drawing implications from earlier computerization eras for the emerging era of ubiquitous computing and for research and practice.

This book includes chapters by 32 authors from the U.S., Canada, and Europe. The authors were specifically commissioned to apply CM theory and concepts to their work for this book. Therefore, this book is the single largest collection of research on CMs to date.

Although some specific CMs such as automated underwriting in the mortgage banking industry extend over several eras, nearly all the CMs described in this book have been fueled by the rise of the Internet and are contemporary. The free Internet and Web technologies have made a larger number of applications possible, helped them to reach millions of potential CM participants, and enabled many of them to flourish as a result of such broad reach. The technological action frames of "death of distance," "democratization," and "freedom/information rights" can all be attributed to the vast array of Web information and applications that have become available on a global scale over the last 10 to 15 years.

Another change is that the technological action frames or themes of earlier CMs have extended into later CMs and computerization eras, although sometimes defined in different ways. For example, the theme "productivity" referred to labor savings in the mainframe era, to "greater output for the same labor" in the PC era, and to "productivity in collaboration among distributed teams" in the Internet era. In addition, subsequent CMs adopt more than one theme such that a contemporary CM might encompass all that have gone before. This can be seen in the Virtual Teams CM (Kiesler et al., Chapter 9, this volume) in which both organizational and individual productivity are promoted through the use of virtual teams with sophisticated networking technology.

A major change in the nature of CMs is scope of influence and the rapidity with which they can influence vast numbers of people to invest time and money into new technology promoted by CMs. For example, consider the latest handheld device, the BlackBerry, in comparison to the "old" CM that promoted AI technology. The AI CM started in the 1960s in academic circles. Businesses began investing in expert system development and implementation in the 1970s. AI was transformed into a CM in the 1980s when mainstream business magazines (e.g., *Fortune*, *Business Week*) and noted academics began to write stories about AI applications that aggressively promoted a fantasy vision of powerful and accessible AI being "here today." Thus, AI technology moved slowly over the course of a 20-year period before becoming a CM. In contrast, BlackBerry PDAs first came on the market in 1999 and by 2006 (only seven years later), there were nearly 5 million people acting as active proponents and users of BlackBerrys for reading and sending e-mail "anytime, anywhere."

Not only can CMs generate membership faster than in previous decades, CMs have taken on a global aspect to their mobilization for membership. Even third world countries are exploring ways to leverage hand-held technologies (PDAs, smart phones, miniPCs) and open software such as Linux as a means of providing computing capabilities to impoverished populations. The Shuttleworth Foundation (www.tsf.org.za) funds efforts to educate people in Africa by sponsoring F/OSS projects that enable more people to have computers and Internet connections. One recent project entails the implementation of kiosks in libraries and other public places in areas where Internet connections are too expensive or impossible. All people need is a CD to take advantage of these kiosks which offer "free" downloads of F/OSS software for people who otherwise would not have access to such products of the F/OSS CM.

A final change in the nature of CMs is that they are starting to merge as suggested by Scacchi (Chapter 14, this volume) and Clement and Hurrell (Chapter 12, this volume), and the influence of specific CMs will not only continue to reach membership on a global scale, but increase in size and potential impact.

Implications

The studies and cases in this book suggest several implications for designers, managers, users and scholars in the ubiquitous computing era.

Designers

People designing ubiquitous computing devices, applications and systems need to be aware that the utopian visions of much, if not most, CM rhetoric rarely becomes reality. Unrealistic visions may not do well in the market and represent an opportunity cost for the vendor. Designers also need to be more aware of the negative aspects of their designs, such as the addictive nature of IM, interactive gaming, and other problematic activities enabled by mobile devices (Middleton & Cukier, 2006). Privacy issues should also be considered when designing ubiquitous computing devices, especially devices that are part of sensor laden environments and "wearable" computing that may intentionally or unwittingly assault individual privacy in the name of security or health (Jarvenpaa, Lang, & Tuunainen, 2005). Designers also need to pay attention to the complexities inherent in Web-based technology and political implications must be carefully considered in the design of future systems.

Managers and Professionals

Executives, managers, and professionals need to be more sophisticated consumers of computing rather than simply responding to vendor and media discourse regarding the "next big thing" in computing. Technology professionals along with users can conduct careful analysis of the fit of new technology with particular individuals and groups in the organization, perhaps even investing in experimental uses, before a broad commitment. Managers considering investment in ubiquitous computing devices such as BlackBerrys or MP3 phones should be aware of the addictive nature and possible misuse of these technologies, such as the potential for identity theft (Mazmanian, Orlikowski, & Yates, 2005; Middleton & Cukier, 2006). Middleton & Cukier (2006) conducted a study of Blackberry usage patterns finding them to be both negative—dangerous, distracting, anti-social and infringing on work-life boundaries—and at the same time, positive—increasing efficiency, enabling multi-tasking, improving response time to managers, and providing freedom to work "anytime, anywhere." Middleton and Cukier (2006) suggested that businesses and individuals need to be cautious of negative consequences when using BlackBerry devices, and consequently, to try and determine which work practices really warrant being connected "any time, anywhere."

Given the potential problems with these devices, managers, executives, and professionals might want to consider measures such as clearly de-limiting their use for work, home, and home–work life connections. Even when there is a clear fit of technology with the organization's activities, managers need to consider how assimilation will occur as the cases in this book illustrate that some people may not be able to easily adapt to new technologies without adequate preparation or training (Kiesler, et al., Chapter 9, this volume; Mark, Chapter 10, this volume).

Organizational Users

Organizational users have the most at stake in understanding CMs because they make the investments in technology. They need to become sophisticated consumers of computing and communications technologies and skeptical of utopian claims for the technology. In the emerging era of ubiquitous computing, they need to be aware that Ubicomp devices and applications that enable work connections "anytime, anywhere" will involve frequent replacement during this period of radical innovation with many different kinds of products, and continuing support for a wide variety of products. These devices may also have problematic side effects such as addiction, intrusion of personal work time, obnoxious disregard for social etiquette, and intrusion of work life into home life.

CM Scholars

Academic and industry researchers have a tremendous opportunity to apply CM analysis and concepts to the emerging Ubicomp devices. In doing so, it would be useful to engage in more historical analysis of previous technologies and to bring knowledge about the effects and implications of previous technologies to bear on predictions about new technologies. The insights and tools used in such analysis and prediction might form the basis for educational programs aimed at training a new generation of social analysts and practitioners who can do useful technology assessment in both vendor and user organizations.

At the most recent IFIP workshop on ubiquitous computing, Yvonne Rogers (2006) published a very significant paper suggesting that the technically oriented research and design efforts in ubiquitous computing needs a new direction. She identified three areas of current ubiquitous computing research and their key limitations:

- Context-Aware Computing – Detecting, identifying, and locating people's movements, routines, or actions with the purpose of assisting people with this information. For example, the military originated the term "augmented cognition" to assist human cognition in the sensing of what is happening around them with recommended actions. Context-aware computing works best in highly constrained environments given the complexity and difficulty in modeling predictable human behavior, and thus, it is unlikely to be effective on a grand scale.

- Ambient/Ubiquitous Intelligence – Computational intelligence involving both physical and digital worlds where "smart devices" will be capable of predicting people's needs and reacting accordingly. Ambient and ubiquitous intelligence has proven equally difficult to implement in workable systems on a large scale.
- Recording/Tracking and Monitoring – Ubiquitous computing systems with sensors for alerting caregivers concerning the whereabouts and health of the elderly and physically and mentally disabled individuals. Privacy and ethical problems arise when using such systems that are not easy to resolve. Rogers (2006) suggests that ubiquitous computing researchers change the direction of such work, given the limited success of current research. Rather than attempt to resolve these grand challenges, she suggests that researchers pursue more limited goals focused on specific activities performed by people in bounded locations. This requires that researchers move "from a mindset that wants to make the environment smart and proactive to one that enables people, themselves, to be smarter and proactive in their everyday and working practices."

Finally, there is another mindset that might warrant change on a broader scale. It is an inherent problematic of the utopian rhetoric of a positive future from technology-driven change even in the face of evidence to the contrary. There is too much of a tendency in the computer, information, and communications communities to follow the "preachin," "accentuate the positive," and "eliminate the negative" suggested by Johnny Mercer in his popular song from 1944, "Ac-Cent-Tchu-Ate the Positive," shown in the selected lyrics that follow:

> You've got to accentuate the positive
> Eliminate the negative
> And latch on to the affirmative
> Don't mess with Mister In-Between

References

Bullen, C., & Bennett, J. L. (1991). Groupware in practice: An interpretation of work experiences. In C. Dunlop & R. Kling (Eds.), *Computerization and controversy: Value conflicts and social choices* (pp. 257–287). San Diego, CA: Academic Press:

Castells, M. (2000). *The rise of the network society* (2nd ed.). Oxford: Blackwell.

Danziger, J., Dutton, W. H., Kling, R., & Kraemer, K. L. (Eds.). (1982). *Computers and politics*. New York: Columbia University Press.

Dourish, P., & Friday, A. (Eds.). (2006). *UbiComp 2006: Ubiquitous computing*. New York: Springer.

Franz, C. R., Roby, D., & Koeblitz, R. R. (1986). User response to an online information system: A field experiment. *MIS quarterly*, 10, 29–42.

Gleeson, J. (2004, October). The picture is clear: Struggling Kodak shifts focus to digital imaging as film industry fades. *The Journal News*, p. 18, 1D.

Grove, A. (1996). *Only the paranoid survive: How to explain the crisis points that challenge every company and career*. New York: Doubleday.

Iacono, S., & Kling, R. (2001). Computerization movements: The rise of the Internet and distant forms of work. In J. A. Yates & J. Van Maanen (Eds.), *Information technology and organizational transformation: History, rhetoric and practice* (pp. 93–136). Thousand Oaks, CA: Sage Publications.

Jabloner, P. (2006). Selling the Computer Revolution. Retrieved from www.computerhistory.org

Jarvenpaa, S., Lang, K., & Tuunainen, V. (2005). Friend or Foe? The ambivalent relationship between mobile technology and its users. *IFIP* 8.2, Cleveland, OH.

Kling, R., & Iacono, S. (1988). The mobilization of support for computerization: The role of computerization movements. *Social Problems*, 35(3), 226–242.

Leavitt, H. J., & Whisler, T. L. (1958). Management in the 1980s. *Harvard Business Review*, 36, 41–48.

Mantovani, G. (1994). Is computer-mediated communication intrinsically apt to enhance democracy in organizations? *Human Relations*, 47(1), 45–62.

Mattern, F. (2001). The vision and technical foundation of ubiquitous computing. *Upgrade*, 2(5), 2–6.

Mazmanian, M. A., Orlikowski, W. J., & Yates, J. (2005). CRACKBERRIES: The social implications of ubiquitous wireless e-mail devices. In C. Sorensen, Y. Yoo, K. Lyytinen, & J. I. DeGross (Eds.), *Designing ubiquitous information environments: Socio-technical issues and challenges* (pp. 337–344). Cleveland, OH: Springer.

Middleton, C. A., & Cukier, W. (2006). Is mobile email functional or dysfunctional? Two perspectives on mobile email usage. *European Journal of Information Systems*, 15, 252–260.

Quan-Haase, A., & Wellman, B. (2006). Hyperconnected net work: Computer mediated community in a high-tech organization. In C. Heckscher & P. Adler (Eds.), *Collaborative Community in Business and Society* (pp. 281–333). New York: Oxford University Press.

Raymond, E. S. (2001). *The cathedral & the bazaar: Musings on Linux and Open Source by an accidental revolutionary*. Sebastopol, CA: O'Reilly & Associates.

Roehrs, J. (1998). *A study of social organization in science in the age of computer-mediated communication*. Unpublished doctoral thesis, Nova Southeastern University.

Rogers, Y. (2006). Moving on from Weiser's vision of calm computing: Engaging UbiComp experiences. In P. Dorish & A. Friday (Eds.), *Ubicomp 2006: Ubiquitous computing*. New York: Springer.

Sørensen, C., Yoo, Y., Lyytinen, K., & DeGross, J. I. (2005). *Designing ubiquitous information environments: Socio-technical issues and challenges*. Cleveland, OH: Springer.

Sproull, L. S., & Kiesler, S. B. (1991). *Connections: New ways of working in the networked organization*. Cambridge, MA: MIT Press.

Weiser, M. (1991, September). The computer for the twenty-first century. *Scientific American*, 94–110.

Wilke, John. (1993). Computer links erode hierarchical nature of workplace culture. *Wall Street Journal*, December 9, pp. A-1, A-7.

Zack, M. H., & McKenney, J. L. (1995). Social context and interaction in ongoing computer-supported management groups. *Organization Science*, 6(4), 394–422.

About the Contributors

Mark S. Ackerman is Associate Professor of Electrical Engineering and Computer Science and School of Information at the University of Michigan. He conducts research in the areas of Computer Supported Cooperative Work (CSCW), collaborative technologies, and Human–Computer Interaction (HCI). Dr. Ackerman heads the SocialWorlds Research Group, which conducts research in information access, privacy, and virtual communities. The theoretical focus of his research group's work is on considering the interplay of the social world with computational systems. He is interested in how to consider incorporating elements of the social world within software systems (such as with collaborative systems) and how these systems will affect their social settings in return. In some cases, such as privacy, it is important to consider *co-design spaces*—where one must design both the technical and social simultaneously (often along with regulatory systems). This research requires a dual emphasis on both the technology and the social structures of its use. Dr. Ackerman holds a Ph.D. in Information Technologies from the Massachusetts Institute of Technology. Mark Ackerman can be reached at ackerm@umich.edu.

Jonathan P. Allen is Assistant Professor of Information Systems at the School of Business and Management at the University of San Francisco. His research examines the organizational and social consequences of information technology (IT), including the value conflicts and social choices embedded in particular information technologies, change in socio-technical systems, the evolution of emerging IT, and helping general managers make better IT choices in the context of larger organizational systems. Dr. Allen holds a Ph.D. in Information and Computer Science from the University of California, Irvine. Jonathan Allen can be reached at jpallen@usfca.edu.

Wai Fong Boh is Assistant Professor at the Nanyang Business School, Nanyang Technological University in Singapore. Her research interests are in the areas of knowledge management and organizational learning, and the management industry and organizational standards. She has articles published or forthcoming in *Organization Science*, *Journal of Management Information Systems*, and *Communications of the ACM*. Dr. Boh has also presented at the International Conference of Information Systems (ICIS) and Academy of Management (AoM) Meetings, and published in the AoM Best Papers Proceedings. In 2002, she won an award for the ICIS Runner-Up to Best Theme-Related Paper Award. Her dissertation won the 2005 OCIS Best Dissertation Award, and was a Newman Award nominee for the Academy of Management Meetings. Dr. Boh holds a Ph.D. from the Tepper School of Business at Carnegie Mellon University. Wai Fong Boh can be reached at awfboh@ntu.edu.sg.

John M. Carroll is Edward M. Frymoyer Chair Professor of Information Sciences and Technology at Pennsylvania State University. His research interests include methods and theory in human–computer interaction, particularly as applied to networking tools for collaborative learning and problem solving, and design of interactive information systems. Recent books include *Making Use* (MIT Press, 2000), *HCI in the New Millennium* (Addison-Wesley, 2001), *Usability Engineering* (Morgan-Kaufmann, 2002) and *HCI Models, Theories, and Frameworks* (Morgan-Kaufmann, 2003). He serves on several editorial and advisory boards and is Editor-in-Chief of the *ACM Transactions on Computer–Human Interactions*. He received the Rigo Award and CHI Lifetime Achievement Award from the Association for Computing Machinery (ACM), the Silver Core Award from the International Federation of Information Processing (IFIP), and the Alfred N. Goldsmith Award from the Institute of Electrical and Electronics Engineers (IEEE). He is a fellow of the ACM, the IEEE, and the Human Factors and Ergonomics Society. Dr. Carroll holds a Ph.D. in Psychology from Columbia University. John Carroll can be reached at jmcarroll@psu.edu.

Andrew Clement is Professor of Information Studies at the University of Toronto. His research, teaching, and consulting interests are in the social implications of information technology and human-centered systems development. Dr. Clement has written papers and co-edited books in such areas as computer supported cooperative work, participatory design, workplace surveillance, privacy, women, work and computerization, end-user computing, and the "information society." His recent research has focused on public information policy, Internet use in everyday life, digital identity constructions, public participation in information/communication infrastructures development, and community networking. Dr. Clement holds a Ph.D. in Computer Science from the University of Toronto. Andrew Clement can be reached at andrew.clement@utoronto.ca.

Mary J. Culnan is the Slade Professor of Management and Information Technology at Bentley College. Her current research focuses on the privacy implications of electronic marketing, and she also teaches on information privacy. She has published in a number of academic journals and has testified before Congress and other government agencies on a range of privacy issues. In 1997, Dr. Culnan served as a Commissioner on the President's Commission on Critical Infrastructure Protection. She is also the author of the 1999 Georgetown Internet Privacy Policy Survey, which the FTC used to make recommendations to Congress about Internet privacy. In March 1999, *Business Week*'s e-biz Web site profiled her as a "Mover & Shaker." She was employed for seven years as a systems analyst by the Burroughs Corporation. Dr. Culnan holds a Ph.D. in Management from UCLA. Mary Culnan can be reached at mculnan@bentley.edu.

Jason Dedrick is Senior Research Fellow at the Center for Research on Information Technology and Organizations (CRITO), and Executive Director of the Personal Computing Industry Center at the University of California, Irvine. His research interests include the globalization of computer production and use, national technology policies, and the productivity impacts of information technology. Dr. Dedrick holds a Ph.D. in Management from the University of California, Irvine. Jason Dedrick can be reached at jdedrick@uci.edu.

Andrew Dutta is Senior Lecturer in Organizational Behavior and Human Resources area at ICFAI University, India. He did postgraduate work in Business Finance at the University of Calcutta and was awarded a Gold Medal for ranking first in his University in 1999. In 2004–2005, Andrew was a Visiting Research Scholar at Bentley College. Andrew has published many papers in reputed journals and magazines of India. Presently, he is finishing his doctoral dissertation titled "Understanding the Role of Features in Information Technology Use" at ICFAI University. Andrew Dutta can be reached at andrewdutta@gmail.com.

William Dutton is Director of the Oxford Internet Institute, Professor of Internet Studies, University of Oxford, and Professorial Fellow of Balliol College, Oxford. He was previously a Professor in the Annenberg School for Communication at the University of Southern California, which he joined in 1980, where he was elected President of the Faculty. In the U.K., Dr. Dutton was a Fulbright Scholar (1986–1987), and was national director of the U.K.'s Programme on Information and Communication Technologies (PICT) from 1993 to 1996. Dr. Dutton holds a Ph.D. in Political Science from SUNY Buffalo. William Dutton can be reached at Director@oii.ox.ac.uk.

Hamid R. Ekbia is Associate Professor of Information Science at the School of Library and Information Science, Indiana University. His current research focuses on how knowledge is developed, represented, transformed, and shared in and among individuals, organizations, and communities. He has written on this topic in the areas of Artificial Intelligence, Decision Support Systems, Knowledge Management, and Free/Open Source Software. He has consulted on various regional and national projects. Dr. Ekbia holds a Ph.D. in Computer Science and Cognitive Science from Indiana University. Hamid Ekbia can be reached at hekbia@indiana.edu.

Les Gasser is Professor at the Graduate School of Library and Information Science at the University of Illinois at Urbana-Champaign. His current research investigates the social and technical aspects of large-scale distributed information systems. He works on social informatics, multi-agent systems, computational organization modeling/simulation, and information quality/reliability. Dr. Gasser has published more than 70 technical papers and five books in these areas. Known worldwide as a key figure in the field of Multi-Agent Systems and Distributed Artificial Intelligence, he has given invited lectures and served on program and organizing committees of the major international AI and DAI conferences and serves on the editorial boards of several journals. He is currently President of the International Foundation for Multi-Agent Systems (IFMAS). Dr. Gasser has consulted and taught extensively in Europe and Japan for over 15 years. He has significant project management, leadership, and entrepreneurial experience and has been a principal or advisor with a number of technology startup firms. Dr. Gasser holds a Ph.D. in Computer Science from the University of California, Irvine. Les Gasser can be reached at gasser@uiuc.edu.

David Gibson is a consultant with the international management consultancy firm Accenture, and is based in London, U.K. He is a part of the Human Performance Global Service Line specializing in Organization Change Strategy, and has most recently worked with clients such as Telstra Australia, Airbus France, and the U.K. Prime Minister's Delivery Unit. Prior to joining Accenture, Dr. Gibson worked with a product and service innovation consultancy based in London, which used consumer ethnography to improve and innovate upon new/existing products and services for blue chip multi-nationals. Dr. Gibson's research focuses upon knowledge worker efficiency through developing more robust ICT offerings. He is also actively engaged in teaching entrepreneurial and business skills to underprivileged youth in countries such as South Africa, Romania, and the U.K. Dr. Gibson holds a M.Sc. in Design, Analysis, and Management of Information Systems from the London School of Economics. David Gibson can be reached at d.gibson@accenture.com.

Christie Hurrell is a graduate of the Joint Master's program in Communication and Culture at York and Ryerson Universities. Her Master's research focused on citizen engagement and electronic government, using a case study of a national foreign policy consultation hosted by the Canadian government. Her work and research since then have covered the areas of community networking, knowledge translation, and health risk communication. Currently, she is based at the University of British Columbia's Centre for Health and Environment Research where her work is directed toward transferring the results of occupational and environmental health research to various stakeholders. Christie Hurrell can be reached at christie.hurell@gmail.com.

Suzanne Iacono is Acting Division Director of the Computer and Network Systems Division of the Computer and Information Sciences and Engineering Directorate of the National Science Foundation. She serves as the chair of the Interagency Social, Economic, and Workforce (SEW) Implications of Information Technology and Information Technology Workforce Development Coordinating Group, which gives policy, program, and budget guidance on federal SEW IT R & D. Previously, Dr. Iacono held a faculty position at Boston University and was a Visiting Scholar at the Sloan School, Massachusetts Institute of Technology. She is Associate Editor for *The Information Society* and *Management Information Systems Quarterly*. She has written many journal articles, book chapters, and conference papers on the social implications of IT. Recent examples include "Best Paper" in the Telemedicine Journal for 1999 and invited commentary in 2001 on the state of IT research in Information Systems Research journal. Dr. Iacono received her Ph.D. in Information Systems from the University of Arizona. Suzanne Iacono can be reached at siacono@nsf.gov.

Sara Kiesler is Hillman Professor of Computer Science and Human-Computer Interaction at Carnegie Mellon University. She applies behavioral and social science to technology design and tries to understand how technology changes individuals, groups, and organizations. She was among the first to conduct scientific studies of computer-mediated communication.

With Lee Sproull, she has authored a book and has collaborated extensively within CMU and with colleagues elsewhere on social aspects of the Internet. Dr. Kiesler continues to study the social impact of the Internet on families, problems associated with multidisciplinary and complex forms of collaboration, geographically dispersed science and project work, information sharing, and the design of human-robot interaction. Dr. Kiesler holds a Ph.D. in Psychology from Ohio State University. Sara Kiesler can be reached at kiesler@cs.cmu.edu.

Rob Kling passed away in May 2003. From 1993–2003, he was Professor of Information Science and Information Systems at Indiana University, Bloomington. At Indiana, he founded and directed the Center for Social Informatics, later renamed the Rob Kling Center for Social Informatics. This center is run jointly by Indiana's Graduate School of Library and Information Science and the School of Informatics. Dr. Kling received his doctorate in 1971, specializing in artificial intelligence, from Stanford University. He held his first professorship in Computer Science at the University of Wisconsin, Madison between 1970 and 1973. He was on the faculty of the University of California, Irvine (UCI) from 1973–1996 and, while there, held professorial appointments in the Department of Information and Computer Science, the Center for Research on Information Technology and Organizations, and the Graduate School of Management. From the early 1970s to the early 2000s, Dr. Kling studied the social opportunities and dilemmas of computerization for managers, professionals, workers, and the public. He examined computerization as a social process with technical elements, studying how intensive computerization transforms work and how computerization entails many social choices. When he passed away in 2003, he was studying the effective use of electronic media to support scholarly and professional communication. Some of that work was posthumously published in a volume he co-edited, *Designing Virtual Communities in the Service of Learning* (Cambridge University Press, 2004).

Dr. Kling contributed to the publication of several books. To name just a few, he was the co-author of *Computers and Politics: High Technology in American Local Governments* (Columbia University Press, 1982), the co-editor of *Computerization and Controversy: Value Conflicts & Social Choices* (Academic Press, 1991) (later, in 1996, Dr. Kling was the sole editor of the 2nd edition of *Computerization and Controversy*), and the co-editor of the posthumously published *Understanding and Communicating Social Informatics: A Framework for Studying and Teaching the Human Contexts of Information and Communication Technologies* (Information Today, Inc., 2005). In addition, Dr. Kling's research was published in more than 85 journal articles and book chapters. He was editor-in-chief of *The Information Society* and served on the editorial and advisory boards of several other scholarly and professional journals. He presented numerous conference papers, gave invited lectures at many major universities, and gave keynote and plenary talks at conferences in the United States, Canada, and Western Europe. Throughout his career, he received many awards. Following his death, the Association of Information Systems named him the 2004 Leo Award winner for his substantial contributions to information systems research. A full bibliography of his work is available at: rkcsi.indiana.edu/index.php/rob-kling-bibliography.

Roberta Lamb passed away on November 29, 2006. At the time of her death, she was Associate Professor in the Donald Bren School of Information and Computer Sciences at the University of California, Irvine. Roberta joined the Informatics Department as Associate Professor in April 2006, coming from the University of Hawaii. For the past 12 years, she had been researching online technology use, and was engaged in two streams of related research: an ongoing study of intranets in commercial organizations, and a study of collaborative networking among university and industry scientists that also involved simulation of collaborating social actors. She was a deputy editor for *The Information Society*, a special issue editor for *Information Technology and People*, and Social Aspects theme editor for the *Journal of Digital Information*. Dr. Lamb held a Ph.D. from the University of California, Irvine. She will be missed greatly. Remembrances can be found at www.ics.uci.edu/community/events/lamb. *The Information Society (TIS)* journal will be having a special issue in her memory. See the *TIS* Web site for announcement.

Gloria Mark is Professor in the Department of Informatics in the Donald Bren School of Information and Computer Sciences at the University of California, Irvine. Her research focuses on the design and evaluation of collaborative systems. Her primary research interest is in developing and evaluating technologies to improve virtual collocation. Her current projects include studying technology use and group-to-group collaboration in space mission design, virtually collocated teams at Intel, and collaborative technology adoption in large distributed organizations. Dr. Mark also runs a groupware usability lab where she conducts experiments. She has examined the usability of a number of leading edge collaborative technologies including a collaborative hypermedia authoring system, an electronic shared workspace, application-sharing, and collaborative virtual environments. Dr. Mark holds a Ph.D. in Computer Science from Columbia University. Gloria Mark can be reached at gmark@ics.uci.edu.

M. Lynne Markus is the John W. Poduska, Sr. Professor of Information Management at the McCallum Graduate School of Business at Bentley College. Professor Markus conducts research on enterprise and inter-enterprise systems, knowledge management, and IT-enabled organization change. She is the author of three books and numerous articles in journals such as *MIS Quarterly*, *Information Systems Research*, *Journal of Management Information Systems*, *Organization Science*, and *Management Science*. She was named Fellow of the Association for Information Systems in 2004. In 2006 she served as the Fulbright—Queen's Visiting Research Chair in The Management of Knowledge-Based Enterprises at the Monieson Centre at Queen's Business School (Kingston, Ontario, Canada). Dr. Markus holds a Ph.D. in Organizational Behavior from Case Western Reserve University. M. Lynne Markus can be reached at mlmarkus@bentley.edu.

Eric T. Meyer is a research fellow at the Oxford Internet Institute. He received his Ph.D. from the School of Library and Information Science at Indiana University in Bloomington. His dissertation examined how marine biologists have seen significant changes in their work practices as they switched from film photography to digital photography. He has published and presented conference papers on the topics of scholarly communication networks, the digital divide, communication regimes, socio-technical interaction networks, manipulation of digital photographs, and photoblogging. Eric Meyer can be reached at eric.meyer@oii.ox.ac.uk.

Mark Poster is Professor at the University of California, Irvine in the History Department, the Department of Film and Media Studies, and the Critical Theory Institute. His fields of interest lie within European intellectual and cultural history, critical theory, and media studies. Dr. Poster has courtesy appointments in the Department of Information and Computer Science and the Department of Comparative Literature. Some of his recent publications are *What's the Matter with the Internet?* (University of Minnesota Press, 2001), *The Second Media Age* (Blackwell, 1995), *The Mode of Information* (University of Chicago Press, 1990) and *Cultural History and Postmodernity* (Columbia University Press, 1997). A collection of pieces old and new with a critical introduction by Stanley Aronowitz is published as *The Information Subject* (G & B Arts International, 2001). He continues his study of the social and cultural theory of electronically mediated information with a work in preparation to be titled *Information Please: Politics and Culture in the Age of Digital Machines*. Dr. Poster holds a Ph.D. from New York University. Mark Poster can be reached at poster@uci.edu.

Anabel Quan-Haase is Assistant Professor of Information and Media Studies and Sociology at the University of Western Ontario. Her research investigates how information and communication technologies transform organizations, communities, and educational settings. She currently holds a Social Science and Humanities Research Council of Canada grant to study how young people have integrated communication technologies into their everyday life. The focus of the project is on instant messaging and how it transforms the way young people stay connected. Dr. Quan-Haase holds a Ph.D. in Information Science from the University of Toronto. Anabel Quan-Haase can be reached at aquan@uwo.ca.

Yuqing Ren is a Postdoctoral Fellow in the Human-Computer Interaction Institute at Carnegie Mellon University. Her research aims to understand ways through which individuals collaborate to share information, integrate knowledge, and participate in communities of practice. Her specific areas of interest include teams and groups, knowledge management, distributed collaboration, online community, and computational modeling of social and organizational systems. Dr. Ren's work has been or will be published in journals such as *Management Science*, *Organization Science*, and *Organization Studies*. Dr. Ren holds a Ph.D. in Organization Science from Carnegie Mellon University. Yuqing Ren can be reached at yren@andrew.cmu.edu.

Walt Scacchi is Senior Research Computer Scientist and research faculty member at the Institute for Software Research and director of research for the Laboratory for Game Culture and Technology at the University of California, Irvine. He joined ISR in 1999 after serving on the faculty at the University of Southern California for eighteen years. From 1981 to 1991 Dr. Scacchi founded and directed the USC System Factory, and from 1993 to 1998 he directed the USC ATRIUM Laboratory. His interests include open source software development, software process engineering, software acquisition and electronic commerce, and organizational studies of system development. He is an active researcher with more than 100 research papers, and consults widely to clients in industry and government agencies. Dr. Scacchi holds a Ph.D. in Information and Computer Science from the University of California, Irvine. Walt Scacchi can be reached at wscacchi@ics.uci.edu.

Carsten Sørensen is Senior Lecturer in Information Systems at The London School of Economics and Political Science. He specializes in how mobile ICT shapes and is shaped by emerging social practices and organizational forms. He has been involved in research on mobile computing since the mid-1990s. In 2001 Dr. Sorensen initiated the mobility@lse research network in mobile interaction (mobility.lse.ac.uk). He is actively engaged in executive education and has consulted for a range of organizations, such as Microsoft, orange, PA Consulting, CA, EDS, and Siemens. He has extensive EU research project experience and is currently Associate Editor of *The Information Systems Journal* and *The e-Service Journal*, on the editorial board of *Information and Organization*, and a member of the Advisory Board for *Scandinavian Journal of Information Systems*. Dr. Sørensen holds a Ph.D. in Information Systems. Carsten Sørensen can be reached at c.sorensen@lse.ac.uk.

Charles W. Steinfield is Professor in the Department of Telecommunication, Information Studies, and Media at Michigan State University and recipient of MSU's Distinguished Faculty Award and its Teacher-Scholar Award. He has been a visiting professor and researcher at the Institut National des Télécommunications in France, Delft University of Technology in the Netherlands, Bellcore, and the Telematica Instituut in the Netherlands. He has published five books and numerous articles in journals such as *Organization Science*, *Information Systems Research*, *Communication Research*, *Electronic Markets*, and the *Journal of Computer-Mediated Communication*. Dr. Steinfield holds a Ph.D. in Communication Theory and Research from the Annenberg School for Communication at the University of Southern California. Charles Steinfield can be reached at steinfie@msu.edu.

Suzanne Weisband is Associate Professor in Management and Information Systems at the University of Arizona. She places a strong emphasis on the unintended, social, and behavioral effects of information and communication technologies and the importance of organizational and social context for understanding these effects. Her current research interests include laboratory experiments of communication and information sharing in groups and field studies on distributed team collaboration and its implications for leadership and performance. Dr. Weisband holds a Ph.D in Social and Decision Sciences and Policy Analysis from Carnegie Mellon University. Suzanne Weisband can be reached at weisband@eller.arizona.edu.

Barry Wellman is Professor of Sociology at the University of Toronto. His research examines virtual community, the virtual workplace, social support, community, kinship, friendship, and social network theory and methods. Based at the University of Toronto, he directs NetLab, teaches at the Department of Sociology, does research at the Centre for Urban and Community Studies, the Knowledge Media Design Institute, and the Bell University Laboratories' Collaborative Effectiveness Lab, and is a cross-appointed member of the Faculty of Information Studies. Dr.

Wellman is also the chair of the Community and Information Technologies section of the American Sociological Association. He has been a Fellow of IBM's Institute of Knowledge Management, a consultant with Mitel Networks, a member of Advanced Micro Devices' Global Consumer Advisory Board, and a committee member of the Social Science Research Council's (and Ford Foundation's) Program on Information Technology, International Cooperation, and Global Security. He is the co-author of more than 200 articles, co-authored with more than 80 scholars, and is the co-editor of three books. Dr. Wellman holds a Ph.D. in Sociology from Harvard University. Barry Wellman can be reached at wellman@chass.utoronto.ca.

Joel West is Associate Professor of Technology Management at the Department of Organization and Management in the College of Business at San Jose State University. His research, teaching, and industry experience center on the sort of global high-technology industries that have been the lifeblood of Silicon Valley for the past 40 years. His research focuses on the effect of technological change on industry structure over time. His teaching focuses on strategy, particularly in technology-based industries. At UC Irvine, Dr. West developed a new course in technology strategy and wrote new cases on standards competition and intellectual property rights, which have been published and adopted at "top 25" business schools. He has won best paper awards for tracks of the Academy of Management and HICSS conferences, and has been active in service to the research community. Dr. West holds a Ph.D. in Management from the University of California, Irvine. Joel West can be reached at joel.west@sjsu.edu.

Rolf T. Wigand is Maulden-Entergy Chair and Distinguished Professor of Information Science and Management at the University of Arkansas at Little Rock. He is the past director of the Center for Digital Commerce and the Graduate Program in Information Management at Syracuse University. Wigand researches Information Management, Electronic Commerce and Markets, IS standards, and the strategic deployment of information and communication technology (ICT). His research interests lie at the intersection of information and communication business issues, the role of newer ICTs and their impact on organizations, industry, and society, as well as their strategic alignment. His research has been supported by the NSF, the German NSF (DFG), the Volkswagen Foundation, the International Social Science Council, Rome Laboratory, and other agencies. He has authored five books and more than 110 articles and book chapters, having appeared in such journals as *MIS Quarterly*, *Journal of MIS*, *Journal of Information Technology*, and *Electronic Markets*. Dr. Wigand holds a Ph.D. in Organizational Communication from Michigan State University. Rolf Wigand can be reached at rtwigand@ualr.edu.

About the Editors

Margaret S. Elliott is a Research Specialist at the Center for Research on Information Technology and Organizations (CRITO), Paul Merage School of Business, University of California, Irvine. She is also affiliated with the Institute for Software Research (ISR) in the Donald Bren School of Information and Computer Science, University of California, Irvine. Her current projects include the study of computerization movements and their influence on technological diffusion; the study of free/open source software development communities as occupational communities; and the study of the influence of organizational culture on the adoption of court technology. She received her Ph.D. in Information and Computer Science in 2000, joined the Institute for Software Research in 2001, and started working for CRITO in 2004. Prior to entry into graduate school, she worked for 10 years as a software engineer and project manager in software development for consulting firms and aerospace engineering, and as a principal investigator in research and development for aerospace engineering. Her research interests include open source software development, virtual organizations, computer-supported cooperative work, occupational communities, organizational culture, court technology, and failures of large-scale software systems. She is an active researcher and has published more than 30 papers. Margaret S. Elliott can be reached at melliott@ics.uci.edu.

Kenneth L. Kraemer is the Taco Bell Professor of Information Technology for Management at the Paul Merage School of Business at UC Irvine. He is also Director of the Center for Research on Information Technology and Organizations (CRITO), as well as Director of the Personal Computing Industry Center. He has conducted research on the management of computing in organizations for more than 40 years. Dr. Kraemer is currently studying the globalization of knowledge work and innovation, the offshoring of new product development, the dynamics of computing in organizations, and the business value of IT and national policies for IT production and use. He is the author or co-author of 15 books, including recently published titles such as *Global E-Commerce: Impacts of National Environment and Policy*, and *Asia's Computer Challenge: Threat of Opportunity for the U.S. and the World?* He has written more than 165 articles, many on the computer industry and the Asia-Pacific region, which have been published in journals such as *Communications of the ACM, MIS Quarterly*, *Management Science*, *Information Systems Research*, *The Information Society*, *Public Administration Review*, *Telecommunications Policy*, and *Policy Analysis*. Dr. Kraemer has also been a consultant on IT policy to major corporations, the federal government, the National Academy of Sciences, the National Academy of Engineering, and the governments of Singapore, Hong Kong, Indonesia, Malaysia, and China. He was the Shaw Professor in Information Systems at the National University of Singapore from 1990 to 1991. Dr. Kraemer holds a Ph.D. from the University of Southern California. Kenneth Kraemer can be reached at kkraemer@uci.edu.

Index

C

D

E

H

I

J

K

L

M

N

O

P

Q

R

S

T

U

V

W

X

Y

Z

More Titles of Interest from Information Today, Inc.

Understanding and Communicating Social Informatics

A Framework for Studying and Teaching the Human Contexts of Information and Communication Technologies

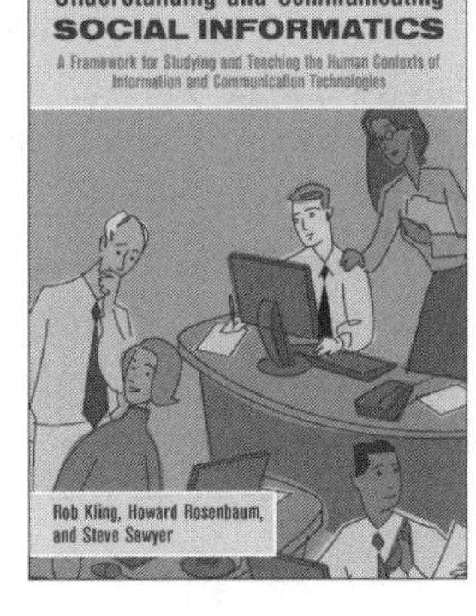

By Rob Kling, Howard Rosenbaum, and Steve Sawyer

Here is a sustained investigation into the human contexts of information and communication technologies (ICTs), covering both research and theory. The authors demonstrate that the design, adoption, and use of ICTs are deeply connected to people's actions as well as to the environments in which ICTs are used. They offer a pragmatic overview of social informatics, articulating its fundamental ideas for specific audiences and presenting important research findings.

240 pp/hardbound/ISBN 978-1-57387-228-7/$39.50

Theories of Information Behavior

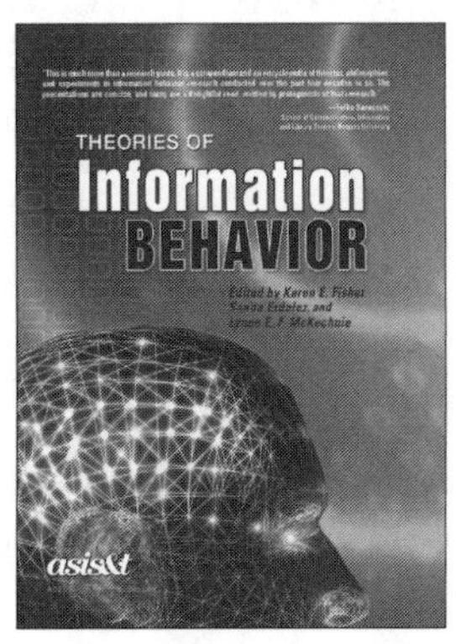

Edited by Karen E. Fisher, Sanda Erdelez, and Lynne (E. F.) McKechnie

This unique book presents authoritative overviews of more than 70 conceptual frameworks for understanding how people seek, manage, share, and use information in different contexts. Covering both established and newly proposed theories of information behavior, the book includes contributions from 85 scholars from 10 countries. Theory descriptions cover origins, propositions, methodological implications, usage, and links to related theories.

456 pp/hardbound/ISBN 978-1-57387-230-0
ASIST Members $39.60 • Nonmembers $49.50

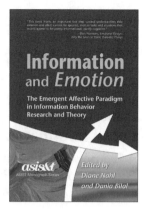

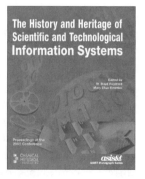

Intranets for Info Pros

Edited by Mary Lee Kennedy and Jane Dysart
Foreword by Tom Davenport

The intranet is among the primary landscapes in which information-based work occurs, yet many info pros continue to view it with equal parts skepticism and dread. In *Intranets for Info Pros*, editors Mary Lee Kennedy and Jane Dysart and their 10 expert contributors provide support and encouragement to the information professional responsible for implementing or contributing to an intranet. Chapters demonstrate the intranets strategic value, describe important trends and best practices, and equip info pros to make a key contribution to their organization's intranet success.

304 pp/softbound/ISBN 978-1-57387-309-3 $39.50

ARIST 42
Annual Review of Information Science and Technology

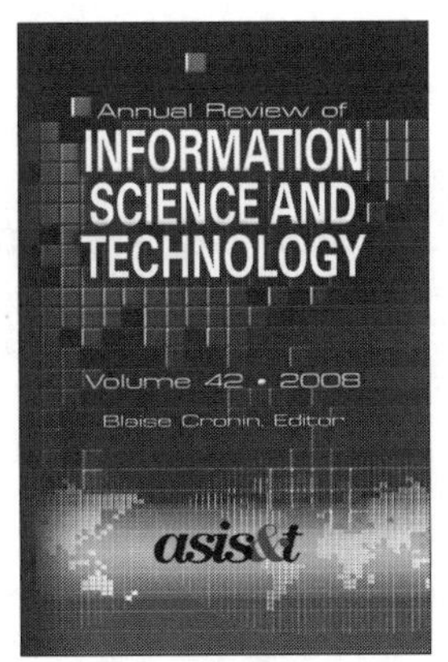

Edited by Blaise Cronin

ARIST, published annually since 1966, is a landmark publication within the information science community. It surveys the landscape of information science and technology, providing an analytical, authoritative, and accessible overview of recent trends and significant developments. The range of topics varies considerably, reflecting the dynamism of the discipline and the diversity of theoretical and applied perspectives. While *ARIST* continues to cover key topics associated with "classical" information science (e.g., bibliometrics, information retrieval), editor Blaise Cronin is selectively expanding its footprint in an effort to connect information science more tightly with cognate academic and professional communities.

712 pp/hardbound/ISBN 978-1-57387-308-6
ASIST Members $99.95 • Nonmembers $124.95

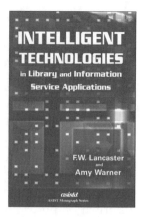

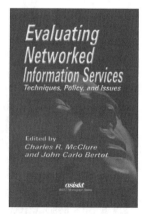

Knowledge Management Lessons Learned

What Works and What Doesn't

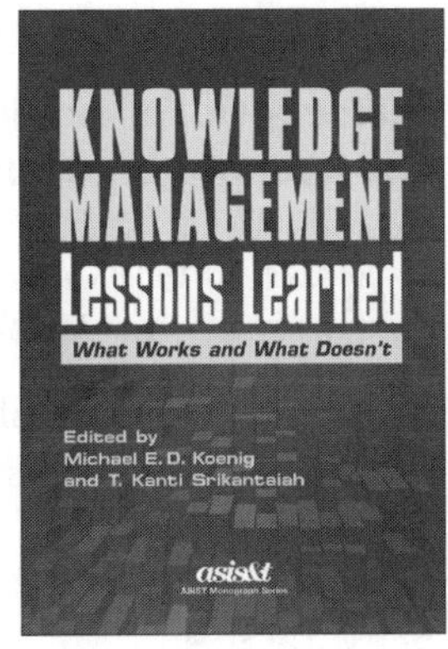

Edited by Michael E. D. Koenig and T. Kanti Srikantaiah

A follow-up to Srikantaiah and Koenig's ground-breaking *Knowledge Management for the Information Professional*, this new book surveys recent applications and innovations in KM. More than 30 experts describe KM in practice, revealing what has been learned, what works, and what doesn't. Includes projects undertaken by organizations at the forefront of KM, and coverage of KM strategy and implementation, cost analysis, education and training, content management, communities of practice, competitive intelligence, and much more.

624 pp/hardbound/ISBN 978-1-57387-181-5
ASIST Members $35.60 • Nonmembers $44.50

Knowledge Management in Practice

Connections and Context

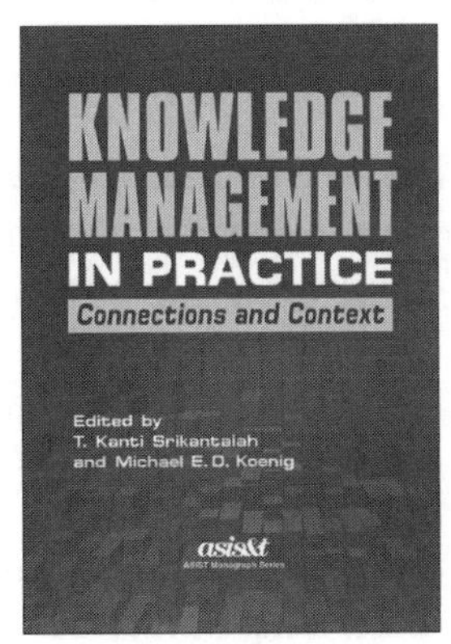

Edited by T. Kanti Srikantaiah and Michael E. D. Koenig

This third entry in the ambitious, highly regarded KM series from editors Srikantaiah and Koenig features 26 chapters contributed by more than 20 experts from around the globe. The book not only looks at how KM is being implemented in organizations today, but is unique in surveying the efforts of KM professionals to extend knowledge beyond their organizations and in providing a framework for understanding user context. *Knowledge Management in Practice* is a must-read for any professional seeking to connect organizational KM systems with increasingly diverse and geographically dispersed user communities.

544 pp/hardbound/ISBN 978-1-57387-312-3
ASIST Members $47.60 • Nonmembers $59.50

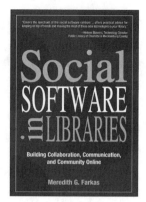

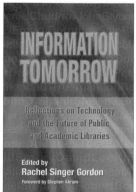